GUIDE TO CHINA BUSINESS CONTACTS—
COMPANIES, PLACES AND MARKETS

GUIDE TO
CHINA BUSINESS CONTACTS
COMPANIES,
PLACES AND
MARKETS

by

Marshall Sittig

NOYES PUBLICATIONS
Park Ridge, New Jersey, U.S.A.

Library of Congress Catalog Card Number: 95-22726
ISBN: 0-8155-1385-2
Printed in the United States

Published in the United States of America by
Noyes Publications
Mill Road, Park Ridge, New Jersey 07656

Transferred to Digital Printing, 2011

Printed and bound in the United Kingdom

Library of Congress Cataloging-in-Publication Data

Sittig, Marshall.
        Guide to China business contacts : companies, places, and markets
    1995 / by Marshall Sittig.
                p.   cm.
        Includes bibliographical references and index.
        ISBN 0-8155-1385-2
        1. China--Commerce--Directories. 2. Investments, Foreign--China
    -Directories. 3. Industries--China--Directories. 4. Business
    enterprises--China--Directories. I. Title.
HF3833.S58   1995
338'.0025'51--dc20   95-22726
                                                                  CIP

PREFACE

"Eighty-two percent of the world's people live in the new expanding markets outside the traditional markets of North America, Europe, Japan and Australia" as pointed out by Louis R. Hughes, president of G.M. Europe at the General Motors annual meeting in May 1994. He went on to point out that "Asian markets are nearing near-explosive growth..."

Of these Asian markets, the #1 potential growth area is China.

As Donald H. Kohnken, executive vice president and chief of staff at W.R. Grace, Boca Raton, FL, says: "When you look at North America, you see 1 to 2% (economic) growth, with the same thing in Europe. In Latin America, you are looking at something in the 4 to 7% range. But when you get to the Asia-Pacific region, with all those people, you go from China with its 14% growth down through various growth levels in other countries. But generally, you are dealing with growth in the 7-14% range. For that reason alone, you can't turn your back on the region" (1).

SRI International, the Menlo Park, California-based research and consulting firm, predicts growth of GDP in the region, excluding China, at about 7.0% per year through 1998. China, which it calls the fastest growing economy in the world, is expected to boost its GDP to about 12% in 1994, settling down to 9.7% by 1997.

In the first half of 1993, China's GDP surged at an annualized 14% clip; in Guangdong Province adjacent to Hong Kong the rate may be as high as 30%. Not since Japan just after World War II has a major economy seen such a growth explosion. Already, China's economy is the world's third-largest behind the U.S. and Japan, indicates the International Monetary Fund. "By 2010," declares the Washington-based U.S.-China Business Council, "China's economy may be the world's largest."

So torrid has been China's growth, in fact, that the economy has become dangerously overheated, forcing the Chinese government to slow it down. As of January 1995, however, the inflation rate still remained above 20% on an annual basis. The perpetual dilemma for policymakers is how to curb credit and cool upward pressure on prices without shutting down money-losing state enterprises and throwing millions out of work. If the government takes an austere line and tries to shut off its cash spigot to frail state firms, inflation may drop, but social chaos could result. But if the government continues to pump out subsidies, the flood of money chasing goods will spur inflation. Another problem is that the optimistic growth figures cited above must be viewed with caution. The mistake can be to confuse need with demand. Demand implies an ability to pay. Chinese people know they will have to struggle just to feed, clothe and offer even a minimal education to the majority of those imaginary consumers.

Another area of concern in Chinese trade development is the alleged piracy of computer software and compact disks which can constitute a serious problem in American-Chinese trade. China's entrance into the 1995 World Trade Organization may, indeed, hinge on a resolution to this problem.

The idea that it may be too late for many foreign companies to enter China seems absurd according to the Economist (London), April 16, 1994. They point out that every year the country needs to construct the equivalent of 100 small power stations, connect another 10 million people to the telephone and build hundreds of miles of railways and roads. As the purchasing power of its 1.2 billion people increases, so does demand for televisions, refrigerators, cars and the rest. Yet worries that some markets have already been tightly sewn up are increasing—particularly now that those firms already operating in the country are being given a helping hand from Beijing.

Tariffs may constitute another problem area in trade development with China. Importing a foreign car or a fax machine into China today means essentially paying for it twice—once to the dealer, and an equal or greater amount to the tariff collector. The price of a domestic airline ticket for a foreign traveller is 50 to 60 percent greater than that charged to a Chinese traveler. It even costs a foreigner double the standard admission fee to take a stroll in the parks of Chinese cities.

Indeed, in the last year, China's powerful State Planning Commission has appeared to be adding—not subtracting—protectionist measures with its "pillar industries" plan to develop state-owned conglomerates under preferential policies that would protect them from both foreign ownership and foreign competition.

Pillar industries will include the automobile industry, petrochemicals, telecommunications and transportation. The issues and potential implications of China's Application for GATT Accession have been reviewed by the U.S. Department of Agriculture experts (53).

Thus, the timely pursuit of Chinese trade opportunity is of the essence and, hopefully, this volume will speed such pursuit to successful conclusions.

*   *   *   *

The preparation of this volume was stimulated by a month in China in 1988 when the author had a booth at a biotechnology exposition in Shanghai that led to many contacts including a visit to the China desk at the U.S. Department of Commerce. Their publications are available through the National Technical Information Service (N.T.I.S.) in Springfield, Virginia. The essence of some dozens of their publications have been incorporated into this volume. That same skeleton has been fleshed out by items from the current U.S. business press and by data obtained directly from China.

Further, a very comprehensive and recent publication by the Economic and Social Commission of Asia and the Pacific of the United Nations has been cited frequently as valuable background material (2).

Then the skeleton has been interspersed with specific citations to possible government and industrial contacts in China drawn from various directories imported from China.

A brief review of China's plans for the development and expansion of several key industries reveals the scope of the commercial opportunities now emerging in China (58).

-- **Electric Power (Thermal):** The Ministry of Electric Powers plans to add 15,000 MW per year to China's power generation capacity over the next ten years. Central and provincial expansion plans include the construction of over thirty-five power stations between 1992 and 1996.

-- **Electric Power (Hydro):** Most hydro-power projects are joint endeavors between the Ministry of Power and the Ministry of Water Resources.

Current plans envision the construction of four huge projects: Three Gorges, to be the largest hydro-power dam in the world, in Hubei Province; Xiaolongdi in Henan Province; Longtan in the Guangxi Autonomous Region; and Ertan in Sichuan Province.

-- **Railways:** China is receiving loans from the World Bank, the Asian Development Bank and the OECF to build and expand six rail lines and to import communications networks, intermodal container transportation and loading systems, computer and signaling systems, software and track maintenance equipment.

-- **Air Traffic Control and Airport Construction:** The Civil Aviation Authority of China (CAAC) is in the midst of a major airport upgrade plan, financed by the OECF. In the summer of 1993, CAAC completed a tender that supplied fifty-two airports all over China with new radar, instrument landing and communications systems. A second tender for more radar, weather radar, satellite network communication systems and other equipment was conducted last year. A third OECF tranche for air traffic control is expected later this year.

-- **Municipal Transportation:** There are at least four major subway projects now either underway or in the planning stages: Although American companies won only a small portion of the Guangzhou Metro, there are still new systems on the way: the Shanyang Light Rail, a new Qingdao Metro, a new subway for Nanjing and an expansion of the Beijing Metro system.

-- **Telecommunications:** The Ministry of Posts and Telecommunications plans to install 12 million new telephone lines per year, for a total of 100 million by the year 2000; plus 1.2 million long distance circuits by 1995, and 3.5 million by the year 2000. Other plans for the next five years include the installation of 32,000 km of optical cable lines.

-- **Metallurgy:** The target under China's Eighth Five-Year Plan for steel production this year is between 78 and 80 million tons. Production is to be raised to 100 million tons per year by 2000 and to 120 million tons per year by 2005. To help achieve these goals, the government has approved the construction of three new steel complexes at Jinan, Jilin Province, Zhanjiang, Guangdong Province and Ningbo, Zhejiang Province. Three existing plants have been approved for expansion: Baoshan in Shanghai, Anshan in Liaoning Province and Capital Iron and Steel in Beijing.

-- **Energy:** One of the major threats to China's ability to sustain its current high-speed growth is the chronic shortage of energy. It is no wonder then, that one of the highest priorities of all development planning is the efficient exploitation of China's energy resources. The Government will be looking increasingly to foreign companies for investment, technology and equipment. In addition to the offshore exploration blocks already open to foreign companies, the Chinese government has opened important areas for onshore exploration and development, including the most important of all, the Tarim

Basin in Xinjiang Province.

-- **Building Materials:** In order to increase the production of cement to fill China's ever expanding construction industry, three plant expansion projects have been approved, at Yichang, the site of the Three Gorges project; at Zhicheng, near Wuhan in Hubei Province; and at Wanxian, Sichuan Province.

-- **Environmental Protection:** China still lacks the financial strength to undertake strict enforcement of environmental standards. Nevertheless, there are some significant environmental projects planned mainly for air pollution control and for municipal water treatment and purification. Sixteen water treatment projects are planned for several points along the Yangzi River alone. An experimental incinerator is being built in Guangzhou and various clean coal technologies are being included on a trial basis in power projects in several provinces. MOEP is planning to use $200 million from Asian Development Bank to raise the efficiency and environmental protection standards in a large matrix of power plants in the Northeast.

-- **Factory Renovations:** China's traditional state-owned heavy industrial base is in serious need of technological renovation. Central government approval has been granted for the renovation and expansion of hundreds of industrial enterprises in Harbin in Heilongjiang Province, Shenyang in Liaoning Province, Shanghai and Chongqing in Sichuan Province. These enterprises have been authorized either to import new technology and equipment directly or to enter into joint ventures with foreign companies.

The Author and Publisher express their thanks to Elaine's Computer Service of Barboursville, VA, for typesetting this book.

CONTENTS

List of Figures

INTRODUCTION

This volume will attempt to conduct a survey of China in these stages -

- a survey of the current states' various industrial areas and geographical zones.
- annotation of these various areas with news notes of recent developments.
- industry-by-industry summaries of the potentials of the various industrial areas for U.S. exports as set forth by experts in the U.S. Department of Commerce [3].
- interspersed with names, addresses and telephone numbers of useful contact organizations for more specific and timely information leading to personal communications and/or contacts with Chinese organizations for current information and future planning.

In recent years, the People's Republic of China (PRC) has been one of the fastest growing economies in the world. Its gross national product (GNP) increased 12.8 percent in 1992 and is projected to grow at 8-9 percent annually in the remainder of the 1990s. Foreign trade as a percentage of China's GNP has risen from about 10 percent int he late 1970s to 38 percent in 1992. Certain regions in China are booming, and many people are becoming affluent. Guangdong province, the most open region with a population of 65 million, has benefitted from neighboring Hong Kong's free-wheeling capitalist economy and the movement of Hong Kong's manufacturing sector into the province has created probably the most dynamic economy in the world (5).

This dynamic growth can be attributed largely to China's policy of reforming its economy and opening up to the outside world, which began in 1979. The pace of reform has quickened in the wake of senior leader Deng Xiaoping's call, made in early 1992 during a tour of southern China, for more rapid growth, greater openness, and stepped-up reform. Deng's policies were endorsed by the Fourteenth Congress of the Chinese Communist Party (CCP) in October 1992, by the Eighth National People's Congress in March 1993, and against by the Third Plenum of the CCP's Fourteenth Central Committee in November 1993. The Third Plenum adopted a decision of steps needed to transform the Chinese economy into a market system with a number of new reform initiatives. Priority areas for reform activity include the state-owned enterprises, banking and taxation, foreign trade, social security, and the rural economic structure.

Rapid economic growth, bold reform measures, and massive infrastructure plans point to enormous market potential in China. The eighth five-year plan (1991-95) calls for spending $70-80 billion a year on imports. Recently, China announced 210 large projects in 23 industries seeking foreign technology and equipment between 1993 and 2000. The cost of imports for the projects is expected to total $30 billion. Additional spending on infrastructure could amount to as much as $200 billion by the year 2000. As China gives priority to infrastructure development, business opportunities appear especially promising in the energy, telecommunications, and transport sectors (5).

1

GEOGRAPHY

Size: The area of China is about 9.6 million square kilometers; the east to west distance about 5,000 kilometers, from the Heilong Jiang (Amur River) to Pamir Mountains in Central Asia; the north to south distance approximately 4,050 kilometers from Heilongjiang Province to Hainan Island in the south.

Topography: The main topographic features include Qing-Zang (Qinghai-Tibet) Plateau 4,000 meters above sea level and Kunlun, Qin Ling, and Greater Hinggan ranges. The longest of the country's numerous river, Chang Jiang (Yangtze River) and Huang He (Yellow River), extend for some 6,300 and 5,400 kilometers, respectively.

Climate: Most of the country is in a temperate belt. Complex climatic patterns exist, ranging from cold-temperate north to tropical south. Precipitation varies regionally; temperatures range from minus 30°C in north in January to 28°C in south in July. There are alternating wet monsoons in summer, dry monsoons in winter.

Administrative Divisions: The country is divided into three governmental tiers. In 1987 twenty-nine provincial units comprise twenty-one provinces, five autonomous regions, and three centrally governed special municipalities; a middle tier consists of autonomous prefectures, counties, autonomous counties, cities, and municipal districts; and a basic level comprises townships, and villages.

Table 1 is a list of the administrative divisions. It also indicates which of the administrative divisions are involved in the Special Economic Zones, which will be treated in detail later in this volume.

The map in Figure 1 shows the whole country and the location of the various provinces. Then, as each province is discussed in the text which follows, a map will be repeated showing the position of that province within the country.

The following tabulation gives the names, addresses, telephone numbers and fax numbers of the principal ministries of the Chinese government as given in a recent reference (58). The department concerned with foreign affairs or foreign cooperation is cited in each case.

TABLE 1

Principal Administrative Divisions in China

1.	Anhui Province	22.	Ningbo (Ningpo) City and Development Zone
2.	Beijing Municipality		
3.	Dalian City and Development Zone	23.	Ningxia Hui region
4.	Fujian Province	24.	Qingdao City and Development Zone
5.	Fujhou City and Development Zone	25.	Qinghai Province
6.	Gansu Province	26.	Shaanxi Province
7.	Guangdong Province	27.	Shandong Province
8.	Guangxi-Zhuang Autonomous Region	28.	Shanghai Municipality
9.	Guangzou (Canton) City	29.	Shantou City and Development Zone
10.	Guizhou Province	30.	Shangxi Province
11.	Hainan Province	31.	Shenzen Development Zone
12.	Hebei Province	32.	Sichuan Province
13.	Heilongjiang Province	33.	Tianjin (Tientsin) Municipality
14.	Henan Province	34.	Xiamen Development Zone
15.	Hubei Province	35.	Xinjiang Uygur (Sinkiang) Autonomous Region
16.	Hunan Province		
17.	Jiangsu Province	36.	Xizang (Tibet) Autonomous Region
18.	Jiangxi Province	37.	Yantai City and Development Zone
19.	Jilin Province	38.	Yunnan Province
20.	Liaoning Province	39.	Zhejiang Province
21.	Nei Mongol (Inner Mongolia) Autonomous Region	40.	Zhuhai Development Zone

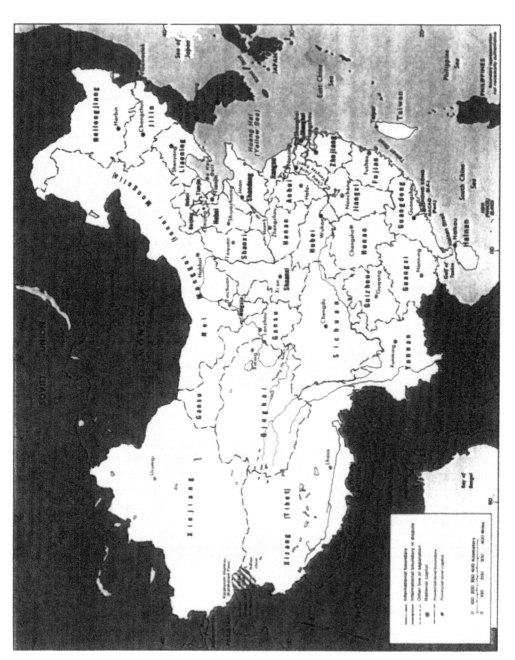

Figure 1:   Map of China - from "China—A Country Study" (4)

Ministry of Foreign Affairs
American and Oceanian Affairs Office
225 Chaoyangmennei Dajie, Beijing 100701
Tel: 513-5566 x4524, 552-167   Fax: 512-3237

Ministry of National Defense
Foreign Affairs Office
25 Huangsidajie, Deshengmenwai, Beijing 100011
Tel: 201-8305   Fax: 201-8356

Ministry of Public Security
Foreign Affairs Office
14 Dongchang'anjie, Dongcheng District
Beijing 100741
Tel: 512-1176

Ministry of State Security
Foreign Affairs Office
14 Dongchang'anjie, Dongcheng District
Beijing 100741
Tel: 524-4702/823-2340

Ministry of Civil Affairs
Foreign Affairs Office
147 Beiheyuan Dajie, Beijing 100721
Tel: 601-2629

Ministry of Justice
Foreign Affairs Office
11 Xizhuangli, Sanyuanqiao, Chaoyang District
Beijing 100016
Tel: 467-7144   Fax: 467-7351

Ministry of Finance
Foreign Affairs Office
3 Nansanxiang Lane, Sanlihe, Xicheng District
Beijing 100820
Tel: 852-8371   Fax: 851-3428

Ministry of Personnel
Foreign Affairs Office
12 Hepinglizhongjie, Dongcheng District, Beijing 100708
Tel: 421-3431, x525/421-8719   Fax: 318-8350

Ministry of Labor
Foreign Affairs Office
12 Hepinglizhongjie, Dongcheng District
Beijing 100716
Tel: 421-3431 x703/421-1624   Fax: 421-1624

Ministry of Geology and Mineral Resources
International Cooperation Office
64 Funeidajie, Beijing 100812
Tel: 601-8170   Fax: 601-7791

Ministry of Construction
Foreign Affairs Office
Xijiao Baiwanshuang, Beijing 100835
Tel: 832-3296   Fax: 839-3333

Ministry of Power Industry
International Cooperation Office
137 Fuyoujie, Xicheng District
Beijing 100031
Tel: 602-3816, 602-3879   Fax: 601-6077

Ministry of Coal Industry
Foreign Affairs Office
211 Hepingli Beijie, Beijing 100713
Tel: 421-3949   Fax: 601-6077

Ministry of Machine Building Industry
International Cooperation Office
46 Sanlihe, Xicheng District
Beijing 100823
Tel: 859-4970, 859-4962   Fax: 851-3867

Ministry of Electronics
International Cooperation Office
Wanshou Road, Beijing 100846
Tel: 822-1838   Fax: 822-1835

Ministry of Metallurgical Industry
Foreign Affairs Office
46 Dongsixi Dajie, Beijing 100711
Tel: 513-3322 x2107, 4107

Ministry of Chemical Industry
International Cooperation Office
Building 16, Hepingli Qiqu, Dongcheng District
Beijing 100013
Tel: 421-5693   Fax: 421-5982

Ministry of Railways
Foreign Affairs Office
10 Fuxingjie, Haidian District, Beijing 100844
Tel: 326-0990, 324-1855   Fax: 327-1295

Ministry of Communications
Foreign Affairs Office
10 Fuxinglu, Haidian District, Beijing 100845
Tel: 326-5544 x2421   Fax: 327-3943

Ministry of Posts and Telecommunications
Foreign Affairs Office
13 Xichanganjie, Beijing 100804
Tel: 602-0540   Fax: 601-1370

Ministry of Water Resources
Foreign Affairs Office
1 Baiguanglu'ertiao, Xuanwu District
Beijing 100761
Tel: 326-0192   Fax: 326-0365

Ministry of Agriculture
International Cooperation Office
11 Nongzhanguang Nanlu, Beijing 100026
Tel: 500-4363   Fax: 500-2448

Ministry of Forestry
Foreign Affairs Office
18 Hepingli Dongjie, Dongcheng District
Beijing 100714
Tel: 421-3278

Ministry of Internal Trade
Foreign Affairs Office
45 Fuxingmennei Dajie, Xicheng District
Tel: 839-1216   Fax: 601-8207

Ministry of Foreign Trade and Economic Cooperation
American and Oceanian Affairs Office
2 Dong Chang'anjie, Dongcheng District
Beijing 100731
Tel: 519-8328   Fax: 512-9568

Ministry of Culture
External Relations Office
Jia 83 Dong Anmenbeijie, Beijing 100722
Tel: 401-3157   Fax: 401-3149

Ministry of Radio, Film and Television
Foreign Affairs Office
2 Fuxingmenwai Dajie, Beijing 100866
Tel: 851-2176   Fax: 851-2174

Ministry of Public Health
Foreign Affairs Office
44 Houhai Beiyan, Xicheng District
Beijing 100725
Tel: 403-4433   Fax: 401-4331

People's Bank of China
Foreign Affairs Office
410 Fuchengmen Dajie, Beijing 100034
Tel: 601-1829   Fax: 601-4096

State Administration for Industry and Commerce
Foreign Affairs Office
8 Sanlihe Donglu, Xicheng District
Beijing 100820
Tel: 834-4246   Fax: 851-3394

Civil Aviation Administration of China
Foreign Affairs Office
155 Dongsixidajie, Beijing 100710
Tel: 401-2233   Fax: 401-6918

State Pharmaceutical Administration
Foreign Affairs Office
38A Beilishilu, Beijing 100810
Tel: 831-3344   Fax: 831-5648

General Administration of Customs
Foreign Affairs Office
6 Jianguomenwai Dajie, Beijing 100730
Tel: 519-5244   Fax: 512-6020

National Environmental Protection Agency
Foreign Affairs Office
115 Xizhimennei Nanxiaojie, Xicheng District
Beijing 100035
Tel: 601-5642   Fax: 601-5641

OPEN CITIES, DEVELOPMENT ZONES, AND REGIONAL ECONOMIES

Open Cities and Development Zones   One central element of China's open economic policy throughout the period since 1979 has been a gradual opening of certain designated areas, especially in the coastal Provinces, where foreign trade and investment has been promoted through preferential measures.   In 1979, the government decided to set up four special economic zones (SEZs)—Shenzhen, Zhuhai, and Shantou in Guangdong Province, and Xiamen in Fujian Province.   In 1988, Hainan Island was also designated an SEZ.   In these SEZs, foreign investors are provided with preferential treatment, including tax holidays, low corporate income tax rates, and other favorable tax provisions (5).

In April 1984, the government announced the opening of fourteen coastal cities to foreign investment, with preferential treatment similar to the SEZs.   The fourteen coastal cities are Dalian, Qinhuangdao, Tianjin, Yantai, Qingdao, Liangyungang, Nantong, Shanghai, Ningbo, Wenzhou, Fuzhou, Guangzhou, Zhanjiang and Beihai.   Since 1985, economic and technical development zones (ETDZs) have been set up within these cities to encourage the establishment of technologically advanced and export-oriented foreign-invested enterprises. (5)

In 1985, the government designated the Zhujiang (Pearl) River Delta, the Changjiang (Yangtze) River Delta, and the Southern Fujian Triangle as coastal economic development areas, and in 1988, these areas were expanded to cover Shandong Peninsula and Liaoning Peninsula.   These economic development areas encompass a large number of cities and counties, and are primarily aimed at developing export-oriented industries.

In 1989, the government announced a development project for Pudong in Shanghai—the Pudong New Area.   This area with a population of 1.4 million comprises a triangular area of 350 square kilometers across the Huangpu River.   Under current plans, the area will consist of five zones with different development objectives: finance and commerce, export processing, free trade, heavy industry, and science and education.   The Shanghai municipal government has issued a series of regulations ont he development of the Pudong New Area, including the Regulations of Shanghai Municipality for the Encouragement of Foreign Investment, which set forth the incentives for foreign companies to invest in Pudong. Basically, these incentives are identical to those available to foreign investors in the SEZs and ETDZs.

Free Trade Zones   Since September 1990, the government has approved the establishment of free trade zones in the coastal cities. A free trade zone, similar to an export processing zone in many countries, is an enclosed area where investors are exempt from import and export duties and domestic taxes if their products are sold outside the country. Besides export processing operations, investors are allowed to set up trading companies, banking and insurance services, and warehouses. These zones are still in the experimental stage, and few laws and regulations governing these zones have been issued by the government. As of March 1993, thirteen free trade zones have been approved by the government—Shatoujiao, Fujian, Guangzhou, Shantou (all in Guangdong), Fuzhou, Xiamen (both in Fujian), Waigaoqiao (in Shanghai), Dalian (in Liaoning), Zhangjiagang (in Jiangsu), Haikou (in Hainan), Qingdao (in Shandong), Ningbo (in Zhejiang), and Tianjin.

Although the most important function of these zones is to encourage export processing, it is common for Chinese enterprises to use the zones as a way to import foreign goods into the China market. U.S. companies interested in exporting to China through the zones should contact the city or zone administration directly.

Growing Economic Regions   China's twenty-nine Provinces, autonomous regions, and municipalities differ greatly in resource endowment and population distribution resulting in different degrees of economic development. The open economic policy pursued by the Chinese Government since 1979 focuses on the coastal areas which account for 40 percent of the country's population and over 50 percent of its gross national product. As a result, foreign investment activities over the past fifteen years have been concentrated in the Provinces and municipalities along the coast. Foreign direct investment in inland regions has been relatively low and is concentrated in a few areas, including Beijing and cities in Sichuan and Jilin (5).

The South Coast region (Guangdong, Fujian, and Hainan) is the leading recipient of foreign investment in China. Since 1979, Guangdong Province has absorbed about one-third of total foreign capital, success of market-oriented economic reforms, and geographic proximity to Hong Kong have enabled Guangdong to become perhaps the fastest growing economy in the world. Although less dynamic than Guangdong, Fujian Province has attained double-digit growth rates in recent years largely due to growing capital inflows from Taiwan. Hainan remains less developed, but with its enormous resources has great potential to become an economic center for foreign investors.

At present, U.S. companies have approximately 150 joint ventures and representative offices in Guangdong, with half of them in Guangzhou and one-third in Shenzhen. The number of U.S. investment projects in Fujian is relatively small (fewer than twenty), and most of them are in the Xiamen SEZ.

The East Coast region (Shanghai, Jiangsu, and Zhejiang) also has attracted large amounts of foreign capital in recent years. With highly market-oriented economies, Jiangsu and Zhejiang Provinces have grown about as quickly as Guangdong even without an external partner such as Hong Kong. Shanghai, the most advanced industrial city in China, has embarked upon an ambitious development program. Shanghai is slated to become a major trade, commercial, and financial center for Asia by the year 2010. Foreign investment and trade associated with the opening of Shanghai's Pudong New Area is likely to lead to accelerated growth in the whole East Coast region.

At present, Shanghai has 800 registered U.s. investment projects and over 200 representative offices. While many of the investments are small, approximately ninety of the Fortune 500 have activities there. To date, contracted U.S. investment in Shanghai is $1.57 billion.

The Northeast region (Liaoning, Jilin, and Heilongjiang) is a heavy industrial center with substantial petroleum, metallurgical, coal, chemical, and building materials industries.

In recent years, Japanese investors have been active there, but U.S. investors have not taken full advantage of the region's opportunities. Currently, U.S. companies have about sixty investment projects and twenty representative offices in the Northeast, most of which are in Liaoning Province, especially Dalian and Shenyang (5).

The Beijing—Tianjin region has become a growing economic and commercial center attracting large amounts of foreign investment. The ETDZ in Tianjin has been very successful in attracting foreign investors. Beijing is the headquarters of all key state trading corporations. Currently, U.S. companies have about 200 joint ventures and representative offices in Beijing.

POPULATION:

The 1982 census reported the total population of China to be 1,008,180,738; the official estimate at end of 1986 was nearly 1.1 billion with 1.4 percent annual rate of increase. Urban population was officially estimated at 382 million by end of 1985, or 37 percent of total. About 94 percent of population lives on approximately 36 percent of land.

Population estimates and projections in millions/are (49)

1950	1970	1990	2010	2025
554.7	830.7	1,139.0	1,395.3	1,512.6

The demographic statistics for China are in a class of their own. In size, China has the largest population of any country in the world: over 1.1 billion in 1992 according to the latest census whose data is just becoming available (1990). China accounts for over 1 in 5 inhabitants of the world, and 1 in 3 people in Asia. Despite its success in reducing family size, by 2025 China will still account for nearly one fifth of the world population.

EDUCATION:

In 1985, about 96 percent of primary school age children attended school as compared with about 20 percent before 1949. About 136 million students enrolled in more than 832,000 primary schools. The secondary level middle schools were divided into junior and senior stages; the majority of schools were at a lower level. About 48.6 million students attended some 104,800 secondary level institutions. Technical education emphasized. Intense competition exists for admission to more than 1,000 colleges and universities; there are about 1.7 million students in various higher educational institutions. Beijing and Qinghua universities and more than 100 other key universities are most sought after by college entrants (4).

HEALTH:

The level of health and medical care in China is improving. There is a system of national, provincial-level, and local facilities in urban and rural areas plus a network of industrial and state-enterprise hospitals. Traditional and Western medicine are both practiced. The average life expectancy was sixty-nine years in 1985. Many once widespread epidemic diseases now under control or eradicated.

DEFENSE ESTABLISHMENT

China's defense industrial complex produced weapons and equipment based predominantly on Soviet designs of the 1950s and 1960s. Because of a lack of foreign exchange, low short-term threat perception, and an emphasis on the other three of the Four Modernizations (agriculture, industry, and science and technology), China had decided to develop its defense industries gradually. It would rely primarily on domestic production, importing foreign technology only in areas of critical need.

The defense industries produced a wide range of military material. Large quantities of small arms and tanks were produced, and many were exported to Third World countries such as Iran. China had upgraded Soviet aircraft and was developing nuclear powered ballistic missile submarines, intercontinental ballistic missiles, and tanks equipped with infrared night vision gear and laser range finders.

Because defense was assigned the lowest priority in the Four Modernizations int eh 1970s, China's large defense sector has devoted an increasing amount of its resources to civilian production. For example, in the mid-1980s approximately one-third of the ordnance industry's output was allocated to civilian production, and the share was expected to rise to two-thirds by 1990. The defense sector produced a wide variety of products, ranging from furniture to telescopes, cameras to heavy machinery.

Despite the military's contribution to the industrial sector, in 1987 Chinese industry lagged far behind that of the industrialized nations. Much of industrial technology was seriously outdated. Severe energy shortages, transportation bottlenecks, and bureaucratic interference also hindered modernization. Although output was high in a number of industries, quality was often poor. However, China's industrial sector has made considerable progress since 1949. Output of most products has increased dramatically since the 1950s, and China now produces computers, satellites, and other high-technology items. The reform program introduced in the late 1970s brought an era of more rational economic planning and laid the groundwork for more balanced and sustained industrial growth. As of 1987 China's leaders were aware of the need for greater industrial efficiency and productivity and were striving to achieve these goals (4).

ARMED FORCES:

In 1987 the combined strength of combat support units of the People's Liberation Army (PLA) was just under 3 million. Ground forces were estimated at 2.1 million, the world's largest standing army. The Air Force was estimated at 390,000, the Navy estimated at 350,000, including those assigned to Naval Air Force, Coastal Defense Forces, and Marine Corps. The Strategic Missile Force was estimated at 100,000. In 1987 ground forces consisted of thirty-five main force armies comprising 118 infantry divisions, thirteen armored divisions, and thirty-three artillery and anti-aircraft divisions; seventy-three regional force divisions, about seventy main and regional force independent combat and combat support regiments. Major weapons systems included Type 34, Type 59, and Type 69 main battle tanks, Type 62 and Type 63 light battle tanks; various caliber howitzers and guns and anti-aircraft artillery. Air Force equipment included nearly 5,200 combat aircraft. Navy equipment included five nuclear powered submarines (three attack and two ballistic missile launching), 110 diesel attack submarines, forty-six major surface combatants (destroyers and frigates), 877 fast-attack craft (armed with guns, missiles, or torpedoes), nearly 900 other combatant and support ships and boats, and 780 Naval Air Force combat aircraft. The Strategic Missile Force included fifty medium-range ballistic missiles (range of 650 nautical miles), sixty intermediate-range ballistic missiles (range of 1,620 nautical miles), four limited-range intercontinental ballistic missiles (range of 3,780 nautical miles), and two full-range intercontinental ballistic missiles (range of 8,100 nautical miles) (4).

The position of the Chinese military has now been complicated by the fact that the military has become China's biggest business empire. Nurtured on privilege and largely exempt from civilian controls, military-run businesses have flourished as a virtual state within a state. They are using their connections to win business licenses, form profitable joint ventures with foreigners and even stretch the law by skirting taxes or dodging import duties. "They're in such a powerful position that no one dares touch them," says a Western diplomat in Beijing. Even the rapidly declining revenues from overseas sales of Silkworm anti-ship missiles, F-7 fighters and ballistic missiles appear to be financing science and technology research academies, not military procurement, the analysts say.

Today, China's military runs a pharmaceutical empire with earnings of $1 billion a year; it produces satellite television dishes and cellular phones as well as food, clothing, trucks, boats, motorcycles and contact lenses.

FOREIGN TRADE:

Small by international standards but growing rapidly in size and importance, foreign trade represented 20 percent of GNP in 1985. Trade is controlled by Ministry of Foreign Economic Relations and Trade and subordinate units and by Bank of China, foreign exchange arm of the central bank. Substantial decentralization and increased flexibility in foreign trade operations has been seen since late 1970s. Textiles constitute the leading export category. Other important exports included petroleum and foodstuffs. Leading imports included machinery, transport equipment, manufactured goods, and chemicals. Japan has been the dominant trading partner, accounting for 28.9 percent of imports and 15.2 percent of exports in 1986. Hong Kong has been the leading market for exports (31.6 percent) but the source of only 13 percent of imports. In 1979 United States became China's second largest source of imports and in 1986 was third largest overall trade partner. Western Europe, particularly the Federal Republic of Germany is also a major trading partner (4). The RMB (renminbi) yuan is inconvertible and may not be exported. The symbol for yuan is ¥. The official exchange rate was 5.79 ¥/$US in June 1993. Swap market exchange rates were in the range of 8.5-9¥/$ at the time. Current rates should always be checked.

THE HONG KONG-CHINA CONNECTION

China and Hong Kong have greatly intensified their economic interaction in recent years. According to Hong Kong government statistics, China is now Hong Kong's major market for exports (29.6 percent of total exports) and major supplier of imports (37.1 percent of total imports). The territory has developed a huge re-export trade, which now accounts for almost 75 percent of its total exports. Hong Kong's position as entreport to the world and a window on China is becoming increasingly more important as much of its manufacturing facilities are moving across the border into southern China to take advantage of lower labor and land costs. The shift in Hong Kong's economy is illustrated by the fact that the number of people employed by manufacturing establishments dropped by 25 percent between 1980 and 1991 while the number of trading entities almost quintupled in the same period—mostly to handle China's trade (5).

Based on publicly available figures on foreign direct investment, China is the number one foreign investor in Hong Kong. More and more Chinese companies are listing locally in order to access the territory's financial markets. According to PRC statistics, Hong Kong receives 47 percent of China's exports and supplies 25 percent of its imports, making Hong Kong China's most valuable trading partner. Meanwhile, Hong Kong is the largest foreign investor in China. While China exhibits double-digit economic growth, Hong Kong traders and investors are able to ride the wave of economic expansion.

For American firms operating in China, the importance of Hong Kong as an entreport has increased greatly in recent years. Some $2.3 billion of U.S. goods were re-exported to China through Hong Kong in 1992. Moreover, China has relied heavily on Hong Kong for its exports to the U.s. market. In 1992, about $18 billion of Chinese goods were transshipped to the United States through Hong Kong, accounting for 70 percent of China's exports to the United States.

In Hong Kong, many of the 38,000 registered Hong Kong trading companies are eager to represent U.S. companies and products in China. In general, Hong Kong trading companies are small and tend to be specialized, both in the type of activities involved and in the number of products handled. They specialize in importing or exporting or re-exporting, and mostly do not mix these activities. They generally handle very few products, and many of them specialize in just one or two products. Export trading companies usually serve as a risk buffer between overseas buyers and local manufacturers—guaranteeing quality and on time delivery, for example. Import trading companies serve primarily as marketing agents for brand name overseas manufacturers, with whom they usually develop and maintain strong relationships.

Many companies begin their foray into the China market by first establishing operations in Hong Kong. The headquarters of many international firms, Hong Kong is a highly competitive modern service economy offering a complete spectrum of companies available to assist foreign firms in conducting China trade. Although China has become much more accessible to foreign business people in recent years, many continue to rely on Hong Kong as a base of operations due to its well-developed offices representing Chinese industrial, financial, and provincial interests, its proximity to two of China's special economic zones—Shenzhen and Zhuhai, and the territory's close economic and commercial ties with the Pearl River Delta, one of the most dynamic economic regions in the world.

Many companies are also establishing hybrid operations whereby their expatriate staff reside in Hong Kong and commute to plants or technical centers across the border in Guangdong Province. The new-to-market exporter should consider whether or not a potential agent/distributor in Hong Kong should represent his firm in the PRC.

In 1997, Hong Kong will become a "Special Administrative Region" of China. The Chinese Government has stated that Hong Kong's economic system will not change for 50 years after 1997. While it is difficult to predict Hong Kong's future, indications are that the territory will continue to thrive after 1997. China's growing investment in Hong Kong is predicted on the assumption by the Chinese Government that its capital will continue to generate income well beyond 1997. China needs Hong Kong's infrastructure to sustain its current policy of fostering economic growth. Moreover, the current Chinese leadership has pointed with prided to the economic growth of the southern regions of China—a direct result of Hong Kong investment and management. All in all, post-1997 Hong Kong will likely continue to play a pivotal role in China's trade and investment relations with the outside world.

Gordon Wu (Princeton University - class of 1957) is bullish on the future of Hong Kong and as Hong Kong born Chinese entrepreneur of great success is probably as entitled to such an opinion as anyone alive. He says: "I know exactly what will happen after 1997-1998," he said. "China has tried every possible economic policy since 1949, the Great Leap Forward, central planning, the Cultural Revolution, you name it, private plots, communes, all sorts of things. And finally they tried this little pitch called open door and reform. Now look at the refrigerators and color TV's. I don't think they want to change. And actually, it is that reason I have so much confidence."

CHANGING INTERNATIONAL TRADE PATTERNS

During the 1950s China's primary foreign trading partner was the Soviet Union. In 1959 trade with the Soviet Union accounted for nearly 48 percent of China's total. As relations between the two countries deteriorated in the early 1960s, the volume of trade fell, decreasing to only just over 7 percent of Chinese trade by 1966. During the 1970s trade with the Soviet Union averaged about 2 percent of China's total, while trade with all communist countries made up about 15 percent. In 1986, despite a trade pact with the Soviet Union, Chinese-Soviet trade, according to Chinese customs statistics, amounted to only 3.4 percent of China's total trade, while trade with all communist countries fell to 9 percent of the total (4).

By the mid-1960s Japan had become China's leading trading partner, accounting for 15 percent of trade in 1966. Japan was China's most natural trading partner; it was closer to China than any other industrial country and had the best transportation links to it. The Japanese economy was highly advanced in those areas where China was weakest, especially heavy industry and modern technology, while China was well endowed with some of the important natural resources that Japan lacked, notably coal and oil. In the 1980s Japan accounted for over 20 percent of China's foreign trade and in 1986 provided 28.9 percent of

China's imports and 15.2 percent of its exports. Starting in the late 1970s, China ran a trade deficit with Japan.

Beginning in the 1960s, Hong Kong was consistently the leading market for China's exports and its second largest partner in overall trade. In 1986 Hong Kong received 31.6 percent of Chinese goods sold abroad and supplied about 13 percent of China's imports. Hong Kong was a major market for Chinese foodstuffs and served as a transshipment port for Chinese goods re-exported to other countries.

The United States banned trade with China until the early 1970s. Thereafter trade grew rapidly, and after the full normalization of diplomatic and commercial relations in 1979, the United States became the second largest importer to China and in 1986 was China's third largest partner in overall trade. Most American goods imported by China were either high-technology industrial products, such as aircraft, or agricultural products, primarily grain and cotton.

Western Europe has been important in Chinese foreign trade since the mid-1960s. The Federal Republic of Germany, in particular, was second only to Japan in supplying industrial goods to China during most of this period. China followed a policy of shopping widely for its industrial purchases, and it concluded deals of various sizes with nearly all of the West European nations. In 1986 Western Europe accounted for nearly 18 percent of China's foreign trade, with imports exceeding exports.

Third World countries have long served as a market for Chinese agricultural and light industrial products. In 1986 developing countries purchased about 15 percent of Chinese exports and supplied about 8 percent of China's imports.

There are serious problems in U.S. trading with China in areas involving patent infringement and intellectual property rights. Pirated Chinese editions of books and computer software are being scrutinized carefully and could well constitute a serious impediment to China's entrance into the new World Trade Organization in 1995.

As of early 1995, however, China agreed to a number of antipiracy areas covering audiovisual and published products aimed at China's entry into the WTO.

CHAPTER 1

PLACES—PROVINCES, CITIES AND ECONOMIC ZONES

The following area-by-area summary of the characteristics and trends has been drawn from various sources with heavy emphasis on a United Nations publication (2).

It is interesting to note that China is exporting products and know-how to a wide variety of both underdeveloped and developed countries.

1. ANHUI PROVINCE

Situated on the lower reaches of the Yangtze River, Anhui Province is a producer of rice, rapeseed, cotton, tobacco, hemp, tea and silk; and it has deposits of coal, iron, copper and other minerals. The Yangtze flows through the province, and on it are the river ports of Anqing and Wuhu that are open to foreign investment and trade.

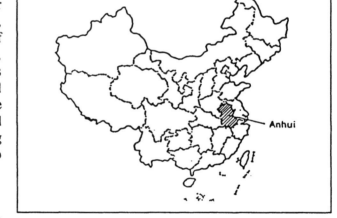

Provincial capital: Hefei
Total Area: 139,000 sq km
Population: 54,600,000 at year-end in 1989

Foreign Trade

The total export and import volume of Anhui Province in 1990 amounted to $US 740 million, an increase of 5.7 percent over $US 700 million in 1989.

The total purchase and purchase on commission basis of commodities for export went up to RMB 3.61 billion yuan, an increase of 10.1 percent against RMB 3.28 billion yuan in 1989.

Exports for the year 1990 totalled $US 654 million, an increase of 14.7 percent against $US 570 million in 1989. Export took up 5.3 percent of the provincial GNP of RMB 58.8 billion yuan, accounting for 1.3 percent of the national export. Export commodities were classified as agricultural, light industrial and heavy industrial products. The export of agricultural and sideline products amounted to $US 160 million, making up 24.5 percent of the total export; that of the light industrial products was $Us 326 million, 49.8 percent of the total; that of the heavy industrial products was $US 168 million, 25.7 percent of the total. As compared with the figures of 1989, the agricultural exports dropped by 2.1 percentage points, the light industrial exports dripped by 1.2 percentage points, and the heavy industrial exports rose by 3.4 percentage points. As classified according to international trade standards, the primary products valued at $US 303 million, accounting for 53.7 percent of the total. As compared with the figures of 1989, the value of primary products, dropped by 2.1 percentage points while the finished products rose by 2.1 percentage points.

There are 810 export commodities. In them, fourteen commodities exceeding $US 10 million were frozen pork, canned food, bean cake, tea, feather, filature silk, cotton yarn, cotton cloth, singlets and vests, silk cloth, garments, steel products, coal, petroleum products. The total value of the fourteen commodities reached $US 281 million. Thirteen commodities each valued between $US 5 million and 20 million were rice, sesame seed, honey, dried sweet potato, cotton seed cake, rape seed cake, rabbit hair yarn, down quilts, synthetic fiber yarn, synthetic fiber cloth, bath towels, black and white TVs and motors. The total value of the thirteen commodities was $US 85 million. Putting the above twenty-seven commodities together, the total value was $US 366 million, making up 56 percent of the export.

These exports were sold to 114 countries and regions; 27.1 percent valued at $US 177 million to Hong Kong and Macau; 17.6 percent at $US 115 million to Japan; 14.4 percent at $US 94 million to European Community; and 7.8 percent at $US 51 million to the United States and Canada.

Total imports for 1990 were $US 83 million, 37 percent less than $US 131 million in 1989, in which technological equipment took up 24.1 percent at $US 20 million; industrial raw materials took up 51.8 percent at $US 43 million; commodities for agricultural production took up 10.8 percent at $US 9 million; market commodities took up 13.3 percent at $US 11 million. As compared with those of 1989, the import of technological equipment dropped by 10.3 percentage points; industrial raw materials dropped by 5.3 percentage points, commodities for agricultural production rose by 9.6 percentage points and market commodities rose by 72 percentage points.

The major imports were: $US 21 million from Japan, accounting for 25.3 percent of the total; $US 17 million from European Community, making up 20.5 percent; $US 15 million from Hong Kong, making up 18.1 percent; $US 8 million from the United States and Canada, making up 9.6 percent; $US 8 million from Australia, making up 9.6 percent; $US 4 million from the former Soviet Union and Eastern European countries, making up 4.8 percent of the total.

Utilization of Foreign Capital

Seventy contracts were approved for the utilization of foreign capital, with a contracted foreign capital value of $US 87.21 million, up 64.9 percent over $US 52.89 million in 1989. Ten contracts were on foreign loans, involving $US 66.67 million; fifty-three contracts on direct investment, with a capital value of $US 9.2 million; seven contracts on other foreign investment, involving $US 1.34 million. The actual value of utilization of foreign capital in the year was $US 50.27 million, a drop of 39.2 percent as compared with $US 82.65 million in 1989. In the utilization of foreign capital, foreign loans were $US 36.73 million, foreign direct investment was $US 9.61 million, other foreign investment was $US 3.93 million.

Among the fifty-three projects on foreign direct investment, there were forty-six equity joint ventures with a contract foreign capital value of $US 16.89 million; one contractual joint venture involving $US 50,000; and six wholly foreign-owned enterprises involving $US 2.26 million. These investment projects were all productive enterprises, covering ten sectors, such as textile, machinery, electronics, agriculture and communication. The foreign capital came from Switzerland, Australia, Italy, the United Kingdom, Canada, the United States, Japan, Hong Kong and Taiwan Province. The value of exports, including exports on commission basis, from operating enterprises with foreign investment amounted to $US 14.18 million, an increase of 89.1 percent against $US 7.5 million of 1989.

Technology Import and Export

Eighty-one contracts were signed on import of technology and equipment with a contract value of $US 33.69 million, an increase of 33 percent against $US 25.34 million in 1989. The imported projects mainly covered the fields of light industry, textile, machinery, chemistry and electronics, which came from the United States, Japan and European Community, etc.

Thirty-seven contracts were signed on export of technology, in a value of $US 17.81 million, an increase of 1.5 times against $US 7.11 million in 1989. The export projects included electronic dust removal technology and equipment for electrical furnaces, establishment of pottery and porcelain plants, plastic plants, technical service for the construction of cement plants and island planning, transfer of Chinese medicine technology, cooperative development of computer software. The market of technology export had been expanded to twenty-three countries and regions, such as the United States, Germany, France, the United Kingdom and Japan, etc.

Foreign Economic Cooperation

Sixteen contracts for undertaking overseas contracted projects and labor service were signed with a contracted value of $US 30.42 million, an increase of 66.3 percent against $US 18.29 million in 1989; a turnover of $US 6.34 million was achieved, an increase of 7.3 percent against $US 5.91 million in 1989; at the end of 1990, there were 213 personnel working abroad. The main contracted projects were: the construction of the Sri Lanka Pilot Plant for Manufacture and Popularization of Rice-based Products, the design of a dam in Iran, the construction of the Population and Health Center in Burundi and the Expansion of the Bujumbura Textile Factory in Burundi, etc. The main projects of labor service cooperation were: provision of cooks on Chinese dishes to Finland, Tunisia and Sri Lanka; provision of engineers and agronomists to factories and farms in the United States, Germany,

Tunisia and Nigeria.

*   *   *   *

The Beijing office of the Province is located at:

17 Beisanhuan Donglu
Beijing 100029
Tel: 4217647, 4218783
Fax: 4239505

Another China contact which may be helpful to users of this volume is:

The Commission of Foreign Economic Relations & Trade of Anhui Province
162 Jinzhai Road, Hefei, China
Tel: 331788   Fax: 0551-331872

2. BEIJING MUNICIPALITY

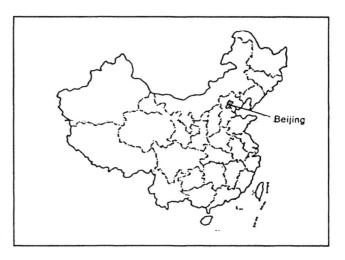

Beijing, capital of the People's Republic of China is situated in the northern part of the North China Plain. It is a city directly under the jurisdiction of the Central Government and the political and cultural center of the country. This ancient city has grown into one of the nation's biggest manufacturing centers in the decades after the inception of the People's Republic. Greater Beijing spreads over and area of 16,807.8 sq km and has a population of 10,211,000 at year-end in 1989. Beijing's gross industrial output ranks second (behind Shanghai's) among municipalities in China. There are more than fifty institutes of higher education, including Beijing University and Qinghua University. Qinghua University is a center for scientific research. The city has designated a high-tech zone near Beijing University that is attracting foreign computer makers.

Foreign Trade

In 1990, the export and import value of Beijing totalled $US 1.74720 billion, decreased by 1.34 percent over $US 1.77094 billion in 1989.

The value of purchase for foreign trade was RMB 5.587 billion yuan, an increase of 13.97 percent over RMB 4.902 billion yuan in 1989.

The total export value amounted to $US 1.32290 billion, an increased of 13.89 percent over $US 1.16157 billion in 1989, and accounted for 12.76 percent of the municipal GNP. It also accounted for 2.54 percent of the nation's export value, ranking No. 10 in the country.

There were forty-four items of commodities each with export value exceeding $US 5 million, and their combined value was $US 670.77 million, accounting for 50.70 percent of the total. Among them were 21 items of commodities each with export value exceeding $US 10 million, including cotton cloth, cotton-polyester blended fabrics, singlet and vests, sweaters and trousers, woolen sweaters, acrylic sweaters, cotton garments, chemical fiber garments, woolen garments, down products, carpets, radio cassette recorders, color TV sets, enamel, limitation antiques, gold ornaments, steel products, coals, coke, automobiles and tools. These commodities were exported to 125 countries and regions. The total import value amounted to $US 424.30 million, a decrease of 30.37 percent over $US 609.37 million.

The import structure was as follows: means of production with the value of $US

386.8 million, accounting for 91.6 percent of the total; means of livelihood $US 37.50 million, 8.84 percent. Classified by international trade standards, primary products were valued at $US 80.88 million, accounting for 19.06 percent of the total; industrial manufactured products $US 343.42 million, 80.94 percent.

The major imports were: various fabrics, valued at $US 48.76 million, machinery and spare parts $US 34.91 million, wool $US 33.81 million, gold $US 31.19 million, non-ferrous metals $US 11.98 million, chemical fertilizer $US 11.30 million, silk $US 10.69 million, steel products $US 10.32 million, synthetic fiber $US 8.01 million, and building and decorating materials $US 5.13 million. The total value of these products was $US 206.10 million, accounting for 48.57 percent of the total.

The commodities were imported from thirty-five countries and regions.

Utilization of Foreign Capital

Some 283 contracts on utilization foreign capital were signed and approved with the contract value of $US 234.94 million, an increase of 22.05 percent over $US 192.495 million in 1989. Among these contracts, thirty-three were of foreign loans amounting to $US 116.90 million; 241 were of foreign direct investment $US 116.88 million and nine were of other foreign investment $US 1.16 million.

The foreign investment actually utilized was $US 406.41 million, a decrease of 17.91 percent over $US 495.068 million in 1989. Among the actually used foreign investment, foreign loans were $US 127.43 million, foreign direct investment $US 276.96 million and other foreign investment $US 2.02 million.

Of 241 projects of foreign direct investment, 210 were equity joint ventures, one was contractual joint venture and thirty were exclusively foreign-owned enterprises. Of these enterprises, 216 projects were productive and twenty-five were non-productive. Classified by trades, thirty-three were involved in textile, eighteen in chemical industry, fifty in electronics, eight in machinery, eight in instruments and meters, eighty-six in other industries, six in agriculture, forestry, animal husbandry fishery and water conservancy, three in construction, one in transportation, eight in house property and public facilities, eight in tourism and twelve in restaurants and catering trade.

The foreign investment was from eighteen countries and regions. The major investment came from the following countries and regions: 108 from Hong Kong with the value of $US 37.81 million; thirty-two from Taiwan Province, $US 25.20 million; forty-four from the United States, $US 10.66 million; twenty-nine from Japan, $US 8.92 million.

By the end of 1990, 382 foreign-invested enterprises had been put into operation, of which, 165 were put into production in 1990. The output value of the year totalled RMB 5,125.61 million yuan, the income from sales was RMB 5,823.44 million yuan with the total value of profits amounting to RMB 247.03 million yuan, and the foreign exchange earnings reached $US 103.28 million. The balance of income and expenditure of foreign exchange was achieved with the surplus amounting to $US 68.89 million.

Technology Import and Export

Some eighty-five contracts of technology and equipment import were signed and approved with the contract value of $US 71 million, a decrease of 34.26 percent over $US 108 million in 1989.

Technology and equipment were introduced from seventeen countries and regions. They were mainly from Germany with the value of $US 15.02 million, accounting for 21.15 percent of the total; from Hong Kong, $US 12.01 million, 16.90 percent; from France, $US 11.17 million, 15.73 percent; from the United States, $US 9.17 million, 12.92 percent; from Finland, $US 4.70 million, 6.62 percent and from Japan, $US 3.41 million, 4.80 percent.

The imported technology and equipment were mainly involved in such industries as municipal facilities construction, energy, communications, textile, automobile, chemical industry, electronics, light industry, machinery and metallurgy. About 100 projects were put into operation in 1990, and the investments realized amounted to RMB 1.2 billion yuan. The increased output value would reach RMB 1.3 billion yuan after the operation of these projects with the profits and taxes amounting to RMB 300 million yuan, and the foreign exchange earnings would reach $US 60 million. Most of these projects were the ones for export and foreign exchange earning.

166 contracts of technology export were signed and approved with the contract value of $US 40 million, a decrease of 20 percent over $US 50 million in 1989. $US 29.7 million were earned in 1990, increased by two times over $US 10 million in 1989. The technology export mainly covered mature industrial technology and complete plant, and products of high and new technology. For example, the technology and complete plant for rods and bars productions were exported to Indonesia with the value of $US 3.9 million.

Foreign Economic Cooperation

In 1990, 109 contracts were signed on foreign contracted projects and labor service with the contract value of $US 37.56 million, in increase of 78.94 percent over $US 20.99 million in 1989. The business turnover achieved was $US 10.56 million, an increase of 3.83 percent over $US 10.17 million in 1989. Altogether 364 people for labor service were sent abroad, and 336 people remained abroad at the end of the year. The labor service personnel were sent to thirty-two countries and regions such as the United States, Japan, the former Soviet Union, Germany, Australia, Tanzania, Tunisia, Mozambique, Norway, Bolivia and Hong Kong. The major contracted projects included the resident buildings in Zanzibar, veterinary school in Rwanda, the children's playground in Guinea, and the Buddhist pagoda in Sri Lanka. The completed project was the House of the Youth in Tunisia.

Beijing undertook eight projects for foreign aid, all were construction ones. There were six recipient countries, i.e. Tunisia, Mauritania, Zaire, Tanzania, Sri Lanka and Mozambique, 120 people for foreign aid were sent abroad, and twelve people remained abroad at the end of the year.

Beijing received one item of aid from a United Nations organization and one bilateral aid item with the value totalling $US 1.98 million. They were Beijing Training Centre of

Communications Administration and the Vocational Education Centre of Chaoyang District in Beijing. Twenty-eight recipient projects were under performance with the value of $US 52.33 million. Five projects had been completed with the value of $US 2 million. All the completed recipient projects achieved good social and economic results, of which the laser safety testing and researching item filled int he gaps in China's laser testing field.

Beijing has ten newly established overseas enterprises, of which, the Chinese investment amounted to $US 3.6 million, all were investments in materials. These enterprises were: Li Guo International Trade and Transportation Co., Ltd., Da Yan Inc., Ltd., and Soft Ware Know-how Co., Ltd., in Japan; the Beanflower Restaurant, Inc. in the United States; the Salon-Qi Nu Li Co., Ltd., Beijing; Duo Ji Restaurant and Xin Ji Foodstuffs Co., Ltd. in Russia; Canberra-Beijing Dong Lai Shun Hotel in Australia; Bei Luo Foodstuffs Co., Ltd. in Italy and Xi Da Computer-Sinology Co., Ltd. in Germany. In 1990, the total business turnover of overseas enterprises, were $US 224 million, equivalent to that of 1989.

Some data on import and export markets for Beijing are summarized in Tables 2-4 (2).

* * * *

A China contact which should be helpful to users of this volume is:

Beijing Foreign Economic Relations & Trade Commission
3 Nan Li Shi Road Tou Tiao, Beijing
Tel: 862015, 866511, Fax: 8010353

Table 2. Export Commodity Structure - Beijing

Classified by agriculture, light and heavy industries				*Classified by international trade standard*			
Category	Export value ($US million)	Percentage of the total		Category	Export value ($US million)	Percentage of the total	
		1990	1989			1990	1989
Agricultural and sideline products	57.01	4.30	7.10	Primary products	160.65	12.14	10.04
Light industrial products	958.98	72.50	68.30				
Heavy industrial	306.91	23.20	24.60	Industrial manu-factured products	1,162.25	87.86	89.96

Table 3. Main Import Markets - Beijing

Country/region	Import value ($US million)	Percent of the total
Hong Kong	135.47	31.93
United States	91.97	21.68
Japan	80.03	18.86
Singapore	13.27	3.13
Germany	12.11	2.85
Australia	9.97	2.35
Thailand	7.33	1.73
Switzerland	5.51	1.30

Table 4. Main Export Markets - Beijing

Country/region	Export value ($US million)	Percent of the total
Hong Kong	289.06	21.85
Japan	185.12	13.99
United States	164.28	12.42
Germany	82.36	6.23
Former Soviet Union	44.24	3.34
Australia	43.41	3.28
Singapore	41.23	3.12
Canada	31.98	2.42
Italy	29.10	2.20
The Netherlands	27.35	2.07

3. DALIAN CITY & DEVELOPMENT ZONE

The city of Dalian, located on the south of the Liaodong Peninsula, is the economic trading base on the sea for the northeastern region of China and the eastern region of the Inner Mongolian Autonomous District. It is the largest harbor and the largest industrial and tourist city in northern China (8). See Figure 3, page 191 and Figure 4, page 193.

Dalian is situated at a longitude from 120 degrees, 58 minutes E. to 123 degrees, 31 minutes E. and at a lattitude from 38 degrees, 43 minutes N. to 40 degrees, 10 minutes N. Across the sea to the south, it faces the Shandong Peninsula. It connects to the vast northeastern continent in the north and reaches the Yellow Sea in the east and the Bohai Sea int he west. The urban area of Dalian is 2,415 sq. km. and the area of the whole city is 12,574 sq. km. Since Dalian is surrounded by threes seas, it has features of ocean climate weather. However, it has four distinct seasons with temperate and monsoon weather. The average temperature in Dalian during the year is 10°C. and it is free of frost for 180 to 210 days. The average volume of rain during the year in Dalian is between 600 and 1,000 mm.

Dalian controls the Lushun zone, the Ganjiangzi zone, the Shahekou zone, the Xigang zone, the Zhongshan zone, the Jinzhou zone, the Wafangdian city, the Zhuanghe prefecture, the Xinjin prefecture and the Changhai prefecture. The urban population of Dalian is 2.4 million people and the population of the whole city is 5.18 million people.

Dalian has rich mineral resources. It has good quality limestone with reserves totalling approximately 1.1 billion tons. Dalian also has reserves of over 10 million tons of different minerals such as silica, magnetite, quartz mineral and dolomite. In addition, there are reserves of barite, asbestos, diamond, copper, lead, mica, phosphorus and marble. Dalian has inexhaustible resources of architectural sandstone which can be provided as a raw material to the architectural and the other industries.

At present, Dalian has a total of over 3,400 different industrial enterprises and it has 680,000 industrial employees. Dalian has developed various industries such as mechanics, metallurgy, petroleum chemical engineering, building materials, textiles, light industry, electronics and the food processing industry. Its exports include ships, diesel locomotives, precision machine tools, electronics, metallurgical mining products, petroleum, chemical engineering products, textile products, apparel and arts and crafts (8).

Agriculture

Dalian, which has rich agricultural resources, is the most important area for fruit and seafood products in China. The coastline in Dalian is 898 km. and the aquaculture area is 1.2 million acres. Because the coastline is very broad, the production conditions for the fishing industry are particularly favorable. The seafood products include fish, shrimp, trepan, abalone, fan shell, clams, etc. The city of Dalian has a superior capability in ocean fishing, artificial cultivation, seafood processing and fishing machine production.

Science and Education

The scientific technology and education are very advanced in the city of Dalian. Currently, Dalian has over 200 different types of scientific research and development institutes and over 110,000 researchers. Dalian has a large capacity for the absorption of scientific technological development, important project research and advanced skills. It has thirteen high level universities with 36,000 students. The China Industrial Scientific Technology Management Training Center in Dalian that was organized by China and the U.S.A. is located at Dalian Science and Engineering University. In addition, the economic development division of the United Nations and the International Marine Organization set up a marine training center in the Dalian Marine Institute.

Labor

The resources and the quality of labor are superior in Dalian. The total number of middle-level technicians comprises two-fifths of the total number of laborers. The high level of universities, job training colleges, business high schools and the other types of middle high schools serve various classes of laborers totalling 32,000 each year in Dalian. In order to raise the quality of its labor pool, the city emphasizes on-the-job training before taking a job, and it creates over 400 various training classes that educate over 12,000 people every year.

Legal Climate

While it is improving the fundamental environment, Dalian also pays a lot of attention to the supplemental environment. In order to protect the legal rights of foreign investors, in addition to current China laws and policies, Dalian makes many local laws and policies involving taxes, land, expenses, and employee hiring. Dalian has also established foreign law firms specializing in trade and a legal development information center. To provide legal services for foreign economic activities and to promote efficiency and the standard of service, the city and townships have created an external economic cooperative technology control center that coordinates and unifies all businesses in the city involved in foreign economic technological cooperation. It provides a good service, a production data market, a labor market, a capital market, and an information market to foreign investors.

Water, Power, Gas

The power supply in Dalian has been improved. In addition to a rebuilt power plant, Dalian has constructed a 500 kv. transformer project from Haichang to Dalian and added two 350,000 kw. generators from the Huanan Dalian Power Plant.

The water supply in the city has been improved. In 1983, Dalian finished the first project to channel the Biliu River to Dalian City. At present, the second project of the water transportation system is in progress and the transportation capacity is over 230,000 tons for daily requirements.

The gas supply is also developed in Dalian City. The capacity of supply in the whole city is 470,000 cubic meters and the accessibility of gas and liquefied gas has reached 81%.

Telecommunications

Dalian has developed a 40,000 line digital phone system. It also has 1,000 long distance digital exchanges that allow telephone direct dialing for domestic and international use. The urban area and three northern prefectures can direct dial to major cities in China and to over ten countries and regions of the world. Dalian has express mail services to over 150 cities in China and to over 100 countries. The city has also established some facilities such as a 500 line digital telegram automatic switching machine, a post office building and a post transportation pier.

Air Transport

The Dalian Zhoushuizi Airport is an important aviation center in the northern area of China. It is one of sixteen international airports open to the world. This airport has over ten routes to major domestic cities such as Beijing, Shanghai, Guangzhou, Harbin, Xian, and Wulumugi. In addition, it has three regular direct flights per week from Dalian to Hong Kong. Regular international flights from Beijing to Dalian and to Tokyo have been opened for three years and are running very well. In 1988, it also established the air cargo flights from Dalian to America, Romania, Holland and Canada.

Land Transport

Dalian's railroad and freeway are also very advanced. The railroad is connected to the Northeast and Huabai Railroad networks. The density of the freeways in Dalian is 32 km. per 100 sq. km. The Dalian Highway which was developed in September 1990 is 375 km. long and has greatly improved the transportation capacity in Dalian.

Sea Traffic

Dalian is a pivotal area for water and land transportation in the northern region of china, and it is also an external economic trading base for the Helongjiang Province, the Liaoning Province, the Jilin Province and the eastern region of Inner Mongolia. In order to expand the handling capacity in the Dalian Harbor, it has increased its number of berths to fifty-eight. Twenty-nine of the berths are deep sea berths and serve shipments of 10,000 tons or more. Another three berths which served over 10,000 ton shipments are floating tube berths. The 100,000 ton oil tankers and 50,000 ton cargo ships can be moored at any time to load and unload the products. At present, the Dalian Harbor has a mechanized system for loading and unloading loose cargo and has over 500 whole container loading and unloading machines. The Dalian Harbor has engaged in trading activities that involve over 140 countries and regions. It has over 2,000 commercial ships to get in and out of the harbor.

The Dalian Harbor has three international goods transportation ships with ten scheduled trips to and from Kobe and Yokohama in Japan, Hong Kong, Hamburg, and Rotterdam. In 1991, the Dalian Harbor had a handling capacity of 54.72 million tons. Much effort has gone into the zone construction of the Daya Bay New Harbor. In 1991, the four common berths and 25,000 to 30,000 tons of whole containers were built bringing the annual handling capacity to 2.6 million tons.

Economic and Technological Development Zone

The Dalian Development Zone has built a 45 km. inner freeway and a cross-sea freeway. It also has a pure water plant serving 50,000 tons of water every day, 54,000 digital telephone switching systems, a 63,000 voltampere transformer and a liquefied gas station which can supply 5,200 tons of gas annually. A disposal plant with a daily handling capacity of 15,000 tons of polluted water is under construction. The basic installation in the 5 sq. km. area have been developed and the services reach a 9 sq. km. area. While the Dalian Development Zone is constructing its basic and residential facilities, it is also paying attention to the supplemental investment environment. It has improved the policies and rules that include several preferential treatments, foreign economic contracts, enterprise registration, labor wages and land usage.

By the end of 1991, the Dalian Development Zone approved 257 foreign investment enterprises to be established. The figure of total investment is over USD 900 million of which USD 350 million has been used. The foreign investment amount is approximately 70% of the gross investment amount.

Dalian Port

The port is in Dalian Bay at 38°56'N, 121°39'E. The port has thirty-five berths, twenty-eight of which are for ships of 10,000 tons and more cargo work is done with ships berthed alongside. Its largest oil terminal can handle oil tankers of up to 100,000 tons. The port currently handles forty-five million tons a year.

The port is equipped with cranes and various types of mobile machines, belt conveyers, floating cranes and large-sized installation for loading and unloading. The maximum lifting weight is 600 tons.

Tugboats, lighters, oil boats and water boats are available. Wharves are rail served, so that cargo can be handled directly between ship and train and through transport between land and sea which is expected. There is a shipyard in the locality and general repairs can be carried out on foreign vessels.

Some of the characteristics of Dalian City and its seaport are reviewed in the following table. (Table 5.)

Table 5. Dalian - Salient Statistics (2)

Area (sq. km.)	12,574	20 (special economic zone alone
Population	2,368,500 (urban)	
Economic situation	Industrial production in 1989	
	Light industry:	6,237.78 (mil. yuan)
	Heavy industry:	9,865.54 (mil. yuan)
	Value of export:	$US 564.17 mil
	Harbor's handling volume:	5,092 (10 thousand tons)
	Investment in capital assets:	2,874.81 (mil. yuan)
	Total value of industrial production:	16,089.42 (mil yuan)
Utilization of foreign capital	Utilization of foreign capital in 1988	
	Contract number:	222
	Foreign contractual value:	$US 255.91 mil.
	Effected foreign investment:	$US 213.46 mil.
	Number of foreign direct investment:	128
	Total foreign direct investment:	$US 74.88 mil.
	Utilization of foreign capital in 1989	
	Contract number:	243
	Foreign contractual value:	$US 388.86 mil.
	Effected foreign investment:	$US 167.38 mil.
	Number of foreign direct investment:	144
	Total foreign direct investment:	$US 66.37 mil.
	Up to end of 1989	
	Joint ventures:	242
	Contractual joint ventures:	39
	Foreign wholly-owned enterprises:	17
	Total:	298
	Japanese enterprises:	56 (up to the end of 1988)
Infrastructure:	Port:	forty-eight berths for production, including twenty-three above 10,000 ton berths.
	Power:	Electric supply capacity: 9 mil. KWH
	Water:	Daily supply capability: 600,000 tons.
	Telecommunication:	Equipped with advanced facilities, direct domestic and international call.

Land use and work-site development fee in the economic and technological development zone:

	I	II
Land for production	7	6
Land for non-production	10	8

The export and technologically-advanced enterprises shall be exempted from the land use fee within five years.

Labor service charge
(Unit: yuan/month)

250 (average)
120% of the real wages of state-owned enterprises of the same trade in the locality.

Other fee

Water: 0.22 yuan/ton
Electricity: 0.21 yuan/kwh

Priorities

Machinery, petrochemistry, shipbuilding, light and textile industry, metallurgy, building materials.

Local preference

The income tax rate on joint venture in economic and technical development zone is 15%. A newly established joint venture can be exempted from income tax in the first two profit-making years, and allowed a 50% reduction of income tax in the third, fourth and fifth years. After the tax exemption period expires, technologically-advanced enterprises subject to a rate of 10% for another three years and export enterprises shall pay income tax at reduced rate of 10% provided that their value of export products in that year amounts to 70% or more of the value of their products for that year. Joint ventures shall be exempted from local income tax within seven years.

Official department in charge is:

Dalian Municipal Committee of Foreign Economic Relations and Trade
20, Bai Yu Street, Zhongshan District, Dalian
Telephone: (0411) 237925

4. FUJIAN PROVINCE

Situated on the south-eastern Chinese coast, Fujian province is separated from Taiwan Province by a strait of the same name. It has an area of 121,400 sq. km. and a population of 28,960,000 by year end in 1989. Fujian has a 3,320 km. of coastline with many deep harbors. More than 40 percent of Fujian is forested, and such deposits as quartz, pyrophyllite, kaolin clay, marble, iron, tungsten, niobium, tantalum and barite have been discovered in different parts of the province. The major ports on the coast are Xiamen and Fuzhou, the provincial capital (2).

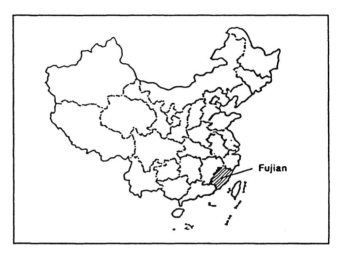

Fujian ranks second after Guangdong province, in attracting foreign capital. Fujian is known for its food processing and other light industries.

It is a predominantly mountainous area, rich in timber. The subtropical climate allows rice, sweet potatoes, tea and citrus fruit to grow in the valleys. Fishing has always been the chief occupation but the subsistence lifestyle forced many people to emigrate to Southeast Asia and, in the 19th century, to Hawaii and California.

Foreign Trade

In 1990, the total export and import of Fujian Province was valued at $US 3.171 billion, an increase of 32.29 percent against $US 2.397 billion in 1989.

The year's total volume of export goods purchased was RMB 7.599 billion yuan, which increased by 85.25 percent as compared with that of RMB 4.102 billion yuan in 1989.

The whole export valued at $US 2.238 billion, 34.67 percent higher than $US 1.662 billion in 1989, taking up 14.31 percent of the Province's GNP and 4.20 percent of the country's total export volume. It ranked the 7th among the nation's total export volume.

The export commodities included $US 248 million for farm and sideline products, taking up 11.08 percent of the total export volume, $US 1.617 billion for light industrial goods, 72.25 percent, and $US 373 million for heavy industrial products, 16.67 percent. The proportion of farm and sideline products decreased by 1.29 percentage points as against 1989, while the proportion of light industrial products and heavy industrial products increased by 1.09 percentage points and 0.20 percentage points respectively. According to the classification of international trade standard, primary products were $US 487 million, accounting for 21.76 percent and industrial finished products were $US 1.751 billion, taking up 78.24 percent.

There were twenty-four varieties of staple commodities each with its export value over $US 10 million, and their export value amounted to $US 819 million, accounting for 36.60 percent of the total export. Fourteen commodities each with export value over $US 20 million were color TV receivers, sports shoes, gold jewelry, canned mushrooms, nylon bags, canned asparagus, plastic slippers, frozen prawn, nylon umbrellas, PV shoes, Oolong tea, electronic watches, stone carved goods, and cement, the export value of which amounted to $US 716 million, taking up 31.99 percent of the total export.

The markets for the Province's export goods covered 125 countries and regions, and the major ones were: Hong Kong, $US 1.057 billion, Japan, $US 286 million, the United States, $US 268 million, Germany, $US 105 million, Singapore, $US 56 million, and Taiwan Province, $US 65 million. The volume of export to these countries and regions totalled $US 1.837 billion which took up 82.08 percent of the Province's whole export.

The total import of the Province was $US 933 million, which increased 26.94 percent as against that of $US 735 million in 1989. Of the import goods, means of production valued $US 667 million while means of subsistence valued $US 266 million, taking up 71.49 percent and 28.51 percent of the total import respectively. The major import commodities were gold, $US 57.15 million, electronic parts and components, $US 55.16 million, chemical fiber fabric, $US 49.95 million, and palm oil, $US 48.53 million, the import value of which totalled $US 211 million, taking up 22.62 percent of the Province's whole import.

The markets for the Province's import commodities were forty-three countries and regions, of which the major ones were: Hong Kong, $US 457 million, Japan, $US 152 million, the United States, $US 58 million, Singapore, $US 39 million, Malaysia, $US 22 million, Germany, $US 17 million, Indonesia, $US 13 million, the former Soviet Union, $US 11 million and Taiwan Province, $US 45 million, and totally there were $US 814 million worth of import from these countries and regions, which took up 87.25 percent of the total import.

Utilization of Foreign Capital

With the approval of the provincial authorities concerned, $US 1.236 billion worth of contracts for utilization of foreign capital were concluded in the year, a 28.62 percent increase over that of $US 961 million in 1989, in which, foreign loans were $US 58.53 million. The number of foreign direct investment projects was 1,043 with a contracted value of $US 1.162 billion. Other foreign investment was $US 15.99 million.

The actually-utilized foreign capital was $US 380 million, a 2.81 percent decrease as compared with that of $US 391 million in 1989, in which, foreign loans were $US 58.53 million, foreign direct investment amounted to $US 290 million and other foreign investment valued $US 31.13 million.

Of 1,043 foreign direct investment projects, 432 were equity joint ventures with a contracted value of $US 285 million, ninety-four were contractual joint ventures with a value of $US 73 million, and 517 were wholly foreign-owned enterprises with a value of $US 804 million. And of the total foreign direct investment, productive projects took up 90 percent and more. In terms of sectors and business lines, there were forty-two in agriculture, 930 in industry, one in construction, five in transportation, ten in commerce, forty-six in real estates, two in culture and arts and seven in other lines.

The foreign investments were mainly from Hong Kong, Japan, the United States and other Southeast Asian countries and regions, among which, 607 projects were from Hong Kong with a contracted value of $US 565 million, 380 from Taiwan Province with $US 462 million, five from the United Kingdom with $US 22 million, twenty-four from Japan with $US 23.96 million, fourteen from the United States with $US 20.40 million and eight from Singapore with $US 10.37 million.

In the year, enterprises with foreign investment which had been put into operation realized an industrial output value of RMB 8.447 billion yuan, 46.52 percent higher that that of RMB 5.765 billion yuan in 1989, taking up 28 percent of the total industrial output value. Export from these enterprises amounted to $US 797 million which increased by 71.03 percent as against $US 466 million in 1989, taking up 35.61 percent of the Province's whole export value (2).

Technology Import and Export

The Province signed fifty-six contracts to import technologies and equipment with a contracted value of $US 29.82 million, an increase of 6.39 percent as compared with that of $US 28.03 million in 1989. The imports were mainly from Japan, the United States, Germany and Taiwan Province of China, among which, twenty-two projects from Japan with a contract value of $US 8.56 million, eight projects from the United States ($US 5.71 million), five projects from Germany ($US 4.15 million), two projects from Italy ($US 2.67 million) and five projects from Taiwan Province of China ($US 2.48 million). The main projects were precision casting production line, technical equipment for polyurethane production, electric spark machining equipment, and bicycle circle-forming equipment. In the year, 181 projects were put into running. When these projects yield economic results, a new output value of RMB 1.87 billion yuan, a new profits and tax of RMB 520 million yuan and export earnings of over $US 50 million yuan can be raised.

Foreign Economic Cooperation

Some 1,167 contracts for undertaking overseas engineering projects and labor service cooperation were signed in the year with a contracted value of $US 176 million, a decrease of 5.38 percent as against that of $US 186 million in 1989. The Province realized a turnover of $US 161 million, an increase of 12.59 percent over $US 143 million in 1989. In the year, 7,640 labor service workers were sent abroad. At the end of the year, 9,686 persons worked abroad. They were mostly dispatched to thirty countries and regions such as Macau, Singapore, Saipan of the United States, Hong Kong, Taiwan Province, etc., and the projects which the Province had undertaken were: the Drainage Works at Tian Suiwai Road, Hong Kong, Hong Kong Zai Road Project, Hualong Building and Huadu Hotel in Macau.

The Province had undertaken five China-aided projects by way of supplying complete sets of equipment, which were mainly the projects in agriculture, water and electricity, municipal engineering, etc., with its recipients of Antigua and Barbuda, Benin, Algeria, Sierra Leone and Equatorial Guinea, sixty-five technicians were sent to the projects and there were 149 technicians remained working outside by the end of the year.

The Province received nine projects with $US 12 million grant from international organizations and bilateral or multilateral organizations mainly for public health for women and babies in the exemplary counties, planned immunity, training for primary and nursery teachers, and disaster relief.

There were two overseas approved for establishing in Argentina and Thailand, with the Chinese investment of $US 1.12 million.

*   *   *   *

The Beijing office of the province is located at:

Madian, Beitaipingzhuang
Beijing 100088
Tel: 2011311
Fax: 2011307

Another China contact which may be helpful to users of this volume is:

Fujian Foreign Economic Relations & Trade Committee
17 Hualin Road, Fuzhou
Tel: 572707
Fax: 556133

Fujian Foreign Economic Relations & Trade Committee
23 Wushan Road, Fuzhou 35001
Tel: 555308
Fax: 55732

5. FUZHOU CITY & DEVELOPMENT ZONES

Fuzhou City is the capital of Fujian Province which faces Taiwan across the sea. Fuzhou City is located on the southeast coast of China at a latitude of 119 degrees, 17 minutes E. and a longitude of 26 degrees, 4 minutes. The city is located on the Fuzhou Basin, the biggest basin in this province, measuring 489 sq. km. and surrounded by mountains. The Ming River flows through this basin from west to east then flows into the East Ocean (8).

Fuzhou has a subtropical monsoon—oriented humid climate. The winter is warm and short. The summer is hot with a comparably long rainy season. The average annual temperature is 19.6 c. The average rainfall volume is 1,300 mm. and average number of days with frost is ten. The direction of the wind which is often influenced by typhoons is from the southeast for the majority of the time and occasionally from the northwest.

The total population of Fuzhou City is 5.4 million people and the total area is 11,968 sq. km. which includes three city districts, one suburb and one port that controls eight towns. The downtown has an area of 1,043 sq. meters and a population of 1.3 million people of which the majority are from the Han tribe and some other small tribes.

Natural Resources

The essential natural resources in Fuzhou are: (1) Minerals such as potassium, aluminum, porcelain clay, river sand, granite, green-stone plank and certain amounts of rare metals (e.g. uranium, etc.) (2) Natural energy such as water power, wind power and ocean tide power. (3) Hot springs. (4) Seafood. (5) Agriculture including flowers, fruits (litchi, longan, orange, banana, etc.) tea leaves, peanuts, sugar cane, etc.

Industry

Fuzhou City has a well-developed foundation in metallurgy, machinery, light industry, electronics, textiles, chemistry, plastic materials, food, pharmacology, building materials, arts and crafts, automobiles, etc. The city's industry includes approximately 3,000 products within 138 sectors of sixteen industrial categories produced by 2,800 companies. There are at least 300 popular items exported to more than 100 countries or areas worldwide.

With one-fourth of the total industrial production and one-fifth of the total revenue of Fujian Province, Fuzhou is the strongest in the province. It also provides an ideal environment for financial investment, tourism and a lot of other services for foreign investors and tourists.

Foreign Investment

From 1979 to 1991, after Fuzhou was totally opened to foreign investment, the city had received 986 contracts involving foreign investment with USD 800 million, of which USD 500 million was used. By 1990, there were 160 Taiwanese investment parties involved.

The categories which foreign parties invest in include industry, garments, business, tourism, real estate, public facility construction and other services. The investment for production is 98% of the total investment. Among the existing 387 companies which fall into three types; joint ventures, contractual ventures and foreign investment, the majority are technical-export and fund-accumulating enterprises.

Transportation

Fuzhou City is in the most important position for transportation in Fujian Province. Fuzhou's port has twenty-six berths including three for ships exceeding 10,000 tons and two for 5,000 tons. Ships go to every major domestic port and more than thirty foreign ports. The distance from Fuzhou to Taiwan is 130 nautical miles and from Fuzhou to Hong Kong is 488 nautical miles. It take twenty minutes to travel to Taiwan by airplane and eight hours by ship. There are six berths being built for both classes of 10,000 ton ships and 5,000 ton ships including facilities from 80,000 to 100,000 container transfers in the Fuzhou Port and more 5,000 ton wharves scouting locations outside the Ming River. There are twenty-one inland sailing routes with a total mileage of 556 km. The Fuzhou Airport now owns twenty-two domestic or overseas air routes and averages eighty flights per week. Its railroad connects to the whole country after the construction of the Outside-Fu Railroad Line was finished, the total transportation capacity doubled. The whole country is accessible by car and there will even be express transportation to Guangzhou, Shanghai and Hong Kong.

Telecommunications

The digital telephone system has 50,000 lines directly connected to the major domestic cities and forty-one overseas locations. The capacity was increased by an additional 20,000 lines at the end of 1991. Fuzhou City now has 130 overseas long distance phone lines to 120 locations and international express delivery service to twenty-two locations. The major post facilities have been established and the telecommunications system has been planned and built. At the end of 1990, the exchange stations were built.

Water, Electricity, Gas

Fuzhou now has twenty-three electric transformer stations with a capacity of over 1 million kw, which provide 210 million kw. hours per year. By the end of 1992, the construction of the Huanan Thermoelectric plant and the Shuako Hydraulic power plant which will each provide 1.4 million kw. will be finished. There are seven waterworks which provide 600,000 tons of water daily and are being expanded. The gas plant started to operate at the end of 1990. It is estimated that the production of liquefied gas provides 100,000 households.

Financial Institutions

Fuzhou has most of the financial institutions which represent 704 organizations of the whole province. These include eighteen foreign exchange and foreign affair institutions, one insurance company engaged in business with foreign countries, one foreign exchange adjustment center and foreign or joint venture banks branch offices.

Educational Institutions

Fuzhou is the educational center for the whole province. There are twelve colleges, 380 high schools including vocational schools and secondary technical schools, and adult teacher colleges and a variety of short-term vocational training schools including forty public institutions and twenty-six private training schools which service 590,000 technical professionals.

Human Resources

Fuzhou contains a multitude of professionals and skilled laborers. Every year, there are 4,000 college graduates, 10,000 high school graduates, 5,000 graduates from secondary technical school, and 8,000 students in school. Concurrently, there are many people trained in short-term adult vocational schools which prepare them for careers suitable for the foreign investors' needs such as finance, radio, accounting, electricity, image tube, car repair, fresh water seafood cultivation, driving, tourism, cooking, etc.

Economic and Technological Development Zones

Maweiqingzhou, on the north coast at the end of the Ming Ring River has a developed area of 4.4 sq. km. In the past five years, this area has become well established to enable foreign investors to access services and resources easily. So far, seventy-seven projects including fifty-four projects invested by foreign investors have been approved to be produced in this zone. Sixty-five enterprises have been established int he zone including twenty-nine with Taiwanese or foreign investment. Manufacturing facilities have been set up for more than 150 products in the following areas: optics, mechanics, electricity, light industry, food, metallurgy, building materials, animal feed, etc. Transportation by railroad, ship and airplane are very convenient in this region. Also, the digital exchange system has been set up for 2,000 lines. There is a thermo power plant which provides 1.4 million km. of energy and a hydraulic plant which provides 65,000 tons of water daily. Fresh water can be obtained directly from the Ming River.

Starting in May 1989, the State Council approved the following areas for Taiwanese investment: The Haicang and Xinglin in the Xiamen Special Economic zone and the undeveloped area in the Mawei Economic Technological Development Zone (about 1.8 sq. km.).

The Fujian Province faces Taiwan across the sea and has the same people and culture in both areas. This area is especially suitable and convenient for Taiwan's investors.

Haicang Taiwanese Investment Zone This port is located on the west side of Xiamen facing the old city of Xiamen and to the north coast at the point where the Kowloon River empties into the ocean. The Haoyu Harbor of this town and the First Harbor of old Xiamen are the two most important shipping points. Xinglin is in the north of this town and Longhai County is in the west. The remaining areas of this town are surrounded by the sea. The depth of the water is about 12 to 15 meters so that many berths which can accommodate 50,000 ton to 100,000 ton ship could be built in this area. Haichan has the Dowchang Expressway to Changchow and the Yensho Railroad within 6 km. of the town. The distance from downtown to the Xiamen Airport is 10 km.

The population of Haicang is about 34,000 people. The total area of the town is 61.23 sq. miles and most of the area is flat. The undeveloped available area is approximately 40 sq. km. There are fifteen dams which provide 3.3 million sq. The construction of the Haoyu Thermo Power Plant which will provide 600 kw. of energy will be finished by 1993.

Xinglin Taiwanese Investment Zone This area is located in the middle of Xiamen to the north of Haicang, southeast of Kuko, and north west of the sea. It has an area of 65.41 sq. km. and a population of 56,000 people. From 1985, this zone began to be established an industrial area and it now has more than ten middle-sized factories in the following industries: glass, textiles, sugar-making, artificial fiber, artificial fertilizers, building materials, etc. In 1988, this zone became a formal district.

Xinglin has two harbors which can accommodate 1,000 ton ships, the Yensha Railroad and the Shazhang Expressway. In addition, there are four more expressways and two railroad stations (Xinglin & Qianchang). The distance is only 5 km. from this area to the Xiamen International Airport. There are also twelve dams and two thermo power plants.

The Fujian government is now planning to provide Taiwanese investors the option of renting land or buying shares. The government will establish the regulations, laws and related institutions to provide the best service for interested Taiwanese investors.

* * * *

Useful contacts in Fuzhou City include:

Fuzhou Chemical Industry Bureau
Tel: 86 591 556312 Fax: 251271

Fuzhou ETDZ Administration
Tel: 86 591 368 2253 Fax: 368 2346

6. GANSU PROVINCE

Lying on the upper reaches of the Yellow River, Gansu is a land locked province in Northwest China through which ran the ancient Silk Roak that linked China with West Asia.

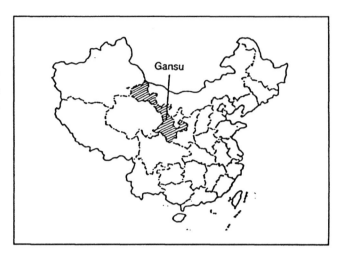

Total Area: 453,700 sq. km.

Population: 21,719,000

Capital: Lanzhou

Foreign Trade

The total volume of Gansu's exports and imports reached $US 202.14 million in 1990, up 8.25 percent over $US 186.74 million in 1989.

The volume of goods purchased for 1990 amounted to RMB 1,040.38 million yuan, an increase of 23.45 percent over the figure of RMB 844.17 million yuan in 1989.

Its export volume was $US 185.67, up 21.05 percent over $US 153.38 million in 1989, making up 4.18 percent of the Provincial GNP, 0.36 percent of the national total exports.

In the composition of export commodities, farm and sideline products were valued at $US 43.59 million, making up 23.48 percent of the total export volume, its proportion reduced 0.42 percentage point over 1989; light industrial products were valued at $US 56.56 million, making up 30.46 percent of the total export value, it proportion reduced 1.94 percentage points over 1989; heavy industrial products were valued at $US 85.52 million, making up 46.06 percent of the total export value, its proportion rose 2.36 percentage points over 1989. Classified by SITC system, primary products were valued at $US 91.6 million, making up 49.33 percent of the total export volume; industrial manufactured goods were valued at $US 94.07 million, making up 50.67 percent of the total export volume (2).

Table 6. Commodities each with export value above $US 3 million - Gansu Province

Value Range	Commodity	Export Value ($US million)	Percent of total export
Above $US 10 million, 2 items	Ferrosilicon and handmade carpet	22,34	12,03
Between $US 5-10 million, 2 items	Zinc ores and garments	10.96	5.90
Between $US 3-5 million, 5 items	Sodium sulphate anhydrous, radio recorder set, oil pump, lentil beans, bearings	20.22	10.89

The commodities were exported to fifty-eight countries and regions. Among them, $US 54.82 million were sold to Hong Kong, making up 29.53 percent of the total export value; $US 38.31 million were sold to Japan, making up 20.63 percent; $US 29.09 million were sold to Western Europe, making up 15.67 percent; and $US 14.12 million were sold to the United States, making up 7.6 percent.

The total value of imports amounted to $US 16.47 million, down 50.63 percent from the figure of $US 33.36 million in 1989. All the import commodities were means of production. Among them, primary products amounted to $US 5.5 million, making up 33.39 percent of the total import value; industrial manufactured goods amounted to $US 10.97 million, making up 66.61 percent. The major import commodities were: complete sets of equipment, $US 3.46 million, making up 21.01 percent of the total import value; steel sheet, $US 3.3 million, making up 20.04 percent; chemical materials, $US 1.43 million, making up 8.68 percent. The major import markets were: Hong Kong, $US 8.37 million, making up 50.82 percent of the total import value: Japan, $US 3.46 million, making up 21.01 percent.

Utilization of Foreign Capital

In 1990, nineteen contracts for the utilization of foreign capital were approved, involving contracted foreign funds of $US 21.04 million, down 64.12 percent from $US 58.64 million in 1989. Of these, two on foreign loans involving foreign funds of $US 4.5 million; eight on foreign direct investment with $US 2.92 million; nine on other foreign investment with $US 13.62 million. $US 4.71 million was actually used, up 26.7 times over 1989, among which, $US 2.4 million were foreign loans, $US 1.54 million for foreign direct investment, $US 770,000 for other foreign investment.

Out of the eight foreign direct investment projects, seven were for equity joint ventures, and one for wholly foreign-owned enterprise, and seven for the productive projects. They were involved in the trades such as machinery, chemical industry, medicine, food, service, etc.

The foreign funds were from six countries and regions such as the United States, Switzerland, Hong Kong, Japan, etc. Of the projects, three from the United States with contracted foreign funds of $US 9.23 million; two from Switzerland with $US 2.44 million; and eight from Hong Kong with $US 3.1 million.

Technology Import and Export

The Province signed thirteen contracts for importing technology and equipment, costing $US 12.57 million, an increase of 35.60 percent over $US 9.27 million in 1989. It actually used $US 9.4 million, up 182 percent over $US 3.33 million in 1989.

Technology was imported from the following countries: five contracts with Japan, two with the United States, two with Germany, and four with Hong Kong. The imported technology and equipment were used in petrochemicals, machinery, light and textile industries, electronics, post and telecommunications, metallurgy, etc.

Foreign Economic Cooperation

The Province signed twenty-two contracted projects and labor service contracts, with the value of $US 135.75 million, up 32.66 percent over $US 102.323 million in 1989. The turnover reached $US 41.7 million, up 2.6 times over $US 11.70 million in 1989. All the year 403 people were dispatched abroad. By the end of 1990, 363 people worked abroad. The major constructing projects were: the international technical training center and highway engineering in Zimbabwe, the bleachers of the Independence Square in Ghana, the well digging and water supply engineering in Cameroon, the Huizhou 26-1 engineering in Singapore, etc.

The Province implemented six economic aid programs in foreign countries covering medical care and health, civil construction, etc. The recipient countries were: Zimbabwe, Madagascar, Togo, Cape Verde and Tanzania. In the year 118 people were sent abroad. By the end of the year, 122 people worked abroad. One aid project was completed in the year.

The Province implemented forty-four multilateral and bilateral aid projects with $US 16.9 million. They were mainly from the international organizations such as UNFPA, UNCF, UNDP and WFP as well as Canada, Japan and Australia, etc. The main aid projects included the comprehensive economic developing project of Huining county from the Government of Canada, the cultural relics' preservation project in Dunhuang from Japan and the agricultural system research project from Australia, etc.

Two enterprises were set up abroad involving $US 790,000 of Chinese investment. They were Longxin Company Ltd. in Singapore and Nanfang Feilong Company Ltd. in Australia.

* * * *

The Beijing office of the province is located at:

17 Beisanhuandonglu, Chaoyang District
Beijing 100029

Tel: 4223878 Fax: 4214020

Another useful China contact for users of this volume might be:

**Gansu Provincial Foreign Relations & Trade Commission
188 Dingxi Road, Lanzhou, China
Tel: (0931) 417915 Fax: (0931) 418083**

7. GUANGDONG PROVINCE

Guangdong

Situated on the South China coast, adjacent to Hong Kong and Macao, Guangdong is one of the richest and most economically developed provinces in China. It is a producer of rice, freshwater fish, sugarcane, pineapples, bananas, litchis, oranges and other subtropical fruits. It has three special economic zones—Shenzhen, Zhuhai and Shantou, two coastal open cities—Guangzhou and Zhanjiang and three open areas on the deltas of the Pearl, Hanjiang and Jianjiang rivers.

Total area:	178,000 sq. km.
Population in 1989:	60,249,800
Provincial capital:	Guangzhou City

The annual Guangdong (formerly Canton) Trade Fair, held in the provincial capital of Guangzhou, was for many year Western executives' first window into the Chinese market. The province, one of the first to actively seek overseas investment, has maintained a distance from Beijing, helped partly by its proximity to Hong Kong and partly by the Cantonese dialect, incomprehensible to many northern Chinese.

Guangdong has been the recipient of the largest amount of foreign investment in China, most of it coming from the transfer of light manufacturing from Hong Kong. However, it has a poorly developed chemical industry compared with Shanghai. Although a major refining center, it has major gaps in its petrochemical production chain, and many of its downstream chemical companies lack economy of scale.

China's two potentially largest chemical projects—Shell's refinery and petrochemical complex and Amoco's purified terephlalic acid plant—are planned in the region. In addition, under the country's latest five year plan, two major ethylene projects are being developed by local enterprises, and they are seeking foreign partners for downstream projects.

The most ambitious foreign investment plan so far is the Shell project—a $6 billion refinery and petrochemical complex at Huizhou, near Shenzhen.

Foreign Trade

In 1990, the total export and import volume of Guangdong Province amounted to $US

16.309 billion, increased by 25.46 percent over $US 12.999 billion in 1989.

The total volume of export commodities purchased was RMB 23.423 billion yuan, with an increase of 10.25 percent over RMB 21.245 billion yuan in 1989.

The total export volume of Guangdong Province was $US 11.018 billion, up 34.89 percent against $US 8.168 billion in 1989, accounting for 37.38 percent of GNP of the province of RMB 141 billion yuan, and 21.16 percent of the total volume of export of the whole country, ranking the first in all the provinces, regions and cities of the country.

Of the province's total export volume, specialized foreign trade corporations was $US 3.518 billion; industry and trade corporations, $US 364 million; local foreign trade corporations, $US 2.294 billion; foreign trade corporations under the ministries and commissions of the State Council, $US 457 million; enterprises with foreign investment, $US 3.724 billion; and earnings by processing with supplied materials, manufacturing with supplied samples, assembling with supplied parts, and compensation trade, $US 661 million. Besides the export undertaken by the subsidiary foreign trade corporations under ministries and commissions of the State Council in Guangdong, the export value of the province was $US 10.56 billion.

Export commodities were sold to 161 countries and regions, of which #US 8.543 billion to Hong Kong, accounting for 80.90 percent of the total export volume; $US 403 million to the United States, accounting for 3.82 percent; $US 288 million to Japan, accounting for 2.73 percent, $US 166 million to Macau, accounting for 1.57 percent; $US 140 million to Singapore, accounting for 1.33 percent.

Import commodities totalled $US 5.749 billion, increased by 19.00 percent against $US 4.831 billion in 1989. Of them, the volume of primary products was $US 1.033 billion, accounting for 17.97 percent of the total import volume; the industrial finished products $US 4.716 billion, accounting for 82.03 percent; the imports for the means of production, goods in shortage and imported technology and equipment and key spare parts accounting for 81 percent. The main import commodities were complete equipment, various kinds of mechanical and electronic equipment, chemical fertilizer, agricultural chemical, steel products, rubber and chemical industrial materials and grain, etc.

Utilization of Foreign Capital

Guangdong signed and approved 7,196 contracts on utilizing foreign capital, with contract value at $US 3.168 billion, decreased by 12.56 percent against $US 3.623 billion in 1989. Of them, 47 foreign loans with a value of $US 303 million; 3,042 were foreign direct investment, with a value of $US 2.69 billion; 4,107 were other foreign investment, with a value of $US 175 million.

The actual use of foreign capital was $US 2.023 billion, decreased by 15.67 percent against $US 2.399 billion in 1989. Of them, the foreign loans were $US 441 million; foreign direct investment was $US 1,460 billion; and other foreign investment was $US 122 million.

Among the 3,042 foreign direct investment projects, there were 1,213 equity joint ventures, 1,018 contractual joint ventures, and 811 wholly foreign-owned enterprises. Of them, the productive projects accounted for more than 90 percent of the total projects with foreign direct investment. They scattered in the following fields: industry, 2,907 projects; transportation, telecommunication and post communication, 25 projects; farming, forestry, animal husbandry, fishery and water conservancy, 47 projects; and other fields, 63 projects.

Foreign direct investment mainly come from Hong Kong, Macau Taiwan Province, Japan, Philippines, Thailand, Malaysia, Singapore, Indonesia, Kuwait, United Arab Emirates, Republic of Korea, Germany, France, Belgium, United Kingdom, Peru, Bolivia, Canada, the United States, Australia, etc. Among them, 2,432 projects were invested by Hong Kong enterprises with the volume 2,109 billion, accounting for 78.40 percent of the total foreign investment.

By the end of 1990, 7,079 foreign investment enterprises had been put into operation, 810 had been confirmed as export-oriented enterprises and 114 technologically advanced enterprises. The export volume of the year was $US 3.724 billion, increased by 63.56 percent over that of 1989, accounting for 35.26 percent of the total export volume of the province. The number of the "processing with supplied materials, manufactured with supplied samples, assembling with supplied parts, and compensation trade" enterprises had reached 20,000, with 1.37 million employees.

The province has become so economically independent from Beijing that central government funding for provincial investment had dropped from 80% in 1979 to only 2%.

Technology Import and Export

Some thirty-four contracts on import of technology and equipment were signed, with a contract value or $US 70.2617 million, decreased by 62.43 percent against that of 1989. The import projects were mainly from the following countries: the United States, $US 22.7613 million; Switzerland, $US 16.527 million; Germany, $US 13.193 million; Japan, $US 11.118 million. The expenditure of the import projects of energy, transportation, post and telecommunications, and raw materials was $US 39.95 million, accounting for 56.86 percent of the total.

Seventy-six projects were contracted for technology export, with a contract value of $US 29.352 million, 1.26 times over $Us 12.9992 million in 1989. Of them, technology export amounted to $US 22.824 million, and technological products export $US 6.528 million.

Foreign Economic Cooperation

Some 997 contracts on foreign projects and labor service abroad were signed with a contract value of $US 97.63 million. The business turnover was $U 107 million. By the end of the year, 8,812 labor service personnel were working abroad.

Guangdong undertook fourteen foreign economic aid projects in eleven countries including Zaire, Papua, New Guinea, Mauritius, Antigua and Barbuda, Madagascar, Sri Lanka, Somali, Zambia, the Congo. The above mentioned projects were involved in light industry, agriculture, transportation, hydropower, etc. Eighty-five sets and 2,340 mechanical and electrical products were provided for foreign aid projects. By the end of the year, 244 engineers and technicians were carrying out the projects abroad.

In 1990, a joint venture was established in Brazil, with the investment of Chinese side $US 300,000.

There were 248 items of commodities each with export volume exceeding $US 5 million, totalling $US 6.82536 billion, accounting for 64.63 percent of the total export volume.

Table 7. Composition of export commodities—Guangdong Province

Classified by agriculture, light and heavy industries			Classified by international trade standard		
Item	Export value ($US million)	Percentage of total export 1990 1989	Item	Export value ($US million)	Percentage of total export 1990 1989
Agriculture and sideline products	1.068	10.12 12.84	Primary products	2.037	19.29 24.91
Light industrial and textile products	7.668	72.61 69.04			
Heavy industrial products	1.823	17.27 18.12	Industrial manu-factored products	8.523	80.71 75.09

Table 8. Main export commodities—Guangdong Province

Value Classifications	Commodities	Export value ($US billion)	Percentage total
13 commodities each with export value over $US million	Garments, cotton cloth, color TV sets, electronic components, radio cassette recorders, leather shoes, pottery and porcelain, toys, drawn-works, bicycles, ceiling fans, leather rubber shoes, oil products.	2.719	25.75
20 commodities each with export value $US 50-100 million	Frozen prawn, silk and satins, pharmaceutical raw materials, tea, furniture, steel products, cotton polyester fabrics, leather rubber shoes, knit grey, sugar, cotton yarn, cotton singlet and vest, other sport shoes, ships, battery, telephone sets, ornaments, live pigs, live chickens, undershirt cloth.	1.246	11.80

10 commodities each with export value $US 10-50 million	Live pond fish, cigarettes, electric fans, rattan work, artificial flowers, cement, tools, plate glass, down garments.	2.115	20.03

* * * *

The Beijing office of the province is located at:

32 Beiwalu, Balizhuang, Haidian District
Beijing 100037
Tel: 8418506, 8415059
Fax: 8415047

Another useful China contact for users of this volume might be:

Guangdong Province Foreign Economic Relations & Trade Commission
305 Dongfeng Road C., Guangzhou
Tel: 330860-4916 Fax: 344112

8. GUANGXI—ZHUANG AUTONOMOUS REGION

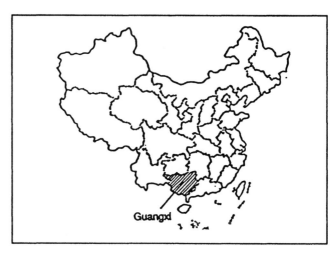

Situated on the South China coast, this autonomous region has an area of 236,000 sq. km. and a population of 41,510,000—14,000,000 of whom are people of the Zhuang Nationality. Paddy, sugarcane, oranges and pineapples are extensively cultivated int his autonomous region which has a subtropical climate. The capital of the Guangxi Zhuang Autonomous Region is Nanning. This region is on the north of the Gulf of Tonking, bordering Vietnam.

Foreign Trade

In 1990, the import and export value of Guangxi Zhuang Autonomous Region was $US 867.99 million, increased by 15.06 percent compared with 1989's value of $US 754.35 million.

The volume on the purchase of export commodities totalled RMB 1834.02 million yuan, increased by 14.18 percent compared with 1989's RMB 1606.25 million yuan.

The export volume was $US 729.44 million, up by 24.84 percent over 1989's $US 594.30 million, accounting for 9.50 of the region's GNP of RMB 36.708 billion yuan, and 1.40 percent of the nation's export total.

The import value totalled $US 138.55 million, declined by 18.52 percent compared with 1989's $US 170.05 million. Among the commodities imported, materials for production valued $US 114.58 million, accounting for 82.70 percent of the import total; materials for livelihood valued $US 23.97 million, accounting for 17.30 percent of the total. If classified according to international trade standard, the value of primary products was $US 33.32 million, accounting for 24.05 percent of the import total; that of manufactured goods was $US 105.23 million, accounting for 75.95 percent of the total.

The major commodities imported were, chemical fertilizer, sugar, diesel oil, trucks, crude oil, steel products, chemical raw materials, cotton, paper pulp and sheets, etc., the value of which amounted to $US 92.7579 million, accounting for 66.95 percent of the import total.

The imported commodities came from twenty-three countries and regions, out of which there were eight major markets. The value of the above mentioned items amounted to $US 119.1068 million, accounting for 85.97 percent of the import total.

Utilization of Foreign Capital

Contracts signed and approved amounted to 133 with a foreign investment of $US 137.47 million, increased by 2.97 times compared with 1989's $US 34.67 million, among which, there were 114 contracts of foreign direct investment with an amount of $US 125.21 million. Foreign investment of the rest nineteen contracts amounted to $US 12.26 million.

The utilization of foreign capitals in real terms for the whole year was $US 35.63 million, percent less than that of 1989. Out of it, $US 28.66 million was of foreign direct investment, $US 6.97 million was of other foreign investment.

Among the 114 contracts of foreign direct investment, fifty-seven were joint ventures, thirty-one contractual joint ventures, twenty-six solely foreign-invested projects. Out of the 114 projects, 107 contracts were for productive projects, and seven contracts were for non-productive projects. If classified according to line of business, thirty-three contracts were for light industry, seventeen for textile and garment, eleven for food industry, ten for electronic industry, seven for machinery, seven for mining, five for agriculture, forestry, animal husbandry and fishery, three for pharmaceutical industry, and twenty-six for others.

Foreign capitals mainly came from: Hong Kong, eighty-two projects; Taiwan Province, nineteen; the United States, seven; and Japan, one project.

In 1990, foreign exchanges earned by foreign-invested enterprises amounted to $US 44.60 million, 33.04 percent more than 1989's amount of $US 33.57 million.

Technology Import and Export

Contracts signed for technology import amounted to nineteen with a value of $US 21 million, the actual utilization of foreign exchange was $US 50 million. The technologies and equipments were mainly imported from Germany, the United States, Italy, Japan, Austria, Sweden, the United Kingdom, and Canada, which involved machinery, post and telecommunications, construction materials, mines, light industry, printing, tobacco, electronics, etc. Thirty projects with imported technology and equipments had entered into operation.

One contract for technology export was signed with a value of $US 140,000. It was a set of edible oil refinery equipment exported to Bangladesh by the Guangxi Machinery and Equipment Import and Export Corporation (2).

Foreign Economic Cooperation

Thirty-seven contracts for project contracting and labor services cooperation were signed with a value of $US 26.98 million, reduced by 69.95 percent from 1989's $US 89.79 million. The turnover was $US 23.2196 million, increased by 72 percent over 1989's $US 13.50 million. Personnel sent abroad for labor service cooperation totalled 421. The projects involved industry, agriculture, road construction, construction of facilities for sports and public health and were distributed in countries and regions such as Somalia, Angola, Guinea, Bangladesh, Gambia, Pakistan, Jordan, Rwanda, Papua New Guinea, Chad, Guam and Saipan of the United States and Hong Kong.

Six projects under Chinese aid were undertaken int he following four countries: Gabon, Burundi, Chad and Gambia. They are agricultural, public health, cultural and sports projects. A twenty-nine member medical team was dispatched to Niger. One project was completed, and three were to be continued. Two projects were for technical cooperation. Personnel dispatched for foreign aid totalled 229.

Table 9. Export commodity structure—Guangxi Province

Classified by agriculture, light and heavy industries			Classified according to international trade standard		
Item	Export value (*$US million*)	Percentage of export total 1990 1989	Item	Export value (*$US million*)	Percentage of export total 1990 1989
Agricultural and sideline products	163.21	22.38 19.61	Primary products	324.00	44.42 49.38
Light and industrial textile products	365.54	50.11 46.85			
Heavy industrial products	200.69	27.51 33.54	Manufactured products	405.44	55.58 50.62

There were thirty-two kinds of commodities each with the export value surpassing $US 5 million, the export total of which amounted to $US 455.17 million, accounting for 62.40 percent of the total export volume.

The export commodities were sold to ninety-one countries and regions, out of which there were ten major markets.

The export volume amounted to $US 632.201 million, accounting for 86.67 percent of the total export volume.

Table 10. Commodities each with the export value surpassing $US 5 million— Guangxi Province

Classified by value (*million $US*)	Item	Export value (*$US million*)	Percentage of total
Over 30 m. (2 items)	Sugar, canned food	97.8449	13.41
20-30 m. (5 items)	Cement, rosin, tin ingot, fireworks, cotton fabrics	117.7568	16.14

| 10-20 m. (6 items) | Barite (lumps, fines), aquatic products, live pigs, bamboo products, garments, antimony ingot | 91.3143 | 12.52 |
| 5-10 m. (19 items) | Tea, silicon, goose and duck down, talcum (lumps and powder), awn products, tin ore, cotton knitwear, Chinese cinnamon, gold jewelry, down products, electronic components, cotton manufactured goods, corrugated paper, rice, mulberry silk, silk, silks and satins, fennel oil, cotton yarn, dried cassava slice | 148.2574 | 20.32 |

Table 11. Major export markets—Guangxi Province

Country/region	Export value ($US million)	Percentage of the export total
Hong Kong, Macau	382.4068	52.42
United States	61.1978	8.39
Japan	55.3347	7.59
Saudi Arabia	41.4831	5.69
Germany	24.346	3.34
The Netherlands	19.2713	2.64
United Kingdom	13.4724	1.85
Singapore	11.6931	1.60
France	11.5619	1.59
Yemen	11.439	1.57

Table 12. Major import markets—Guangxi Province

Country/region	Import value ($US million)	Percentage of the import total
Hong Kong	65.1784	47.04
Former Soviet Union	9.7634	7.05
Brazil	9.0991	6.57
United States	8.7809	6.34
Malaysia	7.5395	5.44
Norway	6.7323	4.86
Venezuela	6.2132	4.48
Oman	5.80	4.19

* * * *

The Beijing office of the region is located at:

6 Shuanghuayuan, Dongsanhuanzhonglu
Beijing 100022
Tel: 7715604, 7715603

A useful China contact for users of this volume could be:

Guangxizhuang Autonomous Region Foreign Economic Relations
& Trade Commission
Seven-Star Road, Nanning, China
Tel: 25581, 20676 Fax: 0771-25581

9. GUANGZHOU (CANTON) CITY

Guangzhou is the largest city in south China and the capital of Guangdong Province.

Guangzhou is situated in the central area of Guangdong Province, north of the Pearl (Zhu Jiang) River delta at a longitude from 112 degrees, 33 minutes E. to 114 degrees, 35 minutes E. and a latitude of 22 degrees, 36 minutes N. to 24 degrees, 18 minutes N. The East River, West River and North River connect at Guangzhou and flow into the sea. Guangzhou which is near the South China Sea and borders Hong Kong and Macao, has an area of 7,434.4 sq. km., of which the area of the urban district is 1,443.6 sq. km. It is in a subtropical region and has marine monsoon climate. There is neither intense heat in the summer nor severe cold in the winter. Its average annual temperature is 21.6°C. with a relative humidity of 29% and temperature difference of 15°–17°C. Precipitation averages 2,165 mm. per year with plenty of rainfall, and a non-frosting period of 300 to 341 days.

Guangzhou is rich in natural resources and agricultural products such as rice, sugar cane, peanuts, vegetables, as well as various tropical fruits such as litchi, oranges, bananas, pineapples, etc. Its water power resources total approximately 360,000 kw. and it has dozens of mineral products such as coal, iron, lead, zinc, copper, bismuth, niobium, tantalum, silica, dolomite, jade-like stone, barite, refractory clay, mirabilite, phosphorus, marble, gypsum, etc. (8).

Guangzhou is advanced in science, technology, culture and education. It has become the center of culture, education and scientific research in south China. There is quite a pool of talent in Guangzhou among 435 scientific research organizations, 130,000 employees engaged in various scientific research, and twenty-five colleges and universities possessing great strength in education and scientific research.

Guangzhou has succeeded in foreign trade, export and in foreign economic and technical cooperation. By 1991, 2,373 contracts were signed covering foreign investment, joint ventures, cooperative ventures, international leasing agreements and compensation trade. Of the contracted foreign investment worth USD 3.8 billion, USD 1.5 billion was actually used. The contracts covered industry, agriculture, commerce, transportation, post and telecommunications, tourism, energy, environmental protection, construction, culture, education and sanitation etc. Using a combination of available equipment and foreign capital, some items have been improved. For instance, in a partnership with the French Peugeot Company, Guangzhou Automobile Factory has manufactured buses and trucks of various types which are in short supply domestically; in cooperation with the American Singer Sewing Machine Company, Huanan Sewing Machine Factory has produced industrial sewing machines, most of which are for export. Today, more than 600 enterprises using foreign capital, joint ventures and cooperative ventures have started production.

Post and Telecommunications

Guangzhou has well developed post and telecommunication services. The Telecommunications Bureau undertakes such business as domestic, international, Hong Kong and Macao telegrams and domestic and long distance calls. The total capacity for telephone installation is 260,000. People in Guangzhou can dial direct to 154 countries and districts including Hong Kong and Macao and to 421 cities in China. There is also express mail service to 130 domestic cities.

Transportation

Guangzhou which is located in the lower reaches of the Pearl River is the crossing point for the railways from Beijing to Guangzhou, Guangzhou to Kowloon and Guangzhou to Guangsan. It is also central to the highways in the province and the major airlines within the area of south central China thus constituting a traffic pivot to home and abroad for the combined transportation of sea, land and air.

The Guangzhou Railway Station is the biggest passenger station in south China. There are eleven train tracks and four huge platforms. Everyday there are forty-two round train trips (sixty round trips during a peak day) which transport over 100,000 passengers.

Guangzhou is the center of the highway network in the province. From Guangzhou to Shantou, Shenzhen, Haifeng, Zhongshan and to Shaoguan, there are five main lines which stretch to the east, west, south and north and connect all counties in the province and neighboring provinces. At present, an expressway connecting Guangzhou, Shenzhen and Zhuhai is under construction. When it is completed, it will greatly improve the traffic situation and transportation.

Guangzhou is also the aviation center connecting provinces in south China. The Baiyun Airport is one of three international airports in the whole country. Guangzhou Civil Aviation Administration Bureau possesses seventy-three aircrafts of various types and specialties and manages seventy-six aviation lines. Aircrafts take off and land almost 200 times daily. There are domestic air routes between Guangzhou and the major cities in northeast, northwest, north and east and southwest China and international routes to Manila, Bangkok and Singapore, etc. Passengers may also link up with the major international airlines of the world via Hong Kong.

There are two harbors in Guangzhou. One is called Guangzhou Harbor and the other is called Huangpu Harbor. Guangzhou Harbor is mainly used for inland water shipping, and is well connected with the big and small towns and cities in the Pearl River delta. There is a 4,287 meter long pier with ninety berths of which thirty-five have a capacity exceeding 1,000 tons. Huangpu Harbor is mainly used for the coastal and ocean shipping because of the spacious river banks and the silence of the waves. The pier is more than 4,000 meters long and has thirty berths. Sixteen of which have a capacity of 10,000 tons and one of them accommodates the container. The harbor is well-linked with China's major ports such as Dalian, Qinhuangdao, Tianjin, Shanghai and Xiamen, etc., for coastal shipping. For ocean shipping, it is well-connected with more than 500 ports and harbors in 110 countries and regions located on five continents. Passenger transportation is also available between Guangzhou and Hong Kong by hovercrafts and steamships.

Some of the major characteristics of Guangzhou Harbor and City are summarized in Table 13.

Table 13. Guangzhou—Salient Statistics (2)

Area (sq. km.)	16,657 (special economic zone alone) 9.6
Population	3,543,900 (urban), 6,000,000 (total)
Economic situation	Industrial production in 1989

Light industry:	17,343.48 (mil. yuan)
Heavy industry:	8,465.70 (mil. yuan)
Value of export:	$US 1,054.19 mil.
Harbor's handling volume:	4,649 (10 thousand tons)
Investment in capital assets:	6,228.10 (mil. yuan)
Total value of industrial production:	25,809.18 (mil. yuan)

Utilization

Utilization of foreign capital in 1988

Contract number:	2,120
Foreign contractual value:	$US 526,.5 mil.
Effected foreign investment:	$US 255.19 mil.
Number of foreign direct investment	289
Total foreign direct investment: $US	134.31 mil.

Up to the end of 1989

Joint ventures:	384
Contractual joint ventures:	182
Foreign wholly-owned enterprises:	37
Total:	603
Japanese enterprises:	4 (up to end of 1988)

Infrastructure:		
	Port:	30 berths, including 16 above 10,000 ton berths, one container berth
	Power:	Yearly supply capacity 4,200 mil. KWH
	Water:	Daily production capability: 21,100 mil. ton
	Telecommunication:	Well-developed telecommunication network, direct domestic and international call

Labor service charge (Unit: yuan/month)	250-300 (average)

Other fees	Water:	0.20 yuan/ton
	Electricity:	0.295 yuan/kwh

Priorities	Light industry, foodstuffs, machinery, electronics, textile, rubber, medicine, chemistry, paper, shipbuilding, metallurgy, building materials
Local preference	The income tax rate on joint venture in economic and technical development zone is 15%. A newly established joint venture can be exempted from income tax in the first two profit-making years, and allowed a 50% reduction of income tax in the third, fourth and fifth years.

Economic and Technological Development Zone

The Economic and Technological Development Zone is in eastern Guangzhou and is 30 km. from the city center. The planned area is 9.6 sq. km. of which 3 sq. km. has been exploited and construction has been completed in an area of 577,000 sq. meters. The aim for the Guangzhou Development Zone is to supply excellent services for investment and it has established a system of management, examination and service. It persists in its policy to legislate early and rule the zone by law. It has formulated and published sixty administrative and economic rules and regulations. Within six years of the establishment of the economic zone, more than 300 contracts for different projects were signed with investment exceeding RMB 2 billion. Over 100 enterprises with foreign investment were set up. The value of their contracts was USD 200 million of which USD 70 million was actually used. Businessmen investing in this area came from the United States, Canada, Australia, Germany and Hong Kong, etc. Presently, there are eight industrial projects whose investment each totals over USD 10 million. Most of the projects including some whose investment is from major international consortium like the American P&G Company and Pepsi Cola Company have had beneficial results. For example, Meile Container Co., Ltd. has been in production for two years and has accomplished a total industrial value of more than RMB 700 million and made more than RMB 100 million profit. It was ranked first for foreign investment enterprises, joint ventures and cooperative ventures for two years in a row (8).

* * * *

Official department in charge:

Guangzhou Municipal Committee for Foreign Economic Relations and Trade
Address: 4#, No. 1, Fu Qian Road, Guangzhou
Telephone: (020) 330360 Fax: (020) 340362

10. GUIZHOU PROVINCE

Guizhou that forms the eastern part of the Yunnan-Guizhou highlands is a very mountainous province in southwestern China. It has an area of 176,000 sq. km. and a population of 31,710,000, about 1/3 of which is made up of people of the Miao, Bouyei, Dong, Yi, Sui, Tujia, Hui, Yao, Zhuang and three other ethnic minorities. The provincial capital is Guiyang, a communication hub with railways and highways radiating to Sichuan, Yunnan and Hunan provinces and the Guangxi Zhuang Autonomous Region (2).

Guizhou is a mineral-rich province with deposits of phosphorus, aluminum, coal, antimony, manganese, mercury, rare-earth, silicon, barite, marble and limestone. Its hydro-power resources are estimated at 18.74 million kw. Already discovered are 2,500 plant species and 1,500 kinds of grass.

Foreign Trade

The total import and export value of Guizhou Province in 1990 topped $US 213.69 million, an increase of 15.13 percent over $US 185.6 million in 1989.

The purchasing value for exports amounted to RMB 727 million yuan, a rise of 2.83 percent over RMB 707 million yuan in 1989.

The export value totalled $US 153.05 million, an increase of 15.93 percent over $US 132.01 million in 1989, taking up 1.86 percent of the Province's GNP and 0.29 percent of the nation's total export.

The composition of the export commodities was: agricultural and sideline products, $US 21.60 million, accounting for 14.11 percent of the total; light industrial products, $US 36.41 million, 23.79 percent; heavy industrial products, $US 95.04 million, 62.01 percent. According to Standard for International Trade Classification, primary products were valued at $US 55.36 million, accounting for 36.17 percent of the total; industrial manufactures, $US 97.69 million, representing 63.83 percent.

Commodities each with export value over $US 5 million were six kinds including bauxite, abrasive, kidney beans, crude zinc, barite, bearings with total export value of $US 26.05 million, accounting for 17.02 percent. Of the total export bauxite was $US 15.89 million and, abrasive was $US 10.16 million.

Exports were mainly sold to fifty-seven countries and regions.

The import value totalled $US 60.65 million, a 13.16 percent increase over $US 53.59 million in 1989. Of that, means of production was $US 55.53 million, accounting for 91.57 percent of the total import; means of livelihood, $US 51.12 million, taking up 8.43 percent. According to SITC, primary products were valued at $US 11.21 million, representing 18.48 percent of the total import; industrial manufactured products, $US 49.44 million, accounting for 81.52 percent.

The major import commodities were: cellulose, filter tip, natural rubber, packaging machine and parts, plant equipment, equipment for light industry, wire communication equipment, kinescope, cord fabric and chemical machine and parts, etc., their import value totalled $US 41.77 million, accounting for 68.87 percent.

The imports were mainly from nineteen countries and regions.

Table 14. Major export markets—Guizhou Province

Country/region	Export value ($US million)	Percentage of the total
Hong Kong	43.35	28.32
Japan	32.09	20.97
United States	18.94	12.38
Germany	8.98	5.87
The Netherlands	7.99	5.22
Former Soviet Union	6.35	4.15
Singapore	5.91	3.86
Total	123.61	80.77

Table 15. Major import markets—Guizhou Province

Country/region	Import value ($US million)	Percentage of the total
Hong Kong	28.16	46.43
Japan	8.44	13.92
Germany	6.24	10.29
Italy	3.52	5.80
Singapore	3.10	5.11
The Netherlands	2.92	4.81
United States	2.53	4.17
Austria	1.09	1.80
Total	56.00	92.34

Utilization of Foreign Capital

Twenty-four contracts utilizing foreign capital were signed and approved with a contractual value $US 37.34 million, a 0.35 percent down over $US 37.47 million in 1989. Of that, there was one foreign government loan, with a value of $US 12.77 million; twenty-one foreign direct investment, with a value of $US 16.32 million; two other foreign investments, with a value of $US 8.25 million.

Actually used foreign investment amounted to $US 29.83 million, an increase of 16.25 percent over $US 25.66 million in 1989. Of that, the foreign loans were $US 19.25 million, the foreign direct investment was $US 4.68 million, and other foreign investment was $US 5.90 million.

Out of twenty-one foreign direct-funded projects, fifteen were equity joint ventures, three were contractual ventures and three were solely foreign-owned enterprises. Twenty-one projects were all productive enterprises. Major industries covered were medicine, food processing, timber processing, chemical industry machinery, leather and fur, non-metal selecting, ferrous metal smelting, printing, rubber products and textiles.

Foreign funds were mainly from four countries and regions. Of the total, eighteen projects were from Hong Kong with $US 21.10 million, three from Taiwan Province with $US 1.94 million, one from the United States with $US 1.18 million, and one from Australia with $US 350,000.

The foreign-owned enterprises int he Province achieved turnover of RMB 101 million yuan, export value of $US 8.10 million in the year.

Technology Import and Export

Eleven contracts on introducing technology and equipment were signed with a contractual value of $US 7.63 million, 4.12 fold increase over $US 1.49 million in 1989; actual foreign exchange spending was $US 3.93 million, 1.64 fold increase over $US 1.49 million in 1989.

Introduced projects came from five countries and regions: Japan with $US 1.85 million, the United Kingdom with $US 3.70 million, Germany with $US 870,000, Ital with $US 1.14 million, and Hong Kong with $US 80,000. The projects covered such industries as post and telecommunications, electronics, machinery, light industry and textile, chemistry and foodstuffs.

Four projects were already put into production in 1990.

Foreign Economic Cooperation

Contracts on contracting engineering projects and labor service cooperation were continuously carried out in 1990, turnover of $US 4.57 million was obtained, 226 personnel were sent abroad and 139 persons remained abroad at the end of the year. Countries where the labor service personnel were sent were Algeria, Yemen, Iraq, etc.

Four assistance projects in foreign countries were undertaken, recipient countries were

Ecuador, Cameroon, Rwanda, Sierra Leone. The industries involved were building, water and electricity, planting, etc. Thirty-two persons were sent abroad, and fifteen persons remained abroad at the end of the year. Moreover, 1,310 units (sets) of machinery and electric products for foreign aid were completed.

Seven international organizations and bilateral aid projects were received, with a total value of $US 24.03 million. Funds were from the United Nations Development Programme, Population Fund, Children Fund, Japanese Government, Canadian Cooperative Council and New Zealand Government (2).

* * * *

The Beijing office of the province is located at:

Hepinglixijeibeikou
Beijing 100101
Tel: 4214965
Fax: 4214110

Another useful China contact for users of this volume might be:

Guizhou Foreign Economic Relations & Trade Committee
21 Beijing Road, Guiyang, Guizhou Province 550004
Tel: 627128 ext. 669   Fax: 0851-626059

11. HAINAN PROVINCE

Hainan Island which had been part of Guangdong Province, became a province and the nation's largest special economic zone in April 1988 with National Peoples' Congress approval. Consisting of the main island of Hainan and upwards of 200 islets and coral reefs including the Xisha, Nansha and Zhongsha islands in the South China Sea. It is the second largest island of China after Taiwan. Hainan Province has a land area of 34,000 sq. km. inhabited by 6,388,000 people of the Han, Li, Miao and other nationalities. The provincial capital is Haikou, a port on the island's northern coast. Coffee and rubber plantations are being developed in the interior, and oil exploration is underway offshore. The whole island is a special economic zone.

Some characteristics of Hainan are summarized in Table 14.

Table 16. Hainan Province—Salient Statistics (2)

Area (sq. km.)	34,000
Population	6,777,900
Economic situation	Industrial production in 1989

Light industry:		1,662.05 (mil. yuan)
Heavy industry:		862.40 (mil. yuan)
Value of export:	$US	354 mil.
Harbor's handling volume:		895 (10 thousand tons)
Investment in capital assets:		2,192 (mil. yuan)
Total value of industrial production:		2,524.45 (mil. yuan)

Utilization of foreign capital	Utilization of foreign capital in 1988

Contract number:	489
Foreign contractual value:	$US 398.68 mil.
Effected foreign investment:	$US 127.71 mil.
Number of foreign direct investment:	463
Total foreign direct investment:	#US 114.21 mil.

Utilization of foreign capital in 1989

Contract number:	378
Foreign contractual value:	$US 280.6 mil.
Effected foreign investment:	$US 109.43 mil.
Number of foreign direct investment:	378
Total foreign direct investment:	$US 109.43 mil.

Up to the end of 1989

Joint ventures:	271
Contractual joint ventures:	106
Foreign wholly-owned enterprises:	290
Total:	667
Japanese enterprises:	12 (up to the end of 1988)

Infrastructure:	Port:	Haikou Port, Shanwu Port and Basou Port
	Power:	Installed capacity: 500 MW
	Water:	Rich water sources
	Telecommunication:	Direct domestic and international call
Priorities	Tropical plant, animal husbandry, mining, oil refining, chemistry, light industry, building materials, tourism	
Local preference	The income tax rate on joint venture is 15%. A newly established joint venture can be exempted from income tax in the first two profit-making years and allowed a 50% reduction of income tax in the third, fourth and fifth years. Export enterprises subject to a reduced rate of 10%	

Development Areas

Because of its regional resources and its proximity to the sea, the Hainan Government divided the whole island into five economic developing areas with their own distinguishing features.

1. **Haikou Economic Developing Area**

This area which centers around Haikou, an international outward-looking coastal city under development, also includes four counties such as Qiongshan, Chengmai, etc. The emphasis for this zone will be on the development of the light, textiles, foodstuffs, machinery, electronics and rubber industries.

2. **Sanya Economic Developing Area**

This area which centers on Sanya, an international tourist city under development, includes four municipalities and counties such as Tongshi, Baoting, etc. The development of the tourist industry will be stressed here.

3. **Yangpu Economic Developing Area**

In the area with its center in Yangpu and including three counties such as Lingao in which foreign investment plays a big role, the development will be mainly based on the petrochemicals and the building materials industries.

4. Basuo Economic Developing Area

This area which centers around the harbor city Bashuo, includes two counties Dongfang and Changjiang. The development of iron and steel, natural gas chemistry and the building materials industries will be stressed here.

5. Qinglan Economic Developing Area

The center of this area is in Wenchang County, the hometown for overseas Chinese. It includes three counties such as Qionghai. The development will focus on agriculture, processing of agri-by-products, foodstuffs, the light, textile and electronic instrument industries as well as the tourist industry.

Biological Resources

The planting area for Hainan tropical crops covers more than 1.1 million acres. The main crops are rubber, coconut palm, pepper, coffee, tea, cashew nuts, cocoa, and citronella, etc. (8).

Hainan is China's biggest production base of natural rubber, which has been growing there for about eighty years. Hainan presently has a planting area of 914,270 acres with an annual output of dry rubber of about 160,000 tons. This accounts for 60 percent of China's total dry rubber output.

Coconut palm in Hainan covers more than 49,420 acres and has an annual coconut production output of over 60 million pieces. Hainan's history for coffee planting is over seventy years old. The fields cover 19,768 acres and produce an annual output of coffee beans of over 770 tons.

Hainan is also an ideal place for tea planting. The tea picking period lasts ten months each year and the output per unit is 30 percent higher than in other provinces. Tea, with its 18,780 acres of planting area, has become one of the agricultural products which is exported in a large volume.

In Hainan, there are 172,970 acres of farm land suitable for pepper growth. Its output ranks number one in China. Hainan's cashew nut is one of the four most famous dried fruits in the world. Hainan has arable land which covers more than 74,130 acres for cashew nut planting. At present, the plantation covers 24,710 acres with an annual output of up to 500 tons. Ledong County is the biggest production base in the whole province.

The fruit harvest comes earlier in Hainan. Among its rich variety and special products, there are mainly litchi, longan, mango and pineapple, etc. The annual production for fruit is 150,000 tons. Even in mid-winter, hundreds of varieties of fruits and vegetables can still be grown in Hainan giving a full supply to both domestic and foreign markets.

Hainan Island is one of the two largest tropical virgin forests left in China. Occupying over 1.5 million acres and covering up to 24 percent, its timber collection volume is 30 million cubic meters. There are twenty or more valuable trees which have been listed as special preserves by the state (8).

The whole province has more than 2,000 different kinds of pharmaceutical plants of which over fifty can be indicated to fight cancer. Hainan is one of the three major planing areas in China for medicinal herbs. It has thirty-four production bases with plants covering 84,014 acres. There are 178 major products such as betelnut, alpinia oxyphylla mig, morindae, amoum villosum lour, alpinia katsumadai hayata, agalloch, codonopsis convolvulacca kurz, honeysuckle and kapok of which seventy-eight are available for export.

Mineral Resources

Three offshore oil and natural gas fields with great potential have been discovered in the sea surrounding the Hainan Island. Oil has been explored offshore to the east of Wenchang County, while two natural gas wells with a daily output of one million cubic meters have been exploited in the Yingge Sea. Oil and gas have also been found in the dry land of the north.

There are more than fifty kinds of minerals which have been discovered in Hainan Island of which thirty or more are worth exploring. Main products are iron, copper, radium, zirconium, titanium, ruby, sapphire, etc. Among these, the reserves of rich iron ore, titanium, zirconium and crystal rank first in China.

Hainan's iron mine is located in Changjiang County, west of the island. It is China's biggest open pit iron mine and also one of the eight biggest mines in Asia. Its reserves are about 3 hundred million tons and the ore content averages 51.2 percent with some as high as 67 percent.

Titanium ore spans the southeastern coast of the island with its reserves accounting for 70 percent of the whole country. In addition, Hainan is also rich in limestone, refractory clay, dolomite, granite, marble and quartzite which are all good for the development of the building materials industry.

Aquatic Products and Salt Resources

Hainan Island has a 1,528 km. coastline and sixty-eight natural harbors and gulfs. There are 63,294 acres of shallow intertidal area which can be used to breed aquatics. The inland water area is 90,420 acres. The fish farm in the 200 meter deep continental shelf covers an area of 65,600 sq. mi. of which 22,400 sq. mi. are located in Xisha, Nansha and Zhongsha Archipelagos, constituting a favorable condition for the development of ocean catching and the breeding industries.

A thousand varieties of fish can be caught during a fishing period, and the annual catching capacity can be up to 100,000 tons. There are over forty varieties of fish which have commercial value such as rock fish, spanish mackerel, pomfret, abalone, shark, prawn, lobster and sea jelly, etc.

More than twenty high-valued aquatics can be cultivated in the shallow intertidal area. Great success has also been made in the cultivation of rock fish, prawn and pearl shells by means of net cages. The pearl which is cultivated from he white butterfly shell in Xincungang, Lingyong County is the most famous and precious one of the pearl family. Each pearl is about 10 mm. in diameter and is worth over USD 10,000 per kilogram.

In Hainan, there are seventy-two types of fish cultivated in fresh water such as chub, carp, scale, water eel and snakeheaded fish, etc. Hainan is also noted for its natural salt works. The southern part of the island is most suitable for salt basking due to its sufficient sunshine, strong wind, little rainfall and high density of sea water. The Yingge Sea, Yuya and Dongfang are the three major salt works in Hainan. The province has salt pits covering 12,355 acres, with an annual output up to 270,000 tons.

Water Supply

A water supply construction has been accelerated in Haikou, Sanya, Yangpu and other developing areas. In Haikou, a ground water plant with daily production of 150,000 tons of water is now under construction. Another water plant with 100,000 tons of daily production will be built in Yongzhuang and will provide water to the Xiuying and Haixiu developing areas. Sanya is now building a water resource pool of 13 million cubic meters which can supply daily water needs of 50,000 tons. The next plan in Sanya is to build a water plant which can provide 200,000 tons of water daily. There are also ample underground water resources in Yangpu. The daily water intake there will not be less than 80,000 tons.

Energy

The generating equipment in Hainan has a total electrical power output of 800,000 kw. There are four thermal power stations and fifty-three hydroelectric power stations. Owing to a loan from the WorldBank, the Daguang Dam Hydroelectric Power Station which has a generating capacity of 240,000 kw. has been inaugurated for construction.

The Macun Thermal Power Station is currently the biggest one in Hainan with a generating capacity designed for 1.1 million kw. At present, the generating equipment which has had a capacity of 400,00 kw. in the first and second engineering periods has been operating, while the third engineering period with equipment capable of using 700,000 kw. is getting under way. The Yangpu Harbor Thermal Power Station, another station under construction, will have an output capacity of 1 million kw. It is expected that in 1992 the total capacity of generating equipment in the whole province will reach 2.1 million kw. A power grid of 110 kv. has bee preliminarily set up in the province. However, there is still a lot of work necessary to transform the old powder grid and build the new one which will be carried out in a planned way (8).

Telecommunications

Of the nineteen cities and counties in the province, sixteen have widely used the dial telephone system. IDD is even available in Haikou and Tongshi cities. There are 37,400 local telephone sets and 17,000 digital international telephone sets in the province.

In February 1990, an investment of USD 560,000 was made to introduce Japanese equipment in order to increase the long distance digital switchboard in Haikou City by 1,200 lines. In addition, RMB 1.2 million was invested in Haikou to build up the 128 line telegraph automatic vehicle system, and USD 450,000 was invested to introduce equipment from Finland for the construction of an optical cable transmission system. Haikou, with 27,000 digital telephone sets, is accelerating a project to expand the submarine cable capacity in order to increase 300 long distance lines. Another project which is being prepared for construction in Haikou is a B-grade satellite ground station. After completion, it will total 432 satellite long distance transmission lines, thus increasing the direct lines to Beijing from 10 to 120.

Transportation

Highways and Railways: The highways in Hainan total 3,000 km. and are accessible to every town and village. The layout of the east, middle and west sides which from north to south and four horizontal routes which from east to west. A new 259 km. expressway is under construction from Haikou to Sanya.

Hainan has a railway which is 214 km. and runs the Sanya Harbor to the town of Shilu via Basuo. The capacity of the freight transportation is 4.23 million and its passenger transportation is 460,000 people.

Airlines: There are two airports in Hainan. One airport is in Haikou and the other one is in Sanya. The Haikou Airport has a runway of 60 x 2,500 meters and is well equipped with service facilities and excels in navigating management. Under any conditions, full assurance is given to the take off and landing of any jumbo and mid-size planes such as the Boeing 737 and Boeing 757. There are airlines with routes from Haikou to the mainland and road and eighty-six flights a week. Twelve of the flights go directly to Honk Kong. Air transportation is also available to Singapore and Bangkok by chartered planes.

Sanya is building a new international airport in order to accommodate the MD-82 and Boeing 767 passenger planes. It is scheduled to complete the project within two and a half years.

Harbors: There are sixty-eight harbors and gulfs of varying surrounding the island. Twenty newly build harbor have available berths of which six berths can accommodate 000 ton ships and handle a capacity totalling 11 million tons. The major harbors are Haikou, Basuo, Sanya, Qinglan and Macun. Yangpu Harbor, located in the west side of the island, is a huge harbor under construction and has more than ten deep water berths. At present, berths with a 20,000 ton capacity and one working pier with a capacity of 3,000 tons have been completed. Macun Harbor is a pier supporting the Macun factory. It has two berth containing a capacity of 20,000 tons.

Foreign Trade

In 1990, the total export and import value of Hainan Province reached $US 937.38 million. 4.62 percent against $US 869 million in 1989.

The total value of goods purchased for export reached RMB 2.41 billion yuan, up 7.59 percent over RMB 2.34 billion yuan in 1989.

The export value totalled $US 471.38 million ($US 501.38 million including the export value the corporation under the central ministries and commissions), up 30.64 percent over $US 360 million in 1989, accounting for 23.6 percent of Hainan Province's GNP.

The import value of the specialized foreign trade corporations and industrial corporations under Hainan Provincial Trade Department amounted to $US 43.38 million, down 49.79 percent against $US 86.39 million in 1989. The import commodities were feeding stuffs, TV sets and sound equipment, western medicine, synthetic fiber, plywood and kinescopes from sixteen countries and regions.

There were fourteen commodities each with export value over $US 5 million, and they were ornaments, tin ore, leather working gloves, shapes and sections steel, mild steel square bars, rayon, carpets, new decor porcelain, frozen prawn, vegetables, silk, firecrackers and fireworks, cloth, manioc slices.

These commodities were sold to forty-nine countries and regions.

Utilization of Foreign Capital

Two hundred and fifty-two contracts on foreign direct investment were signed and approved with the value of $US 128.82 million, down 53.48 percent against $US 279.61 million in 1989. In these contracts, ninety-eight were for equity joint ventures with the value of $US 38.53 million. Thirty were for contractual joint ventures with the value of $US 11.88 million, and 124 were for wholly foreign-owned enterprises with a value of $US 78.41 million. The amount of actual utilization of foreign capital was up 18.03 percent over that in 1989.

In the 252 contracts, 186 were for productive enterprises and sixty-six for non-productive enterprises, which were in such sectors as agriculture, forestry, animal husbandry and fisher, industry, communication and transportation, real estate management, public service, and culture and education. The main sources of foreign capital include fifteen countries and regions, such as Hong Kong, Macau, Taiwan Province, Japan, the United States, Singapore, Switzerland, Argentina, and the Russian Federation. One hundred and fifty-nine projects were from Hong Kong with foreign capital of $US 108.89 million; fifty from Taiwan Province with $US 23.5 million, four from Singapore with $US 20.28 million; twelve from Japan with $US 7.07 million; and one from the Russian Federation with $US 5 million.

Table 17. Structure of export commodities—Hainan Province (2)

Item	Export value ($US million)	Percentage of total export 1990	1989
Primary products	162.377	37.01	39.70
Manufactured industrial products	276.323	62.99	60.30

Table 18. Major export markets—Hainan Province

Country/region	Export value ($US million)	Percentage of total
Hong Kong	351.80	80.19
Japan	32.50	7.31
Sri Lanka	8.35	1.90
Thailand	6.80	1.55
Germany	6.40	1.46
United States	5.78	1.32
The Netherlands	3.12	0.71
United Kingdom	1.97	0.45

Table 19. Major import markets—Hainan Province

Country/region	Import value ($US million)	Percentage of total
Hong Kong	29.53	68.08
Singapore	6.50	14.98
Peru	4.15	9.57
Japan	0.87	2.01
Malaysia	0.82	1.89
Thailand	0.66	1.52
United States	0.61	1.41
Total	**43.41**	**99.49**

* * * *

Official department in charge:

Bureau of Economic Cooperation of Hainan Province
Address: Niu Long Pai, Haikou
Telephone: (0750) 42744

The Beijing office of the province is located at:

172 Xizhimen Dajie, Xicheng District
Beijing 100035
Tel: 6014173 Fax: 6016816

12. HEBEI PROVINCE

Hebei Province has a population of 58,810,000 according to a year-end count in 1989. It has 6.6 million hectares of farmland on which grow wheat, maize, cotton and other crops. The province has big reserves of coal, petroleum, iron another minerals and a fairly developed economy. The provincial capital is Shijiazhuang, an important industrial center and a railway hub 270 km. south of Beijing.

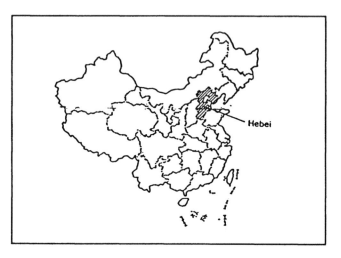

Hebei encircles the cities of Beijing and Tianjin. Its broad industrial sector includes machinery, pharmaceutical, electronics and chemicals. A major port, Qinghuangdao, handles large amounts of bulk cargo.

The climate is extreme. The winters are bitterly cold; the summers are uncomfortably hot and sometimes bring disastrous droughts. Despite its harsh environment, Hebei is densely populated, particularly in the lowland areas, where wheat and cotton are grown.

Foreign Trade

In 1990, the total export and import value of Hebei Province was $US 1.952 billion, showing an increase of 3.4 percent over $US 1.888 billion of 1989.

The purchasing value of export commodities was RMB 6.076 billion yuan, increased by 40.68 percent over RMB 4.319 billion in 1989.

The export value reached $US 1.737 billion, a rise of 6.11 percent over $US 1.637 billion of 1989, accounting for 7.25 percent of the Province's GNP and 3.34 percent of the country's total export value, ranking the ninth.

There were twenty-two commodities each earning over $US 10 million, the value totalling $US 1.206 billion taking up 69.43 percent of the total export value. They were crude oil, cotton piece goods, cotton, cotton polyester blended fabrics, coal, cotton yarn, garments, cotton knitwear, carpet, maize, canned goods, frozen prawn, chestnuts, pottery and porcelain, etc.

Commodities were exported to 125 countries and regions, of which Japan, Hong Kong, the United States, Germany, former Soviet Union, Singapore, the Netherlands, Republic of Korea, the United Kingdom, and Czechoslovakia were ten major exporting countries. The markets each with importing China's commodities over $US 100 million included Japan, $US 701 million, taking up 40.36 percent of the total export value; Hong Kong, $US 341 million, 19.63 percent; the United States, $US 120 million, 6.91 percent.

The import value was $US 215 million which was 14 percent less than $US 250 million of 1989. Of the imports, means of production took up 94.88 percent, totalling $US 204 million; means of subsistence, 5.12 percent, $US 11 million. Classified by international trade standard, the primary products took up 58.60 percent, totalling $US 126 million; industrial finished products, 41.40 percent, $US 89 million. The main imports covered fertilizers, chemical raw materials, cotton, electronic instruments, steel products, complete sets of equipment, light industrial machinery, and chemical industrial machinery, etc., with a value reaching $US 152 million, accounting for 70.70 percent of the total import. The goods were imported from twenty-seven countries and regions, some nine major importing countries among which were Japan, the United States, Hong Kong, Germany, and Canada, etc., with a value of $US 180 million, accounting for 83.72 percent.

Utilization of Foreign Capital

One hundred and twenty-nine contracts on using foreign capital were signed and approved, the contract value of foreign capital being $US 131.42 million, 8.70 percent less than $US 143.94 million of 1989. Of those, there were nine contracts on foreign loans, valuing $US 42.50 million; 110 contracts were on foreign direct investments valuing $US 85.93 million; and ten contracts were on other investments, valuing $US 2.99 million.

The actual input of foreign capital was $US 86.97 million, 19.66 percent less than $US 108.25 million of 1989, of which foreign loans were $US 42.5 million, foreign direct investment was $US 37.57 million, and other foreign investment was $US 6.9 million.

Out of 110 foreign direct investment projects, 102 were joint ventures, one was contractual joint venture, and seven were solely foreign-funded enterprises. In terms of sectors, fifty-four projects were in light industry, eighteen in machinery, twelve in textiles, twelve in electronics, six in building materials, five in chemical industry, one in agriculture, one in pharmaceutical, and one in metallurgy.

The investors were mainly from nine countries and regions including Hong Kong with seventy-one projects in the amount of $US 51.12 million, Taiwan Province with fifteen projects in the amount of $US 13.63 million, Panama with one project in the amount of $US 7.83 million, Japan with six projects int he amount of $US 1,37 million, and the United Kingdom with one project in the amount of $US 1.34 million.

Up to the end of 1990, 158 foreign-funded enterprises had been put into production and turned out RMB 830 million yuan. The revenue of the goods sold was RMB 774 million yuan and the foreign exchange generated through export were $US 45.34 million, keeping a balance of the income and the expenditure (2).

Technology Import and Export

Some sixty-four contracts on import of technology and equipment were signed, the contractual value being $US 58.82 million, an increase of 2.91 percent over $US 57.16 million of 1989; actual use of foreign funds recorded $US 87.13 million, an increase of 62.78 percent over $US 53.53 million of 1989. The importation was mainly from Japan, Germany, the United States, Italy, and Hong Kong, etc., covering textiles, light industrial products, machinery, electronics, and pharmaceutical, etc.

Foreign Economic Cooperation

Fourteen contracts on undertaking contracting projects and providing labor service abroad were signed, contract value being $US 8.5 million, up 15.42 percent over $US 7.36 million of 1989; business turnover was $US 6.34 million, 35.41 percent less than $US 9.81 million of the previous year. Eighty-three people were sent abroad to provide labor service in the year, and by the end of the year, 188 people were working in Bangladesh, Congo, Mali, Nepal, Bolivia, Ethiopia, Canada, the United States, Hungary, Kuwait, and the United Arab Emirates, etc. One foreign aid project in Ethiopia was undertaken. The following foreign aid projects were completed in 1990: Bangladesh Aquatic Water Conservancy Project, Nepal Reclamation Area, Bolivia Water Ditch Repairing Project, two Water Supply Projects in Congo. Thirty-three people were sent abroad to provide aid in the year and eighty-five people were working by the end of the year. Two productive enterprises were set up in Australia and the United States, and the Chinese investment amounted to $US 700,000.

Table 20. List of the main exports—Hebei Province

Classified by agriculture, light and heavy industries			*Classified by international trade standard*		
Item	*Export value ($US million)*	*Percentage of the total* 1990 1989	*Item*	*Export value ($US million)*	*Percentage of the total* 1990 1989
Farm and sideline products	328.63	18.92 19.74	Primary products	936.24	53.90 49.94
Light industrial products	662.24	38.12 43.34			
Heavy industrial products	746.21	43.96 36.92	Industrial finished products	800.84	46.10 50.00

* * * *

The Beijing office of the province is located at:

**1 Zhuiba Hutong, Huanghuamenjie, Dianmen
Dongcheng District
Beijing 100009
Tel: 4031116-262 4031302
Fax: 4031302**

Another China contact which should be helpful to users of this volume is:

**Foreign Economic Relations & Trade Commission of Hebei Province
58 Beima Road, Shijiazhuang, China
Tel: 744842**

13. HEILONGJIANG PROVINCE

Lying in the northernmost part of China, Heilongjiang Province bordering Siberia is the sixth largest province in China. It has an area of 454,600 sq. km., and according to a year-end count, the population was 34,424,000 in 1989. China's largest oil field, the Daqing field, is located in this province that abound in coal, petroleum, graphite, gold, uranium and other minerals. Heilongjiang is the most heavily forested province in China with a timber reserve of 1,485 million cubic meters. The province is a producer of wheat, sorghum, soya bean and other crops. The provincial city is Harbin, a river port and railway hub on the Songhuajiang. Its climate and soil are similar to those of Alberta, Canada, and, like the Canadian prairie province, the Chinese province is a major wheat-growing region. Because of this, farms are larger and more mechanized than in the rest of the country.

Foreign Trade

In 1990, Heilongjiang's total volume of export and import was amounted to $US 1.49 billion, an increase of 5.65 percent against $US 1.41273 billion in 1989.

The total value of commodities purchased for export was RMB 6.66 billion yuan, up 5.71 percent over RMB 6.3 billion in 1989.

The export value reached $US 1.08659 billion with a growth of 5.77 percent over $US 1.02732 billion in 1989 accounting 8.6 percent of the Province's GNP, and 2.09 percent of China's total export, and ranking the 12th in the country.

The composition of export commodities was agricultural and sideline products amounting to $US 380.91 million, accounting for 35.06 percent of the total export value; light industrial products $US 427.37 million, 39.33 percent; and heavy industrial products $US 278.31 million, 25.61 percent. Compared with that in 1989, the proportion of agricultural and sideline products in export commodities dropped by 19.44 percentage points, while that of light industrial products and heavy industrial products rose by 11.03 percentage points and 8.41 percentage points respectively. By SITC system, primary products valued $US 533.27 million, taking up 49.08 percent of the total export, and manufactured industrial products, $US 553.32 million, 50.92 percent.

There were eighteen commodities each with export value over $US 10 million, which include soybean, corn, bean expellers, garments, fine linen cloth, tools, canned beef, frozen beef, beet pulp, cotton fabrics, cotton/polyester yarn, radio recorder sets, industrial bearings, ship overhaul, down garments, etc. The combined export value of these commodities reached $US 530.31 million, accounting for 48.80 percent of the total export. There were twenty commodities each with export value of $US 5-10 million, which include embroidered articles, cotton polyester, blended fabrics, fur garments, woolen blankets, cotton rubber shoes, paraffin wax, sanitary chopsticks, wool knitwear, bristles, automobiles, tires, aluminum products, crystalline flake graphite, broken soybean cakes, etc. The combined export value of these commodities amounted to $US 137.77 million, accounting for 12.68 percent of the total export.

The commodities were exported to eighty-seven countries and regions. The countries and regions to which the export value exceeding $US 10 million include Hong Kong, Japan, the former Soviet Union, Republic of Korea, Thailand, Malaysia, Singapore, Indonesia, Germany, and the United States. The combined value of export to the above-mentioned countries and regions was $US 933.69 million, 85.93 percent of the total export, of which the former Soviet Union was $US 358.95 million, taking up 33.03 percent of the Province's total export; Hong Kong, $US 175.09 million, 16.11 percent; Japan, $US 172.09 million, 15.84 percent; and Republic of Korea, $US 76.3 million, 7.02 percent.

The total import value was $US 405.89 million, 5.31 percent more than $US 385.41 million in 1989. Of the import commodities, means of production valued $US 366.31 million, accounting for 90.25 percent of the total, and means of livelihood $US 39.58 million, 9.75 percent. The main import commodities include machinery equipment, raw materials for industry, agricultural goods, and mean of livelihood from twenty-nine countries and regions, such as the former Soviet Union, Japan, the United States, Republic of Korea, and Hong Kong. The countries and regions from which the commodities were imported with the value over $US 5 million include Hong Kong, Japan, Republic of Korea, the former Soviet Union, and the United States. Among them, the former Soviet Union took up $US 282.52 million, 69.61 percent of the total import; Japan, $US 41.06 million, 10.12 percent; and Hong Kong $US 34.07 million, 8.39 percent.

In 1990, the total border trade with the former Soviet Union reached SF 179.85 million, increased by 26.19 percent over SF 570.47 million in 1989. Among the total, import valued SF 375.88 million, 60.61 percent more than SF 234.03 million in 1989; and export valued SF 343.97 million, 2.24 percent more than SF 336.44 million in 1989. The major import commodities include chemical fertilizer, timber, steel products, cement, aquatic products, medical care articles, chemical products, garments, textiles, furniture, etc. The export commodities were light industrial products, textiles, farm and sideline products, machinery equipment, transportation tools, building materials, electromechanical instruments, etc. One hundred and seventeen economic and technological cooperation contracts were signed upon barter trade, with a total value of SF 232.79 million. Among these contracts, forty-three were actually fulfilled with a value of SF 26.15 million, including twenty-two contracts for vegetable planting, ten for construction, and eleven for others, 10,957 labor service personnel were sent abroad. By the end of 1990, the province had established economic and trade relations with about 600 former customers from thirty-one states in nine

Republics, five frontier Regions and six Autonomous Republics in the former Soviet Union.

Utilization of Foreign Capital

Eighty-six contracts on using foreign capital were signed and approved with the contract value of $US 77.89 million, down 11.35 percent against $US 87.86 million in 1989. Among them, two contracts were of foreign loans, valuing $US 46.83 million; seventy-six contracts were of foreign direct investment, valuing $US 27.13 million; and eight contracts were of other foreign investment, valuing $US 3.93 million. The actual use of foreign capital was $US 63.2 million, down 17.68 percent against $US 76.77 million in 1989. Of this, $US 28169 million was of foreign loans, $US 30.58 million of foreign direct investment, and $US 3.39 million of other foreign investment.

Out of seventy-six foreign direct investment projects, fifty-nine were equity joint ventures, two were contractual joint ventures, and fifteen were wholly foreign-owned enterprises. Classified by trade, sixty-three were in industry, seven were in catering service, and four were in agriculture. One each in communication and transportation, and TV and broadcasting. The investors mainly came from sixteen countries including the former Soviet Union, the United States, Japan, Canada, Singapore, Thailand, the Republic of Korea, Taiwan Province, and Hong Kong. Forty-three projects were from Hong Kong with foreign investment of $US 10.99 million; two from Thailand with $US 3.09 million; four from Taiwan Province with $US 3.09 million; and nine from the Republic of Korea with $US 1.49 million (2).

Technology Import and Export

One contract was signed for importing technical knowhow and equipment of formaldehyde production line from the United States, valuing $US 2.55 million.

Seven contracts for technology export were signed with a total value of $US 7.96 million, 24.76 percent increase over $US 6.38 million in 1989.

Foreign Economic Cooperation

The Province signed six contracts on contracting engineering projects with the former Soviet Union, involving contract value of $US 11.91 million; seven contracts on labor service cooperation with the former Soviet Union, Italy, and Equatorial Guinea involving contract value of $US 5.01 million. In 1990, 1,604 engineers, technicians and labor service personnel were sent abroad.

* * * *

The Beijing office of the province is located at:

5 Fuxingmen Beidajie
Beijing 100045
Tel: 8033322 Fax: 8033203

Some other China contacts which should be helpful to users of this volume include:

Heilongjiang Province Foreign Economic Relations & Trade Commission
55 Heping Road, Harbin 15001
Tel: 221704

Harbin Municipal Foreign Economic Relations & Trade Commission
102 Tong Jiang Street, Daoli District, Harbin, China 150010
Tel: 418139, 417832 Fax: 0451-416661

14. HENAN PROVINCE

Lying on both banks of the Yellow River west of Shandong Province, Henan is one of China's banner foodgrain and cotton producers. It has 7 million hectares of land growing tobacco, jute, soya bean, peanut and other crops. The province has big deposits of coal, petroleum, natural gas, aluminum, gold, silver, molybdenum, perlite and other minerals.

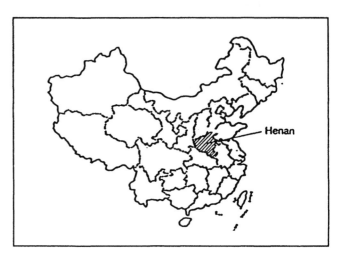

It covers 160,000 sq. km. (62,000 sq. miles) in central China. Henan is a major wheat area and also produces tobacco, jute, soybean, sesame, rapeseed and peanuts. The floods that used to plague the province have been ended by river control schemes, particularly along the Huang He (Yellow River). Its population is 71,890,000.

The Provincial capital is Zhengzhou.

Foreign Trade

The total export and import value of Henan Province in 1990 was $US 979.71 million, 8.74 percent increase over the $US 900.96 million in 1989.

The purchase value of export commodities was $US 5.35223 million, 14.73 percent increase over the $US 4.66509 million of 1989.

The total export value was $US 866.89 million, 5.58 percent increase over the $US 818.97 million in 1989, 4.69 percent of the GNP of the province and 1.68 percent of the total value of national exportation.

The composition of the export commodities was: agricultural and sideline products at $US 3.15.49 million, 36.39 percent of the total export value; light industrial products at $US 372 million, 42.91 percent of the total; heavy industrial products at $US 179.4 million, 20.7 percent of the total. Compared with 1989, the proportion of agricultural and sideline products increased by 0.26 percentage points, light industrial products decreased by 2.7 percentage points, and heavy industrial products increased by 2.44 percentage points. According to the standard categories of international trade, primary products were at $US 419.11 million, 48.35 percent of the total export value, 1.27 percentage points more than the previous year; the industrial manufactured products at $US 447.78 million, 51.65 percent of the total, 1.27 percentage points less.

The export market was further expanded. Commodities were sold in 100 countries and regions, six countries more than that of 1989. According to the regional breakdown, countries in Asia were at $US 506.67 million, 58.45 percent of the total export value; EC countries at $US 107.49 million, 12.40 percent of the total; the former Soviet Union and Eastern European countries at $US 124.27 million, 14.34 percent of the total; North American countries at $US 56.78 million, 6.55 percent of the total; South American countries at $US 7.4 million, the oceanic countries at $US 5 million, and African countries at $US 3.41 million.

Major markets each with export value above $US 10 million included fourteen countries and regions, in which Hong Kong was at $US 305.37 million, 35.22 percent of the total export value; Japan at $US 96.3 million, 11.11 percent of the total; the former Soviet Union at $US 77.68 million, 8.96 percent of the total; the United States at $US 49.46 million, 5.71 percent of the total.

Goods imported were at $US 112.82 million, 37.6 percent increase over the $US 81.99 million of 1989.

Composition of the import commodities was: means of livelihood at $US 40.13 million, 35.5 percent of total import value; means of production at $US 72.69 million, 64.43 percent of the total. According to the standard categories of international trade, primary products were at $US 64.8 million, 57.5 percent of the total import value; industrial manufactured products at $US 47.95 million, 42.5 percent of the total. Major commodities included cigarette auxiliaries, fertilizer, complete plant chemical auxiliaries, animal oil and vegetable oils.

The imported goods were from twenty-one countries and regions, including mainly; Hong Kong at $US 48.18 million, 42.71 percent of the total import value; the United States at $US 22.04 million, 19.5 percent of the total; Germany at $US 5.52 million, 4.89 percent of the total; Norway at $US 4.1 million, 3.64 percent of the total.

Utilization of Foreign Capital

Fifty-four new contracts on utilizing foreign capital were signed with approval, with the total contracted value of foreign investment at $US 24.3 million, 90.04 percent less than the $US 244 million of 1989. Among the contracts, one was foreign loan project with the contracted value at $US 2.37 million; fifty-five were foreign direct investment with the investment value at $US 21.06 million; three were other foreign investment with the contracted value at $US 870,000. The actually used of foreign capital in the year was at $US 13.73 million, 70.19 percent less than that of 1989.

Among the fifty projects of foreign direct investment, thirty-nine were joint ventures, with the contracted value of foreign investment at $US 13.1 million; one contractual joint venture, with the contracted value at $US 2.54 million, ten solely foreign-owned projects, with the total contracted value at $US 5.42 million. Forty-nine of these projects were of productive type, in which three were in the field of textile industry, five in electronics and communication, and six in chemical industry (2).

The foreign investors were from seven countries and regions. Among them, businessmen from Hong Kong invested in twenty-five projects, with the total contracted value at $US 9.33 million; Taiwan Province in twelve projects at $US 4.04 million; Japan in four projects at $US 3.07 million; the United States in six projects at $US 2.94 million.

Thirteen foreign investment enterprises went into production in the year, playing a positive role for the economic development for the province. For example, the Zhongyuan Fertilizer Factory financed by the World Bank Loan, after it was launched into production, the production capacity of synthetic ammonia in the factory increased by 400,000 tons. The Anyang Color Kinescope Glass Case Factory jointly owned by the Chinese side and foreign businessmen, has already reached the annual production capacity of 4.6 million sets. During the year, the exportation of products by the foreign investment enterprises reached $US 20.06 million.

Technology Import and Export

In 1990, $US 8.28 million in foreign exchange was used for the importation of technology and equipment, 45.92 percent less than the $US 15.31 million of the previous year. Thirty-eight contracts were signed with fifteen countries and regions for the exportation of technology, with the total contracted value at $US 13.98 million, 6.68 times increase over the $US 1.82 million of 1989. Among the contracts, one was on the exportation of technology, with the contracted value at $US 9.96 million; twenty-five were on the exportation of technical products, with the contracted value at $US 4.02 million.

Foreign Economic Cooperation

Thirty-eight contracts were signed for contracting engineering projects and labor service within the year, with the contracted value at $US 25.4 million, 10.15 percent more than the $US 23.06 million of 1989. Among them, twenty-four were of contracted projects, with a total value of $US 22.81 million; fourteen were of labor service, with a total value of $US 2.59 million. The business turnover completed was $US 24.67 million, 2.68 percent less than the $US 25.35 million of the previous year. Eight hundred and seventy technical and engineering and labor service personnel were dispatched abroad in the year. By the end of the year, there 1,266 people working abroad in thirty-four countries and regions. Major projects included: Housing Estate Development Project in Hong Kong, Power Transmission Line Project in Pakistan, and Banjul City Water Supply Project in Gambia.

Seven foreign aid projects were undertaken within the year, including station rehabilitation, highway, and water conservancy projects in Guinea, Senegal and Nepal, as well as technical cooperation projects in culture and sports. Three of the projects have already been completed.

From the United Nations agencies like UNFPA and UNICEF, $US 3.58 million worth of assistance was received for the training of primary and kindergarten teachers, and health protection projects for women and children.

One chemical production enterprise was approved to be established in Germany, with the investment from the Chinese side at $US 0.81 million.

Table 21. Commodities each with export value above $US 5 million—Henan Province

Value/category	Export commodities	Export value ($US million)	Percentage of the total export value
Above $US 50 million, 1 item	Cotton	68.19	7.87
Above $US 10 million, 17 items	Cotton cloth and its garments, cotton polyester cloth, cotton manufactured goods, cotton knitwear, cotton yarn, embroidered articles, feed stuffs, live pigs, maize, goat skins, frozen beef, coal, rolling bearings, steel products, pottery and ceramics, shoes.	429.79	49.58
Above $US 5 million, 15 items	Flue-cured tobacco, garlic, silk garments, silk, leather products, canned food, bee honey, carpets, down filled garments, bauxite, casings, soy beans, timber, chemical fiber yarn, paper and pulp.	101.48	11.71

* * * *

The Beijing office of the province is located at:

117 Guangqumen Neidajie, Chongwen District
Beijing 100062
Tel: 5112296, 7015768-3194
Fax: 7014503

Another useful China contact for users of this volume might be:

Henan Foreign Economic Relations & Trade Committee
115, Wenhua Road, Zhengzhou, China
Tel: 332821, 332786 Fax: 0371-336261

15. HUBEI PROVINCE

Known as a land of lakes, and with the important Yangtze port of Wuhan as its capital, Hubei Province is a major producer of rice and fish in China. It covers an area of 185,900 sq. km. and has a population of 52,238,900 made up of people of the Han, Tujia, Hui, Miao and Manchu nationalities. Its steel plant in Wuhan is one of the biggest in the country, and located in Shiyan in northwestern Hubei is the No. 2 Automotive Works, one of the largest in China. The climate is moist and warm and the soil is fertile, making Hubei an important producer of rice, soya beans, wheat, maize, tea and cotton.

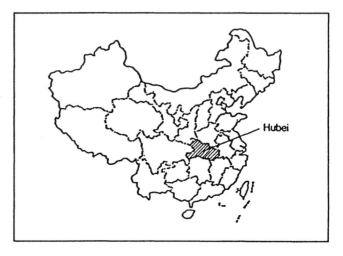

Foreign Trade

In 1990, Hubei's total export and import value stood at $US 1.18968 billion, down by 4.46 percent from $US 1.24525 billion of 1989.

Hubei's purchase for export totalled RMB 5.469 billion yuan, up 3.17 percent over RMB 5.301 billion yuan in 1989.

The total export value increased by 4.40 percent to $US 1.07180 billion from $US 1.02662 million last year, accounting for 7.18 percent of the provincial GNP and 2.06 percent of the nation's total export value.

The export commodities and their value concluded in 1990 are as follows: $US 1;83.93 million for the export of agricultural and sideline products, 17.16 percent of the total export; $US 707.22 million for light industrial products, 65.98 percent of the total; $US 180.65 million for heavy industrial products, 16.86 percent of the total; according to the classification of international trade standard, $US 274.43 million for primary products, accounting for 25.6 percent of the total; $US 797.37 million for finished industrial products, 74.4 percent of the total.

There were thirty kinds of major export commodities each with an export value over $US million, and their export amounted to $US 471.14 million, 43.96 percent of the total export.

The commodities were exported to 144 countries and regions including Hong Kong, Japan, the Soviet Union, the United States, Germany, Singapore, among which the export to Hong Kong reached $US 478.2 million, taking up 44.62 percent of the total; Japan, $US 92.56 million, 8.64 percent; the former Soviet Union, $US 83.83 million, 7.82 percent; and the United States, $US 61.18 million, 5.0 percent; Germany, $US 34.14 million, 3.19 percent; and Singapore, $US 19.34 million, 1.8 percent.

The import value totalled $US 117.88 million, down by 46.08 percent from $US 218.63 million in 1989, of which $US 105.23 million was for means of production, 89.27 percent of the total, $US 12.65 million for means of subsistence, 10.73 percent. Among the major imports were $US 16. million for fabrics; $US 8.154 million for tobacco and cigarette auxiliaries; $US 6.11 million of animal oils and vegetable oils; $US 6.06 million for western medicine; $US 6.01 million for chemical raw materials; $US 4.426 million for synthetic fiber; $US 3.02 million for rubber and its products; $US 2.96 million for TV receivers and sound equipment; $US 2.15 million for paper; $US 1.99 million for telecommunication equipment; $US 1.34 million for embroidered articles raw materials. The total value was $US 58.50 million, accounting for 49.63 percent of the total value of importation.

The main import markets were Hong Kong, the United States, Japan, Singapore, Macau, Germany, the United Kingdom, etc., of which with $US 67.75 million import from Hong Kong, taking up 57.47 percent of the total; $US 13.98 million from the United States, 11.86 percent; and $US 12.40 million from Japan, 10.52 percent.

Utilization of Foreign Capital

One hundred and eighty-five contracts on utilizing foreign capital were signed and approved with a contract value of foreign investment standing at $US 61.73 million, a drop of 55.98 percent from $US 140.22 million of 1989. Of the contracts, three were on foreign loans involving $US 11.26 million; ninety-nine on foreign direct investment with $US 39.47 million; and $US 11.00 million of other foreign investment.

Out of the ninety-nine projects of foreign direct investment, seventy-five were equity joint ventures, seven were contractual joint ventures, and seventeen were wholly foreign-owned enterprises, including eighty-seven productive projects and twelve non-productive projects. By the end of 1990, 284 were foreign direct investment enterprises, among which 242 were productive projects, and forty-two were non-productive projects. Foreign investment mainly comes from Hong Kong, the United States, Taiwan Province, the Netherlands, Macau, Australia, Singapore and Germany.

In 1990, the foreign-invested enterprises earned $US 25.30 million from their export, 56.37 percent up against $US 16.18 million in 1989.

Technology Import and Export

Some twenty-seven contract for import of technology and equipment were signed with a contract value standing at $US 39.1515 million, down by 34.15 percent from 1989. The imports mainly came from the United States, Japan, Hong Kong, Belgium, Germany, Republic of Korea covering machinery, electronic industries, and textiles as well as light and chemical industries (2).

One contract was signed for the export of China's technology, totalling $US 3 million.

Foreign Economic Cooperation

Twenty-five contracts for foreign projects and labor service cooperation were concluded with a contract value of $US 180 million, 4.80 times up against the amount of $US 31.06 million in 1989. The turnover of the year was $US 79.80 million, increasing by 11.84 percent over $UFS 71.35 million of 1989, and a total of 2,658 labor service personnel were working abroad for these projects. The number of experts working abroad by the end of the year stood at ninety-eight. Twelve aid projects were undertaken. Recipient countries include Nepal, Algeria, Cameroon, Thailand, Mozambique, covering highway, traffic, medicine and health as well as agricultural science and technology. The number of experts working abroad by the end of the year stood at 426.

Eleven projects involving aid from the United Nations Population Fund and UNICEF were accepted, amounting to $US 34.91 million, which will be completed within five years of 1990-1994.

In the year, one enterprise was established abroad, namely International Leather Processing Company, Ltd (Thailand) with China's investment of $US 720,000. By the end of 1990, eleven enterprises were established abroad with a contract value of $US 10.17 million and Chinese investment of $US 4.06 million. The main projects include Australia Hao Di-Chinese Investment Co., Ltd., America CHB Co., Ltd., Macau Jianxinglong Enterprise Co., Ltd., with total profit of $US 4.37 million.

Table 22.   Commodities each with export value exceeding $US 5 million
—Hubei Province (2)

Exported commodities classified by value	Commodity Name	Export value ($US million)	Percentage of the total
Over $US 30 million (5 items)	Cotton cloth, cotton garments, cotton, cotton polyester fabrics, live pigs.	210.93	19.68
$US 10-30 million (10 items)	Cigarettes, cotton yarn, bath towels, polyester garments, singlets & vests, ramie garments, vegetable feedstuffs, billet, steel plate, cotton ramie blended yarn.	156.43	14.60
$US 5-10 million (15 items)	Fresh eggs, tea, flue-cured tobacco, gallnut, raw lacquer, bristles, feather down garments, ramie yarn, thermos, sport shoes, tires, industrial bearing, sesame, machinery, bean expellers.	103.78	9.68

* * * *

The Beijing office of the province is located at:

44.A Beishiqiaolu, Haidian District
Beijing 100081
Tel: 8314488-2111 Fax: 8314488

Another China contact which might be helpful to users of this volume is:

Hubei Provincial Foreign Economic Relations & Trade Commission
8, Jianghan North Road, Hankou, Wuhan, China
Tel: 562821 Fax: 561149

16. HUNAN PROVINCE

Hunan is situated in the north of Guangdong Province and south of the Yangtze River. It has an area of 210,000 sq. km. and a population of 60,094,000 made up of the Han, Tujia, Miao, Dong, Yao and Zhuang nationalities. The provincial capital is Changsha, a city on the Beijing-Guangzhou Railway, the nation's major north-south trunk line. The province is quite rich in natural resources, and its antimony reserves are the biggest

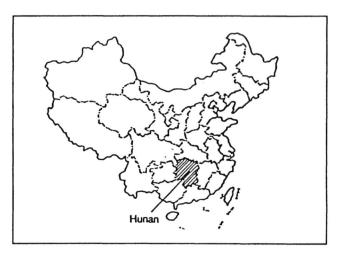

in the world and hydropower resources are estimated at more than 15 million kw. Because of its warm, humid climate and fertile soils, it developed rapidly into a major rice area. Today, it supplies one-sixth of the country's rice, mainly from the densely settled lowlands around Dongting and the Xiang floodplain. The province also produces tungsten, used for lamp filaments and steel production, and other metal ores.

Foreign Trade

In 1990, the total value of export and import of Hunan Province was $US 935.48 million, 4.56 percent increase over the $US 894.72 million of 1989.

The total purchase value of export commodities was RMB 4.11 billion yuan, 12.70 percent increase over RMB 3.647 billion yuan of 1989.

Total value of exportation was $US 805.52 million, 21.02 percent more than $US 665.63 million of 1989, 5.87 percent of the GNP of the province and 1.56 percent of the total value of national exportation.

Among the export commodities: agricultural and sideline products accounted for $US 161.01 million, 19.99 percent of the total value of exportation, 2.43 percentage points less than 1989; light industrial products accounted for $US 369.35 million, 45.85 percent of the total, 4.06 percentage points more; heavy industrial products accounted for $US 275.16 million, 34.16 percent of the total, 1.63 percentage points less. According to the standard categories of international trade: primary products accounted for $Us 254.29 million, 31.57 percent of the total amount of exportation, 3.2 percentage points less than 1989; manufactured products accounted for $US 551.23 million, 68.43 percent of the total, 3.2 percentage points more.

Commodities each with export value above $US 3 million were fifty-three items, with the total export value at $US 610.73 million, 75.82 percent of the total value of exportation.

Export commodities were sold to 108 countries and regions, mainly to the five major markets of Hong Kong and Macau, Japan, the United States, EC, and the former Soviet Union and Eastern Europe. Export value amounted to $US 654.91 million, 81.30 percent of the total.

The value of import goods totaled $US 129.96 million, 43.27 percent less than $US 229.09 million of 1989.

Table 23. Commodities each with the export value above $US 5 million
—Hunan Province

Amount/category	Commodities	Export value ($US million)	Percentage of total export value
Over $US 10 million (16 items)	Live pigs, ramie & ramie products, firecrackers & fireworks, pottery, antimony products, garments, tea, frozen pork, leather & its products, iron alloy, feed stuffs, feather down & its products, hard alloy, cotton cloth, chemical fiber, blended cloth, shoes.	402.82	50.01
$US 5-10 million (21 items)	Rice, lithopone, light diesel oil, steel products, tools, cotton knit-wear, industrial bearings, metal products, cotton manufactured products, tungsten ore, ammonium paratungstate, canned food, suckling pigs, eggs, silk and silk products, lead, silicon, foundry products, mini complete plant, hand em-broidered articles.	150.21	18.65

Table 24. Major markets each with the export value above $US 20 million
—Hunan Province

Country/region	Export value ($US million)	Percentage of the total
Hong Kong and Macau	558.03	44.45
The United States	71.55	8.88
Japan	68.47	8.50
The former Soviet Union	38.77	4.81
Germany	36.69	4.55
Thailand	20.72	2.57

The composition of import commodities was: means of production, valuing $US 117.61 million, accounting for 90.5 percent of total import value; means of subsistence, $US 12.35 million, 9.5 percent. Categorized according to standard of international trade, primary products were $US 37.9 million, 29.19 percent of the total import value; and industrial manufactured products, were $US 92.0 million, 70.81 percent.

Commodities each with the import value above $US 5 million were eight items, i.e. paper, cigarette auxiliaries, light industry machinery, urea, complete plant and technical import, metal minerals, crude oil, industrial chemical raw materials, etc., valuing $US 84.70 million, 65.17 percent of the total import value.

The import commodities came from major import markets in nineteen countries and regions; Hong Kong and Macau at $US 65.71 million, accounting for 50.56 percent of the total import value; Italy at $US 16.37 million, 12.60 percent; Japan at $US 8.34 million, 6.42 percent; the United States at $US 5.48 million, 4.22 percent; Australia at $US 4.35 million, 3.35 percent; and Indonesia at $US 3.? million, 2.92 percent.

Utilization of Foreign Capital

In 1990, 127 contracts on utilizing foreign capital had been signed with approval, with the total contracted value at $US 49.86 million, 67.08 percent less than the $US 151.46 million of 1989. Among the contracts signed, one was a foreign loan project, with the contracted value at $US 8.75 million; forty-five were foreign direct investment projects, with contracted value of foreign investment at 26 million; and eighty-one were other foreign investment projects, with foreign investment value at $US 14 million.

The actually-used foreign investment was $US 177.80 million, 45.29 percent more than $US 122.38 million of 1989, in which $US 158.75 million were foreign loans; $US 11.16 million were foreign direct investment; and $US 7.89 were other investments.

Among the forty-five projects of foreign direct investments, thirty-two were joint ventures; seven were contractual joint ventures; and six were solely foreign-owned projects. They can be divided into forty-four productive projects and one non-productive project. Categorized according to the field of activities, six were electronics and machinery and garments, three each of metallurgy, transportation, food, light industry and textile, two each of chemicals and geology and minerals, one each of agriculture, construction materials, biology, medicine and service, and three of other fields.

Foreign direct investment came from six countries and regions, of which: Hong Kong accounted for $US 13.96 million, Taiwan Province—$US 6.42 million, Belgium—$US 4.60 million, Japan—$US 1 million, Australia—$US 0.4 million, and the United States—0.36 million.

In 1990, foreign investment enterprises already in business operation had earned $US 24.? million, realizing a profit of RMB 35.99 million yuan.

Technology Import and Export

Seventeen contracts on the importation of technology were signed with approval in

1990, with a contracted value at $US 15.67 million, 42.14 percent less than the $US 27.0802 million of 1989. The actually-used amount of foreign exchange were $US 8 million, 58.22 percent less than the $US 19.? million of 1989.

The introduced projects mainly came from Japan, the United States, Italy, Switzerland, Germany and other developed countries. These projects were mainly in fields of tobacco industry and post and telecommunications.

Sixteen contracts were signed for the exportation of technology, with the total contracted value at $US 25.40 million, 120 percent over the $US 11.67 million of 1989. The actual foreign exchange earnings were $US 6.41 million. The export of technology was mainly composed of complete plant and key equipment, exported to the countries and regions like Bangladesh, Pakistan, Thailand and Hong Kong.

Foreign Economic Cooperation

Eighty-seven contracts for projects and labor service abroad were signed with a total value of $US 13 million, 47.14 percent more than the $US 8.84 million of 1989. Business turnover completed was $US 18.79 million, 2.3 times more than the $US 5.66 million of 1989. Three hundred and nine labor service personnel were dispatched abroad and the number reached 623 by the end of the year. The projects were located in countries and regions like Thailand, Ghana, Burkina Faso, Zaire, Liberia and the United States. Fields of cooperation mainly included building, highway, bridge, machinery, electronics, non-ferrous metals, metallurgy, textile, tailoring, painting, papering with qigong, embroidery, weaving with bamboo, grass and willow twig, and food and drink services.

In 1990, ten external aid projects were undertaken for their continuation; two medical teams were sent abroad; 220 personnel were dispatched. By the end of the year, the number of people sent to work abroad was 284. The number of recipient countries was twelve. Four projects of technical cooperation were completed in the year.

Nineteen United Nations and bilateral aid projects were received, with a total worth of $US 26.2165 million. They mainly included: Comprehensive Agricultural Development of Wuyi Mountainous Region, Development of Balanced Fertilizer Spraying Technology, Supervision of Children's Nutrition, Training for Women Development, Training of Teachers, etc.

In 1990, overseas investment enterprises were established, one each in Germany and United Arab Emirates, with the total investment from the Chinese side at $US 0.74 million. By the end of 1990, thirty-seven overseas enterprises were established in fifteen countries and regions, with the total investment value from the Chinese side at $US 8.36 million and the accumulated profits at $US 12.5973 million.

*   *   *   *

The Beijing office of the province is located at:

Madian, Beitaipingzhuang
Beijing 100088
Tel: 2011133-2717, 2019380
Fax: 2019333

Another China contact which might be helpful to users of this volume is:

Hunan Foreign Economic Relations & Trade Commission
4 Wuyi Road E., Changsha, Hunan Province
Tel: 442147, 449208 Fax: 0731-442891

17. JIANGSU PROVINCE

Situated on a very fertile alluvial plain in the lower Yangtze River Valley, Jiangsu Province is the most densely populated chinese province, where very intensive farming is practiced to make the most of the land. The province has also fairly developed industry turning out a wide spectrum of products ranging from automobiles, TV sets and silks and satins to arts and crafts (2).

Total area: 102,600 sq. km.
Population: 65,350,000
Capital: Nanjing, a port on the Yangtze.

Jiangsu's industrial output accounts for 13% of the nation's total, which places it first among the provinces. The province is particularly strong in textiles, machinery, chemicals, food and other light manufacturing.

Jiangsu province is the site of the industrial city of Wuxi. The Jiagnan semiconductor plant there has received equipment from numerous Japanese and American companies.

Foreign Trade

The total value of export and import of Jiangsu Province in 1990 reached $US 3.69452 billion, an increase of 11.73 percent over $US 3.30674 billion in 1989.

The export commodities purchased totaled RMB 22.64 billion yuan, up by 33.46 percent over RMB 16.964 billion yuan in 1989.

The total export value was $US 2.94995 billion, increasing by 20.84 percent against $US 2.44111 billion in 1989, accounting for 10.72 percent of the Province's GNP and 5.67 percent of the total national export and ranking fifth of the whole nation.

Among the export commodities, agricultural and sideline products reached $US 217.15 million taking up 7.36 percent of the total, light industrial products, $US 2.04847 billion, 69.44 percent heavy industrial products, $US 684.33 million, 23.2 percent. Compared with that in 1989, the proportion of agricultural and sideline products as well as light industrial products in the total export decreased by 0.6 percentage points and 2.25 percentage points respectively while that of heavy industrial products rising by 2.85 percentage points. According to the international trade standard classification, the export of primary products was $US 602.76 million, accounting for 20.43 percent the export; industrial manufactured goods $US 2.34719 billion, 79.57 percent. Compared with that of 1989, the proportion of primary products decreased by 1.27 percentage points and industrial manufactured goods increased by 1.27 percentage points.

Eleven items of commodities each with the export value exceeding $US 30 million totalled $US 1.06302 billion, accounting for 36.04 percent of the total export; twenty-nine items of commodities with the export value each between $US 10 to 30 million totalled $US 496.59 million, 16.83 percent; thirty-three items of export commodities each with value of $US 5 to 10 million totalled $US 241.42 million, 8.18 percent. Nine items commodities each with value over $US 50 million included silk and satins, cotton cloth, petroleum products, cotton-polyester blended garments and fabrics, raw silk, knitwear and cotton knitwear, amounting to $US 989.78 million altogether and taking up 33.35 percent of the total export.

Goods were exported to 148 countries and regions.

Table 25. Major export markets—Jiangsu Province

Country/region	Export value ($US million)	Percentage of the total export
Hong Kong	653.63	22.16
Japan	587.91	19.93
European Community	463.12	15.7
United States	385.44	13.06
Former Soviet Union	110.74	3.75
5 Eastern European Countries	77.19	2.62
Total	**2278.03**	**77.22**

The total import value reached $US 744.57 million, down by 13.99 percent against $US 865 million in 1989. Among them, the import of means of production was $US 743.06 million, accounting for 99.8 percent and that of means of livelihood $US 1.51 million, 0.2 percent. If the imports were divided by the international trade standard classification, primary products were $US 120.32 million, 16.16 percent and industrial manufactured products $US 624.25 million, 83.84 percent.

The main items of imports were chemicals, timber, stable rayon, synthetic fiber, spare parts, components of TV sets and sound equipment, telecommunication equipment, complete sets of equipment. The total import value reached $US 484.1 million, accounting for 65.02 percent of the total imports.

The main commodities came from thirty-six countries and regions.

Table 26. Main import markets—Jiangsu Province

Country/region	Import value ($US million)	Percentage of the total import
United States	272.12	36.55
Japan	169.22	22.73
Hong Kong	114.26	15.34
European Communities	64.02	8.6
Singapore	23.23	3.12
Total	**642.85**	**86.34**

Utilization of Foreign Capital

The province signed 512 contracts on the utilization of foreign capital, amounting to $US 456.08 million, up by 15.62 percent over $US 394.48 million in 1989. Among them, thirty-four were foreign loans valued at $US 144.94 million, 393 were foreign direct investment with $US 285.61 million, and eighty-five were other forms of foreign investment with $US 25.53 million.

The actual utilization of foreign capital was $US 283.7 million, increasing by 19.47 percent, compared with $US 237.46 million in 1989, of which, $US 155.34 million was foreign loans, $US 104.38 million was foreign direct investment and $US 23.98 million was other foreign investment. Of the 393 foreign direct investment contracts, 352 were equity joint ventures, twelve were contractual joint ventures and twenty-nine were wholly foreign-owned enterprises. Among those projects, 388 were productive and five were non-productive. According to division of trade, they were classified as follows: 148 were in light industry, ninety-nine in textile and garment industry, fifty-nine in electronics and electric appliances, thirty-one in metallic products, twenty-three in medicines and health products, fifteen in machinery products, thirteen in agriculture, animal husbandry and cultivation, two in real estate, two in hotel and funfair and one in consultancy.

The investors were mainly from eighteen countries and regions, of which, Hong Kong and Macau with 233 projects, $US 159.0565 million; the United States, thirty-one projects, $US 56.51 million; Taiwan Province, sixty projects, $US 28.4135 million; Japan, thirty-six projects, $US 12.4179 million; the Netherlands, one project, $US 11.2332 million; Singapore, twelve projects, $US 8.389 million; and Australia, four projects, $US 1.158 million.

By the end of 1990, 525 foreign-invested enterprises went into operation. The total annual industrial output value reached RMB 4.58472 billion yuan and sales income was RMB 4.11885 billion yuan; direct export value amounted to $US 193.14 million, increasing 1.2 times over that in 1989. There was surplus in foreign exchange balance.

Technology Import and Export

Two contracts on technology import were signed, valued at $US 960,000. The projects covered technology of machinery and light industry from the United States and the United Kingdom.

Foreign Economic Cooperation

Some 121 contracts were signed on overseas engineering and labor service cooperation with value of $US 75.89 million, down by 2.24 percent against $US 77.63 million in 1989. The total turnover reached $US 83.89 million, up by 8.46 percent over $US 77.35 million in 1989. At the end of the year 2,965 labor service personnel remained abroad. The major projects contracted were Benin highway teaching buildings in Kenya and construction engineering of ground satellite receiving station in Nepal.

The province undertook thirteen projects involving Chinese government assistance, of which, eight were completed items and five were technical and other cooperation. The nine recipient countries were Tanzania, Senegal, Ecuador, Mozambique, Somalia and Barbados with projects in agriculture, water conservancy, geology, construction and electricity. The first phase technical cooperation of Senegal Dam and the consolidation and winding up of canal in Somalia have been concluded. One hundred and fourteen people were sent out and 213 remained abroad at the end of the year. One project was carried out with assistance by the United Nations Industrial Development Organization with the aid valued at $US 605,000 and the first phase scheme was being undertaken. Jiangsu established seven productive enterprises involving Chinese investment of $US 1.21 million in the United States, Australia, Antigua and Babuda, Bolivia and Malaysia (2).

*   *   *   *

A contact which should be helpful to users of this volume is:

Jiangsu Foreign Economic Relations & Trade Commission
29 East Beijing Road, Nanjing 210008
Tel: 712136   Fax: 025-712072

18. JIANGXI PROVINCE

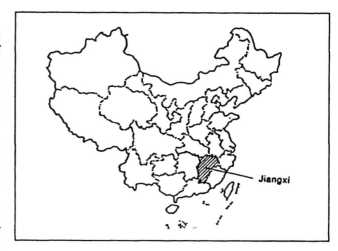

Situated on the south bank of the Yangtze River and west of Fujian Province, Jiangxi covers an area of 166,900 sq. km. and has a population of 36,950,000 at year end in 1989. The provincial capital is Nanchang.

Known as the "homeland of non-ferrous metals," Jiangxi Province has the richest reserves of copper tantalum, cesium, thallium, scandium, uranium and thorium in China. Its deposits of tungsten, selenium, tellurium rubidium and lithium are the second biggest in the country. There are also rare earth, China clay and marble deposits (2).

The climate is warm and moist and its fertile soil is used to grow rice, tea and cotton. Coal is mined at Pingxiang and clay at Gaoling mountain near Jingdezhen.

Foreign Trade

In 1990, the total export and import volume of Jiangxi Province was $US 631.18 million, increased by 7.48 percent over $US 587.26 million in 1989.

The total value of commodities purchased for export reached RMB 2.7 billion yuan, an increase of 9.18 percent over RMB 2.473 billion yuan in 1989. Of the total, 96.04 percent were directly exported by the Province totalling RMB 2.593 billion yuan, and 3.96 percent were allocated for export to other port provinces totalling RMB 107 million yuan.

The total export volume reached $US 561.47 million, an increase of 8.86 percent over $US 5.5.77 million in 1989, accounting for 6.31 percent and 1.08 percent of the Province's GNP and the nation's total export respectively.

The structure of export commodities was specified as follows: agricultural and sideline products and heavy industrial products, decreased by 1.07 percentage points and 1.46 percentage points respectively compared with those of 1989. Light industrial products increased by 2.53 percentage points. Industrial manufactured goods increased by 5.77 percentage points, of which, the percentage occupied by machinery and electronic products in the total export increased from 7.21 percent to 9.25 percent.

There are 745 items of export commodities, of which the export value of eighty items each with export value exceeding $US 1 million respectively. Their total value reached $US 475.28 million, accounting for 84.65 percent of the total export. Of these, the export value of fourteen items of commodities each exceeding $US 10 million respectively, totalled $US

262.26 million, accounting for 46.71 percent of the total. They are garments, porcelain, synthetic blended fabrics, tungsten ores, rice, ammonium paratunstate, live pigs, firecrackers and fireworks, cotton piece goods, canned goods, feedstuffs, automobiles, tea, and down products. The export value of fourteen items of commodities ranged from $US 5-10 million. Their value reached $US 93.05 million, accounting for 16.57 percent of the total. They are honey, cotton manufactured products, ramie cloth, resin, ramie yarn, cotton knitwear, steel products, rare earth, color TV sets, cement, ferromanganese, spun rayon knitwear, silk and drawnworks.

The Province exported its commodities to eighty-four countries and regions. There were forty-three countries and regions, to which the export value exceeded $US 1 million each, totalling $US 522.16 million and accounting for ninety-three percent of the total.

The total imports valued at $US 69.71 million, a decrease of 2.49 percent from $US 71.49 million in 1989.

The structure of import commodities was means of production valued at $US 69.17 million, accounting for 99.23 percent of the total; and means of livelihood at $US 540,000, accounting for 0.77 percent of the total. Classified by international trade standard, primary products valued at $US 32.49 million, accounting for 46.61 percent of the total; and industrial manufactured products at $US 37.22 million, accounting for 53.39 percent.

There were forty-one import commodities such as chemical fertilizer amounting to $US 14.23 million, accounting for 20.41 percent of the total import value; spun rayon cloth $US 6.63 million, 9.51 percent; chemical raw materials $US 4.85 million, 6.96 percent; synthetic fiber $US 3.28 million, 4.71 percent textile and garment subsidiary materials $US 3.09 million, 4.43 percent.

Commodities were imported from thirteen countries and regions. The value of imported goods from Hong Kong, Japan, Macau and the former Soviet Union accounted for 36.26, 32.78, 12.75 and 6.48 percent of the total respectively.

Utilization of Foreign Capital

In 1990, Jiangxi Province signed and approved 101 contracts on utilizing foreign capital with the contract value of $US 122.92 million, an increase of 38.24 percent over $US 88.9158 million in 1989. Of these contracts, five were involved in foreign loans totalling $US 92.11 million; fifty-four were in foreign direct investment totalling $Us 28.55 million; forty-two were in other foreign investment totalling $US 2.26 million. The value of foreign capital actually utilized reached $US 51.41 million, an increase of 33.05 percent over $US 38.64 million in 1989. Of the total utilized foreign capital, foreign loans reached $US 42.03 million, foreign direct investment $US 6.21 million, other foreign investment $US 3.17 million.

Among the fifty-four projects receiving foreign direct investment, forty-two were equity joint ventures, seven were contractual joint ventures, and five were exclusively foreign-owned enterprises. Of these, fifty-two were productive enterprises, and two were non-productive. The foreign investment projects were involved in the fields of agriculture, forestry, animal husbandry and fishery, water conservancy, industry communications and service. Foreign investment came from countries and regions such as Hong Kong, Taiwan, Province, Japan, France, Liberia, etc., of which, thirty-four items were from Hong Kong, the value amounted to $US 13.83 million, accounting for 48.44 percent of the foreign direct investment. Fourteen were from Taiwan Province, the value reached $US 390,000, accounting for 32.89 percent.

By the end of 1990, 183 foreign-invested enterprises had been approved, 144 of which were equity joint ventures, thirty were contractual joint ventures, and nine were exclusively foreign-owned enterprises. In 1990, the output value of fifty-eight foreign-invested enterprises which had been put into operation and production reached RMB 398.55 million yuan, the foreign exchanges earned through export were $US 25.30 million, an increase of 138.23 percent over that of 1989. The profit achieved was RMB 29.68 million yuan, an increase of 58.04 percent over that of 1989. And the taxes turned over amounted to RMB 11.62 million yuan, an increase of 16.08 percent over that of 1989.

Technology Import and Export

Ten contracts were signed for the import of technology and equipment with the contract value of $US 5.076 million, a decrease of 62.50 percent from $US 12.851 million in 1989. The foreign exchanges actually used amounted to $US 12.437 million, a decrease of 39.42 percent from $US 20.5 million in 1989. The items of technical import came from Italy, the United States, Switzerland, Japan, Germany, Hong Kong and Taiwan Province, of which, the projects from Italy and the United States accounted for 32.18 percent and 26.47 percent of the total contract value respectively. The introduced projects were mainly involved in four trades of electronics, machinery, metallurgy and light industry. In 1990, eleven introduced projects were put into production.

Foreign Economic Cooperation

Nine contracts of contracting foreign projects and labor service were signed with the contract value of $US 6.86 million, an increase of 59.16 percent over $US 4.31 million in 1989. $US 7.2 million of the turnover was achieved, a decrease of 21.58 percent from $US 9.22 million in 1989. In the year of 1990, 414 people for labor service were sent to countries and regions such as Libya, Japan, Zambia, Jordan, Saipan (the United States), Germany, Hong Kong, Iraq and Kuwait to undertake contracted engineering projects and also to provide labor service in sewing and cooking. By the end of the year, 534 people remained abroad.

In 1990, the Province undertook four foreign aid projects and sent abroad seventy foreign aid persons. The major projects were involved in the construction of a hospital in Equatorial Guinea and three technical cooperation projects such as a hydroelectric station in Sierra Leone, the M'pourie Farm in Mauritania and a hydroelectric station in the Congo.

The Province received two donations from UNDP and UNICEF, which were used for the development of Shanjiang Lake, health care for women and children, export planning of tractors and porcelain. The total value of donations amounted to $US 2.25 million, of which, $US 2.37 million were actually received.

* * * *

The Beijing office to the province is located at:

Madian, Beitaipingzhuang
Beijing 100088
Tel: 2029039   Fax: 2011070

Table 27. Export commodity structure—Jiangxi Province (2)

Classified by agriculture, light and heavy industries			*Classified by international standard*		
Categories	*Export value ($US million)*	*Percentage of the total* *1990 1989*	*Category*	*Export value ($US million)*	*Percentage of the total* *1990 1989*
Agricultural and sideline products	131.72	23.46 24.53	Primary products	224.98	40.07 45.84
Light industrial products	280.74	50.00 47.47			
Heavy industrial products	149.01	26.54 28.00	Industrial manu-factured products	336.49	59.93 54.16

Table 28. Major markets with the export value exceeding $US 10 million each—Jiangxi Province (2)

Country/region	*Value ($US million)*	*Percentage of the total in 1990*	*Percentage of the total in 1989*
Hong Kong	208.86	37.20	36.22
Japan	52.50	9.35	11.35
Former Soviet Union	40.32	7.18	5.96
Germany	30.24	5.39	8.48
Singapore	27.24	4.85	2.61
United States	26.57	4.73	6.96
United Kingdom	15.73	2.80	2.31
Thailand	15.58	2.77	2.23

Another China contact which may be helpful to users of this volume is:

Foreign Economic Relations & Trade Department of Jiangxi Province
60 Zhanqian Road, Nanchang 330002
Tel: 226611, 227281 Fax: 225234

19. JILIN PROVINCE

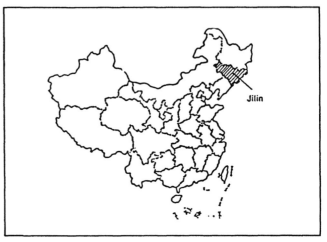

          This Northeast China province that borders on the Democratic People's Republic of Korea and the Maritime Territory of the former Soviet Union spreads over an area of 187,000 sq. km. in which dwell 24,027,000 people of the Han, Korean, Mongolian, Hui, Manchu and Xibe nationalities. The provincial capital is Changchun, where China's biggest automotive works are located.

          In eastern Jilin Province are Changbaishan Mountains and coniferous forests where the largest nature reserve in China is located. In the Changbaishan Mountains ginseng is cultivated or grows wild, and there are white cranes, swans, Manchurian tigers and sika deer. In central Jilin Province is the Song-Liao fertile plain—one of the biggest granaries in China. The west is an extensive, and flat grassland for grazing of beef cattle and fine wool sheep.

          Unlike the neighboring provinces of Heilongjiang and Liaoning, mineral resources are scant in Jilin. Agriculture is the main occupation; it is China's leading producer of soya beans and also grows wheat, millet and sugar beets.

Foreign Trade

          The total value of export and import of Jilin Province in 1990 reached $US 952.71 million, a 2.28 percent increase from $US 931.50 million in 1989.

          The purchasing value for export commodities totalled RMB 3.235 billion yuan, an increase of 9.22 percent over RMB 2.962 billion yuan of 1989.

          Its total export value was $US 751.71 million, an increase of 11.96 percent over $US 671.38 million in 1989, accounting for 10.04 percent of the provincial GNP and 1.44 percent of the total value of national export.

          There were eight export commodities with the value over $US 10 million, including maize, bean expellers, garment, frozen beef, cultivated ginseng, automobiles, castorseed and canned beef, the total value amounted to $US 401.47 million, marking up 53.41 percent of the total export.

          The commodities with the value ranging from $US 5 million to $US 10 million were beet pulp, silicon manganese alloys, soya bean, canned pork, jackets, gym shoes, cement, woolen piece goods, kidney beans, bath towels, totalled $US 60.60 million, accounting for 8.06 percent of the total export.

Goods were exported to seventy-seven countries and regions.

Table 29. Structure of export commodities—Jilin Province

Classified according to agriculture, light industry and heavy industries			Classified according to international trade standard		
Item	Export value ($US million)	Percentage in total 1990 1989	Item	Export value ($US million)	Percentage in total 1990 1989
Farm and sideline products	410.61	54.62 56.70	Primary products	487.71	64.88 65.50
Light industrial and textile products	194.61	25.89 23.10			
Heavy industrial products	146.49	19.49 20.20	Industrial manufactured goods	264.00	35.10 34.50

Table 30. Main markets for export—Jilin Province

Markets for export	Export value ($US million)	Percentage of the total (percent)
Hong Kong	215.23	28.63
Japan	180.64	24.03
Former Soviet Union	160.86	21.40
Singapore	21.06	2.80
United States	19.74	2.63
Korea DPR	18.52	2.46
Cuba	13.70	1.82
The Netherlands	10.45	1.39

The import value totalled $US 200.99 million, decreased by 22.73 percent from $US 260.12 million in 1989. The imports of means of production cost $US 187.50 million, taking up 93.29 percent of the total value, and the means of livelihood cost $US 13.49 million, accounting for 6.71 percent of the total. Classified according to international trade standard, primary products, with the value of $US 19.44 million, accounted for 9.67 percent of the total import, and industrial manufactured goods, with the value of $US 181.55 million, accounted for 90.33 percent of the total.

Its main imports were auto parts, with the value of $US 33.85 million, chemical fertilizers with $US 30.27 million, chrome ores with $US 23.83 million, auto spare parts with $US 8.10 million and machines with $US 7.46 million. All of them amounted to $US 103.51

million, taking up 51.50 percent of the total imports.

The import markets were scattered in twenty-three countries and regions.

Table 31. List of the main import markets—Jilin Province

Country/region	Import value ($US million)	Percentage of total import
Germany	37.43	18.62
Former Soviet Union	31.80	15.82
Japan	31.70	15.77
Hong Kong	28.63	14.24
United States	14.08	7.01
Korea DPR	13.19	6.56
India	6.76	3.36
France	5.03	2.50

The province's border barter trade annual value amounted to SF 259.24 million, decreased by 16.58 percent from SF 310.77 million in 1989. Among them, import value reached SF 124.05 million, down 10.85 percent against SF 139.14 million in 1989, and export value reached SF 135.19 million, 21.23 percent decrease from SF 171.62 million in 1989. Major import goods contain chemical fertilizer, cement and chemical materials; and major export goods contain maize, canned goods, leather shoes and gym shoes.

Utilization of Foreign Capital

Some eighty-two contracts signed for using foreign capital were approved, with a contract value of $US 92.35 million, 43.13 percent more than $US 64.52 million in 1989, thirteen contracts of which were in foreign loan, with a value of $US 56.31 million: fifty-two were foreign direct investment, with a contract value of $US 20.81 million; and seventeen were other foreign investment, with a value of $US 15.23 million.

Foreign investment actually used was $US 28.62 million, a decrease of 20.66 percent against $US 36.08 million in 1989, $US 8.28 million of which were in foreign loans. $US 17.60 million in foreign direct investment, $US 2.74 million in other foreign investment.

Among the fifty-two projects with foreign direct investment, there were forty-three equity joint ventures, six contractual joint ventures and three wholly foreign-owned enterprises. Thirty-two were productive projects and twenty were non-productive projects. Classified in line, thirty-two were on industrial projects, three on electronics projects, one each on textile and construction, eight on commercial and service projects, and seven on other projects.

The investors mainly came from: Hong Kong with twenty-three contracts, $US 6.71 million; Taiwan Province with eleven contracts, $US 6.12 million; Japan with nine contracts, $US 4.09 million; the United States with five contracts, $US 3.50 million; Republic of Korea with three contracts, $US 0.25 million; and Canada with one contract, $US 0.14 million.

Twenty foreign investment enterprises were put into production and started their operation. The annual output value of foreign investment enterprises was fulfilled at a value of RMB 231.49 million yuan, and foreign exchange earning was $US 8.57 million (2).

Technology Import and Export

Thirty-six contracts for introduction of technology and import of equipment were concluded, with a contract value of $US 42.14 million, 10.34 percent less than $US 47.00 million in 1989. Foreign exchange actually used were $US 30.40 million, up by 22.48 percent over $US 24.82 million. Import items mainly were: four from former Soviet Union, valued at $US 11.74 million; thirteen from Japan, valued at $US 8.42 million; one from Austria, valued at $US 8.35 million; two from Switzerland, valued at $US 5.66 million; and three from Italy, valued at $US 3.22 million. The imports were mainly used in the fields of light industry, textiles, telecommunications, medicines, machinery, chemicals, agriculture, forestry, electronics and metallurgy.

The province signed seven technology export contracts, with a value of $US 5.88 million, up 5.7 times over $US 880,000 in 1989.

Major items were exports to the former Soviet Union, Iran and Iraq of plastic injection shapings, equipment and technology of hydrogen peroxide solution, design technology and full set of equipment for brickyard with the annual output of 5 million pieces.

Foreign Economic Cooperation

Seventy-two contracts for contracting overseas projects and labor service were signed, worth $US 42.17 million, an increase of 1.2 times over $US 19.00 million in 1989; turnover was achieved to 22.44 million, an increase of 73 percent more than $US 19.00 million in 1989. Workers sent abroad reached 3,428 persons, 2,483 persons being abroad at the end of the year. Workers were distributed to countries and regions such as the former Soviet Union, the United States, Japan, Spain, Singapore, Thailand, Canada, Germany, the United Arab Emirates, Libya, Niger and Turkey. Major contractual items cover Sudan Main Bridge and Dam in Niger, etc.

Jilin undertook three foreign aid projects in Niger, Sudan and Vanuatu, chiefly on physical installation, bridge construction and medical services.

Six bilateral and international organizations assistance projects were accepted from the United Nations, Japan and Canada, with a value of $US 21.51 million.

One non-trade enterprise was established abroad, with a total investment of $US 437,000 from Chinese side.

* * * *

The Beijing office of the province is located at:

Madian, Beitaipingzhuang
Beijing 100088
Tel: 2011085, 2019321   Fax: 2011084

Another China contact which should be helpful to users of this volume is:

Jilin Province Foreign Economic Relations & Trade Commission
81 Stalin Street Changchun, Jilin Province 130021
Tel: 828077, 827011   Fax: 824772

20. LIAONING PROVINCE

Bordering on the Democratic People's Republic of Korea, Liaoning, one of the most economically developed provinces in China, boasts such large industrial centers as Shenyang, the steel center of Anshan and the mining center of Fushun, where an open-cut mine with coal seams 90 m. thick is located. It has an area of 147,380 sq. km. and a population of nearly 40 million. The provincial capital is Shenyang (2).

The province accounts for 40% of the nation's coal production and has China's third largest oil field, the Liaohe Oil Field. The port city of Dalian is the center of Japanese manufacturing investment in China.

Tobacco, apples and pears are grown in the province, which is unusually well endowed with minerals. The great coal fields of Fushun, Fuxin and Benxi are among the largest and richest in China. There is iron ore at Anshan, Benxi and Liaoyang, and there is also valuable reserve of manganese and molybdenum, used in steel production. As a result, Liaoning is China's leading producer of iron and steel, aluminum and heavy machinery.

Foreign Trade

The value of export and import of Liaoning Province in 1990 totalled $US 6.295 billion, an increase of 18.02 percent over $US 5.334 billion in 1989.

The foreign trade purchase value was RMB 12.501 billion yuan, in increase of 6.87 percent over RMB 11.697 billion yuan in 1989.

The export value totalled $US 5.6 billion, an increase of 25.96 percent over $US 4.446 billion in 1989, accounting for 10.76 percent of the national total export and ranking the second in the country, representing 27.61 percent in GNP of the Province.

The structure of export commodities was: agricultural and sideline products at $US 622 million, accounting for 11.17 percent of the total export; light industrial products at $US 881 million, accounting for 15.73 percent of the total export; heavy industrial product at $US 4.097 billion, representing 73.16 percent of the total. Comparing with 1989, the proportion of agricultural and sideline products and light industrial products decreased 2.86 and 1.81 percentage points respectively; and heavy industrial products increased by 4.67 percentage points.

The products were exported to more than 121 countries and regions. The main markets were: Japan, $US 2.255 billion, accounting for 40.27 percent of the total export; the United States, $US 1.052 billion, accounting for 18.79 percent; Singapore, $US 499 million, accounting for 8.91 percent; and Hong Kong, $US 471 million, accounting for 8.41 percent.

The export of border trade was $US 5.31 million, a decrease of 48 percent over $US 10.21 million in 1989.

The import value was $US 695 million, a decrease of 21.56 percent over $US 886 million in 1989. The main import products were complete sets of equipment and technology, steel products, chemical raw materials, light industrial machinery, electrical equipment and textile products, etc. The main import markets were Japan, $US 274 million; Hong Kong, $US 138 million; the United States, $US 52 million; and Germany, $US 29 million.

Utilization of Foreign Capital

Six hundred and forty-one contracts of utilizing foreign capital were signed and approved with a total contract value of $US 764 million, a decrease of 16.78 over $US 918 million in 1989. Of them, thirty-seven contracts were foreign loans, totalled $US 210 million; 371 contracts were foreign direct investment, a total contract value of $US 496 million; and 233 contracts were other foreign investment, valued $US 58.4 million.

The actually utilized foreign capital totalled $US 961 million, of which, foreign loans were $US 310 million; foreign direct investment were $US 600 million; other foreign investments were $US 51 million. The investors were mainly from Hong Kong, Japan and the United States.

Among 371 foreign direct-invested projects, 287 were Sino-foreign equity joint ventures, thirty-four were contractual joint ventures, and fifty were wholly foreign-owned enterprises.

The industrial output of foreign-funded enterprises in the province amounted to RMB 3.134 billion yuan. Foreign exchange earnings reached $US 218 million, $US 138 million of which was earned from export of products, an increase of 57.97 percent over the year 1989.

Technology Import and Export

Eighty-five contracts were signed for importing technology and equipments with a total contract value of $US 58.96 million, a decrease of 33.62 percent over $US 88.82 million in 1989. Of those, two were technology contracts with total value of $US 0.5 million; seventeen were production lines and key machines with total value of $US 22.01 million; and sixty-six were separate machines with $US 36.45 million. Major industries involved were metallurgy, chemical industry, textile industry, communication, etc. The imported projects were mainly from Japan, Germany, Italy and the United States.

Seventy-nine contracts for exporting technological products were signed with a total contract value of $US 81.5 million. Of them, technical licensing was $US 0.23 million; technical information and service was $US 2.74 million; technical cooperation was $US 0.21

million; and complete plants and production line were $US 78.32 million. The export of technology went to twenty-two countries and regions which mainly involved Bangladesh, Pakistan, Thailand, Indonesia, Chile, India, the former Soviet Union, Japan and Hong Kong.

Foreign Economic Cooperation

Ninety-four contracts on contracting overseas projects and providing labor service were concluded with a total contract value of $US 244.19 million, an increase of 96.66 percent over $US 124.17 million in 1989, and the turnover reached $US 81.66 million, an increase of 1.05 times over $US 39.76 million in 1989. The projects mainly scattered in the former Soviet Union, Japan and the Middle East, etc. Some 13,810 persons were sent abroad and 6,346 persons were being abroad at the end of the year. Ten complete plant projects for foreign economic aid were undertaken, eight projects for the United Nations system and bilateral aid were continuously carried out with a transaction value of $US 26.69 million. Three projects were completed by the end of the year with an actual value of $US 2.11 million.

Nine non-trade equity joint ventures were established abroad with the Chinese investment of $US 3.67 million.

* * * *

The Beijing office of the province is located at:

1 Deshengmen Waidajie, Liaoning Hotel
Beijing 100088
Tel: 2015588, 2014676

Another China contact which should be helpful to users of this volume is:

Liaoning Provincial Commission of Foreign Economic Relations
and Trade Department
45-1 Beiling Street, Huanggu District, Shenyang
Tel: 692479   Fax: 693858

21. NEI MONGOL AUTONOMOUS REGION (INNER MONGOLIA)

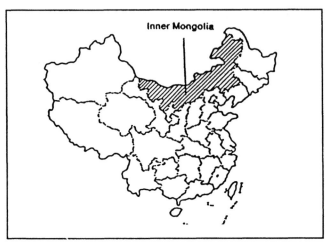

Lying in China's northern frontier areas, Inner Mongolia occupies an area of 1.183 million sq. km., or 12.3 percent of China's total territory. It has a 4,200 km. common boundary with the former Soviet Union and the Mongolian People's Republic (MPR). The autonomous region was established on 1 May, 1947—two years before the founding of the Chines People's Republic.

Eastern Inner Mongolia has the second biggest timber reserve in China. The Hulun Buir Grassland in central Inner Mongolia is one of the nation's five biggest livestock-raising regions. Its total verified coal reserves are estimated at more than 200 billion tons, accounting for 1/4 of the national total. It has rich deposits of petroleum, iron, copper, lead, zinc, gold, silver, rare earth and other minerals (2).

The autonomous region's capital is Hohhot, a rising city with a well-developed woolen industry.

Inner Mongolia has a population of 21,222,300, comprising members of the Mongolian, Han, Manchu, Hui and other nationalities. The Mongol population is 3,073,000, making up for 14.4 percent of the total population (21,222,300).

Foreign Trade

In 1990, the total export and import value of the Inner Mongolia Autonomous Region amounted to $US 465 million, an increase of 7.41 percent compared with $US 432.92 million in 1989.

The purchasing value for export commodities was RMB 1,731.84 million yuan, a decrease of 6.27 percent from 1,847.71 million yuan in 1989.

The export value totalled $US 324.64 million, a decrease of 3.47 percent from $US 336 million in 1989, accounting for 5.47 percent of the Region's GNP and 0.62 percent of the nation's total export.

The structure of export commodities was specified as follows: agricultural and sideling products amounted to $US 101.61 million, accounting for 31.30 percent of the total; light industrial products $US 146.64 million, accounting for 45.17 percent; heavy industrial products $US 76.39 million, making up 23.53 percent. Compared with that of 1989, the export value of agricultural and sideline products decreased by 8.57 percentage points, light industrial products increased by 7.94 percentage points, heavy industrial products increased by 0.63 percentage points. According to the specification of the international trade standard, the export value of primary products amounted to $US 123.33 million accounting for 37.99 percent of the total; that of industrial manufactured products $US 201.31 million, making up 62.01 percent.

There were twelve items of commodities, the export value of each item exceeded $US 5 million respectively. They earned $US 120.05 million, representing 36.98 percent of the total. Of the twelve items commodities each with export value over $US 10 million were: dehaired goatwool $US 27.4 million, accounting for 8.44 percent of the total; frozen beef $US 12.37 million, accounting for 3.81 percent; carpet $US 12.05 million, accounting for 3.71 percent, and soybean $US 10.55 million, accounting for 3.25 percent.

The export commodities were sold to sixty-one countries and regions. There were fifteen countries and regions to which the export value was more than $US 2 million.

Table 32. List of the main export markets - Inner Mongolia (2)

Country/region	Export value ($US million)	Percentage of the total export
Former Soviet Union	98.53	30.35
Japan	59.41	18.30
Hong Kong	52.34	16.12
United Kingdom	24.69	7.61
United States	12.74	3.92
Italy	10.62	3.27
Mongolia	9.34	2.88
France	5.43	1.67
Germany	5.27	1.62
Switzerland	3.88	1.20
Total	**282.25**	**86.94**

The total import value reached $US 140.36 million, an increase of 45.27 percent over $US 96.62 million of 1989. The structure of import commodities was stated as follows: the import of means of production amounted to $Us 122.74 million, accounting for 87.45 percent of the total, a decrease of 2.38 percentage points compared with that of 1989; means of livelihood reached $US 17.62 million, accounting for 12.55 percent of the total, an increase of 2.38 percentage points in comparison with that of 1989.

The major import goods were chemical fertilizer with the value of $US 54.73 million, accounting for 38.99 percent of the total; steel products $US 10.15 million, 7.23 percent; timber $US 9.6 million, 6.84 percent; non-ferrous metal $US 6.66 million, 4.74 percent; electronic computers $US 4.03 million, 2.87 percent; electronic components $US 3.6 million, 2.56 percent; cellulose fiber $US 2.68 million, 1.91 percent; medicines and pharmaceutical raw materials $US 2.51 million, 1.79 percent.

The goods were mainly imported from twenty-two countries and regions.

Utilization of Foreign Capital

Fourteen contracts of using foreign capital were approved with the contract value of $US 19.46 million, an increase of 5.19 percent over $US 18.50 million in 1989. All these were foreign direct investment projects. Actually used foreign investments were $US 10.64 million, an increase of 128 percent over $US 4.67 million in 1989.

Among fourteen foreign direct-funded projects, eight were equity joint ventures, three were contractual joint ventures, three were exclusively foreign-owned enterprises. Of the total, thirteen were productive enterprises and one was non-productive. The fields covered were as follows: six projects in garment processing, two in chemical industry, and one each in animal husbandry, textile industry, building materials, electronics, automobile maintenance and public catering trade, respectively.

Classified by regions, eight projects were from Hong King with the contract foreign investment value reaching $US 11.20 million; one from Singapore with the value of $US 4.95 million; one from Taiwan Province with the value of $US 1.83 million; one from the former Soviet Union with the value of $US 1.26 million; one from Macau with the value of $US 130,000; one from Japan with the value of $US 50,000; and one from the United States with the value of $US 40,000.

The foreign exchange earning of enterprises with foreign investment was $US 14.50 million in 1990.

Technology Import and Export

Seven contracts were signed to introduce technology and equipments with contract value of $US 4.1312 million, a decrease of 76.87 percent from $US 17.86 million in 1989. The actual expense of foreign exchanges totalled $US 5.17 million, a decrease of 21.07 percent from $US 6.55 million in 1989. The projects introduced came from Japan, the United States, Taiwan Province, Germany, France and the United Kingdom. The main technology and equipments introduced were: the equipment for technical transformation of small-sized oxidic film resistance and a wool weaver warping, brick production lines as well as key equipment for the production of leather and high grade cosmetics.

One project was put into operation in the year. The increased output value amounted to RMB 12.77 million yuan. Profit and tax was RMB 5.01 million yuan, and export earnings were $US 400,000. One product was newly developed.

Foreign Economic Cooperation

Fifty-nine contracts for foreign contracting projects and labor service were signed with the contract value of $US 29.7066 million, a decrease of 45.73 percent from $US 54.74 million in 1989. The turnover achieved was $US 20.4847 million, an increase of 3.29 times over $US 4.78 million in 1989. Some 1,605 people for labor service were sent abroad, and fifty-eight people remained abroad at the end of the year.

Table 33. List of the main import markets - Inner Mongolia

Country/region	Export value ($US million)	Percentage of total import
Former Soviet Union	85.00	60.56
United States	13.61	9.70
Japan	8.13	5.79
Hong Kong	7.97	5.68
Mongolia	7.67	5.46
Singapore	4.92	3.51
Taiwan Province	2.66	1.90
Thailand	2.38	1.70
Hungary	2.07	1.47
United Kingdom	1.85	1.32
Total	**136.26**	**97.08**

The total import and export value of the border trade with the former Soviet Union was SF 230.29 million, an increase of 28.01 percent over SF 179.90 million in 1989. Of the total, export value reached SF 105.18 million, import value was SF 125.11 million. The main export commodities were fruits, various kinds of canned meats, frozen beef, garments, down filled products, cotton knitwear, vacuum flasks, etc. The main import commodities were chemical fertilizer, steel products, timber, chemical raw materials, non-ferrous metals, agricultural and animal husbandry machinery, etc.

The total import and export value of the border trade with the People's Republic of Mongolia amounted to SF 26.56 million, an increase of 59.62 percent over SF 16.64 million in 1989. Of the total, export value was SF 10.47 million; import value reached SF 16.09 million. Major export commodities were nationality goods, computers, canned goods, garments, shoes, articles of daily use, etc. Major import commodities were chemical fertilizer, timber, woolen overcoats, waste metals, etc.

* * * *

The Beijing office of the region is located at:

47 Chongneidajie, Chongwen District
Beijing 100005
Tel: 5137679   Fax: 5136517

Another China contact which should be helpful to users of this volume is:

Inner Mongolia Autonomous Region Foreign Economic Relations & Trade
Department
24 Zhong Shan Road W, Huhhot 010020
Tel: 667398   Fax: 662138

22. NINGBO (NINGPO) CITY & DEVELOPMENT ZONE

Ningbo City has historically been a famous commercial center handling goods and resources for eastern Zhejiang Province.

The port of Ningbo is situated at 20°53'N, 121°33'E on the southeastern part of the Yangtze delta, where Yongjiang, Yaojiang and Fenghuajiang meet. It is located at the south coast of Hangzhou Bay of the East China Sea. At present it is composed of the three port areas, i.e., the Old Port Area, Beilun Area and Zhenhai Area.

The Port of Ningbo was opened in 1844, and has to date a history of more than 140 years. In the period of the Sixth Five-Year Plan, three deepwater berths (one for unloading iron ore of 100,000 dwt ship and the other two for ships of 25,000 dwt) were completed in Beilun Area. And in Zhenhai Area, two berths, one of which is being used for vessels of 10,000 dwt and above, were completed.

At the end of 1985, there were altogether twenty-one berths, four of which are deepwater berths for vessels of 10,000 dwt and above. The annual throughput capacity was 26.7 million tons.

In addition, a radar navigation system (first used in China) was also completed and put into use. They include three radar stations, i.e., Xiaqi, Qitou and Daxie, covering the whole entrance channel of thirty nautical miles long and the whole water area of the Port.

The Ningbo Economic and Technological Development Zone is located in the northeast of the old Ningpo urban area. This small port area is located southeast of where the Pu River and the ocean join, 20 km. away from downtown and 10 km. from the deep water Beilun Harbor. It covers approximately 3.9 sq. km. of which 2.38 km. have been developed int eh early stage. So far, it has built a superior investment facility. By 1990, the amount of basic construction and investment reached RMB 256 billion of which RMB 148 billion was spent on basic facilities and RMB 108 billion was spent on above ground construction. In addition, there is a network of underground facilities for water, electricity, roads, communications, sewers, etc.

Some of the characteristics of Ningbo port and city are summarized in Table 34.

Table 34. Ningbo City—Salient Statistics (2)

Area (sq. km.)	9,397 3.9 (Economic Development Zone alone)	
Population	1,073,500 (urban)	
Economic situation	Industrial production in 1989	
	Light industry:	9,502.72 (mil. yuan)
	Heavy industry:	6,555.51 (mil. yuan)
	Harbor's handling volume:	2,230 (10 thousand tons)
	Investment in capital assets:	1,544.19 (mil. yuan)

| | Total value of industrial production: | 16,058.23 (mil. yuan) |

Utilization of foreign capital

Utilization of foreign capital in 1988

Contract number:	70
Foreign contractual value:	$US 41.54 mil.
Effected foreign investment:	$US 8.5 mil.
Number of foreign direct investment:	62
Total foreign direct investment:	$US 6.89 mil.

Utilization of foreign capital in 1989

Contract number:	71
Foreign contractual value:	$US 61.97 mil.
Effected foreign investment:	$US 32.18 mil.
Number of foreign direct investment:	64
Total foreign direct investment:	$US 15.57 mil.

Up to the end of 1989

Joint ventures:	139
Contractual joint ventures:	19
Foreign wholly-owned enterprises:	8
Total:	166
Japanese enterprises:	8

Infrastructure:

Port: 42 berths, including one 100,000 ton berths, nine above 10,000 ton berths.

Power: One of power supply centers of the East China power network. Zhenhai Power Plant has a total installed capacity of 1.05 mil. KW.

Water: Rich water source, daily production capability: 986,300 tons.

Telecommunication: Equipped with advanced facilities, direct domestic and international calls.

The export and technologically-advanced enterprises shall be exempted from the land use fee within five years, and allowed a 50% reduction for another five years.

Labor service charge
(Unit: yuan/month)

Managers: 200-300 (average)
Staff members: 150-250 (average)
125% of the real wages of state-owned enterprises of the same trade in the locality.

Other fees:

Water: 0.20 yuan/ton

	Electricity: 0.17-0.40 yuan/kwh *0.148-2.33
Priorities	Machinery, chemistry, foodstuffs, textile, light industry, building materials, electronics, instruments and meters.
Local preference	The income tax rate on joint venture in economic and technical development zone is 15%. A newly established joint venture can be exempted from income tax int he first two profit-making years, and allowed a 50% reduction of income tax in the third, fourth and fifth years. After the tax exemption period expires, technologically-advanced enterprises subject to a rate of 10% for another three years, and export enterprises shall pay income tax at a reduced rate of 10% provided that their value of export products in that year amounts to 70% or more of the value of their products for that year. Joint ventures shall be exempted from local income tax within five years. The export enterprises shall be exempted from it within eight years.

Official department in charge:

Ningbo Municipal Committee of Foreign Economic Relations and Trade
182, Jiefang South Road,
Ningbo, 315000
Tel: (0574) 62544, 63181

Most manufacturing industries in Ningpo traditionally have been small scale, light and integrated. A few recently established large and medium-size manufacturers have large production capacity such as crude oil processing which totals 2.5 million tons per year, ammonia which processes 520,000 tons per year, synthetic ammonia which produces 300,000 tons at Zhenhai Petrochemical Plant with a 650,00 kw. capacity at Zhenhai's Electricity Plant. The industrial network mainly consists of textiles, machinery, petroleum, chemicals and electricity and was coordinated with electronics, medicine, metals, building supplies, transportation and arts and crafts. The entire city currently has 7,966 manufacturers and 610,000 employees (8).

Ningpo's industry is comprehensive and varied with 145 categories of products. The major products which are important either for domestic use or export are petrochemicals, chemical fertilizers, pesticides, internal combustion engines, converters, tractors, water meters, washing machines, refrigerators, radios, recorders, valves, cotton yarn, cotton fabric, knitting wear, cigarettes, canned goods, garments, aluminum products, furniture sets, etc.

Ningpo is supported by cotton and food production, and a variety of industries in the townships and towns. Its agriculture, forestry, farming, breeding and fishing industries are being developed. It is a commercial zone for agriculture with integrated operations. It has been named "Country of Fish and Rice." The plain's major produce includes aquatic rice, cotton, rapeseed, lima beans, etc.. Its mountain areas are full of firewood, bamboo, pinewood, tea, oranges, arbutus, peaches, pear trees, etc.

Ningpo City is vigorously developing science and technology. It has established fifteen natural science research institutes administered by the city, including chemical engineering, electronics, agricultural machinery, agricultural technology, medicine, fishery, econometrics, stereography, mechanics, environmental protection, etc. There are science and technology centers administered by the city and its counties. The entire city's science and technology team constantly grows bigger and stronger. There are 40,000 scientists and technical workers in the natural and social sciences.

23. NINGXIA HUI AUTONOMOUS REGION

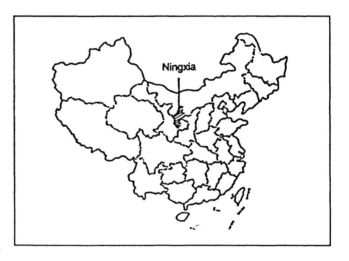

One of the five autonomous regions in China, this is a region between Nei Mongol and the province of Gansu, stretching south from the Huang He river. The regional capital is Yinchuan, a city with many mosques and a large Moslem population. The Ningxia Hui Autonomous Region spreads over an area of 66,400 sq. km. and has a population of 4,548,000; 1,497,000 of whom are Hui people who are followers of Muhammad.

With an elevation of 1,100-2,200 miles above sea level, the autonomous region is divided into two parts, the highlands in the south and the Ningxia Plain irrigated by water from the Yellow River in the north. Rice, wheat, beets, melons, red peppers and Chinese wolfberries, which are very rich in vitamins, are cultivated in the agricultural districts, while sheep and cattle are pastured in the highlands.

There are deposits of coal, phosphorus, gypsum, petroleum, quartz, barite, marble and silica. Coal, with a total reserve of 30 billion tons, is found in all fourteen counties in the autonomous region (2).

Foreign Trade

The total export and import value of Ningxia Hui Autonomous Region in 1990 was $US 83.24 million, 10.37 percent more than $US 75.42 million in 1989.

Export commodity purchasing value was RMB 350.84 million yuan, 47.91 percent more than RMB 237.20 million yuan in 1989.

The total export value was $US 75.13 million, 26.44 percent more than 1989's $US 59.42 million, accounting for 5 percent of the region's GNP and 0.14 percent of the total export value of the country.

There were fifteen export commodities with export value each exceeding $US 1 million, namely, coal, ferro silicon, foodstuffs, feedingstuffs, cashmere, woolen blankets, industrial bearings, cotton yarn, tires, drilling machines, cotton bleached cloth, ramie cloth, spun rayon piece goods, pseudo-ephedrine HCI, and pulses, with the combined export value of $US 53.46 million, accounting for 71.16 percent of the total export value.

The export commodities were sold to thirty-five countries and regions.

The total import value was $US 8.11 million, 49.31 percent lower than that of $US

16 million in 1989. The imports included means of production valued at $US 7.51 million, taking up 92.60 percent of the total import and means of subsistence valued at $US 0.6 million, occupying 7.40 percent. According to the international trade classification standard, primary products amounted to $US 1.19 million, taking up 14.69 percent of the total import, and industrial manufactured products were $US 6.92 million, accounting for 85.33 percent.

The major imports included electric power equipment with $US 1.68 million, accounting for 20.72 percent of the total import value; tire cord fabric $US 1.36 million, 16.79 percent; chemical machinery, $US 0.46 million, 5.61 percent; light industry equipments, $US 0.43 million, 5.36 percent. The main import markets were the United States ($US 5.20 million, taking up 64.08 percent of the total import), Hong Kong ($US 1.78 million, 21.91 percent), Japan ($US 0.56 million, 6.86 percent), and Germany ($US 0.55 million, 5.55 percent).

Utilization of Foreign Capital

Seven contracts for utilizing foreign funds were signed and approved with a total contractual foreign investment value of $US 7.35 million, a 5.91 percent increase compared with $US 6.94 million in 1989. Among them, three were for government loans of $US 6.33 million; four were for foreign direct investment of $US 1.02 million. The foreign capital actually used amounted to $US 13.37 million, 3.84 percent more than that of 1989, among which government loans were $US 12.34 million and foreign direct investment were $US 1.03 million. Of all four contracts for foreign investment from Hong Kong, three were equity joint ventures and one was contractual joint venture. They were all productive projects.

By the end of 1990, fifteen foreign investments were approved by the Autonomous Region, ten were in operation, earning $US 0.52 million foreign exchange through export, 3.5 times more than that of 1989.

Technology Import and Export

Nine contracts were signed for technology and equipment import with a value of $US 13.46 million, an increase of 47.59 percent over the $US 9.12 million in 1989. Technologies and equipments were from Spain ($US 4.67 million), Germany ($US 2.83 million), Switzerland ($US 2.38 million), Denmark ($US 1.97 million), the Netherlands ($US 0.77 million), Taiwan Province ($U 0.65 million), covering light industry, garment making, foodstuffs, printing, chemical fiber, etc. (2).

Foreign Economic Cooperation

Last year a turnover of $US 8.12 million was earned through contracted projects and labor service cooperation. Two hundred and fifty-seven people were dispatched abroad in the year, most of them were dispatched to Yemen, Egypt, United Arab Emirates, Uganda and Kuwait, etc. Up to the end of the year, 524 people were working abroad.

The residence building and maintenance projects in Yemen, Egypt, and United Arab Emirates, the barracks projects in Uganda and labor service cooperation project in Kuwait were the main contracted projects.

One project for foreign aid, project of maintenance, the government office building of Sierra Leone, was undertaken. Thirty people were sent to work abroad in the year, up to the end of which, thirty people were working abroad.

The region implemented four international organization's and bilateral aid projects with an amount of $US 2.30 million. The main projects were Ningxia Nurse School and Science and Technology Hall equipments, each was provided $US 1 million by the Japanese Government in the form of gratuitous aid; the woman project of Gu Yuan county was given the amount of $US 0.27 million gratuitously by the United Nations Population Funds. $US 2.27 million had already been completed.

Table 35. Export commodity composition - Ningxia Hui Region (2)

Exports classified by farm products, light industrial products and heavy industrial products			*Classified by international trade standard*		
Item	Export value ($US million)	Percentage of total export value 1990 1989	Item	Export value ($US million)	Percentage of total export value 1990 1989
Farm and sideline products	15.11	20.11 22.3	Primary products	36.75	48.92 62.5
Light industrial products	16.58	22.07 21.3			
Heavy industrial products	43.44	57.82 56.4	Industrial manu-factured products	38.38	51.08 37.5

Table 36. Main export markets - Ningxia Hui Region (2)

Country/region	*Export value ($US 10,000)*	*Percentage of the total export value*
Hong Kong	2566	34.15
France	1168	15.55
Japan	874	11.63
Belgium	612	8.14
Former Soviet Union	424	5.64
United States	287	3.82
Korea DPR	191	2.54
United Kingdom	136	1.81

* * * *

The Beijing office of the region is located at:

**15 Fensiting Hutong, Anneidajie, Dongcheng District
Beijing 100009
Tel: 4035587**

Another useful China contact for users of this volume might be:

**Ningxia Foreign Economic Relations & Trade Bureau
199 Jiefang Street W, Yincuan 750001
Tel: 43337, 43338 Fax: 0951-448833**

24. QINGDAO CITY & DEVELOPMENT ZONE

This is a major city and port of Shandong (Shantung) province on the Yellow Sea (Huang Hai). It was a German treaty port from 1898 to 1914 and is now Shandong's biggest city. German influence is kept alive in the Qingdao brewery. Other industries include the manufacture of locomotives and railway rolling stock.

Qingdao has a big open and flat area which includes 7.5 million acres of cultivated land, 1.9 million acres of forest, 560,000 acres of tidal land and 860,000 acres of shallow ocean water. The area produces provisions, peanuts, cotton, fruit, vegetables, a variety of livestock, seafood and more than thirty mineral resources such as gold, graphite, marble, granite, etc. (8).

Qingdao has well-developed technical and educational systems. There are 111 scientific and technical institutions and approximately 170,200 technicians. The majority of the technicians specialize in ocean study and are aided by fifteen ocean study institutions. Qindao has 3,100 schools with 1,000,000 students including seven colleges with 15,000 students.

An economic and technological development zone occupies 15 sq. km. area which is located on the west of the Jiaoji Bay and on the south of the newly built Qiangang Bay, faces the old downtown and is separated by the sea with a distance of 2.26 miles.

The Qindao port is the fourth largest in the whole country and does not freeze in the winter. The port of Qingdao is situated in Jiaozhou Bay at 36°04'N, 120°20'E on the southern coast of the Shandong Peninsula. Dagang wharves have a frontage of 3,000 meters. There are altogether thirty-two berths, sixteen berths of which are for 10,000 ton ships. Cargo work is done with ships berthed alongside. There is also an oil terminal at Huangdao which can berth one 50,000 ton oil tanker.

The port is equipped with lifting machinery, a mechanized conveying system for loading coal, and various kinds of mobile machines. The maximum lifting weight is 250 tons. Tugboats, lighters and harbor workcraft are available. Wharves are rail served. There is a shipyard in the locality, and temporary repairs can be carried out on foreign ships. The cargo throughput in 1985 was 26.1 million tons.

Table 37 summarizes some of the salient facts about the city and port.

Table 37. Qingdao City—Salient Statistics (2)

Area (sq. km.)	10,654, 15 (Economic Development Zone alone)
Population	2,036,300 (urban)
Economic situation	Industrial production in 1989

Light industry:	10,908.52 (mil. yuan)
Heavy industry:	6,759.64 (mil. yuan)
Value of export:	$US 277.97 mil.

Harbor's handling volume:	3,145 (10 thousand tons)
Investment in capital assets:	2,305.11 (mil. yuan)
Total value of industrial production:	17,668.16 (mil. yuan)

Utilization of foreign capital

Utilization of foreign capital in 1988

Contract number:	101
Foreign contractual value:	$US 144.46 mil.
Effected foreign investment:	$US 39.78 mil.
Number of foreign direct investment:	29
Total foreign direct investment:	$US 12.33 mil.

Utilization of foreign capital in 1989

Contract number:	102
Foreign contractual value:	$US 151.68 mil.
Effected foreign investment:	$US 108.15 mil.
Number of foreign direct investment:	44
Total foreign direct investment:	$US 58.01 mil.

Up to the end of 1989

Joint ventures:	87
Contractual joint ventures:	19
Foreign wholly-owned enterprises:	5
Total:	111
Japanese enterprises:	19

Infrastructure

Port:	Nine docks, fifty-five berths, including twenty-one above 10,000 ton berths.
Power:	Electric capacity: 497,000 KWH
Water:	Daily supply capability: 294,000 tons.
Telecommunication:	Equipped with advanced facilities, direct domestic and international calls.

Land use fee and work site development fee in the economic and technological development zone:

industrial use	5.8-8.8
commercial use	8.0-9.0

Labor service charge (Unit: yuan/month)

300-350 (average)
120% of the real wages of state-owned enterprises of the same trade in the locality.

Other fees

Water:	0.40 yuan/ton
Electricity:	0.17 yuan/kwh

Priorities

Textile and garment, machinery, rubber, chemistry light industry, foodstuffs, instrument and meters.

Local preference

The income tax rate on joint venture is 15%. A newly established joint venture can be exempted from income tax in the first two profit-making years and allowed a 50% reduction of income tax in the third, fourth and fifth years.   After the tax exemption period expires, export and technologically-advanced enterprises subject to a reduced rate of 50% for another three years, and all exempted from local income tax.

Joint ventures shall be exempted from the local income tax within five years, and allowed a 50% reduction for another five years.

Official department in charge:

Qingdao Municipal Committee of Foreign Economic Relations and Trade
17, Hu Bei Road
Qingdao
Tel: (0532) 279930   Fax: (0532) 336036

25. QINGHAI PROVINCE

With an elevation exceeding three kilometers, Qinghai Province on the northeastern part of the Tibet-Qinghai Plateau is known as the "cradle" of mighty rivers. The Yangtze, Yellow River and Mekong rise in this province that spreads over an area of 720,000 sq. km. and has a population of 4,400,000 made up of the Han, Tibetan, Hui and other nationalities. The provincial capital is Xining, an ancient city and a rising industrial center (2).

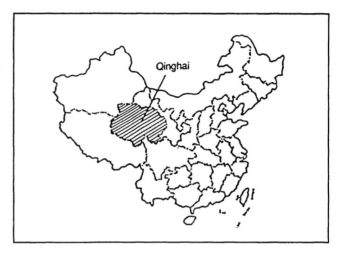

There are many lakes in the province that abound in potash, bromine, asbestos, selenium, sulphur, Glauber's salt, boron and other deposits. China's largest salt lake, Lake Qinghai, is situated in the province. Salt is so plentiful that highway roadbeds in some localities are built on it.

The breeding of yaks, sheep and horses provides the mainstay of the economy. The province is also rich in coal and oil.

Foreign Trade

The total volume of export and import of Qinghai Province in 1990 came to $US 70.27 million, showing an increase of 8.31 percent against $US 64.88 million in 1989.

The purchasing value of export commodities reached RMB 421.64 million yuan, an increase of 25.15 percent over RMB 336.92 million yuan in 1989.

The total export volume was $US 68.05 million, an increase of 16.34 percent over $US 58.49 million, and accounting for 5.24 percent and 0.13 percent respectively of the Province's GNP and the total export volume of China.

Among the export commodities, farm and sideline products came to $US 20.91 million, accounting for 30.73 percent of the Province's total export, 5.9 percentage points down as compared with that of 1989; light industrial products, $US 12.14 million, accounting for 17.85 percent, and 0.14 percentage point up; and heavy industrial products, $Us 35 million, accounting for 51.43 percent, and 5.73 percentage points up. To classify according to the international standard for trade, primary products amounted to $US 24.42 million, accounting for 35.89 percent of the total export, 6.66 percentage points down; and manufactured industrial products amounted to $US 43.63 million, accounting for 64.11 percent, 6.66 percentage points up.

The export commodities with export value of more than $US 2 million each were silicon iron, amounting to $US 18.47 million; carpet, $US 5.03 million, metal silicon, $US 4.36 million; frozen beef, $US 3.66 million; zinc concentrate ore, $US 3.29 million; cordycepts, $US 3.07 million; horsebeans, $US 2.94 million; and dehaired goatwool, $US 2.63 million.

The export commodities were sold to thirty-three countries and regions. The major buyers were Japan with its purchase amounting to $US 34.48 million, accounting for 50.67 percent of the Province's total export; Hong Kong, $US 9.01 million, accounting for 13.24 percent; the former Soviet Union, $US 6.46 million, accounting for 9.49 percent; Singapore, $US 3.84 million, accounting for 5.64 percent; Italy, $US 3.04 million, accounting for 4.47 percent; France, $US 2,83 million, accounting for 4.16 percent; and the United States, $US 1.72 million, accounting for 2.53 percent.

The total volume of import came to $US 2.22 million, a decrease of 65.26 percent from $US 6.39 million in 1989. The imports included means of production valuing $Us 1.03 million, taking up 46.04 percent of the total import; and means of livelihood valuing $US 1.19 million, taking up 53.60 percent. To classify according to the international standard of trade, $US 110,000 for primary products, accounting for 4.95 percent of the total import; and $US 2.11 million for manufactured industrial products, accounting for 95.05 percent. The major import commodities were: western medicine valued at $US 320,000, accounting for 14.41 percent of the total import; photographic paper valued at $US 310,000, 13.96 percent; bearings valued at $US 300,000, 13.51 percent; medical apparatus and instruments valued at $US 280,000, 12.61 percent; and sound equipment and materials valued at $US 120,000, 5.41 percent. The imports mainly came from Hong Kong ($US 1.66 million, accounting for 74.77 percent of the total import); and Japan ($US 490,000, accounting for 22.07 percent).

Utilization of Foreign Capital

Two contracts were signed and approved for the use of foreign capital. The contract value amounted to $US 6.1 million, an increase of 369.23 percent over $US 1.3 million in 1989. The foreign capital was loaned from the Swiss and German Governments, respectively used for importing key equipment in Qinghai Mafang Flour Mill and reconstruction of earthquake disaster area in Hainan.

Foreign Economic Cooperation

Two contracts were signed for economic aid, involving medical and health program and railway construction. The recipient countries included Burundi and Tanzania. Both were fulfilled on schedule. In 1990, twelve persons were sent and remained abroad at the end of the year.

In 1990, the Province received twenty-three aid programs with the value of $US 2.9534 million provided by UNICEF, UNFPA, Canadian Government, etc.

* * * *

The Beijing office of the province is located at:

Hepingli Xijiebeikou
Beijing 100029
Tel: 4223870   Fax: 4223871

Another useful China contact for users of this volume might be:

Qinghai Foreign Economic Relations & Trade Department
120 Shulinxiang, Xining 810007
Tel: 76722, 76965   Fax: 76805

26. SHAANXI PROVINCE

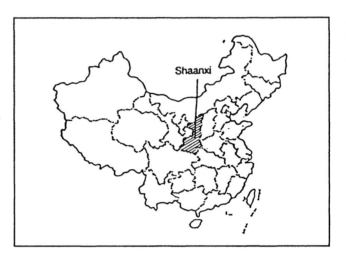

Situated in the middle reaches of the Yellow River some 800 km. west of the East China coast, Shaanxi Province spreads over an area of 205,600 sq. km. and has a population of 31,910,000, according to a year-end count in 1989. The provincial capital of Xi'an, where the terra cotta warriors and battle steeds of Emperor Qin Shihuang have been excavated, is an ancient Chinese capital and an industrial city now building aircraft and TV tubes (2).

The province abounds in coal, petroleum, molybdenum, antimony and mercury. Its coal reserve estimated at 146.4 billion tons is the third largest in China after that of Shanxi Province and Inner Mongolia. Such rare animals as the giant panda and golden haired monkey are found in the southern part of the province bordering Sichuan Province.

Foreign Trade

The total export and import volume in Shaanxi Province in 1990 was $US 541.88 million, an increase of 28.27 percent over $US 422.44 million in 1989.

The total export commodity purchasing volume was RMB 1.84206 billion yuan, in increase of 34.63 percent over RMB 1.36823 billion yuan.

The total export volume reached $US 460.59 million, an increase of 47.30 percent over $US 312.68 million in 1989, accounting for 5.89 percent of the Province's GNP and 0.09 percent of the total export volume of the country.

Table 38. Export commodity pattern - Shaanxi Province (2)

Classified by agriculture, light and heavy industries			Classified by the standard of international trade		
Category	Export value ($US million)	Percentage of total export value 1990 1989	Category	Export value ($US million)	Percentage of total export value 1990 1989
Agricultural and sideline products	45.39	9.85 20.74	Primary products	95.87	20.81 36.95

Light industrial products	275.69	59.86	56.71			
Heavy industrial products	139.51	30.29	22.55	Industrial manufactured products	364.72	79.19 63.05

There were twenty items of export commodities worth of $US 233.30 million, accounting for 50.6 percent of the total export value; seven items of export commodities each with the export value over $US 10 million were: cotton, cotton polyester fiber cloth, cotton yarn, garments, medicines, steam coal, mulberry silk, etc., with the total value of $US 152.57 million, accounting for 33.12 percent of the total export volume.

The commodities were exported to seventy-seven countries and regions. The major markets for export were concentrated in ten countries and regions including Hong Kong, Japan and Germany.

Table 39. Major markets of export Shaanxi Province (2)

Country/region	Export value ($US million)	Percentage of the total export value
Hong Kong	140.12	30.42
Japan	68.92	14.96
United States	27.39	5.95
Germany	13.05	2.83
Former Soviet Union	11.13	2.42
Belgium	10.15	2.20
Singapore	9.47	2.06
United Kingdom	8.96	1.95
The Netherlands	8.78	1.91
France	5.53	1.20
Total	**303.50**	**65.89**

The total import volume amounted to $Us 81.29 million, down 25.94 percent from $US 109 million in 1989, of which, the import value of means of production was $US 60.73 million, making 74.71 percent of the total import value; the means of livelihood, $US 20.56 million, making up 25 percent. Classified by the standard of international trade, primary products amounted to $US 21 million, accounting for 26.27 percent of the total import value; industrial manufactured products, $US 59.69 million, making up 73.43 percent.

Nine major import commodities were: electronic computers, chemical raw material, cotton, visa staple rayon, thin copper plate, electronic industrial equipment, telecommunications equipment, western medicines, TV sets and sound equipment, etc., with a total amount of $US 66.16 million, accounting for 81.39 percent of the total import value.

The import commodities came from seventeen countries and regions. The major markets were: Japan, with value of $US 40.93 million; Hong Kong, with a value of $US 22.21 million; Germany, with a value of $US 3.41 million; Italy, with a value of $US 3.19

million; the United States, $US 2.14 million, and Belgium, $US 1.44 million. The total value was $US 73.32 million, accounting for 90.20 percent of the total import value.

Utilization of Foreign Capital

Some twenty-nine contracts of foreign investment were approved and signed in 1990, with a total value of $US 197.71 million, down 25.06 percent from $US 263.84 million in 1989. Of the total, five contracts were foreign loans, with a value of $US 187.15 million; and twenty-four were foreign direct investment, with a value of $US 10.56 million.

The actually utilized foreign capital amounted to $US 115.66 million, down 27.84 percent from $US 160.29 million in 1989, of which, $US 68.38 million was from foreign loans, $US 41.88 million was foreign direct investment, and $US 5.40 million was other foreign investment.

Among the twenty-four foreign directly invested projects, twenty-one were joint ventures, one was a contractual joint venture, two were solely foreign-owned enterprises, twenty were productive projects, and four were non-productive enterprises. The industries these projects involved were textiles, electronics, food, restaurant and drink, decorating, forwarding and light industry.

Investors were mainly from: Hong Kong, seventeen projects worth $US 9.19 million; Japan, five projects worth $US 970,000; and the United States, two projects worth $US 400,000.

By the end of 1990, seventy-six foreign-funded enterprises were put into operation, accounting for 45 percent of the total approved. The sales volume of the whole year was RMB 547.35 million yuan, with a profit of RMB 31.95 million yuan, an export value of $US 21.56 million.

Technology Import and Export

Sixteen contracts for import of technology and equipment were signed in 1990, with a contract value of $US 8.53 million, dropped by 72.42 percent compared with $US 30.93 million in 1989. The actually utilized capital was $US 14.74 million, down 32.91 percent from $US 21.97 million in 1989. The imported technology and equipment were from: Japan, Hong Kong, the United States, Germany and so on. The industries involved were in machinery and electronics, light industry, textiles and energy, etc. Eight imported projects were completed and put into operation in that same year, and the annual output value could be increased by RMB 242.98 million yuan, profits by RMB 27.34 million yuan, tax revenue by RMB 12.93 million yuan.

Six contracts for export of technology and technological products were signed with a contract value of $US 14.89 million, 4.1 times more than $US 2.92 million in 1989.

Foreign Economic Cooperation

In 1990, sixteen contracts were signed for foreign contracting engineering and labor service cooperation with a total value of $US 32.06 million, 9.69 times more than $US 3 million in 1989; the turnover fulfilled was $US 24.22 million, down 2.77 percent from $US 24.91 million in 1989; in that same year, 1,217 labor service personnel were dispatched abroad, and there were 900 people working abroad by the end of that year. They were mainly dispatched to Japan, Hong Kong, Cameroon, etc. The major contracting engineering projects were in the fields of construction, electric power, medical treatment, water conservancy and agriculture, etc.

There were six aid projects in foreign countries undertaken by Shaanxi, of which, the new projects were: the project of consulting services on electric power prospecting and electric power development in Antigua and Barbuda; the survey, designing and purchasing of equipment and materials for the project of farmland water conservancy and irrigation in Defa, the Niger, had been completed. In that same year, fifty people were dispatched to the foreign countries, and there were ten people working abroad by the end of that year.

Twenty-six projects financed from international organizations and for bilateral assistance had been performed (fourteen were newly signed in 1990). The amount from foreign assistance was more than $US 3.70 million. The funds mainly came from UNICEF, UNFPA, WFP, Canada, Sweden and European Community, etc. The industries involved were in water conservancy, agriculture, culture and education, health, medical treatment, pharmaceuticals, family planning, milk, dairy products, professional training, and so on.

Establishing the "Chinese Food Center" in Malaysia was newly approved. It mainly handled medicinal meals. The Chinese side invested $US 1.50 million.

27. SHANDONG PROVINCE

With an 80 million-plus population, Shandong, situated on the coast where the Yellow River empties into the sea, is China's third most populous province. The province has an area of 153,000 sq. km. It abounds in coal, petroleum, iron and other minerals. The Shengli Oilfield, the second biggest in China, is located in the province, a big producer of wheat, cotton, maize and other crops.   Its peanut output is the biggest in China.

The provincial capital is Jinan. Shandong has long been famous for its fine quality silk cloth—known in English as shantung. The Shengli oilfield, close to the estuary of the Huang He, is the second largest in China after Daqing. It has some of the best infrastructure in China, including a modern expressway network that branches out from the port of Qingdao.

Foreign Trade

The total export and import value of Shandong Province in 1990 was #US 4.186 billion, an increase of 3.92 percent over $US 4.028 billion in 1989.

The total value of commodities purchased for export came to RMB 11.14 billion yuan, an increase of 11.07 percent over RMB 10.03 billion yuan in 1989.

The total export value amounted to $US 3.496 billion, up 14.14 percent against $US 3.063 billion in 1989. It accounted for 12.76 percent of the Province's GNP and 6.71 percent of the nation's total export, ranking fourth in the nation.

The export commodity composition was: $US 1.201 billion of farm and sideline products, making up 34.3 percent of the total export, down 1.6 percentage points over 1989 in proportion; $US 988 million of light industrial products, making up 28.3 percent, down 0.5 percentage points; $US 1.037 billion of heavy industrial products, making up 37.4 percent, up 1.9 percentage points in proportion. Classified according to international trade standards, the export of primary products was $US 1.748 billion, making up 50 percent of the total export; that of finished industrial products was $US 1.748 billion, making up 50 percent.

Commodities each with the export value exceeding $US million included: maize, beans, edible oils, frozen pork, aquatic products, vegetables, canned goods, beer, vermicelli, ground nut products, feedstuffs, flue cured tobacco, timber, Chinese crude drugs, silk, cotton, cotton yarn, cotton piece goods, cotton manufactured goods, silks and satins, garments, drawnworks, carpets, footwear, color TV sets, grass and willow plaited products, rolled steel, hardware, cement, graphite, coal, crude oil, dyestuff, rubber products, medicines, machines tools, auto spare parts, ceramics and so on, totalling 55 varieties. Their export value came to $US 2.75 billion, accounting for 78.66 percent of the total export (2).

The commodities were exported to 142 countries and regions. The major markets were: Japan, $US 920 million, making up 26.32 percent of the total export; Hong Kong and Macau, $US 590 million, making up 16.88 percent; EC, $US 400 million, making up 11.44 percent; Singapore, $US 350 million, making up 10.01 percent; the United States, $US 260 million, making up 7.44 percent; Republic of Korea, $US 180 million, making up 5.15 percent; former Soviet Union and East Europe, $Us 160 million, making up 4.58 percent.

The value of imported commodities that arrived in China was $US 690 million, down 28.87 percent against $US 970 million in 1989. Among them, means of production was $US 660 million, taking up 95.65 percent of the total import; while means of subsistence was $US 30 million, taking up 4.35 percent. Classified according to international trade standard, the import of primary products was $US 290 million, taking up 42.03 percent of the total import and that of finished industrial products was $US 400 million, taking up 57.97 percent.

The major imports were: complete set of equipments and technologies, light industrial machineries, computers, cars and motorcycles, medical apparatus and instruments, TV sets and audio equipments, rolled steel, non-ferrous metals, rubber and products, chemical fertilizer, wool, synthetic fibers, animal fats and vegetables oils (oilseeds).

The imports came from twenty-four countries and regions. The major sources were: Japan, $US 150 million, taking up 21.74 percent of the total; Hong Kong, $US 120 million, taking up 17.39 percent; the United States, $US 98.60 million, taking up 14.29 percent; Germany, $US 59 million, taking up 8.55 percent; Singapore, $US 35.80 million, taking up 5.19 percent; France, $US 34.60 million, taking up 5.01 percent; Italy, $US 28 million, taking up 4.06 percent.

Utilization of Foreign Capital

The Province signed 663 contracts for utilizing capital with a contract value of $US 407.01 million, down 10.40 percent against $US 454.26 million in 1989. Of these contracts, eighteen were for foreign loans with a value of $US 140.94 million, 366 for foreign direct investment with a value of $US 23.83 million; 297 for other foreign investments with a value of $US 33.24 million.

$US 259.68 million of foreign funds was actually used, down 12.89 percent against $US 298.11 million in 1989, in which, $US 73.98 million was foreign loans; $US 150.84 million was foreign direct investment and $US 34.86 million was other foreign investment.

In 366 projects of foreign direct investment, 309 were equity joint ventures, seventeen were contractual joint ventures and forty were wholly foreign-owned enterprises. Of these projects, 95 percent were productive ones and 5 percent were non-productive. In terms of lines, 308 were industrial projects, two were transportation projects, two were catering projects, two were construction projects, three were projects for public health and welfare, and four were projects of literature and education.

Investors came from seventeen countries and regions including Hong Kong, ninety-nine projects, involving $US 119.55 million of investment; Taiwan Province, forty-eight projects, $US 31.65 million; Japan, thirty-one projects, $US 26.25 million; the United States, forty-seven projects, $US 25.42 million; and the Republic of Korea, twelve projects, $US 22.07 million.

Up to the end of 1990, 387 foreign-invested enterprises were put into operation or production. An output value of RMB 2.026 billion yuan and a turnover of RMB 1.878 billion yuan was fulfilled in the year. RMB 116 million yuan of taxes and profits was realized. The export earning came to $US 137 million.

Technology Import and Export

One hundred and sixty-two contracts were signed on the import of technologies and equipments with a contract value of $US 350 million, 2.5 times more than $US 99.72 million in 1989. 80.77 percent of it was paid for equipments, 9.51 percent for technologies and 9.49 percent for other items. $US 88.62 million was actually used, up 1.78 percent over $U 87.07 million in 1989. The projects were mainly imported from Japan, the United States, Germany, Italy, the United Kingdom, Belgium, Switzerland, Hong Kong and other countries and regions, mainly involving the sectors as textiles, chemical industry, chemical fibers, machinery, plastic products, oil processing, building materials, non-metal mines, electronics, post and telecommunication, printing, tobacco processing, food industry and environment protection, etc.

In 1990, twenty-nine projects were put into production. After these projects started production, RMB 400 million yuan output value and RMB 80.54 million yuan of taxes and profits could be increased. $US 55.23 million could be earned from export.

In 1990, thirty-one contracts were signed on technology export with a contract value of $US 28 million.

Foreign Economic Cooperation

Some ninety-one contracts were signed for contracting projects and supplying labor service with a contract value of $US 33.77 million, 1.4 times more than $US 13.89 million in 1989; $US 17.12 million of turnover was fulfilled, up 71.23 percent over $US 10 million in 1989. By the end of the year, 1,462 people were abroad. Sectors of cooperation covered engineering construction, seamen service, medical and health care, fruit tree plantation, water supply projects, ocean fishing, food service and garment processing, etc. The projects contracted were scattered in the countries and regions of the United States, Papua New Guinea, Western Samoa, Gambia, Mauritania, Nigeria, Zanzibar, Yemen, Greece, Japan, the former Soviet Union, and Hong Kong, etc.

The Province undertook five projects of foreign aid, covering fruit tree cultivation, medical and health care, cane weaving techniques, dam project and water supply project, etc. The recipient countries were Ecuador, Western Samoa, Papua New Guinea, Yemen,

Mauritania, etc.

The Province carried out twenty-eight projects utilizing aid provided by international organizations or through bilateral agreements with a total value of $US 19.60 million. The aid was used in agriculture, animal husbandry, cultural and educational projects, etc.

Six non-trade enterprises were set up abroad with a Chinese investment of $US 4.894 million.

* * * *

The Beijing office to the province is located at:

Madain, Beitaipingzhuang
Beijing 100088
Tel: 2011064 Fax: 2011066

28. SHANGHAI MUNICIPALITY

Shanghai, situated not far south of the Yangtze River Estuary, is one of the world's largest ports and China's biggest manufacturing center. It turns out a long catalogue of products, including steel, aircraft, automobiles, ocean-going ships, machinery, electronic products, electrical household appliances and countless consumer items. It has several economic and technical development zones, and is going to open up the 177 sq. km. new Pudong Development Zone. Shanghai is the nations biggest foreign trade port, and it is trading with upwards of 160 countries and regions around the globe. Greater Shanghai, consisting of twelve urban districts and nine countries spreads over an area of 6,340 sq. km. and has a population of 12,764,000 (2).

On the east bank of the river, facing the Bund, old Shanghai's Art Deco waterfront of banks, trading houses and hotels, the skyline is dominated by Asia's tallest television tower, a 1,500-foot-tall architectural Goliath. The tower, has a center spine that pierces two giant "pearls," one of them a geodesic dome housing an elevated shopping mall.

With Beijing's help, Shanghai has an ambitious plan to develop six "pillar industries"—steel, autos, petrochemicals, energy, telecommunications and computer products. These industries would replace the city's traditional base of light industry, especially textiles, which lately have been unprofitable.

Beijing has invested several billion dollars to create the country's leading steel manufacturer in Shanghai, called Baoshan Iron & Steel Complex. Combined with smaller, locally-funded steel plants, Shanghai's steel production will soon reach 17 million tons a year, making it China's largest producer.

Shanghai Volkswagen, a Sino-German joint venture that makes 200,000 cars a year, will soon raise that by a third. It is already the largest foreign-funded manufacturer in China.

The city's petrochemical industry got a boost when the country's leading producer, Shanghai Petrochemical Corp., was selected as one of several companies to issue stock abroad in 1993. Through combined offerings in Shanghai, Hong Kong and New York, Shanghai Petrochemical raised more than $500 million.

Meanwhile, the city's goal of becoming China's leading center for service industries has borne fruit. The service sector now represents 38% of local gross domestic product, up from 30% in 1990. By the turn of the century, the proportion should reach 45%.

That surge is largely the result of the central government's designation of Shanghai as the country's future financial center. The city is home to China's leading stock market, ten commodity exchanges and a nationwide foreign-exchange center. Mr. Huang says total volume on the city's financial markets reached 1.1 trillion yuan in 1993 ($127 billion), making it one of Asia's largest financial centers.

Foreign Trade

In 1990, the total export and import volume of Shanghai City was $US 7.427 billion, a decrease of 5.36 percent from $US 7.848 billion in 1989.

The value of purchased goods for export was RMB 18.418 billion yuan, an increase of 6.89 percent over RMB 17.23 billion yuan in 1989.

The total export was $US 5.317 billion (including export of the corporations under the central ministries and commissions, the total export of the whole city was $US 5.524 billion), an increase of 5.66 percent over $US 5.032 billion in 1989, accounting for 34.46 percent of the City's GNP and 10.21 percent of the total export of the nation, and ranking the third in the country.

Export goods structure was: agricultural and sideline products, $US 662 million, accounting for 12.45 percent of the total export; heavy industrial products, $US 1.268 billion, 23.85 percent; and light industrial products, $U 3.387 billion, 63.70 percent. As compared with 1989, the export of agricultural and sideline products decreased by 2.46 percentage points, that of heavy industrial products increased by 0.62 percentage points, and that of light industrial products increased by 1.84 percentage points.

There were 101 kinds of commodities each with export value over $US 10 million, totalling $US 3.129 billion, accounting for 58.85 percent of the total export. Among them, the following twelve items with an export value of over $US 50 million were: cotton polyester blended fabrics, cotton cloth, steel products, hardware, toys, petroleum products, medicine raw materials, silk piece goods, chemical raw materials, tea, bicycles, and tools, totalling $US 1.129 billion, accounting for 21.23 percent of the total export.

The export commodities were sold to 167 countries and regions.

The total import value was $US 2.11 billion, a decrease of 25.07 percent from $US 2.816 billion in 1989, of which, $US 2.028 billion was for means of production, taking up 96.11 percent; and $US 82 million for means of livelihood, 3.89 percent.

There were twelve kinds of import commodities each with a volume of over $US 50 million, summing to $Us 1.292 billion, accounting for 61.23 percent of the total import. These commodities were steel products, chemical raw materials, auto parts, cotton, knitwear, light industry machinery and their parts and accessories, synthetic fibers, cellulose fibers, complete sets of equipment and import of technology, vegetable oil and animal fat, wool, and non-ferrous metal.

The import commodities came from fifty-two countries and regions.

Utilization of Foreign Capital

Two hundred and sixty-nine contracts on using foreign capital were signed and approved, involving $US 588 million, a decrease of 51.08 percent from $US 1.202 billion in 1989.

Out of the 201 foreign direct investment projects, 190 projects were industrial productive with foreign capital of $US 360.25 million, accounting for 94.53 percent and 96.16 percent of the total number of foreign direct investment projects and the total value respectively.

By the end of 1990, Shanghai had altogether approved 910 foreign investment enterprises, 742 of which were equity joint ventures, involving $US 1.442 billion; 126 were contractual joint ventures, $US 1.152 billion; and forty-two were wholly foreign-owned enterprises, $US 288 million. The foreign investment enterprises were mainly distributed in eight fields: 717 were industrial projects, 106 were house property, public utilities and consulting projects, twenty-two were construction projects, and others were commerce and catering, farming, forestry, water conservancy, communications, post and telecommunications, health and sports projects.

Foreign direct investment were from twenty-four countries and regions. The major investors came from Hong Kong involving in 444 projects, valued at $US 772.54 million; the United States, 122 projects, $US 715.43 million; Japan, 128, $US 407 million; Germany, eleven, $US 154.36 million; and Singapore, thirty, $US 79.18 million.

Till the end of 1990, 527 foreign investment enterprises had already started production, accounting for 57.91 percent of the total approved. Of the 527 enterprises, 294 were export-oriented enterprises, and fifty-seven were technologically advanced enterprises. The export earning of the foreign investment enterprises amounted to $US 299 million.

Economic and Technological Development Zone

In April 1990, the State Council decided to develop and open Shanghai Pudong New Area. Pudong New Area is a delta zone of about 350 square kilometers east of Huangpu River, southwest of the mouth of the Yangtze River, and north of the Chuanyang River. It is the largest development zone in China. In September, nine policies and regulations for encouraging foreign investment in Pudong New Area were promulgated, marking the beginning of a new phase in development and construction of Pudong New Area. Till the end of 1990, there were fifty-five foreign investment enterprises in Pudong New Area. The contract value was $US 264 million. Out of the fifty-five enterprises, eighteen were approved after April 1990.

Some of the characteristics of the Pudong are summarized in the following table.

Table 40. Pudong Special Economic Zone—Salient Characteristics (2)

Opened date for Special Economic Zone (SEZ)	18 April 1990
Area (sq. km.)	350
Population	700,000 (new area)
Economic situation	Industry by the end of 1990: 2,500 Industrial enterprises, mainly include petrochemistry, shipbuilding, iron and steel, construction materials, machinery, textiles and light industries. Industrial output value: 10% of the total of Shanghai. Agricultural output value: 10% of the total of Shanghai.
Infrastructure	Water supply: present capacity is 800,000 tons daily, four new water works providing 400,000 tons daily will be constructed to make supply ability to 1.2 million tons daily. Power: sufficient gas and electric power to meet present demand, a new power station with 3.6 million kilowatts circular network will be constructed. Telephone: 20,000 lines of switching capacity. Ports: four new berths and dig in harbor pool will be built in addition to the existing berths, to handle 20-26 million tons annually.
Bonded territories	Foreign business agencies are allowed to carry out trans-shipment trade and import and export for the enterprises in the new area.

Official department in charge:

Pudong Development Office under the Shanghai Municipality Government

Besides Pudong New Area, the original three economic and technological development zones have also made stable progress.

Technology Import and Export

One hundred and ninety-three contracts on import of technology and equipment were signed with a value of $US 143 million, a decrease of 43.30 percent from $US 261 million in 1989.

To calculate according to value, the import from the United States took up 29.96 percent; Japan, 26.0 percent; Hong Kong, 8.83 percent; Italy, 6.76 percent; and Germany, 6.01 percent.

In 1990, sixty-nine import projects were completed and put into production. The output value was $US 948 million.

Thirty-nine contracts on technology export were signed with a value of $US 69.57 million.

Foreign Economic Cooperation

Seventy-eight contracts for contracting engineering projects and labor service cooperation were signed with a value of $US 60.1 million, a decrease of 16.46 percent from $US 71.94 million in 1989. The business turnover was $US 51.13 million, a decrease of 16.42 percent from $US 61.39 million in 1989. Nine hundred and eighty-nine people for labor service were dispatched abroad, a decrease of 51.23 percent from that of 1989. They were distributed in sixty-five countries and regions. At the end of the year, 2,041 people were still abroad.

The City undertook nine foreign aid projects. Nine countries including Sudan, Surinam, Ethiopia, Burkina, Faso, Benin, Egypt, etc. received the aids. One hundred and fifty people were sent abroad, and ninety-seven were still abroad at the end of the year.

The City accepted two aid projects from the United Nations organization and Japan, valuing $US 10.7 million. Twenty-eight international economic aid projects of various kinds were undertaken in 1990.

The City funded seven productive enterprises abroad in 1990 and the Chinese side invested $US 9.89 million.

Table 41. Major export markets - Shanghai (2)

Country/region	Export value ($US million)	Percentage of the total export
Hong Kong	1,029.61	19.36
Japan	759.08	14.28
United States	745.33	14.02
Germany	229.76	4.32
Singapore	182.11	3.43
Former Soviet Union	173.64	3.27
Italy	127.01	2.39
United Kingdom	115.07	2.16
Australia	102.37	1.93
Canada	91.79	1.73

Table 42. Major import markets - Shanghai (2)

Country/region	Import value ($US million)	Percentage of the total import
Hong Kong	529.83	25.11

Germany	345.35	16.37
United States	280.72	13.30
Japan	158.89	7.53
Australia	107.80	5.11
United Kingdom	48.19	2.28
Singapore	37.30	1.77
Italy	29.95	1.42
Malaysia	28.46	1.35
Switzerland	22.27	1.06

Table 43. Economic and technological development zones in 1990 - Shanghai (2)

Name of economic and and technological zones	Number of foreign funded enterprises	Use of foreign capital ($US million)	Foreign exchange earning ($US million)
Minhang	68	147.69	67.50
Caohe	29	193.03	19.22
Hongqiao	10	381.95	6.86

Table 44. Utilization of foreign capital - Shanghai (2)

Project	1990			1989		
	Number of contracts	Contract value ($US million)	Used value ($US million)	Number of contracts	Contract value ($US million)	Used value ($US million)
Total	269	**588.05**	**779.70**	326	**1,201.80**	**1,169.09**
Foreign loans	21	196.97	588.52	52	835.34	746.97
Business credit	15	148.21	543.22	46	642.81	672.27
Export credit	6	48.76	7.98	4	31.54	36.90
Other forms			37.32	2	150.99	37.80
Foreign direct investment	201	374.63	177.19	199	359.75	422.12
Equity joint ventures	159	198.00	107.17	175	185.91	327.52
Contractual joint ventures	12	40.25	67.46	15	26.29	94.60
Wholly foreign-owned enterprises	30	136.38	2.02	9	147.55	
Other foreign	47	16.45	13.99	75	16.71	

The port of Shanghai has about 181 berths, fifty-five are able to receive 10,000 ton freighters. Each year, more than 2,000 foreign freighters from more than 160 countries and regions pass through Shanghai, in addition to over 10,000 Chinese freighters. The port has modern facilities to handle bulk liquid and powder form of chemicals.

With cargo handling capacity of over 146 million tons in 1989, the port is the largest in China, accounting for over 30 percent of the country's international trade. But the port can only receive freighters of up to 30,000 dwt.

Satellite ports are being built nearby so that cargoes can be broken down and carried on to Shanghai by smaller vessels. Foreign freighters will also be able to sail directly into China's largest river—the Yangtze River.

Electronic remote control and television monitoring have been introduced at the harbor.

The port of Shanghai is situated in the lower stream of the Huangpu River, at 31°14'N, 121°30'E.

Some of the characteristics of Shanghai City and port are summarized in Table 45.

Table 45. Shanghai Municipality—Salient Statistics (2)

Area (sq. km.)	6,186. Minhang: 2.13	Honggiao: 0.652
	Caohejing: 5	Pudong: 350
Population	7,777,900 (urban)	
Economic situation	Industrial production in 1989	
	Light industry:	56,557 (mil. yuan)
	Heavy industry:	46,352 (mil. yuan)
	Value of export:	$US 7,710.52 mil.
	Harbor's handling volume:	15,604 (10 thousand tons)
	Investment in capital assets:	17,478.61 (mil. yuan)
	Total value of industrial production:	102,909 (mil. yuan)
Utilization of foreign capital	Utilization of foreign capital in 1988	
	Contract number:	328
	Foreign contractual value:	$US 1,054.73 mil.
	Effected foreign investment:	$US 1,322 mil.
	Number of foreign direct investment:	219
	Total foreign direct investment:	$US 364 mil.
	Utilization of foreign capital in 1989	
	Contract number:	326
	Foreign contractual value:	$US 1,201.8 mil.
	Effected foreign investment:	$US 1,169 mil.
	Number of foreign direct investment:	199
	Total foreign direct investment:	$US 422 mil

Up to the end of 1989

Joint ventures:	583
Contractual joint ventures:	114
Foreign wholly-owned enterprises:	12
Total:	709
Japanese enterprises:	95

Infrastructure

Port: 113 berths, including fifty-five above 10,000-ton berths, four container berths, harbor length 16 km. long.

Power: sufficient electric power

Water: rich water resources

Telecommunication: one of the major centers of China's international and domestic postal and telecommunication services.

Land use fee
(Unit: yuan/year sq. m.)

	A	B	C	D	E	F
Industry:	60-100	50-90	30-70	15-30	5-20	4-12
Commerce:	60-100	50-90	40-80	30-60	20-30	12-20
Residential commercial building:	50-90	45-80	35-70	20-50	12-30	8-14

Export and technologically-advanced enterprise can be exempted from the land use fee in the first three years, and allowed a 50% reduction in the following years.

Labor service charge
(Unit: yuan/month)

450 (average)
150% of the real wages of state-owned enterprise of the same trade in the locality.

Other fees

Water: 0.12 yuan/ton
Electricity: 0.058 yuan/kwh

Priorities

Machinery, electronics, textile, light industry, chemistry, instruments and meters, building materials, shipbuilding, automobiles, pharmaceutical metallurgy, optical fiber communication, biology.

Local preference

The income tax rate on joint venture in economic and technical development zone is 15%. A newly established joint venture can be exempted from income tax in the first two profit-making years, and allowed a 50% reduction of income tax in the third, fourth and fifth years.

Export and technologically-advanced enterprises can be exempted from local income tax during the period for the exemption for income tax. After the exemption period expires, those enterprises shall be exempted from local income tax for three years, and subject to a reduced rate of 505 for another three years.

Official department in charge:

Shanghai Municipal Committee of Foreign Economic Relations and Trade
33, Zhong Shan Road, E.1
Shanghai
Tel: (021) 3232200   Fax: (021) 3233798

*   *   *   *

The Beijing municipal office of the city is located at:

7 Qianzhai Hutong, Beichang Street, Xicheng District
Beijing 100031
Tel: 6012852, 6016894   Fax: 3099772

29. SHANTOU CITY & DEVELOPMENT ZONE

The city of Shantou is in Guangdong province, 220 miles northeast of Hong Kong. The Shantou Special Economic Zone was set up in 1981. About 80% of the foreign investment projects are light manufacturing, such as garments, electronics, toys and building materials. Hong Kong is by far the leading investor.

Situated at the point where the Han River, Rong River and Lian River merge, with the south and Hong Kong and Macau nearby, the Shantou Special Economic Zone covers 52.6 sq. km. Some of the salient characteristics of Shantou City and port are summarized in Table 46 which follows.

Table 46. Shantou City—Salient Characteristics (2)

Area (sq. km.)	52.6	
Population	526,800	
Economic situation	Industrial production in 1989	
	Light industry:	4,840.59 (mil. yuan)
	Heavy industry:	1,695.31 (mil. yuan)
	Value of export:	$US 747.29 mil.
	Harbor's handling volume:	618 (10 thousand tons)
	Investment in capital assets:	1,209.23 (mil. yuan)
	Total value of industrial production:	6,535.90 (mil. yuan)
Utilization of foreign capital	Utilization of foreign capital in 1988	
	Contract number:	524
	Foreign contractual value:	$US 192.67 mil.
	Effected foreign investment:	$US 97.44 mil.
	Number of foreign direct investment:	221
	Total foreign direct investment:	$US 43.70 mil.
	Utilization of foreign capital in 1989	
	Contract number:	1000
	Foreign contractual value:	$US 256.13 mil.
	Effected foreign investment:	$US 157.41 mil.
	Number of foreign direct investment:	285
	Total foreign direct investment:	$US 93.65 mil.
	Up to the end of 1989	
	Joint ventures:	187
	Contractual joint ventures:	457

	Foreign wholly-owned enterprises:	148
	Total:	792
	Japanese enterprises:	9

Infrastructure	Port:	12 berths
	Power:	Installed capacity: 225 MW
	Water:	Daily supply capability: 320,000 tons.
	Telecommunication:	Equipped with advanced facilities, direct domestic and international calls.

Labor service charge
(Unit: yuan/month)

Managers:	600 (average)
Staff members:	360 (average)

120% of the real wages of state-owned enterprises of the same trade in the locality.

Other fees

Water:	0.30 yuan/ton
Electricity:	0.44 yuan/kwh

Priorities

Textile, petrochemistry, chemistry, metals light industry, foodstuffs, agriculture.

Official department in charge:

Development Bureau of Shantou Economic Special Zone
Shantou Economic Special Zone
Qingdao
Tel: (0754) 260540

Shantou Municipal Committee of Foreign Economic Relations and Trade
3, Da Hua Road, Shantou
Tel: (0754) 275473 or 274251   Fax: (07054) 271037

30. SHANXI PROVINCE

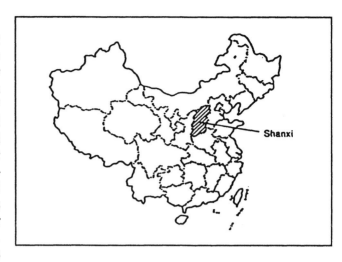

Shanxi, China's banner coal producer, is situated on the middle reaches of the Yellow River in North China. It has a verified coal reserve of 257 billion tons, which is mined and then moved out of Shanxi province by trains and lorries, or converted into electricity at "pithead" power plants and carried by high-voltage transmission lines to Beijing, Tianjin and other industrial cities in North China. Shanxi produces 1/3 of China's annual total coal output. The provincial capital is Taiyuan, a big industrial city.

Total area: 156,300 sq. km.

Population: 27,930,000 at the end of 1989

It is a fertile area, but the soil erodes easily and needs careful management. Rainfall is light and variable, and Shanxi is vulnerable to drought. Maize, wheat and cotton are grown.

Foreign Trade

In 1990, the total export and import value of Shanxi Province was $US 521.12 million, up 12.82 percent over $US 461.89 million in 1989.

The export commodity purchasing value was RMB 2.17273 billion yuan, increasing 14.22 percent over RMB 1.90228 billion yuan in 1989. The variety of commodities purchased for export was 496, of which, industrial and mineral products were RMB 1.67834 billion yuan, representing 77.25 percent of the export purchase value while agricultural and sideline products were RMB 494.39 million yuan, taking up 22.75 percent.

The export value totalled $US 458.11 million, up by 14.52 percent over $US 400.01 million in 1989, taking up 5.83 percent of the Province's GNP and 0.88 percent of the national export.

The structure of export commodities was: farm and sideline products amounting to $US 45.81 million, representing 10 percent of the total export; light industrial products, $US 103.57 million, 22.61 percent; heavy industrial products, $US 308.73 million, 67.39 percent. Compared with that in 1989, the proportion of farm and sideline products, heavy industrial products decreased by 2.82 percentage points and 7.06 percentage points respectively, while that of light industrial products increased by 9.88 percentage points. If the exports were divided according to the international trade standard classification, the export of primary products was $US 314.64 million, taking up 68.68 percent of the total, while manufactured industrial products was $US 143.47 million, 31.32 percent.

The Province exported 486 varieties of products, among which, fifty items with an export value exceeding $US 1 million, totalling $US 379.23 million which represented 82.78 percent of the total export value. Eleven kinds of commodities with export value exceeding $US 5-10 million, included maize, aluminum, pig iron, cotton yarn, mulberry silk, flange plate, ferro-silicon, mung ben furfural, walnut meat and frozen rabbit. Their total export value was $US 300.92 million, taking up 65.69 percent. Three kinds of commodities with export value exceeding $US 10 million were coal, coke and cotton cloth. Their export value totalled $US 228.2 million, representing 49.81 percent. In 1990, the export of machinery and electronic products reached $US 36.4 million, representing 7.95 percent of the total export and increasing by 39.46 percent over $US 26.1 million in 1989.

The Province exported commodities to eighty-two countries and regions. The markets with export value over $US 5 million covered Hong Kong, $US 147.74 million, taking up 32.25 percent of the total export; Japan, $US 136.74 million, 29.85 percent; the United States, $US 22.55 million, 4.92 percent; Germany, $US 19.5 million, 4.26 percent; the former Soviet Union, $US 14.81 million, 3.23 percent; the Netherlands, $US 10.39 million, 2.27 percent; France, $US 10.33 million, 2.25 percent; Singapore, $US 7.96 million, 1.74 percent; United Kingdom, $US 6.22 million, 1.36 percent; and Taiwan Province, $US 5.67 million, 1.24 percent. The exports to the above-mentioned countries and regions amounted to $US 381.91 million, taking up 83.37 percent.

The total import value reached $US 63.01 million, increasing 1.83 percent over 61.88 million in 1989. Among them, direct import value was $US 44.04 million and the value for import by trust was $US 18.97 million.

The structure import commodities were means of production, $US 42.02 million, 66.69 percent; means of livelihood, $US 20.99 million, 33.31 percent. Divided by the international trade standard classification, the import of primary products was $US 15.19 million, 22.11 percent; and industrial manufactured goods, $US 47.82 million, 75.89 percent. The major import commodities covered light industrial products, complete sets of equipment and technology, instruments, metals and minerals, cereals, oils and foodstuffs, textiles, arts and crafts, amounting to $US 47.94 million, 76.08 percent of the Province's import.

The imports mainly came from nineteen countries and regions, such as Hong Kong, $US 16.27 million, accounting for 36.94 percent of direct imports; Japan, $US 8.75 million, 19.87 percent; the United States, $US 5.63 million, 12.78 percent; Germany, $US 5.38 million, 12.22 percent; Australia, $US 1.8 million, 4.09 percent; Sweden, $US 1.65 million, 3.75 percent; Taiwan Province, $US 1.08 million, 2.45 percent.

Utilization of Foreign Capital

Twenty-nine contracts of utilizing foreign capital were approved with a total value of $Us 52.59 million up by 1.85 times over $US 18.45 million in 1989. Among them, two projects were in the form foreign loans with a value of $US 36.4 million; twenty-five projects in foreign direct investment, $US 12.02 million and two in other forms of foreign investment,

$US 4.17 million.

The actual use of foreign capital was $US 12.1 million, increasing by 23.34 percent again $US 9.81 million in 1989, of which foreign loans were, $US 8.7 million and foreign direct investment was $US 3.4 million.

Of the twenty-five projects involving foreign direct investment, twenty-three were joint ventures and two were wholly foreign-owned enterprises. Among them, twenty-two were production-oriented and three were non-productive ones. If dividing them by lines, eight projects were for light industry, and four were for metallurgy and for industry respectively, one each for coal, chemical industry, textiles, garments, machinery and electronic industry respectively, and three for other sectors.

The sources of foreign investment were: Hong Kong, twenty projects; the United States, two; one each from Thailand, Japan and Canada respectively.

By the end of 1990, fifty-six foreign-invested enterprises have been put into operation and a total output value of RMB 195 million yuan were realized. The turnover was RMB 107.24 million yuan and foreign exchanges earned were $US 15.10 million.

Technology Import and Export

There were twelve contracts signed for technology and equipment import with contract value of $UFS 11.98 million, down by 21.02 percent compared with $US 15.1688 million in 1989.

Among the imported items, five were for machinery, three were for light industry, and four were electronics. The sources of the imports were: Italy, three items, $US 4.45 million; Hong Kong, three items, $US 3.86 million; Spain, one item, $US 1.13 million; Sweden, one item, $US 990,000; Germany, two items, $US 740,000; Japan, one item, $US 570,000; and Switzerland, one item, $US 240,000.

Foreign Economic Cooperation

Eleven contracts for contracted projects and labor service were signed with contract value of 1.86 million, increasing by a large extent compared with that in 1989. The turnover was $US million, down by 77.82 percent against that in 1989; 122 labor service personnel were dispatched abroad and eighty-seven still remained outside China by the end of 1990, scattering in countries and regions including Hong Kong, the former Soviet Union, Germany, Iraq, Central Africa, Chad, Equatorial Guinea, Papua New Guinea, Mauritius, Cameroon, Yemen, Zambia. The contracted projects were houses and buildings maintenance of Primary School in San Tome and Principe, construction of Out Building of Cooperation Ministry as well as Embassy Building Construction.

Five projects involving aid to other countries were completed, among which, one was construction and maintenance, one for agriculture and three for engineering supervision and management. The recipient countries were San Tome and Principe, Central Africa, Chad, Zambia and Equatorial Guinea. Twenty-seven people in aid to foreign countries were sent abroad and twenty-seven remained there at the end of the year. Furthermore, 143 sets (items) of machinery and electronic products were provided for fifteen projects in countries of Asia, Africa and Latin America (2).

Three overseas enterprises were set up with approval in Mongolia, Thailand and Australia, involving $US 1.3 million from the Chinese side.

*   *   *   *

A China contact which should be helpful to users of this volume is:

Shanxi Provincial Bureau of Foreign Economic Relations and Trade
6 Xinjian Road, Taiyuan 030002
Tel: 441722   Fax: 0351-440733

31. <u>SHENZHEN DEVELOPMENT ZONE</u>

Situated in the south of Guangdong Province with Donguan and Huiyang to its north, Hong Kong to its south and Daya Bay to its east, Shenzhen Special Economic Zone is a part of Shenzhen City. It is 49 km. long from east to west, 7 km. wide from north to south and occupies 327.5 sq. km. The Guangzhou-Kowloon Railway goes straight through the special economic zone and is 32 km. from Kowloon and Hong Kong and 147 km. from Guangzhou. The total residential population at the end of 1991 was 732,000 with 432,000 people living in the urban area (8).

Shenzhen is the largest of the country's "special economic zones" set up to attract investment from overseas. Shenzhen has almost become an extension of Hong Kong, which it borders. The most developed industries are electronics, toy, food processing, textiles and garments (56).

Some of the important facts regarding Shenzhen are summarized in Table 47.

Table 47. Shenzhen Special Economic Zone—Salient Characteristics (2)

Area (sq. km.)	327.5 Shekou: 4.5	
Population	1,026,900 Permanent residents: 362,000	
Economic situation	Industrial production in 1989	
	Light industry:	8,348.53 (mil. yuan)
	Heavy industry:	3,297.04 (mil. yuan)
	Value of export:	$US 2,174.28 mil.
	Harbor's handling volume:	956 (10 thousand tons)
	Investment in capital assets:	4,539.25 (mil. yuan)
	Total value of industrial production:	11,645.25 (mil. yuan)
Utilization of foreign capital	Utilization of foreign capital in 1988	
	Contract number:	694
	Foreign contractual value:	$US 487.39 mil.
	Effected foreign investment:	$US 444.29 mil.
	Number of foreign direct investment:	591
	Total foreign direct investment:	$US 287.16 mil.
	Utilization of foreign capital in 1989	
	Contract number:	711
	Foreign contractual value:	$US 489.04 mil.
	Effected foreign investment:	$US 458.09 mil.
	Number of foreign direct investment:	647
	Total foreign direct investment:	$US 292.52 mil.

Up to the end of 1989

Joint ventures:	1,757
Contractual joint ventures:	607
Foreign wholly-owned enterprises:	221
Total:	2,585
Japanese enterprises:	62

Infrastructure

Port: Xingang, Dongtoujiao Shangbu, Meisha, Shekou, Chiwan, Mawan and Yantian Ports for operation

Power: Supplied by Guangdong Power Network and Hong Kong Electric System

Water: Daily supply capability: 570,000 tons

Telecommunication: Equipped with advanced facilities, direct domestic and international calls.

The technologically-advanced projects shall be exempted from it within five years and allowed a 50% reduction for three years.

Labor service charge
(Unit: yuan/month)

Managers: 1,000 (average)
Staff members: 500 (average)
120% of the real wages of state-owned enterprises of the same trade in the locality.

Other fees

Water:	0.20 yuan/ton
Electricity:	0.43 yuan/kwh

Priorities

Textile and garment, machinery, petrochemistry light industry, foodstuffs, electronics, building materials

Local preference

The income tax rate on joint venture is 15%. A newly established joint venture can be exempted from income tax in the first two profit-making years and allowed a 50% reduction of income tax in the third, fourth and fifth years. After the tax exemption period expires, technologically-advanced enterprises subject to a reduced rate of 50% for another three years, and export enterprises shall pay income tax at the rate of 105.

Official department in charge:

Shanzhen Municipal Economic Development Bureau
8, Shang Bu Middle Road
Shenzhen
Tel: (0755) 223211

32. <u>SICHUAN PROVINCE</u>

This most populous province in China, which has a population of 107.143 million of 1/10 of the Chinese population, sprawls over an area of 570,00 sq. km. on the upper reaches of the Yangtze River in Southwest China. In the center of the province is a flat alluvial plain. The climate is humid and temperate and its soils are unusually fertile. Rice, wheat, millet, sugar cane and citrus fruits are grown. So far, foreign investment is small. But such major cities as Chengdu and Chongqing are trying to attract high-tech manufacturers to form partnerships with China's military-owned electronics factories.

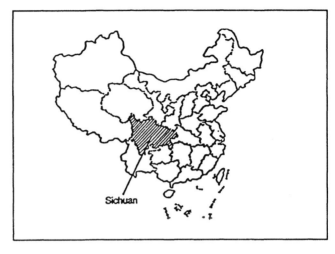

Foreign Trade

In 1990, the total export and import volume of Sichuan was $US 1.363 billion, an increase of 6.24 percent over $US 1.283 billion in 1989.

The total export purchasing volume was RMB 5.686 billion yuan, an increase of 16.3 percent over RMB 4.889 billion yuan in 1989.

The total export volume was $US 1.116 billion, an increase of 17.6 percent over $US 94 million in 1989, accounting for 5.85 percent and 2.14 percent of the Province's GNP and the total export volume of the whole country respectively.

The structure of the export commodities was: agricultural and sideline products, valuing $US 104.92 million and accounting for 9.4 percent of the total export; light industrial products, $US 573.8 million, 51.4 percent; and heavy industrial products $US 437.42 million, 39.2 percent. By SITO system, primary products valued $US 389.43 million, accounting for 34.9 percent of the total export and manufactured industrial products, $US 726.77 million, 65.1 percent.

The export commodities were sold to 112 countries and regions. The first ten major export markets were Hong Kong, Japan, Germany, the former Soviet Union, the United States, Italy, Thailand, Singapore, the Netherlands and France, totalling $Us 891.17 million, accounting for 79.84 percent of the total export.

The total import volume was $US 247 million, a decrease of 25.93 percent from $US 333.49 million in 1989. Of which, $US 193.08 million was for means of production, accounting for 78.17 percent of the total import; and $US 53.92 million for means of livelihood, 21.83 percent. By SITO system, $US 41.05 million was for primary products, accounting for 16.62 percent of the total import and $US 205.95 million for manufactured industrial products, 83.38 percent.

The main import goods were: steel products, automobiles, and motorcycles (accessories) chemical raw materials, cotton, complete sets of equipment, electronic components, metals ores, kinescope, pharmaceutical raw materials, palm oil, light industrial machinery, power equipment, medical apparatus, video recorders, etc., totalling $US 184.9 million, and accounting for 74.86 percent of the total import.

The import commodities came from twenty-six countries and regions. The main import markets were the following ten countries and regions: Japan, Hong Kong, Australia, the United States, Germany, Mozambique, Singapore, Canada, Italy and the United Kingdom, totalling $US 223.12 million, accounting for 90.33 percent of the total import value.

Utilization of Foreign Capital

One hundred and seventy-two contracts on utilizing foreign capital were signed and approved, valuing $US 317.04 million, an increase of 2.5 times over $Us 90.5 million in 1989. Of them, ten were foreign loans with a total value of $US 137.79 million; 134 were foreign direct investment, $US 100.56 million; and twenty-eight were foreign investment in other forms, $US 78.69 million.

In 1990, the actually used foreign funds was $US 183.36 million, an increase of nineteen times over $US 9.09 million in 1989, of which, $US 158.57 was foreign loans, $US 16.04 million was foreign direct investment, and $US 8.75 million was other foreign investment.

Among the 134 direct investment projects, sixty-eight were equity joint ventures, thirty-five were contractual joint ventures, and thirty-one were wholly foreign-owned enterprises. One hundred and twenty-seven were productive enterprises, and seven were non-productive projects. They were involved in such trades as communications, chemical industry, pharmacy, building materials, electromechanics, light industry and textile, garments, etc.

The foreign direct investment came from the following countries and regions: Hong Kong, France, the United States, Japan, Singapore, Taiwan Province and the Republic of Korea.

By the end of 1990, 280 foreign-invested enterprises went into operation, $US 35.21 million was earned from export in 1990.

Technology Import and Export

Some fifty-three contracts on import of technology and equipment were signed with a total value of $US 57.86 million, an increase of 60.19 percent over $US 36.12 million in 1989. $US 43.53 million was actually used, a decrease of 0.91 percent from $US 43.93 million in 1989. The import projects came from eleven countries and regions such as Japan, Germany, the United States, France, Switzerland, the United Kingdom, Italy, Australia, and

Hong Kong. They were involved in such trades as light industry and textile, electromechanics, communications, machinery, electronics, and pharmacy.

Foreign Economic Cooperation

Some 110 contracts for contracting projects and labor service cooperation were signed with a total contract value of $US 228.85 million, an increase of 38.10 percent over $UFS 165.71 million in 1989. The business turnover was $US 166.18 million, an increase of 53.60 percent over $US 108.19 million in 1989. About 3,631 people for contracting projects and labor service were dispatched abroad, and 5,375 people were still working abroad at the end of the year. They were sent to fifty-two countries and regions including the former Soviet Union, Pakistan, Indonesia, Bangladesh, Yemen, Nepal, Germany, etc. The contracting projects were installation of the 210,000 KW generator sets and construction of a 300,000 ton chemical fertilizer plant in Bangladesh, and erection of 500,000 KW power transmission line in Pakistan.

The Province undertook nine foreign aid projects, involving in road construction, geological prospecting, building, agriculture, telecommunications, etc. Countries that received aids were Nepal, Benin, Kenya, Vanuatu, Ethiopia, Mali, etc. Four hundred and fifty-seven people were dispatched abroad for foreign aid projects, and 767 people were abroad at the end of the year.

The province received thirty-seven foreign aid projects with $US 5.2 million of foreign-invested funds from the United Nations and other countries. Among them, four were provided by UNFPA, nineteen by UNICEF, five by UNDP, one by WHO, five by other countries, and three by friendly non-governmental organizations.

Some thirteen enterprises were set up abroad. The Chinese side invested $US 5.74 million.

Table 48. List of commodities each with the export value of over $US 10 million
- Sichuan Province (2)

Classified by value	Name of commodities	Export value ($US million)	Percentage of total export
Over $US 15 million (10 kinds)	Raw silk, steel products, frozen pork, silk piece goods, electronic components, chemical raw materials, garments, Chinese crude drugs, aluminum plates, ferroalloy	368.07	32.98
Between $US 10-15 million (7 kinds)	Canned pork, antibiotics, canned vegetables, mulberry silkworm cocoon, vegetables, cotton grey cloth, feather and down	85.98	7.70

*   *   *   *

The Beijing office of the province is located at:

5 Gongyuan Toutiao, Jianguomen
Beijing 100005
Tel: 5122277-206, 5122568   Fax: 5122361

Another useful China contact for users of this volume might be:

Sichuan Province Commission for Foreign Economic Relations & Trade
Tel: 334033, 332372   Fax: 028-334675

33. TIANJIN (TIENTSIN) CITY

The city of Tianjin (Tientsin) is one of three special municipalities that are controlled directly by the Central Government in China. It is a very important harbor city and a comprehensive industrial base int he coastal area. Tianjin is a distribution center for the northern ten provinces and cities. With newly added dockside facilities, Tianjin's new harbor now handles 24 million tons of cargo a year. The city has also a

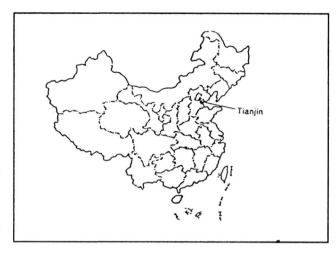

large sized economic and technological development zone where many foreign-funded operations have been, or are being established. Tianjin and the adjacent counties, over which it exercises jurisdiction, have an area of 11,305 sq. km. and a population of 8,523,500 at year-end in 1989.

Tianjin is China's third most populous city and fourth largest retail center (after Shanghai, Beijing and Guangzhou). Tianjin's major exports are garments, textiles, footwear, carpets, household electrical appliances and machinery. The city also is developing a hugh zone for the petrochemical industry.

The underground resources in Tianjin are very rich. The annual production of petroleum, natural gas and oil from the famous Dagang oil field are 4.7 millions tons of crude oil and 370 million cubic km. of natural gas. The Bohai oil field under exploration and development by China and Japan is one of the natural gas and oil fields at the bottom of the sea that is the main development project in China.

Tianjin has thirty-five types of metal and non-metal minerals. It also has coal, iron, molybdenum, manganese, purple sand pottery clay and marble.

Foreign Trade

The total value of export and import in Tianjin in 1990 was $US 2.21 billion, decreasing by 0.18 percent over $US 2.214 billion in 1989.

The export commodity purchasing value was RMB 6.487 billion yuan, increasing by 17.33 percent over RMB 5.529 billion yuan in 1989.

The export value was $Us 1.786 billion (including the export of the companies of central ministries and commissions in Tianjin, the total export value of the city was $US 1.92 billion) up 5.93 percent as compared with $Us 1.686 billion in 1989 representing 28.76 percent of the city's GNP and 3.43 percent of the total national export value, ranking the eighth.

The structure of the export commodities was: agricultural and sideline products, with total amount of $US 301 million, accounting for 16.85 percent of the total export value; light industrial products, $US 821 million, 45.47 percent; heavy industrial products, $US 673 million, 37.68 percent. As compared with that in 1989, the proportion of agricultural and sideline products, and heavy industrial products in the total exports increased by 0.6 percentage points and 1.78 percentage points respectively, and the proportion of light industrial products decreased by 2.48 percentage points. If divided according to the international trade standard classification, the export value of primary products was $US 343 million, accounting for 19.2 percent of the total; and of industrial manufactured products was $US 1.443 billion, 80.8 percent.

There were forty kinds of commodities each with the export value over $US 10 million, including garments, carpets, synthetic blending fabrics, cotton cloth, color TV sets, cotton knitwear, dyestuffs, prawn, refractories material, Chinese herbs, machinery equipment, chemical raw materials. The total value was $US 1.015 billion, taking up 56.83 percent.

The markets for the export commodities were over 158 countries and regions.

The import value totalled $US 424 million, down by 19.7 percent over $Us 528 million in 1989. the structure of import commodities was: means of production, with the import value of $US 354 million, accounting for 83.49 percent of the total; means of livelihood, $US 70 million, 16.51 percent. If divided by the International Trade Standard Classification, primary products, with the total amount of $US 114 million, took up 26.89 percent of the import value; and industrial manufactured products, $Us 310 million, 73.11 percent.

The main import commodities were TV sets and audio systems equipment, $US 45.31 million; cotton, $US 44.24 million; rolled steel, $US 42.93 million; raw materials for chemical industry, $US 26.86 million; synthetic fabrics and cotton knitwear, $U 25.23 million; animal oils and vegetable oils, $US 24.92 million; wool, $Us 17.47 million; electronic computers, $US 12.55 million; and motorcars and motorcycles, $US 13.07 million. The import value reached $US 252.58 million, accounting for 59.57 percent of the total import commodities coming from thirty-six countries and regions (2).

Utilization of Foreign Capital

One hundred and thirty-six contracts for the utilization of foreign capital were approved and the contract value was $US 178.54 million, down by 15.84 percent as compared with $US 212.14 million in 1989. Among them, two projects were in the form of foreign loans with the value of $US 45; million; 129 projects were in foreign direct investment with $US 131.65 million; five projects were in other forms of foreign investment with $US 1.89 million.

The actual utilization of foreign investment was $US 83.63 million, decreasing by 74.85 percent against $US 160.36 million in 1989. Among them were, foreign loans, $US 46.7 million; foreign direct investment, $US 34.93 million; other foreign investment, $US 2 million. Over twenty countries and regions have invested in Tianjin and there are over 400 joint ventures, cooperative enterprises and sole ownerships that have been approved. The OTIS, Motorola and IBM Companies in America, Yamaha, Seiko, and NEC in Japan and Germany have established companies in China.

Among the 129 projects with foreign direct investment, seventy were equity joint ventures, two were contractual joint ventures and fifty-seven were wholly foreign-owned enterprises. Of these projects, 118 were industrial productive enterprises and eleven projects were in commerce, service trade, transportation and agriculture, etc.

The investments were mainly from countries and regions, such as Hong Kong, sixty-seven projects; Japan, twelve projects; the United States, thirteen projects; Taiwan Province, seventeen projects; and Republic of Korea, five projects.

By the end of 1990, 550 foreign-invested enterprises were approved with the total contract value of $US 582.63 million. Among them, 431 were equity joint ventures, twenty-five were contractual joint ventures, and ninety-four were wholly foreign-owned enterprises. Of these projects, 447 were industrial productive enterprises, fifty-five were in line of commerce and service trade, ten in transportation, ten in agriculture, eleven in building industry and seventeen in other fields. At present, 236 foreign-invested enterprises started operation in the city. The total annual turnover reached RMB 2.058 billion yuan and foreign exchange earning was $US 90.98 million.

Technology Import and Export

One hundred and twenty-seven contracts on import of technology and equipment were signed with a total value of $US 91.17 million, up by two times over $Us 30.89 million in 1989.

The imports mainly came from fifteen countries and regions, such as the United States, $US 30.12 million; Germany, $US 10.79 million; Austria, $US 10.73 million; Japan, $US 10.21 million; France, $US 6.55 million; totalling $US 68.4 million, accounting for 75.02 percent of the total value for technology and equipment imports.

The import of technology and equipment has gone into fields like machinery, electronics, metallurgy, chemical industry, textiles, food industry, light industry, pharmaceuticals, post and telecommunications, etc. Ninety-six projects were completed and put into operation in 1990, with output value of RMB 248 million yuan.

Eighteen contracts on the technology export were signed with the contract value of $US 19.37 million, increasing 241 times against $US 80,000 in 1989.

Foreign Economic Cooperation

One hundred and ninety-eight contracts for projects and labor service abroad were signed with contract value of $US 57.38 million, up 1.2 times over $US 26.23 million in 1989. Business turnover was $US 28 million, up 43.52 percent against $US 19.51 million in 1989. Some 3,176 labor service personnel remained abroad by the end of the year, covering countries and regions such as Japan, the United States, Hong Kong, Singapore, Germany and former Soviet Union.

Four hundred and fifty-five sets of mechanical and electrical equipment were provided for thirty-one projects in twenty-three recipient countries.

Four overseas enterprises were established last year, involving $US 5.6 million investment from Chinese side. The main projects were Seagull Precision Timer Corporation Ltd. and a fishery company in Indonesia, the Pacific Shipping Company Ltd in Panama and Friendship Corporation in the former Soviet Union.

Table 49. Main markets for Tianjin's export (2)

Country/region	Import value ($US million)	Percentage of the total
Hong Kong	351.63	19.69
Japan	244.93	13.17
United States	227.46	12.74
Germany	101.23	5.67
Former Soviet Union	62.55	3.50
Singapore	57.74	3.23
The Netherlands	46.96	2.63
United Kingdom	42.66	2.38
France	35.29	1.98
Italy	34.21	1.92

Table 50. Main import markets

Country/region	Import value ($US million)	Percentage of the total
Hong Kong	183.80	43.35
Japan	104.75	24.71
United States	20.70	4.88
France	13.49	3.18
Germany	11.68	2.75
New Zealand	10.88	2.57
United Kingdom	8.30	1.96
Australia	6.52	1.54
Malaysia	5.00	1.18
Italy	4.03	0.95

Tianjin (Xingang) Port

Xingang situated at 39°00'N, 117°43'E, is the main port on the eastern shore of Bohai Sea in northeast China. It serves as the main port of the industrial city of Tianjin and also serves as the major port of entry to the capital city of Beijing, which is about 175 kilometers away from Xingant Port.

The port as thirty-nine berths, twenty-nine of which are capable of accommodating ships of 10,000 tons or above with a total annual cargo throughput of about 20 million tons. The first specialized container berth is almost 400 meters long and can accommodate vessels carrying 1,300 containers each. Container services have been started with the United States, Japan, Australia and Hong Kong. Yard stacking provides storage for up to 6,828 containers.

Another modern container berth capable of handling 100,000 standard containers annually and two general cargo berths capable of handling 670,000 tons are in operation at Tianjin Harbor. After its completion in 1985, the Port can now handle between 300,000 and 400,000 containers a year, and some are being refrigerated. Now the Port is equipped with cranes, floating cranes, conveyers and mobile cargo-handling machinery. The maximum lifting weight is 150 tons.

A computer system is now employed. Wharves, particularly container wharves, are rail served. There is a shipyard in the locality, and temporary repair services can be rendered to foreign vessels.

Economic and Technological Development Zone

The economic and technological development zone is located in eastern Tianjin, approximately 50 km. from the urban area, neighboring Tungu which is by the shore and the Tianjin Harbor. It is one of the major components of the strategy to encourage Tianjin's industries to move to the shore area.

Transportation in the zone is very good. The new harbor which spans 2 km. in the southeast is connected with the zone by highways. The Tianjin Airport, across the Beijing-Harbin Railroad, is 38 km. to the west. In addition, three highways connect the zone with China's highway network. The highway from Beijing through Tianjin to Tungu traverses the zone. After it is completed, it will take one hour to drive from the zone to Beijing.

The zone is able to facilitate the establishment of modern factories. It has built sufficient plants and factories totalling approximately 300,000 sq. meters for fifty manufacturers. There are roads which equal 24 km. long. Its facilities also provide communications, water, electricity, heat and gas. 80,000 sq. meters of matching construction which has been completed int he residential area provide investors with a very good environment. Currently, the zone has signed 128 joint venture contracts with parties from fourteen countries and regions such as the United States, Japan, Germany, France, Belgium, Denmark, Singapore and the Philippines. Eighty firms have invested and started to produce goods.

The zone continuously improves its investment environment which can be profitable for domestic or foreign investors. It has published a series of regulations that provide legal protection for foreign investment.

Completion of the zone which will total 3 sq. km.. is planned within thirty years. The zone emphasizes the development of industries such as building supplies, medicine, electronics, textiles, light industries, chemical engineering and product processing. There are joint and cooperative ventures between Chinese and foreign investors and sole foreign investment.   The projects are knowledge and technology intensive and generate foreign currency from export.   The zone's economy is trade-oriented.   It also provides preferential treatment to the projects that utilize advanced technology and that the most needed domestically.

Some of the statistics concerning the city and the special economic zone are summarized in Table 51 which follows.

Table 51. Tianjin (Tientsin) City - Salient Statistics (2)

Area (sq. km.)	11,305 33 (special economic zone only)	
Population	5,697,700 (urban)	
Economic situation	Industrial production in 1989	
	Light industry:	20,261 (mil. yuan)
	Heavy industry:	17,264 (mil. yuan)
	Value of export:	$US 1,683.51 mil.
	Harbor's handling volume:	2,437 (10 thousand tons)
	Investment in capital assets:	6,854 (mil. yuan)
	Total value of industrial production:	37,525 (mil. yuan)
Utilization of foreign capital	Utilization of foreign capital in 1988	
	Contract number:	101
	Foreign contractual value:	$US 309.76 mil.
	Effected foreign investment:	$US 344.01 mil.
	Number of foreign direct investment:	94
	Total foreign direct investment:	$US 62.44 mil.
	Utilization of foreign capital in 1989	
	Contract number:	112
	Foreign contractual value:	$US 242 mil.
	Effected foreign investment:	$US 430.24 mil.
	Number of foreign direct investment:	97
	Total foreign direct investment:	$US 16.72 mil.
	Up to the end of 1989	
	Joint ventures:	362
	Contractual joint ventures:	22
	Foreign wholly-owned enterprises:	37
	Total:	421
	Japanese enterprises:	67
Infrastructure	Port:	50 berths, harbor length: 8,862 m. long

	Power:	4 large and medium-sized electric power plant supplied by the network linked to Beijing and Tangshan.
	Water:	Yearly supply capacity: 714.73 mil. tons
	Telecommunication:	Direct domestic and international calls for export and technologically-advanced enterprises

	B	C	D	E	F	G
industry	3	2.5	2	1.5	1	0.5

Labor service charge   480 (average)
(Unit: yuan/month)

120% of the real wages of state-owned enterprise of the same trade in the locality

Other fees   Water: 0.35 yuan/ton
              Electricity: 0.14 yuan/kwh

Priorities   Petroleum, electronics, textiles, light industry chemistry, foodstuffs, paper, automobiles, generating equipment, metallurgy

Local preference   The income tax rate on joint venture in economic and technical development zone is 15%. A newly established joint venture can be exempted from income tax in the first two profit-making years, and allowed a 50% reduction of income tax in the third, fourth and fifth years. Joint ventures approved by the end of 1990 shall be exempted from local income tax.

Official department in charge:

**Tianjing Municipal Committee of Foreign Economic Relations and Trade
55, Chong Qing Avenue, Heping District
Tianjing
Tel: (022) 302837, 304032**

* * * *

The Beijing municipal office of the city is located at:

**5 Building, 12 Qu, Heipingjie, Dongcheng District
Beijing 100013
Tel: 421482**

34. <u>XIAMEN DEVELOPMENT ZONE</u>

The Port of Xiamen in the south of Fujian province is situated at Jinmen Bay, at 24°27'..118°04'E. It was opened up in 1683 and developed into a trading port in 1843. Xiamen is in southern Fujian province and was designated a special economic zone in 1984. Xiamen owes much of its recent economic growth to that huge influx of investment from Taiwan, where people speak the same dialect.

In the period of the Sixth Five Year Plan, Dongdu, located between Shuangshishan Hill and Niutoushan Hill, was chosen as the site for a new port area. The project of the first phase which was completed in 1984, was to build four deep water berths for vessels of 10,000 dwt and above with an annual throughput of 2.09 million tons.

Many of the salient features of Xiamen are summarized in Table 52.

Table 52. Xiamen Special Economic Zone—Salient Statistics (2)

Area (sq. km.)	131, excluding Xinlin & Haichang Development Zone: 126.64 sq. km.
Population	1,076,800
Economic situation	Industrial production 1989

	Light industry:	3,692.16 (mil. yuan)
	Heavy industry:	1,760.29 (mil. yuan)
	Value of export:	$US 646.78 mil.
	Harbor's handling volume:	513 (10 thousand tons)
	Investment in capital assets:	972.44 (mil. yuan)
	Total value of industrial production:	5,452.45 (mil. yuan)

Utilization of foreign capital	Utilization of foreign capital in 1988

	Contract number:	180
	Foreign contractual value:	$US 157 mil.
	Effected foreign investment:	$US 49 mil.
	Number of foreign direct investment:	180
	Total foreign direct investment:	$US 48.01 mil.

Utilization of foreign capital in 1989

	Contract number:	323
	Foreign contractual value:	$US 834.96 mil.
	Effected foreign investment:	$US 238.22 mil.
	Number of foreign direct investment:	225
	Total foreign direct investment:	$US 209.8

Up to the end of 1989

	Joint ventures:	239
	Contractual joint ventures:	28
	Foreign wholly-owned enterprises:	201
	Total:	468
	Japanese enterprises:	12

Infrastructure	Port:	37 berths, including 4 above 10,000 ton berths
	Power:	Supplied by the Power Network of Fujian
	Water:	Rich water sources
	Telecommunication:	Equipped with advanced facilities, direct domestic and international call.

Labor service charge
(Unit: yuan/month)

Managers: 450-600 (average)
Staff members: 350-400 (average)
150% of the real wages of state-owned enterprises of the same trade in the locality.

Other fees	Water:	0.30 yuan/ton
	Electricity:	0.33 yuan/kwh

Priorities

Textile and garment, machinery, chemistry light industry, foodstuffs, electronic, building materials, sea chemistry, biology

Local preference

The income tax rate on joint ventures is 15%. a newly established joint venture can be exempted from income tax in the first two profit-making years and allowed a 50% reduction of income tax in the third, fourth and fifth years. After the tax exemption period expires, technologically-advanced enterprises subject to a reduced rate of 10% for another three years, and export enterprises shall pay income tax at the rate of 10%.

Official department in charge:

**Xiamen Municipal Committee of Foreign Economic Relations and Trade
11th and 12th floor, Information Mansion, Hu Li Industrial Zone
Xiamen 361006
Tel: (0592) 41902 Fax: (0592) 621901**

35. XINJIANG UYGUR (SINKIANG) AUTONOMOUS REGION

Spreading over an immense area of 1.6 million sq. km. or 1/6 the total territory of China, this autonomous region in far west China has a population of 14,541,600, of whom 6,827,300 are Uygur, 5,531,600 are Han, and 1,087,900 are Kazak. The rest numbering 1,094,800 is made up of people of the Hui, Mongolian, Kirgiz, Tajik, Xibe, Manchu, Tatar, Russian and other ethnic groups. The regional capital is Urumqi, a city situated in almost the very center of the Euro-Asian landmass and more than 2,500 km. from the east Chinese coast.

Xinjiang is a vast land which abounds in minerals. The principal minerals are petroleum, coal, aluminum and non-ferrous metals of all kinds. Rich petroleum reserves have been found in Xinjiang's Junggar and Tarim basins. The region produces plenty of melons, seedless raisins, wool and long-stapled cotton and has extensive tracts of grassland (2). A railway connects the region with Gansu province and northern China, but the successful development of Xinjiang's mineral riches will depend on further improvements in communications.

Foreign Trade

Xinjiang's total export and import value in 1990 was $US 410.86 million, a decrease of 15.53 percent over 1989's $US 486.39 million.

Goods purchased for export totalled RMB 889.01 million yuan, up 16.96 percent as against RMB 760.1 million yuan in 1989.

The total export value reached $US 335.91 million, a decrease of 6.93 percent compared with 1989's $US 360.94 million. The export value took up 6.38 percent of the Autonomous Region's GNP of RMB 25.188 billion yuan and 0.65 percent of the total export value of the whole country.

There were forty-three items of major products each with an annual export value exceeding $US 1 million each. Among the forty-three varieties, there were twelve items each with export value over $US 5 million. They were cotton, cotton yarn, cashmere sweaters, woolen sweaters, cotton cloth, casings, canned tomato ketchup, carpets, lithium carbonate, licorice root ointment, cotton polyester frocks and down clothes, totalling $US 217.97 million which took up 64.89 percent of the total export value. Commodities were exported to forty-two countries and regions.

Table 53. Composition of export commodities - Xinjiang Uygur (2)

Classified according to agricultural industrial product				Classified according to international trade standard			
Item	Export value ($US million)	Percentage of the total 1990	1989	Item	Export value ($US million)	Percentage of the total 1990	1989
Agricultural & sideline products	182.42	54.31	57.2	Primary products	201.41	59.96	60.00
Agricultural & sideline manu- factured products	104.41	31.08	28.5				
Industrial & mineral products	49.08	14.61	14.3	Industrial manu- factured products	134.50	40.04	40.00

Table 54. Major export markets Xinjiang Uygur (2)

Country/region	Export value ($US million)	Percentage of the total
Japan	106.05	31.57
Former Soviet Union	72.81	21.68
Hong Kong	57.68	17.17
Germany	13.34	3.97
America	13.15	3.92
Czechoslovakia	11.26	3.35

Imported goods were $US 74.95 million, a decrease of 40.26 percent as against $US 125.46 million in 1989. Of the imported goods, means of production totalled $US 66.26 million, making up 88.41 percent of the total imports; and materials of livelihood reached $US 8.69 million, making up 11.59 percent. According to the classification for international trade standard, primary products were $US 1.76 million, taking up 2.34 percent of the total imports, whereas the industrial manufactured products amounted to $US 73.20 million, making up 97.66 percent.

Major imports covered ten varieties, such as, ammonium phosphate, diammonium phosphate, thick steel plate, then steel plate, section steel, auto parts, urea, kinescope, medical appliances, etc., totalling $US 62.52 million, making up 83.42 percent of the import value.

Commodities imported came from thirteen countries and regions.

Table 55. Major import markets - Xinjiang Uygur (2)

Country/region	Import value ($US million)	Percentage of the total
Former Soviet Union	47.36	63.19
Hong Kong	14.39	19.20
Japan	8.77	11.70
United States	1.54	2.05

Xinjiang's total trade with the former Soviet Union was $US 120.17 million, almost the same as that of 1989, making up 29.25 percent of Xinjiang's total trade. Of the total with the former Soviet Union, the export was $US 72.81 million, and import was $Us 47.36 million.

1990 saw the total border trade of $US 71.38 million; that with the Soviet Union was $US 69.81 million (of which, the export was $US 34.65 million), and that with Pakistan was $US 1.57 million (of which, the export totalled $US 1.14 million). Of the border trade, the major exports were thermos bottles, garments, knitwear, woolen sweaters, etc., and major imports were chemical fertilizers, steel products, automobiles, etc.

Utilization of Foreign Capital

In 1990, nine contracts were signed and approved for utilization of foreign capital with a contracted foreign investment of $US 264.46 million, 6.6 times more than 1989's $US 34.76 million. Of the said contracts, two were foreign loans with a value of $US 206.06 million; six were involved with foreign direct investment totalling $US 57.61 million; one was involved in other foreign investment valuing $US 79,000. The actual utilization of foreign capital amounted to $US 17.21 million, a decrease of 61.59 percent as against $US 44.735 million in 1989. Of the total actually-utilized foreign capital, foreign loans involved $US 10.54 million; foreign direct investment, $US 5.95 million; and other foreign investment, $US 72,000.

Of the six contracts with foreign direct investment, five were joint ventures and one was wholly foreign-owned enterprise. Sectors invested were production-oriented, and mainly covered: textile industry, four; building materials, one; and fodder, one. The foreign capital came from Canada and Spain.

In 1990, the export value of foreign-invested enterprises that were in operation was $US 19.61 million, constituting 5.84 percent of Xinjiang's total export.

Technology Import and Export

Eight contracts were signed for introduction of technology and import of equipment with a contracted value of $US 5.73 million, a decrease of 40.35 percent compared with $US 9.60 million in 1989. The projects mainly imported from Japan, the United States, Germany, Italy, and the former Soviet Union.

Foreign Economic Cooperation

Some nineteen contracts were signed involving contracting projects and labor service, with a contracted value of SF 4.09 million and SF 4.09 million, and the turnover was realized in the year. Some 1,100 technicians and labor service workers were sent abroad, and 290 remained working abroad in the end of the year.

Projects executed were: residence and hotel construction and maintenance projects in the former Soviet Union and a cement factory in Mongolia.

In 1990, two non-productive enterprises were set up in the former Soviet Union with Chinese capital of $Us 1.20 million.

In 1990, Xinjiang received an amount of $US 1.25 million from the United Nations Population Fund for women's participation and development and two aid given gratis from the Japanese Government involving 1.519 billion Japanese Yen.

* * * *

The Beijing office of the region is located at:

7 Sanlihelu, Xicheng District
Beijing 100044
Tel: 8318561 Fax: 8354579

36. XIZANG (TIBET) AUTONOMOUS REGION

Spreading over an area of 1,228.400 sq. km. north of Bhutan, Sikkim and Nepal.

The population at year-end in 1989 was 2,150,000. Lhasa is the regional capital.

Highland barley and other crops are cultivated in the sheltered valleys of eastern Tibet, while sheep, cattle and yak, an ox-like, hairy animal, are pastured on the vast grasslands in northern Tibet. Many mineral deposits have been discovered,

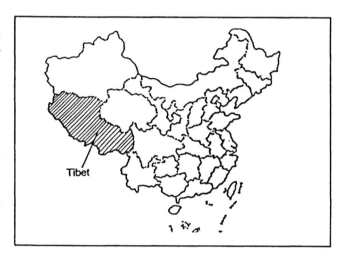

and the ones with the biggest reserves are chromite, copper, boron and gypsum. There are also deposits of lithium, known as the aristocrat of metals used in nuclear reactions and metallurgy. Tibet has the biggest reserve of geothermal energy in China, some of which are being harnessed to generate electricity.

Tibet, which has no industry a few decades ago, produced goods worth RMB 330 million in 1989. Cement production reached 120,000 tons, almost enough to meet local needs (2).

Foreign Trade

In 1990, the total value of import and export of Tibet Autonomous Region reached $US 30.2192 million, a decrease of 1.5 percent compared to the $US 30.67 million in 1989.

The purchase value of export commodities amounted to RMB 69.18 million yuan, a decrease of 37.34 percent against RMB. 110.41 million yuan in 1989.

The total value of export was $US 13.94 million, a decrease of 10.35 percent against $US 15.55 million in 1989, accounting for 2.97 percent GNP in Tibet Autonomous Region, 0.03 percent of national export value.

Table 56. List of export commodities structure - Tibet (2)

Classified by agriculture, light and heavy industries				*Classified by standard of international trade*			
Category	Export value ($US million)	Percentage of the total export value 1990	1989	Category	Export value ($US million)	Percentage of the total export value 1990	1989
Agricultural and sideline products	12.78	91.67	91.44	Primary products	12.81	91.92	95.88
Light industrial products	1.10	7.92	3.99				
Heavy industrial products	0.06	0.41	4.57	Industrial manufactured products	1.13	8.08	4.12

The commodities each with export value exceeding $US 1 million were sheep wool, dehaired goatwool, cordiceps sinensis, totalling $US 11.29 million, making up 80.99 percent of the total export value.

The commodities were mainly exported to the following countries and regions: Hong Kong, Japan, Thailand, Malaysia, Nepal, Singapore, Germany, France, the Netherlands, Italy, the United Kingdom, Switzerland and the United States.

The total import value amounted to $US 16.28 million, up 7.67 percent over $US 15.12 million of 1989, among which, $US 9.98 million of means of production made up 61.28 percent of the total import value; $US 6.30 million of means of livelihood made up 38.72 percent. Classified by standard of international trade, the primary products reached $US 250,000 making up 1.51 percent of the total import value; $US 16.03 million for industrial manufactured products, accounting for 98.49 percent.

The imported goods were mainly as follows: $US 5.29 million for automobile and its components, making up 32.51 percent of the total import value; $US 3.11 million for steel products, accounting for 19.10 percent; $US 1.73 million for pesticide, occupying 10.64 percent; $US 1.08 million for textile products, making up 6.63 percent.

The main import markets were Japan, Nepal, Hong Kong, and Brazil with total value of $US 15.89 million, making up 97.62 percent of the total import value.

In 1990, the total value of import and export in Tibet's border trade amounted to $US 9.02 million, a decrease of 18.15 percent compared with $US 11.02 million in 1989. The main export commodities were animal by-products, native produce, textile products, and light industrial products. The main import goods were cereals, oils and foodstuffs, articles for minority nationality, household electrical appliances, etc.

Utilization of Foreign Capital

In 1990, one contract was approved to utilize foreign investment with a value of $US

150,000. This project was processing of animal by-products. The investment came from Nepal.

Foreign Economic Cooperation

Tibet Autonomous Region accepted five projects of international aid with a total value of $US 6.78 million. Among them, three projects were from the United Nations Children's Fund and other international organizations with a total value of $US 5.40 million; and two projects were from the bilateral aid with a total value of $US 1.38 million. The above-mentioned projects have been performed completely.

*   *   *   *

The Beijing office of the region is located at:

149 Gulou Xidajie, Dongcheng District
Beijing 100009
Tel: 4018822, 4019831   Fax: 4019831

37. YANTAI CITY & DEVELOPMENT ZONE

Yantai City is a very important industrial, agricultural, fishing and foreign trade merchandise production center in Shandong Province. It is one of the most advanced areas in economic development in the whole country. The city is a seaport specializing in electronics, machinery, light industry, food, textiles, silk, chemistry, gold and the building materials industry. It is also a seaport for foreign trade and tourism. Yantai City is an ideal place for foreign investors due to its excellent location and environment, abundant resources, strong production base and developed transportation (8).

Yantai City is located on the eastern Shandong Peninsula at a latitude of 37 degrees, 30 minutes N. and a longitude of 120 degrees, 24 minutes E. The city borders the Bohai Sea in the north where you can see the Liaodong Peninsula across the ocean, the Yellow Sea in the south and Qingdao and Weifang Cities to the west.

Yantai City's industrial foundation is very solid. It has already established advanced industrial production systems in light industry, food, textiles, machinery, building materials, silk, electronics, instruments, chemistry, gold, coal, etc. Yantai City is one of the most important industrial bases of Shandong Province. It has over 2,500 city industries or businesses which is higher than the country's average. It also has over 2,000 major industrial products and over 200 multi-industrial products which are exported to other countries. Port wine, cans, wooden clocks and locks are Yantai's four most famous traditional industrial products. Automobiles, mobile machines, air conditioner-related products and synthetic leather, etc., are newly developed products.

Some major features of Yantai City are summarized in the following table.

Table 57. Yantai City—Salient Statistics (2)

Area (sq. km.)	18,900 10 (Special Economic Zone only)
Population	794,600 (urban)
Economic situation	Industrial production in 1989
	Light industry:
	Heavy industry:
	Value of export:
	Harbor's handling volume:
	Investment in capital assets:
	Total value of industrial production:
Utilization of foreign capital	Utilization of foreign capital in 1988
	Contract number:
	Foreign contractual value:
	Effected foreign investment:

Light industry: 5,757.94 (mil. yuan)
Heavy industry: 4,454.3 (mil. yuan)
Value of export: $US 151.22 mil.
Harbor's handling volume: 1,225 (10 thousand tons)
Investment in capital assets: 1,010.26 (mil. yuan)
Total value of industrial production: 10,212.24 (mil. yuan)

Contract number: 104
Foreign contractual value: $US 75.12 mil.
Effected foreign investment: $US 22.77 mil.

Number of foreign direct investment:	63
Total foreign direct investment:	$US 22.77 mil.

Utilization of foreign capital in 1989

Contract number:	128
Foreign contractual value:	$US 73.46 mil.
Effected foreign investment:	$US 20.99 mil.
Number of foreign direct investment:	63
Total foreign direct investment:	$US 11.40 mil.

Up to the end of 1988

Joint ventures:	47
Contractual joint ventures:	4
Foreign wholly-owned enterprises:	5
Total:	56
Japanese enterprises:	6

Infrastructure

Port:	13 berths, yearly harbor handling capacity: 13 million tons
Water:	Daily supply capability: 100,000 tons
Telecommunication:	Direct domestic and international call in the economic and technological development zone:
industrial use	1-1.3
commercial use	11-15
residential bldg.	4-6

Labor service charge
(Unit: yuan/month)

150-180 (average)

120% of the real wages of state-owned enterprises of the same trade in the locality.

Other fees

Water:	0.38 yuan/ton
Electricity:	0.22 yuan/kwh

Priorities

Textile, machinery, chemistry, energy, electronic light industry, foodstuffs

Local preference

The income tax rate on joint venture is 15%. A newly established joint venture can be exempted from income tax in the first two profit-making years and allowed a 50% reduction of income tax in the third, fourth and fifth years. After the tax exemption period expires, technologically-advanced enterprises subject to a reduced rate of 10% for another three years, and export enterprises shall pay income tax at a reduced rate of 10% provided that their value of export products in that year amounts to 70% or more of the value of their products for that year.
Joint ventures shall be exempted from local income tax within ten years.

Official department in charge:

Yantai Municipal Committee of Foreign Economic Relations and Trade
17-2, West Yu Huang Ding Road
Yantai
Tel: (0535) 243389

Yantai City's fruit industry is so flourishing that it has gained the reputation of the "Country of Fruit." It is one of China's most important export bases for fruit. It has a 263,040 acre growing area which produces many types of fruit such as apples, Laiyang pears, Changba pears, grapes, haw, big cherries, chestnuts, etc. The Yantai apple has a long history and a special taste and has over 100 different varieties. The growing area for grapes is 14,796 acres with an annual production of 75,000.

Yantai City's countryside has an abundant labor supply which includes 1.2 million people involved in industrial or secondary production. The countryside has over 53,000 businesses covering over thirty different kinds of business which hire almost 800,000 employees. Their production is over 50% of the city's total industrial and agricultural output. The machinery industry, the agricultural by-products processing industry and the building materials industry are the three major rural businesses in the city.

Economic and Technological Development Zone

The Yantai Economic and Technological Development Zone is located west of Yantai City across the river from the old city. It is designed to cover as much as 10 sq. km. but at present, 4 sq. km. contain basic and living service facilities which qualify for plant openings and investment. Over 100 domestic and foreign businesses have been established here. The zone has flat land, a stable ground structure, convenient transportation, ample utilities, advanced communications and complete facilities in trade, travel and the service industry. The Yantai Science and Technical Industrial Institute is located in the zone. The institute possesses special privileges to enable it to achieve scientific results as meaningful as from renowned international and domestic institutions and undergo product research and development to promote the city's products.

38. YUNNAN PROVINCE

Yunnan, a very mountainous province in southwestern China, has a common border of 4,060 km. with Myanmar, Lao People's Democratic Republic and Viet Nam. It covers an area of 394,000 sq. km. with 36.48 million people of the Han nationality and the Yi, Bai, Hani, Zhuang, Dai, Miao and eighteen other ethnic minorities. It is a mountainous area, embracing the western half of the Yungui Plateau. While the plateau surface enjoys a mild, temperate climate, the south is subtropical and tropical. The mountains contain some bizarre scenery—including a "forest" of tree-shaped 30 m. (100 ft.) high limestone crags, pitted with caves. They are also a botanist's paradise, with more than 15,000 plant species. The best agricultural land is around the city of Kunming, where rice, wheat and maize are grown.

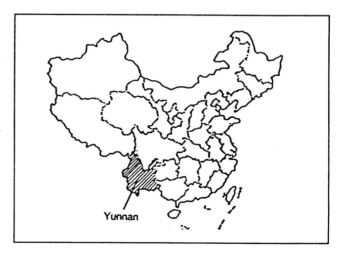

Foreign Trade

The import and export volume of Yunnan Province in 1990 totalled $US 751.14 million, decreased by 6.35 percent from $US 802.09 million in 1989.

The value of products purchased for export was RMB 2.344 billion yuan, increased by 12.69 percent over RMB 2.08 billion yuan in 1989.

The export volume totalled $US 562.41 million, increased by 4.41 percent over $US 538.63 million in 1989, accounting for 6.91 percent of the Province's GNP and 108 percent of the national export value.

Table 58. Export commodity structure - Yunnan Province (2)

Classified by agriculture, light and heavy industries			*Classified by international trade standard*		
Category	*Export value ($US million)*	*Percentage of the total* 1990 1989	*Category*	*Export value ($US million)*	*Percentage of the total* 1990 1989
Agricultural & sideline products	65.53	11.65 18.6	Primary products	233.37	41.49 31.3

Light industrial products	288.10	51.23	48.7			
Heavy industrial products	208.78	37.12	32.7	Industrial manu-factured products	329.04	58.51 68.7

There were fifty-one items of commodities, with export value of each item exceeding $US 1 million. The total value of these commodities amounted to $US 367.68 million, accounting for 65.38 percent of the total. Of them, the export value of cigarettes exceeding $US 30 million, amounted to $US 140.95 million, accounting for 25.06 percent of the total. The export value of tin, tea and machine tools ranged from $US 10-30 million respectively, totalling $US 87.88 million and accounting for 15.63 percent of the total. The export value of phosphorous ore, jade ornaments, garments, kidney beans, calcium magnesium phosphate, phosphor, flue-cured tobacco, antimony ingots and telescopes ranged from $US 5-10 million, totalling $US 58.03 million and accounting for 10.32 percent of the total.

The commodities were exported to sixty-nine countries and regions, nine countries more than that of 1989.

Table 59. Main export markets - Yunnan Province (2)

Country/region	Export value ($US million)	Percentage of the total
Myanmar	142.73	25.38
Hong Kong	96.28	17.12
Japan	68.45	12.17
United States	22.12	3.93
Former Soviet Union	19.12	3.40
Singapore	9.33	1.66
Thailand	9.28	1.65
United Kingdom	8.18	1.45

The total import volume was $US 188.73 million, a decrease of 28.36 percent from $US 263.46 million in 1989. Of the total, means of production were valued at $US 89.06 million, accounting for 47.19 percent of the total; means of livelihood $US 99.67 million, 52.18 percent. Classified by international trade standard, the value of primary products amounted to $US 78.57 million, accounting for 41.63 percent of the total; and the value of industrial manufactured products was $US 110.16 million, 58.37 percent.

Major imports were agricultural products with the value of $US 68 million, accounting for 36.03 percent of the total; tobacco and cigarette subsidiary materials, $US 22.4 million, 11.90 percent; technology and complete equipment, $US 22.37 million, 11.85 percent; various kinds of machinery, $US 14.05 million, 7.45 percent; and raw materials for arts and crafts $US 10.14 million, 5.40 percent.

The commodities were imported from twenty-two countries and regions.

Table 60. Main import markets - Yunnan Province (2)

Country/region	Import value ($US million)	Percentage of the total
Myanmar	72.92	38.64
Hong Kong	29.43	15.59
United States	21.64	11.47
Germany	12.36	6.55
Japan	11.14	5.90
Finland	7.83	4.15
France	6.81	3.61
Australia	6.58	3.49
United Kingdom	6.17	3.27

Yunnan's total import and export value of the border trade was $US 202.72 million, a decrease of 20.38 percent from $US 254.62 million in 1989. Of the total, the export value amounted to $US 127.92 million, and the import value amounted to $US 74.80 million. The total import and export value of the border trade with Myanmar reached $US 195.72 million, accounting for 96.54 percent of the total border trade value (export value, $US 123.52 million and import value, $US 72.20 million). The total import and export value of the border trade with the Lao People's Democratic Republic was $US 7 million, accounting for 3.46 percent of the total (export value, $US 4.4 million and import value, $US 2.6 million).

Utilization of Foreign Capital

Thirty-six contracts on using foreign capital were signed and approved with the contract value of $US 4.51 million, an increase of 3.38 percent over $US 4.3626 million in 1989. Of the total, eleven were contracts of foreign direct investment with the total value of $US 2.53 million; twenty-five were of other foreign investment with the total value of $US 1.98 million.

The foreign investment actually utilized was $US 7.38 million, a decrease of 6.25 percent from $US 7.872 million in 1989, of which, the amount of foreign direct investment was $US 2.61 million, and other foreign investment was $US 4.77 million.

Among eleven projects of foreign direct investment, seven were equity joint ventures, and four were exclusively foreign-owned enterprises. All of them were productive. Of these projects, two were involved in plantation, two in chemical industry, one in garment processing, casting, photographic plate making and food processing, respectively. The investors mainly came from Hong Kong, Taiwan Province, Singapore and the United States.

Technology Import and Export

Fourteen contracts of technology and equipment import were signed and approved with the contract value of $US 63.926 million, increased by 1.23 times over $US 28.6271 million in 1989. The foreign exchange actually used amounted to $US 22.38 million, decreased by 30.90 percent from $US 32.39 million in 1989. The major projects were involved in cigarette packing lines, cigarette machines, tray fillers, soft packing machines, compound filler up production lines, printing machinery, etc., three of them were introduced from Germany with the value of $US 29.18 million; four from the United Kingdom, $US 24.00 million; and one from Italy, $US 5.90 million.

Foreign Economic Cooperation

Twenty-three contracts of foreign engineering contracting and labor service were signed and approved with the contract value of $US 6.8674 million, a decrease of 2.05 percent from $US 7.0113 million in 1989. The turnover was $US 4.561 million, an increase of 30.81 percent over $US 3.4525 million in 1989. At the end of the year, ten people remained abroad. Yunnan mainly undertook the construction of a teaching building of a university and Point Monies Bridge in Mauritius, the water treatment project in Pakistan, the second resident building in Maldives, and the runway transformation project of Nam That Airport in the Lao People's Democratic Republic.

Yunnan Province undertook five projects of foreign aid in Mauritius, Cameroon and Maldives. Twenty-three people for foreign aid were sent abroad. At the end of the year, thirty-five people remained abroad.

The Province received eleven assistant projects from international organizations and bilateral-aid projects with the value of $US 17 million.

Eight enterprises were approved to be set up in Mauritius, Bolivia, Myanmar, the United States, Tanzania and Australia. The total Chinese investment amounted to $US 2.1 million.

*   *   *   *

The Beijing office of the province is located at:

17 Beishanhuandonglu, Chaoyang District
Beijing 100029
Tel: 4216514   Fax: 4217364

Another useful China contact for users of this volume might be:

Yunnan Foreign Economic Relations & Trade
576 Beijing Road, Kunming 650011
Tel: 28175, 35001   Fax: 35107

39. ZHEJIANG PROVINCE

Lying on the East China coast south of the Yangtze River Estuary, Zhejiiang Province is land of rice and fish, and is well-known for its silk and tea. Off its long coastline are 2,164 islands, the most famous ones being the Zhoushan - one of China largest fishing grounds. The important ports along the coast are Ninbbo and Wenzhou. The province occupies an area of 101,800 sq km and has a population exceeding 40,000,000.

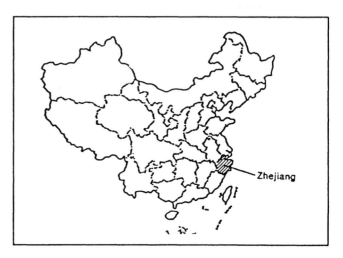

The provincial capital is Hangzhou, a tourist center with its picturesque West Lake. Zhejiang is a mountainous province on the east coast that is now getting the attention of foreign investors. The coastal city of Wenzhou may be the most entrepreneurial spot in China. The port of Ningbo is drawing money from Hong Kong shipping interests, who see it as a transshipment point for cargo coming down the Yangtze River.

Hills and mountains make up more than 70 per cent of the province, and cultivated land is restricted to valleys and the narrow coastal plains. Rice, tea, maize, sugar cane and tangerines are grown in the subtropical province. Dense forests of pine, spruce, and bamboo cover the mountainsides in the interior, and they are exploited to serve a flourishing timber and paper industry.

Zhejiang is a major area of importance for textile equipment and facilities. Zhejiang together with Shanghai and Jianjsu are the main silk production centers in China.

Zhejiang coastal plain is a natural gas producing area of some importance.

The total export and import volume of Zhejiang Province in 1990 was $US 2.55 billion, an increase of 9.49 per cent over $US 2.329 billion in 1989.

The export commodities purchasing value was RMB 13.891 billion yuan, an increase of 27 per cent over RMB 10.938 billion yuan in 1989.

The export value was $US 2.259 billion, an increase of 20.22 per cent over $us 1.879 billion in 1989, accounting for 13.16 per cent of the province's GNP and 4.34 per cent of the total export of the whole country, and ranking sixth in China.

Table 61. Structure of export commodities - Zhejiang Province (2)

By agriculture, light and heavy industries			*By SITC system*		
Item	*Export value (\$US million)*	*Percentage of* total export 1990 1989	*Category*	*Export value (\$US million)*	*Percentage of* total export 1990 1989
Agricultural & sideline products	305.71	13.5 14.4	Primary products	627.52	27.8 32.1
Light industrial products	1,645.94	72.9 69.1			
Heavy industrial	307.69	16.5 16.5	Manufactured industrial products	1,631.82	72.2 67.9

The export commodities were sold to 134 countries and regions. Of them, twenty-one countries bought commodities valuing more than \$US 10 million each, totalling \$US 1.955 billion, and accounting for 86.54 percent of the total export.

Table 62. Commodities each with export value over \$US 5 million - Zhejiang Province (2)

Classification by value	*Name of commodities*	*Export value (\$US million)*	*Percentage of total export*
Over \$US 100 million (4 kinds)	Garments, silk and satins, mulberry silk, tea.	630.29	27.90
Between \$US 50-100 million (3 kinds)	Cotton cloth, aquatic products, canned goods.	234.46	10.38
Between \$US 10-50 million (30 kinds)	Hardware, cotton knitwear, knitwear, cotton manu- factured goods, vegetables, petroleum products, cotton/ polyester blended fabrics, straw products, wool knitwear, B/W TV sets, gasoline, tools, leather garments, down products, color bulbs, small sized complete sets of equipments, art shoes, silk knitwear, fluorspar in lumps (in powder), artificial silk pro-	630.86	27.93

ducts, cement, locks, nylon um-
brellas, bearings, cotton yarn,
rabbit hair, pesticides, and toys.

Total	**1,495.61**	**66.21**

Table 63. Major export markets - Zhejiang Province (2)

Country/region	Export value ($US million)	Percentage of total export
Hong Kong	659.83	29.21
Japan	345.19	15.28
United States	226.63	10.03
Germany	137.20	6.07
Former Soviet Union	94.94	4.20
Italy	67.53	2.99
Singapore	67.46	2.99
France	53.50	2.37
Switzerland	36.78	1.63
Morocco	36.76	1.63
Total	**1,725.82**	**76.40**

The total import value was $US 290.81 million, a decrease of 35.39 percent from $US 450.12 million in 1989, of which, $US 277.96 million was for means of production, accounting for 95.58 percent of the total import; and $US 12.85 million was for means of livelihood, accounting for 4.42 percent. By SITC system, $US 105.44 million was for primary products, accounting for 36.26 percent of the total; and $US 185.37 million for manufactured industrial products, 63.74 percent.

Major import commodities were: chemical raw materials valuing $Us 38.77 million; cotton, $US 36.46 million; complete sets of equipment and various kinds of machinery, $US 18.40 million; electronic computers and various kinds of instruments, $US 18.13 million; synthetic fiber, $US 15.63 million; ores, $US 11.27 million; and rubber, $US 10.24 million. The sum was $US 148.9 million, accounting for 50.12 percent of the total import value.

Table 64. Major import markets - Zhejiang Province (2)

Country/region	Import value ($US million)	Percentage of total import
Hong Kong	135.19	46.49
Japan	58.52	20.12
United States	29.40	10.11
Germany	16.03	5.51
Australia	10.99	3.78

Taiwan Province	7.30	2.51
Malaysia	4.51	1.55
The Netherlands	3.63	1.25
Macau	3.50	1.20
Singapore	3.02	1.04
Total	**272.09**	**93.56**

Utilization of Foreign Capital

Three hundred and seventeen contracts on using foreign capital were signed and approved. Contract value was $US 164.91 million, a decrease of 48.34 percent from $US 319.23 million in 1989, of which, $US 30.03 million were foreign loans, $US 133.13 million were foreign direct investment for 294 projects, and $US 1.76 million were other foreign investment for twenty-three projects.

The actually used foreign funds was $US 79.17 million, a decrease of 71.77 percent from $US 280.45 million in 1989, of which, foreign loans was $US 30.02 million, foreign direct investment was $US 48.44 million, and foreign investment in other forms was $US 710,000.

Among the 294 foreign direct investment projects, 249 were Chinese-foreign equity joint ventures, fifteen were contractual joint ventures, and thirty were wholly foreign-owned enterprises. Or 287 were productive enterprises and seven were non-productive projects. To classify by trade, ninety-two were for textile and garments, fifty for machinery and electronics, thirty-five for arts and crafts, twenty for light industry, eleven for chemical industry, five for culture and education, five for instruments and meters, four for building materials, three for transportation and storage, two for agriculture, one for scientific research and technical service, and seventy-six for others.

The investment came from sixteen countries and regions. The major investors were Hong Kong, involving in 169 projects, valuing $US 69.8 million; Taiwan Province, sixty projects, $US 30.09 million; Singapore, five projects, $US 12.41 million; the United States, twenty-two projects, $US 6.92 million; Japan, eighteen projects, $US 4.5 million; Canada, three projects, $US 1.15 million; and Macau, three projects, $US 740,000.

By the end of 1990, 407 foreign investment enterprises went into operation. The business turnover was RMB 2.36 billion yuan, the profit was RMB 90.07 million yuan, and the export earning was $Us 149 million.

Technology Import and Export

One hundred and forty-three contracts on import of technology and equipment were signed with a value of $US 72.12 million, an increase of 1.13 times over $US 33.81 million in 1989.

Ten contracts on export of technology were signed with a value of $US 17.21 million. Major exports were power machinery, electric power generating equipment, pharmaceutical equipment, heavy machinery, etc.

Foreign Economic Cooperation

The Province signed 68 contracts for contracting engineering projects and labor service cooperation, valuing $Us 24.05 million, an increase of 25.20 percent over $US 19.21 million in 1989. The business turnover was $US 15.43 million, a decrease of 17.71 percent from $Us 18.75 million in 1989. Some 2,700 people were dispatched abroad in 1990, and 1,352 people were still abroad at the end of the year. Most of them were sent to countries and regions such as Kuwait, Iran, Yemen, Japan, Hong Kong, Austria, Germany, Fiji, Sierra Leone and Australia, and coastal countries of West Africa. Main contracting projects were construction of villas and apartment buildings in Kuwait City, Chinese Gardens in Japan, Esfahan Hydropower Station in Iran, and Fiji hydroelectric project, etc.

The Province undertook ten foreign aid projects, involving in hydropower, construction, agriculture, etc. More than 100 people were sent abroad for foreign aid. Countries that received aid were Fiji, Sierra Leone, Mayanmar, Mali, Uganda, and Central Africa. The 47 km. 11KV power transmission line of Power Network in Fiji and the Mayanmar Cultural Theatre were completed.

The Province received eighteen foreign aid projects with $US 2.61 million of foreign funds from international organizations and other countries, of which, $US 2.11 million was from international organizations and $US 500,000 was from other countries.

Two overseas enterprises were approved and established. The Chinese side invested $US 760,000. By the end of 1990, ten enterprises went into operation, with a total Chinese investment of $US 4.99 million. These enterprises scattered in Canada, the United Arab Emirates, Japan, Thailand, Singapore, Australia, etc.

* * * *

The Beijing office of the province is located at:

Madian, Beitaipingzhuang
Beijing 100088
Tel: 2032376   Fax: 2011323, 2019436

Another China contact which should be helpful to users of this volume is:

Foreign Economic Relations & Trade Bureau of Zhejiang Province
216 Yan'an Road, Hangzhou 310006
Tel: 557532   Fax: 0571-554131

40. ZHUHAI DEVELOPMENT ZONE

The city of Zhuhai is located in the southern province of Guangdong on the right bank of the Pearl River. Across 36 nautical miles of the Pearl River, it faces Hong Kong and Shenzhen in the east, connects to Macao in the south, neighbors with the Xinhui and Taishan prefectures in the west, and connects to Zhongshan City in the north. Zhuhai which is about 15 km. from Guangzhou has about 144 islands. The urban population of Zhuhai is approximately 270,000 and the population of the whole city area is 520,000.

Zhuhai with its pleasant weather and rich seafood resources is a beautiful place and a famous tourist center (8).

Originally, Zhuhai was an undeveloped poor fishing village. The city was built in March, 1979, and was established as a special economic district in August, 1980. The district has been expanded to 121 sq. km. A comparison of the city's development before and after 1989 reflects a tremendous change in Zhuhai. By the end of 1991, the city had finished the basic construction costing RMB 8.2 billion. In a 30 sq. km. developed city area, it has built the basic installations like harbors, piers, telecommunications and roads. By the end of 1991, the total amount of contracted foreign investment was USD 3.3 billion of which USD 1 billion was actually used to establish 600 foreign investment companies. Zhuhai also cooperated with other provinces, cities, and autonomous zones to create 900 domestic companies. Since in 1991 the figure for gross production in Zhuhai was over RMB 6 billion, the total revenue of people in the city was over RMB 3.9 billion and the total revenue of people in the trading was over USD 2 billion, the cost of living for people in Zhuhai has obviously been raised.

Jiuzhou Harbor is the main harbor of Zhuhai. It has eleven piers. Three piers are for passenger transportation to and from Hong Kong and Shekou. Eight piers are for goods transportation, two of which serve 10,000 ton shipments, and four of which serve 5,000 ton shipments. Jiuzhou Harbor has a 7,480 sq. meter warehouse and a 140,000 sq. meter loading area. The annual handling capacity of Jiuzhou is 2.5 million tons.

Some of the principal statistics concerning Zhuhai are given in Table 65.

Table 65. Zhuhai Special Economic Zone—Salient Statistics (2)

Area (sq. km.)	121
Population	270,000, permanent residents: 200,000
Economic situation	Industrial production in 1989

	Light industry:	2,244.11 (mil. yuan)
	Heavy industry:	675.54 (mil. yuan)
	Value of export:	$US 365.08 mil.
	Harbor's handling volume:	231 (10 thousand tons)

Investment in capital assets:	957.84 (mil. yuan)
Total value of industrial production:	2,919.65 (mil. yuan)

Utilization of foreign capital　　Utilization of foreign capital in 1988

Contract number:	1,251
Foreign contractual value:	$US 311.87 mil.
Effected foreign investment:	$US 217.62 mil.
Number of foreign direct investment:	252
Total foreign direct investment:	$US 47.40 mil.

Utilization of foreign capital in 1989

Contract number:	1,395
Foreign contractual value:	$US 241.82 mil.
Effected foreign investment:	$US 169.47 mil.
Number of foreign direct investment:	225
Total foreign direct investment:	$US 53.28 mil.

Up to the end of 1988

Joint ventures:	169
Contractual joint ventures:	32
Foreign wholly-owned enterprises:	13
Total:	214
Japanese enterprises:	6

Infrastructure

Port:	Jiuzhou Port is an above 10,000 ton deepwater port.
Power:	Supplied by Guangdong Power Network
Water:	Daily supply capability: 60,000 tons
Telecommunication:	Equipped with advanced facilities, direct domestic and international call.

Joint ventures shall be exempted from it within three years and allowed a 50% reduction for three years. Export enterprises shall be exempted from it within five year and allowed a 50% reduction for five years.

Labor service charge
(Unit: yuan/month)

Managers: 450 (average)
Staff members: 300 (average)
120% of the real wages of state-owned enterprises of the same trade in the locality.

Other fees

Water:	0.12 yuan/ton
Electricity:	0.25-0.35 yuan/kwh

Priorities

Textile and garment, light industry, foodstuffs, electronics, building materials

Local preference	The income tax rate on joint venture is 15%. A newly established joint venture can be exempted from income tax in the first two profit-making years and allowed a 50% reduction of income tax in the third, fourth and fifth years.

Official department in charge:

Zhuhai Municipal Committee of Foreign Economic Relations & Trade
Xiangzhou District, Shenzhen
Tel: (0756) 222143, 222570

CHAPTER 2

INFRASTRUCTURE

As with all developing countries (and even with some developed countries), an area of major problems lies in getting goods and services from the point where they are produced to the point where they are needed.

An interesting study on the relations between transport and territorial development in China from 1949 to 1985 has been published in Canada (6).

Closely allied to the infrastructure problem is the question of future city planning in China.

There is a stated policy of reducing the proportion of Chinese living in the countryside from today's 87% (a disputed figure) of its 1.2 billion population to 50% by 2040. that means moving 440 million people—the population of America and Russia combined—into cities.

But while it is true that there is not nearly enough land to keep a billion peasants busy, the cities are not ready to absorb them either. A case in point is the railway station in Guangzhou, in southern China, where thousands of country folk who took the train to the boom town now live and sleep.

Urban planners in China say that the answer is to build lots of new cities, perhaps 200 of them. In a typical Chinese puzzle, the question of now that is to be done, or where, is hidden from view. Different bureaucracies in Beijing are drawing up plans, but there is no agreed map setting out where the new and expanded cities will be. There is no apparent means of financing the scheme, and the planners are authorized to do nothing but plan.

China's economy expanded at an astounding 13 percent in 1992 and 1993, leaving its relatively rudimentary infrastructure in the dust. The government responded with dramatic plans to expand highways, railroads, ports, airports and even subways. But big plans cost big money, and China doesn't have a lot of cash to spare. That's what has major financiers around the world salivating.

Beijing has spent very little on building roads and rails in recent years. According to World Bank estimates, transport investment amounted to only 1.4 percent of China's gross national product from 1985 to 1990, compared with 2.5 percent in India. As a result, the emerging highway system is barely developed, and China's city streets are jam packed.

The situation is similar in rail transport: With only enough railcars to meet 60 percent of total freight demand, delays in coal deliveries alone cost the nation an estimated 400 billion yuan (US $70 billion) in 1992, the Coal Ministry says. Thanks largely to breakdowns in the system, China's transportation network hauled 0.5 percent less freight and 10.3 percent fewer passengers in the first half of 1993 than in the same period a year before.

The government has taken several steps to address these problems. Its current five-year plan, ending in 1995, calls for building 180 additional shipping berths and 90,000 kilometers or railways. In November 1993, Beijing unveiled a blueprint for expanding the country's expressway network—now 659 kilometers—to 3,000 kilometers by the year 2000. And in April 1993, it took the wraps off a plan to build four transnational highways, an effort involving a 14,500 kilometer-long link among 100 major cities and ports.

TRANSPORTATION

Transportation is a major factor in China's national economy. For most of the period since 1949, however, transportation occupied a relatively low priority in China's national development. Inadequate transportation systems hindered the movement of coal from mine to user, the transportation of agricultural and light industrial products from rural to urban areas, and the delivery of imports and exports. As a result, the underdeveloped transportation system constrained the pace of economic development throughout the country. In the 1980s the updating of transportation systems was given priority, and improvements were made throughout the transportation sector (see figure 2).

Figure 2. Railroads and Major Air and Sea Ports, 1987
From Reference (4)

In 1986, China's transportation systems consisted of long distance hauling by railroads and inland waterways and medium distance and rural transportation by trucks and buses on national and provincial-level highways. Waterborne transportation dominated freight traffic in east, central, and southwest China, along the Chang Jiang (Yangtze River) and its tributaries, and in Guangdong Province and Guangxi-Zhuang Autonomous Region, served by the Zhu Jiang (Pearl River) system. All provinces, autonomous regions, and special municipalities, with the exception of Xizang Autonomous Region (Tibet), were linked by railroads. Many double-track lines, electrified lines, special lines, and bridges were added to the system. Subways were operating in Beijing and Tianjin, and construction was being planned in other large cities. National highways linked provincial-level capitals with Beijing and major ports. Roads were built between large, medium, and small towns as well as between towns and railroad connections. The maritime fleet made hundreds of port calls in virtually all parts of the world, but the inadequate port and harbor facilities at home still caused major problems. Civil aviation underwent tremendous development during the 1980s. Domestic and international air service was greatly increased. In 1985, the transportation system handled 2.7 billion tons of goods. Of this, the railroads handled 1.3 billion tons; highways handled 762 million tons; inland waterways handled 434 million tons; ocean shipping handled 65 million tons; and civil airlines handled 195,000 tons. The 1985 volume of passenger traffic was 428 billion passenger kilometers; road traffic, for 17.4 billion passenger kilometers; and air traffic, for 11.7 billion passenger kilometers (4).

Ownership and control of the different elements of the transportation system varied according to their roles and their importance in the national economy. The railroads were owned by the state and controlled by the Ministry of Railways. In 1986, a contract system for the management of railroad lines was introduced in China. Five-year contracts were signed between the ministry and individual railroad bureaus that were given responsibility for their profits and losses. The merchant fleet was operated by the China Ocean Shipping Company (COSCO), a state-owned enterprise. The national airline was run by the General Administration of Civil Aviation of China (CAAC). Regional airlines were run by provincial-level and municipal authorities. Highways and inland waterways were the responsibilities of the Ministry of Communications. Trucking and inland navigation were handled by government-operated transportation departments as well as by private enterprises.

Transportation was designated a top priority in the Seventh Five-Year Plan (1986-90). Under the plan, transportation-related projects accounted for 39 of 190 priority projects. Because most were long-term development projects, a large number were carried over from 1985, and only a few new ones were added. The plan called for an increase of approximately 30 percent in the volume of various kinds of cargo transportation by 1990 over 1985 levels. So each mode of transportation would have to increase its volume by approximately 5.4 percent annually during the five year period. The plan also called for updating passenger and freight transportation and improving railroad, waterways, and air transportation. To achieve these goals, the government planned to increase state and local investments as well as to use private funds.

Railroads China's first railroad line was built in 1876. In the seventy-three years that followed, 22,000 kilometers of track were laid, but only half were operable in 1949. Between 1949 and 1985, more than 30,000 kilometers of lines were added to the existing network, mostly int he southwest or coastal areas where previous rail development had been concentrated. By 1984, China had 52,000 kilometers of operating track, 4,000 kilometers of which had been electrified. All provinces, autonomous regions, and special municipalities, with the exception of Xizang Autonomous Region, were linked by rail. Many double-track lines, electric lines, special lines, and railroad bridges were added to the system. Railroad technology also was a upgraded to improve the performance of the existing rail network. There still were shortcomings, however. Most of the trunk lines were old, there was a general shortage of double-track lines, and Chinese official admitted that antiquated management techniques still were being practiced. There were plans in the late 1980s to upgrade the rail system, particularly in east China, in the hope of improving performance.

China's longest electrified double-track railroad, running from Beijing to Datong, Shanxi Province, was opened for operation in 1984. One of the world's highest railroads, at 3,000 meters above sea level in Qinghai Province, also went into service int he same year, and improved double-track railroads, some of them electrified, offered a fast way to transport coal from Shanxi Province to the highly industrialized eastern part of the country and the port of Qinhuangdao for export.

Production and maintenance of modern locomotives also made an important contribution to increased rail capacity. Manufacturing output in the mid-1980s increased significantly when production of electric and diesel locomotives for the first time exceeded that of steam powered ones. China hoped, in the long run, to phase out its steam powered locomotives. In the mid-1980s, China had more than 280,000 freight cars and about 20,000 passenger cars. The country still was unable, however, to meet the transportation needs brought about by rapid economic expansion (4).

Railways have been the mainstay of China's transport network and now carry 60 percent of national passenger traffic and 70 percent of all freight. Railway development is an important factor in the growth of the national economy and raising people's living standards (2).

China has the total railway lines of 53,340 kilometers, 6,900 kilometers of which are electrified and 9,000 kilometers are suitable for diesel locomotives. All provinces, municipalities and autonomous regions except Tibet, Taiwan and Hainan, are incorporated int he national rail network.

The volume of rail movements has been expanding rapidly in recent years. In 1990, 957 million passengers and 1.46 billion tons of cargo were recorded with the turnover freight reaching 1,322 billion tons-kilometers. Since the adoption of the open policy in 1979, the railway network has grown rapidly. The present growth rate means an extra 70 million passengers and 50 million tons of freight per year. Practically, all the major coastal cities have rail connections with the interior. More than 200 million tons of goods pass in and out of each of these ports by rail each year; this figure is increasing at an annual rate of 10 million tons.

In 1990, China invested RMB 6.717 yuan in railway construction and built 285.5

kilometers railways; 248.7 kilometers of railways were double-tracked and 551 kilometers were electrified. Construction of nineteen major railway-related projects under the State are also conducted.

Container transportation moved by railway has been introduced, but in a small capacity. By 1990, China has a total of 264,000 containers handled by 318 stations and forty-three international container mail lines.

China has also entered into cooperation with several foreign countries and international organizations for railway construction projects, the majority of which are for upgrading existing lines and construction new lines with foreign loans. So far, some agreements have already been signed. Some are about to be signed with the World Bank, Asian Development Bank, the and Japanese Bank.

However, railway transport is mainly for China's domestic trade and only a small capacity is used internationally.

It comes under two categories:

      (i)   International railway transport from China to East European countries and the Democratic People's Republic of Korea (known as SMGS);

      (ii)   International railway container transport via Siberia to European countries and the Islamic Republic of Iran (known as TSR).

The conversion turnover was 1,340.7 ton/km. in 1990. An average of 72,919 wagons were loaded daily. The coal turnover made up over 40 percent of the overall railway turnover. An average of 28,479 coal wagons were loaded daily. The coal turnover was 105 percent of the overall annual plan, reaching 608.91 million tons in 1989, an increase of 7.8 percent or 44.11 million tons over the previous year. Its growth rate was higher than that of freight turnover. Of the total coal turnover, 168.9 million tons were shipped out of Shanxi Province, accounting for 100.7 percent of the annual planned target, an increase of 10.87 percent of 16.48 million tons over the previous year.

As pointed out by one international consultant, the Chinese badly need nuclear power to lessen the burden of coal movement on the rail system. Meanwhile, transport of key materials such as oil, cement, chemical fertilizer, salt and phosphate had all fulfilled or overfulfilled the country's targets (2).

In 1990, China's railway also moved 5.38 million containers of 9.47 million tons of goods, up 6 percent and 11 percent. China built 200,000 one-ton and 6,500 ten-ton containers in 1989 and moved 46,223 international containers in the same year.

In the next three years, authorities plan to build the following rail lines: Beijing-Kowloon; the Lanzhou-Xinjiang; the Baoji-Zhongwei; the Houma-Yueshan; the Zhejiang-Jiangxi; the Beijing-Guangzhou; the Datong-Qinhuangdao; the Chengdu-Kunming; and the Xian-Ankang. These lines will speed the development of many rural areas, support agricultural trade with neighboring countries, for example, Xinjiang Province's trade with Kazakhstan, provide access to phosphorous deposits in southwest China, and encourage agricultural production by making inputs more accessible and providing greater access to markets.

Figure 3 shows the principal railways in China (48).

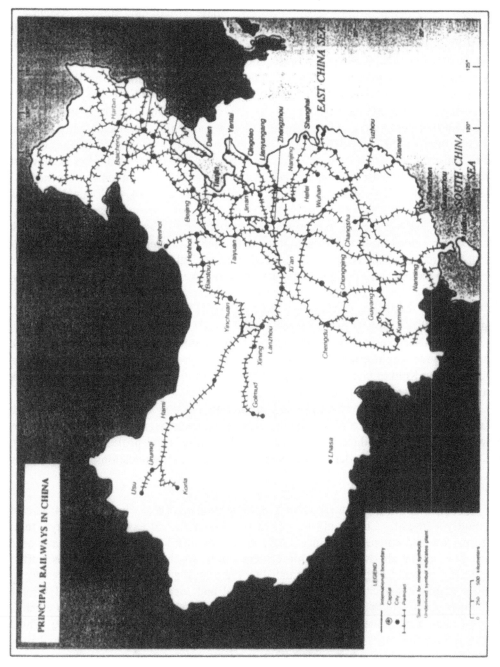

Figure 3: Principal Railways in China (48)

Subways China's first subways opened to traffic in Beijing in 1970, and Tianjin in 1980, respectively, and subway systems were planned for construction in Harbin, Shanghai, and Guangzhou beginning in the 1980s. In its first phase, the Beijing subway system had 23.6 kilometers of track and seventeen stations. In 1984, the second phase of construction added 16.1 kilometers of track and twelve stations, and in 1987 additional track and another station were added to close the loop on a now circular system. In 1987, there were plans to upgrade the signaling system and railcar equipment on 17 kilometers of the first segment built. The subway carried more than 100 million passengers in 1985, or about 280,000 on an average day and 450,000 on a peak day. In 1987, this accounted for only 4 percent of Beijing's 9 million commuters. The Beijing subway authorities estimated that passenger traffic would increase 20 percent yearly. To accommodate the increase in riders, Beijing planned to construct an extension of a 7 kilometer subway line under Chang'an Boulevard, from Fuxing Gate in the east to Jianguo Gate in the west. The Tianjin subway opened a 5 kilometer line in 1980. The Shanghai subway was planned to have 14.4 kilometers of track in its first phase (4).

Robert S. O'Neil, chief executive of the engineering firm De Leuw, Cather & Company, which helped build the Washington, D.C. subway system, has looked out across China's backward urban landscape and counted nineteen subway systems and eighty-two airports that are moving into design, construction or reconstruction phases in the next few years.

"We know there is a market here for us," Mr. O'Neil said. His firm has been working on Shanghai's subway project since 1987.

Little of this has been easy. Last winter, his negotiators were close to winning a huge contract to provide engineering services for the subway system in Guangzhou, when Chancellor Helmut Kohl of Germany "came over here with his concessionary loans and took the contract away from us," Mr. O'Neil said.

His firm, a subsidiary of the Parsons Corporation, has now formed a consortium with other American companies like Motorola and General Railway Signal to compete better by tailoring their integrated products and systems to what China's rail projects are not able to develop domestically, like modern train control systems, communications and operating systems.

Roads Roads in China total about 1 million kilometers and carry about 14 percent of the country's freight. China only has about 600 kilometers of express highways, most roads are narrow and congested. Since 1949, thousands of kilometers of roads have been built each year so that almost all township centers can be reached by truck and bus traffic. The emphasis is on building better roads funded by the central government (it will use surplus food grains to pay construction workers), provincial and local governments, and foreign capital. Plans call for building four limited access highways: Beijing-Guangzhou-Zhuhai; Tongjiang-Dalian-Yantai-Shenzhen; Lianyungang-Xinjiang; and Shanghai to Chengdu. These new highways and the roads built and improved by local governments will greatly aid rural development.

Figure 4 shows the principal roads in China (48).

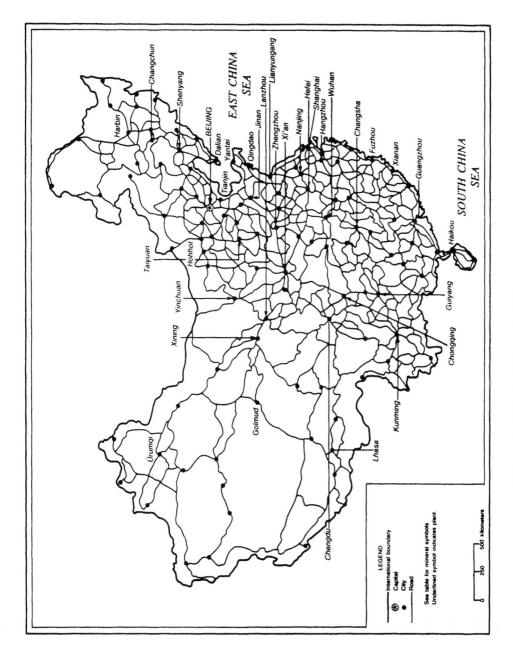

Figure 4: Principal Roads in China (48)

In 1986, China had approximately 962,800 kilometers of highways, 52,000 kilometers of which were completed between 1980 and 1985. During this period, China also rebuilt 22,000 kilometers of highways in cities and rural areas. Nearly 110,000 kilometers of roads were designated part of a network of national highways, including roads linking provincial-level capitals with Beijing and China's major ports.

Provincial-level and local governments were responsible for their own transportation and road construction, some with foreign expertise and financing to hasten the process. Most financing and maintenance funds came from the provincial level, supplemented in the case of rural roads by coal labor. In line with the increased emphasis on developing light industry and decentralizing agriculture, roads were built in large, medium-sized, and small towns and to railroad connections, making it possible for products to move rapidly between cities and across provincial-level boundaries. In 1986, approximately 780,000 kilometers of the roads, or 81 percent, were surfaced. The remaining 19 percent (fair weather roads) were in poor condition, hardly passable on rainy days. Only 20 percent of the roads were paved with asphalt; about 80 percent had gravel surfaces. In addition, 60 percent of the major highways needed repair (4).

China's highways carried 660 million tons of freight and 410 million passengers in 1985. In 1984, the authorities began assigning medium-distance traffic (certain goods and sundries traveling less than 100 kilometers and passengers less than 200 kilometers) to highways to relieve the pressure on railroads. Almost 800 national highways were used for transporting cargo. Joint provincial-level transportation centers were designated to take care of cross-country cargo transportation between provinces, autonomous regions, and special municipalities. A total of about 15,000 scheduled rural buses carried 4.3 million passengers daily, and more than 2,300 national bus services handled a daily average of 450,000 passengers. The number of trucks and buses operated by individuals, collectives, and families reached 130,000 in 1984, about half the number of state-owned vehicles. In 1986, there were 290,000 private motor vehicles in China, 95 percent of which were trucks. Most trucks had a four to five ton capacity.

The automobile was becoming an increasingly important mode of transportation in China. The automotive industry gave priority to improving quality and developing new models rather than increasing production. Nevertheless, as a result of the introduction of modern technology through joint ventures with advanced industrialized countries, Chinese automobile production for 1985 surpassed 400,000 units.

Although cars and trucks were the primary means of highway transportation, in the mid-1980s carts pulled by horses, mules, donkeys, cows, oxen, and camels still were common in rural areas. Motor vehicles often were unable to reach efficient travel speeds near towns and cities in rural areas because of the large number of slow-moving tractors, bicycles, hand and animal drawn carts, and pedestrians. Strict adherence to relatively low speed limits in some areas also kept travel speeds at inefficient levels.

Priority was also given to highway construction. China planned to build new highways and rebuild existing highways to a total length of 140,000 kilometers. At the end of the Seventh Five-Year Plan (1986-1990), the total length of highways was to be increased to 1 million kilometers from the existing 940,000 kilometers (4).

One of the major factors in superhighway construction have been the efforts of Gordon Wu, the Hong Kong developer. In mid-1994, Mr Wu opened China's first superhighway, a $1.1 billion, six-lane toll road running seventy-seven miles from the border of Hong Kong to Guangzhou, the commercial hub of southern China. Work on a second highway, from the Portuguese colony of Macao to Guangzhou, has started, and Mr. Wu hopes to finish a 400 mile highway stretching from Guangzhou to Changsha, the capital of Hunan Province in central China, before the end of the century.

Bridges In the late 1980s, China had more than 140,000 highway bridges. Their length totaled almost 4,000 kilometers. Among the best known were the Huang He (Yellow River) Bridge in Nei Mongol Autonomous Region (Inner Mongolia), the Liu Jiang Bridge in Guangxi-Zhuang Autonomous Region, the Ou Jiang Bridge in Zhejiang Province, the Quanzhou Bridge in Fujian Province, and four large bridges along the Guangzhou-Shenzhen highway. Five major bridges—including China's longest highway bridge—were under construction during the mid-1980s, and a 10,282 meter long railroad bridge across the Huang He on the Shandong-Henan border was completed in 1985 (4).

Tunnels China plans to build a road and rail link across the Bo Hai strait, which divides the Bo Hai and Yellow seas between China and the Koreas. A Beijing-backed newspaper said the 83 mile crossing would have the world's longest undersea tunnel.

Construction of the $10 billion connection between Shangdong and Liaodong peninsulas in northeastern China is to begin in 1994 and could be completed by 2010, the Wen Wei Po Paper in Hong Kong said. Bridge sections as long as 4.4 miles will hopscotch across ten islands and connect to a 36 mile tunnel, outdistancing the world's longest underwater tube, the 33.5 mile Seikan rail tunnel between Japan's Honshu and Hokkaido islands.

The Chinese project would cut 620 miles from the land journey between the northeast and eastern points near Tianjin, a Bo Hai Sea port city, and Beijing.

This could save $910 million in transportation costs annually, serving 80 million tons of rail cargo and 7.5 million vehicles according to the Wall Street Journal for August 9, 1994.

Air Transport By the end of 1990, China had opened 378 air routes, linking China's ninety-four large, medium and small cities as well as remote regions and areas, totalling 472,000 kilometers in length. There are direct routes between Beijing and each province and municipality on the mainland (2).

China has signed civil aviation agreements with more than thirty countries and developed airline business with more than 100 countries and regions. It has also established forty-four international routes to thirty-seven cities in twenty-eight countries and regions.

China has air service connections with the Democratic People's Republic of Korea, Pakistan, France, Germany, the United States of America, the United Kingdom, Ethiopia, Switzerland, Romania, Yugoslavia, Albania, Japan, the Islamic Republic of Iran, Myanmar, the Philippines, Thailand, and Australia, etc. Although the volume of cargo moved by air is small and the air freight rate is high as compared with ocean and rail transport, air transport is particularly attractive for high-value goods, perishable and fresh goods, small packages and goods that are urgently needed.

Air China National Foreign Trade Transportation Corporation cargo service is a safe and speedy mode rendered by the China National Foreign Trade Transportation Corporation (SINOTRANS) dealing with cargo to Europe, North America, Japan, and Southeast Asia. SINOTRANS also deals with air courier service having branches throughout China and a worldwide network of agents handling express parcels to and from more than eighty countries and 350 cities.

China has now joint ventures with foreign countries to provide express parcels service from China to other parts of the world to meet the needs if international trade.

In 1987, China's civil aviation system was operated by the General Administration of Civil Aviation of China (CAAC). By 1987, China had more than 229,000 kilometers of domestic air routes and more than 94,000 kilometers of international air routes. The more than 9 million passengers and 102,000 tons of freight traffic represented a 40 percent growth over the previous year. The air fleet consisted of about 175 aircraft and smaller turboprop transports. CAAC had 274 air routes, including thirty-three international flights to twenty-eight cities in twenty-three countries, such as Tokyo, Osaka, Nagasaki, New york, San Francisco, Los Angeles, London, Paris, Frankfurt, East Berlin, Zurich, Moscow, Istanbul, Manila, Bangkok, Singapore, Sydney, and Hong Kong. Almost 200 domestic air routes connected such major cities as Beijing, Shanghai, Tianjin, Guangzhou, Hangzhou, Kunming, Chengdu, and Xi'an, as well as a number of smaller cities. The government had bilateral air service agreements with more than forty countries and working relations with approximately 386 foreign airline companies. CAAC also provided air service for agriculture, forestry, communications, and scientific research (4).

The staff of CAAC was estimated at approximately 50,000 in the 1980s. The administration operated three training colleges to educate future airline personnel. In a bid to improve CAAC's services, more ticket offices were opened in major cities for domestic and international flights.

In the mid-1980s, regional airlines began operations under the general aegis of CAAC. Wuhan Airlines, run by the Wuhan municipal authorities, started scheduled passenger flights to Hubei, Hunan, Guangdong, and Sichuan provinces in May 1986. Xizang also planned to set up its own airline to fly to Kathmandu and Hong Kong.

In the 1980s, the central government increased its investment in airport construction, and some local governments also granted special funds for such projects. Lhasa Airport in Xizang, Jiamusi Airport in Heilongjiang Province, and Kashi and Yining airports in Xinjiang-Uygur Autonomous Region were expanded, and new airports were under construction in Xi'an, Luoyang, and Shenzhen. An investment of ¥500 million was planned for expanding runways and building new terminals and other airport facilities. In 1986, China has more than ninety civilian airports, of which eight could accommodate Boeing 747s and thirty-two could accommodate Boeing 737s and Tridents (4).

Inland Waterways About 136,000 kilometers of navigable rivers, streams, lakes, and canals carried 44 percent of freight traffic in 1986, only slightly less than railroads. Rapid growth. Principal system Chang Jiang and its tributaries in central and east China; major freight artery. Secondary system Zhu Jiang (Pearl River) and its tributaries in south (4).

Inland navigation is China's oldest form of transportation. Despite the potential advantages of water transportation, it was often mismanaged or neglected in the past. Beginning in 1960, the network of navigable inland waterways decreased further because of the construction of dams and irrigation works and the increasing sedimentation. But by the early 1980s, as the railroads became increasingly congested, the authorities came to see water transportation as a much less expensive alternative to new road and railroad construction. The central government set out to overhaul the inefficient inland waterway system and called upon localities to play major roles in managing and financing most of the projects. By 1984, China's longest river, the Chang Jiang, with a total of 70,000 kilometers of waterways open to shipping on its main stream and 3,600 kilometers on its tributaries, became the nation's busiest shipping lane, carrying 72 percent of China's total waterborne traffic. An estimated 340,000 people and 170,000 boats were engaged in the water transportation business. More than 800 shipping enterprises and 60 shipping companies transported over 259 million tons of cargo on the Chang Jiang and its tributaries in 1984. Nationally, in 1985 the inland waterways carried some 434 million tons of cargo. In 1986 there were approximately 138,600 kilometers of inland waterways, 79 percent of which were navigable.

The Cihuai Canal in northern Anhui Province opened to navigation in 1984. This 134 kilometer canal linking the Ying He, a major tributary of the Huai He, with the Huai He's main course, had an annual capacity of 600,000 tons of cargo. The canal promoted the flow of goods between Anhui and neighboring provinces and helped to develop the Huai He Plain, one of China's major grain producing areas.

Figure 5 shows China's inland waterways (4).

Figure 5. Principal Improved Inland Waterways, 1987.

China has more than 50,000 rivers, most of them are ice-free year round. It offers favorable conditions for inland water transport (2).

The Yangtze River has a navigation channel of 6,300 kilometers long and its waterway depth is currently expanded from 2.1 meters to 2.9 meters at the river's Chongqing-Yichang section, and from 2.5 to 4.0 meters at Wuhan-Anqing section, and from 1.7 to 3.2 meters at Yichang-Wuhan section, and the section from Nanjing downwards the Yangtze River Mouth is 10.5 meters. The Chongqing-Yibin section of the river is now being dredged to allow ships of up to 1,000 deadweight tons to navigate.

The project to enlarge the Yawosha Channel at the Yangtze estuary, the only way for ships to enter the river or the sea, began in November 1989 and was completed and put into operation in March 1990. The new channel, 4,250 meters long, 250 meters wide and 7.3 meters deep, makes the navigable conditions much better than before.

Waterway transport has been China's important transport system. In 1990, China's total dead weight tons reached 37.5 million (dwt), doubling the 1978 figure, and the waterway freight transported totalled 830 million tons. The volume of goods transported through waterways accounted for one-fifth of the nation's total.

According to statistics, steamers and barges in the country carried a total of 222 million passenger/trip in 1990, an 8.5 percent drop from the previous year, and 582 million tons of cargo, down 1.9 percent. In other words, they shipped 17.546 billion persons per kilometer, down 7.7 percent, and 1,090.445 billion tons of cargo per kilometer, up 10.8 percent.

In 1990, main coastal ports handled about 480 million tons of cargo, a 5.5 percent increase over the previous year. Shanghai Port alone handled 145.6 million tons, one-fifth of the nation's total, setting a record high for six consecutive years. Inland harbors handled more than 700 million tons of cargo, of which, main harbors along the Yangtze and Heilongjiang rivers handled 150 million tons, up 2.5 percent over the previous year (2).

Ocean Transport and Ports China has a coastline of 18,000 kilometers along some twenty large and medium-sized developed coastal cities covering across ten provinces and autonomous regions. Over the last ten years, China invested a substantial amount in improving and expanding port facilities to meet the growing needs of foreign trade expansion. In 1989, China built and put into operation twenty-seven deepwater berths and sixty-eight medium-sized and small berths, adding a total annual handling capacity of 48 million tons of cargo. By the end of 1990, there was a total of 251 deepwater berths in China (2).

China has also heavily invested in expanding and modernizing its ocean going fleets. Now ocean transportation system has played a major role in moving foreign trade cargoes. In 1990, 90 percent of the country's foreign trade amounting to 160 million tons of import and export cargo was moved through the seaports.

The transport network for fuels, passengers, and import and export alike is constantly working at full capacity. With the opening of the coastal cities and Hainan Province, and the expanding development of the special economic zones, trade and economic exchanges with other countries are bound to increase. Pressure on the ports is rising steadily.

The following ports are open for direct handling of foreign trade: Shanghai, Dalian, Tianjin (Xingang), Qingdao, Huangpu, Qinghuangdao, Beihai, Fuzhou, Guangzhou, Longkou, Wenzhou, Yingkou, Yantai, Ningbo, Shantou, Basuo, Fangcheng, Zhangjiang, Haikou, Xiamen, Zhangjiagang, Nantong, Shijiu, Weihai.

The reader is also referred to the section on "Port Development" in Chapter 4 later in this volume.

The country wants to build three hub ports—in Dalian, in northern Lianoning Province; Ningbo, in eastern Zhejiang Province, and Shenzhen, in southern Guangdong Province—designed to handle huge new generation container vessels, thus tripling its container capacity to 9 million standard cargo containers by 2000.

Wharf Holdings is building a container port in Wuhan, on the upper reaches of the Yangtze, and a rail link from Wuhan to Hong Kong. Hutchison Whampoa will upgrade a container port in Shanghai. Both projects will cost over $1 billion.

China ranks ninth among merchant marine nations. About 15 percent of its domestic freight is carried by ship. In the past few years, ports at Nanjing, Wuhu, and Wuhan on the Yangzi River have been opened to foreign ships. Ports at Heishantou and Shiwei in Inner Mongolia along the Erhkuna River (tributary to the Heilongjiang [Amur] River) have been opened to Russian border trade. Ports at Heihe, Qike, Fuyan, Tongjiang, and Harbin on the Heilongjiang and the Songhua Rivers have been opened. Corn and soybeans can now be shipped via these rivers through Russia to the Pacific.   Opening these ports to foreign shipping and constructing docks, warehouses, container and grain handling facilities, and grain silos support China's bid to expand agricultural trade.

There is a rapidly growing merchant fleet; 600 vessels of various kinds in 1984, total cargo capacity over 16 million tons. Major ports include Shanghai, Dalian, Qinhuangdao, Qingdao, Tianjin, and Huangpu.

During the early 1960s, China's merchant marine had fewer than thirty ships. By the 1970s and 1980s, maritime shipping capabilities had greatly increased. In 1985, China established eleven shipping offices and jointly operated shipping companies in foreign countries. In 1986, china ranked ninth in world shipping with more than 600 ships and a total tonnage of 16 million, including modern roll-on and roll-off ships, container ships, large bulk carriers, refrigerator ships, oil tankers, and multipurpose ships. The fleet called at more than 400 ports in more than 100 countries (4).

The container ship fleet also was expanding rapidly. In 1984, China had only fifteen container ships. Seven more were added in 1985, and an additional twenty-two were on order. By the early 1980s, Chinese shipyards had begun to manufacture a large number of ships for their own maritime fleet. The China Shipping Inspection Bureau became a member of the Suez Canal Authority in 1984, empowering China to sign and issue seaworthiness certificates for ships on the Suez Canal and confirming the good reputation and maturity of its shipbuilding industry. In 1986, China had 523 shipyards of various sizes, 160 specialized factories, 540,000 employees, and more than 80 scientific research institutes. The main shipbuilding and repairing bases of Shanghai, Dalian, Tianjin, Guangzhou, and Wuhan had fourteen berths for 10,000-ton-class ships and thirteen docks.

The inadequacy of port and harbor facilities has been a longstanding problem for China, but has become a more serious obstacle because of increased foreign trade. Beginning in the 1970s, the authorities gave priority to port construction. From 1972 to 1982, port traffic increased sixfold, largely because of the foreign trade boom. The imbalance between supply and demand continued to grow. Poor management and limited port facilities created such backups that by 1985 an average of 400 to 500 ships were waiting to enter major Chinese ports on any given day. The July 1985 delay of more than 500 ships, for instance, caused huge losses. All of China's major ports are undergoing some construction. To speed economic development, the Seventh Five-Year Plan called for the construction by 1990 of 200 new berths—120 deepwater berths for ships above 10,000 tons and 80 medium-sized berths for ships below 10,000 tons—bringing the total number of berths to 1,200. Major port facilities were developed all along China's coast.

The characteristics of a number of ports are given under specific locations in Chapter 2. Data on some specific port developments not covered there are covered here by way of introduction, however (7).

They are as follows:

1.   Behai
2.   Fencheng
3.   Fuzhou

4. Huangpu
5. Lianyungang
6. Longkou
7. Nanjing
8. Nantong
9. Qinhuangdao
10. Shijiu
11. Wenzhou
12. Yingkou
13. Zhangjiagang
14. Zhanjiang
15. Zhenjiang

Table 66.
1. Behai Port—Salient Statistics (2)

Area (sq. km.)	275.
Population	194,650 (urban)
Economic situation	Industrial production in 1989

Light industry:	585.44 (mil. yuan)
Heavy industry:	121.38 (mil. yuan)
Value of export:	$US 87.94 mil.
Harbor's handling volume:	121 (10 thousand tons)
Investment in capital assets:	106.42 (mil. yuan)
Total value of industrial production:	706.82 (mil. yuan)

Utilization of foreign capital	Utilization of foreign capital in 1988

Contract number:	24
Foreign contractual value:	$US 22.87 mil.
Effected foreign investment:	$US 1.94 mil.
Number of foreign direct investment:	23
Total foreign direct investment:	$US 1.72 mil.

Utilization of foreign capital in 1989

Contract number:	7
Foreign contractual value:	$US 6.3 mil.
Effected foreign investment:	$US 1.8 mil.
Number of foreign direct investment:	7
Total foreign direct investment:	$US 1.8 mil.

Up to the end of 1989

Joint ventures:	28
Contractual joint ventures:	26
Foreign wholly-owned enterprises:	4
Total:	58

Infrastructure

Port:	2 above 10,000 ton berths, 6 above 5,000 ton berths
Power:	Installed capacity 170 MW
Water:	Daily supply capacity: 120 tons
Telecommunication:	Direct domestic and international call

Other foreign investment projects:

	I	*II*	*III*
class one	127.5	112.5	97.5
class two	112.5	97.5	81

Land charge criterion for undeveloped land
Overseas Chinese, Taiwan, Hong Kong, Macau investment project: 27.9
Other foreign investment project: 27

Export and technologically-advanced enterprises shall be exempted from land use fee. Other joint ventures pay land fee at 1 yuan/year sq. m.

Land service charge
(unit: yuan/month)

Manager: 240 (average)
Staff member: 230 (average)
129% of the real wages of state-owned enterprises of the same trade in the locality.

Other fees

Water:	0.26 yuan/ton
Electricity:	0.30 yuan/kwh

Priorities

Petrochemistry, foodstuffs, building materials, water product processing, sea industry

---

Official department in charge:

Beihai Municipal Committee of Foreign Economic Relations and Trade
East Bei Bu Wan Road
Beihai
Tel: (07891) 23530, 23381

2. Fengcheng Port

The Port of Fengcheng on the north coast of Beibu Bay, is situated at 21°37'N, 108°21'E. It is one of the newly-developed deepwater ports in the southwest of China in the period of the Sixth Five-Year Plan. Two deepwater berths for vessels of over 10,000 dwt were completed and put into use in October 1983. And then, in 1985, another deepwater berth for ships of 15,000 dwt was completed.

Four berths for ships of 15,000-25,000 dwt and above were completed in 1986. Now there are eight berths, seven of which are deepwater berths with an annual throughput capacity of 4.7 million tons.

Table 67

3. Fuzhou Port (located in the southeastern part of China) Statistics (2)

Area (sq. km.)	11,968	*4.4
Population	1,269,000 (urban)	
Economic situation	Industrial production in 1989	
	Light industry:	4,976.78 (mil. yuan)
	Heavy industry:	2,778.33 (mil. yuan)
	Value of export:	$US 141.24 mil.
	Investment in capital assets:	1,601.75 (mil. yuan)
	Total value of industrial production:	7,755.11 (mil. yuan)
Utilization of foreign capital	Utilization of foreign capital in 1988	
	Contract number:	168
	Foreign contractual value:	$US 117.81 mil.
	Effected foreign investment:	$US 36.63 mil.
	Number of foreign direct investment:	168
	Total foreign direct investment:	$US 23.55 mil.
	Utilization of foreign capital in 1989	
	Contract number:	214
	Foreign contractual value:	$US 151.56 mil.
	Effected foreign investment:	$US 65.36 mil.
	Number of foreign direct investment:	214
	Total foreign direct investment:	$US 50.35 mil.
	Up to the end of 1988	
	Joint ventures:	131
	Contractual joint ventures:	17
	Foreign wholly-owned enterprises:	9

| | Total: | 157 |
| | Japanese enterprises: | 11 |

Infrastructure	Port:	3 ports, including 2 above 10,000 ton berths in Mawei Port.
	Power:	Supplied by Northern Electric Power Network of Fujian.
	Water:	Daily supply capacity: 300,000 tons.
	Telecommunication:	Equipped with advanced facilities, direct domestic and international call.

| Labor service charge (Unit: yuan/month | 250-300 (average) |

| Other fees | Water: | yuan/ton |
| | Electricity: | yuan/kwh |

| Priorities | Foodstuffs, machinery, electronics, chemistry, textile, light industry, metallurgy, pharmaceutics |

Local preference
The income tax rate on joint venture in economic and technical development zone is 15%. A newly established joint venture can be exempted from income tax in the first two profit-making years, and allowed a 50% reduction of income tax in the third, fourth and fifth years. After the tax exemption period expires, technologically-advanced enterprises subject to a reduced rate of 50% for another three years, and export enterprises shall pay income tax at a reduced rate of 10% provided that their value of export products in that year amounts to 70% or more of the value of their products for that year. Joint ventures are all exempted from local income tax.

Official department in charge:

Fuzhou Municipal Committee of Foreign Economic Relations and Trade
34, W Shan Road
Fuzhou
Tel: (0591) 56176

4. Huangpu Port

The Port of Huangpu is situated in the mouth of the Pearl River at 23°06'N, 113°26'E, 31.5 kilometers southeast of the city of Guangzhou. The total length of frontage of the wharves is 2,200 meters. There are altogether twenty-eight berths, twenty-two of which are deepwater berths for 10,000 ton ships. Cargo work is carried out alongside or by lighters.

The port is equipped with cranes, belt conveyers, grain suckers and various kinds of mobile machines. The maximum lifting weight is 250 tons. Tugs, lighters, and launches are available. Wharves are rail served. General temporary repairs can be affected to foreign ships.

5. Lianyungang Port

The Port of Lianyungang is situated at the south end of Haizhou Bay of the Yellow Sea and the east end of Longhai Railway Line, at 34°45'N, 119°27'E. The Port was opened in 1933. The cargo throughput in 1985 was 9.29 million tons.

In the period of the Sixth Five-Year Plan, the newly built pier No. 3 with four general cargo berths for ships of 10,000 dwt and above was built. A new area, Miaoling, was developed and would be completed in the period of the Seventh Five-Year Plan.

Some general characteristics of Lianyungang Port are summarized in the following table.

Table 68
Lianyungang Port—Salient Statistics (2)

Area (sq. km.)	6,265	*3
Population	508,500 (urban)	
Economic situation	Industrial production in 1989	
	Light industry:	1,957.44 (mil. yuan)
	Heavy industry:	1,049.56 (mil. yuan)
	Harbor's handling volume:	1,126 (10 thousand tons)
	Investment in capital assets:	661.82 (mil. yuan)
	Total value of industrial production:	3,007 (mil. yuan)
Utilization of foreign capital	Utilization of foreign capital in 1988	
	Contract number:	17
	Foreign contractual value:	$US 27.68 mil.
	Effected foreign investment:	$US 20.24 mil.
	Number of foreign direct investment:	10
	Total foreign direct investment:	$US 2.46 mil.
	Utilization of foreign capital in 1989	
	Contract number:	9
	Foreign contractual value:	$US 11.33 mil.
	Effected foreign investment:	$US 10.47 mil.
	Number of foreign direct investment:	6
	Total foreign direct investment:	$US 7.36 mil.

Up to the end of 1988

Joint ventures:	11
Total:	11
Japanese enterprises:	3

Infrastructure

Port:	11 berths, including 7 above 10,000 ton berths
Power:	Two electric power plants with capacity of 480 MW
Water:	Rich water source
Telecommunication:	Direct domestic and international call.

Labor service charge
(Unit: yuan/month)

Manager:	300 (average)
Staff member:	240-250 (average)

125% of the real wages of state-owned enterprises of the same trade in the locality.

Other fees

Water:	0.36 yuan/ton
Electricity:	0.20 yuan/kwh

Priorities

Textile, machinery, electronic, chemistry, light industry, foodstuffs, building materials, agriculture.

Local preference

The income tax rate on joint venture is 15%. A newly established joint venture can be exempted from income tax in the first two profit-making years, and allowed a 50% reduction of income tax in the third, fourth and fifth years.

Export and technologically-advanced enterprises shall be all exempted from local income tax.

Official department in charge:

Lianyungang Municipal Committee of Foreign Economic Relations and Trade
Xin Pu Hai East Road
Lianyungang
Tel: (01518) 32854

6. Longkou Port

The port, located in Shangdong Province, has one 10,000 ton class coal berth, one 10,000 ton class sundry berth, one 10,000 ton class passenger/sundry berth, and one 5,000 ton class passenger, to handle 2.2 million tons of cargo including 1.5 million tons of coal annually.

7. Nanjing Port

The total annual cargo handling capacity of Nanjing Port comes to 42 million tons, after No. 35 wharf handling two million tons put into operation in 1989. In 1990, two 10,000 ton class deepwater berths, three 1,000 ton class berths and six 15,000 ton class berths and seven medium sized berths were completed at Nanjing Port, increasing the wharf's annual handling capacity to 6.44 million tons, making it the largest wharf on the Yangtze River.

Featured with deepwater and wide water surface, the Yangtze River mouth can allow 10,000 dwt ocean going ships to sail straight to Nanjing, a 5,000 dwt ship to Wuhan, and a 1,000 dwt ship passing through the Three Gorges to Chongqing. Along the Yangtze River ports, four international routes have been opened to link the Yangtze River.

8. Nantong Port

The Port of Nantong is situated at 32°01'N, 120°49'E. It is a river port at the down stream (north bank) of the Yangtze River. It is roughly in the middle part of China's coastal area and facing the city of Shanghai. The port was opened up in 1904. At present, it is composed of three stevedore districts: Tiansheng, Nantong and Langshan.

In the period of the Sixth Five-Year Plan, one newly-built general cargo berth for vessels of 25,000 dwt and one transhipment platform for ships of 35,000 dwt were built.

There are not fourteen berths, three of which are deepwater berths for ships of 10,000 dwt and above. The cargo throughput in 1985 was 10.29 million tons. It is now one of the important sea-river-transhipment terminals.

Some of the characteristics of Nantong port are summarized in the following table.

Table 69
Nantong Port—Salient Statistics (2)

Area (sq. km.)	8,000	
Population	449,000 (urban)	
Economic situation	Industrial production in 1989	
	Light industry:	9,479.02 (mil. yuan)
	Heavy industry:	4,714.52 (mil. yuan)
	Value of export:	$US 76.21 mil.
	Harbor's handling volume:	2,520 (10 thousand tons)
	Investment in capital assets:	767.16 (mil. yuan)
	Total value of industrial production:	14,193.54 (mil. yuan)
Utilization of foreign capital	Utilization of foreign capital in 1988	
	Contract number:	60

Foreign contractual value:	$US 69.35 mil.
Effected foreign investment:	$US 27.47 mil.
Number of foreign direct investment:	22
Total foreign direct investment:	$US 10.53 mil.

Utilization of foreign capital in 1989

Contract number:	40
Foreign contractual value	$US 30.60 mil.
Effected foreign investment:	$US 34.31 mil.
Number of foreign direct investment:	21
Total foreign direct investment:	$US 6.83 mil.

Up to the end of 1989

Joint ventures:	72
Contractual joint ventures:	9
Foreign wholly-owned enterprises:	
Total:	81
Japanese enterprises:	11

Infrastructure	Port:	Twelve berths, including four 10,000 ton berths
	Power:	Two power plants have a total capacity of 1,024 MW.
	Water:	Daily supply capability of 300,000 ton
	Telecommunication:	National and international direct dialing.

Enterprises with foreign investment shall be exempted from the land use fee within six years. The product export & technologically advanced enterprises shall be exempted from it within ten years.

Labor service charge (Unit: yuan/month)	Manager:	300 (average)
	Staff member:	220 (average)

125% of the real wages of state-owned enterprise of the same trade in the locality.

Other fees	Water:	0.23 yuan/ton
	Electricity:	0.38 yuan/kwh

Priorities — Machinery, electronics, textile, light industry, chemistry, instrument, building materials, pharmaceutical products.

Local preference — The income tax rate on joint venture in economic & technical development zone is 15%. A newly established joint venture can be exempted from income tax in the first two profit-making years, and allowed a 50% reduction of income tax in the third, fourth and fifth years.
Joint ventures in the development zone are all exempted from local surtax.

Official department in charge:

Nantong Municipal Committee of Foreign Economic Relations & Trade
51, Gongnong Road
Nantong
Tel: (0513) 512291, 517864

9. Qinhuangdao Port

The Port of Qinhuangdao is situated at 39°54'N, 119°, 37'E, was built in the Gulf of the Bohai Sea in 1903. It is the third largest port in China. It offers a larger capacity for taking in and discharging cargo than the railway.

Qinhuangdao is an ice-free port with deep and broad water. It handles more coal exports than any other port in China (80 percent of China's coal for export). Each year it deals with over 30 million tons of outgoing coal, 80.3 percent of which is for export, mainly to Japan.

Now the Port has been changed into a comprehensive one with 10,000 dockers and twenty-nine berths and twenty-two are deepwater berths for sending out energy resources. Its oil wharf alone is a mile long.

Qinhuangdao is a major glass manufacturing center. Also, the first oil pipeline in China was laid from Daqing to Qinhuangdao in 1974.

Some of the characteristics of the port are summarized in the following table.

Table 70
Qinhuangdao Port—Salient Statistics (2)

Area (sq. km.)	7,752 *1.9
Population	489,400 (urban)
Economic situation	Industrial production in 1989

Light industry:	939.08 (mil. yuan)
Heavy industry:	1,174.85 (mil. yuan)
Harbor's handling volume:	6,563 (10 thousand tons)
Investment in capital assets:	946.32 (mil. yuan)
Total value of industrial production:	2,113.93 (mil. yuan)

Utilization of foreign capital	Utilization of foreign capital in 1988

Contract number:	18
Foreign contractual number:	$US 9.42 mil.
Effected foreign investment:	$US 5.25 mil.
Number of foreign direct investment:	18
Total foreign direct investment:	$US 5.25 mil.

Utilization of foreign capital in 1989

Contract number:	11
Foreign contractual value:	$US 14.52 mil.
Effected foreign investment:	$US 6.91 mil.
Number of foreign direct investment:	11
Total foreign direct investment:	$US 6.91 mil.

Up to the end of 1989

Joint ventures:	31
Contractual joint ventures:	2
Total:	33
Japanese enterprises:	3

Infrastructure	Power:	Supplied by Beijing, Tianjing and Tangshan Electric Power Network
	Water:	Rich water sources
	Telecommunication:	Equipped with advanced facilities, direct domestic and international call.

Labor service charge (Unit: yuan/month)

200 (average)

120% of the real wages of state-owned enterprises of the same trade in the locality.

Other fees	Water:	0.026 yuan/ton
	Electricity:	0.15 yuan/kwh

Priorities

Textile and garment, machinery, glass products, light industry, foodstuffs, instrument and meters, building materials, arts and handicrafts.

Local preference

The income tax rate on joint venture is 15%. A newly established joint venture can be exempted from income tax in the first two profit-making years, and allowed a 50% reduction of income tax in the third, fourth and fifth years.

Official department in charge:

Qinhuangdao Municipal Committee of Foreign Economic Relations and Trade
30, Wen Hua Road
Qinhuangdao
Tel: (0335) 35625

10. Shijiu Port

The port of Shijiu is situated on the coast of the Yellow Sea at the intersection between the Shandong Peninsula and the Subei shoals, being 35°33'N, 119°25'E. It is a newly developed open sea deepwater port in the period of the Sixth Five-Year Plan. In the first phase, two deepwater berths were newly built (one for bulk coal carriers of 100,000 dwt, and the other for carriers of 25,000 dwt (in fact, two carriers of 100,000 dwt could also be berthed), with a total berth length of 452 meters and a water depth of 17 meters. The designed annual exporting capacity is 15 million tons of coal.

Table 71
11. Wenzhou Port (located at the south part
of Zhejiang Province)—Salient Statistics (2)

Area (sq. km.)	11,784
Population	557,800 (urban)
Economic situation	Industrial production in 1989
	Light industry: 3,095.38 (mil. yuan)
	Heavy industry: 2,273.53 (mil. yuan)
	Value of export: $US 2.67 mil.
	Harbor's handling volume: 430 (10 thousand tons)
	Investment in capital assets: 428.41 (mil. yuan)
	Total value of industrial production: 5,368.91 (mil. yuan)
Utilization of foreign capital	Utilization of foreign capital in 1988
	Contract number: 14
	Foreign contractual value: $US 4.61 mil.
	Effected foreign investment: $US 1.04 mil.
	Number of foreign direct investment: 14
	Total foreign direct investment: $US 1.04 mil.
	Utilization of foreign capital in 1989
	Contract number: 28
	Foreign contractual value: $US 8.96 mil.
	Effected foreign investment: $US 5.74 mil.
	Number of foreign direct investment: 28
	Total foreign direct investment: $US 5.74 mil.
	Up to the end of 1988
	Joint ventures: 8
	Contractual joint ventures: 1

	Foreign wholly-owned enterprises:	2
	Total:	11
	Japanese enterprises:	1 (up to the end of 1988)

Infrastructure	Port:	Thirty berths, yearly with harbor's handling capability of 2.4 million tons
	Power:	Supplied by East China power network
	Telecommunication:	Direct domestic and international call, rate of 50% within five years.

Labor service charge (Unit: yuan/month)	200 (average) 120% of the real wages of state-owned enterprises of the same trade in the locality.

Other fees	Water:	0.18 yuan/ton
	Electricity:	0.17 yuan/kwh

Priorities	Machinery, chemistry, metallurgy, shoes, garment and textile industry, metallurgy, building materials.

Official department in charge:

**Wenzhou Municipal Committee of Foreign Economic Relations and Trade
45, Fu Xue Xiang
Wenzhou
Tel: (0577) 6262**

12. Yingkou Port

The port is situated at 40°18'N, 122°06'E and has two 10,000 ton class sundry berths with an annual cargo handling capacity of about six million tons of goods. The port is in Liaoning Province. The coal berth for self-unloading ships of 30,000 dwt and four deepwater berths were built in 1986.

13. Zhangjiagang Port

The Port of Zhangjiagang is situated at 31°58'N, 120°24'E. It is a new port located on the south bank of the downstream of the Yangtze River. The construction of the Port began in 1968. In 1970, two floating pontoon wharves (one for ships of 10,000 dwt and above, and another for ships of 5,000 dwt) were completed.

In the period of the Sixth Five-Year Plan, two general berths for ships of 10,000 dwt and above were completed, thus providing an additional throughput capacity of 0.7 million tons. Now, the Port has a total throughput capacity of 2.8 million tons and has become one of the important terminals for sea-river-canal transhipment purpose.

Table 72. 14. Zhangjiang Port—Salient Statistics
(located in the west of Guangdong Province and a port city in the farthest south of China) (2)

Area (sq. km.)	12,472. *2	
Population	1,012,300 (urban)	
Economic situation	Industrial production in 1989	
	Light industry:	2,960.2 (mil. yuan)
	Heavy industry:	842.12 (mil. yuan)
	Value of export:	$US 129 mil.
	Harbor's handling volume:	1,555 (10 thousand tons)
	Investment in capital assets:	697.74 (mil. yuan)
	Total value of industrial production:	3,802.32 (mil. yuan)
Utilization of foreign capital	Utilization of foreign capital in 1988	
	Contract number:	117
	Foreign contractual value:	$US 80.56 mil.
	Effected foreign investment:	$US 40.35 mil.
	Number of foreign direct investment:	80
	Total foreign direct investment:	$US 21.93 mil.
	Utilization of foreign capital in 1989	
	Contract number:	80
	Foreign contractual value:	$US 47.08 mil.
	Effected foreign investment:	$US 33.94 mil.
	Number of foreign direct investment:	49
	Total foreign direct investment:	$US 25.64 mil.
	Up to the end of 1989	
	Joint ventures:	65
	Contractual joint ventures:	305
	Foreign wholly-owned enterprises:	5
	Total:	375
	Japanese enterprises:	6
Infrastructure	Port:	Twenty-two berths for production, including seventeen 10,000 ton berths, one 50,000 ton oil berth.
	Power:	Supplied by Guangdong Electric Power
Network		
	Water:	Daily supply capability of 200,000 ton.

	Telecommunication:	Equipped with advanced facilities, direct domestic and international call.

Labor service charge (Unit: yuan/month)	350 (average)	

Other fees	Water:	0.20 yuan/ton
	Electricity:	0.295 yuan/kwh

Priorities	Energy, foodstuffs, machinery, electronics, textile, electric home appliances, fishing and agriculture.

Local preference	The income tax rate on joint venture in economic and technical development zone is 15%. A newly established joint venture can be exempted from income tax in the first two profit-making years, and allowed a 50% reduction of income tax in the third, fourth and fifth years. Joint ventures in the development zone are all exempted from local surtax.

Official department in charge:

**Zhanjiang Municipal Committee of Foreign Economic Relations and Trade
31, South Road, Chikan District,
Zhanjiang
Tel: (0759) 338893**

15. Zhenjiang Port

The Port of Zhenjiang is situated at 32°10'N, 119°39'E, where the Yangtze River and the Grand Canal meet.

In the period of the Sixth Five-Year Plan, four deepwater berths for seagoing ships of 25,000 dwt and eight medium and small sized berths were completed in Dagang Area. The total cargo throughput was 5.85 million tons in 1985.

The Port of Zhenjiang is composed of an old port area and a new port area and became one of the most important sea-river-canal transhipment terminals.

Multimodal Transport and Containerization To promote foreign trade and economic interchanges between China and foreign countries, international multimodal transport and cargo consolidation, especially Hanger Container, have been introduced in China in recent years. Multimodal transport has been applied to cargo movement to Japan, the United States, Canada, West Europe, North Europe, Mediterranean, East Africa, Middle East, Far East, Australia and others.

Containerization is a very important technical innovation in transport. Having the merits of high efficiency in cargo handling, quick turn around, reducing shortages and damage, economical packing, low labor intensity and simplified formalities etc., it is now being extensively applied to sea, land and air transport throughout the world. China first introduced containerization to sea-borne export goods in 1973. In recent years, China has, together with the departments of communication, put in great efforts in developing movement of containers by sea. A number of container yards and container freight stations have been set up by China. By now, major ports are connected with fourteen regular container routes, and the number of containers moved inward and outward have been increasing by folds yearly.

In China has also been rapidly developing movement of containers by other modes of transport. In 1980, it started to move containers over the Trans-Siberian Railway Landbridge (TSR) to the Islamic Republic of Iran and to seventeen European countries. Over the past eleven years, the number of containers has been increasing fairly and quickly and the result proved satisfactory. The variety of commodities has also increased. There are now more than twenty loading stations in fourteen provinces and cities handling TSR containers.

In the past few years, Hong Kong and Fujian-Hong Kong direct highway container services were put into operation. Services are provided to issue bills of lading, arrange customs clearance and negotiate payment locally for customers. As formalities are simplified, services upgraded and freight charges lowered, these services are appreciated by customers at home and abroad.

Multimodal transport is a combination of at least two of the modes of transport by sea, land and air. Because of its simplified formalities, a single bill of lading being used for the whole passage, safety, promptness, and "door-to-door" service, its advantages are becoming more and more apparent in international trade. In 1976, China started using this mode of transport, mainly a land-sea combination via Hong Kong. It was only after 1980 that China began to move containers by multimodal transport. This movement is being expanded.

With further diversification of international trade, conventional single-mode transport can no longer meet the needs of trade development. The extensive adoption of advanced means of transport and techniques in organization, comprehensive utilization of various modes of transport, selection of best routing and planning and rendering better services for foreign trade have become new challenges for China.

Containers which have been employed on twelve international shipping routes include:
- Huangpu-Japan route
- Shanghai-Japan route
- Singang-Japan route
- Dalian-Japan route
- Shanghai-Australia route
- Xiangang-Australia route
- China-Persian Gulf route
- China-the United States route
- China-Europe route
- China-Mediterranean route
- China-Hong Kong route

- China-Southeast Asian route, including Singapore, Thailand, Malaysia, Indonesia, etc.

ELECTRIC POWER

From 1949 to the mid-1980's, China pursued an inconsistent policy on the development of electric power. Significant under-investment on the readjustment period, starting in 1979, caused serious power shortages into the mid-1980s. Although China's hydroelectric power potential was the world's largest and the power capacity was the sixth largest, 1985 estimates showed that demand exceeded the supply by about 40 billion kilowatt hours per year. Because of power shortages, factories and mines routinely operated at 70 to 80 percent capacity, and in some cases factories only ran for three or four days a week. Whole sections of cities were frequently blacked out for hours.

China's is the world's fourth largest power producer. But the average Chinese consumes less than 650 kilowatt hours, barely enough to burn a 75-watt light bulb year round. And about 120 million rural Chinese—one-tenth of this enormous country's population—live without electricity in their houses or villages.

China's leaders began to acknowledge the seriousness of the power shortage in 1979. The government took no positive steps until the mid-1980s, when it announced import of 10,000 megawatts of thermal power plant capacity to serve the east's large population centers. It also launched a nationwide campaign to create an additional 5,000 megawatts of electric power capacity. Under the Seventh Five-Year Plan, China planned to add 30,000 to 35,000 megawatts of capacity, a 55 to 80 percent increase over previous Five-Year plans. In 1994, it was stated that the Chinese want to add 17,000 megawatts per year over the next ten years. Their installed capacity is 175,000 megawatts, so they want to increase 10 percent per year for the next ten years.

A major factor in electric power development in Southern China is the work of Hong Kong developer, Gordon Wu and his company, Hopewell Holdings which in 1994 spun off Consolidated Electric Power Asia to manage power projects.

China is scheduled to invest 11 billion yuan ($1.9 billion) in rural electrification projects in 1991-95. About 60 percent of the expansion will come from new hydropower stations built in south China. The money will be raised by local governments and residents. Authorities look favorably upon the development of hydropower because it has ecological advantages. For example, farmers will burn less timber to meet their energy requirements.

With economic growth of nearly 12 percent predicted this year, China is failing to meet its goals for adding power generation. Blackouts are plaguing the largest industrial centers like Shanghai, and shortages are cutting deep into productivity nationwide.

But instead of accelerating a program to build power plants with foreign financing, the Chinese leadership has refused to approve a single joint venture power plant since late in 1992, when Gordon Y.S. Wu signed an agreement for this last power project in Guangdong Province in the south.

Nearly fifty projects involving foreign partners are now on hold in China, power industry officials say. Large American power companies like Mission Energy, Wing

International, Entergy and General Electric have been negotiating joint venture deals for months to build power stations, but the local authorities have not been able to get approval from the central government in Beijing.

An outstanding example of China power development is Huaneng Power, a company listed on the New York Stock Exchange in late 1994. Huaneng Power is one of the world's largest independent power producers. It owns and operates five power plants in China's five most populous provinces. Huaneng Power's 1993 revenue totaled more than $500 million, a 24% increase from the previous year.

The company plans to use proceeds from the offering for expansion, particularly to buy foreign equipment. Almost half of all thermal power plant generating equipment imported into China from Western countries from 1985 to 1993 was installed in plants owned by Huaneng Power or its controlling shareholder, Huaneng International Power Development Corporation.

The four coal-fired power plants are powered by units supplied by either a General Electric Company-led consortium, or a consortium of companies in Japan's Mitsubishi group.

Coal-fired Power Generation The Chinese leadership decided to build thermal power plants to meet the country's electricity needs, because such plants were relatively inexpensive and required construction lead times of only three to six years. In 1985 approximately 68 percent of generating capacity was derived from thermal power, mostly coal-fired, and observers estimated that by 1990 its share would increase to 72 percent. The use of oil-fired plants peaked in the late 1970s, and by the mid-1980s most facilities had been converted back to coal. Only a few thermal plants were fueled by natural gas. Hydroelectric power accounted for only about 30 percent of generating capacity. Observers expected that during the Seventh Five-Year Plan, China would continue to emphasize the development of thermal power over hydroelectric power because of the need to expand the power supply quickly to keep pace with industrial growth. However, in the long term, hydroelectric power gradually was to be given priority over thermal power.

In 1986 China's total generating capacity was 76,000 megawatts: 52,000 from thermal plants and 24,000 from hydroelectric power sources. China planned to construct large generators having capacities of 100 to 300 megawatts to increase thermal power capacity. The new, larger generators would be much more efficient than generators having capacities of only fifty megawatts or less. With the larger generators, China would only have to increase coal consumption by 40 percent to achieve a 54 percent increase in generating capacity by 1990. Foreign observers believed that as China increased its grid network, it could construct power plants close to coal mines, than run power lines to the cities. This method would eliminate the costly and difficult transportation of coal to smaller urban plants, which had already created a significant pollution problem (4).

Oil-fired Power Generation China has been self-sufficient in all energy and coal and petroleum have been exported since early 1970s. Coal reserves are among world's largest; mining technology was inadequately developed but improving in late 1980s. Petroleum reserves are very large but of varying quality and in disparate locations. Suspected oil deposits in northwest and offshore tracts are believed to be among world's largest; exploration and extraction have been limited to scarcity of equipment and trained personnel; twenty-seven contracts for joint offshore exploration and production by Japanese and Western oil companies were signed by 1982, but by late 1980s only a handful of wells were producing. Substantial natural gas reserves exist in the north, northwest, and offshore. Hydroelectric potential is the greatest in world, it is the sixth largest in capacity. Very large hydroelectric projects are under construction, others are in planning stage. Thermal power, mostly coal-fired, produced approximately 68 percent of generating capacity in 1985; expected to increase to 72 percent in 1990. Emphasis on thermal power in late 1980s seen by policy makers as quick, short-term solution to energy needs; hydroelectric power is seen as long-term solution. Petroleum production growth is to continue in order to meet needs of nationwide mechanization and provide important foreign exchange but domestic use is to be restricted as much as possible (4).

Gas-fired Power Generation China has a temporary energy deficit, and despite its copious reserves of good quality coal, recently imported Australian coal into Shanghai; but in the long run China could not require imports of energy materials. It could, however, be an exporter of LNG (Liquefied Natural Gas).

Gaz de France has set up a joint company with French equipment manufacturers directed at the internal Chinese market. Chinagaz is made the Gaz de France representative in China, Shooter. Current members specialize in providing equipment for distribution, but it is eventually hoped to include gas transport companies as well. Half of China's gas consumption is currently based on town gas, 30% on butane-propane and 20% on natural gas.

Nissho Iwai of Japan, Atlantic Richfield of the U.S. and the National Offshore Oil Corporation of China jointly announced a plan to produce LNG from a field of Hainan Island in southern China. If all goes as planned, production should begin in late 1996.

The three partners plan to complete feasibility studies on the project by early next year when it is hoped the approval for development work can be granted. This would be the first LNG project emanating from China with production being sent to Japan or South Korea. Production is expected to be approximately 1.5 MMT/Y.

In light of the current upheaval in world energy markets, a gas project from the Far East is becoming relatively more attractive when one compares it to Middle Eastern oil. Projections of LNG demand for the remainder of the century in Japan, South Korea and Taiwan are rising and the possibility of an LNG project from China is becoming more reasonable.

The Yacheng 13-1 gas field, sixty-five miles south of Hainan Island, was discovered by Atlantic Richfield Co., (Arco) in 1983. In 1985, Arco signed an agreement with China National Offshore Oil Corporation (CNOOC) to develop the Yacheng gas field. This project has been delayed due to the fall in the price of gas, which forced Arco and CNOOC to renegotiate their partnership terms. They then started negotiations through Nissho Iwai Corporation (NIC) for export of the gas to Japan as LNG. The discussions were suspended due to the Tiananmen Square incident in summer 1989.

In January 1990, NIC and CNOOC announced they would again study the project.

Recoverable reserves were reported at some 65 bcm. An LNG export project would involve a single-train liquefier with a capacity of 1.5 MM tons/yr. and a single 125,00 m3 LNG carrier. The companies hoped to start commercial production in 1995, with plans to sell LNG to Japan. The cost of the project was estimated at $1 billion. Equity shares in the joint venture company would be held by CNOOC (50%), Arco (30%) and NIC (20%).

For more information, one might contact:

China National Offshore Oil Corporation
29-31 Dong Changan Jie
Beijing 3113
China
Tel: 55-2031, 55-5225

<u>Hydroelectric Power</u> From 1949 to 1986, China built at least twenty-five large, 130 medium, and about 90,000 small-sized hydroelectric power stations. According to the Ministry of Water Resources and Electric Power, China's 1983 annual power output was 351.4 billion kilowatt hours, of which 86 billion kilowatt hours were generated by hydroelectric power. While construction of thermal plants was designed as a quick remedy for alleviating China's power shortages, the development of hydroelectric power resources was considered a long-term solution. The primary areas for the construction of hydroelectric power plants were the upper Huang He (Yellow River), the upper and middle stream tributaries and trunk of the Chang Jiang, and the Hongshui He in the upper region of the Zhu Jiang Basin. The construction of new hydroelectric power plants was expected to be a costly and lengthy process, undertaken with assistance from the United States, Canada, Kuwait, Austria, Norway, France, and Japan (4).

The reader is also referred to the section "Hydroelectric Power" in Chapter 4 on Industrial Markets for further information on this topic.

A major project in the planning stage is the Three Gorges Dam on the Yangtze River. China hasn't attempted a project of this scale since the Great Wall and the Grand Canal. Named for the scenic stretch of the Yangtze River it will irrevocably alter, the dam has taken on nearly sacred importance for Chinese leaders, a monument to the greatness of modern China.

It would be the largest hydroelectric dam in the world, a 1.2 mile stretch of concrete creating a narrow inland sea, 370 miles long, as a reservoir. The daunting feat of engineering would displace 1.2 million people and cost more than virtually any other single construction project in history—all of which seems to add to its allure.

With early construction under way, the price tag continues to soar. One critic contends the real cost could total $17 billion, a sum so great the extravagance could damage, instead of showcase, China's recent economic miracle. The dam is scheduled to be completed in 2009.

Other obstacles loom. The Three Gorges, China's equivalent of the Grand Canyon, is one of the cradles of Chinese civilization.

And technical problems abound. River-borne silt, the natural enemy of all dams, may prove more troublesome and costly then planners initially acknowledged. Resettling a huge and poor population has proved more expensive and politically sensitive than expected. And some analysts—including onetime supporters—believe inflated cost have already made the project a money-losing proposition.

Supporters say the dam would help solve two of China's more vexing problems. In a nation where many factories can't operate long shifts because of energy shortages, the turbines would generate 18,000 megawatts of electricity—as much as 10 average-size nuclear power plants. And the dam would protect the densely populated downstream reaches of the Yangtze from heavy flooding.

Nuclear Power   To augment its thermal and hydroelectric power capacity, China was developing a nuclear energy capability. China's nuclear industry began in the 1950s with Soviet assistance. Until the early 1970s, it had primarily military applications. In August 1972, however, reportedly by directive of Premier Zhou Enlai, China began developing a reactor for civilian energy needs. After Mao Zedong's death in 1976, support for the development of nuclear power increased significantly. Contracts were signed to import two French-built plants, but economic retrenchment and the Three Mile Island incident in the United States abruptly halted the nuclear program. Following three years of "investigation and demonstration," the leadership decided to proceed with nuclear power development. By 1990 China intended to commit between 60 and 70 percent of its nuclear industry to the civilian sector. By 2000 China planned to have a nuclear generating capacity of 10,000 megawatts, accounting for approximately 5 percent of the country's total generating capacity (4).

In 1986 a 300 megawatt domestically designed nuclear power plant was under construction at Qinshan, Zhejiang Province, with completion planned for 1989. Although most of the equipment in the plant was domestic, a number of key components were imported. This, China's first nuclear power plant, designed and built by China in coastal Zhejiang Province, has been in trial operation for two years.

Another plant, with two 900 megawatt reactors, was under construction at Daya Bay in Guangdong Province. The Daya Bay project was a joint venture with Hong Kong, with considerable foreign loans and expertise. The second of the Daya Bay plant's 900 megawatt reactors came on line in 1994, marking the completion of the seven-year project.

The plant, located only thirty miles north of Hong Kong, is a joint venture between China's Guangdong provincial government and the Hong Kong Nuclear Investment Company, a subsidiary of Hong Kong's China Light and Power Company. Electricite de France designed the Daya Bay plant, and Framatome, another French company, supplied its two reactors. The plant will generate 1,800 megawatts of electricity, with about 70 percent going to Hong Kong.

The Seventh Five-Year Plan called for constructing two additional 600 megawatt reactors at Qinshan.

As pointed out elsewhere in this report, China badly needs nuclear power development to ease the huge burden of coal movement which occupies a major portion of the freight movement on the nation's railways.

U.S. nuclear plant producers, including Westinghouse Electric Corporation, are keen to compete for Chinese orders, but are prohibited from doing so by the U.S. But, Canadian reactors could be supplied by a group of companies possibly including the Canadian subsidiaries of General Electric Company and Westinghouse. But for U.S. companies, participating in a Canadian group is less attractive than winning their own order from China.

POSTAL SERVICES

Postal service is administered by the Ministry of Posts and Telecommunications, which was established in 1949 and re-established in 1973 after a two year period during which the postal and telecommunications functions had been separated and the ministry downgraded to a subministerial level. Although postal service in China goes back some 2,500 years, modern postal services were not established until 1877 by the Qing government. Development was slow; by 1949 there was only one post office for every 370 square kilometers (4).

Since then the postal service has grown rapidly. In 1984 China had 53,000 post and telecommunications offices and 5 million kilometers of postal routes, including 240,000 kilometers of railroad postal routes, 624,000 kilometers of highway postal routes, and 230,000 kilometers of airmail routes. By 1985 post offices were handling 4.7 billion first-class letters and 25 billion newspapers and periodicals. In 1987, after a six year hiatus, six digit postal codes were ordered to be put into use.

TELECOMMUNICATIONS

In 1987, China possessed a diversified telecommunications system that linked all parts of the country by telephone, telegraph, radio, and television. None of the telecommunications forms were as prevalent or as advanced as those in modern Western countries, but the system included some of the most sophisticated technology in the world and constituted a foundation for further development of a modern network.

When the People's Republic was founded in 1949, the telecommunications facilities in China were outdated, and many had been damaged or destroyed during the way years. In the 1950s, existing facilities were repaired, and, with Soviet assistance, considerable progress was made toward establishing a long distance telephone wire network connecting Beijing to provincial-level capitals. In addition, conference telephone service was initiated, radio communications were improved, and the production of telecommunications equipment was accelerated. Growth in telecommunications halted with the general economic collapse after the Great Leap Forward (1958-60), but revived in the 1960s after the telephone network was expanded and improved equipment was introduced, including imports of Western plants. An important component of the Fourth Five-Year Plan (1971-75) was a major development program for the telecommunications system. The program allotted top priority to scarce electronics and construction resources and dramatically improved all aspects of China's telecommunications capabilities. Microwave radio relay lines and buried cable lines were constructed to create a network of wideband carrier trunk lines, which covered the entire country. China was linked to the international telecommunications network by the installation of communications satellite ground stations and the construction of coaxial cables linking Guangdong Province with Hong Kong and Macao. Provincial-level units and municipalities rapidly expanded local telephone and wire broadcasting networks. Expansion and modernization of the telecommunications system continued throughout the late 1970s and early 1980s, giving particular emphasis to the production of radio and television sets and expanded broadcasting capabilities (4).

In 1987, the Ministry of Posts and Telecommunications administered China's telecommunications systems and related research and production facilities. Besides postal services, some of which were handled by electronic means, the ministry was involved in a wide spectrum of telephone, wire, telegraph, and international communications (see Postal Services, this chapter). The Ministry of Radio and Television was established as a separate entity in 1982 to administer and upgrade the status of television and radio broadcasting. Subordinate to this ministry were the Central People's Broadcasting Station, Radio Beijing, and China Central Television. Additionally, the various broadcasting training, talent search, research, publishing, and manufacturing organizations were brought under the control of the Ministry of Radio and Television. In 1986, responsibility for the movie industry was transferred from the Ministry of Culture to the new Ministry of Radio, Cinema, and Television. The Chinese Communist Party's Propaganda Department coordinates the work of both telecommunications-related ministries.

As of 1987, the quality of telecommunications services in China had improved markedly over earlier years. A considerable influx of foreign technology and increased domestic production capabilities had a major impact in the post-Mao period.

The primary form of telecommunications in the 1980s was local and long distance telephone service administered by six regional bureaus: Beijing (north region), Shanghai (east region), Xi'an (northwest region), Chengdu (southwest region), Wuhan (central-south region), and Shenyang (northeast region). These regional headquarters served as switching centers for provincial-level sub-systems. By 1986, China had nearly 3 million telephone exchange lines, including 34,000 long distance exchange lines with direct, automatic service to twenty-four cities. By late 1986 fiber optic communications technology was being employed to relieve the strain on existing telephone circuits. International service was routed through overseas exchanges located in Beijing and Shanghai. Guangdong Province had coaxial cable and microwave lines linking it to Hong Kong and Macao (4).

To put China's telephone service into worldwide perspective, the following table shows projected trends for various countries.

	Millions of phone lines added, 1993-2000	Percent increase in lines	Investment $ billions
China	35.5	19.3%	$53.3
Russia	15.5	6.7	23.3
India	9.1	11.2	13.7

Brazil	6.8	6.4	10.2
Mexico	6.3	8.5	9.4
Thailand	4.3	16.7	6.6
Malaysia	3.1	11.9	4.6
Poland	2.7	6.7	4.0
Indonesia	2.6	13.6	3.9

With only two lines for every 100 people, China has one of the lowest densities of telephones in the world. In America, by contrast, there is one line for every two people. China wants to increase its telephone capacity to ten lines per 100 people by 2000, an enormous task that some analysts think will cost the country about $100 billion.

Foreign firms doubt that China will be able to complete such an undertaking on its own. But their efforts to help build, finance and run some of the new networks have been blocked by China's Ministry of Posts and Telecommunications (MPT). It has steadfastly defended its monopoly and warned of the threat to national security should foreign devils ever be allowed to sell telecom services.

Luckily, not everyone in China believes that the MPT should have its own way. With the backing of twenty-six state institutions, including the ministries of electronic industries, power and railways, the city governments of Beijing, Shanghai and Tianjin, and a powerful group of mainland Chinese investors, a second telecom network is now being formed: Liantong (more awkwardly in English, China United Telecommunications Corporation). Liantong plans to spend $12 billion over the next five years improving its biggest shareholders' internal telephone networks. By 2000 it also wants to carry 10% of China's long distance calls and 30% of its mobile calls.

The large, continuously upgraded satellite ground stations, originally installed in 1972 to provide live coverage of the visits to China by U.S. president Richard M. Nixon and Japanese prime minister Kakuei Tanaka, still served as the base for China's international satellite communications network in the mid-1980s. By 1977, China had joined Intelsat and, using ground stations in Beijing and Shanghai, had linked up with satellites over the Indian and Pacific oceans (4).

In April 1984, China launched an experimental communications satellite for trial transmission of broadcasts, telegrams, telephone calls, and facsimile, probably to remote areas of the country. In February 1986, China launched its first fully operational telecommunications and broadcast satellite. The quality and communications capacity of the second satellite reportedly was much greater than the first. In mid-1987, both satellites were still functioning. With these satellites in place, China's domestic satellite communication network went into operation, facilitating television and radio transmissions and providing direct dial long distance telephone, telegraph, and facsimile service. The network had ground stations in Beijing, Ürümqi, Hohhot, Lhasa, and Guangzhou, which also were linked to an Intelsat satellite over the Indian Ocean.

Telegraph development received lower priority than the telephone network largely because of the difficulties involved in transmitting the written Chinese language. Computer technology gradually alleviated these problems and facilitated further growth in this area. By 1983, China had nearly 10,000 telegraph cables and telex lines transmitting over 170 million messages annually. Most telegrams were transmitted by cables or by shortwave radio. Cut-microwave transmission also was used. Teletype transmission was used for messages at the international level, but some 40 percent of county and municipal telegrams still were transmitted by Morse code.

Apart from traditional telegraph and telephone services, China also had facsimile, low-speed data transmission, and computer-controlled telecommunications services. These included on-line information retrieval terminals in Beijing, Changsha, and Baotou that enabled international telecommunications networks to retrieve news and scientific, technical, economic, and cultural information from international sources.

High-speed newspaper-page facsimile equipment and Chinese-character-code translation equipment were used on a large scale. Sixty-four channel program-controlled automatic message re-transmission equipment and low- or medium-speed data transmission and exchange equipment also received extensive use. International telex service was available in coastal cities and special economic zones.

The Central People's Broadcasting Station controlled China's national radio network. Programming was administered by the provincial-level units. The station produced general news and cultural and educational programs. It also provided programs for minority groups in the Korean, Manchurian, Zang (Tibetan), Uygur, and Kazak languages, as well as programs directed toward Taiwan and overseas Chinese (see Glossary) listeners. Radio Beijing broadcast to the world in thirty-eight foreign languages, *putonghua* (see Glossary), and various dialects, including Amoy, Cantonese, and Hakka. It also provided English-language news programs aimed at foreign residents in Beijing. Medium-wave, shortwave, and FM stations reached 80 percent of the country—over 160 radio stations and 500 relay and transmission stations—with some 240 radio programs (4).

The nationwide network of wire lines and loudspeakers transmitted radio programs into virtually all rural communities and many urban areas. By 1984 there were over 2,600 wired broadcasting stations, extending radio transmissions to rural areas outside the range of regular broadcasting stations.

In 1987, China Central Television (CCTV), the state network, managed China's television programs. In 1985, consumers purchased 15 million new sets, including approximately 4 million color sets. Production fell far short of demand. Because Chinese viewers often gathered in large groups to watch publicly owned sets, authorities estimated that two-thirds of the nation had access to television. In 1987 there were about 70 million television sets, an average of twenty-nine sets per 100 families. CCTV had four channels that supplied programs to the over ninety television stations throughout the country. Construction began on a major new CCTV studio in Beijing in 1985. CCTV produced its own programs, a large portion of which were educational, and the Television University in Beijing produced three educational programs weekly. The English-language lesson was the most popular program and had an estimated 5 to 6 million viewers. Other programs included daily news, entertainment, teleplays, and special programs. Foreign programs included films and cartoons. Chinese viewers were particularly interested in watching international news, sports, and drama.

Currently, only China's state-owned CCTV and Mr. Murdoch's Hong Kong-based

Star TV broadcast Mandarin programming by satellite to China. There may well be room for more: CCTV's programming is staid at best, and Star has had to contend with Beijing's efforts to restrict the reach of foreign broadcasters, including the regulation of television reception by satellite dishes.

Hong Kong-based TVB International Ltd. hopes to beam to China its Mandarin satellite channel. TVB International, owned by Sir Run Run Shaw's Television Broadcasts Ltd. hopes to add more Mandarin channels later. Star will replace its channel devoted to British Broadcasting Corporation's BBC World Service with a Mandarin movie channel.

In addition, CIM Ltd., publisher of Hong Kong's Ming Pao newspaper, plans to provide news and information on at least two Mandarin-language satellite channels by the end of the year. Turner Broadcasting System, Inc. also wants to start broadcasting two channels to China later this year, including some programming in Mandarin. Other U.S. media companies are lining up to broadcast to China, too.

The reader is also referred to the section on "Telecommunications Equipment" in Chapter 4 on Industrial Markets for further information.

CHAPTER 3

RESOURCES

MINERAL

After 1949 geological exploration discovered deposits of more than 130 useful minerals. China is among the world leaders in proven deposits of tungsten, antimony, rare earth metals, molybdenum, vanadium, titanium, pyrite, gypsum, barite, copper, tin, lead, zinc, aluminum, mercury, manganese, nickel, phosphorus, asbestos, fluorite, magnetite, and borax. Of these, China exported antimony, tin, and tungsten in significant quantities. In general, mineral extraction was inadequate for industrialization because of transportation bottlenecks and shortages of modern equipment for mining, smelting, and refining.
A number of important mineral products were imported despite large domestic deposits, including aluminum, copper, and zinc (4).

Among the rare earth metals and ferroalloys, beryllium, tungsten, molybdenum, barium, manganese, mercury, niobium, zirconium, and titanium were present in large reserves and were extracted in adequate quantities. Deficiencies existed in chromium, platinum, and gold.

China produced sufficient quantities of most non-metallic minerals to meet domestic needs. Barite, fluorite, salt, and talc were available in massive reserves and were exported in large quantities. Graphite, magnetite, phosphates, and pyrite were less abundant but generally satisfied domestic demand. Sulfur deposits were large, but quality was low and imports were necessary.

China is rich in uranium and has favorable geological conditions for the formation of uranium deposits. The ore is easy to mine and dress because of its relatively simple physical composition.

Figure 6 is a map of China showing mineral resources (48). Underlined symbols indicate a plant location (4).

China is the world leader in proven reserves of antimony, barite, molybdenum, rare earths, titanium, tungsten, and vanadium. China has 55 billion tons of iron ore, albeit with an average grade of only 30% to 35% elemental content. Moreover, only 5% of the ore reserves contain 35% to 50% iron. Major deposits occur in Anhui, Hebei, Liaoning, and Nei Mongol. Major gold deposits are in Hebei, Heilongjiang, Henan, Hunan, Jilin, Nei Mongol, and Shandong. Bauxite deposits occur in Guangxi, Guizhou, Henan, and Shandong. Lead and zinc deposits are in Fujian, Gansu, Guangdong, and Guangxi.

With the exception of some commodities such as chromium, copper, and potash, China produces significant quantities of a wide array of minerals and metals, based on its production and/or export capability for these commodities.

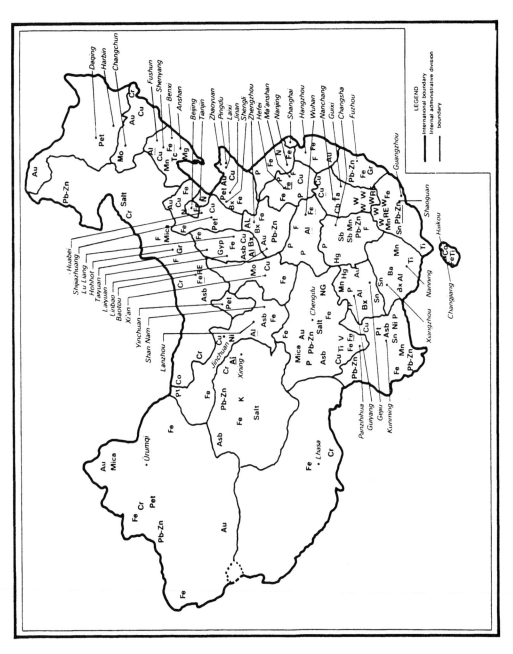

Figure 6: China - Mineral Resources (48)

Antimony As noted above, there is among the world leaders in proven deposits of antimony.

The largest antimony deposit in the world is stated to be in Hunan Province. Hunan's exports account for nearly three fourths of China's total antimony exports. Reserves have been estimated at 2 million tons.

Guangxi Province has reserves ranking second in China and also has a number of smelters with an annual output of perhaps 5,000 tons.

Gansu Province has mines with an annual prospected production capacity of 3,000 tons.

Other Provinces with major deposits include:

- Guizhou Province with reserves estimated at 100 million tons.
- Hubei Province with reserves estimated at 20 million tons.

Bauxite Bauxite as a raw material for aluminum production is another important mineral asset in China.

The largest bauxite deposits in China are in Guangxi Province. The reserves are estimated at 1 billion tons and mining operations were reported as 300,000 tons/year with planned expansion to 1 million tons/year by the year 2000.

Hunan Province has a large number of deposits with reserves in the area of hundreds of millions of tons. Current production of ore containing 60-70% of alumina is several hundred thousand tons per year with most of it designated for export.

Shanxi Province is a third province with large estimated reserves and active mining installations.

Coal In the first half of the twentieth century, coal mining was more developed than most industries. Such major mines as Fushun, Datong, and Kailuan produced substantial quantities of coal for railroads, shipping, and industry. Expansion of coal mining was a major goal of the First Five-Year Plan. The state invested heavily in modern mining equipment and int he development of large, mechanized mines. The "longwall" mining technique was adopted widely, and output reached 130 million tons in 1957.

During the 1960s and 1970s, investment in large mines and modern equipment lagged, and production fell behind the industry's growth. Much of the output growth during this period came from small local mines. A temporary but serious production setback followed the July 1976 Tangshan earthquake, which severely damaged China's most important coal center, the Kailuan mines. It took two years for production at Kailuan to return to the 1975 level (4).

In 1987 coal was the country's most important source of primary energy, meeting over 70 percent of total energy demand. The 1984 production level was 789 million tons. More than two-thirds of deposits were bituminous, and a large part of the remainder was anthracite. Approximately 80 percent of the known coal deposits were in the north and northwest, but most of the mines were located in Heilongjiang Province and east China because of their proximity to the regions of highest demand.

Although China had one of the world's largest coal supplies, there still were shortages in areas of high demand, mainly because of an inadequate transportation infrastructure. The inability to transport domestic coal forced the Chinese to import Australian coal to south China in 1985. The industry also laced modern equipment and technological expertise. Only 50 percent of tunneling, extracting, loading, and conveying activities were mechanized, compared with the 95 percent mechanization level found in European nations.

Figure 7 is a map of China showing the locations of coal resources and mining areas (48).

China is the world's largest coal producer, but its coal is being used inefficiently and with no environmental controls. The British Government's Overseas Development Administration awarded a contract worth $1.7 million to a British Coal consortium to investigate coal used in power generation, industry, and in homes; coal carbonization to produce gas; wastewater treatment and reuse; computer modeling of energy use; and investment finance and training in Taiyan Shi, Shanxi Province. This project has the potential to be of enormous benefit to the environment. Recommendations will be put forward in Taiyuan, and they will be used as guidelines in thirty other cities in China (48).

China National Coal Corp. (CNCC), China Northeast and Nei Mongol Coal Corp. (CGCC) are three major corporations involved with coal production in China and are administrated by the Ministry of Energy. In the restructuring ministries and commission of the State Council during the eighth NPC conference, the Ministry of Energy was abolished and replaced by the Ministry of Coal Industry and the Ministry of Power Industry. The general manager of CNCC became the Minister of the Ministry of Coal Industry.

In China, coal enterprises employed a total of 7.6 million people to produce 1.1 billion tons of coal in 1992. With such a massive work force, it is difficult to cut production costs and raise efficiency. Therefore, CNCC planned to close thirty inefficient mines in 1993 and was expected to lay off more than 30,000 workers and shift 70,000 people to its non-coal subsidiary companies. The corporation employed more than 3 million people and produced more than 370 Mmt of coal in state-owned mines in 1992. The corporation hopes to move a total of 400,000 workers out of coal mining by the end of 1995. CGCC also was to transfer about 400,000 redundant coal miners to other industries in the next three years to improve efficiency. It will build 100 coal mines that can produce 30% of its existing total output. The corporation also is trying to develop an international coal market. CGCC produced 365 Mmt of coal in 1992 and vowed to shut down inefficient and unprofitable coal mines. East Coal also is planning a massive layoff to increase efficiency.

China has completed its prospecting study on the Large Dabaodang Coalfield, near Yulin Shi and Shenmu Xian, in the northern part of Shaanxi Province. The field has a proven reserve of 24.8 billion tons of high grade coal, and about 80% of the reserves were buried less than 600 m below the surface. It is suitable for large scale mechanized mining. The overall development plan is under draft. The Shaanxi Provincial government invested more than $12.5 million in the construction of a methanol plant, with a designed annual output of 300,000 tons, to utilize its rich natural gas project are expected to help in developing the region's economy.

Shanxi Province, the leading coal producer in China, planned to exploit coal deposits in the Luliang Shan area. The plan calls for the completion of the Liliu Mine in the year

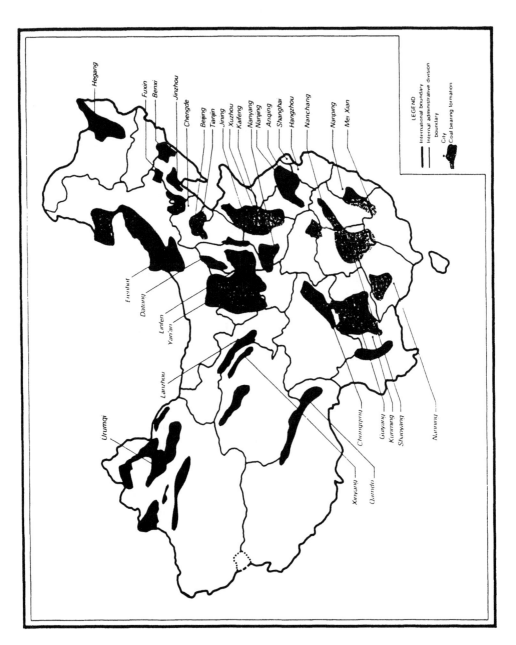

Figure 7: Coal Resources in China (48)

2005. The mine is expected to have an annual production capacity of 15 Mmt of coking coal. The Liliu Mine covers five xians in Luliang Prefecture. There is a coal-bearing area of 4,842.5 m^2 with an estimated coal reserve of 50 billion tons with low ash and sulfur content. Construction of the 116 km Liliu railway began in 1986 and was completed in November 1992. Other infrastructural facilities being built include an expressway, a power plant with a capacity of 1.2 MkW, a fiber optic cable between Taiyuan, capital of the Province, to Lishi, and a coal dressing plant (48).

CNCC and the Shanghai government are preparing to set up a coal trading center in the Pudong area. In the first stage, only spot trading will be permitted. Future trading is expected to start later. Trading policies include contract trade, market prices, and commissions, allowed by market members.

Copper Anhui Province has reserves of copper ore estimated at 20 million tons.

Gansu Province is a major producer. The Balyin mine was said to be the largest copper producer in the 1970's and was then the only mine with its own smelter and refinery. A second important copper producer in Gansu Province is the Jinchuan complex at Lanzhou which features nickel sulfide deposits containing copper and joint production of copper and nickel.

Jiangxi Province has proven reserves which are estimated to be one fifth of China's total and one of the world's largest—perhaps over 8 million tons. Potential annual output from the mines is perhaps 200,000 to 300,000 tons.

Shanxi Province is also a major producer of copper ore—perhaps a million tons of ore per year.

In 1992, China's supply of copper continuously fell short of demand; therefore, China has banned exporting copper metal and its alloys beginning in 1993. The booming industry demand for copper led to the import of more than 200,000 tons of copper ore in 1992. In addition, the country also imported more than 400,000 tons of copper and its alloys during the year. In the second half of 1992, the demand of copper became very tight because the price hike in the world market restrained the import of copper to a certain degree. In addition, the expansion of automotive, machine building, and electronic sectors increased copper use (48).

China North Industries Corp. signed an agreement with Philcopper Gold Mining Co., Philippines, that would guarantee the purchase of part of Philcopper's future copper production. Under the agreement, China will buy 30% of the future copper concentrate with contained gold, silver, pyrites, and rare metals for a period of thirty years. The two sides also are negotiating a loan package to finance a joint venture for a copper and gold beneficiation plant. An agreement was being based on the exchange of Chinese mining and milling equipment for copper concentrate for a period of time.

Japan agreed to spend $16 million during the next six years for China to look for copper deposits along the Chang Jiang. It includes geological studies and drilling. The study will cover two regions, each about 1,000 km^2, one near Kunming in Yunnan Province and the other in Xian in Shaanxi. The project was expected to start in June 1993.

The third stage of construction of Jiangxi Copper Corp.'s Dexing copper mine is under way. After completion, the mine would have a daily capacity of 90,000 tons of ore by 1996. Also, the extension of the Guixi smelter is under construction. After the completion, smelter capacity will increase from the current level of 110,000 tons to 200,000 tons in 1996.

CNNC reached an agreement with Udokan Mining Co. (UMC) of Russia with Chita Minerals Co. (Hong Kong-based company) owned 45%; Andrei Chuguyevsdy's Arter Group, 35%; the Chita Geological Committee, 15%; and the Chita government, 5%, on the construction of a large copper mine int he Chita region of Russia. Copper content of the ore is more than 1% and ore reserves are estimated at least 1.2 billion tons. Under the agreement, UMC will sell no less than 260,000 tons of 400,000 tons of refined copper yearly for twenty-five years to CNNC when it comes on-stream in 1997. The concentrate will be shipped by the Baikul-Amur railway from Udokan to China. A smelter will be built specifically to treat the high sulfur concentrates. The $1.74 billion project will be financed by the Bank of China, Outokumpu of Finland, and General Electric of the United States (48).

Fluorspar   Active production of fluorspar is carried out in Anhui and Gansu Provinces with some 40-50 mining centers reported in Guangdong Province, also. Jiangxi Province is also an active mining area.

The largest reserves are reported in Nei Mongol however, with verified reserves of 50 million tons.

Gold   Shandong Province leads China in both reserves and annual production. Over a million tons of ore are produced with actual gold production of several hundred thousand troy ounces.

Shaanxi Province also has attractive potential with both alluvial deposits and vein mines.

Under the current regulations, gold information is considered a state secret. Chinese Government does not reveal its geological reserves of gold nor statistical data on gold production. However, this may change if certain gold deposits need high technology and funds for development. In the past two decades, China devoted more than 50% of its mineral exploration and development funds to search for gold (48).

Graphite   Heilongjiang Province is the location of the largest known graphite deposits in China with reserves in the hundreds of millions of tons, much of it suitable for open-pit mining.

Another considerable source of graphite reserves and a major graphite producer is Shandong Province.

In Inner Mongolia, there is also production of natural scaly graphites. For additional information, one might contact:

Xinghe Graphite Mine
Xinghe
Ulangab Meng
Inner Mongolia 013659
China
Cable: Xinghe 1075

Iron Ore China had iron ore reserves totaling approximately 44 billion tons in 1980. In the mid-1980s, however, China relied on import because of domestic transportation and production problems. Sizable iron ore beds are distributed widely in about two-thirds of China's provinces and autonomous regions. The largest quantities are found in Liaoning Province, followed by Sichuan, Hebei, Shanxi, Anhui, Hubei, Gansu, Shandong, and Yunnan provinces and Nei Mongol Autonomous Region (4).

In the mid-1980s mines lacked modern excavation, transportation, and ore-beneficiation equipment. Most of the ore mined had a low iron content and required substantial refining or beneficiation before use in blast furnaces. Most mines lacked modern plants for converting low-grade iron ore into concentrated pellets.

It is interesting that foreign sources are being exploited to supplement domestic sources. In Peru, for example, a China company, the Shougang Corporation bought the state iron company for $270 million in cash and investments. There are also iron ore purchases from Western Australia.

Figure 8 is a map of China showing major iron ore deposits and iron and steel works.

In 1992, China imported about 25 million tons of iron ore, mainly from Australia, Brazil, and India. The total output of iron ore was 197 million, which accounted for only 70% of the country's need in 1992. Most of the iron ore used by Baogang, Chongqing Iron and Steel Works, and Wugang is imported. Even after the completion of the new mines, the output of iron ore still would not be able to meet the rising demand by the steel industry. China expected to import annually more than 50 million tons of iron ore in the Ninth Five-Year Plan (1996-2000). At the same time, China is focusing efforts on developing mines overseas. Delegations and research teams have been sent to Brazil, India, Peru, Russia, and Vietnam to pursue the possibility of setting up a joint venture to mine iron ore in these countries. Average iron content in ores produced from mines of these countries is about double those in China, which averages only about 30% iron content (48).

Lead-Zinc In Gansu Province, the Changba Lead & Zinc Mine feeds the Baiyin smelter, operated by the Baiyin Non-Ferrous Corp. For further information, one could contact:

Baiyin Non-Ferrous Metal Co.
Baiyin
Gansu Province, China 730900
Tel: 22560

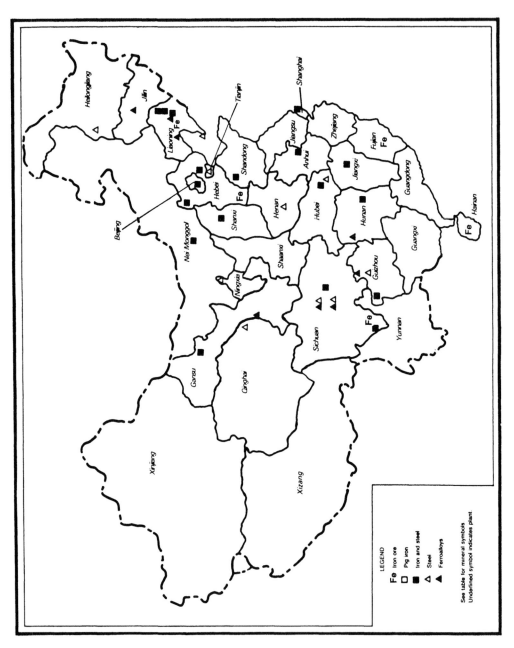

Figure 8: Location of Major Iron Ore Deposits and Iron and Steel Works in China (48)

Ore reserves of several million tons are reported. A slurry pipeline has been considered to transport ore concentrate to the nearest rail line. Cooperation in a zinc smelter was to involve Teho Zinc of Japan.

In Guangdong Province, the Fankou Lead-Zinc mine is reported to be adjacent to two main ore bodies containing some 30 million tons of ore. Ore production is to be 3,000 tons/day and production capacity is targeted for 150,000 tons/year of metal. For further information, one could contact:

Fankou Lead & Zinc Mine
Renhua County
Shaoguan, Guangdong Province
China 512325
Tel: 880531

In Hunan Province, there are a number of ore deposits and mines. The Shuikoushan Mine is stated to be the most important zinc producer in China. The adjacent Zhuzhou smelter has a production capacity of 70,000 tons of zinc per year. For further information, one could contact:

Zhuzhou Metal Smeltery
North District
Zhuzhou, Hunan Province 412004
China
Tel: 31431

In Liaoning Province, the mine at Fushun produces copper and zinc. The smelter at Shenyang is reported to produce 20,000 tons of zinc annually. For further information, one might contact:

Shenyang Metal Smeltery
Tiexi, Shenyang
Liaoning Province 110025
China
Tel: 551411

In Qinghai Province, the Qaidam basin is reported to contain proven reserves of some 30 million tons. There are gold, silver, and tin also present in the ore body.

Asia Minerals, a private company in Vancouver, Canada, signed an agreement with Chinese authorities to acquire up to a 60% equity in the Qiandongshen lead and zinc project in Shaanxi Province. Asia Minerals retained Cominco Engineering Services to complete a feasibility study on the project. The deposit is believed to have a total reserve of 12 million tons, including 6.4 million tons grading 1.6% lead, 8.3% zinc, and 23 g silver per ton. Drilling indicated that there was a potential for a further 5 to 6 million tons of similar grade reserves. Capital costs were estimated at $28 million, allowing for a capital payback of 2.5 years from start up. The mine will have an output of 1,200 thousand tons/day of ore. Mine life was estimated at seventeen years (48).

Construction of the opencast Lanping lead and zinc mine, Yunnan Province, began in 1992. The mine has verified reserves of 14.3 million tons of lead and zinc. Ore content is 85% zinc, grading 9.63%. Apart from lead and zinc, the ore also contains cadmium, silver, and thallium.

Limestone There are many areas in China where deposits in excess of 100 million tons are reported.
These include:

- Anhui Province
- Liaoning Province
- Nei Mongol
- Shanxi Province
- Shandong Province
- Shangxi Province

Lithium Xizang Province has salt lakes in the northern part of the province which reportedly account for nearly 50% of the world's total lithium salts.

Salt lakes in Qinghai Province also contain huge amounts of mixed salts including lithium salts.

Magnesium Liaoning Province and particularly Yingkou County is the site of deposits of over a billion tons of ore with a magnesium oxide content of 40-45%. The largest magnesium/magnetite deposit in China is said to be at Dashiqiao. The total annual production is 3 million tons with export going through the port at Dalian. For further information, one might contact:

Liaoning Magnesium Corp.
Yong'anlu, Haicheng
Lianing 114200
Tel: 25620-2251

Manganese Guangxi Province contains the largest deposit (estimated to exceed 100 million tons) of manganese in the country. The mine in Daxin County is being developed. The Baiyi manganese mine is also under development.

Hunan Province also has large reserves—estimated at 25 million tons.

In Qinghai Province, as much as a billion tons of manganese chloride are contained in Qarhan Salt Lake in Qaidam basin.

Mercury Guizhou Province is estimated to contain 80% of China's mercury reserves.

There are also mercury deposits being worked in:
- Guangdong Province
- Guanxi Province
- Hunan Province
- Qinghai Province
- Shaanxi Province
- Sichuan Province

Molybdenum Liaoning Province is a major participant in the Chinese molybdenum industry. The Xinhun deposit is said to contain 46 million tons of ore having 0.22% molybdenum content. It is planned to produced 2,000 tons of ore per day.

China's largest molybdenum mine is said to be in Shaanxi Province at Jinduicheng. It is hoped to process 15,000 tons of ore per day to give 12,000 tons of concentrate per year.

Nickel There are a number of provinces in China with significant nickel deposits.

In Anhui Province, there is production of copper, nickel, and cobalt by Tongling Non-Ferrous Metal Co. For more information, one might contact:

Tongling Non-Ferrous Metal Corp.
Tongguanshan, Tongling
Anhui Province 244001
China
Tel: 34367

In Gansu Province, the largest nickel-producing center in China which is believed to contain the largest deposits of nickel sulfide in the world is located in Jinchang municipality of Yongshan County. Nickel production here is about 80% of China's total; the nickel content of the ore exceeds 5% and the ore contains some 20 different metals. For more information, one might contact:

Jinchuan Non-Ferrous Metal Co.
Jinchuan, Jinchang
Gansu Province 737100
China
Tel: 5230

Also in Gansu Province, at Banin, there is an open-pit mine with large nickel sulfide deposits of about 1.5% nickel content. For more information, one might contact:

Baiyin Non-Ferrous Metal Co.
Baiyin, Gansu Province 316101
China
Tel: 53912

The above contact is also cited under "Lead-Zinc."
    In the southern region of Hebei Province, there is an ore body containing nickel, copper, and cobalt in an iron ore. For more information, one might contact:

Xingtai Iron & Steel Works
Qiaoxi, Xingtai
Hebei Province 054027
China
Tel: 223927

    In Hubei Province, there is substantial production of copper, nickel, and cobalt from the Tonglushan mine. For more information, one might contact:

Daye Non-Ferrous Metal Co.
Xialu, Huangshi
Hubei Province 435005
China
Tel: 392027

Also in Hubei Province, both nickel and cobalt are produced by electrolysis at Wuhan.
    In Jilin Province, there are major ore bodies in Panshi County. The Panshi Nickel Mine & Fertilizer Plant has been producing since 1982.
    Other large nickel deposits occur in:
* Nei Mongol
* Shaanxi
* Sichuan
* Xinjiang
* Xizang

Oil and Natural Gas Before 1949 China imported most of its oil. During the First Five-Year Plan it invested heavily in exploration and development of wells. In 1959 vast reserves were discovered in the Songhua Jiang (Sungari River)-Liaohe Basin in northeast China. The Daqing oil field in Heilongjiang Province became operational in 1960. Daqing was producing about 2.3 million tons of oil by 1963, and it continued to lead the industry through the 1970s. Further important discoveries, including the major oil fields of Shengli (in Shangdong Province), and Dagang (in Tianjin special municipality) enabled China to meet domestic needs and eliminate nearly all imports by the mid-1960s. In 1973, despite a steadily growing internal demand for petroleum products, output was large enough to export 1 million tons of crude oil to Japan. Exports increased to 6.6 million tons in 1974 and reached 13.5 million tons in 1978. In 1985 exports of crude oil amounted to approximately 20 million tons, roughly 16 percent of total production. The majority of 1985 exports were to Japan, but the government also had released increasing quantities on the spot market and sent some to Singapore for refining. Although the government temporarily abandoned its drive to broaden its oil export base in 1986, 130.7 million tons of crude oil still were produced, an increase of 5.8 million tons over 1985 (4).

Oil reserves are large and widely dispersed. In general, development is concentrated on deposits readily accessible from major industrial and population centers. Deposits in remote areas such as the Tarim, Junggar, and Qaidam basins remain largely unexplored. The quality of oil from the major deposits varies considerably. A few deposits, like the Shengli field, produce low-quality oil suitable mainly as fuel. Most of the oil produced in China from the big fields in the north and northeast is heavy, is low in sulfur, and has a very high paraffin content, making it difficult and expensive to extract and to refine.

Offshore and drilling were first undertaken int he early 1970s and became more widespread and advanced as the decade progressed. Chinese and foreign oil experts believed that offshore deposits were extensive and could equal onshore reserves. Offshore operations relied heavily on foreign technology. In 1982 thirty-three foreign oil companies submitted bids for offshore drilling rights; twenty-seven eventually signed contracts. By the mid-1980s, when offshore exploration results were disappointing and only a handful of wells were actually producing oil, China began to emphasize onshore development. To continue offshore exploration, China established the China National Offshore Oil Corporation to assist foreign oil companies in exploring, developing, extracting, and marketing China's oil.

Offshore exploration and drilling were concentrated in areas in the Sough China Sea, Gulf of Tonkin, and Zhu Jiang (Pearl River) Delta in the south, and the Bo Hai Gulf in the north. Disputes between China and several neighboring countries complicated the future of oil development in several promising offshore locations.

Natural gas was a relatively minor source of energy. Output grew rapidly in the 1960s and 1970s. By 1985 production was approximately 12 billion cubic meters—about 3 percent of China's primary energy supply. The following year, output increased by 13 billion cubic meters. Sichuan Province possesses about half of China's natural gas reserves and annual production. Most of the remaining natural gas is produced at the Daqing and Shengli oil fields in the northeast. Other gas-producing areas include the coastal plain in Shanghai and in Jiangsu and Zhejiang Provinces; the Huabei complex in Hebei Province; and the Liaohe oil field in Liaoning Province.

The exact size of China's natural gas reserves was unknown. Estimates ranged from 129 billion to 24.4 trillion cubic meters. The Chinese hoped for a major discovery in the Zhongyuan Basin, a 5,180 square kilometer area along the border of Henan and Shandong provinces. Major offshore reserves have been discovered. If successfully tapped, these could increase gas output by 50 percent. The largest unexploited natural gas potential is believed to be in Qinghai Province and Xinjiang-Uygur Autonomous Region (4).

Figure 9 is a map of China showing oil and natural gas resources (48).

Figure 10 is another map showing oil basins yet to be exploited—both onshore (Tarim

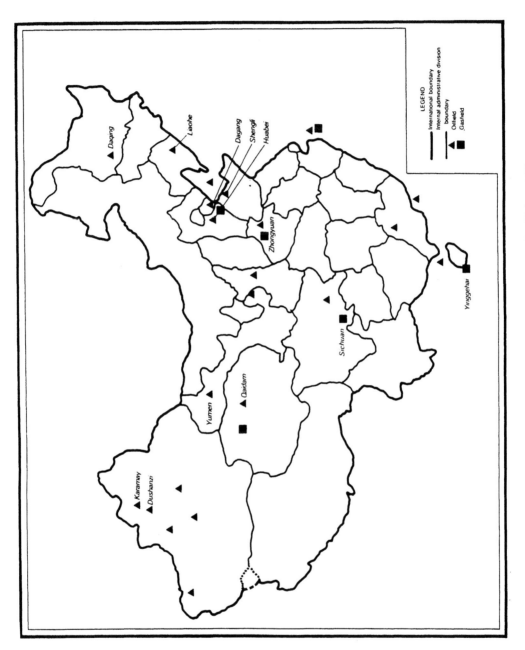

Figure 9: Oil and Natural Gas Resources in China (48)

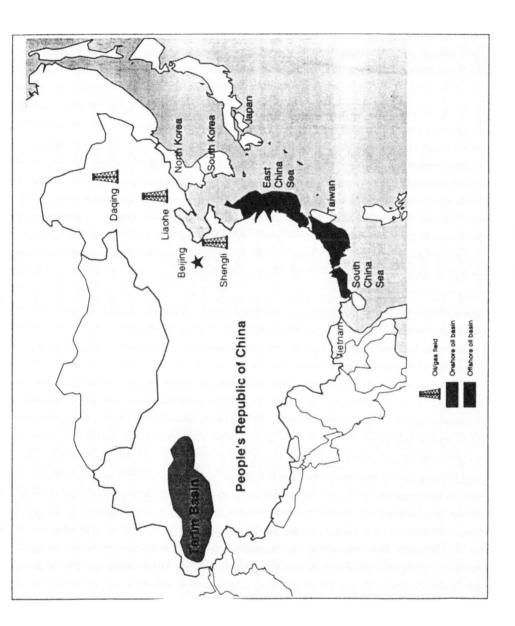

Figure 10: Oil Basins in China (47)

Basin) and offshore (47).

There is the potential for serious international conflict in the South China Sea area and in the area around the Spratly Islands in particular.

The Spratlys—comprising twenty-one islands and atolls, fifty submerged land spits and twenty-eight partly submerged bits of rock and reef spread out over 340,000 square miles—are considered by some to be a sacred and inviolable part of Chinese territory.

The Spratly Islands, are claimed entirely by China, Vietnam and Taiwan and in part by Malaysia, the Philippines and Brunei. Military forces of all but Brunei, occupy the scattered islets, cays and rocks of the archipelago.

China triggered the latest tit-for-tat taunts when it signed an exploration contract in May 1992 with Crestone Energy Corporation. The agreement covers a block near the Spratlys that Vietnam says is on its continental shelf. At the time, Crestone declared that China is prepared to use its navy to defend the company. In spring 1994, Vietnam leased a block containing the promising Blue Dragon structure, just west of Crestone's concession, to a consortium that includes Mobil Corporation of the U.S. Should fighting ever erupt, the U.S. could feel compelled to enter the fray to keep open a strategic waterway. International sea lanes passing near the Spratlys Islands—an archipelago in the South China Sea—carry more than 705 of Japan's oil imports. China's oil sector is eager to raise output and tap potential reserves. With the approval of the Government, China National Petroleum Corp. (CNCP) announced it is opening inland areas to foreign oil companies for exploitation. China opened the Nan Hai (South China Sea) and Bo Hai to foreign oil exploration and development fourteen years ago, followed by the opening of eleven provinces in south China five years ago and the Dong Hai (East China Sea) in 1992 (48).

The newly opening areas include nine provinces and autonomous regions and one municipality in northern China—Hebei, Henan, Hubei, Gansu, Nei Mongol, Ningxia, Qinghai, Shandong, Xinjiang, and Tianjin Shi. The area covers about 420,000 km², and the untapped resources in those areas are estimated to be 8.2 billion tons of oil and 2.5 trillion m³ of natural gas. The bidding areas for enhancement of oil recovery include fourteen blocks in ten oil fields of Daqing, Dagang, Henan, Huabei, Jianghan, Jiangsu, Jilin, Liaohe, Shengli, and Zhongyuan. The bidding on the southeastern part of Tarim Basin, Xinjiang Uygur Zizhiqu, began in March 1993. This section divided into five blocks covering 72,730 km². Construction of roads through the deserts of Tarim Basin is expected to completed within years. Foreign companies that are to undertake risk exploration will share oil reserves. CNCP stressed that contracting on joint oil development between China and foreign companies will comply with international conventional standards. Other areas opened bidding in early 1994.

Chinese geologists estimated total oil reserves in the Tarim Basin at 10 billion tons. CNPC spent more than $20 million drilling discovery wells in the past two years. In 1991, CNPC signed an agreement with Japan National Oil Corp. to explore an area of 30,000 km² in the southwestern part of Tarim Basin. In 1992, the corporation signed an agreement with Exxon of the United States to act as technical contractor for exploration work in Xinjiang. The Chinese Government also is putting a considerable effort into developing infrastructure in the area. Getting the oil from Tarim Basin to the marketplace requires the construction of a pipeline to the eastern part of China.

China Offshore Oil Nan Hai East Corp., a subsidiary of China National Offshore Oil Corp. (CNOOC), planned to develop nine offshore oil fields in the next five years to achieve annual production of 7 million tons/year by 1997. In 1992, the two offshore oil fields, Huizhou 21-1 and Huizhou 26-1, produced 2.58 million tons of oil, accounting for two-thirds of China's offshore output. About 40% of the crude oil was exported. Lufeng 13-1 was put into production in August 1993. The oil field is a joint venture between CNOOC and the JHN (Japan Petroleum Exploration Co., Huanan Oil Development Co., and Nippon Mining Co.) oil group of Japan. Xijiang 24-2 and Xijiang 302 are scheduled to be in operation in 1994. These two oil fields are a joint development among CNOOC, Phillips Petroleum International Corp., Asia, and Pecton Orient Co. of the United States. Other wells that are under development are Huizhou 32-2 and Huizhou 32-3 by ACT [Agip (Overseas) Ltd. of Italy, Chevron Overseas Petroleum, and Texaco Petroleum Maatshappij (Netherland) B.V Co.] and CNOOC (48).

In 1992, CNPC also has expanded its international activities. The corporation has negotiated either buying or forming joint ventures in Canada, India, Indonesia, Papua New Guinea, Peru, Russia, Turkmenistan, and Venezuela. CNPC also will extend its business from merely developing oil fields to downstream industries such as oil refining and petroleum products.

Currently, China exports more than 23 million tons of crude oil while importing 10 million tons of oil, including the re-import of oil products processed abroad. Because of booming economic growth, the country will become a net importer in 1995. During the past several years, the rate of oil output could not keep up with the rate of growth in demand. The main oil fields that went into operation in the 1960's and 1970's have entered the late stages of their stable yield. Output by the main oil fields is progressively decreasing (48).

The reader is also referred to the section on "Petroleum in Chapter 4 on "Industrial Markets."

Phosphates Guizhou Province is the site of a number of large deposits of phosphate rock.

Hanan, Hebei, Hubei, and Hunan Provinces are also the locations of major deposits. There are an estimated 20 billion tons of phosphate rock in Yunnan Province.

Rare Earths Rare earth deposits are found in:
- Anhui Province
- Gansu Province
- Guangdong Province
- Hunan Province
- Jiangxi Province
- Nei Mongol

The largest rare earth production line in China is at a plant in Gansu Province.
A major mining operation is located at Bayon Obo in Nei Mongol. For more

information, one might contact:

Baotou Steel & Rare Earth Co.
Hondcon, Baotou
Inner Mongolia 014010
China
Tel: 82873

Salt   There are huge salt deposits in many parts of China—some in the form of underground mines and some in the form of salt lakes or brine deposits.

The Qaidam basin in Qinghai Province contains 50% of the country's reserves—some 60 billion tons. The Qarhan salt lake contains soluble manganese in addition to sodium and potassium. Production of one million tons per year is planned. Caka Salt Lake in the same area is stated to contain 40% of the country's boron, over 90% of the country's potassium plus abundant lithium.

Tin   The largest tin field in China is located at Gejiu, in Yunnan Province, with both underground and surface placer sites. For more information, one might contact:

Yunnan Tin Industrial Co.
Geiju City, Yunnan Province 661400
China
Tel: 6152

The tin reserves in Guangxi Province are the largest in China and production of ore is second. Production in the area is estimated at one million tons/year of refined tin. For more information, one might contact:

Dachang Mining Bureau
Nandan County, Hechi,
Guanxi Province 315301
China
Tel: 285832

Titanium   China claims that its titanium reserves account for more than 20% of the world's total.

There are large ilmenite deposits in Guangxi Province and also in Hainan.

In Hebei Province, there are titanium mines. For more information, one might contact:

Chengde Iron & Steel Works
Shangluan District
Chengde, Hebei Province 067002
China
Tel: 444901

There are also large deposits in Sichuan Province. The iron ore complex there as a billion tons of iron ore containing 11.6% titanium dioxide and 0.3% vanadium pentoxide; it is said to contain 80% of China's vanadium. For more information, one might contact:

Panzhihua Iron & Steel Corp.
East District, Panzhihua
Sichuan Province 617067
China
Tel: 4261

or possibly the following:

Panzhiua Mining Administration Bureau
West District, Panzhihua
Sichuan Province 617066
China
Tel: 617066

<u>Tungsten</u> China's reserves account for more than 50% of the world's total.
Guangdong Province is a major location. The Nanling mountains may contain 80% of the country's reserves.
Hunan Province is also very important. Xikuang mountain in the Wuling range in Hunan is reported to have the largest deposit in the country.
Jianxi Province is probably second in importance as regards tungsten deposits.

AGRICULTURAL

China has the world's largest agricultural economy and one of the most varied. The nation stands first among all others in the production of rice, cotton, tobacco, and hogs and is a major producer of wheat, corn, millet, tea, jute, and hemp. This wide range of crops is possible because of the country's varied climate and agricultural zones. China participates on a large scale in international agricultural markets, both as an exporter and as an importer (4).
A successful agricultural sector is critical to China's development. First, it must feed more than 1 billion people, and 21 percent of the world's population, using only 7 percent of the world's arable land. Second, it must provide raw materials for the industrial sector.

Third, agricultural exports must earn the foreign exchange needed to purchase key industrial items from other countries (4).

While this book is primarily concerned with industrial production, markets and trade, agricultural markets and trade are also of obvious importance. China's best agricultural market prospects for U.S. companies in the 1994-95 period, in order of estimated importance (based on size and growth potential), are set forth below (58):

Rank	Description
1	Wheat
2	Cotton
3	Logs
4	Hides and Skins
5	Poultry Meat
6	Tree Nuts (Pistachios)
7	Dried Fruits (Raisins)
8	Snack Foods

Barley Barley is a major grain produced in the lower Chang Jiang Basin. It is used for direct human consumption, livestock feed, and increasingly is in great demand as a feedstock to produce beer (4).

Corn Corn is grown in most parts of the country, but is most common in areas that also produce wheat. Corn production has increased substantially over time and in some years has been second only to production of rice. Consumers have traditionally considered corn lies desirable for human use than rice or wheat. Nevertheless, it frequently yields more per unit of land than other varieties of grain, making it useful for maintaining subsistence. As incomes rose in the early 1980s, consumer demand for corn as a food grain decreased, and increasing quantities of corn were allocated for animal feed (4).

Corn ranks third behind rice and wheat among China's top grain crops. Corn is raised in almost all provinces, is a major food and feed grain, and was imported and exported during the 1980's. The first scenario assumes that cultivated and sown area are under reported, that yields are valid, and that output is considerably above reported output by China. The second assumes that area is up but yields are lower and output is unchanged from official reported output (46).

Cotton Cotton is China's most important fiber crop. The crop is grown on the North China Plain and in the middle and lower reaches of the Chang Jiang Valley. In the 1970s domestic output did not meet demand, and significant quantities of raw cotton were imported. Production expanded dramatically in the early 1980s to reach a record 6 million tons in 1984. Although production declined to 4.2 million tons in 1985, China was still, by far, the largest cotton producer in the world. In the 1980s raw cotton imports ceased, and China became a major exporter of cotton (4).

Before 1983, China was one of the world's largest importers of raw cotton. These imports averaged around 100,000 tons annually, but climbed to a peak of nearly 900,000 tons in 1980. A dramatic increase in domestic cotton production filled domestic demand, and exports exceeded imports in 1983. In 1985, China shipped nearly 500,000 tons of raw cotton to Asian and European markets (4).

China's 1993/94 cotton output fell 17 percent to 3.74 million tons due to bollworms and flooding. This contributed to a 4 percent decline in consumption. Area is expected to increase in 1994/95, but still fall short of the government's 6 million hectare target. Imports are expected to remain about unchanged in 1994/95 as we continue to exceed production. The exact level will depend on the success of the government in regaining control over cotton procurement and distribution (53).

U.S. cotton exports to China in 1993 fell to 179 tons from the 133,500 metric tons the previous year. The reduced cotton exports were basically responsible for the decline in the value of U.S. agricultural exports in China. In fact, China's cotton production in 1992 and 1993 dropped sharply from the 1991 output because of bollworm infestations, particularly in Shandong, Hebei, and Henan. However, high stocks and success in reducing natural fiber use in yarn and textile manufacturing allowed the country to reduce cotton imports to below 10,000 tons, compared with 280,000 tons imported in 1992. Consequently, the value of U.S. cotton exports to China decreased to less than $200,000 in 1993, substantially lower than the $186 million in 1992. However, China began to buy U.S. cotton in the first quarter of 1994 because of a domestic cotton shortage for textile use and the questionable quality of the remaining stocks. Cotton prices are high in the world market and how much cotton China will buy from foreign sources remains to be seen (53).

As of 1995, China's fast growing domestic and export demand for cotton fabric has finally pushed China into a perpetual deficit situation. Currently, the expansion of the textile industry is constrained by lack of resources. Chinese cotton production is limited by insect infestations, and is highly susceptible to weather anomalies. Therefore, China will continue to be a buyer of cotton for the foreseeable future. Note: the table below does not account for cotton held as stocks (58).

Cotton is the second best agricultural trade prospect for the U.S. and the following data show total markets, total imports, U.S. imports and exports (all in millions of $US).

	1993	1994	1995
Total Market Size	4,684	4,500	4,700
Total Local Production	4,508	3,500	4,200
Total Exports	140	140	140
Total Imports	53	250	300
Total Imports from U.S.	31	200	250

Unit: 1,000 metric tons

Fruit Temperate, subtropical, and tropical fruits are cultivated in China. Output expanded from 2.6 million tons in 1955 to more than 11 million tons in 1985. Reforms in the early 1980s encouraged farmers to plant orchards, and the output of apples, pears, bananas, and citrus fruit was expected to expand in the late 1980s (4).

The seventh ranking agricultural export from the U.S. to China is dried fruit, primarily raisins.

Raisin data is presented immediately below as representative of the dried fruit area. Although there are no official statistics on China's raisin production, domestic production is likely to exceed 100,000 metric tons (total grape production in 1993 was 1.36 million metric tons). Imports in 1993 surged by 49 percent, with U.S. market share increasing from 28 percent in 1992 to 47 percent. Other dried fruits, especially prunes, are showing similar growth. Market research indicates that California raisins are widely recognized for their high quality in value. Market value in millions of $U.S. are follows (58):

	1993	1994	1995
Total Market Size	n/a	n/a	n/a
Total Local Production	n/a	n/a	n/a
Total Exports	1,749	2,000	2,400
Total Imports	2,820	3,500	4,000
Total Imports from U.S.	1,330	1,800	2,500

Meat   Meat output was a record 33 million tons in 1992, 7 percent above the previous year and surpassed the 1995 official target of 30 million tons. Pork output rose 1.8 million tons to 26.4 million. Excellent grain and oilseed crops in 1991 and 1992 and large grain stocks will maintain feed supplies and promote continued growth in meat output in 1993 (46).

In 1987, China had the largest inventory of hogs in the world. The number increased from about 88 million in 1955 to an estimated 331 million in 1985. Hogs are raised in large numbers in every part of China except in Muslim areas in the northwest. Most hogs are raised in pens by individual farm households, but in the mid-1980s the Chinese were constructing large mechanized feeding operations on the outskirts of major cities. Before the 1980s, the state's major goal was to increase output with little regard to the ratio of meat to fat. In the 1980s, consumers became more conscious of fat content, and breeders and raisers were shifting to the production of leaner hogs (4).

China's livestock sector experienced another year of robust growth in 1993. Bumper grain harvests during the last five years, liberalized grain prices, the decline in the ratio of government to free market meat procurement, and increased consumer demand for meat fostered rising livestock inventories and meat output. Higher quality feeds, better herd management, sustained market and distribution reforms, and breed improvement programs were also factors in China's growth in meat production (53).

According to the 1994 China Statistical Summary, pork, beef, mutton, and poultry output continued their rapid growth, increasing 8.3, 29.6, 9.9, and 13.6 percent, respectively, from 1992. Responding to the government's policy of increasing the consumption share of beef and poultry relative to pork, the 1993 increase in beef and poultry meat output was higher than pork. Despite no government meat subsidies for urban consumers in 1991, which increased retail meat prices, overall meat consumption continued to rise rapidly and swelling producer profits stimulated supply.

China's hog sector continues to be dominated by relatively small backyard producers. However, the number of larger, more efficient specialized livestock households and commercial operations is rising. Likewise, improved hybrid breeds are more widespread as consumers demand leaner cuts of pork. The significance of these two trends is that improved hog breeds are increasing feeding efficiency, while the additional commercial hog operations are expanding hogs on commercial grain-based feeds (versus non-grain feeds primarily used by backyard producers).

The hog slaughter rate (beginning inventory divided by total slaughter) in 1993 was 98 percent, up from 95 in 1991, though still well below the 150 percent or more reported in many developed countries. In 1993, hog slaughter reached 378 million head, surpassing the state hog slaughter target for the year 2000 by more than 78 million head. The central government continues to push for higher hog slaughter weights, slower inventory growth, and increased slaughter rates.

Cattle inventory underwent another year of dramatic growth, particularly in farming areas where the availability of forage and feedstuffs has increased. Year end inventory reached more than 113 million head, up from 108 million in 1992. Government policy continues to promote the development and use of non-grain feedstuffs, including ammoniated straw and green fodder stalks. In 1993, forty additional counties were added to the existing ten that receive special government aid to promote this policy. In addition to the jump in cattle inventory, beef production surged nearly 30 percent over 1992 in response to larger average carcass weights, an estimated higher slaughter rate, and increased consumer demand for beef and veal.

Sheep inventory increased dramatically in 1992 after three consecutive years of flat-to-declining numbers. Mutton and goat meat also increased, rising 9.9 percent over 1992 to nearly 1.4 million tons. Mutton production and consumption is mostly concentrated in a few northern and western provinces. Rising slaughter weights and rates have kept mutton and goat meat output on the upswing, even during the years of low or declining inventory growth, in large part because of central and provincial government policies aimed at settling nomadic herders, improving herd management, and improving breeding programs. In addition, government policy was also a factor in the drastic reduction in winter lamb kill by encouraging the use of winter shelters, and thereby dramatically improving returns to the herder.

Continuing a trend begin in 1990, China's live cattle and beef exports declined in 1993 because of improved domestic demand and a government policy of exporting more value-added meat products. China imported 2.1 millions tons of beef in 1993, mainly high-quality beef from Australia to supply hotels and restaurants. Beef exports are exported to continue to decline in 1994, while imports are likely to reach 4 million tons. Beef imports would be growing even faster were it not for China's high tariffs and very difficult inspection system.

China's live hog exports, almost solely to Hong Kong, have remained fairly steady over the last five years, hovering between 2.7 and 3.0 million head. An export quota restricts hog shipments, so despite additional demand in Hong Kong, exports are not expected to change much. Fresh pork exports increased slightly in 1993, but are still far below the 1990 peak of 124,000 tons, due to reduced imports to Russia and Hong Kong. China apparently does not allow fresh pork imports, though no published prohibition has been identified. Live hog imports continue to be severely restricted by fierce quarantine regulations and are not expected to rise much under the current quarantine regime.

China's long-term meat trade will likely evolve slowly. Beef imports, particularly higher quality fresh, frozen, or chilled should continue to modestly but constantly increase as personal incomes grow. Fresh, frozen, or chilled poultry meat imports, including certain high-demand parts like paws (chicken feet), should see continued strong growth. U.S. export prospects are improving, but China's trade laws and practices continue to inhibit U.S. sales. Assuming China stays on the path of liberalizing trade, U.S. meat and animal exports will likely accelerate (53).

One further aspect of the meat category which might be considered is that of hides and skins. There are no reliable statistics on China's production and thus total market size of cattle hides and skins. Unofficial estimates indicate that about 10 million cattle hides are produced each year. The rapid growth of China's leather manufacturing industry, fueled largely by investors from Taiwan, Hong Kong, and more recently, South Korea, are generating the demand for raw hides and skins. While U.S. product quality is highly regarded, Australia is an effective price competitor. The rapid increase in both exports and imports in 1994 and 1995 is reflected in first quarter data. U.S. trade data also shows U.S. exports in the first two months of 1994 at an eight-fold increase over the same period in 1993 (58). Some data for recent years on the hide and skins trade areas follows (figures in millions of $U.S.).

	1993	1994	1995
Total Market Size	n/a	n/a	n/a
Total Local Production	n/a	n/a	n/a
Total Exports	1,396	10,000	12,000
Total Imports	4,645	20,000	25,000
Total Imports from U.S.	1,549	5,000	10,000

China is a net exporter of poultry meat, but because its export and import markets are disjointed, imports are expected to exhibit double-digit growth through the end of the century. Exports are dominated by live bird exports to Hong Kong and chicken pieces to Japan. The import sector consists of primarily of "moving parts," i.e.: paws, wings, wing tips, and legs. Rapid rise of the fast food industry in China, both domestic and foreign, bodes well for continued strong demand for imported poultry meat (58). Some poultry market figures are given below (all figures in millions of $U.S.).

	1993	1994	1995
Total Market Size	5,224	6,005	6,705
Total Local Production	5,300	6,100	6,800
Total Exports	175	220	240
Total Imports	100	125	145
Total Imports from U.S.	69	87	101

Unit: 1,000 metric tons

Oilseed China is an important producer of oilseeds, including peanuts, rapeseed, sesame, seed, sunflower seed, and safflower seed. Oilseed output in 1955 was 4.8 million tons. Output, however, did not expand between 1955 and 1975, which meant per capita oilseed availability decreased substantially because of population growth. Production from 1975 to 1985 more than tripled, to 15.5 million tons, but China continues to have one of the world's lowest levels of per capita consumption of oilseeds (4).

Area sown to oilseeds in 1994 is expected to increase slightly or remain the same as the previous year. The increases in area sown to rapeseed and cottonseed crops are expected to be somewhat more than offsetting the decline in area sown to soybean and peanut crops. After a sharp increase in area in 1993, soybean production is not expected to have another significant area expansion in 1994. Even if soybean prices remain high, limited cultivated area will constrain additional gains. Any area expansion in a crop is at the expense of another crop. In 1993, area sown to cotton dropped by more than 1.8 million hectares and allowed soybean area to increase significantly. However, in 1994/95, cotton area will likely increase about 10 percent over the previous year after the bollworm infestation in 1992 and 1993. With strong domestic demand for soybeans, as reflected by the prevailing high prices, increased soybean output in 1994 will likely come from yield advances. However, soybean output in 1994 is expected to be lower, around 14 million tons, assuming a return to more normal yields.

Similarly, record peanut output of 8.4 million tons in 1993 is not expected to be surpassed easily in the near future because of the record unit yield (2.49 tons/ha) and area required. As in the case of soybeans, the increase largely resulted from a shift in area from cotton, particularly in Shandong Province. In 1994, increased cotton area suggests a slight decline in peanut area. Assuming a more normal yield of 2.3 tons per hectare and area sown to peanuts remaining at 3.3 million hectares, peanut production in 1994 will reach about 7.5 million tons, down 11 percent from last year's record crop.

China's rapeseed area will likely rise slightly in 1994. Rapeseed output, assuming the same yields as in 1993, is expected to be more than 7.5 million tons. Cottonseed production is also expected to improve in 1994, because of a higher area and unit yield. It is generally expected that insect infestation will not be as damaging as in 1992. Finally, sunflower seed production in 1994 is likely to remain roughly the same as its average over the last three or four years, at around 1.3 million tons (53).

After very impressive growth in oilseed crop production in the last fifteen years, China's edible vegetable oil consumption is still very low compared with world averages and with the per capita consumption levels observed in neighboring countries or regions, such as South Korea, Japan, Taiwan, and Hong Kong. China's per capita consumption of edible vegetable oil is only about half of that of South Korea and much lower than Japan and their cousins in Taiwan and Hong Kong (53).

Based on the experiences of other developing countries, China's per capita edible vegetable oil consumption will expand significantly as rapid economic growth continues. In general, an increase of 1 kilogram of edible vegetable for each person in China can be translated into an increased demand of more than 1 million tons per year. With limited cultivated area and a large population, China will either need to import more oilseed or more edible oil to make up the likely deficit, particularly if China's trade regime is liberalized as the country is admitted into GATT. Assuming a more open trading system, China's current under used crushing facilities (including joint ventures) suggest that the country will likely import more beans in the future, because the residuals or meal produced after oil extraction can be used in feed manufacturing to meet the expected rapid growth in livestock output (53).

Oilseed production in 1994 is likely to decline slightly or remain unchanged after increasing 16 percent in 1993 to a record 38.3 million tons. Enormous increases in soybean and peanut output in 1993 offset declines in other oilseeds. Because of rapid economic growth and population increases, China's long-run domestic demand for edible vegetable oil and soybean meal will continue rising (53).

Potatoes Both Irish and sweet potatoes are grown in China. In the 1980s, about 20 percent of output came from Irish potatoes grown mostly in the northern part of the country. The remaining 80 percent of output came primarily from sweet potatoes grown in central and sough China (cassava output was also included in total potato production). Potatoes are generally considered to be a somewhat lower quality food grain. Per capita, consumption has declined through time. Potatoes are also used in the production of vodka and as a livestock feed (4).

Rice In 1987 China was the world's largest producer of rice, and the crop make up a little less than half of the country's total grain output. In a given year, total rice output came from four different crops. The early rice crop grows primarily in provinces along the Chang Jiang and in provinces in the south; it is planted in February to April and harvested in June and July and contributes about 34 percent to total rice output. Intermediate and single crop late rice grows in the southwest and along the Chang Jiang; it is planted in March to June and harvested in October and November and also contributed about 34 percent to total rice output in the 1980s. Double crop late rice, planted after the early crop is reaped, is harvested in October to November and adds about 25 percent to total rice production. Rice grown in the north is planted from April to June and harvested from September to October; it contributes about 7 percent to total production.

All rice cultivation is highly labor intensive. Rice is generally grown as a wetland crop in fields flooded to supply water during the growing season. Transplanting seedlings requires many hours of labor, as does harvesting. Mechanization of rice cultivation only minimally advanced. Rice cultivation also demands more of other inputs, such as fertilizer, than most other crops.

Rice is highly prized by consumers as a food grain, especially in south China, and per capita consumption has risen through the years. Also, as incomes have risen, consumers have preferred to eat more rice and less potatoes, corn, sorghum, and millet. Large production increases in the early 1980s and poor local transportation systems combined to induce farmers to feed large quantities of lower quality rice to livestock.

China is one of the world's largest rice exporters, annually shipping out about 1 million tons. Rice exports go primarily to Asian and East European countries and to Cuba (4).

Rice output for 1993 was 177.7 million tons (paddy basis), down 4.6 percent from he 186.2 million ton 1992 crop. The primary reason for the decrease stemmed from a 5.4 percent decrease in area from 32.1 million hectares in 1992 to 30.4 million hectares in 1993. In the south, farmers increased the area sown to high quality Indica rice and in the north they grew more high quality Japonica rice. These increases, however, were more than offset by the reduced area sown to low quality, early rice crops in south China. Rice yields in 1993 rose 0.9 percent.

Consumers in urban areas are eating less rice and more meat, fruits, vegetables, and wheat products. The opening of rural and urban free markets in the early 1980's and the announced ending of the planned purchase and planned supply system in April 1993 allowed farmers to respond to market signals and consumers to purchase rice in open markets. This set the stage for a revolution in rice consumption patterns. Previous policy stressed increasing rice output with little regard for quality. With open markets, consumers in south China bid up the price for high quality intermediate and late crop rices at the expense of the low quality early rice. Urban consumers pay top prices for specialty rices such as jasmine Thai rice.

USDA estimates rice stocks for 1993 at 24.89 million tons. Farm families generally try to keep six months to two years worth on hand for their own requirements and as a kind of insurance policy against crop failures, breakdowns in the transportation system, and ill health. Enterprises from the old Grain Bureau try to keep about a three month stock of rice on hand to supply urban residents. Some rice stocks are also held in the State Council's controlled strategic grain reserves.

In most years, China is a rice importer and exporter. China's exports climbed from 933,000 tons in 1991/92 to 1.5 million tons in 1993/94. China shipped 1.04 million tons of japonica rice to Japan. Lower quality rice was shipped to Cuba, Europe, and Africa. Imports have steadily fallen from 1 million tons in 1988/89 to 400,000 tons in 1993/94. Most imports come from North Korea and Thailand and some from Vietnam (not recorded in custom data) (53).

Seafood Aquatic production increased slowly after 1950s, reaching 6.2 million tons in 1985. Output is composed of both marine and freshwater fish, shellfish, and kelp. Marine products contributed 63 percent to total aquatic production. Fishermen collected more than 83 percent of marine output from the open seas. The remaining 17 percent of output came from sea farms along China's coasts (4).

The freshwater catch accounted for 37 percent of total aquatic output in the mid-1980s. Fish farming in ponds accounted for 80 percent of the total freshwater catch; only 20 percent was collected in natural rivers, lakes, and streams. Fish from all sources provides consumers with an important source of protein and added variety in their diet (4).

China, which farmed fish 5,000 years ago, has more than 90 percent of world aquaculture production, but indoor Chinese systems are mainly hatcheries. This could be an interesting focus for future development, given the huge potential market.

Soybeans Soybeans, a leguminous crop, are also included in China's grain statistics. The northeast has traditionally been the most important producing area, but substantial amounts of soybeans are also produced on the North China Plain. Production of soybeans declined after the Great Leap Forward, and output did not regain the 10 million ton level of the late 1950s until 1985. Population growth has greatly outstripped soybean output, and per capita consumption has fallen. Soybeans are a useful source of protein and fat, an important consideration given the limited amount of meat available and the grain- and vegetable-based diet. Oilseed cakes, by-products of soybean oil extraction, are used as animal feed and fertilizer (4).

Soybeans have been a major foreign exchange earner for most of this century. Static production and rising domestic demand for soybeans and soybean products meant a decline in exports until the early 1980s. For example, in 1981, Argentina and the United States shipped more than 500,000 tons of soybeans to China; these two countries and Brazil also exported soybean oil to China. Domestic production expanded in the early 1980s, however, and by 1985 soybean imports fell and exports exceeded 1 million tons. Also in the early 1980s, China began to ship soybean meal to Asian markets.

Sugar Sugarcane accounted for about 83 percent of total output of sugar crops in 1985. Major producing provinces include Guangdong, Fujian, and Yunnan Provinces and Guangxi-Zhuang Autonomous Region. Production has grown steadily through the years from about 8 million tons in 1955 to over 51 million tons in 1985.

Sugar beet production accounted for the remaining 17 percent of total output in 1985. Major producing provinces and autonomous regions include Heilongjiang, Jilin, Nei Mongol, and Xinjiang. Sugar beet production rose from 1.6 million tons in 1955 to 8.9 million tons in 1985. Despite these impressive increases in output, per capita consumption was still very low, and large quantities were imported.

Sugar imports to China come primarily from Australia, Cuba, the Philippines, and Thailand. Quantities imported climbed steadily from 100,000 tons in 1955 to 500,000 tons in the mid-1970s and continued to rise dramatically to a peak of more than 2 million tons in 1985.

China's 1993/94 (October/September) sugar output is expected to fall 18.1 percent from the previous year to 6.8 million tons raw value. Marketing and price reforms introduced in 1991 and 1992, combined with record output in 1991/92, caused sugar crop and refined sugar prices to fall in 1992/93. Cane and beet production were also affected by rising input costs, the use of IOUs by sugar mills in some regions, and increased returns from competing crops. China's State Statistical Bureau reported 1993/94 beet production falling 20 percent to 12 million tons and cane output declining 12 percent to 64.2 million tons (53).

Although lower retail sugar prices played a role in reduced 1993/94 crop output, beet production was seriously affected by low returns relative to other competing crops under the new liberalized system of government non-intervention in planting and procurement pricing decisions. Farmers were free to choose what crop they preferred to plant, while mills were forced to purchase beets based on the expected returns for refined sugar on the open market. Low sugar prices, lower returns relative to cane production, and the memory of delayed payments during the previous year's beet procurement season all combined to dramatically reduce sugar crop production.

Though sugar beet area only fell 9.2 percent, production fell 20 percent, declining from 15.1 million tons in 1992/93 to 12 million in 1993/94. Beet sugar output also declined, falling to 1.17 million tons (table 10). Reduced profits for beet production even prompted area to decline in what had been a rapidly expanding beet area, the Xinjiang Autonomous Region. Major competing crops for beet area in the Northeast include grains and soybeans.

Cane area and production also fell in 1993.94 because of low returns, particularly in Guangdong Province. Cane sugar production declined as well, falling from 6.65 million tons in 1992/93 to an estimated 5.63 million in 1993/94. Low procurement prices, reduced incentives, the increased competition for area from non-agricultural projects (roads, factories, houses) caused Guangdong can area and production to fall sharply. Cane production fell more modestly in the other two major cane producing provinces, Guangxi and Yunnan. Guangxi retained its position as the number one producing province. Guangdong cane output fell more than 6.6 million tons to 17.1 million, while Guangxi production fell less than 500,000 tons to 23.1 million. The reduction of Guangdong cane area and production is likely to be permanent.

The precipitous decline in refined sugar availability and rising consumer prices reduced China's 1993/94 sugar consumption by 12 percent to 6.9 million tons. Although the government moved to increase supply by expanding import quotas and releasing sugar from state reserves, it was not enough to counter the decline in domestic production. Increased supply in 1994/95 is expected to raise consumption 7 percent to 7.4 million tons—though still well short of the 1992/93 record of 7.8 million.

Rising consumer incomes and rapid growth in the food processing and beverage industry will support continued increases in per capita consumption well into the next century. Sugar officials in China estimate that between 1979/80 and 1992/93, the share of total sugar supply utilized by the food and beverage industry increased from 30 percent to 65 percent. China's sugar production is expected to increase in the future in response to this demand, though China will still need to gradually increase imports to supply the burgeoning food processing industry (53).

Timber Forests were cleared in China's main agricultural areas centuries ago. Most timber, therefore, comes from the northeast China and the less densely populated parts of the northwest and southwest. The yield totalled around 60 million cubic meters in 1985. Bamboo poles and products are grown in the Chan Jiang Valley and in south China, and output reached 230 million poles in 1985.   Rubber trees are cultivated in Guangdong Province; output rose steadily from 68,000 tons in 1975 to 190,000 tons in 1985.   Other important forestry products include lacquer, tea oilseed, tung oil, pine resin, walnuts, chestnuts, plywood, and fiberboard (4).

The area covered by forests amounted to some 12 percent of total land area, which officials hoped to increase over the long term to 30 percent.   Afforestation campaigns are carried out annually to re-establish forest, plant shelter belts, and set up soil stabilization areas.   But because of continued overcutting of forests and low seedling survival rates in newly planted sections, China's forests are in a precarious situation.   Better management and increased investment over a long period of time will be required to increase output of valuable forest products (4).

China is perpetually in short supply of wood.   This shortage is becoming especially acute in light of China's unprecedented building boom.   Wood is required for use in both housing and infrastructure development.   Therefore, exports of logs to China will always be a major opportunity for the United States.   U.S. softwood logs have come under heavy competition from cheaper tropical hardwood from southeast Asia.   However, that trend is now reversing itself as many southeast Asia countries recognize the value of preserving their rain forests, and China must once again look north for wood supplies.   Recent competition is coming from Russia, but fortunately Chinese buyers are familiar with U.S. wood, and are willing to pay a premium for it due to its superior quality.   In addition to logs, the market for hardwoods and panel products is also bright in China, but so far these markets are not as well developed as the market for logs (58).   Some data on dollar values of the log trade in millions of $U.S. are as follows:

	1993	1994	1995
Total Market Size	55,050	57,000	58,000
Total Local Production	52,000	53,000	53,500
Total Exports	100	100	100
Total Imports	3,150	3,900	4,400
Total Imports from U.S.	1,316	2,000	2,200

Tobacco   China is the world's largest producer of leaf tobacco.   Farmers produce many kinds of tobacco, but flue-cured varieties often make up more than 80 percent of total output.   Major producing areas include Henan, Shandong, Sichuan, Guizhou, and Yunnan provinces (4).

Another bumper tobacco harvest in 1992 prompted government calls for reducing production and area.   Growth in cigarette output and factory profits continues to slow as the government tobacco monopoly reigns in unauthorized cigarette output and rampant smuggling of foreign brands.   Cigarette supply continues to outstrip demand, particularly at the low end of the market 46).

<u>Vegetables</u> China is the world's largest producer and consumer of vegetables and is the fifth leading exporter. In 1991, China's farmers were estimated to have produced more than 170 million tons of vegetables compared with U.S. vegetable output of 28 million tons. In 1993, the United States exported $1.5 million worth of vegetables to China while importing $103 million from China. In the coming decade, U.S. vegetable exports to China will expand but imports from China will also grow. Competition between the U.S. and China producers and processors for foreign vegetable markets likely will be keen (53).

In 1992, china exported 3.1 million tons of vegetables worth 1.3 billion. With the introduction of modern processing and packaging equipment, and the development of storage, handling, transportation, and retailing facilities, China could become a formidable competitor in international vegetable markets, but at the same time, China's vegetable imports likely will increase as well (53).

<u>Wheat</u> In 1987, China ranked third in the world as a producer of wheat. Winter wheat, which in the same year accounted for about 88 percent of total national output, is grown primarily in the Chang Jiang Valley and on the North China Plain. The crop is sown each fall from September through November and is harvested in May and June the subsequent year. Spring wheat is planted each spring in the north and northeast and is harvested in late summer. Spring wheat contributes about 12 percent of total wheat output.

Wheat is the staple food grain in north China and is eaten in the form of steamed bread and noodles. Per capita consumption has risen, and the demand for wheat flour has increased as incomes have risen. Wheat has been by far the most important imported grain.

Wheat had been imported nearly every year since the early 1950s. These imports averaged about 5 million tons in the 1960s and 1970s, but rose to a peak of more than 13 million tons in 1982. Wheat imports fell as wheat output expanded rapidly, so that by 1985 imports fell to just under 5.5 million tons. Argentina, Australia, Canada, France, and the United States have been major sources of China's wheat imports (4).

U.S. wheat exports to China declined only slightly, from 3.0 million tons in 1992 to 2.7 million in 1993, despite the 40 percent decline in China's overall wheat imports. The United States was successful in maintaining exports, in value terms, and increasing share because of higher wheat prices. Wheat export value rose nearly 2 percent to $278 million in 1993. Wheat has always been a leading U.S. agricultural commodity to China, accounting for 74 percent of total value in 1993. U.S. 1994 wheat exports to China are forecast to remain near 1993 because China has reaped bumper grain harvests for four consecutive years and has large grain stocks (53).

Wheat output for 1994 is projected at 103 million tons, more than 3 million tons below the record 1993 crop. Wheat prices rose in the last few months of 1993, which heightened growers enthusiasm to grow wheat. Retail flour prices in open markets rose from 1,593 RMB per ton in December 1993 to 1,750 RMB in April 1994, a ten percent increase (5). But the rising prices were not sufficient to motivate farmers to boost area. Wheat area is projected at 29.6 million hectares, down more than 635,000 ha from last year. Some very dry, hot weather in the North China Plains could limit yield growth in 1994, and yields are projected at 3.5 tons per ha.

Wheat imports for the June/July 1994/95 year are projected to reach 10 million tons because of the projected lower 1994 crop and because the overly large wheat stocks of the past will be worked down. Imports will help meet consumer demand for higher quality and specialty wheats, and to overcome domestic transportation constraints.

China remains a major importer of U.S. wheat, despite the recent decline in purchases. The underlying demand factors, i.e.: limited land, increasing population, wider variety of wheat, and basic food products, indicate that China will continue to be a major consumer and importer of wheat.   Imports continue to be controlled by the central government and purchases are handled by a grain monopoly (58).

Wheat production in 1993 reached a record 106.4 million tons, 4.7 percent above 1992, as area decreased 0.9 percent to 30.2 million hectares, and yields increased 5.6 percent to 3.5 metric tons per hectare because of efficient use of inputs and good weather. Both winter and spring wheat regions had favorable growing conditions in 1993 resulting in a good quality wheat crop.

Rising incomes and population increases were the primary forces supporting demand for wheat. Wheat consumption rose steadily over the last decade, but the rate of increase slowed in 1992 and 1993. Urban consumers in north China continue to eat more high quality baked goods, cookies, and instant noodles. But urban consumers in south China also are changing their tastes from traditional rice to wheat products.

With the growing importance of open retail markets and the government's decision to end the grain rationing system in April 1993, consumers are demanding higher quality wheat products. Consumers used to have little recourse to poor quality rationed flour, but open markets now offer different brands of high quality flour.

Wheat imports for the July 1993/June 1994 year are estimated at 4.5 million tons, down from the 6.7 million tons imported in 1992 and 15.8 million tons in 1991. There are several factors behind the decline in imports. In 1992 and 1993, farmers harvested back-to-back record wheat crops. In April 1993, the government announced the end of its planned supply system in which it guaranteed urban residents wheat rations. This policy, along with the government's reorganization of the Grain Bureau, in which the government reduced its subsidies for wheat stocks, led many enterprises in the grain economy to evaluate wheat stock positions. These enterprises found they were holding larger wheat stocks than they could afford and took measures to reduce stocks. These actions led to a temporary bulge in available supplies, and hence, less demand for imported wheat. After some period of time the wheat stock issue will be resolved and normal wheat trade should continue (53).

China's rising consumption may some day turn it into a giant food importer like Japan and place enormous strains on the world's grain supplies. This nightmare could happen if an abrupt decline in China's ability to feed itself coincides with grain shortages that could force the U.S. and other exporting countries to impose export restrictions or even outright embargoes.

This crisis is seen brewing in China's booming economy and its effects on eating habits and land use. Pork consumption per person in China has risen to the level of industrial countries, pushing China ahead of the U.S. as the world's leading consumer of red meat. At the same time, China is suffering from a massive loss of crop land similar to what Japan,

Taiwan and South Korea have experienced. By 2030, China could have a grain shortage of 216 million tons, which would exceed the world's entire 1993 grain surplus of 200 million tons.

CHAPTER 4

INDUSTRIAL MARKETS

China's industrial sector has shown great progress since 1949, but in the late 1980s it remained undeveloped in many respects. Although the country manufactured nuclear weapons and delivery systems and could launch domestically produced satellites, many of its industries used technologies of the 1950s. Although China was one of the world's largest producers of fuel in the mid-1980s and had the world's largest hydroelectric power potential, frequent energy shortages caused lengthy factory shutdowns. Despite massive coal reserves in north China, transportation deficiencies necessitated coal imports to south China. Research institutes developed sophisticated industrial technologies, but bureaucratic and political obstacles impeded implementation.

To solve these and other problems, the Chinese leadership initiated sweeping economic reforms in the late 1970s. Although specific industrial reforms were not clearly defined, broad goals included loosening bureaucratic controls on enterprises and managers to promote a decentralization of authority. Other broad goals were to increase worker productivity by offering incentives; to give market forces greater influence on output mix, purchases, sales, and hiring; to make enterprises operate more efficiently and be responsible for profits and losses; and to restructure the price system to reflect supply and demand more accurately.

Another major goal of the reform program was development of light industry. Beginning with the First Five-Year Plan (1953-57), China adopted the Soviet model of economic development, stressing a heavy industrial base. However, this emphasis seriously strained China's resources and capital and led the leadership in the late 1970s to shift to development of light industry. Because light industry is labor intensive, this shift helped to alleviate unemployment. It also satisfied growing consumer demand, which had not been met because of overemphasis on heavy industry. Another reason for diversification into light industry was the desire to increase exports to obtain much-needed foreign currency.

By the mid-1980s, industrial reforms had achieved substantial success in some areas. Industrial output was about twenty-five times that of 1952. A wide range of modern industries had been established, and the country was one of the world's leading producers of coal, textiles, and bicycles. There were major plants in almost every key industry, and a strong effort had been made to introduce manufacturing into undeveloped and rural areas. Light industry output of consumer goods had increased dramatically. In some cases, enterprises reduced operating costs, managers were able to exercise greater autonomy, and technical innovations were implemented to increase efficiency.

Despite these bright spots in the 1980s, overall results were disappointing to Chinese economic planners. Major problems included failure to reform the price system, interference of local cadres in the managers' operation of enterprises, and perpetuation of the life tenure, "iron rice bowl" system for workers. Rapid industrial growth made energy shortages one of the most critical problems facing the economy, limiting industrial enterprises and mines to 70 or 80 percent of capacity. According to China's energy planners, the country would have to quadruple electricity production to meet the gross value of industrial and agricultural output target for the year 2000. For a quick increase in output, the industry emphasized short-term development of thermal power plants. For the long term, China planned to rely on its vast hydroelectric power potential and nuclear power to meet electricity demand.

In the 1980s, large scale, centrally controlled plants dominated manufacturing. These large plants were supplemented with many small scale town and township enterprises, which accounted for significant percentages of national output of coal, construction materials, and leather products.

TRENDS IN INDUSTRIAL PRODUCTION

The shifts in economic policy typical of the People's Republic of China since 1949 have strongly affected industrial production. In the period of recovery from World War II and the Chinese civil war of 1945-49, industrial output more than doubled as plants were repaired and employment rose. The First Five-Year Plan concentrated on constructing plants and equipment for heavy industry, much of it with Soviet assistance. The machinery, iron and steel, and mining industries all built their foundations on this period. The increases in productive capacity resulted in a second doubling of output.

The Great Leap Forward (1958-60) saw production surge by 45 percent in 1958 as new plants went into operation, facilities operated beyond capacity, and great numbers of small local plants were established. But the overambitious plan to revamp China's economy soon encountered problems of misallocation and overextension of resources. The demands of the Great Leap Forward left the work force physically exhausted. As the overburdened economy began to collapse, growth fell to 22 percent in 1959 and 4 percent in 1960. Output dropped precipitously in 1961 because of the earlier withdrawal of Soviet technicians, misallocation of resources, and a serious food shortage. In 1962, with the restoration of planning and coordination, production began to recover. Industrial priorities were transferred from production of industrial goods to agricultural inputs and consumer goods. By 1965, most sectors of industry had regained their 1957 production levels.

In the early stages of the Cultural Revolution (1966-76), production declined when civil disturbances disrupted factories and transport in the big industrial cities. In 1967 output fell, and it remained below the 1966 level in 1968. After order was restored, production recovered in 1969 and grew by 18 percent in 1970. With resumption of growth and the beginning of the Fourth Five-Year Plan (1971-75), output grew by over 10 percent in 1971 and 1972 and by 13 percent in 1973. A wide-ranging program of investment in plants and equipment, including foreign imports, raised industrial capacity. Throughout the 1970s thousands of new, small-scale plants added significantly to levels of production, especially in coal, chemical fertilizer, cement, and electricity, although there were some setbacks. In the mid-1970s, the influence of the Gang of Four and disruption by the succession struggle again reduced industrial output. Political activities in factories and uncertainty of managers and planners caused growth to fall to 4.4 percent in 1974. Growth recovered to 10.3 percent in 1975 but fell to zero in 1976 in the uncertainty surrounding the deaths of Mao Zedong and Zhou Enlai, the second fall of Deng Xiaoping, and the destruction caused by the Tangshan earthquake.

In 1977 and 1978, the Four Modernization effort began in earnest. Growth reached 14 percent in 1977, when political stability was restored and plants resumed full operation. The high growth rate in 1977 and 1978 caused a serious overheating of the economy, however. At the end of 1978, the leadership introduced a comprehensive economic reform. In 1979 the economy entered a period of readjustment, emphasizing a slower, more rational rate of growth. Policy stressed development of light industry and gave priority to the textile and consumer industries in supplying raw and unfinished materials, power, fuel, and finances. Capital investment in light industry increased from 5.4 percent in 1978 to about 8 percent in 1980. Between 1978 and 1981, the proportion of light industry in gross industrial output value increased by about 9 percent. The rate of capital construction decreased, and the government initiated a major drive to correct imbalances in the economy by gearing production to consumer needs and improving efficiency.

In 1983 the government took measures to economize on fuel, energy, raw materials, and working capital. The policy experimentally granted enterprises more autonomy. It introduced new kinds of contracts, permitting limited competition among enterprises serving the same markets. The government began to allow market forces to determine production. At the Third Plenum of the Twelfth National Party Congress Central Committee in October 1984, the party officially reiterated its commitment to reform the urban economy, signaling a high priority for industrial modernization.

The Seventh Five-Year Plan (1986-90) called for greater responsiveness to consumer demand, increased efficiency, and a further assimilation of modern technology. The plan sought to accelerate development of the energy and raw materials industries and control growth of manufacturing industries, making the two sectors develop more proportionately. Development of the transportation and communications sectors received high priority, and plans called for expanding the building industry. The leadership hoped to speed development of tertiary industry, such as restaurants and small shops, to meet consumer needs.

The best prospects for sales by the U.S. to the P.R.C. have been reviewed in some detail by the International Trade Administration, Office of the PRC and Hong Kong of the U.S. Department of Commerce and are abstracted here, category by category.

The best prospects are summarized in Tables 73 and 74 which follow—the first in alphabetical order and the second in the order of estimated importance (3).

The various industry market segments will be discussed here in alphabetical order. Where available, detailed analysis os the various sectors will be abstracted from the many documents published by the International Trade Administration of the U.S. Department of Commerce.

The most effective way to promote a product in China is through personal, face-to-face contact with a potential customer. This will not only enable the seller to demonstrate the merits of his product but will also enable him to establish the personal relationship with the buyer that is necessary for any long term negotiation or sales. The best way to meet the most number of people in both the industry and the appropriate government offices is to participate in a trade exhibition. This will also have the added benefit of providing up-to-date exposure to market trends and preferences as well as enable the exhibitor to get a feel for some of his competition.

Table 73

China Markets for U.S. Industry (in order of importance) (3)

Rank	Code	Description
1	AIR	Aircraft and Parts
2	AGC	Agricultural Chemicals
3	ICH	Industrial Chemicals
4	OGM	Oil and Gas Field Machinery and Services
5	CPT	Computers and Peripherals
6	MIN	Mining Industry Equipment
7	TEL	Telecommunications Equipment
8	ELP	Electric Power Systems
9	APG	Airport and Ground Support Equipment
10	AGM	Agricultural Machinery
11	CHM	Chemical Production Machinery
12	PMR	Plastic Materials and Resins
13	PTE	Power Transmission Equipment
14	APS	Automotive Parts and Service Equipment
15	LAB	Laboratory Scientific Instruments
16	PME	Plastics Production Machinery
17	FPP	Food Processing/Packaging
18	PKG	Packaging Equipment
19	TXM	Textile Machinery
20	CSF	Computer Software
21	MED	Medical Equipment
22	TXF	Textile Fabrics
23	EIP	Electronics Production and Test Equipment
24	PAP	Paper/paperboard
25	MTL	Machine Tools/Metalworking Equipment
26	CSV	Computer Services
27	CON	Construction Equipment
28	BLD	Building Products
29	FOD	Foods, Processed
30	PCI	Process Controls—Industrial
31	PVC	Pumps, Valves and Compressors
32	ACE	Architectural/Construction/Engineering Services

33	PUL	Pulp/paper machinery

Other Best Prospects: Not updated for 1993, but considered attractive markets. (In alphabetical order.)

--	APP	Apparel
--	DNT	Dental Equipment
--	DRG	Drugs and Pharmaceuticals
--	ELC	Electronic Components
--	MHM	Materials Handling Equipment
--	PGA	Printing/Graphics
--	POL	Pollution Control Equipment
--	PRT	Port and Shipbuilding Equipment
--	RRE	Railroad Equipment
--	WRE	Water Resources Equipment
--	YAR	Yarns

China's best commercial market prospects for U.S. companies in the 1994-95 period, in order of estimated importance (based on size and growth potential), are set forth below (58).

Rank	Description
1	Aircraft and Parts
2	Electric Power System
3	Computers and Peripherals
4	Telecommunications Equipment
5	Automotive Parts and Service Equipment
6	Agricultural Chemicals
7	Industrial Chemicals
8	Plastic Material and Resins
9	Chemical Production Machinery
10	Building Products
11	Pumps, Valves, and Compressors
12	Electronic Components
13	Machine Tool Equipment
14	Oil and Gas Field Machinery Service
15	Medical Equipment
16	Laboratory Scientific Instruments
17	Electronic Production and Test Equipment
18	Mining Industry Equipment
19	Construction Equipment
20	Process Controls - Industrial
21	Insurance

22	Pulp/Paper and Paper Machinery	
23	Pollution Control	
24	Computer Software	
25	Food Processing/Packaging	
26	Pharmaceuticals	
27	Agricultural Machinery	
28	Telecommunication Services	

Table 74

China Markets for U.S. Industry (in alphabetical order) (3)

Rank	Code	Description
33	ACE	Architectural/Construction/Engineering Services
2	AGC	Agricultural Chemicals
10	AGM	Agricultural Machinery
1	AIR	Aircraft and Parts
--	APP	Apparel
14	APS	Automotive Parts and Service Equipment
9	APG	Airport and Ground Support Equipment
28	BLD	Building Products
11	CHM	Chemical Production Machinery
27	CON	Construction Equipment
20	CSF	Computer Software
5	CPT	Computers and Peripherals
26	CSV	Computer Services
--	DNT	Dental Equipment
--	DRG	Drugs and Pharmaceuticals
23	EIP	Electronics Production and Test Equipment
--	ELC	Electronic Components
8	ELP	Electric Power Systems
30	FOD	Foods, Processed
17	FPP	Food Processing/Packaging
3	ICH	Industrial Chemicals
15	LAB	Laboratory Scientific Instruments
21	MED	Medical Equipment
--	MHM	Materials Handling Equipment
6	MIN	Mining Industry Equipment
25	MTL	Machine Tools/Metalworking Equipment
4	OGM	Oil and Gas Field Machinery and Services
24	PAP	Paper/paperboard
31	PCI	Process Controls—Industrial

--	PGA	Printing/Graphics
18	PKG	Packaging Equipment
16	PME	Plastics Production Machinery
12	PMR	Plastic Materials and Resins
--	POL	Pollution Control Equipment
--	PRT	Port and Shipbuilding Equipment
13	PTE	Power Transmission Equipment
34	PUL	Pulp/paper machinery
32	PVC	Pumps, Valves and Compressors
--	RRE	Railroad Equipment
7	TEL	Telecommunications Equipment
22	TXF	Textile Fabrics
19	TXM	Textile Machinery
--	WRE	Water Resources Equipment
--	YAR	Yarns

The above tabulations refer to industrial markets. In a recent report (58), agricultural market prospects have also been surveyed.

China's best agricultural market prospects for U.S. companies in the 1994-95 period, in order of estimated importance (based on size and growth potential), are set forth below.

Rank	Description
1	Wheat
2	Cotton
3	Logs
4	Hides and Skins
5	Poultry Meat
6	Tree Nuts (Pistachios)
7	Dried Fruits (Raisins)
8	Snack Foods

AGRICULTURAL CHEMICALS (INCLUDING FERTILIZER)
The Department of Commerce review of this market segment is given in Table 75.

Table 75

Review of Agricultural Chemicals (including Fertilizers) (3)

A)	Three-letter ITA industry sector code:		AGC
B)	Est. total market size (USD Million):		
	1991 -		$7,000
	1992 -		$7,350
	1993 -		$7,717
	1994 -		$8,180
	1995 -		$8,670
C)	Est. 1992-4 annual market growth rate:	5%	
D)	Est. total imports (USD Million):		
	1991 -		$2,000
	1992 -		$2,140
	1993 -		$2,918
	1994 -		$2,790
	1995 -		$2,600
E)	Est. annual total import growth rate:	5%	
F)	Est. imports from U.S. (USD Million):		
	1991 -		$600
	1992 -		$660
	1993 -		$762
	1994 -		$754
	1995 -		$748 (58)
G)	Est. annual growth of imports from USA:	10%	
H)	China's receptivity to U.S. Products in this sector (5 - High/1 - Low):		3
I)	Competition from local/third-countries for U.S. firms (5 - Low/1 - High):		2
J)	Chinese market barriers to U.S. sales in this sector (5 - Few/1 - Many):		3

K) Comments - Factors for increased U.S. sales:

- U.S. fertilizer exports to CHINA jumped 81% from 1990 to 1991. Fertilizer accounts for most of the ag-chemicals market; more than 20% is imported (one of China's largest import categories).
- Phosphate & Potassium demand is growing fast.
- About 40% of China's pesticides/herbicides are imported.
- New patent law and U.S-China agreement on intellectual property protection will reduce rampant piracy offering new opportunities; investment in JV's may be an attractive strategy.

L)	MOST PROMISING SUB-SECTORS	1992 MARKET SIZE
	1. High-grade (urea) nitrogen fertilizer	$2,000 million
	2. Potassium & phosphate fertilizer	$1,000 million
	3. Selective pesticides	$ 500 million

With one-fifth of the world's population concentrated in just 7% of the world's arable land, agricultural space is at a premium in China, necessitating wide use of fertilizers. the country is already the third largest fertilizer manufacturer. But 76% of its production is nitrogen, which tends to be overused. Production of phosphate and potash fertilizers will develop as infrastructure projects allow extraction of the minerals. But for the time being it is often cheaper for China to import, and the amount of foreign purchases is high, running about equal to the country's 20 million m.t./year fertilizer capacity.

There are plans to build a number of new units and transform older plants to build capacity to 26 million m.t./year by 1995 and 30 m.t./year by 2000. Under the eighth Five-Year Plan (1991-95), capacity will be increased to 7.36 million m.t./year and to 3.7 million m.t./year in the ninth plan (1995-2000). Under the current plan, a better balance is sought in production of nitrogen (76% of the domestic total), phosphate (23%), and potash (1%).

Fertilizer production and use for 1994 likely will grow slowly because energy, labor, and raw material costs will be higher and farmers' profit margins will be reduced. In 1993, fertilizer production was down slightly. The state fixed price of urea rose from 538 RMB per ton before October 1, 1992, to 660 RMB after that date. By March 1993, the price rose again to 1,000 RMB and another 11 percent by May 1994. The rapid rise in fertilizer prices during the last half of 1993 dampened prospects for fertilizer use in 1994 even though grain prices in the last quarter of 1993 rose in some provinces. Fertilizer prices rose much faster than grain prices so that fertilizer sales in the first half of 1994 have been below the previous year. Retail market prices for urea fluctuated even more radically than state prices. Areas with healthy financial reserves are attempting to build up strategic fertilizer reserves to dampen fluctuations in prices (53).

In the past few years, China chemical fertilizer use on a product weight basis has been 120 to 130 million tons. About 105 million tons, or 87.5 percent of total supply, was produced domestically and 15 million tons or 12.5 percent was imported. China's Customs Administration reported imports of 10.2 million tons (product weight) of chemical fertilizers in 1993, down 45 percent from 1992. Urea fertilizer imports decreased by 52 percent while imports of compound fertilizers dropped to 3.6 million tons, a decrease of 45 percent.

The State Council set the domestic chemical fertilizer production target for the end of the eighth 5-Year Plan (1991-1995) at 125 million tons. Authorities plan to expand capacity by 20 million metric tons in the next two years. That target is to be composed of 92.2 million tons of nitrogen fertilizer, 32.3 million tons of phosphorous fertilizers, and 420,000 tons of potassium fertilizers. Here we have an interesting insight into some elements of current economic policy making. On the one hand, we see evidence that state planners have been active in setting physical output targets for chemical fertilizer production. Yet on the other hand, we see that market forces have created conditions in which fertilizer plants have over capacity—they can produce more fertilizers than farmers are willing to purchase at current market prices.

In August 1993, the State Council adopted "China's Agricultural Development Program for the 1990's." By the year 2000, investments will be made to expand chemical fertilizer capacity to produce 150 million tons. Specifically, the government plans to transform small chemical fertilizer plants and introduce new kinds of fertilizers (53).

Domestic pesticide production in 1993 decreased to 249,000 tons, down 12.3 percent from 1992. Demand and, subsequently, output fell because rising input costs pushed pesticide prices above what many farmers were willing to pay given slowly rising agricultural product prices. Stocks built up and producers reduced output.

Usually output and use data of various kinds of chemical pesticides are aggregated together, but recently published documents reveal several facets of China's pesticide use. In 1991, the aggregate domestically manufactured pesticide output was composed of 77.5 percent insecticides, 13.8 percent fungicides, and 7.9 percent herbicides. Total supply of pesticides from domestic production and imports rose from 104,000 tons in 1960 to a peak of 618,000 tons in 1979. High pesticide use in this period was dictated by commune agricultural technology specialists who had abundant supplies at relatively low prices. Under the economic reforms, farmers applied pesticides on a benefit cost basis, and use dropped sharply so that supply in 1987 was only 171,000 tons. Since then farmers have sought more effective pesticides which are less dangerous to use and are more environmentally sound.

Since economic reforms began in 1979, about 10 percent of pesticide supplies have come from imports. Over the past seven years (a period in which there is PRC trade data), insecticides accounted for 59 percent of total imports; herbicides, 33 percent; fungicides, 7 percent; and disinfectants and rodenticides, 1 percent. In 1992, China imported $203 million worth of pesticides, mostly insecticides and herbicides, of which the United States accounted for $44 million (53).

Some useful contacts in the agricultural chemicals sector include:

Gangzhou Chemical Fertilizer Plant
Yunhe, Gangzhou
Hebei Province 061000
Tel: 223511

Guangzhou Nitrogenous Fertilizer Factory
Tianhe District, Guangzhou
Guangdong Province 510661
Tel: 5515792

Guizhou Chishui Natural Gas Fertilizer Factory
Chishui County, Zunyi Area
Guizhou Province 564700

Hubei Fertilizer Plant
Zhijiang County, Yichang Area
Hubei Province 443200
Tel: 22012

Kunming Sodium Tripolyphosphate Plant
Xishan, Kunming
Yunnan Province 650117
Tel: 90319

Liaohe Chemical Fertilizer Plant
Shuangtaizi, Panjin
Liaoning Province 124021
Tel: 551298

Luzhou Natural Gas Chemical Plant
Luzhou, Sichuan Province 646300
Tel: 22423

Panjin Natural Gas Chemical Plant
Shuangtaizi District, Panjin
Liaoning Province 124021
Tel: 551421

Puyang Zhongyuan Chemical Fertilizer Plant
Puyang, Henan Province 457000
Tel: 44731

Shandong Pesticide Factory
Zhangdian, Zibo
Shandong Province 255009
Tel: 213042

Shijiazhuang Chemical Fertilizer Plant
Chang'an District, Shijiazhuang
Hebei Province 050041
Tel: 649921

Suzhou Agrochemicals Group Corporation
Canlang District, Suzhou
Jiangsu Province 215007
Tel: 551605

Yunnan Natural Gas Chemical Plant
Shuifu County, Zhaotong
Yunnan Province 657800
Tel: 22941

AGRICULTURAL MACHINERY

The Department of Commerce review of this segment is given in Table 76 (3).

The farm machinery market in 1993 showed moderate growth (46). Restrictions on the use of small farm tractors for short distance hauling likely will decrease the demand for these tractors. On the other hand, the demand for farm use trucks, trailers, and small passenger buses will increase. The Information Center of the China National Agricultural Machinery Corporation forecasted that 1993 sales of small, four-wheeled tractors would decrease by 10 to 15 percent. Sales of large farm tractors and implements would rise. The Center noted that there would be a brisk market for heavy duty (crawler type) tractors because of the construction and road-building boom. The Center forecasted that 1993 combined sales would increase slightly to 8,000 units. In 1993, the state planned to reduce by half its mandatory production quotas for farm machinery to help prepare the industry for more open market competition.

Table 76

Review of Agricultural Machinery Market Sector (3)

A)	Three-letter ITA industry sector code	AGM
B)	Est. total market size (USD Millions)	
	1991 -	$ 5,800
	1992 -	$ 6,000
	1993 -	$ 8,999
	1994 -	$ 9,854
	1995 -	$10,791 (58)
C)	Est. 1992-4 annual market growth rate: 10%	
D)	Est. total imports (USD Millions)	
	1991 -	$ 165
	1992 -	$ 180
	1993 -	$1,471
	1994 -	$1,559
	1995 -	$1,652 (58)
E)	Est. annual total import growth rate:	6%
F)	Est. imports from U.S. (USD Millions):	
	1991 -	$15
	1992 -	$18
	1993 -	$30
	1994 -	$32
	1995 -	$34 (58)
G)	Est. annual growth of imports from USA: 5%	
H)	China's receptivity to U.S. products in this sector (5 - High/1 - Low):	3
I)	Competition from local/third-countries for U.S. firms (5 - Low/1 - High):	2

J)   Chinese market barriers to U.S. sales
      in this sector (5 - Few/1 - Many):   2
K)   Comments - Factors for increased U.S. sales:
      •   During the 8th Five-Year Plan, agriculture will be given high priority.
      •   The Chinese government intends to make large investments to improve grain storage
           facilities and update farm machinery; this will create good opportunities for U.S.
           exporters and manufacturers in this field.
      •   U.S. exports are very competitive. Major competition comes from Japan because
           of the soft loans provided by the Japanese Government. Small size tractors are the
           most promising sales prospects.

L)   <u>Most promising sub-sectors</u>   <u>1992 market size</u>
      1.   Grain storage facilities $200 Million
      2.   General farm machinery $100 Million
      3.   Pesticides (note overlap with $ 50 Million
            Agricultural chemicals category above)

Overview Agricultural reforms introduced in China ten years ago dissolved most collective farming areas into household plots. Since then, most farm machinery and equipment sales have been geared to satisfy the needs of small scale production and basic transportation. Specific development projects funded by international development agencies, however, have continued to offer opportunities for large scale equipment sales. Foreign exchange limitations have often made joint venture manufacturing arrangements or technology transfer agreements the only option available for businesses seeking to participate in the China market. Protection of the domestic industry has limited the variety of foreign products that may be introduced into the market. U.S. companies must also compete for a small market with third country manufacturers that are frequently assisted by government supported concessioner financing arrangements.

Agricultural mechanization is a high priority status in the Chinese government's development plans for the near and medium-term future. In order to feed its population, China has taken many modernizing steps to increase agricultural output. Another important goal of the Chinese government is to export an agricultural surplus. With a stated commitment from the central government toward these ends, many opportunities present themselves for U.S. manufacturers as demand for agricultural machinery grows.

Table 77 give statistical data on the agricultural machinery industry (53).

Farm machinery sales slumped 30 to 40 percent in the last half of 1993. While grain prices rose in the last quarter of the year, machinery prices rose even faster. For example, from January 1993 to January 1994, prices of tractors and equipment rose 20 percent while the price of diesel fuel and gasoline rose 80 percent.

Government authorities lifted price controls on a number of key industrial commodities, which resulted in rising prices for farm machinery. In 1993, China's leaders told firms that, with the upcoming accession to the GATT, no special protection would be granted to enterprises in the farm machinery sector. But recently, the government implemented a new consumption tax measure. Some salesmen took advantage of the new measure to raise farm machinery prices. To prevent further such fraudulent practices the China Tax Administration issued a ruling stating that the new consumption tax would not apply to farm machinery sales.

Large tractor production fell from 57,000 in 1992 to 37,000 in 1993 and output of small tractors decreased from 1,391,000 in 1992 to 866,000 in 1993. But aggregate motive power for farm machinery in 1993 rose to 318 billion kwh, an increase of 4.8 percent. Yet the machine-plowed area estimated at 51.4 million hectares remained unchanged from 1991. There are several reasons for this phenomenon. First, many farmers purchased tractors not to plow their fields but to earn cash by hauling freight and passengers on short local hauls. Second, with the rapid rise in diesel fuel prices, farmers tended to use their tractors less and only when they could make a good profit.

During the fifteen years after reforms were initiated (1979-1993), China's farm machinery development can be summarized as follows. The quantity of motive power on farms increased 1.6 times. The number of tractors owned by farm households rose 3.4 times and the number of farm-use trucks expanded 8.5 times. Even with this rapid expansion during the reform period, most of China's farm operations continue to be accomplished with hand labor. For example, in 1991 (the latest year for which there is this kind of data), 34 percent of the sown area was plowed by tractors, 17 percent was machine sown, and only 8 percent was machine harvested.

The State Council's "Agricultural Development Program for the 1990's" notes that by the year 2000, authorities expect farm machinery enterprises will be able to annually produce 200,000 large tractors, 500,000 small tractors, 10,000 combines, and internal combustion engines with a total of 80 million horsepower (53).

Table 77

Statistical Data on the Agricultural Machinery Industry (53)

	1991	1992	1993	Estimated annual real growth over the next 3 years
Import Market	91	180	191	6%
Local Production	6,000	7,900	8,900	10%
Exports	132	151.8	174.5	15%
Total Market Demand	5,959	7,928	8,917	10%
Imports from US	17	27	28.4	5%

Exchange rate used: 5.7 Yuan/$

Future inflation rate assumed: 15%

Estimated 1991 Import Market Shares:

> USA.................18%
> Japan...............40%
> Canada..............7%
> France..............5%
> Germany.............5%
> Italy................. 5%
> Russia...............5%
> South Korea.........5%
> UK.................. 5%
> Ukraine............. 5%

Receptivity code (1-5): 3

Scale: 5 = extremely receptive
          4 = very receptive
          3 = fairly receptive
          2 = somewhat receptive
          1 = not receptive

(The receptivity code represents the degree to which American products are favored in the given market. Although Chinese agricultural producers greatly favor American machinery, generally higher American prices slightly reduce the U.S. receptivity code. American manufacturers face stiff competition from other nations' agricultural machinery manufacturers which present low prices and soft loans granted by their own governments.)

Market Assessment

Market Demand   The Chinese government's agricultural policy places great importance on modernization. At the last National People's Congress, convened on March 15, 1994, the Prime Minister, Li Peng, stated as one of China's new economic goals that the structure of agricultural production must be readjusted (from manual to mechanized labor) in order to develop more efficient farming and greater yields. The National People's Congress also issued a declaration that the current five-year plan (1991-1995) support the agricultural sector, calling this sector the "Foundation of the National Economy." In numerical terms, these policy statements translate into a projected annual 4% rate of growth for agricultural production (53).

In order to achieve ever increasing agricultural production, the Chinese government encourages farmers to increase their level of mechanization. Currently, Chinese agriculture lacks modern agricultural techniques, and is very labor intensive. This labor intensive system reveals itself when one compares percentage of total population engaged in food production, only 1-2% in the United States as opposed to 75-80% in China. The Chinese government recognizes the need to mechanize so that agricultural production maybe raised to the point required to feed the country's huge population.

However, great plans need money to back them up. The Chinese government does not have any funds specifically designated for agricultural mechanization. Rather, following the general decentralizing trend over the past fourteen years, the Chinese government relies on the agricultural producers themselves to purchase and import their own machinery. This decentralization of purchasing decisions has led to much freer controls on import procedures. By looking into the regional markets and not just to the central government agencies in Beijing, U.S. agricultural machinery manufacturers may find fairly promising prospects.

Estimates place the total market demand at $US 7.9 billion for 1992. Most of the goods on this market are produced domestically. Chinese farmers would like to purchase American machinery very much, but costs are often simply too high. The only alternative is buying domestic machinery, which frequently lacks in quality. However, much of the domestic machinery available suits well the needs of most Chinese agricultural producers. Nevertheless, a niche market (the state farms) definitely exists for American equipment.

Long-term prospects for selling on the China market look good. The demand for American agricultural machinery will most likely grow with the continued mechanization trend.

Industrialization will also play a significant factor as agricultural laborers seek manufacturing jobs, having more room in the agricultural sector for increased capital-to-labor ratios.

However, the agricultural sector in China currently faces some serious problems. With central and local government agencies and officials enraptured with the economic reforms that are sweeping the country, agriculture has taken a back seat to industrial modernization. Government funds are short in supply and are directed elsewhere away from agriculture. The Chinese government now pays farmers IOUs for their crops, an unpopular policy that cannot last much longer. In addition, local officials have been assessing all sorts of extra levies on the peasant population. These extra taxes are collected for such activities as funding local officials' own investment schemes and maintaining their relatively high standard of living. Only in recent weeks (from the time of writing this report) has the central government stepped in to try to prevent such abuses.

When able to make import purchases, Chinese agricultural producers are attracted to soft loans attached to the purchase by the foreign exporter's home government. Chinese resources note that all foreign suppliers of agricultural machinery and equipment, with the noted exception of the United States, offer some sort of soft loans to Chinese buyers when purchasing machinery made in their respective countries.

End-user Profile End-users of agricultural machinery & equipment consist of the following: private farmers, collective organizations, farmers' cooperatives, and state farms.

After de-collectivization in the late seventies and early eighties, private farmers are by far the largest of these groups. Their numbers reach an astounding 900 million nationwide. However, due to such a high population and limited arable land, the average size plot of land per family is only 0.5 hectares, or 1.25 acres. This does not leave much room for large scale, machinery-intensive farming. Smaller scale machinery suits itself well to such an environment. In fact, 90% of all tractors in China are under 20 hp. Private farmers also own 76% of all agricultural machinery in the country. This group of end-users presents a large market for small-scale farm tools and equipment.

Collective organizations make up the second largest group of end-users, owning about 18% of total machinery nationwide. The most prominent type of collective organization is the agricultural machinery public service system. This system is a network of stations at the local level designed to help promote mechanization in the countryside. Their services include machinery repair, instruction on proper equipment use, machinery storage, and using the station's own machinery to help other farmers in crop planting and harvesting. These machinery service stations provide good opportunities for exporters as they have a wide range of machinery, including larger scale equipment.

The third largest type of end-user, the state farms, offer the best prospects for U.S. exports. These farms can be thought of as large agri-businesses. They occupy very expansive tracts of land, and primarily use large scale machinery. These farms are also directly funded by the Chinese government, and export a portion of their yields, giving them greater access to foreign exchange than the average private farmer. The areas of the country where most large state farms are located are Heilongjiang, Jilin, Liaoning (in the northeast), and Xinjiang (in the northwest). Consequently, these areas also have the highest concentration of agricultural mechanization in the nation. Many other state farms are located near Beijing in Shandong and Hebei Provinces. Large scale farming in the rest of the country is inhibited by either high population density or unaccommodating terrain.

The last type of end-user is the farmers' cooperative organizations, owning only 1% of total agricultural equipment. This type of organization consists of small groups of local private farmers helping each other with the planting and harvesting of each person's plot. Whereas collectives are state-sponsored, cooperatives are not.

Competitive Situation Domestically produced agricultural machinery by far holds the largest share of the total market. Ninety-eight percent of all machinery owned by Chinese agricultural producers is made domestically. The reason for the high market saturation lies the fact that Chinese farmers tend to be able to afford only domestic products. The consensus among agricultural producers is that American products are unquestionably the best, but the only affordable equipment available is domestically made. A small portion of domestically made Chinese agricultural machinery gets exported. The exports are usually part of counter trade deals with less developed nations (53).

Among imported equipment, Japanese manufacturers hold the largest market share in China at roughly 40%. Japanese companies, such as Mitsubishi, sell their products aggressively in China and keep abreast of new opportunities that become available. Nevertheless, Chinese agricultural producers prefer machinery that comes from the U.S. Some American manufacturers who have sold equipment to the Chinese market include: Caterpillar, Ford, J.I. Case International, and GT. According to estimates, American market share will grow at a rate of 5% over the next three years. This rate of growth, however, does not match the projected growth of the total market. The reason for the slight lag lies in the fact that American machinery fills a niche market, and is somewhat price uncompetitive.

In addition to purchasing machinery from abroad with scarce foreign exchange, China also engages in counter trade arrangements with Russia and Ukraine. China swaps primarily consumer goods and apparel for agricultural machinery from these two countries. The machinery acquired in these transactions carries the reputation for being better than most domestic machinery, but worse than most other foreign ones. Price is what makes the Chinese attracted to such transactions. However, the amount of agricultural machinery acquired is not great compared to the total import market size.

Price competition is also fierce among the foreign imported machinery as well. U.S. manufacturers rank highest in price of imported equipment. In addition, most other foreign governments allow their manufacturers to grant soft loans to Chinese purchasers when exporting, whereas a Chinese purchaser must pay hard currency in full when buying a U.S. product. One possible way to compensate for other suppliers' soft loans and to be competitive would be to include extra services and training in the sales package.

One way to circumvent the distinct price discrepancy is to produce domestically. A great many Chinese agricultural machinery manufacturers are looking to form joint venture production operations with foreign partners. However, in light of past foreign joint venture experience in China, this option is not without its own risks and difficulties and would require considerable preparatory research.

Market Access

Import Climate In recent years, China has moved to a more decentralized import regime. The central authorities in Beijing no longer firmly control all that is imported into the country. Sources indicated that now any import/export company can import agricultural machinery into China. However, there is an important exception, large-sized tractors and combines need central government approval from the Department of Agricultural Mechanization of the Ministry of Agriculture. The specific sizes of "large" tractors and combines remains undefined, so it would be best to make sure that the buyer already has central government approval if needed. All other types of agricultural machinery are free from any sort of central government approval mechanism (53).

Distribution The best entry strategy for this market would be to contact directly both the national and local levels of government to establish contact with appropriate agricultural machinery importers and end-users. A good place to start would be the Ministry of Agriculture's Department of Agricultural Mechanization and the State Farm Bureau.

Selling through an agent or establishing a representative office are two ways of gaining greater exposure to this market. An agent or representative in China would be able to keep abreast of current market demand, and maintain necessary purchaser contacts. Information on finding an agent or setting up a representative office can be obtained from the Foreign Commercial Service at the American Embassy, Beijing. However, be advised that a representative office in China is not allowed to sell products directly.

Financing For many years government sponsored soft loans were available to Chinese customers of European and Japanese firms but not through U.S. companies. Lack of soft loan support, which amounts to a de facto 30%-40% discount, handicapped U.S. suppliers throughout the 1980's. Recently, the OECD members agreed to stop soft loans below the OECD rates unless the bid is for a bonafide, non-profit aid project.

As Chinese buyers often lack the necessary amounts of hard currency for international purchases, soft loans and other credits offered by the seller prove very appealing. This puts American manufacturers at somewhat of a disadvantage, as they compete with other nations' companies that do have the ability to grant such loans. Counter trade provides a solution, but the processes involved are complex. Nevertheless, because the large state farms in the northeast export a portion of their product, thereby generating hard currency, they are better positioned to import machinery than the average Chinese farmer.

Imports into China require import licenses that indicate government approval to spend foreign exchange. However, if the Bank of China issues a letter of credit, then the necessary approvals already have been met.

Bank of China primarily uses sight letters of credit. Payment is made only after the Chinese bank issued the letter of credit receives the import documents. This process can result in a minimum of 10 to 20 days before the U.S. exporter is able to collect payment for delivered goods.

Best Sales Prospects The best sales prospects for American agricultural machinery and equipment lie in the large state-run farms. These "agribusinesses" are characterized as having a fairly high capital-to-labor ratio, as opposed to private family plots which are farmed almost entirely by human hands. The Chinese government is particularly interested in equipment used for large scale production of grain, corn, cotton, and oil-bearing crops. The areas that contain the largest concentration of state-run farms are located in the northeastern provinces of Heilongjiang, Jilin, and Liaoning.

China has a large agricultural machinery market, and competition runs fairly high for those wanting to sell here. The competition comes primarily from the abundant, low cost domestic manufactures. The Chinese implement import substitution as much as possible, however, due to the poor quality of domestically manufactured machinery, some imported equipment must be obtained. U.S. equipment is viewed as high quality and is popularly received among Chinese agricultural producers, provided that the price remains competitive.

There are two potential problems that appear when selling goods to China. First, China lacks a transparent trade system. Part of the reason for this stems from economic reforms and decentralization, resulting in a lack of organization. A market access agreement signed in September of 1992 should alleviate the situation as it is implemented over the course of this year. Second, foreign exchange is usually scarce. However, the large state-run farms, the best potential customers, generally have better access to foreign exchange than most other types of agricultural producers in China.

Some products that Chinese agricultural producers are particularly interested in include:

1)   Tractors of 100-150 hp
2)   Grain sowers, combines, and dryers
3)   Corn combines
4)   Rice transplanters
5)   Cotton harvesters
6)   Plant protection machinery
7)   Irrigation equipment
8)   Gardening machinery (for small-scale use)*
9)   Excavation machinery
10)   Vehicles for product transportation
11)   Any implements that have multi-functional use**

*Gardening machinery suits the small plots of land owned by private farmers, and may sell well on this market.
**Chinese buyers want machinery and equipment that can be used in all types of circumstances and for all kinds of jobs. Since foreign exchange is scarce, making imports expensive, Chinese buyers seek to get as much use as possible for what they buy.

<u>Useful Contacts</u>:

Ministry of Agriculture
11 Nong Zhan Guan Nan Li
Beijing, China 100026
Tel: 5001869   Fax: 5001869

Administrative Department of Agricultural Mechanization
Ministry of Agriculture
No. 11 Nong Zhan Guan Nan Li
Beijing, P.R. China 100026
Tel: (01) 5003366-4822, 4822, 5003861
Fax: (01) 5002448, 5003366

China State Farms Agribusiness Corporation
56 Zhuanta Lane, Xisi
Beijing, China 100810
Tel: 6052031-316   Fax: 6024847

China State Farms Import Export Corporation
56 Zhuanta Lane, Xisi
Beijing, China 100810
Tel: 6015102, 6015101   Fax: 6015102, 6015101

China International Cooperation Company for Agriculture, Livestock & Fishery
56 Zhuanta Hutong, Xisi
Beijing, China 100810
Tel: 6052531-530, 6062571 Fax: 6024548

China National Agricultural Machinery Corporation
Beijing, China 100825
26 Yuetan Nan Jie, Xicheng District
Tel: 8012416, 8523624 Fax: 8012871, 8032123

China Tobacco Import Export Corporation
11 Hu Fang Lu, Xuan Wu District
Beijing, China 100052
Tel: 3013399-2261, 3043620 Fax: 3043640

China National Corporation for the Development of Agricultural
Produce & Native Products
45 Fuxingmen Street
Beijing, China 100801
Tel: 6011833, 6018581 Fax: 6018581

China National Seed Corporation
31 Min Feng Hutong, Xidan
Beijing, China 100032
Tel: 6020954 Fax: 6014770

Heilongjiang Department of Agriculture, Animal Husbandry & Fishery
Wenzhong Jie
Harbin, Heilongjiang Province
Tel: (451) 224522 Fax: (451) 214763

Jiamusi Agricultural Machinery Administration
Zhongshan Jie
Jiamusi, Heilongjiang Province
Tel: (454) 221268 Fax: (454) 221279

Jilin Department of Agriculture
Sidalin Dajie
Changchun, Jilin Province
Tel: (431) 825043 Fax: (431) 825041

Liaoning Agriculture & Animal Husbandry Bureau
Taiyuan Beilu
Shenyang, Liaoning Province
Tel: (25) 2263087   Fax: (24) 2263088

Agricultural Commission, Inner Mongolian Autonomous Region
Wulanchabu Lu
Huhuhaote, Inner Mongolia
Tel: (471) 43343

Hubei Agricultural Machinery Administration
No. 194, Shengli Jie, Hankou
Wuhan, Hubei Province 430014
Tel: (27) 235815, (27) 212202   Fax: (27) 219367

Jiangsu Bureau of Agricultural Machinery
Zhongshan Beilu
Nanjing, Jiangsu Province
Tel: (25) 634024   Fax: (25) 634027

Anhui Bureau of Agricultural Machinery
Huizhou Lu
Heifei, Anhui Province
Tel: (551) 255680   Fax: (551) 255681

Hebei Department of Agriculture
Yuhua Zhonglu
Shijiazhuang, Hebei Province
Tel: (311) 646380   Fax: (311) 646380

Zhengzhou Bureau of Agriculture, Forestry & Agricultural Machinery
No. 30, Tongbai Lu
Zhengzhou, Henan Province 450006
Tel: (371) 448652, (371) 446840   Fax: (371) 446840

Shandong Department of Agriculture
Shimuyuan Dongjie
Jinan, Shandong Province
Tel: (531) 462005

Sichuan Agricultural Machinery Bureau
No. 50 Desheng Lu, Xinhua Da Dao
Chengdu, Sichuan Province 610017
Tel: (28) 676202, (28) 663684   Fax: (28) 663684

Xinjiang Department of Agriculture
Shengli Lu
Wulumuqi, Xinjiang Autonomous Region
Tel: (991) 268455

China Nation Tobacco Corporation
11 Hu Fang Road, Xuanwu District
Beijing, PRC 100052
Tel: 3013399-2263   Fax: 3043619

Liaoning Province Representative Office
1 De Sheng Men Wai Da Jie
Liaoning Hotel
Beijing, China 100088
Tel: 2015588, 2014676   Fax: 2015588

Jilin Province Representative Office
Ma Dian, Bei Tai Ping Zhuang
Beijing, China 100088
Tel: 2011085, 2019321   Fax: 2011084

Hebei Province Representative Office
1 Zhui Ba Hu Tong, Huang Hua Men Jie
Di An Men, Dong Cheng District
Beijing, China 100009
Tel: 4031116, 4031302   Fax: 4031302

Heilongjiang Province Representative Office
5 Fu Xing Men Bei Da Jie
Beijing, China 100045
Tel: 863497   Fax: 8033203

Xinjiang Autonomous Region Representative Office
7 San Li He Lu, Xi Cheng District
Beijing, China 100044
Tel: 8322266, 8318561   Fax: 894579

Shandong Province Representative Office
Madian, Beitaipingzhuang
Beijing, China 100088
Tel: 2011058   Fax: 2011066

In addition to the above contacts in government agencies and the like (53), there are a number of useful points of contact in the agricultural machinery industry within China as follows (8):

Anshan Hongqi Tractor Plant
Lishan, Anshan
Liaoning Province 114042
Tel: 371693

Beijing General Diesel Engine Works
Chaoyang District
Beijing 100022
Tel: 7215588

Changchun Tractor Plant
Erdaohezi, Changchun
Jilin Province 130031
Tel: 42911

Changwei Tractor Plant
Weichang District, Weifang
Shandong Province 261004
Tel: 233931

Changzhou Diesel Engine Works
Zhonglou District, Changzhou
Jiangsu Province 213002
Tel: 603656

Changzhou Tractor Plant
Changzhou
Jiangsu Province   213012
Tel: 600424

Dalian Diesel Engine Factory
No. 49 Dongbei Road, Dalian
Liaoning Province 116011
Tel: 333993

Lishui Farm Use Vehicle Plant
Lishui County, Nanjing
Jiangsu Province 211200
Tel: 3369

No. 1 Tractor Plant, Luoyang
Jiangxi, Luoyang
Henan Province 471004
Tel: 273280

Quanjiao Diesel Engine Works
Quandjiao County, Chuxian Area
Anhui Province 239500
Tel: 82644

Shanghai Diesel Engine Works
Yangpu District
Shanghai 200432
Tel: 5483506

Shanghai Tractor Engine Corporation
Yangpu District
Shanghai 200082
Tel: 5419510

Shijiazhuang Tractor Factory
Chang'an, Shijiazhuang
Hebei Province 050033
Tel: 554132

Tianjin Tractor Works
Nankai District
Tianjin 300190
Tel: 362240

Weifang Diesel Engine Works
Weicheng District, Weifang
Shandong Province 261001
Tel: 224951

Wujin Diesel Engine Works
Wujin County, Changzhou
Jiangsu Province 213161
Tel: 651125

Xinjiang Shiyue Tractor Plant
Shayibake Urumqi
Xinjiang Uygur Autonomous Region 830000
Tel: 550090

Yulin Prefecture Diesel Engine Works
Yulin
Guangxi Province 537005
Tel: 3151

Ziyang Diesel Engine Works
Ziyang County, Neijang
Sichuan Province 641301
Tel: 22228

AIRCRAFT AND PARTS

The Department of Commerce review of this segment is given in Table 78.

Table 78

Review of Aircraft & Parts Market Sector (3)

A)	Three-letter ITA industry sector code:	AIR
B)	Est. total market size (USD Millions):	
	1991 -	$2,400
	1992 -	$3,000
	1993 -	$4,350
	1994 -	$5,105
	1995 -	$5,993 (58)
C)	Est. 1992-4 annual market growth rate:	20%
D)	Est. total imports (USD Millions)	
	1991 -	$1,270
	1992 -	$1,500
	1993 -	$2,300
	1994 -	$2,645
	1995 -	$3,041 (58)
E)	Est. annual total import growth rate:	20%
F)	Est. imports from U.S. (USD Millions):	
	1991 -	$1,081
	1992 -	$1,000
	1993 -	$2,100
	1994 -	$2,415
	1995 -	$2,777
G)	Est. annual growth of imports from USA	15%
H)	China's receptivity to U.S. products in this sector (5 - High/1 - Low):	5
I)	Competition from local/third-countries for U.S. firms (5 - Low/1 - High):	4
J)	Chinese market barriers to U.S. sales in this sector (5 - Few/1 - Many):	5

K)   Comments - Factors for increased U.S. sales:

- Excellent track record of U.S. aircraft companies and their increased familiarity with the market, including aggressive sales.
- China's plans to expand its civilian aircraft fleet.
- Tourism/business travel market is increasing, general travel demand is heavy.
- Plans to upgrade Chinese aircraft will stimulate parts market.
- U.S. aircraft are preferred by Chinese airlines, but the U.S. faces competition from soft loans. Aircraft sales are also subject to political conditions, and bilateral tensions between China and European Countries, or pressure from the governments of these countries, has been known to affect Chinese purchasing decisions.

L)	Most promising sub-sectors	1992 market size
	1. Wide-bodied jet aircraft, 1992	$200 - 300 million
	...Through the mil-1990s.	$1,000 - 3,000 million
	2. 100-200 passenger jet aircraft	$300 million
	3. Aircraft parts	$50 million

In the late 1950s, China began developing its own aircraft, known as the Yun, or Y series. China built 135 civil aircraft between 1981 and 1985 and was scheduled to build hundreds more during the Seventh Five-Year Plan. Civil aircraft and aircraft engines were produced in large plants located primarily in Shanghai, Xi'an, Harbin, and Shenyang. Medium-sized factories produced the necessary test equipment, components, avionics, and accessories. China hoped for eventual self-reliance in all aircraft production, but it still imported aircraft in 1987.

For firms that have been in China for many years, patience is being rewarded. McDonnell Douglas Corp., for instance, first initiated ties with the Chinese in 1975, leading to an aircraft-assembly joint venture in China in 1987. The long-term relationship blossomed fully last year: the firm signed a lucrative contract to build forty MD-80s and MD-90s in China, with the potential for as many as 130 more.

Now, Airbus Industries of France and Boeing and McDonnell Douglas of the U.S. are major players on the China air transport scene.

Some useful contacts in the aircraft and parts sector include:

Changhe Aircraft Manufacturing Plant
Zhushan, Jingdezhen
Jiangxi Province 333002
Tel: 442019

Chengdu Aircraft Industrial Corporation
Huangtianba, Qingyang District
Chengdu, Sichuan Province 610092
Tel: 769461-2535

Harbin Aircraft Manufacturing Corporation
Pingfang, Harbin
Heilongjiang Province 150066
Tel: 801122

Nanchang Aircraft Manufacturing Company
Qingyunpu District, Nanchang
Jiangxi Province 330024
Tel: 251833

Shaanxi Aircraft Manufacturing Company
Chenggu County, Hanzhong
Shaanxi Province 723215
Tel: 212974

Shenyang Aircraft Corporation
Huanggu District, Shenyang
Liaoning Province 110034
Tel: 462591-3916

Xi'an Aircraft Industrial Corporation
Yanliang District, Xi'an
Shaanxi Province 710000
Tel: 61971-4

ALUMINUM

After lifting the restriction of aluminum use for doors and windows, the volume of aluminum consumption increased dramatically. In 1992, the target for aluminum output was set at 950,000 tons. In the first half of 1992, even though the output of aluminum was up 28% compared to that of 1991, the supply still fell short of demand. By the end of June 1992, the stock held in major aluminum plants had been depleted. The domestic market price of aluminum was up as high as $2,500 per ton in July 1992 and maintained at about $2,200 per ton the remainder of the year. The rapid growth of the real estate industry in the coastal areas and newly open inland regions expanded the use of aluminum.

In June 1992, CNNC merged Zhengzhou Aluminum Plant, Zhengzhou Light Metals Research Institute, Zhongzhou Aluminum Plant, and Mining Company to form China Great Wall Aluminum Corporation. It was felt that one large aluminum corporation would strengthen the coordination of the Henan Province's aluminum industry and would eliminate the intraprovincial and interprovincial competition for raw materials between the two large aluminum plants, Zhengzhou and Zhongzhou.

The first phase of construction of the Zhongzhou Aluminum Plant in Jiaozuo, Henan Province, was completed in 1992. Trial runs of the plant began, and the plant was expected to be in full operation in early 1993 with a capacity of 200,000 mt/a of alumina using a sintering process. The second phase was in the planning stage. It will use the Bayer process to output 400,000 mt/a alumina. The ultimate goal was to output 1.2 Mmt/a of alumina in the year 2000.

In 1991, Guizhou Aluminum Plant produced a total of 79,000 tons of aluminum. In 1992, Guizhou Aluminum Plant completed the construction of its combination-mixing process plant and its second 160,000-ampere potline using Soderberg anodes was retired because of excess fluoride emissions. It will be replaced by a 180,000-ampere potline using prebaked anodes with an annual capacity of 120,000 tons of aluminum.

Some useful contacts in the aluminum industry include:

Baotou Aluminum Plant
Baotou
Inner Mongolia 014046
Tel: 71144

Fushun Aluminum Plant
Wanghua District, Fushun
Liaoning Province 113001
Tel: 688471-3425

Guizhou Aluminum Plant
Baiyan District, Guiyang
Guizhou   550058
Tel: 641309

Lanzhou Aluminum Plant
Xigu District, Lanzhou
Gansu Province 730060
Tel: 56511

Lanzhou Liancheng Aluminum Plant
Yongdeng County, Lanzhou
Gansu Province 730335

Nanping Aluminum Factory
Nanping City
Fujian Province 353000
Tel: 24031

Qinghai Aluminum Plant
Datong Autonomous County
Xining, Qinghai Province 810108
Tel: 52923-2485

Qingtonxia Aluminum Factory
Qingtonxia City
Ningxia 751603
Tel: 31028

Shandong Aluminum Plant
Zhangdian District, Zibo
Shandong Province 255052
Tel: 290334

Shanxi Aluminum Plant
Hejin County, Yuncheng
Shanxi Province 43300
Tel: 22665

Southwest Aluminum Processing Factory
Ba County, Chongqing
Sichuan Province 631326
Tel: 812352

Xiangxiang Aluminum Plant
Xiangxiang
Hunan Province 411400
Tel: 71001

Yunnan Aluminum Plant
Chenggong County, Kunming
Yunnan Province 650502
Tel: 79911

Zhengzhou Aluminum Plant
Shanguie, Zhengzhou
Yunnan Province 450041
Tel: 816537

APPAREL

The Department of Commerce review of this segment is given in Table 79 (3).

The reader is also referred to the sections which follow on Textile Fabrics and Textile Machinery.

Table 79

Review of Apparel Sector

A)	Three-letter ITA industry sector code:	APP
B)	Est. total market size (USD Millions):	
	1991 -	$2,000
	1992 -	$2,100
C)	Est. 1992-4 annual market growth rate:	5%
D)	Est. total imports (USD Millions):	
	1991 -	$20
	1992 -	$22
E)	Est. annual total import growth rate:	10%
F)	Est. imports from U.S. (USD Millions):	
	1991 -	$3
	1992 -	$4
G)	Est. annual growth of imports from USA:	33%
H)	China's receptivity to U.S. products in this sector (5 - High/1 - Low):	4
I)	Competition from local/third-countries for U.S. firms (5 - Low/1 - High):	2
J)	Chinese market barriers to U.S. sales in this sector (5 - Few/1 - Many):	3
K)	Comments - Factors for increased U.S. sales:	

- Though US apparel firms face major problems with Chinese piracy, the appeal of casual US styles to the Chinese market is increasing dramatically.
- Specialty items are in particular demand.

L)	Most promising sub-sectors	1992 market size
1.	Western-style blue jeans	$20 million
2.	Leather and blue denim jackets	$10 million
3.	High-end suits and sport clothes	$100 million

Production value of the garment industry reached approximately USD 7 billion in 1990, an increase of 75.9 percent over 1985's figures. In 1990, more than 3 billion garments were produced, double the 1985 figure. The apparel industry employed 1.15 million people in 1985 and 1.65 million in 1990. As of 1990, 17,241 enterprises were engaged in garment or apparel production, according to Chinese statistics. The textile industry sub-council of the China council for the promotion of trade and industry says the number of garment factories has grown to more than 37,000 as of April 1992, employing 2.5 million people with total annual production of USD 9.3 billion. Enterprises range in size from small individually-owned enterprises of a few dozen workers to large scale, state-owned factories employing several thousand. According to the council's figures, more than a thousand foreign funded garment firms had been established by 1992, representing a total of more than USD 500 million in foreign investment.

China's apparel industry is directed at two markets, China's growing domestic market and the international market. The general view is that in ten or twenty years, the importance of China's domestic market will surpass that of the international market. In the near term, the international garment market is an important source of foreign exchange earnings since China exported some USD 16 billion in garments and textiles in 1991, about one-fourth of China's total exports.

A central theme in China's apparel industry is the need to upgrade quality and production capability if China is to compete in the international market and, once foreign competition is permitted, China's domestic market. Chinese officials and factory managers see a definite need to shift to higher value production while at the same time gaining efficiency over what has largely been an inefficient sector.

While technical renovation is an ongoing process which China delayed for many years, technical modernization and investment has caught on in the past few years with the effect that the industry has improved its performance. On the policy side, China's State Council decided, in 1986, to transfer the administration of the garment sector from the ministry of light industry to the ministry of textile industry. The purpose was to unify control over two related industrial sectors: Garments/apparel and textiles. Recently, there has been a trend toward vertically and horizontally integrated conglomerates which have both textile and garment production capabilities as well as downstream services such as trading and marketing.

Problems of apparel industries: While some of the problems facing the apparel industry have been resolved, quality concerns continue to plague the industry. In the five years between 1986 and 1991, five specific problems were identified and targeted for resolution. The five problems were: 1) yarn faults, 2) filling bars, 3) shading, 4) skew weft, and, 5) shrinkage. According to Chinese statistics, quality ratings have improved by 4 to 5 percent per year since 1989. Up about 5 percent from 1990, 94.35 percent of all knitwear passed export quality assessment in 1991.

The need to upgrade technology is apparent. The Ministry of Textiles estimates that only 20 percent of all equipment engaged in garment production can be considered "advanced technology." U.S. textile manufacturers who have inspected China's factories say they see some highly productive 1980's technology, a lot of 1970's equipment begging to be replaced, and a fair amount of 1940's/50's equipment limping inefficiently along awaiting the junkyard.

Garment producers frequently complained that China's indirect trading system, which forces garment sales to pass through authorized trading companies, distanced producers from their buyers and their markets. While a number of structural reforms have expanded the number of trading corporations authorized to conduct the garment trade, this limitation continues to inhibit the rapid transmission of market information to China's producers.

In the past, China's hierarchical structure tended to isolate textile research centers as well. As research centers are being "spun off" from their parent ministries or being told to shift from theoretical to applied research, their efforts are being redirected to real applications in the garment and textile industry. This is especially important in the fast changing world of fashion and fabric design.

Over-production continues to plague the industry, largely due to remnants of Chins's centrally planned economy. When China's textile production overheated in October and November 1991, 593,800 cotton spindles were taken out of production for the final two months, according to press reports. More than 1,200 textile factories stopped production completely or halved production, idling nearly 40 percent of the nation's spindles. The stoppage has also an effort to prevent further additions to already massive and burdensome stockpiles.

Exports: For the first half of 1992, apparel exports exceeded USD 6.5 billion, according to China customs statistics. Because China shifted from its own classification system to the harmonized system on January 1, 1992, comparisons with earlier years risk mixing classifications. With this caveat in mind, China customs figures for 1991 indicate China's garment exports were USD 7.7 billion. According to Chinese statistics, which greatly under-count China's exports through Hong Kong to the U.S., China's garment exports to the U.S. barely exceeded USD 600 million for the first half of 1992. Department of Commerce figures for 1991 show the U.S. imported apparel valued at USD 3.4 billion.

Chinese officials hope to sell USD 10 billion worth of garments in 1995. According to Chinese officials, profits from garment exports declined 58.8 percent in 1991 and garments valued at USD 3.6 billion were gathering dust in warehouses as late as March 1992. The domestic market may make up for some of the decline in profits. Domestic garment sales in China's 200 large and medium-sized cities, a total population of more than 100 million are projected to rise 8.38 percent in 1992 to reach a total of 102 million pieces. Garments made from chemical fibers are expected to capture about 70 percent of all sales. The strongest individual sectors are overcoats, up 42.1 percent, women's shirts, up 11.85 percent, and men's suits, up 10.39 percent.

Imports: China's garment imports are, as might be expected, a fraction of its exports. In the first six months of 1992, China imported approximately USD 400 million in garments or about the same amount as in all of 1991. U.S. garment exports to China for 1991 were put at USD 76 million, according to Chinese customs statistics. The bulk of China's garment imports come from or merely through Hong Kong.

ARCHITECT/CONSTRUCTION/ENGINEERING SERVICES
The Department of Commerce review of this segment is given in Table 80 (3).

Table 80

Review of Architect/Construction/Engineering Service Sector

A)	Three-letter ITA industry sector code:	ACE
B)	Est. total market size (USD Millions):	
	1991 -	$400
	1992 -	$440
C)	Est. 1992-4 annual market growth rate:	10%
D)	Est. total imports (USD Millions):	
	1991 -	$120
	1992 -	$134
E)	Est. annual total import growth rate:	12%
F)	Est. imports from U.S. (USD Millions):	
	1991 -	$4
	1992 -	$8
G)	Est. annual growth of imports from USA:	100%
H)	China's receptivity to U.S. products in this sector (5 - High/1 - Low):	4
I)	Competition from local/third-countries for U.S. firms (5 - Low/1 - High):	
J)	Chinese market barriers to U.S. sales in this sector (5 - Few/1 - Many):	3

K) Comments - Factors for increased U.S. sales:
- Recent major loosening of credit for big projects.
- Emphasis on infrastructure in the Eighth Five-Year Plan, especially ports, power plants and transportation (bridges, roads and railways).
- Solid reputation of U.S. engineering and architectural firms.

L)	Most promising sub-sectors	1992 market size
	1. Power Station ACE	$110 million
	2. Subway ACE	$45 million
	3. Port ACE	$30 million
	4. Transportation (road & railway) ACE	$40 million

AUTOMOTIVE INDUSTRY

The average Chinese family has 1.2 kids, three bicycles—and no car. The world's auto makers are vying with one another to fill that void.

Domestic production of all types of vehicles, including heavy trucks, reached 1.3 million in 1993, up 23% over the previous year. Imports, subject to punishing duties, were 310,000, with as many as 200,000 more vehicles smuggled in. Officials predict confidently that China will manufacture about three million cars and trucks by the end of the century.

Beijing's statisticians say 80 million Chinese families, most of them city dwellers, will buy their first car by 2010, helping push total annual production to about eight million vehicles a year. By designing a small, inexpensive car for sale to average citizens, China's auto industry will replace Japan as the world's second largest, after the U.S., by 2010.

Germany's Porsche AG, presented a prototype, dubbed C88, which was developed from scratch in conjunction with Chinese engineers at the China Family Car Forum in Beijing in November 1994. The curvy-lined C88 sedan won't set speed records: Its 50-horsepower engine reaches sixty miles an hour in twenty-two seconds, a milestone of underachievement for Porsche. But the maker of elite sports cars thinks sales could accelerate at a record pace, to maybe 250,000 C88s each year.

Perhaps the biggest surprise is the eagerness of luxury car maker, Mercedes-Benz, to tap the low end of the world's biggest mass market. Mercedes went to the drawing board to come up with its "FCC," or Family Car China, concept vehicle.

The FCC looks like a squashed minivan. It has a radically raked windshield, hugh square headlights and front wheels only a few short inches from the front bumper. The car stands eight inches higher off the ground than an ordinary passenger car, making it possible to fit the small engine entirely under the passenger compartment. That frees up room in the interior, puts the engine out of collision range and makes for unsurpassed safety standards. Mercedes could build a three-cylinder, 1.3 liter FCC with local parts and even antilock brakes for about $10,000 a vehicle. It would be the slowest car Mercedes ever built and in relative terms, the least expensive.

China's auto industry, with more than 120 plants, is inefficient and needs to be reorganized into large groups. China would consolidate auto makers into three globally competitive giants and three secondary manufacturers by 1997.

The Volkswagen joint venture in Shanghai, a Citroën venture at Shiyan and northeast China's sprawling First Automobile Works, also linked with Volkswagen, were mentioned for the first category.

Likely candidates for the second category are Chrysler's Jeep Cherokee factory in Beijing, Peugeot's Guangzhou plant and Daihatsu's plant in Tianjin.

Foreign auto makers already producing in China include Volkswagen AG of Germany, Peugeot SA and Citroën SA of France, Daihatsu Motor Co. and Suzuki Motor Co. of Japan and Chrysler Corp. of the United States.

China's auto market is small, with domestic production in 1993 of 1.3 million units, up 23 percent from 1992. Official imports last year totaled 310,461 vehicles, up 48 percent over 1993, and thousands more were smuggled in.

With the economy growing at more than 10 percent a year, many foreign producers say this may be the last great undeveloped car market.

China is expected to become the second largest market for autos after the U.S. in the first decade of the next century. The State Planning Commission said three large conglomerates, based on existing joint venture producers in China, would account for most sales in the domestic market by the end of the century.

The government's model plant is its Shanghai factory. It made 100,000 Santana passenger cars in 1993, nine times its 1990 output, and the cars had a local content rate of 81.47 percent, double the rate in 1990. The Santana retails for about 160,000 yuan ($18,000).

Tianjin currently produces 60,000 Charade cars and mini-buses a year with Daihatsu technology.

There is an ambitious effort by leaders of China's Communist Party to double the nation's annual production to three million vehicles, half of them automobiles, by the end of the decade. Increasingly, the cars would go to individual consumers; in the past the emphasis had been on larger vehicles like mini-vans that could move groups of people.

American, Japanese and European auto makers are scrambling for the right to participate in a handful of joint venture partnerships with China's state-owned auto combines to produce several versions of the family sedan.

But many Chinese and Western experts, drawing from what happened in the United States and other industrial nations, contend that a transportation system dominated by the automobile could become a huge mistake in China, which already suffers from traffic congestion, choking pollution and dwindling supplies of oil. A big increase in gasoline consumption in China, they say, could hasten the next worldwide energy crisis.

China's state planners have seized on the auto industry as one of four heavy industries whose growth can help sustain the country's rapid economic expansion over the next two decades. The other three are telecommunications, computers and petrochemicals.

To create a true automobile economy, however, would require a huge investment in roads and highways in China, which today has about as many miles of road as existed in the United States at the end of the 19th century. The few dozen short stretches of modern freeways built in the last decade are almost lost in the a rural landscape where dirt paths and narrow farm-to-market lanes still predominate.

The annual production capacity of China's automobile industry in 1992 was about 650,000 with a variety of medium-duty, light-duty motor vehicles for special purposes. In 1990, China turned out 516,000 automobiles and 970,000 motorcycles. The proportion of heavy duty vehicles grew from 2.77 percent to 3.54 percent of the total annual output from 1989 to 1990; sedans, jeeps from 11.4 percent to 13.39 percent; medium-duty vehicles from 36.94 percent to 40.18 percent and the light-duty vehicles dropped from 33.2 percent to 28 percent (2).

China has imported key technology, equipment and parts from the United States, Germany and Italy and has set up joint venture with Germany and France to upgrade its automobile industry. Now China can make a variety of automobiles to meet most of the present domestic market needs and have exported small quantity to about fifty-seven countries and regions.

The country's total vehicle production in 1994 could reach 1.5 million; about one-tenth the level of the United States or Japan. But China's auto production has been growing at an annual rate of 17 percent since 1979. In 1993, production jumped 22.8 percent, outpacing overall economic growth of 13 percent.

The automotive industry, which grew substantially after 1949, did not keep pace with the demands of modernization. In the early 1980s, demand was still low. A surge in demand resulted in the production of 400,000 vehicles and the importation of another 300,000 vehicles through early 1985. In the second half of 1985, stringent administrative measures curtailed most imports, and in early 1986 domestic production was reduced to 13 percent of that in early 1985. One cause for this was a large surplus created by high production and importation levels in 1984 and 1985. Although 1986 production levels were considered a short-term slowdown, the targets of the Seventh Five-Year Plan were quite low (4).

Overview China's automotive industry production grew nearly 50 percent in 1992, however. This rapid growth in supply, however, was not able to keep up with explosive growth in demand. Thus, imports of autos, CKD or SKD and parts have been increasing rapidly. Detroit's big three and their Japanese, Korean and European competition have all established a presence in China (11).

China's Eighth Five-Year Plan (1990-1995) outlines the future scope and direction of the automotive sector. The Plan emphasizes the further development of the automobile and its parts and components industry. Localization in many joint venture enterprises is steadily increasing and will continue to be encouraged. The manufacturing of both heavy duty and light duty trucks has been designated one of the Chinese government's priority projects in this industry. Automotive parts and service equipment were ranked eleventh in the Department of Commerce's-China's Best Prospects Index for 1992 (3). Furthermore, the production of sedan cars is rapidly expanding as demand greatly exceeds supply.

China's 14th Party Congress branded the Chinese economy as a "socialist-market" economy. This was a significant development in that the Chinese government officially recognized the market rather than central planning as China's main economic driving force. China, with an economic growth rate of 12.8%, is the fastest developing country in the world. Foreign exchange reserves exceed $45 billion. The U.S. trade deficit with China for 1992 was approximately $18.3 billion.

China's automotive industry is loosely under state control. The policy making body directly responsible for the administration of the automotive industry is the China National Automotive Industry Corporation (CNAIC), a deputy-ministry level department. CNAIC states that its responsibilities include: the formulation of policies, laws and regulations for the development of the whole automotive industry; the development of medium and long term programs; the examination and approval of construction projects; the administration of automotive research and development institutions; the coordination of import-export corporations, joint ventures, and international economic and technological cooperation and exchanges.

The Chinese automotive industry is quite dispersed consisting of over 125 plants which manufacture trucks, vans and passenger cars, approximately 600 factories which assemble or overhaul vehicles and over 2,400 factories which manufacture automotive parts. These large numbers attest to fragmentation in the sector which makes CNAIC's task of trying to rationalize the entire automotive industry progressively more difficult. CNAIC's main goal as projected in the Eighth Five-Year Plan is to attain greater efficiency, not scale. It is in China's best interest to streamline its automotive industry. An added variable which further complicates the rationalization process is strong regional forces which are at play in China today. Provincial and Municipal governments are becoming important players in the automotive sector.

Chinese government figures show that for the first time in the history of the Chinese automobile manufacturing industry, production levels in 1992 exceeded one million vehicles. The actual production figures for 1992 were 1.08 million automobiles, a 47% increase from the previous year. This rate of increase may not be sustainable over the longer term. The business cycle may have peaked in 1992.

The main goals projected for the automotive parts and accessories industry is to improve the overall quality of automobile parts and components. One of the greatest weaknesses in the automotive parts industry in China is the lack of technology which adversely affects the quality of the finished product. As China further emphasizes the localization of parts and components for those joint ventures producing vehicles, better quality parts must be produced.

The Eighth Five-Year Plan states that the main task for this sector is to reach a localization of over 90% for those joint ventures which are already firmly established in China. By the end of 1991, the local content for those automobiles produced by joint ventures was as follows: Santana, Shanghai-Volkswagen Automotive Corporation, 70.4%; Cherokee, Beijing Jeep Corporation, 55.1%; Charade, Automotive Industry Corporation, 45.7%; Peugeot 504 and 505, Guangzhou Peugeot, 37.7% and 29.8% respectively; Audi, First Auto Works, 21%, Steyr, 67%; Iveco, Nanjing Auto Works, 44.2%; Daihatsu, Tianjin Minibus Factory, 97%.

Table 81 summarizes some statistics for the automobile industry in China (11).

Table 81

Statistical Data for the Automobile Industry in China

CV = Complete Vehicle; PC = Parts and Components
(US $ Million)   (% Gain Loss)

	1990	1991	1992	Est. Average Annual Growth - Next 3 Years
Import Market:	1203	1660	3305	35%
CV:	766	1077	2434	
PC:	437	583	871	
Local Production:	103	138	185 (est.)	12%
Exports:	178	235	310 (est.)	15%
CV:	93	82		
PC:	84	152		
Total Market:	1128	1563	3180	35%
Imports from U.S.:	64	123	441 (est.)	30%
CV:	36	94	na	
PC:	28	29	na	
U.S. Receptivity Score:		3.5		
Exchange Rates:				
Official:	1:4.8	1:5.4	1:5.8	
Spot:	1:5.6	1:6.0	1:6.6	
Future Inflation Rate Assumed:		15%		

1991 Import Market Share for U.S. and Major Competitors:

Country	Total	CV	PC
Japan	40%	33%	54%
Germany	22%	22%	8%
France	8%	11%	---
U.S.	7%	9%	1%
Other	23%	25%	37%

Market Assessment: With the population of over 1.1 billion, estimates suggest that there were only approximately seven million vehicles in use in China in 1992. Although 1989-90 witnessed a decrease in auto production, statistics show that the development climate in the auto industry in China appears to be quite promising. In 1991, the Chinese automobile industry produced over 708,000 vehicles which included 360,000 trucks and 80,000 sedan cars. This was an increase of 36% over 1990 production figures. Domestic sales for 1991 reached $13 billion. Exports of vehicles and auto components were $235 million. Of the 125 auto manufacturing plants in China, eight produce sedan cars.

It is estimated that the sedan car production for 1992 will be well over 120,000. Chinese government officials estimate that the annual production level for sedan cars in 1993 will reach 250,000 and 600,000 by 1996. These official projections may be overstated. Nonetheless, they are indicative of government plans for this industry. Chinese government officials further estimate that demand for automobiles in China may jump to 1.1 million units in 1993 which is a significant increase from 1992 demand which reached 950,000 units.

Another calculation by the Chinese government estimates that China has 300 million households whose bank saving total $175 billion. Chinese urban areas have a very rapidly growing middle class with substantial savings. If one out of every twenty households each buy one automobile, 1.5 million cars will be needed in the future. Although it is dangerous to make such general projections, this methodology suggests that demand for automobiles and services have the potential to increase dramatically in the future.

Over the past fourteen years, China's automobile industry has experienced three recessions, each being directly linked to a nationwide austerity program launched by the central government. Although economic conditions in the Chinese market seem very promising in general and for the automotive industry specifically, austerity programs aimed at harnessing rampant economic growth could occur in the future. It should be noted that at year-end 1993, many analysts have suggested that the Chinese economy is at the top of the business cycle and that continued growth in aggregate demand may lead to inflation.

Following China's most recent austerity program of 1989-90, the production of cars has increased, sales have surpassed production, inventories have fallen below normal levels, key enterprises have reached their production targets will before the fiscal year's end, and pre-tax profits have greatly increased. There are several reasons for this increase in market demand for automobiles. Investment in fixed assets is increasing which stimulates vehicle production and sales. The automobile industry's replacement market is growing considerably in size. Better quality vehicles with higher efficiency are increasingly in demand. Another factor is that China is gradually facing its urban pollution problems. One of the main obstacles China must overcome in its current bid to host the 2000 Olympic Games in Beijing is air pollution. Factors such as these contribute to the need for more replacement vehicles. The national economy's rapid rate of development is also increasing end-user purchasing power.

End-User Profile Out of the seven million vehicles in use in China, the majority are government-owned either by enterprises, institutions or the military. China's economy has not developed to the point where a significant percentage of the population has acquired the means to individually purchase automobiles. According to Beijing press reports, there are only 37,000 private car owners in China today.

With China's new market reforms steadily gaining ground, individual income disparity is increasing. It is estimated that the per capita income and aggregate savings of over five million people is elevated enough to sustain the purchase of a private automobile. Thus, in the sedan car sector of the automobile industry, demand greatly outweighs supply. Due to long waiting lists, the purchase of sedan cars by individuals is quite difficult. The most significant vehicle end-users, namely town enterprises and the taxi and tourism industries are all developing at an increased rate. (Hertz recently established a joint venture auto rental firm in Shanghai.) Furthermore, China wants to increase the development of public-use vehicles to meet its growing urban transportation needs.

The demand for automotive parts and components is also steadily growing. As the number of automobile production joint ventures increase in China, the need for high quality parts and components is expanding as well. As mentioned above, joint ventures faced with demands for greater localization have an increasing need to obtain high quality parts and components. In this regard, U.S. companies which manufacture parts are encouraged by the Chinese government to establish joint ventures which can supply China's expanding automobile market. There are over thirty joint ventures in China's automotive industry. Over twenty of them produce auto parts and the rest produce complete vehicles.

Competitive Situation:

Domestic Production   According to Chinese customs statistics, the automotive industry's local production figures, although low in dollar value, suggest relatively high production volume. The Chinese automotive industry's domestic production primarily supplies the internal market versus export markets. Chinese estimated exports for 1992 comprised only 19% of the estimated total market value for the same year.

Many of the major automotive companies in China have already established joint ventures with automotive companies from other countries, including Japan, Germany, France and the U.S. The most significant joint ventures in the automotive industry, including their 1991 localization rates, have been listed above. Addresses and contact information are found in a later section of this report.

Concerning the production of complete vehicles, without the establishment of a joint venture, foreign automobile companies, especially the U.S., cannot effectively penetrate the Chinese market. Tariff rates for the importation of complete vehicles are prohibitively high. Those joint ventures already established in China which are producing vehicles are primarily catering to the domestic market. One American joint venture, Beijing Jeep is only now slowly beginning to export locally produced vehicles, mainly to South East Asian countries. Shanghai Volkswagen which has attained a high level of localization is selling car engines back to Germany.

Automobile companies were the three most productive Foreign Invested Enterprises (FIEs) for 1991. They included in descending order of importance, Shanghai Volkswagen, Beijing Jeep, and Guangzhou Peugeot.

Imports   Imports play an important role in meeting total market demand in the Chinese automotive sector.   Please refer to "Statistical Data" for import statistics and the estimated average annual growth rate expected for the following three years.

U.S. Market Position and Share   According to Chinese customs statistics, in 1991 the average total U.S. market share in the automotive industry was 7%.   In 1991 the leading exporters to China (in US$ million) were: U.S. 123, compared to 665 for Japan, 367 for Germany, and 129 for France.

In 1991, the average U.S. market share for complete vehicles (which include CKDs and SKDs) was 9%.   In 1991 complete vehicle exports to China among the contenders (in US$ million) were: 94 for the U.S., compared to 351 for Japan, 238 for Germany and 118 for France.

The U.S. market share for parts and components in 1991 was less than 1%.   Leading exporters to China (in US$ million) during that same year were: 29 for the U.S., compared to 315 for Japan, 129 for Germany, and 10 for France.

Market Access:

Import Climate   On October 10, 1992 the U.S. Trade Representative announced an agreement with China that will provide unprecedented market access for exports to China. Under the agreement, China has committed to dismantle its complex system of non-tariff barriers including import license requirements, quotas, and other non-transparent administrative controls or restrictions on importation of U.S. goods.   The agreement requires elimination of import barriers beginning December 31, 1992 and continuing until December 31, 1997.   During the time in which barriers remain in place for particular products, the agreement calls for the Chinese government to progressively increase access each year until the barrier is removed completely.   While the time frames for liberalization of controls vary for particular products, nearly seventy-five percent of all barriers will be eliminated within two years.   The remaining twenty-five percent will be eliminated by 1997.   Those barriers which affect the auto industry will be eliminated as of December 31, 1992 and include quotas on auto parts imported by U.S. joint ventures in China which are required to meet existing needs and production expansion.

China uses tariffs as one of several tools to protect its domestic industry. Tariff rates on automobiles which are discouraged products are prohibitively high at 250%. Tariff rates on parts and components according to Chinese 1993 General Administration of Customs statistics range from 6% to 80%. China has announced that it will rely increasingly on tariffs as a barrier to imports as it phases out selected non-tariff barriers. Tariffs also vary for the same product, depending on whether the product is eligible for an exemption from the published tariff.   Automobiles granted import licenses may, under certain conditions, be imported at a 50 percent rather than the prohibitive 250 percent advertised by the General Customs Administration.   Joint venture localization rates also have an impact on tariffs. Beginning at 60% localization, joint ventures benefit from reduced tariffs on imports.

Despite the fact that various controls will remain on the importation of passenger vehicles and trucks, the Chinese have agreed to set up major buying missions in the future. In 1992, China purchased an estimated 2004 vehicles for an estimated total of $55 million.

In addition to tariffs, imports are also charged industrial and commercial taxes and value-added taxes. These additional charges add substantially to the official tariff rate. China adroitly uses this combination of tariffs and additional taxes to clamp down on imports that it views as threatening to its domestic industry.

Distribution/Business Practices China does not have an established system of independent agents or distributors, so U.S. companies must use other methods for penetrating China's market. A few "tried and true" practices are listed below:

- Use the services of a U.S. (or third country) trading company. Many of these trading companies are willing to handle American products. Trading companies with offices in China will likely be the most effective.
- Use the services of a Hong Kong-based agent or distributor. Many Hong Kong agents and distributors are very active in China and have an extensive network of Chinese contracts.
- Establish a representative office in China. This is a good, but expensive, way to maintain continued visibility in China. Some U.S. companies form joint ventures with Chinese enterprises to provide after-sales service for the U.S. company's products in China.
- Establish a manufacturing joint venture with a Chinese partner. Note: the U.S. partner will have to consider the special issue of repatriating profits when it considers a joint venture with China.
- Establish a technology transfer relationship with a Chinese partner. Although many U.S. companies have engaged in successful technology transfer arrangements with Chinese enterprises, the U.S. partner should review carefully intellectual property rights protection which China's legal structure offers.

Finally, U.S. companies should be aware that, although China has no requirement for counter trade provisions in imports, a foreign company willing to consider counter trade may sometimes gain the competitive edge.

Financing Importing into China often requires import licenses and approval to spend foreign exchange. However, if the Bank of China (BOC) or another state-owned bank issues a Letter of Credit (LC), the U.S. seller can usually be sure that necessary approvals have been obtained.

Most BOC LC's are sight LCs. Payment is made only after the Chinese bank which issued the LC has received the export documents. This means a minimum 10-20 day wait before the U.S. exporter can collect payment for goods delivered. (For example, a U.S. exporter would arrange for all export documents to be shipped to BOC, and then would have to wait for BOC to review the documents before collecting payment.)

A second common Chinese payment practice affects large equipment sales and technology exports to China. For such sales, Chinese buyers typically make a 10-25% down payment, then pay 70-75% on delivery and the remaining 10-15% on installation. However, at the time of the initial down payment, Chinese buyers often require a Standby Letter of Credit from the seller's bank, guaranteeing the return of the down payment if sales terms are not met. A problem arises when a smaller U.S. exporter does not have a credit line sufficient to cover the required Standby LC. (Note: this special provision does not usually apply to sales of commodities or to sales of simple goods.)

The prospects for straight cash sales to China are limited by shortage of foreign exchange (in the hands of would-be importers) and by government policies that stress developing domestic manufacturing capability over importing finished products. Although there are no legislatively mandated counter trade requirements, common forms of business with China now include counter trade and compensation, trade, leasing, and technology licensing arrangements.

China's Central government exerts strict control over foreign exchange allocation, and foreign exchange controls constitute a significant non-tariff barrier. Most of China's imports and exports are handled by a relatively small number of state-owned trading companies authorized to transact business involving foreign exchange. Moreover, Chinese regulations for foreign-invested enterprises require that the remittance of profits, the purchase of imported components or raw materials, and the payment of compensation to foreign personnel be done in foreign currency. If such a company has a shortage of foreign currency (usually because it is having difficulty exporting its products), it may be unable to carry out these transactions. While foreign invested enterprises can now get foreign currency at local currency swap markets, it involves the payment of a premium which affects the profitability of the firm.

Best Sales Prospects   The most promising areas for the U.S. automotive industry's involvement in China include light truck manufacturing, automotive parts, and the manufacture of compact cars. The introduction of light trucks to the Chines market could prove mutually beneficial for both China and the U.S. Rural areas in China mostly rely on cumbersome road tractors and 5-ton trucks. The replacement market for these vehicles is quite large. The localization capability for light truck manufacture is relatively high, given an intermediate level of technology.

Automotive parts and service equipment have been ranked eleven in FCS-China's Best Prospects Index for 1992. The 1991 estimated market size for this sector was $500 million with an annual market growth rate of 15%. Estimated total imports in 1991 were $583 million with a 15% estimated average annual growth rate for total imports. 1991 estimated imports from the U.S. reached $29 million and the estimated average annual growth rate of imports from the U.S. was also 15%. Sub-sectors which are the most promising among automotive parts and service equipment include special purpose vehicle parts and accessories such as those for concrete mixing, freight, oil tank, chemical, garbage, ambulance, and other such vehicles. The estimated market size for this sub-sector is $10 million. Auto parts and accessories which are most promising include air conditioners, rear axle components, and high technology OEM components. The estimated market size for this sub-sector is $8 million.

Although the U.S. has been more cautious than its European and Japanese counterparts in sedan car manufacture in China, the potential opportunity for U.S. companies to establish joint ventures does exist. Sedan cars are well suited in China for use as light transport vehicles, official cars and taxis. Currently, as mentioned above, the demand for compact cars far exceeds supply.

Useful Contacts Chinese economy does not operate on open market distribution channels which are typically found in free market economic systems. It is difficult to identify prospective sales agents or distributors in China's foreign trade system. The companies listed below are authorized state-owned foreign trade corporations which are buyers' agents, as opposed to sellers' agents.

Aeolux Automotive Industry Import & Export Corporation
(AKA Dong Feng Automotive Plant)
Shiyan, Hubei Province
Tel: 24249, 24700

Aeolux Automotive Industry Import and Export Shenzhen Joint Corporation
Shanbu, Shennan Road Central
Shenzhen, Guangdong Province
Tel: (755) 38483, 38453
Fax: (755) 240-860

China National Automotive Industry Import & Export Corporation (CAIEC)
27-B Liuyin Street
West District, Beijing
Tel: (1) 601-3023
Fax: (1) 601) 1393

China National Automotive Industry Import and Export Corporation,
Beijing Company Ltd.
101 Dongxiaoshi Dajie
Chongwen District, Beijing 100062
Tel: (1) 511-3483, 511-2289, 511-3887, 701-3613
Fax: (1) 701-3614

China National Automotive Industry Import and Export Corporation,
Nanjing Company Ltd.
331 Zhongyang Road
Nanjing, Jiangsu Province
Tel: (25) 636-295
Fax: N/A

China National Automotive Industry Import & Export Corporation,
Shanghai Company Ltd.
390 Wukang Road
Shanghai 200031
Tel: (21) 433-6892
Fax: (21) 433-0518

China National Automotive Industry Import & Export Corporation,
Shenyang Company Ltd.
6/F Jinbei Auto Building
57 Zhonghua Road
Shenyang, 100001, Liaoning Province
Tel: (24) 368-870, 368-974, 372-241, 369-130, 369-194
Fax: (24) 723-736

China National Automotive Industry Import & Export Corporation,
Shenzhen Company Ltd.
Room 1404, Tower No. 3, Tongjian Building
Shennan Road Central
Shenzhen, Guangdong Province
Tel: N/A
Fax: (755) 360-447

China National Automotive Industry Import & Export Corporation,
Tianjin Company Ltd.
78 Yantai Road
Tianjin 300040
Tel: (22) 317-809
Fax: (22) 317-268

China National Automotive Industry Import & Export Corporation,
Wuhan Company Ltd.
727 Jiefang Avenue
Hankou, Wuhan, Hubei Province
Tel: (27) 24216
Fax: (27) 26594

Other Useful Contacts

Beijing Car & Motorcycle Manufacturing Company
Chaoyang District
Beijing 100020
Tel: 5019145

Beijing Coach Company Ltd.
Fengtai District
Beijing 100075
Tel: 722233

Beijing Jeep Company Ltd (Joint Venture)
Shuang Jing, Chaoyang Qu
Beijing, 100022
Fax: 771-1363

Beijing Light Automobile Company Ltd.
Haidian District
Beijing 100044
Tel: 8417722

Changchun Passenger Coach Works
Kuancheng, Changchun
Jilin Province 130062
Tel: 73981

Chengdu Engine Company
Shuangqiaozi, Chengdu District
Chengdu, Sichuan Province 610067
Tel: 443112

China No. 1 Automobile Plant
Chaoyang, Changchun
Jilin Province
Tel: (431) 505-404
Fax: (431) 867-780

China No. 2 Automobile Plant
Shiyan
Hubei Province 442001
Tel: 23460

Chongqing Auto Engine Plant
Shapingba, Chongqing
Sichuan Province 630031
Tel: 662836

Chongqing Automobile Manufactory
Jiulongpo, Chongqing
Sichuan Province 630052
Tel: 623300

Dandong Automobile Works
Zhen'an District, Dandong
Liaoning Province 118008
Tel: 62161

Ford International Business Development Inc., Beijing
Jingguang Office Tower #2612
Beijing 100026
Tel: 501-2058/2059
Fax: 501-2037

General Motors Overseas Corporation
(Automotive/technical assistance in Joint Ventures)
SCITE Tower #403
Beijing 100004
Tel: 512-2288 ext. 403
Fax: 512-3618

Guangzhou Peugeot Automobile Company (Joint Venture)
Hengsha
Huangpu 510700
Tel: 2279704
Fax: 347-484

Jiangxi Automobile Manufactory
Qingyunpu, Nanchang
Jiangxi Province 330001
Tel: 251809

Jinan General Automobile Manufactory
Tianqiao, Jinan
Shandong Province 250031
Tel: 551199

Jinbei Auto Company Ltd.
Tiexi, Shenyang
Liaoning Province 110025
Tel: 454271

Liuzhou Minicar Factory
Liuzhou
Guanxi Province 545007
Tel: 22893

Liuzhou Motor Manufactory
Liuzhou,
Guangxi Province 545005
Tel: 331982

Nanjing Automotive Works
Gulou, Nanjing
Jiangsu Province 210009
Tel: 313551

No. 2 Automobile Complex, Hangzhou Branch
Xiacheng, Hangzhou
Zhejiang Province 310006
Tel: 893324

Shaanxi Automobile Works
Qishan County, Baoji
Shaanxi Province 722408
Tel:

Shanghai Automobile Plant
Jiaxing County
Shanghai 201805
Tel: 9567780

Shanghai Volkswagen Automotive Company Ltd. (Joint Venture)
Luopu Lu, Anting
Jiading County 201805
Tel: (21) 956-7780
Fax: (21) 952-9815

Shijiazhuang Automobile Plant
Qiaodong, Shijiazhuang
Hebei Province 050041
Tel: 647243

Sichuan Automobile Plant
Shuangqiao District, Chongqing
Sichuan Province 630900
Tel: 42124

Tianjin Automobile Manufactory
Beijiro, Tianjin 300401
Tel: 590418

Tianjin Mini Automobile Factory
Xijiao District
Tianjin 300380
Tel: 791845

Xinjiang Automobile Plant
Xinshi District, Urumqi
Xinjiang-Uygur Autonomous District 830011
Tel: 336800

Yizheng Automobile Manufactory
No. 47 Qianjin Road, Yizheng
Jiangsu Province 211400
Tel: 442532

Yunnan Dongfeng Automobile Factory
Xishan, Kunming
Yunnan Province 650106
Tel: 81271

AUTOMOTIVE PARTS & SERVICE EQUIPMENT

Table 82 summarizes some statistics for the automobile parts and service industry (3).

Table 82

Review of Automotive Parts & Service Equipment Industry (3)

A)	Three letter ITA industry sector code:	APS
B)	Est. total market size (USD million):	
	1991 -	$ 7,000
	1992 -	$ 8,000
	1993 -	$ 9,300
	1994 -	$10,170
	1995 -	$11,080 (58)
C)	Est. 1992-4 annual market growth rate:	15%
D)	Est. total imports (USD millions):	
	1991 -	$ 880
	1992 -	$1,000
	1993 -	$5,500
	1994 -	$6,050
	1995 -	$6,655 (58)
E)	Est. annual total import growth rate:	15%
F)	Est. imports from U.S. (USD millions):	
	1991 -	$100
	1992 -	$120
	1993 -	$670
	1994 -	$737
	1995 -	$810 (58)
G)	Est. annual growth of imports from USA:	15%
H)	China's receptivity to U.S. products in this sector (5 - High/1 - Low):	3
I) ·	Competition from local/third countries for U.S. firms (5 - Low/1 - High):	2
J)	Chinese market barriers to U.S. sales in this sector (5 - Few/1 - Many):	3
K)	Comments - factors for increased U.S. sales:	

* Purchases of parts and accessories by US-Chinese joint ventures; JV's are increasingly localizing their parts for motor vehicles.
* The market for special purpose vehicle parts is a stronger market than that for sedan parts.

L)	Most promising sub-sectors	1992 Market Size
	1. Special purpose vehicles' parts accessories (e.g. for cement, freight, oil tank, chemical, garbage, ambulance, and other such vehicles).	$800 Million
	2. Auto and motorcycle parts and accessories (e.g. rear axle components, air conditioning equipment, special/ luxury gear).	$600 Million

Some useful contacts in the automotive parts industry include:

Changsha Automobile Electric Equipment Factory
Changsha, Hunan Province 410005
Tel: 26301

Chengdu Light Automobile Re-Equipment Plant
Gaoshengqiao, Laonanmenwei, Wuhou District
Chengdu, Sichuan Province 610041
Tel: 581667

Guangzhou Battery Factory
Haizhu District, Guangzhou
Guangdong Province 510253
Tel: 4449532

Luoyang Bearing Factory
Jianxi District, Luoyang
Henan Province 471039
Tel: 411244

Shanghai Auto Gear Factory
Jiading County, Shanghai 201800
Tel: 953 0122

Shanghai Battery Factory
Hongkou District, Shanghai 200081
Tel: 6627600

Shanghai Bearing Corporation
Huangpu District, Shanghai 200003
Tel: 3226881

Wafangdian Bearing Plant
Beigongjijie, Wafangdian
Lianing Province 116300
Tel: 3850

Some useful contacts in the tire industry are as follows:

Anhui Tyre Plant
Dongshi, Hefei
Anhui Province 230011
Tel: 482021

Beijing Tyre Plant
Haidian District, Beijing 100085
Tel: 2912244

Chongqing General Tyre Plant
Jiulongpo, Chongqing
Sichuan Province 630052
Tel: 810456

Dongfeng Tyre Plant
Shiyan, Hubei Province 442053
Tel: 51211

Guangzhou Tyre Plant
Hua County, Guangzhou
Guangdong Province 510828
Tel: 66432299

Guizhou Tyre Plant
Guiyang, Guizhou Province 550008
Tel: 42213

Henan Tyre Plant
Jiefang District, Jiaozuo
Henan Province 454159
Tel: 333955

Liaoning Tyre Plant
Longchene, Chaoyang
Liaoning Province 122009
Tel: 210901

Shanghai Rubber & Tyre (Group) Corporation
Huangpu District, Shanghai 200002
Tel: 3290433

Weihai Tyre Plant
Weihai, Shandong Province 264200
Tel: 322771

AVIONICS & AIRLINE GROUND SUPPORT EQUIPMENT INDUSTRY

Table 83 summarizes some statistics for the avionics and airline ground support equipment industry.

Interestingly, in late 1994, the U.S. Secretary of Defense, William J. Perry, made an official visit to Beijing to build ties with the Chinese military establishment. One of the areas he covered was possible U.S.-China cooperation in developing air traffic control systems by channeling some of China's military spending together with U.S. technical assistance to improve China's airline safety.

Table 83

Review of Avionics and Airline Support Equipment Industry (3)

A)	Three letter ITA industry sector code:	APG
B)	Est. total market size (USD millions):	
	1991 -	$300
	1992 -	$375
C)	Est. 1992-4 annual market growth rate:	25%
D)	Est. total imports (USD millions):	
	1991 -	$ 70
	1992 -	$ 88
E)	Est. annual total import growth rate:	25%
F)	Est. imports from U.S. (USD millions):	
	1991 -	$ 35
	1992 -	$ 45
G)	Est. annual growth of imports from USA:	30%
H)	China's receptivity to U.S. products in this sector (5 - High/1 - Low):	5
I)	Competition from local/third countries for U.S. firms (5 - Low/1 - High):	4
J)	Chinese market barriers to U.S. sales in this sector (5 - Few/1 - Many):	4
K)	Comments - factors for increased U.S. sales:	

* Close cooperation between FCS & U.S. firms has helped increase sales, particularly in Guangzhou.
* New airports are being built in China, old ones are being upgraded.
* Controls on sales to China of high tech equipment have been loosened.
* Purchases of aircraft from the U.S. are increasing.

	Most promising sub-sectors	1992 Market Size
L)	1. Navigational aids	$60 million
	2. Radio/radar equipment	$50 million
	3. Communications equipment	$200 million

Overview Air Traffic Control (ATC) and related equipment includes: radars, meteorology equipment, communication, navigation and landing aids, instrument landing systems, terminal area and control center equipment and information systems satellites.

In China's rapidly expanding market, the aviation sector stands to be one of the most promising for US exports. since 1990 China's annual air passenger volume has grown at an average rate of 30%, reaching 28.7 million passengers in 1992. Economic reform, burgeoning tourism and the drag of poor ground transportation on economic growth have led to the rapid expansion of the civil aviation sector. In order to meet this new demand, airports are being constructed and renovated.

During the last fifteen years, air traffic control procurement in China has taken a back seat to fleet expansion. This had led to the relatively backward state of air traffic control in China. Furthermore, the purchasing of modern equipment and technical training has been hindered by a lack of coordination, priority and funding. These factors have contributed to the substandard safety reputation of China's airlines.

In order to remedy this situation, and to demonstrate to the world its commitment to safety and modernization, China has committed itself to the upgrading of its civil navigation system. China's State Council has slated several hundred million of dollars in the coming years for improving and expanding its civil navigation system. The Chinese government plans to invest over one billion RMB (USD 200 million) alone in upgrading its ATC systems during the current Eighth Five-Year Plan (1991-1995). During this period ten new airports in southern and central China have been planned. Nationwide, over the next ten years, forty major airports and forty minor airports are slated to be built anew or modernized. Many of these will require ATC equipment. In addition to central and local government funding, capital will come from several external sources, notably Japan's Overseas Economic Cooperation Fund (OECF). China welcomes foreign investment to help finance its many infrastructure projects including airports.

The Chinese market for ATC and related equipment is projected to expand by 30% annually for the next several years. This estimate is based on production and sales figures provided from major international ATC suppliers, as well as import statistics.

China does not supply its airports with domestic equipment; purchases of most sophisticated equipment come primarily from overseas. Thus, this market is extremely import friendly. If American companies can offer competitive prices, they will be well positioned to capture a substantial share of China's growing market.

Over the next six years, East China's airport development will race to catch up and keep pace with the double digit economic growth which has transformed East China itself. Major Plans include construction of eighteen airports, including two large scale international airports, and improvements on twenty existing airports, including a second runway and a new terminal building for Shanghai's Hong Qiao airport. Estimated value of imported equipment and services is USD 62 million. A proposal for an international airport in Pudong which could require USD 100 million in imports is under study.

Thus, China offers a potentially large market for U.S. manufactured ground support and airport equipment and related services. Transportation in China is still underdeveloped, and air transport and the equipment and services which support it are important. Several major, new airports are being planned and built, and a number of smaller ones are being redesigned and/or upgraded. This market was created and is expanding because of the increasing demand, not only for ground support and airport equipment and services (GSAES), but also for consulting services and equipment covering all aspects of airport development-construction of new buildings, development of airport infrastructure, airfield design and construction, and airspace safety and navigational considerations (12).

The forces which will influence changes in this market vis-a-vis U.S. sales prospects include:

a. U.S. perceptions of whether the Chinese government is prepared to loosen central political and economic controls, thus encouraging more foreigners to visit the PRC and creating an increased demand for GSAES;

b. The U.S. government's willingness to loosen controls on sales to China of certain key, high-tech GSAES equipment; and

c. Availability of funding. The PRC government plays a dominant role in this sub-sector market. The Civil Aviation Leading Group of China, established in 1984, projects the PRC's civil aviation requirements, policies, and priorities. The Civil Aviation Administration of China (CAAC), the organization which oversees and coordinates all of China's national airline companies, is the PRC's principal end-user of airport equipment. There are six airlines under CAAC—Air China, China Eastern Airlines, China Southern Airlines, China Southwest Airlines, China Northern Airlines, and China Northwest Airlines. CAAC's procurement arm is the China Aviation Supply Corporation (CASC), and CASC's First Department is responsible for business with U.S. Companies. If the central government loosens control over GSAES-related purchases and projects, local authorities and enterprises can, if they have the funds, pick up the ball and run more quickly with it.

Market Assessment The Chinese airline industry is growing rapidly. Local demand (generated by increasing numbers of local Chinese traveling inside of China and by increasing air freight) and foreign demand (tourists, business people, and others from abroad) are increasing year by year. The number of passengers flown by China's airlines has grown about 23% per annum from the early 1970's through 1990, and demand in the GSAES sub-sector has increased proportionately. Cargo increases, 1990 to 2005, are expected to average about 22% per annum, and this means a continuing demand in the GSAES sub-sector. Between 1988 and 1993, new airports are being built in many parts of China including Jinan, Shandong Province; Nantong and Nanjing, Jiangsu Province; and elsewhere. Old airports being improved include Hongqiao in Shanghai; Hangzhou in Zhejiang; Xiamen and Fuzhou in Fujian; and Nanchang in Jiangxi. The Sanya Airport, Hainan Island, is another new project. China Southern Airlines is undertaking six projects now—Enshi Airport in Hubei, Tianhe Airport in Wuhan, Fenghuang Airport in Sanya, Fuyong Airport in Shenzhen, Changde Airport in Hunan, and Nanyang Airport in Henan. A new airport is being built in Guilin, Guangxi.

There is a new, ICAO-approved cross-USSR and cross-China air route for which the PRC will need four or five air route surveillance radars (ASR's). When sufficient access roads like the Shenzhen-Guanzhou superhighway are planned and built for new airports, the numbers of passengers will increase a great deal. All kinds of equipment and services in the GSAES sub-sector will probably be needed to serve the increase in consumers.

There are many small, new projects being planned in remote parts of China and Tibet. These include the installation of communications and navigation equipment and the construction of a new terminal building at the Gonggar Airport in Lhasa, Tibet; the importation of about USD two million worth of communications, illumination, navigation, and other equipment, as well as vehicles, for the Guiyuang Airport in Guizhou Province; and the possible establishment of an aircraft maintenance station at the CAAC Flying College in Guanghan, Sichuan Province for Piper/Cheyenne aircraft.

From CAAC's perspective, satellite systems offer two advantages. First, the technology is advanced and very reliable. Second, the transition to satellite systems will be fairly easy in China because, given the present rudimentary ATC system, there will be no need to abandon an extensive existing ground based system.

Any such system must meet international civil aviation organization (ICAO) standards. China is therefore interested in international cooperation. CAAC is currently working with Japan's Civil Aviation Bureau to produce studies on future navigation systems, for example. According to CAAC, Japanese Yen loan allocations, either between now and 1995 or during the Ninth Five-Year Plan (1995-2000), will be used to finance the purchase of 100 satellite ground stations in order to improve the country's satellite navigation capability. This will not be enough to cover the whole of Chinese airspace, but is viewed as an important first step.

Over forty major new airport or airport renovation projects are planned for the next five to ten years. CAAC officials have said that there will be about forty smaller projects undertaken at the provincial level as well, two or three per province. Companies interested in provincial projects should contact the local governments concerned. As a general rule, capital cities and cities in popular tourist or business locations will be likely targets for new or renovated airports. Below is a partial list of the large scale projects:

There are currently five large scale, high priority projects in process:

- **Beijing Airport:** A new terminal building is to be built, in part, with OECF support.
- **Guilin Airport:** Construction of a new runway to accommodate Boeing 747 aircraft. Guilin reportedly has its own foreign exchange for imports.
- **Fuzhou Airport:** Construction of a new runway for 747's. The city is seeking investment to finance the project.
- **Urumuqi Airport:** Construction of a new runway for 747's. This point is to be a key link in the proposed plan to establish an air route from southern China through Russia to Europe.
- **Chengdu Airport:** A renovation project to include a new runway and terminal building.

The feasibility studies for seven more large projects have been approved. They are now in the preliminary design phase:

- **Nanjing Airport:** Construction of a new airport to handle 747's. Discussions are reportedly underway with the Dutch Government which may lead to the provision of a soft loan.
- **Zhengzhou Airport:** A renovation project of unspecified parameters.
- **Harbin Airport:** Construction of a new airport, possibly with a loan from the South Korean Government.
- **Yinchuan (Ningxia Autonomous Region):** Construction of a facility to handle MD-82 aircraft.
- **Dunhuang Airport (Gansu Province):** Construction of a new airport to handle MD-82's.
- **Sanya Airport (Hainan):** A new airport, possibly to be financed with a French Government loan.
- **Guangzhou Airport:** Two plans are under consideration. First, to renovate the existing airport with a new runway. Second, to build an entirely new airport.
- **Haikou Airport (Hainan):** Construction of a new airport.
- **Hangzhou Airport:** Construction of a new airport.

Other important projects either underway or soon to be undertaken are:

- **East China Air Group,** an investment group formed by six regional governments (covering Shandong, Jiangsu, Zhejiang, Anhui, Jiangxi, and Fujian provinces) and China Eastern, one of the largest airlines, plans to invest 10 billion RMB (USD 1.8 million) to expand civil aviation facilities. Twenty new airports are planned by the year 2000.
- **Shanghai's Hongqiao airport** is scheduled for a major expansion beginning in 1994, to be completed in 2005. ATC equipment will be needed. (The expansion includes a second runway and a new terminal area.)
- **New airports** will be built at Zhoushan and Quzhou, in Zhejiang Province.
- **Wuzhou Airport** will build a medium-sized feeder airport. Telecommunications and Navaids will be bought through China Southern Airline's purchasing department.
- **The construction of Liuzhou airport** will require new telecommunications, meteorological, and Navaids equipment.
- **Gaoqi International Airport** (Xiamen special economic zone) is currently undergoing an expansion. (The expansion includes a new taxiway, terminal building, and oil depot.)
- **Hainan Province** is going to build Sanya Fenghuang Airport (Sanya City).
- **Yixu in Fuzhou** will house the country's first instrument guidance system - USD 2.9 million of German equipment has already been installed.
- **Wuhan Tianhe International Airport** will be receiving an OECF loan worth 7.850 billion yen (USD 47.3 million).

Companies should follow plans to build or renovate airports in the following cities: Shenzhen, Xiamen, Dalian, Shantou, Wenzhou, Ningbo, Yantai, Qingdao, Chongqing, Dayong, Zhuhai, Yichang, Yanji, Beihai, and Guiyang.

In East China alone, phenomenal economic growth over the past two years has outpaced growth in infrastructural services, particularly airport capacity. Demand on air services was extreme; airlines doubled, sometimes tripled flights to most destinations and even wet-leased from the Russians to accommodate passenger demand. Estimated passenger volume for 1993 in East China (comprised of Shanghai and the provinces of Zhejiang, Jiangsu and Anhui) is 8 million, serviced by 150 domestic air routes and thirteen international air routes. Shanghai's Hongqiao Airport, completed a two-year expansion in 1991, expecting to accommodate passenger increases through 1997. It reached full capacity, however, last year when its passenger throughput totalled 6.5 million passengers. Overall, passenger and cargo throughput grew 30% in 1992 but airports in East China have limitations in terms of size and equipment. Runway length restricts plane size and related passenger load, while limited navigational and other equipment precludes night flights and all-weather landings. This situation will get worse before it gets better. Continued air traffic growth will put additional strains on East China's congested and poorly equipped airports.

To improve the situation, East China plans to construct eighteen airports within the next five years, providing unlimited opportunities for U.S. exporters of equipment and services. The estimated market for imports is USD 52 million. Improvements on many of East China's existing twenty airport facilities could offer an additional USD 15 million in export opportunities. Construction of two large scale airports, located in Nanjing, Jiangsu Province, and in Shaoshan, Zhejiang Province, will present opportunities for design and construction of terminal buildings as well as overall airport design. Shanghai plans to add another runway and construct a new international terminal building, the latter to replace a facility which opened only two years ago. Construction plans for a massive, almost USD 1 billion international airport in Pudong are on hold, pending completion of the Shanghai second runway project as well as a clearer indication of where Pudong is heading (13).

Competitive Situation

Domestic Production China produces limited amounts of airport equipment, mainly low-end avionics such as radar and also baggage carrousels. Smaller airports prefer local equipment because of its cheaper prices, but this preference may change as smaller airports increase their awareness of aviation safety and their understanding of the more efficient imported equipment. Unless foreign firms provide technology transfers, it is unlikely that China will move beyond its current capability of small-scale, low-end production.

China Electronics Import & Export Corporation, one of China's few air equipment manufacturers, consistently bids lowest or second-to-lowest in international tender offers. They market their own products, Chinatron's products, as well as those of subcontractors. So far they have had limited success with OECF tenders for several reasons. First, while supplying some ATC equipment, they have little experience in and limited capabilities for putting up entire systems. Second, the Chinese government lacks confidence in Chinese technology when compared to that offered by international leaders. Third, when receiving OECF loans they have no special advantages, unlike World Bank loans where they receive a 15% price preference.

In order to develop their industrial capabilities, Chinese companies have sought foreign joint ventures, but with limited success. Chinatron, an electronics manufacturer involved in the production of all types of electronics, is one such company that is very interested in finding an American partner. The head of the company believes that a joint venture with an American company will reduce the costs of production for the American company, especially in the long run. A joint venture project will also receive the approval of the central government, which, it is hoped, will result in more contracts. According to Chinatron, American companies are favored because they are perceived to have superior technology.

Lockheed has a USD 30 million aircraft maintenance facility in Guangzhou. Piper may establish a maintenance station in Guanghan, Sichuan. Another American firm might consider some kind of cooperative arrangement with a Chinese factory to produce semi-advanced systems.

Imports Imports represent a large portion of this sub-sector. Domestic production is an adequate source for some basic equipment, but air traffic control systems are more complex and require very sophisticated equipment, most of which is acquired from foreign companies.

Imports are important in the advanced equipment fields—ASR's, ATC's, navaids, etc. China's more sophisticated airports will require up-to-date and state-of-the-art equipment in these areas as well as lighting, compressors, building controls, measuring equipment, and probably even specialized ground vehicles. Imports from he U.S. in the GSAES sub-sector are (probably) not keeping with Chinese demands. There is probably little sourcing from non-market economies; the USSR gave or sold China some basic radars years ago, and one U.S. company is considering updating them to create new devices.

Large size airports such as Shanghai's Hongqiao, Jiangsu's Nanjing and Zhejiang's Shaoshan have, or will have, a strong preference for imported equipment. Since these large scale airports will each import about USD 8-9 million in equipment, they represent about half the import market.

U.S. Market Position and Share According to industry sources, U.S. equipment enjoys an excellent reputation. Market share reflects this. The estimated U.S. market share is 85%. Canada (fueling equipment), Germany (radar, refueling equipment, trucks), Norway (ILS, PAPI) and Japan (trucks and refueling equipment) are the strongest competitors for U.S. firms. While these countries frequently offer soft loans to their suppliers, East China CAAC noted that they do not like the restrictions involved with tied aid and are willing to pay more for purchasing freedom. Soft loans will continue to cause U.S. suppliers major defeats, however, particularly at cash-starved smaller airports. Japanese firms are becoming increasingly aggressive, in response to the growing market potential for airport equipment.

Only a few American companies have been active in China's ATC market over the past decade. Generally high prices through the 1980s and American export controls which have kept some high-tech firms from making sales, have combined to keep America's market share small. An additional difficulty that U.S. companies face is China's inadequate infrastructure, which lacks the ability to fully absorb the higher technological level of U.S. products. Nevertheless, U.S. firms have maintained a 20-25% share of the Chinese market, and because of recent defense cutbacks in the U.S. and the strength of the Chinese economy, many more American companies are seriously attempting to enter China's market. A barometer of this trend is the level of American participation in the recent OECF tenders. One U.S. company tendered a bid in the 1992 procurement round; eleven were involved in the competition for the 1993 round.

In general, U.S. companies have a competitive advantage in quality, but suffer because of their higher prices. In one case, a U.S. company's equipment was judged to be too expensive and too technically advanced for the targeted airport, and thus it was not considered for purchase. According to CAAC, the situation at this airport did not warrant the more expensive technology the U.S. company offered. The Chinese have traditionally compromised on technology in favor of low prices. Accordingly, much of the equipment purchased has been in the middle to low end of the price spectrum.

Several U.S. companies have adopted a productive strategy which targets projects that require high-tech equipment when compromises cannot be made. Many of the southern airports, especially in the special economic zones (SEZ's), are tremendously busy. Because of their heavy traffic, these airports require extremely sophisticated and reliable equipment, thus making them ideal markets for American ATC companies.

Some trends in U.S. sales of air traffic control equipment to China is given in Table 84.

Table 84

Air Traffic Control Equipment

U.S. Exports to China
in thousands of dollars

		1990	1991	1992
1.	Radio Navigation Aids	8,069	8,415	10,071
2.	Electrical Instrument aeronautical or space navigation	4,422	8,654	5,470
3.	Radio transmitters (for civil aircraft	28	9	125
4.	Radio transceivers (for civil aircraft)	2,692	2,888	5,306
5.	Communications satellites	39,049	NA	77,764
6.	Radar, radio navigation aid antennas	18	366	182

CAAC planners and local airports use four criteria to evaluate equipment for possible acquisition:

a. *Price:*
China is only just beginning ATC modernization, so considerable demand exists for equipment and technology. CAAC has been given approval to acquire as much equipment and technology as possible, but funds are limited. The financial constraints result in purchases of technologically-inferior equipment which CAAC believes is adequate for China's situation. However, CAAC is beginning to consider more carefully the full life-cycle costs of equipment against offer prices received in response to tenders. These calculations are based more on the actual experience of Chinese end-users than any mathematical or technical evaluation. Nevertheless, price is still the most important factor.

b. *Suitable Technology:*
Technology must be suitable for China's conditions. Some less advanced equipment may be suitable for certain areas of China. Questions concerning the capability of ATC personnel to absorb high technology training areas as well. Regional differences play a role in the technology equation. The eastern parts of China re well-endowed with universities and college graduates with English skills are relatively available. The western parts of China are handicapped in the sense that higher education is simply less available. Equipment that may be appropriate in the East may not be in the West. Equipment purchased for the modernization of the eastern route structure will probably be among the world's more advanced models. In the West, equipment will be less advanced, yet reliable in terms of performance.

c. *Potential for Technological Upgrade:*
Taking into account China's goal to develop a nationwide ATC system, and future plans for air traffic management controlled by satellites and ground stations, the capacity for equipment upgrade is an important consideration. As noted, future plans include a possible upgrade to "Mode S" technology and satellite communication. As test cases in satellite communications and radar, CAAC is now using six satellite ground stations to cover gaps in radar tracking along several domestic air routes.

d. *Reliability:*
CAAC wants dependable, long-lasting equipment. Therefore, vendor and product history are important considerations in purchasing decisions. After sales and maintenance assistance from the manufacturer is also essential and carefully evaluated.

An additional note on conditions that affect American companies' competitive position in China concerns the method by which companies structure their tender offers. U.S. companies submit very detailed bids that include spare parts expenses and projected maintenance needs. The original bid considers and accounts for all technical aspects of a project. This method is sound from an engineering point of view, but with all the costs factored in, American prices turn out to be quite high. Other foreign companies, on the other hand, tend to submit vague bids that do not include all the technical and engineering details. Consideration of spare parts is often left for future sales. This enables these companies to offer low initial prices, even though the long-term cost to the end-user is often higher than the original American price.

According to officials, CAAC applies three essential principles in all procurement deliberations:

1. **Technology:** Technology must be the best and most reliable for the price offered.
2. **Price:** Prices must be reasonable given the technology and capability of the equipment.
3. **Service:** After sales service and maintenance assistance from the manufacturer is essential and is evaluated carefully.

Market Access: There are relatively few market access barriers for U.S. exporters of airport equipment because there is really no domestic airport equipment industry to protect, and China wants to develop its airports quickly. This will require China to import equipment and services. In fact, in an attempt to attract foreign funding, China recently began to encourage foreign investment, mainly in terminal construction and operations. China assumes that foreign investors can recoup their investment by operating terminal building concessions.

Distribution/Business Practices - China does not have an established system of independent agents or distributors, so U.S. companies must use other methods for penetrating China's market. To market products and services in China, FCS recommends using the services of a trading company, either from the U.S., Hong Kong or Taiwan. Experience in the China market, as well as product knowledge, are required qualifications.

Importing into China often requires import licenses and approval to spend foreign exchange. However, if the Bank of China (BOC) or another state-owned bank issues a letter of credit, the U.S. seller can usually be sure that necessary approvals have been obtained.

Most BOC LC's are sight LC's. Payment is made only after the Chinese bank which issued the LC has received the export documents. This means a minimum 10-20 day wait before the U.S. exporter can collect payment for goods delivered. (For example, a U.S. exporter would arrange for all export documents to be shipped to BOC, and then would have to wait for BOC to review the documents before collecting payment.)

A second common Chinese payment practice affects large equipment sales and technology exports to China. For such sales, Chinese buyers typically make a 10-25% down payment, then pay 70-75% on delivery and the remaining 10-25% on installation. However, at the time of the initial down payment, Chinese buyers often require a Standby Letter of Credit from the seller's bank, guaranteeing the return of the down payment if sales terms are not met. A problem arises when a smaller U.S. exporter does not have a credit line sufficient to cover the required Standby LC.

The prospects for straight cash sales to China are limited by shortage of foreign exchange (in the hands of would-be importers) and by government policies that stress the development of domestic manufacturing capability over importing finished goods. Although there are no legislatively mandated countertrade requirements, common forms of business with China now include countertrade and compensation trade, leasing, and technology licensing arrangements.

China's Central government exerts strict control over foreign exchange allocation, and foreign exchange controls constitute a significant non-tariff barrier. Most of China's imports and exports are handled by a relatively small number of state-owned trading companies authorized to transact business involving foreign exchange.

Best Sales Prospects

Equipment most needed from abroad includes (14):

A (R) SR's - Air (Route) Surveillance Radar Systems
ATC/NAV/Com - Air Traffic Control/Navigational Aids/Communication equipment
ALS's - Approach Light Systems
ATC/AMS's - Air Traffic Control/Air Space Management Systems
Air Conditioning Systems
Baggage movers
Baggage claim equipment
Customs/security equipment
Computers (for financial data and for operational data)
Cargo equipment - movers, scales, storage equipment
Catering equipment
Closed-circuit TV systems
Escalators and elevators
Fire prevention equipment
Heavy-duty equipment (cranes, bulldozers, sweepers, mowers, compressors)
Handicap services equipment
ILS's - Instrument Landing Systems
Jet-start compressors
Lights - runway and taxiway edge
MLS's - Microwave Landing Systems
MSSR's - Monopulse Secondary Surveillance Radar Systems
Navaids - Navigational Aids
Operations center and control tower equipment
Passenger movers (horizontal)
Refueling trucks
RML's - Remote Microwave Links
Radar systems
PAPI's - runway Precision Approach Path Indicators

Safety and rescue equipment
Telephone systems
Ticketing equipment
Transmitter/receivers
Terminal building controls
Vehicles (trucks, sedans, jeeps, vans, buses)
VOR/DME - Visual Omni-Range/Distance Measuring Equipment
Water purification/filtration equipment

Services most needed from abroad include:

Studies - engineering, consulting, and design,
   a) for airport buildings, infrastructure, administration;
   b) for airfield construction;
   c) for airspace use;
   d) for traveler flows and freight movement flows;
   e) for environmental issues (principally water, but also local impact studies).

Also needed are:

a) Training on financial data and operational data computers
b) Management enhancement program assistance with radar system organization, domestically and internationally
c) Terminal/concession services (e.g., specialty shops, car rentals, western restaurants, banks/currency exchanges, business service centers, telephone/fax services - for major international airport centers only)

Key Contacts:

China Aviation Supplies Corporation
First Department
155 Dong Si Street
West Beijing, China
P.O. Box 612 Beijing 100710
Tel: 401-2233 X8077   Fax: 401-6392

China Chamber of Commerce for Machinery &
Electronic Products Import & Export
67 Jiao Nan Street
P.O. Box 33-2
Beijing, China 100712
Tel: 401-3322 X3505/3507 Fax: 401-9375

CAAC (Civil Aviation Administration of China)
Capital Construction Division
Capital Construction & Airport Department
155 Dong Si Street, West
Beijing, China 100710
Tel: 401-2233 X8758 Fax: 401-4104

Civil Aviation Administration of China
Capital Construction & Airport Department
155 Dong Si Street, West
Beijing, China
Tel: 401-2233 X8723

BANKS

The history of the Chinese banking system has been somewhat checkered. Nationalization and consolidation of the country's banks received the highest priority in the earliest years of the People's Republic, and banking was the first sector to be completely socialized. In the period of recovery after the Chinese Civil War (1949-52), the People's Bank of China moved very effectively to halt raging inflation and bring the nation's finances under central control. Over the course of time, the banking organization was modified repeatedly to suit changing conditions and new policies (4).

The banking system was centralized early on under the Ministry of Finance, which exercised firm control over all financial services, credit, and the money supply. During the 1980s, the banking system was expanded and diversified to meet the needs of the reform program, and the scale of banking activity rose sharply. New budgetary procedures required state enterprises to remit to the state only a tax on income and to seek investment funds in the form of bank loans. Between 1979 and 1985, the volume of deposits nearly tripled and the value of bank loans rose by 260 percent. By 1987, the banking system included the People's Bank of China, Agricultural Bank, Bank of China (which handled foreign exchange matters), China Investment Bank, China Industrial and Commercial Bank, People's Construction Bank, Communications Bank, People's Insurance Company of China, rural credit cooperatives, and urban credit cooperatives.

The People's Bank of China was the central bank and the foundation of the banking system. Although the bank overlapped in function with the Ministry of Finance and lost many of its responsibilities during the Cultural Revolution, in the 1970s it was restored to its leading position. As the central bank, the People's Bank of China had sole responsibility for issuing currency and controlling the money supply. It also served as the government treasury, the main source of credit for economic units, the clearing center for financial transactions, the holder of enterprise deposits, the national savings bank, and a ubiquitous monitor of economic activities.

Another financial institution, the Bank of China, handled all dealings in foreign exchange. It was responsible for allocating the country's foreign exchange reserves, arranging foreign loans, setting exchange rates for China's currency, issuing letters of credit, and generally carrying out all financial transactions with foreign firms and individuals. The Bank of China had offices in Beijing and other cities engaged in foreign trade and maintained overseas offices in major international financial centers, including Hong Kong, London, New York, Singapore, and Luxembourg.

The Agricultural Bank was created in the 1950s to facilitate financial operations in the rural areas. The Agricultural Bank provided financial support to agricultural units. It issued loans, handled state appropriations for agriculture, directed the operations of the rural credit cooperatives, and carried out overall supervision of rural financial affairs. The Agricultural Bank was headquartered in Beijing and had a network of branches throughout the country. It flourished in the late 1950s and mid-1960s, but languished thereafter until the late 1970s, when the functions and autonomy of the Agricultural Bank were increased substantially to help promote higher agricultural production. In the 1980s, it was restructured again and given greater authority in order to support the growth and diversification of agriculture under the responsibility system.

The People's Construction Bank managed state appropriations and loans for capital construction. It checked the activities of loan recipients to ensure that the funds were used for their designated construction purpose. Money was disbursed in stages as a project progressed. The reform policy shifted the main source of investment funding from the government budget to bank loans and increased the responsibility and activities of the People's Construction Bank.

In the mid-1980s, the banking system still lacked some of the services and characteristics that were considered basic in most countries. Interbank relations were very limited, and interbank borrowing and lending were virtually unknown. Checking accounts were used by very few individuals, and bank credit cards did not exist. In 1986, initial steps were taken in some of these areas. Interbank borrowing and lending networks were created among twenty-seven cities along the Chang Jiang and among fourteen cities in north China. Interregional financial networks were created to link banks in eleven leading cities all over China, including Shenyang, Guangzhou, Wuhan, Chongqing, and Xi'an and also link the branches of the Agricultural Bank. The first Chinese credit card, the Great Wall Card, was introduced in June 1986 to be used for foreign exchange transactions. Another financial innovation in 1986 was the opening of China's first stock exchanges since 1949. Small stock exchanges began operations somewhat tentatively in Shenyang, Liaoning Province, in August 1986 and in Shanghai in September 1986.

Throughout the history of the People's Republic, the banking system has exerted close control over financial transactions and the money supply. All government departments, publicly and collectively owned economic units, and social, political, military, and educational organizations were required to hold their financial balances as bank deposits. They were also instructed to keep on hand only enough cash to meet daily expenses; all major financial transactions were to be conducted through banks. Payment for goods and services exchanged by economic units was accomplished by debiting the account of the purchasing unit and crediting that of the selling unit by the appropriate amount. This practice effectively helped to minimize the need for currency.

The following is a list of A) Chinese banks such as those described above and B) American banks doing business in China.

Chinese:

People's Bank of China
Communication Division
32 Chengfang Street
Beijing, China 100800
Tel: (86-1) 601-6705/601-6707
Fax: (86-1) 601-6704

Bank of China (Headquarters)
American & Oceanic Division of the Foreign Affairs Bureau
410 Fuchengmennei Dajie
Beijing, China 100034
Tel: (86-1) 601-1829

Bank of China, Beijing Branch
Business Affairs Office
19 Dong'anmen Dajie
Beijing, China 100006
Tel: (86-1) 519-9114
Fax: (86-1) 512-2177

Agriculture Bank of China
Foreign Affairs Office
40 Fucheng Road, Yulong Hotel 3/F #2301
Beijing, China 100046
Tel: (86-1) 841-5588 x23007-23009/2301
Fax: (86-1) 841-3128

Industrial & Commercial Bank of China
Foreign Affairs Office
26 Xichangan Street
Beijing, China 100031
Tel: (86-1) 603-1062/3262299
Fax: (86-1) 603-1056

People's Construction Bank of China (Headquarters)
Foreign Affairs Office
C 12 Fuxing Road
Beijing, China 100810
Tel: (86-1) 851-4488 x4111/327-2505

People's Construction Bank of China, Beijing Branch
Foreign Affairs Department
Yanjing Hotel 2/F #13226
Tel: (86-1) 835-6688 x13226
Fax: (86-1) 835-7531

Investment Bank of China
Foreign Affairs Office
B11 A Zuo Fuxing Road, Meidiya Hotel Office Building #4455
Beijing, China 100038
Tel: (86-1) 5900
Fax: (86-1) 851-6088

Communication Bank of China
Foreign Affairs Office
12 Tiantan Dongli
Beijing, China 100061
Tel: (86-1) 701-2255 x3206/702-8807/511-2349
Fax: (86-1) 701-6524

Citic Industrial Bank
Foreign Affairs Office
Capital Mansion, 6 Xinyuan Nanli
Beijing, China 100027
Tel: (86-1) 466-0344
Fax: (86-1) 466-1059

State Development Bank
Yulong Hotel, 40 Fucheng Road, Haidian District
Beijing, China 100046
Tel: (86-1) 843-7253
Fax: (86-1) 843-7254

American:

American Express Bank
Beijing Representative Office
Room 2702, China World Trade Centre
Beijing, China 100004
Tel: (86-1) 5052838/5054626
Fax: (86-1) 5054626

Guangzhou Representative Office
CI, G/F, Central Lobby, Guangdong
International Hotel, 339 Huanshi Dong Lu
Guangzhou 510060
Tel: (86-20) 3311771
Fax: (86-20) 3313535

Shanghai Representative Office
Room 205, Ruijin Building, 205 Mao Ming Nan Road
Shanghai 200020
Tel: (86-21) 472-9390/472-7589
Fax: (86-21) 472-8400

Bank of America
Beijing Representative Office
Room 2722-23, China World Trade Centre
Beijing, China 100004
Tel: (86-1) 5053546/5053508/5053545
Fax: (86-1) 5053509

Guangzhou Branch
Room 1325, Dong Fang Hotel, 120 Liuhua Lu
Guangzhou 510016
Tel: (86-20) 6678063/6669900-1325
Fax: (86-20) 6678063

Shanghai Branch
Room 104-107A, Union Building Ground Floor
100 Yanan Dong Lu
Shanghai 200002
Tel: (86-21) 3292828
Fax: (86-21) 3201297

Bank of the Orient
Xiamen Branch
25 Xingsheng Road, Huili Industrial District
Xiamen 361006
Tel: (86-592) 625778
Fax: (86-592) 625798

Bankers Trust Company
Beijing Representative Office
Suite 125, Ground Floor, Lufthansa Center
50 Liangmaqiao Road, Chaoyang District
Tel: (86-1) 463-8-38
Fax: (86-1) 463-8037

Chase Manhattan Bank
Beijing Representative Office
Room 509/512
China Science & Technology Exchange Centre
Beijing, China 100004
Tel: (86-1) 5123457
Fax: (86-1) 5123693

Shanghai Representative Office
Shanghai Centre, Shanghai 200040
Tel: (86-21) 2797022

Tianjin Branch
14/F, Tianjin International Building
75 Nanjing Road, Tianjin 300050
Tel: (86-22) 3395111
Fax: (86-22) 3398111

Chemical Bank
Beijing Representative Office
Room 1205/1812
China Science & Technology Exchange Centre
Beijing 100004
Tel: (86-1) 5123700
Fax: (86-1) 5123771

Shanghai Representative Office
Room 2606, Union Building, 100 Yanan Dong Lu
Shanghai 200002
Tel: (86-21) 3261888/3263888
Fax: (86-1) 3201524

Citibank, N.A.
Beijing Representative Office
Room 1801/1811, Citic Building
Beijing, China 100004
Tel: (86-1) 5004425
Fax: (86-1) 5004425/5127930

Guangzhou Representative Office
Room 1215, Dong Fang Hotel
Guangzhou 510060
Tel: (86-20) 6667150

Shanghai Branch
Suite 509, Union Building, 100 Yanan Road
Shanghai 200002
Tel: (86-21) 328-9661, 328-9662, 320-1988
Fax: (86-21) 273-1317

Shenzhen Branch
38/F, International Financial Building
23 Jianshe Road
Shenzhen 528000
Tel: (86-755) 231138/232338
Fax: (86-755) 231238

Xiamen Representative Office
I/F, Meilihua Hotel, Xiamen 361006
Tel: (86-592) 5621666-818
Fax: (86-592) 621814

Far East National Bank
Beijing Representative Office
Room 5005, Beijing International Hotel
9 Jianguomennei Street
Beijing, China 100005
Tel: (86-1) 5126688-5005
Fax: (86-1) 5129972

First National Bank of Boston
Shanghai Representative Office
6/F, 9 Business Centre, Union Building
100 Yan An Road East
Shanghai 200002
Tel: (86-21) 3290808 x55/57
Fax: (86-21) 320-0244

First National Bank of Chicago
Beijing Representative Office
Room 1605, Citic Building
Beijing, China 100004
Tel: (86-1) 5003281/5003514; 5002255 x1640/41/50
Fax: (86-1) 5003166

Republic National Bank of New York
Beijing Representative Office
Room 2201, Liang Ma Tower, Chao Yang District
Beijing, China 100004
Tel: (86-1) 5066549
Fax: (86-1) 5066943

Security Pacific National Bank
Guangzhou Office
Suite 1350-51, Garden Hotel Office Tower
368 Huanshi Dong Road, Guangzhou
Tel: (86-20) 3338999 x1337-38
Fax: (86-20) 3350706

China International Finance Company, Ltd.
(Security Pacific National Bank JV)
33/F, International Trade Center
Renmin Nan Road
Shenzhen, Guangdong, PRC
Tel: (86-755) 252510/237567
Fax: (86-755) 237566

BEVERAGES

China is a significant market for both alcoholic beverages (especially beer) and for non-alcoholic beverages (such as the cola drinks—in view of the huge population of potential drinkers).

Beer   China is the second largest beer market in the world.   Beer production in hectaliters in 1992 was as follows for major consuming countries:

U.S.	237
China	120
Germany	116
Japan	69
Brazil	57

The beer market in China clearly has great potential. Beer consumption there is growing about 25% a year, and China is expected to become the world's No. 1 beer market, surpassing the U.S. by the year 2000. There's also still lots of room for growth. Currently, China's 1.2 billion people drink an average of only 10 liters of beer a year each, compared with 83 liters a person in the U.S.

Pabst is the leading U.S. producer of beer in China—selling 2.8 million barrels per year and leading other U.S. companies by far. Pabst first entered China in 1990, when it sold and shipped three of its used U.S. breweries to Zhaoqing City and signed a licensing agreement with that community. The city-owned breweries now produce only Pabst. The city has ordered three more breweries, and investors in Shanghai are trying to get a license to brew Pabst as well.

Now it appears that Pabst will get some competition in China. G. Heileman Brewing Company has signed an agreement with an investment group led by Hong Kong Investments, Ltd. to brew, distribute and market its Lone Star beer through twenty-three Chinese breweries. Heileman will get a royalty from beer sales, and Hong Kong Investments will put up money for brewery improvements and training for twenty-three brewmasters at a California brewery school.

In China, though, there is no national market. Food and beverages are a local affair, and it is expensive and difficult to ship beer across provincial borders and break into protectionist regional markets. The largest brewer of Chinese beer, Tsingtao Brewing Company, has only a 2% market share there, according to Swiss Bank Corporation.

Miller High Life is brewed under license in Beijing, and Miller is looking for ways to expand its presence. Anheuser-Busch attacked China in typical fashion—buying a 5% piece of Tsingtao and trying to muscle its way into the market with imports. But other brewers report that both companies have found regional protectionism and antiquated transportation to be big barriers to growth. Philip Morris, the brewers of Miller High Life beer, is looking for investment opportunities.

Heineken is also entering the China beer market by way of Asia Pacific Breweries, Ltd which is a joint venture between Heineken and Fraser & Neave, Ltd. of Singapore. This joint venture has a stake in a Shanghai brewer whose "REEB" brand is said to have 30% of

Shanghai beer sales. In addition, Lion Nathan Company, Ltd. of New Zealand plans to build a $235 million brewery in Suzhou-Singapore township.

China's export beer industry is an especially promising market, for this sector has a good potential for earning foreign exchange through its export sales. The Chinese beer industry is a rapidly growing one. Certain provisions in China's complex price structure favor this industry, so the industry has been able to retain control of its export earnings and to use these earnings to upgrade its facilities. China's beer industry seeks modern technology and equipment, and is very interested in acquiring high quality food additives needed for its export products.

Soft Drinks U.S. exports of soft drinks to China reached $3 million in 1991 and declined to $2 million in 1992, a level which was maintained in 1993 (53).

Coca-Cola Company (U.S.) has taken as partners the Shanxi Bureau of China's Ministry of Coal and the Kerry Group of Malaysia in a venture to build a $25 million bottling plant in Shanxi Province in North China.

Some useful contacts in the beverage industry include:

Bozhou Gujing Winery
Bozhou, Fuyang
Anhui Province 236820
Tel: 22313

Guangdong Sansui Jianlibao Beverage Factory
Sanshui County, Foshan
Guangdong Province 528100
Tel: 732288

Guangzhou Zhujiang Brewery
Haizhu District, Guangzhou
Guangdong Province 510315
Tel: 4451136-449

Jiangsu Sihong Shuanggou Winery
Sihong County, Huaiyin
Jiangsu Province 330001
Tel: 251809

Qingdoa Brewery
Taidong, Qingdao
Shandong Province 266021
Tel: 334047

Shandong Lanlingmei Winery
Cangshan, Linyi
Shandong Province 277731
Tel: 871454

Shanghai Shenmai Beverage & Food Company Ltd.
Minhang District
Shanghai 200240
Tel: 4301250

Shehong Too Pai Winery
Shehong County, Suining
Sichuan Province 629209
Tel: 22216

Shenyang Brewery
Tiexi District, Shenyang
Liaoning Province 110021
Tel: 455688

Shichuan Mianzhu Jinnanchun Distillery
Mianchu County, Deyang
Sichuan Province 618200
Tel: 22206

Tianjin Jinmei Beverage Company Ltd.
Nankai District
Tianjin 300113
Tel: 761501

Xinghuacun Fenjiu Distillery
Fenyang County
Shanxi Province 032205
Tel: 29920

Yibin Wuliangye Winery
Yibin
Sichuan Province 644007
Tel: 226926

BUILDING PRODUCTS & HARDWARE

The building products industry comprises two major categories:

- Building Materials, such as cement and glass, fiberboard and wood.
- Hardware and Fixtures, such as refrigerators and elevators.

China's building materials industry developed rapidly and reached an output value of ¥28.7 billion in 1984. It manufactured over 500 kinds of products and employed approximately 3.8 million people in 1984. These materials were used in the metallurgical, machinery, electronics, aviation, and national defense industries and in civil engineering projects. The main production centers for building materials were Beijing, Wuhan, and Harbin (15).

Modern housing has been in chronic shortage in contemporary China. Housing conditions in 1949 were primitive and crowded, and massive population growth since than has placed great strains on the nation's building industry. According to 1985 estimates, 46 million additional units of housing, or about 2.4 billion square meters of floor space, would be needed by the year 2000 to house every urban family. Adequate housing was defined as an average of eight square meters of living space per capita. As of 1985, however, the average per capita urban living space, for example, was only 6.7 square meters. Housing specialists suggested that the housing construction and allocation system be reformed and that the eight square meter target be achieved in two stages: six square meters by 1990 and the additional two square meters between 1990 and 2000. To help relieve the situation, urban enterprises were increasing investment in housing for workers. In 1985 housing built by state and collective enterprises in cities and towns totaled 130 million square meters of floor space. In the countryside, housing built by farmers was 700 million square meters.

China has embarked on a major program to expand and improve its particle board and fiberboard sectors, and Chinese authorities are encouraging foreign investment and joint ventures in this area. (Both particle board and fiberboard are considered preferable to plywood because of their lower requirements for raw materials.) China wants to integrate particle board and fiberboard production with other timber processing activities, and plans to upgrade and expand sawmills in the nation's forest regions. There are reportedly no plans to expand or upgrade sawmills in the coastal regions, which process most imported logs.

In order to conserve the nations wood resources, current Chinese government policy discourages many uses of wood. For example, the government encourages the use of non-wood materials, such as cement, brick or steel for building construction. During the Seventh Five-Year Plan (1986-1990), the government hopes to save 66 million cubic meters of wood per year through substitution guidelines and wood use restriction.

Table 85 summarizes some salient statistics for the building products industry.

In the paragraphs which follow, the building products industry is discussed with particular emphasis on East China.

Table 85

Some Statistics Regarding the Building Products Industry (3)

A) Three-letter ITA industry sector code: BLD
B) Est. total market size (USD millions):
    1991 - $ 6,000
    1992 - $ 6,050
    1993 - $ 8,524
    1994 - $10,210
    1995 - $12,541 (58)
C) Est. 1992-4 annual market growth rate: 8%
D) Est. total imports (USD millions):
    1991 - $ 560
    1992 - $ 600
    1993 - $1,744
    1994 - $2,005
    1995 - $2,505 (58)
E) Est. annual total import growth rate: 8%
F) Est. imports from U.S. (USD millions):
    1991 - $ 28
    1992 - $ 30
    1993 - $295
    1994 - $339
    1995 - $389 (58)
G) Est. annual growth of imports from U.S.:   2%
H) China's receptivity to U.S. products in
    this sector (5 - High/1 - Low):   2
I) Competition from local/third countries
    for U.S. firms (5 - Low/1 - High):   4
J) Chinese market barriers to U.S. sales
    in this sector (5 - Few/1 - Many):   3
K) Comments - factors for increased U.S. sales:
    * Market for building products is expected to increase with increased emphasis on construction
       projects.
    * Increase in demand for higher technology and higher quality materials and equipment.
    * U.S. exports are very competitive. Major competitors are Japanese, German, and Korean
       (58).

L) <u>Most Promising Sub-sectors</u>   <u>1992 market size</u>
    1. Building hardware and fixtures $100 million
    2. Wood products $ 80 million
    3. Specialty cements $ 50 million

Overview East China's double digit economic growth over the past few years has created strong demand on the building materials industry which now has a total market of over $2 billion, with imports consisting of roughly 25% or $500 million. In 1992, due to a great influx in the number of companies (foreign and domestic) descending on Shanghai to explore business opportunities, vacancies of office and apartment space fell from 15.2% to 1.1%. This situation resulted in rapid developments on the Shanghai construction scene. Domestic producers now find it difficult to provide products of the quality and the quantity demanded by the construction market.

This report focuses on the import market for products needed to support the continuing construction boom in the region. Specifically, it focuses on products used in high-rise buildings, low-rise complexes, interior decoration, and joint venture manufacturing facilities. It excludes furnishings and appliances, construction machinery, as well as other tools necessary for construction. The best prospects in the East China construction market are bathroom fixtures, telecommunication equipment, air conditioning and heating ventilation systems, glass curtain walls and more.

Opportunities for U.S. companies are mainly in two areas: 1) the joint venture and foreign invested projects; 2) the market created by Chinese individuals and companies who desire better living and working accommodations. The U.S. holds a minor share of this market. Although the construction boom will continue for years to come, the number of imported products will decline as the quality of domestically manufactured products increases. Currently, most Chinese do not have the means to research products available from abroad. They largely depend on foreign firms to come to them. Non-U.S. firms are doing that. Few U.S. firms have made such effort. U.S. companies must make themselves known to capitalize on this market.

Market Assessment

Market Demand Shanghai is the focal point of East China's construction materials market. Desiring a modern city, Shanghai plans to both renovate many existing structures, and construct new ones. Accordingly, the city established the Minhang and Hongqiao Economic & Technological Development Zones, the Caohejing Hi-Tech Park, and the Pudong New Area to "promote Shanghai foreign economic cooperation and trade, to further develop new industries and technologies, and to increase exports." Pudong (or East Shanghai) is the most ambitious of these plans, and will involve the construction of a new international city from the ground up. The largest market for U.S. building materials is foreign invested projects or Chinese projects in these Development Zones because materials imported for the projects are exempt from the high tariffs which make products unaffordable.

In 1992, Shanghai approved 200 proposed building projects, 60% in Puxi (West Shanghai) and 40% in Pudong, altogether totaling 20.1 million square meters, more than twice the total area granted in the preceding four years. Sixty of the buildings approved in Pudong were under construction by the end of 1993. In Shanghai, approximately half of the approved construction projects are major foreign invested projects, including high-rise office and apartment towers. For these projects, developers designate approximately 20% of the investment for imported construction materials.

Generally, foreign ventures aim to set up quality facilities to present a proper image and/or attract tenants. The opportunities range from office buildings, apartment high-rises and villas to manufacturing facilities. The majority of the buildings under construction are destined for office use. Analysts expects a glut of vacancies to flood the Shanghai market by 1995. Housing, though, still presents a problems for foreigners and more well off Chinese who desire better living conditions. Furthermore, development plans and corresponding construction continue to spread outward from Shanghai to encompass the East China region as a whole. Excess office space in the Shanghai market should only impact the market for a short interim.

The flourishing Shanghai retail market and building renovation projects will help sustain demand for imports. New foreign name brand outlets and other stores use high quality materials for their interior decor and displays. Also, developers recently completed several large malls, and more are under construction. Some analysts contend that these projects will quickly saturate the market. Those who warn of this suggest that a retail company first open a smaller shop in a hotel or elsewhere rather than reserve space in a mall. This could affect the amount of materials necessitated by the market, however, many existing department stores plan renovation which should sustain the market for high quality materials. Furthermore, hotels, ballrooms, teahouses, karaoke houses and stores in Shanghai "demand magnificent interiors." Foreign, and some Chinese, companies demand "grade A" office space. The Shanghai Interior Design Association forecasts that hotels will spend approximately $200 million over the next five years to renovate some 7000 rooms in the city's deluxe hotels.

With the rise of living standards in the Shanghai area, some individual citizens now look for higher quality kitchen equipment (sinks and ventilation), bathroom fixtures, and decorative materials (wall panelling, flooring, door and window frames, and tile) to renovate their homes. According to reports, a family spends on average $910 for home decoration projects. The domestic market could greatly expand with lower tariffs. This is not to say, however, that duties bar all local consumers from purchasing imported goods.

End-user Profile Large domestic and international banking and insurance firms often contract for high-rise construction projects as a way to publicize their name in an impressive way. Also, many Hong Kong and Taiwan investment companies build high-rise complexes for the return on investment. Many domestic corporations invest in projects in anticipation of Shanghai's re-emergence as China's great international city.

Along with the high-rise projects in the Pudong New Area, ten big infrastructure projects will start soon: bridge construction, port development, sewage systems, power plants, water treatment facilities, telecommunications facilities, storm and flood control systems, metro projects, gas utility systems, and airport facilities. American exporters should contact the Pudong Urban Construction Commission or the Shanghai Building Materials Industry Bureau.

Sino-foreign manufacturing joint ventures construct facilities that range from relying completely on imported construction materials to solely using domestic materials. The main considerations are cost and the intended function of the structure. Often it is the Chinese partner who desires imported products and the foreign partner who decides what is most cost effective.

For those interested in investing in the industry, the Foreign Cooperation Division of the Shanghai Building Materials Industry Bureau actively seeks joint venture partners for the domestic manufacturers. They have comprehensive knowledge of the manufacturing scene and know which factories present the best potential for successful joint ventures. The Shanghai Investment Commission recommends the following areas for foreign investment or joint ventures in the construction materials industry:

- Deep Processing Glass Products
- New Wall Materials
- Special Glass Fiber Products
- Lightweight Board for Construction Use
- Fireproof Sheets
- Coal Ash Ceramsite
- Products of Glass Fiber and Reinforced Plastic
- High Quality Waterproof Materials
- Silicon-Glass Products

Decentralization and Market Economy The improvements in the domestic building materials industry will affect the entire import market. Since 1980, China has spent $3.09 billion to introduce advanced technologies and equipment in order to renovate the production lines of the building materials and upholstery industries. The current strategy focuses on attracting companies to come to the area to create modern production facilities either in the form of a joint venture or through the sale of equipment and technology. The Chinese want to produce high quality goods for both the domestic and export markets. In the future, U.S. manufacturers should expect strong competition from domestic producers.

Another matter to contend with is the entry of goods from Hong Kong. Many construction materials entering China for domestic consumption (not large construction projects) face high tariffs and import duties. As an alternative, companies sell their products to Hong Kong supply companies. These companies then distribute the materials to destinations throughout China along well established, "cost effective," networks which avoid high tariffs. This presents unfair competition to parties attempting to export directly to China.

Competitive Situation

Domestic Production Officials readily admit to the sub-standard quality of many of the Chinese-produced building material products. They accept the need to import limited amounts of high quality products. Imports, however, are generally considered temporary measures. Officials encourage manufacturers to invest here. China focuses on attracting foreign investment and technology to increase the quality of its domestically produced materials. This trend poses the largest challenge to U.S. exports to China.

The Shanghai Yaohua Pilkington Glass Company (U.K.) and the Smith Company (Denmark) both serve as good examples of new joint ventures. Pilkington will soon introduce a second line to further their float glass production. Smith made inroads into China by setting up production lines for cement. The Chinese think highly of both these companies, and appreciate the commitment to the market displayed by both firms.

Imports The import substitution policy which hinders so many other markets is not prevalent in the building materials industry. Previously, the Chinese attempted to protect their market by insisting that developers source construction materials locally. To import, a developer had to justify the need, even to the degree of product by product discussions. Instead of continuing to alienate those wishing to invest and build first-class facilities in China, the Chinese changed tact. Now, Chinese officials do not block entities wishing to import building materials, and the market will remain quite large for some years. Eventually, though, more and more domestic products will replace imports.

U.S. Market Position and Share In this market, two main factors influence the number of U.S. products imported. First, architects and developers of large projects make almost all the decisions regarding product sourcing. To some extent, the nationality of these people influence choice (choosing home country products), but they base the majority of decisions on packages offered from international bids. The second factor is one of distance. Many Chinese considering purchases for local projects or personal use hesitate to seek out U.S. companies due to lack of familiarity with the producers and language. This can be overcome by more active marketing in the country by American firms. Currently, only a very small number of American firms have representation in the Chinese market. This must be cited as the major reason by the market share is so low.

Competitive Factors This section deals solely with sales to major high-rise construction projects in the development zones and to the foreign invested projects elsewhere.

Usually, project developers, architects, and contractors make their procurement decisions outside of China—most often in Hong Kong. Commonly, they contract a material supply company to source or send out invitations for bids for projects. Also, almost all Chinese contractors have Hong Kong trading companies to act as agents when importing materials. Therefore, manufacturers desiring to sell their product for use in Chinese construction projects need to market to these supply companies as well as their domestic counterparts.

For the most part, sales are based on price, quality, and service. Purchasers recommend exporters set up a marketing team in Hong Kong to publicize products to the architects and design companies as well as the relevant procurement agencies for building materials. Aside from product presentation meetings with these entities, companies should place advertisements in technical journals and magazines and include contact information with names, addresses, phone, and fax numbers. Companies should participate in related international exhibitions held in China because they present an excellent opportunity to find agents and distributors. Also, the Chinese depend on exhibitions to find companies interested in, and capable of, selling to the market.

Chinese business people do not travel abroad as frequently as their foreign counterparts. Often their only opportunity to view a product is if it has been used on a project in China. The Chinese do not buy blindly, and a company's first sale to the market will stand as an advertisement. The Chinese will watch to see how it performs. Companies bidding on a project for their first sale to China often offer a low price and a complete service package. Some companies attempting to enter the market have donated the materials and service to have their bid accepted. Manufacturers must ensure their product is installed correctly. Developers advise that "the product is only as successful as its application, and this is the showcase."

Best Sales Prospects (not ranked)

- Bathroom fixtures and facilities (tub, shower, mirrors): Developers and government entities build 6,000,000 sq/m of apartment rooms each year, and use 100,000 to 120,000 sets of bathroom fixtures. Except for Japanese-owned hotels, most import their units from the U.S.
- Telephone systems: Many projects require imported telephone and office automation systems, relays, resistors, switching devices, and wire in order to offer the expected sophisticated services to occupants.
- Escalator and elevator systems: Domestically manufactured ones, including JV products, fill some of the demand, but are not large enough for the new high-rises.
- Air conditioning systems: Again, domestic products do well, but China doe s not yet manufacture very large capacity air conditioning systems.
- Marble stone materials: Currently sourced solely from Italy. Buyers prefer dark to light, because light stains more easily and is more difficult to clean.
- Glass curtain wall: East China does not produce enough high quality float glass to meet demand. In addition, China does not produce large, thick, glass curtain wall.
- Steel: Steel structures use imported I-beams. Chinese I-beams cannot match the combined lightweight and strength of foreign products. The volume required to provide necessary support strength is more expensive than the imported steel.
- Manufacturing facilities: Companies commonly import dock lifts, electrical transformers, air compressors, water heaters, hv/ac and other environmental control equipment.

Other products commonly imported include the following:

- Framing materials for doors and windows
- Fire safety devices and security equipment
- Mirror finished stainless stain
- Lighting equipment
- High quality carpets
- Pipes
- High quality lock systems for doors and windows

- Floor and wall paneling
- Glass fiber insulation
- Sealants

Useful Contacts

Shanghai Municipality

Shanghai Foreign Investment Commission
F17 New Town Mansions
55 Lou Shan Guan Road
Shanghai, China 200335
Tel: (8621) 275-2200   Fax: (8621) 275-4200

Shanghai Foreign Investment Service Center
F14 New Town Mansions
55 Lou Shan Guan Road
Shanghai, China 200335
Tel: (8621) 275-7178/0700   Fax: (8621) 275-6364

Pudong Development Office of Shanghai Municipality
Division of Information and Liaison
141 Pudong Road
Shanghai, China 200120
Tel: (8621) 884-9445 Fax: (8621) 884-9692

Pudong Urban Construction Bureau
No. 1103 Wen Deng Road
Shanghai, China 200127
Tel: (8621) 881-1333   Fax: (8621) 884-9692

Shanghai Construction Commission
Foreign Economic Technical Cooperation Department
220 Sichuan Road (C) #602
Shanghai, China 200002
Tel: (8621) 323-3406, 321-2810 X7603

Material & Equipment Department
53 Fu Zhou Road
Shanghai, China 200002
Tel: (8621) 321-8357, 321-3759

Shanghai Bureau of Building Material Industry
240 Beijing East Road
Shanghai, China 200002
Tel: (8621) 329-0453

Shanghai Foreign Investment Enterprises
Materials Supply Company
235 Chong Qing Road
Shanghai, China
Tel: (8621) 327-1798

Shanghai Construction Materials Trade Center
1344 Lu Jia Bang Road
Shanghai, China
Tel: (8621) 377-2261

China Building Material Industrial Corporation, Shanghai Branch
Import & Export Department
649 San Meng Road
Shanghai, China 2000434
Tel: (8621) 439-3439, 544-4142   Fax: (8621) 544-4256

China Building Equipment & Materials Corporation, Shanghai Branch
Import & Export Department
Rm 307, House No. 1
Lane 183, Nanyang Road
Shanghai, China 200040
Tel: (8621) 247-4917   Fax: (8621) 247-0886

Shanghai Building Materials Scientific & Technological
Information Institute
6/F, 100 Yan An Road (E)
Shanghai, China 200002
Tel: (8621) 321-3414   Fax: (8621) 321-5793

East China Building Technology Development & Research Center
7/F Han Guan Building
271 Henan Zhong Road
Shanghai, China 200002
Tel: (8621) 322-5146 X701, 709   Fax: (8621) 321-4301

Shanghai Interior Decoration Industry Association
Rm 1001, House 293, Yun Nan Nan Road
Shanghai, China 200021
Tel: (8621) 328-3502

Shanghai Belly International Business Service Company, Ltd.
Rm 314, Jing An Commercial House
301 Hua Shan Road
Shanghai, China 200031
Tel: (8621) 248-7453   Fax: (8621) 248-8340

Provinces of Zhejiang, Jiangsu, and Anhui

Economic Planning Commission
Sheng Fu Road
Hangzhou, China 310025
Tel: (571) 752-854   Fax: (571) 752-496

The Foreign Trade Corporation of Zhejiang Province
7 Tian Mu Road, Dong Hai Hotel
Hangzhou, Zhejiang 310007
Tel: (571) 55-0291   Fax: (571) 55-0336/55-6492

Jiangsu

Economic Planning Commission
70 Beijing West Road
Nanjing, Jiangsu 210013

Jiangsu Provincial Foreign Trade Corporation
29 East Beijing Road
Nanjing, Jiangsu 210008
Tel: (25) 71-0103/71-0198   Fax: (25) 71-1532

Anhui

Bureau of Construction Materials Administration
421 An Qing Road
Hefei City, Anhui 230061
Tel: (551) 257-411/257-380   Fax: (551) 255-100

Anhui Import & Export Corporation
13-16/F, Financial Building
256 Jinzhai Road
Hefei, Anhui 230061
Tel: (551) 25-6264/25-3538   Fax: (551) 25-7265

Large scale capital construction has dramatically increased the demand for building materials such as cement. Like the chemical fertilizer industry, cement production featured simultaneous development of small scale plants and large, modern facilities. Widespread construction of small scale cement plants began in 1958. By the mid-1970s, these plants existed in 80 percent of China's counties; in 1984 they accounted for a major share of national cement output. These local plants varied widely in size and technology. In 1983, China produced approximately 108 million tons of cement, second in the world to the Soviet Union. In 1984, production increased 14 percent, to 123 million tons and, except for Xizang (Tibet) and Ningxia-Hui autonomous regions, every province, autonomous region, and special municipality had plants capable of producing 500,000 tons of cement per year. In 1985, cement production increased to almost 146 million tons.

Some useful contacts in the cement industry include:

Fujian Cement Plant
Yong'an
Fujian Province 366014
Tel: 39050

Handan Cement Plant
Feng Fengkuang, Handan
Hebei Province 056200
Tel: 513722

Hebei Jidong Cement Plant
Xin District, Tangshan
Hebei Province 063031
Tel: 241822

Liuzhou Cement Plant
Liuzhou
Guangxi Province 545008
Tel: 22131

Ningauo Cement Plant
Guangde County, Xuancheng
Anhui Province 242312
Tel: 22391

By the mid-1980s, China was one of the world's primary producers of plate glass, a critical building material. Production in 1985 reached 49.4 million cases, and twenty urban glass factories each produced 500,000 cases annually. Three large glass plants, each having a production capacity of 1.2 million standard cases, were scheduled for completion in 1985 in Luoyang, Qinhuangdao, and Nanning.

Shanghai Yaohua Pilkington, a joint venture between Chinese partners, a British glass maker and United Developments, an Israeli trading firm, has a big lead in flat glass production.

Some useful contacts in the glass industry include:

Beijing Glass Group Corporation
Chaoyang District
Beijing 100022
Tel: 7718233

Guangdong Float Glass Company, Ltd.
Shangbu District, Shenzhen
Guangdong Province 518067
Tel: 692135

Luoyang Glass Works
Xigong District, Luoyang
Henan Province 471009
Tel: 337511

Qinhuangdao Yaohua Glass Plant
Haigang, Qinhuangdao
Hebei Province 066013
Tel: 331133

Yaohua Pilkington Glass Company, Ltd.
Nanshi District
Shanghai, China 2000126
Tel: 8801554

Zhongshan Shiqi General Glassworks
Zhongshan
Guangdong Province 528400
Tel: 824141

CHEMICALS

Chemical production in China has achieved considerable success in the recent five years. The production of basic chemicals are expanded, equipment and technology has been gradually advanced. In 1990, the total output value of the chemical industry reached RMB 75.786 billion yuan. Chemical fertilizer output reached 90 million tons in 1990, 4.1 percent, up over previous year; pesticide was 18,000 tons, an increase of 9.5 percent; soda ash output was 3.74 million tons, becoming the third biggest producers in the world; caustic soda output, 3.3 million tons, up by 3.3 percent; sulfuric acid, 11 million tons, up by 2.8 percent; benzene up by 15.2 percent; glacial acetic acid up by 20.8 percent and concentrated nitric acid up by 1.3 percent.

Over the past five years, China heavily invested in petrochemical industry to increase its petrochemical products, some of which are still not enough to meet the domestic demand at present. In the meantime, China warmly invites foreign investors to set up joint ventures for some key chemical industry. The petrochemical industry is also discussed in this section of this report.

Table 97 summarizes some key statistics for the industrial chemicals sector.

Table 97

Statistics for the Industrial Chemicals Sector

A)	Three-letter ITA industry sector code:	ICH
B)	Est. total market size (USD millions):	
	1991 -	$10,000
	1992 -	$12,000
	1993 -	$13,200
	1994 -	$14,520
	1995 -	$16,117
C)	Est. 1992-4 annual market growth rate:	10%
D)	Est. total imports (USD millions):	
	1991 -	$ 2,000
	1992 -	$ 2,200
	1993 -	$ 2,942
	1994 -	$ 3,450
	1995 -	$ 3,800
E)	Est. annual total import growth rate:	8%
F)	Est. imports from U.S. (USD millions):	
	1991 -	$ 800
	1992 -	$ 1,000
	1993 -	$ 432
	1994 -	$ 470
	1995 -	$ 510 (58)
G)	Est. annual growth of imports from U.S.:	6%

H) China's receptivity to U.S. products in
    this sector (5 - High/1 - Low):   3
I) Competition from local/third-countries
    for U.S. firms (5 - Low/1 - High):   2
J) Chinese market barriers to U.S. sales
    in this sector (5 - Few/1 - Many):   4
K) Comments - Factors for increased U.S. sales:
    • Drive for self-sufficiency in basic intermediates and coolness towards direct foreign
      investment spell declining imports and limited investment opportunity.
    • Primary opportunity is in Process Technology Licensing, especially in petrochemicals.
    • Opportunities good in performance (specialty/proprietary) chemicals.
    • New patent law and U.S.-China agreement on intellectual property protection will reduce
      rampant piracy offering new opportunities.

L) <u>Most Promising Sub-sectors</u>   <u>1992 market size</u>
    1. Specialty, fine, proprietary $500 million
    2. Cigarette filter tow $ 10 million

The chemical industry is China's fourth largest, after textiles, machinery and metals. In 1993, the sales of the country's 30,000 chemical firms amounted to 330 billion yuan ($57 billion)—or 9% of GDP. Sales by state-owned chemical producers, the biggest of which is Sinopec, made up just over half of this. China is also the world's biggest producer of chemical fertilizers, the second largest producer of caustic soda and the sixth largest maker of plastics.

By global standards, however, China's chemical industry is still a toddler, accounting for a mere 3% of world production. Even Sinopec, which claims fixed assets of 10 billion yuan, looks a minnow when swimming beside Germany's BASF, Britain's ICI or America's DuPont. According to China's minister for the chemicals industry, the average Chinese person buys just 5 kilograms (11 lbs.) of plastic a year—one-twentieth of the purchases of his American counterpart.

China's chemical industry is inefficient. At first glance, Sinopec's Yanshan factory, just outside Beijing, looks just like its western equivalent. But it employs 47,000 people—perhaps ten times too many by western standards. The government admits that chemical companies in China are overstaffed by 50%, but says it cannot lay people off. And thanks to Mao-era economic planning, raw materials are mostly manufactured in the northeast of the country, whereas most petrochemicals and plastics production is in the southwest. Poor transport mean that plants often run out of supplies.

In 1993, chemical production grew by 8.9%—or four percentage points less than the rest of the economy. Despite being the sixth largest producer, China imports half of its plastics.

Without minimizing the importance of China's overall economic growth and potential, plastics consumption is a good indicator and driver for the chemical industry's overall potential. It is, after all, plastics that drive the demand for chemical raw materials such as olefins and aromatics.

The Eighth Five-Year Plan, which ends in 1995, notes at least 3.5 Mt of plastics production, however, consumption will exceed this by about 2 Mt and therefore require imports to cover the deficit. This deficit could grow even larger by the end of the Ninth Five-Year Plan in the year 2000, creating the need for greater imports. On a per capita basis, this equates to as much as 8 kg of plastics consumption per person. The following paragraph shows this comparison.

Five Year Plan	End Year	Plastics Production Mt	Plastics Consumption Mt	Per Capita, kg
6th	1985	1.2	2.6	2
7th	1990	2.3	3.3	3
8th	1995	3.5	5.5	6
9th	2000	4.0+	7.0-8.0	7-8
World Average			21	19
Industrial Countries			66	60
U.S.			109	99

Compared with the world average of 19 kg/capita, or in the U.S. of 99 kg/capita, China's consumption levels are still quite low. In fact, a multiplier of three or four times the current level is not incomprehensible and could quite easily be obtained in the next 10-20 years. The impact of such a multiplier is tremendous considering China's population size of 1.2 billion people. However, China's overall geography does not warrant that all 1.2 billion people will consume this amount of plastics. With more than half its population residing in rural communities, it would be optimistic to assume that half the population would use this amount of plastics. Even so, half China's population is a huge number to consider, and would be sufficient to drive major structural changes in the future chemical industry (59).

China's chemical industry evolved from a negligible base in 1949, grew substantially in the 1950s and early 1960s, and received major emphasis in the late 1960s and 1970s. In 1984, chemical products served primarily agriculture and light industry. The three main areas of chemical manufacturing were chemical fertilizers, basic chemicals, and organically synthesized products. Chemical fertilizer was consistently regarded as the key to increased agricultural output. The output of many chemical products rose steadily, sometimes dramatically, from 1978 to 1986.

Except for a few items, such as soda ash and synthetic rubber, the great majority of chemical products, including fertilizer, came from small factories. Small-scale plants could be built more quickly and expensively than large, modern plants and were designed to use low-quality local resources, such as small deposits of coal or natural gas. They also minimized demands on the overworked transportation system.

Larger and more modern fertilizer plants were located in every special municipality, province, and autonomous region. In the early 1970s, China negotiated contracts with foreign firms for construction of thirteen large nitrogenous-fertilizer plants. By 1980, all thirteen plants had been completed, and ten were fully operational.

From 1980 to 1984, many inefficient fertilizer plants were shut down, and by 1984 additional plants were being built with the most advanced equipment available. To capitalize on China's rich mineral resources, the new plants were being constructed close to coal, phosphate, and potassium deposits.

Compared with advanced countries, China's chemical fertilizers lacked phosphate and potassium and contained too much nitrogen. To boost supplies of phosphate and potassium, China relied heavily on imports during the Sixth Five-Year Plan.

Basic chemical production grew rapidly after 1949. In 1985, production of sulfuric acid was approximately 6.7 million tons. Major production centers were in Nanjing and Lüda, and large plants were located at many chemical-fertilizer complexes. Soda ash output in 1985 was 2 million tons; production was concentrated near major sources of salt, such as large coastal cities, Sichuan and Qinghai Provinces, and Nei Mongol Autonomous Region. Production of caustic soda was scattered at large facilities in Lüda, Tianjin, Shanghai, Taiyuan, Shenyang, and Chongqing. In 1985, output of caustic soda was 2.4 million tons. Nitric acid and hydrochloric acid were produced in the northeast and in Shanghai and Tianjin.

The chemical industry's organic-synthesis branch manufactured plastics, synthetic rubber, synthetic fibers, dyes, pharmaceuticals, and paint. Plastics, synthetic rubber, and synthetic fibers such as nylon were particularly important in the modernization drive because they were used to produce such basic consumer goods as footwear and clothing. From 1979 to 1985, plastics production grew from 793,000 tons to 1.2 million tons and chemical fibers from 326,300 tons to 947,800 tons. The major centers for organic synthesis included Shanghai, Jilin, Beijing, Tianjin, Taiyuan, Jinxi, and Guangzhou. The industry received large amounts of foreign machinery in the 1970s (4).

There is a regional sectoral report (32) focusing on market opportunities for U.S. petrochemical equipment and technology suppliers in East China. The East China Consular District, comprised of the Shanghai Municipality and the provinces of Jiangsu, Zhejiang and Anhui, contains six of China Petrochemical Corporation's (SINOPEC's) thirteen subsidiaries and the Shanghai Chemical Industrial Bureau's (SCIB's) plants, managed by the Shanghai Municipality. East China spends over USD 100 million annually on imported equipment, technology and services. With continued expansion and technical renovations planned, demand for imported technology and equipment is likely to expand to USD 130 million a year by 1995. These developments make East China a promising market for U.S. production machinery, process technology and engineering services; all areas where the United States is very competitive. The opportunities range from direct sales of equipment and catalysts, to transfer of process technologies and possible joint ventures. The report includes information on East China's principal petrochemical complexes enabling U.S. chemical suppliers, equipment manufacturers, engineering firms and other interested parties to contact Chinese companies directly.

With an output value of USD 2.6 billion in 1991, East China produces about 27 percent of China's total petrochemical output and represents an even larger proportion of the production for some products. For example, East China produces nearly half of China's chemical fibers (767 thousand tons in 1990 for East China). The industry in East China has developed rapidly in the last ten years. Two of the seven petrochemical complexes included in this study only began production in the 1980s; Yangzi Petrochemical, China's newest and one of its largest complexes, began construction in 1984. The expansion has only been possible with the opening up of China to foreign trade after a long period of isolation. The industry has absorbed technology and equipment from all over the world. The United States commands about 25 percent of the market for imported equipment and technology in East China with roughly USD 25 million in annual sales. The Chinese appreciate the quality of American products and welcome contact with U.S. suppliers.

1. Shanghai Petrochemical Complex:

Shanghai Petrochemical Complex (SPC), also known as Jinshan Petrochemical, is a 12 square kilometer complex located south of Shanghai at the Hangzhou Bay of the East China Sea. SPC began operation in 1978 and has 64,000 employees. The Central Government financed SPC's first stage (1972-78) and loaned SPC the funds for the second stage (1978-1986). SPC itself financed the RMB 35 billion third stage (1986-91) borrowing some funds from foreign banks and raising the remainder through the sale of domestic bonds. SPC is China's fifth largest corporation in value of sales and is China's largest producer of polyester fiber. Jinshan exported USD 28 million worth of chemicals in 1989 and USD 44 million in 1990.

Of the sixteen production units in SPC's first stage, seven used Japanese equipment (including one using U.S. technology), eight used Chinese equipment and one used German equipment. Of the ten units in the second and third stages, three employed U.S. technology and Chinese or third country equipment, only one used U.S. equipment. Japanese and Italian export credits and concessional loans funded equipment from those respective countries for the remaining units from

SPC's Annual Production

Ethylene:	450,000 MT
Polypropylene:	140,000 MT
Low Density Polyethylene:	80,000 MT
Polyester Chips:	100,000 MT
Staples:	90,000 MT
Ethylene:	120,000 MT

Plans are underway to increase ethylene production capacity from 300,000 MT per year to 450,000 MT and to renovate the hydrogen cracker and the aromatics stripper. The following new projects are also under consideration (expected annual production in parenthesis): acrylonitrile (150,000 MT), sodium cyanide (20,000 MT), acrylic fiber (60,000 MT), ethylene glycol (100,000 MT), polyethylene (200,000 MT), styrene monomer (80,000 MT), ABS resin (60,000 MT), rubber (60,000 MT), ammonia (12,000 MT).

2. Shanghai Gaoqiao Petrochemical Corporation

Established in November 1981, Shanghai Gaoqiao Petrochemical Corporation (Gaoqiao) covers an area of 312 hectares in the Shanghai Pudong Economic Development Zone and has 22,000 employees. For several years Gaoqiao has been Shanghai's number one exporting enterprise (USD 78 million in 1990). All of Gaoqiao's primary production equipment is China made. In 1991 the assets were RMB 1.1 billion. In 1990 the company also received 600 foreign visitors.

Gaoqiao has an annual crude oil processing capacity of 7.5 million metric tons (MMT) and is integrated with thirty refining units, twenty organic chemical units and a power generating station. Gaoqiao recently completed a 2.5 MMT per year atmospheric and vacuum distillation plant and support facilities. A 50,000 MT per year polybutadiene rubber unit, a 20,000 MT per year polyether unit and a 20,000 MT per year propylene oxide unit are under construction.

Gaoqiao produces 300 products. The main products are gasoline, kerosene, diesel oil, jet fuel, various brands of lubricating oil, wax, petroleum coke, asphalt, ethylbenzene, propylene glycol, phenol, acetone, polybutadiene rubber, industrial detergent, polyether, acrylic fiber, acrylonitrile, and tertiary butanol.

In November 1991, Gaoqiao and CALTEX (a Texas-based corporation formed by Chevron and Texaco) started a USD 2 million joint venture to produce lubricating oil for vehicles and ships. Initial production will be 5,000 MT per year, increasing to 50,000 MT per year by 1995. Gaoqiao has signed a letter of intent with Transworld Oil (USA) to establish an oil refining plant, and is currently conducting a feasibility study on the project. Gaoqia also has joint ventures with German and Hong Kong companies.

Gaoqiao is considering joint ventures to produce normal paraffin (50,000-70,000 MT) to expand production of ion exchange resin (from 4,000 to 10,000 cubic meters); and to produce styrene monomer (100,000 MT) and polystyrene (50,000 MT).

3. Shanghai Chemical Industry Bureau (SCIB)

The Shanghai Chemical Industry Bureau administers 146 industrial enterprises, of which 116 are state-owned. The remaining thirty are smaller, collectively-owned enterprises. SCIB also includes sixteen independent design and research institutes. There are 147,000 employees in the Bureau of which 11,300 (8%) are technical personnel. In 1990, SCIB's total industrial output value was RMB 6 billion yuan (USD 1.1 billion). SCIB turned over 1.5 billion RMB (USD 0.3 billion) in profits and taxes. Total assets are valued at RMB 3.1 billion. Exports in 1990 and 1991 reached USD 173 million and USD 210 million respectively.

SCIB has ten product divisions: chemical raw materials, plastics, dyestuffs, pesticides, coatings and pigments, rubber products, chemical fertilizers, chemical equipment, coking and coal chemistry, and chemical reagents. SCIB offers more than 6,000 products with 30,000 specifications. The main products include: chemical fertilizers, pesticides, organic chemical raw materials, acids and alkalies, inorganic salts, synthetic resins, pigments, and chemical reagents.

Since 1983, SCIB has imported equipment and technology over USD 300 million including more than USD 50 million of American equipment. Six of the SCIB's ten joint ventures are with American companies including: DuPont (pesticides); Cabot (carbon black); and Union Carbide and Allied Signal (molecular sieves). The Bureau is interested in additional relationships with the U.S. chemical industry.

The Bureau plans to construct the following facilities during the Eighth Five-Year Plan:
1. A Plastics Auxiliaries Project (22,000 MT), total investment of RMB 150 MN (USD 30 MN).
2. Acetic Acid Plant (100,000 MT) with a total expected investment of RMB 500 MN (USD 90 MN).
3. A Cellulose Fibers Project, 50,000 MT of Cellulose and 100,000 MT of fine Methanol with a total expected investment of USD 200 MN.
4. A 50,000 MT, USD 1 MN Titanium Dioxide Pigment Project.
5. A Project to produce rubber tires for cars, trucks, agricultural equipment and mining equipment.

4. Yangzi Petrochemical Corporation:

Yangzi Petrochemical (YPC) is SINOPEC's newest and one of its largest complexes. YPC's development and construction has been extremely rapid. The company was formed in September 1983. Construction began in June of 1984 and finished in 1990. YPC has more than 20,000 employees. The complex is composed of ten major sets of production equipment. YPC has its own electric plant and water supply to enable constant operation. Crude oil is piped directly from Shengli Oilfield in Shandong Province. YPC operates its own ten wharf port facility and its own railway depot and link to the Shanghai-Beijing railway line. In 1991, YPC had successful test runs on several of the production lines installed in 1990 and 1991.

First phase projects initiated in 1987 included an ethylene plant (300,000 MT annual capacity), a polyethylene plant (140,000 MT), an ethylene glycol plant (200,000 MT) and an atmospheric and vacuum distillation plant (3 million MT). Second phase projects included an aromatics complex (450,000 MT), a purified terephthalic acid (PTA) plant (450,000 MT), an acetic acid plant (70,000 MT) and a vacuum residue plant.

YPC has purchased equipment and technology licenses from a number of U.S. companies. The ethylene plant uses Lummus technology, the aromatics section uses UOP and Unicorp equipment, MTA uses Amoco technology, the urea plant uses Chevron technology, the pilot plant for polypropylene signed an agreement with Stubbs, Overbeck and Associates for engineering and equipment, the delayed coking plant uses a Dresser pump. In addition, YPC directly imports over USD 1 million per year in catalysts and spare parts from the United States.

With all their basic lines now operating successfully, YPC is looking towards downstream products. The company welcomes joint ventures in new product areas such as jet oil, chemical fibers, PET and SM. YPC is already producing the inputs for these products.

5. Jinling Petrochemical Corporation:

Jinling Petrochemical Corporation (JPC) is located in northeast Nanjing, along the Beijing-Shanghai Railway. It has 23,000 employees and assets of RMB 1.1 billion. In addition to self-raised funds, it receives funds from SINOPEC and local banks. JPC's exports reached USD 105 million worth of products in 1989 and USD 107 million in 1990. JPC imports most of its equipment from Japan, the United States, Canada and Western Europe and imports crude oil from the Middle East. It has no formal purchase or expansion plans.

6. Zhenhai General Petrochemical Works:

Zhenhai General Petrochemical Works (ZGPW) is north of Ningbo in Zhejiang Province, on the coast of the East China Sea. ZGPW has over 8,000 employees, of whom 20 percent are engineers and technicians, on its 11 square kilometers. ZGPW exported USD 59 million worth of products in 1989 and USD 74 million in 1990.

ZGPW annually processes 3 million MT of crude oil and produces 300,000 MT of synthetic ammonia and 520,000 MT of urea. Other products include: 90# Motor Gasoline, Regular Leaded Gasoline for export, 1# Naphtha, 2# Lamp Kerosene, 0# Diesel Oil for export, 10# Building Asphalt and Sulphur.

During the Eighth Five-Year Period the company plans to invest RMB 4.3 billion to develop more downstream production facilities, relying on three sources of funding, ZGPW itself, SINOPEC, and Zhejiang Province.

7. Anqing General Petrochemical Works:

Anqing General Petrochemical Works (AGPW) is situated in Anqing, Anhui Province. AGPW began operation in 1979 and now employs 12,000 people on its 400 hectare site. Major facilities include a crude oil refinery (3 million MT annual processing capacity), a chemical fertilizer plant (300,000 MT of synthetic ammonia and 520,000 MT of urea) and a thermal power plant with an installed capacity of 150,000 KW.

AGPW is constructing China's first catalytic splitting plant, a RMB 2 billion investment. AGPW expects to complete it during the Ninth Five-Year Plan (1996-2000). Anqing is also planning a 50,000 MT acrylonitrile plant to be followed by a 50,000 MT fiber project to process acrylonitrile. Long range plans call for AGPW to construct ABS, SBS and other resin plants.

Key Contacts

China Jinshan Associated Trading Corporation
Jinshan Hotel
Jinshanwei, Shanghai, China 200540
Tel: 86-21-794-0935   Fax: 86-21-794-2248

Director, Foreign Affairs
China Jinshan Associated Trading Corporation
Jinshan Hotel
Jinshanwei, Shanghai, China 200540
Tel: 86-21-794-1888   Fax: 86-21-794-0687

General Manager
Shanghai Gaoqiao Petrochemical International Trade Company
2908 Pudong Da Dao,
Pudong Shanghai, China 200129
Tel: 884-6482 x8831   Fax: 884-6359, 884-6481

Vice General Manager
Shanghai Gaoqiao Petrochemical International Trade Company
2908 Pudong Da Dao
Pudong Shanghai, China 200129
Tel: 884-6482, 884-7636   Fax: 884-6359, 884-6481

General Manager
Nanjing Yangzi Petrochemical International Trading Company
Dachang District, Nanjing
Jiangsu Province, China
Tel: (025) 784329   Fax: (025) 791662

Manager, Senior Engineer
Nanjing Yangzi Petrochemical International Trading Company
Business Department No. 2
Dachang District, Nanjing
Jiangsu Province, China
Tel: (025) 784323   Fax: (025) 791662

Nanjing Yangzi Petrochemical International Trading Company
Business Department No. 1
Dachang District, Nanjing
Jiangsu Province, China
Tel: (025) 784321, 783290   Fax: (025) 791662

Vice General Manager
Jinling Petrochemical Import & Export Corporation
78 Suo Jin Cun
Nanjing, China 210042
Tel: (025) 504361   Fax: (025) 502925

Director of Development
SINOPEC Jinling Petrochemical Corporation
78 Suo Jin Cun
Nanjing, China
Tel: (025) 654567

ZPGW Shanghai Representative Office
Room 503, 33 Jiujiang Road
Shanghai,, China 200002
Tel: 329-0352, 323-1869

Anqing City Government, Shanghai Representative Office
#14 1670 Lane, Huaihai Zhong Road
Shanghai, China 200031
Tel: 4371033

Corporation of Shanghai Chemical Industry
Foreign Economic and Technological Cooperation
110 Hankou Road
Shanghai, China 200002
Tel: 321-7879   Fax: 321-6107

Shanghai Chemical Industry Bureau
Directory, Foreign Trade Office
110 Hankou Lu
Shanghai, China 200002
Tel: 321-0902   Fax: 321-6107

General Manager, First Division
China National Technical Import/Export Corporation
Beijing Exhibition Center Hotel
135 Xi Zhimenwai Street
Beijing, China
Tel: 8316633-5201
CNTIC has been responsible for large scale purchases and World Bank Projects

SINOPEC International Corporation
Liaison Department Manager
No. 2, 5th District
Heping Li
Beijing, China
Tel: 4217744 x318

Some useful contacts in the industrial chemical industry include:

Beijing Chemical Plant
Chaoyang District
Beijing 100022
Tel: 782931-208

Beijing Dongfang Chemical Plant
Tong County
Beijing 101149
Tel: 5761040

Beijing No. 2 Chemical Plant
Chaoyang District
Beijing 100022
Tel: 7712277

Beijing No. 3 Chemical Plant
Fengtai District
Beijing 100075
Tel: 72244, 77412

Beijing Organic Chemical Plant
Chaoyang District
Beijing 100022
Tel: 771 2255-557

Changshou Chemical Plant
Changshou County, Chongqing
Sichuan Province 631220
Tel: 44531

Dagu Chemical Plant
Tanggu District
Tianjin 300455
Tel: 983966

Dalian Chemical Industrial Company
Ganjingzi District, Dalian
Liaoning Province 116032
Tel: 662312-2623

Dalian Dyestuffs Plant
Zhongshan District, Dalian
Liaoning Province 116001
Tel: 805151

Fuzhou No. 2 Chemical Plant
Fujhou, Fujian Province 350011
Tel: 557679

Guangzhouo Chemical Plant
Tianhe District, Guangzhou
Guangdong Province 510655
Tel: 5525305

Hangzhou Electrochemical Plant
Puyanxiang, Xiaoshan
Zhejiang Province 311213
Tel: 652244

Hefei General Daily Use Chemical Plant
Dongshi District, Hefei
Anhui Province 230011
Tel: 482391

Heilongjiang Chemical Plant
Eulan Ergi, Qiqhar
Heilongjiang Province 161041
Tel: 83901

Huainan General Chemical Plant
Tianjia'an, Huainan
Anhui Province 232038
Tel: 44556

Hunan General Daily Use Chemical Plant
Changsha, Hunnan Province 410003
Tel: 20901

Jilin Chemical Industrial Bureau
Longtan, Jinlin
Jilin Province 132021
Tel: 338671

Jinxi General Chemical Plant
Lianshan District, Jinxi
Liaoning Province 121500
Tel: 220301

Kunming Sodium Tripolyphosphate Plant
Xishan, Kunming
Yunnan Province 650117
Tel: 90319

Lanzhou Chemical Industrial Corporation
Xigu, Lanzhou
Gansu Province 730060
Tel: 55981

Nanjing Chemical Industrial (Group) Company
Dachang District, Nanjing
Jiangsu Province 210048
Tel: 792455

Nanjing Chemical Plant
Qixia District, Nanjing
Jiangsu Province 210038
Tel: 501333-01321

Nanning Chemical Industrial Group Corporation
Nanning, Guanxi Province 530031
Tel: 229424

Qingdao Chemical Plant
Cangkou District, Qingdao
Shandong Province 266042
Tel: 45022

Qindao Dyestuffs Factory
Sifang District, Qingdao
Shandong Province 266031
Tel: 332186

Qingdao Soda Plant
Cangkou District, Qingdao
Shandong Province 266043
Tel: 442049

Quzhou Chemical Industrial Company
Kecheng, Quzhou
Zhejiang Province 324004
Tel: 28801

Sanming Chemical Plant
Sanming, Fujian Province 365000
Tel: 222801

Shanghai Chemical Industrial Plant
Yangpu District, Shanghai 200090
Tel: 5419050

Shanghai Chloric Alkali Plant
Minhang District, Shanghai 200241
Tel: 4340000

Shanghai Daily Use Chemical Company
Huangpu District, Shanghai 200002
Tel: 3212433

Shanghai No. 8 Chemical Dyestuffs Plant
Putuo District, Shanghai 200240
Tel: 4358361

Shanghai Tianyuan Chemical Plant
Changning District, Shanghai 200051
Tel: 2595100

Shanghai Wujing Chemical Plant
Minhang District, Shanghai 200241
Tel: 4343040

Shanghai Wusong Chemical Plant
4600 Longwulu, Minhang District
Shanghai 200241
Tel: 4343040

Shashi General Daily Use Chemical Plant
Shashi, Hubei Province 434001
Tel: 213591

Sichuan Dyestuffs Factory
Changshou County, Chongqing
Sichuan Province 631256
Tel: 44601

Sichuan General Chemical Plant
Qingbaijiang District, Chengdu
Sichuan Province 610301
Tel: 22961

Siping United Chemical Plant
Tiedong District, Siping
Jilin Province 136001
Tel: 388445

Southeast (Changzhou) Chemical Industrial Group
Changzhou, Jiangsu Province 213014
Tel: 441413

Taiyuan Chemical Industrial Company
Hexi, Taiyuan
Shanxi Province 030021
Tel: 665206

Tangshan Soda Plant
Fengnan County, Tangshan
Hebei Province 063305
Tel: 229178

Tianjin Chemical Industrial Plant
Hangu District, Tianjin 300480
Tel: 966100

Tianjin Soda Factory
Tanggu District, Tianjin 300450
Tel: 983951

Weifang Soda Ash Factory
Shouguang County, Weifang
Shandong Province 262737
Tel: 331331

Wuhan Daily Use Chemical Group Company
Hanyang District, Wuhan
Hubei Province 430050
Tel: 444908

Wuhan Chemical Industrial Group Corporation
Hongshan, Wuhan
Hubei Province 430078
Tel: 701171

Wuxi Chemical Industrial (Group) Company
Beitang, Wuxi
Jiangsu Province 214041
Tel: 401601

Yancheng Salt Chemical Industrial Bureau
Yuncheng, Shanxi Province 044000
Tel: 222381

Yongxin-Shenyang Chemical Plant (Company, Ltd.)
Tiexi District, Shenyang
Liaonign Province 110026
Tel: 520516

Zhongshan Jingxi Chemical Industry Company, Ltd.
Qingshi Road, Shiqi, Zhongshan
Guangdong Province 528402
Tel: 823007

Zhouzhou Chemical Industry Group Corporation
North District, Zhuzhou
Hunan Province 412004
Tel: 31931-677

Zigong Honghe General Chemical Plant
Dongxingsijie, Ziliujing District
Zigong, Sichuan Province 643000
Tel: 224951

Some useful contacts in the petrochemical industry include:

Anqing Petrochemical Complex
Anqing, Anhui Province 246001
Tel: 375631

Baling Petrochemical Corporation
Yueyang, Hunan Province 414000
Tel: 224512

Beijing Yanshan Petrochemical Corporation
Gangnanlu, Fangshan District
Beijing 102500
Tel: 9332061

Dalian Petrochemical Corporation
Ganjingzi, Dalian
Liaoning Province 116031
Tel: 661371

Daqing Petrochemical Complex
Longfeng, Daqing
Heilongjiang Province 163714
Tel: 331034-63028

Fushun Petrochemical Corporation
Xinfu, Fushun
Liaoning Province 113008
Tel: 222484

Guangzhou Petrochemical Works
Huangpu, Guangzhou
Guangdong Province 510726
Tel: 2279720

Jinling Petrochemical Corporation
Xuanwu, Nanjing
Jiangsu Province 210042
Tel: 654567

Jinxi Petroleum Processing & Chemical Works
Lianshan, Jinxi
Liaoning Province 121500
Tel: 229950

Jinzhou Petrochemical Company
2 Chongqinglu, Jinzhou
Liaoning Province 121001
Tel: 467532

Lanzhou Petrochemical Machinery Works
Qilihe District, Lanzhou
Gansu Province 730050
Tel: 33611

Maoming Petrochemical Corporation
Maoming, Guangdong Province 52511
Tel: 262951

Qilu Petrochemical Corporation
Liazi District, Zibo
Shandong Province 255436
Tel: 711012

Qingdao Petrochemical Plant
Cangkou District, Qingdao
Shandong Province 266043
Tel: 446591

Shanghai Gaoqiao Petrochemical Company
Chuansha, Shanghai 201200
Tel: 8847636

Shanghai Petrochemical Complex
Jinshan County, Shanghai 200540
Tel: 794194

Tianjin Petrochemical Corporation
Shanggulin, Dagang
Tianjin 300271
Tel: 710094

Urumqi Petrochemical Plant
Dongshan, Urumqi
Xinjiang Province 830019
Tel: 440711

Wuhan Petrochemical Plant
Qingshan, Wuhan
Hubei Province 430082
Tel: 663534

Yangzi Petrochemical Corporation
Dachan, Nanjing
Jiangsu Province 210048
Tel: 791112-2946

Zhenhai Petrochemical Complex
Zhenhai, Ningbo
Zhejiang Province 315207
Tel: 355911

Some useful contacts in the paint and coatings industry include:

Beijing Hongshi Coating Corporation
Fengtai District, Beijing 100075
Tel: 7211166

Chongqing Paint Factory
Jiulongpo, Chongqing
Sichuan Province 630051
Tel: 623075

Dalian Paint Plant
Shahekou, Dalian
Liaoning Province 116022
Tel: 402094

Qingdao Paint Factory
Cangkou District, Qingdao
Shandong Province 266043
Tel: 466741-220

Shanghai Coating Corporation
Huangpu District, Shanghai 200032
Tel: 4312149

Tianjin Paint Factory
Beijiao, Tianjin 300400
Tel: 540311

Some useful contacts in the soap and detergent industry include:

Guangzhou Procter & Gamble Ltd.
Yuexlu District, Guangzhou
Guangdong Province 510120
Tel: 3320388

Shanghai Soap Factory
Yangpu District, Shanghai 200090
Tel: 5431130

Shanghai Synthetic Detergent Factory
Xuhui District, Shanghai 200232
Tel: 4364331

Shanghai Toothpaste Plant
Jin'an District, Shanghai 200040
Tel: 2563020

Tianjin Synthetic Detergent Plant
Dongjiao, Tianjin 300300
Tel: 473624

Xuzhou Synthetic Detergent Factory
Xuzhou, Jiangsu Province 221007
Tel: 67069

Some useful contacts in the industrial chemicals field include:

Ministry of the Chemical Industry (Beijing)
Tel: 86–2019933
Science & Technology Dept.; Ext. 739
Foreign Affairs Dept.;
Tel: 86–42102961, Ext. 453

Haohua Chemical Industry Group
Tel: 86–493–3501 Fax: 86–493–3502
Contact: Li Yijie, President

China National Chemical Engineering Corp.
Tel: 86–201–8683 Fax: 86–202–9873

China National Chemical Construction Corp.
Tel: 86–424–2961
Fax: 86–421–5982 86–421–5527

Sinochem
Tel: 86–831–6020 832–3249
Fax: 86–802–1280 831–6026

Sinochem International Chemicals
Tel: 86–841–5588
Fax: 86–841–3120 842–3212

CHEMICAL PRODUCTION MACHINERY

As noted elsewhere in this volume—under Industrial Chemicals and Petrochemicals, for example, chemical products are of great and growing importance in China.

The machinery required to produce the chemicals is a separate industrial category. Table 86 summarizes some of the data concerning the chemical production equipment industry.

Table 86

Statistics Concerning the Chemical Production Machinery Sector(3)

A)	Three-letter ITA industry sector code:	CHM
B)	Est. total market size (USD millions):	
	1991 -	$2,500
	1992 -	$2,800
	1993 -	$3,079
	1994 -	$3,417
	1995 -	$3,783
C)	Est. 1992-4 annual market growth rate:	10%
D)	Est. total imports (USD millions):	
	1991 -	$1,200
	1992 -	$1,400
	1993 -	$1,540
	1994 -	$1,670
	1995 -	$1,837
E)	Est. annual total import growth rate:	10%
F)	Est. imports from U.S. (USD millions):	
	1991 -	$250
	1992 -	$300
	1993 -	$330
	1994 -	$338
	1995 -	$419 (58)
G)	Est. annual growth of imports from U.S.:	10%
H)	China's receptivity to U.S. products in this sector (5 - High/1 - Low):	3
I)	Competition from local/third countries for U.S. firms (5 - Low/1 - High):	3
J)	Chinese market barriers to U.S. sales in this sector (5 - Few/1 - Many):	3
K)	Comments - factors for increased U.S. sales:	

- China is pushing for self-sufficiency in chemical intermediates, especially petrochemicals.
- U.S. strength in process technology and engineering.
- Focus on high-grade and compound fertilizers, and on fine and specialty chemicals, also favors U.S. technical strength.

L)	Most Promising Sub-sectors	1992 market size
	1. Process technology (petrochem & other)	$ 500 million
	2. Petrochemical plants	$1,600 million

CIGARETTES & TOBACCO

As outlined under resources-agricultural, China is the world's largest producer of leaf tobacco. The cigarette industry is widespread and in addition to tobacco is a significant consumer of filter materials (see Table 97 under Industrial Chemicals).

China is a tobacco company's dream: 300 million smokers who consume 1,8 trillion cigarettes a year. Cigarette sales in the major Chinese cities in billions of cigarettes are as follows:

Shanghai	21
Guangzhou	5
Beijing	2
Shenzen	1

These are primarily domestically produced.

When Beijing announced a broad ban on cigarette advertising recently, the international cigarette industry started worrying that its prospects in the vast market were going up in smoke.

International tobacco companies were concerned that the advertising ban could destroy their chance of expanding their minuscule 1% share of the China market.

After studying reports of the new restrictions closely, however, most cigarette makers believe they can continue to attract China's smokers with existing merchandising strategies. That's because their key strategy—sponsorship of events and broadcasts—seems not to be included in the new ban, which affects advertising in television, radio, newspapers, magazines and cinema.

Thus, Britain's B.A.T. Industries PLC, whose 555 brand cigarette is perhaps the best known foreign brand in China, not only sponsors sporting events like the annual Hong Kong-to-Beijing Motor Rally, but also gives money to schools through the B.A.T. Education Foundation.

Cigarette companies figure China's self-interest will preserve their industry. Tobacco spawns huge revenues for Beijing; all tobacco must be sold through the China National Tobacco Company monopoly, and duty on imported cigarettes is nearly 450% of their value. Consequently, tobacco is among the central government's biggest sources of funding, accounting for more than $6 billion a year in income.

Some useful contacts in the cigarette industry include:

Anyang Cigarette Factory
Beiguan District, Anyang
Henan Province 455000
Tel: 422583

Baoding Cigarette Factory
Nanshi, Baoding
Hebei Province 71008
Tel: 222911

Baoji Cigarette Factory
Jintal, Baoji
Shaanxi Province 721008
Tel: 312244

Beijing Cigarette Factory
Chaoyang District
Beijing 100024
Tel: 5762922-245

Bengbu Cigarette Factory
Bengbu
Anhui Province 233010
Tel: 81279

Bijie Cigarette Factory
Bijie
Guizhou Province 551700
Tel: 23540

Changchun Cigarette Factory
Erdaohezi, Changchun
Jilin Province 130031
Tel: 47447

Changde Cigarette Factory
Wuling, Changde
Hunan Province 415000
Tel: 228888

Changsha Cigarette Factory
Changsha
Hunan Province 410014
Tel: 55911

Changdu Cigarette Factory
Chenghua District, Chengdu
Sichuan Province 610051
Tel: 444622

Chenzhou Cigarette Factory
Chanzhou City
Hunan Province 423000
Tel: 222011

Chongquing Cigarette Factory
Nan'an District, Chongqing
Sichuan Province 630061
Tel: 273692

Chuxiong Cigarette Factory
Chuxiong
Yunnan Province 675000
Tel: 22344

Chuzhou Cigarette Factory
Chuzhou
Anhui Province 239001
Tel: 23607

Dali Cigarette Factory
Dali City
Yunnan Province 671000
Tel: 25004

Fuyang Cigarette Factory
Fuyang
Anhui Province 236020
Tel: 264601

Gannan Cigarette Factory
Nankang County, Ganzhou
Jiangxi Province 341400
Tel: 22516

Guangdong Meizhou Cigarette Factory
Meijiang District, Meizhou
Guangdong Province 514000
Tel: 235101

Guangshui Cigarette Factory
Junminlu, Guangshui
Hubei Province 432721
Tel: 4349

Guangzhou No. 1 Cigarette Factory
Haizhou, Guangzhou
Guangdong Province 510310
Tel: 4451271

Guangzhou No. 2 Cigarette Factory
Liwan, Guangzhou
Guangdong Province 510180
Tel: 8812508

Guiding Cigarette Factory
Guiding County, Qiannan
Guizhou Province 551300
Tel: 31035

Guiyang Cigarette Factory
Guiyang
Guizhou Province 550003
Tel: 523023

Hangzhou Cigarette Factory
Jianggan, Hangzhou
Zhejiang Province 310008
Tel: 652044

Harbin Cigarette Factory
Nangang, Harbin
Heilongjiang Province 150009
Tel: 341451

Hefei Cigarette Factory
Jiao District, Hefei
Anhui Province 230031
Tel: 333244

Henan Nanyang Cigarette Factory
Nanyang City
Henan Province 473007
Tel: 22430

Henan Xinzheng Cigarette Factory
Xinzheng, Zhengzhou
Henan Province 451150
Tel:

Hohhot Cigarette Factory
Yuquan District, Hohhot
Inner Mongolia 010020
Tel: 671919

Hong'an Cigarette Factory
Hong'an County, Huanggang
Hubei Province 431500
Tel: 369

Huaiyin Cigarette Factory
Qingpu District, Huaiyin
Jiangsu Province 223002
Tel: 334676

Hubei Dangyang Cigarette Factory
Zilong Road, Dangyang
Hubei Province 444100
Tel: 22248

Hubei Lichuan Cigarette Factory
Lichuan, Exi
Hubei Province 445400
Tel: 22027

Jiangsu Salt Industrial Corporation
Xinpu District, Lianyungang
Jiangsu Province 222001
Tel: 412111

Jinan Cigarette Factory
1 Gongye Beilu, Jinan
Shandong Province 250100
Tel: 44149

Kaifeng Cigarette Factory
Nanguan, Kaifeng
Henan Province 475003
Tel: 221600

Kinming Cigarette Factory
Guandu, Kunming
Yunnan Province 650202
Tel: 50025

Kunming Cigarette Factory (Branch)
Wuhua District, Kunming
Yunnan Province 650033
Tel: 52289

Laifeng Cigarette Factory
Laifeng County, Exi
Hubei Province 445700
Tel: 22641

Lanzhou Cigarette Factory
Changguan, Lanzhou
Gansu Province 720030
Tel: 465311

Lingling Cigarette Factory
Yongzhou, Lingling Area
Hunan Province 425000
Tel: 24291

Liuzhou Cigarette Factory
Liuzhou
Guangxi Province 545005
Tel: 33854

Longyan Cigarette Factory
Longyan City
Fujian Province 364000
Tel: 23250

Luoyang Cigarette Factory
Luoyang
Henan Province 471023
Tel: 337277

Nanchang Cigarette Factory
Xihu, Nanchang
Jiangsi Province 330009
Tel: 51297

Nanding Cigarette Factory
Xuanwu District, Nanjing
Jiangsu Province 210018
Tel: 641456

Nanning Cigarette Factory
Nanning
Guangxi Province 530001
Tel: 332601

Ningbo Cigarette Factory
Jiangdon District, Ningbo
Zhejiang Province 315040
Tel: 332916

Qianjiang Cigarette Factory
No. 64 Jiefang Road, Qianjiang
Sichuan Province 648700
Tel: 22532

Qingdao Cigarette Factory
Taidong, Qingdao
Shandong Province 266021
Tel: 331510

Qingzhou Cigarette Factory
136 Yunmenshan Nanlu
Qingzhou
Shandong Province 262500
Tel: 722012

Qujing Cigarette Factory
Qujing
Yunnan Province 655001
Tel: 22882

Shanghai Cigarette Factory
Yangpu District
Shanghai 200082
Tel: 5418740

Shaoguan Cigarette Factory
Wujing District, Shaoguan
Guangdong Province 512026
Tel: 772269

Shanyang Cigarette Factory
Heping District, Shenyang
Laoning Province 110002
Tel: 226666

Shanzhou Cigarette Factory
Shazoujiao, Shanzhen
Guangdong Province 518020
Tel: 533525

Shifang Cigarette Factory
Shifang County, Deyang
Sichuan Province 618400
Tel: 24451

Shijiazhuang Cigarette Factory
Qiaoxi District, Shijiazhuang
Hebei Province 050051
Tel: 27979

Sichuan Cigarette Factory
Ziyang County, Neijiang
Sichuan Province 641300
Tel: 22679

Taiyuan Cigarette Factory
Nancheng, Taiyuan
Shanxi Province 030012
Tel: 224058

Tianjin Cigarette Factory
Hendong District
Tianjin 300012
Tel: 243858

Wuhan Cigarette Factory
Hanyang Wuhan
Hebei Province 430051
Tel: 442611

Wuhu Cigarette Factory
Matang, Wuhu
Anhui Province 241002
Tel: 32288

Wuming Cigarette Factory
Wuming County, Nanning
Guangxi Province 530100
Tel: 2241

Xiamen China-American Cigarette Factory
Huacheng Road, Huli, Xiamen
Fujian Province 361006
Tel: 623522

Xiamen Cigarette Factory
Kaiyuan District, Xiamen
Fujian Province 361004
Tel: 553090

Xiangfan Cigarette Factory
Xiangfan
Hubei Province 441000
Tel: 224076

Xichang Cigarette Factory
Xichang, Liangshan
Sichuan Province 615042
Tel: 22453

Xinjiang Cigarette Factory
Kuizun, Yili
Xinjiang Province 833200
Tel: 22336

Xuchang Cigarette Factory
Weidu, Xuchang
Henan Province 461000
Tel: 222962

Xuzhou Cigarette Factory
Gulou, Xuzhou
Jiangsu Province 221005
Tel: 24273

Yan'an Cigarette Factory
Yan'an
Shaanxi Province 716000
Tel: 2196

Yanji Cigarette Factory
Yanji, Yanbian
Jilin Province 133001
Tel: 515961

Yinghou Cigarette Factory
Zhanqian, Yingkou
Liaoning Province 115002
Tel: 35259

Yunnan Yun Cigarette Factory
Yuxi City
Yunnan Province 653100
Tel: 222343

Zaoyang Cigarette Factory
Guangwulu, Zaoyang
Hubei Province 441200
Tel: 3070

Zhangjiakou Cigarette Factory
Qiadong, Zhangjiakou
Hebei Province 075000
Tel: 214991

Zhanjiang Cigarette Factory
Chikan, Zhanjiang
Guangdong Province 524033
Tel: 338377

Zhaotong Cigarette Factory
Zhaotong
Yunnan Province 657000
Tel: 24027

Zhengzhou Cigarette Factory
Guancheng, Zhengzhou
Henan Province 450004
Tel: 22918

Zhumadian Cigarette Factory
Zhumadian
Henan Province 463003
Tel: 3359

Zunyi Cigarette Factory
Zunyi
Guizhou Province 563003
Tel: 3946

COAL INDUSTRY

China is the world leader in coal production. Its coal output in 1990 reached 1.08 billion tons, ranking first in the world. In the past decade, the country constructed 220 new coal mines, increasing its annual coal production capacity by 175.63 million tons.

Coal is still China's main energy resource, accounting for 70 percent of total energy consumption. The percentage is expected to hit 76 percent by the year 2000.

The country's export volume of coal in 1990 was about 3.8 times that of 1980. Coal has become one of the ten major exports of the country. At present, China has 7 million coal miners.

Some useful contacts in the coal industry include:

Beijing Coal Mining Bureau
Mentougou District
Beijing 102300
Tel: 9842461

Beijing Coking & Chemical Plant
Chaoyang District
Beijing 100023
Tel: 7719922

Datong Coal Mining Administration Bureau
Mine, Datong
Shanxi Province 037003
Tel: 442001

Dayan Coal Mining Bureau
Ewenki, Hulun Bur
Inner Mongolia 002102

Feicheng Coal Mining Bureau
Beicheng, Tai'an
Shandong Province 271608
Tel: 212525

Fenxi Coal Mining Bureau
Jiexiu County
Shanxi Province 031200
Tel: 2165

Handan Coal Mining Bureau
Contai District, Handan
Hebei Province 056002
Tel: 23927

Hebei Coal Mining Bureau
Shancheng, Hebi
Henan Province 456650
Tel: 21611

Hegang Coal Mining Administration Bureau
Xiangyang, Hegang
Heilongjiang Province 154100
Tel: 33007

Hunan Lianshao Coal Mining Bureau
Loudi
Hunan Province 417000
Tel: 313127

Hunan Lianshao Coal Mining Bureau
Loudi
Hunan Province 417000
Tel: 313127

Huozhou Coal Mining Administration Bureau
Huozhou Cheng
Shanxi Province 031400

Jalai Nur Coal Mining Administration Bureau
Manzhouli, Hulun Buir
Inner Mongolia 021412
Tel: 32051

Jiaozuo Coal Mining Administration Bureau
Jiaozuo
Henan Province 454159
Tel: 225851

Jincheng Coal Mining Bureau
Jincheng
Shanxi Province 048006
Tel: 222135

Liaoyuan Coal Mine
Xi'an District, Liaoyuan
Jilin Province 136201
Tel: 2804

Nantong Coal Mining Bureau
Nantongkuang, Chongqing
Sichuan Province 630802
Tel: 71724

Northwest Coal Mining Machinery Plant
Dawukou District, Shizuishan
Ningxia Province 753001

Panjiang Coal Mining Administration Bureau
Zhongshan District, Liupanshui
Guizhou Province 561617

Pingshuo Coal Industrial Company
Shuozhou
Shanxi Province 038506
Tel: 23666

Pingzhuang Coal Mining Administration Bureau
Yuanbaoshan, Chifeng
Inner Mongolia 024076
Tel: 22318

Shanxi Lu'an Coal Mining Administration Bureau
Xiangyuan County, Changzhi
Shanxi Province 046204
Tel: 23910

Shitanjing Coal Mining Administration Bureau
Dawukou District, Shizuishan
Ningxia Province 753300
Tel: 2934

Tongchuan Coal Mining Administration Bureau
Tongchuan
Shaanxi Province 727000
Tel: 212211

Tonghua Coal Mining Administration Bureau
Badaojiang, Hunjiang
Jilin Province 134300
Tel: 225039

Wanbei Coal Mining Bureau
Suzhou, Juxian
Anhui Province 234001
Tel: 25353

Wuda Coal Mining Bureau
Wuda, Wuhai
Inner Mongolia 016004
Tel: 323519

Xingtai Coal Mining Administration Bureau
Qiaoxi District, Xingtai
Hebei Province 054021
Tel: 223971

Yangquan Coal Mining Administration Bureau
Mine Qangquan
Shanxi Province 045000
Tel: 42843

Yima Coal Mining Administration Bureau
Chaoyanglu, Yima
Henan Province 472300
Tel: 32900

Zaozhuang Coal Mining Administration Bureau
Xuecheng, Zaozhuang
Shandong Province 277100
Tel: 441328

Zhengzhou Coal Mining Administration Bureau
Mi County, Zhengzhou
Henan Province 452371
Tel: 446525

Zibo Coal Mining Bureau
Zichuan District, Zibo
Shandong Province 255120
Tel: 511321

COMPUTERS AND PERIPHERALS

Table 87 summarizes some of the salient statistics concerning the computer and peripherals industry (3).

Table 87

Some Statistics Concerning the Computer and Peripherals Industry

A)	Three-letter ITA industry sector code:	CPT
B)	Est. total market size (USD millions):	
	1991 -	$1,200
	1992 -	$1,300
	1993 -	$1,180
	1994 -	$1,443
	1995 -	$1763
C)	Est. 1992-4 annual market growth rate:	10%
D)	Est. total imports (USD millions):	
	1991 -	$ 700
	1992 -	$ 800
	1993 -	$ 990
	1994 -	$1,213
	1995 -	$1,485
E)	Est. annual total import growth rate:	10%
F)	Est. imports from U.S. (USD millions):	
	1991 -	$ 108
	1992 -	$ 130
	1993 -	$ 842
	1994 -	$1,031 (58)
G)	Est. annual growth of imports from U.S.:	20%
H)	China's receptivity to U.S. products in this sector (5 - High/1 - Low):	4
I)	Competition from local/third countries for U.S. firms (5 - Low/1 - High):	3
J)	Chinese market barriers to U.S. sales in this sector (5 - Few/1 - Many):	4
K)	Comments - factors for increased U.S. sales:	

- Tough Chinese import licensing requirements.
- A sector strongly affected by U.S. export control and Chinese "import substitution" policies.
- Much pent-up demand.
- U.S. exports are highly competitive in both price and quality, and are preferred by Chinese end-users. Major competitors in PC's are Taiwanese, while both Japanese and Taiwanese firms are important in peripherals. Local firms are quickly losing market share and are being forced to tie in with foreign firms to survive (58).

L)	Most Promising Sub-sectors	1992 market size
	1. Work stations	$ 70 million
	2. 386/486 PC's	$ 60 million
	3. Printers	$100 million

COMPUTER SERVICES

Table 88 summarizes some of the important statistics concerning the computer services industry (3).

Table 88

Some Statistics Concerning the Computer Services Industry

A)	Three-letter ITA industry sector code:	CSF
B)	Est. total market size (USD millions):	
	1991 -	$100
	1992 -	$200
	1993 -	$340
	1994 -	$446
	1995 -	$580
C)	Est. 1992-4 annual market growth rate:	12%
D)	Est. total imports (USD millions):	
	1991 -	$31
	1992 -	$35
	1993 -	$28
	1994 -	$45
	1995 -	$59
E)	Est. annual total import growth rate:	13%
F)	Est. imports from U.S. (USD millions):	
	1991 -	$22.5
	1992 -	$30
	1993 -	$27
	1994 -	$43
	1993 -	$56 (58)
G)	Est. annual growth of imports from U.S.:	14%
H)	China's receptivity to U.S. products in this sector (5 - High/1 - Low):	4
I)	Competition from local/third countries for U.S. firms (5 - Low/1 - High):	3
J)	Chinese market barriers to U.S. sales in this sector (5 - Few/1 - Many):	3
K)	Comments - factors for increased U.S. sales:	

K) Comments - factors for increased U.S. sales:
- New laws on intellectual property rights which protect computer software as a literary work will significantly increase the demand for computer services.

L)	Most Promising Sub-sectors	1992 market size
	1. Operating System Services	$10 million
	2. Database Management Services	$10 million
	3. Network Services	$ 8 million

COMPUTER SOFTWARE

Table 89 summarizes some of the statistics of the computer software market in China (3).

The industry is the subject of a Department of Commerce report (16).

Table 89

Some Statistics Concerning the Computer Software Industry

A)	Three-letter ITA industry sector code:	CPT
B)	Est. total market size (USD millions):	
	1991 -	$100
	1992 -	$120
C)	Est. 1992-4 annual market growth rate:	20%
D)	Est. total imports (USD millions):	
	1991 -	$ 90
	1992 -	$110
E)	Est. annual total import growth rate:	20%
F)	Est. imports from U.S. (USD millions):	
	1991 -	$ 70
	1992 -	$ 80
G)	Est. annual growth of imports from U.S.:	15%
H)	China's receptivity to U.S. products in this sector (5 - High/1 - Low):	4
I)	Competition from local/third countries for U.S. firms (5 - Low/1 - High):	4
J)	Chinese market barriers to U.S. sales in this sector (5 - Few/1 - Many):	5

K) Comments - factors for increased U.S. sales:
- Rapid modernizing of product and process technology spurs this market.
- Piracy of software remains a serious problem. Recently, PRC authorities have begun to enforce software protection laws, but the actual impact seems to have been minimal.
- U.S. exports are highly competitive. Major competitors are the Germans and Japanese in manufacturing software and the French in telecommunications software.
- Statistics are difficult because of piracy. Data from the Business Software Alliance, published in the May 1994 China Economic Review reported that over 90% of available software is pirated, available at about RMB 15 per disk (US $1.70).
- Analysts agree that one important key to the China market is the ability to manufacture a Chinese version of your program (58).

L)	Most Promising Sub-sectors	1992 market size
	1. Graphic Work Station Software	$20 million
	2. High Resolution Monitor Software	$ 8 million
	3. CAD/CAM Software	$ 5 million

Overview The IPR Agreement reached between China and the U.S. on January 17, 1992 created a market in China for legitimate U.S. software products when the new laws and regulations were enforced. Previously, most PC software used in China was unauthorized copies of software. Most of it has been adapted for Chinese character input. The fair market value of all the new PC software used annually in China is estimated at USD 8 million. There are currently over 400,000 PCs in China. Beside the operating system software, most have some kind of Chinese character input system and word processing software. About half have database and spreadsheet software.   There are several thousand users of CAD/CAM/CAE, desktop publishing, languages and other specialized software. Software sold in China must be adapted to accept standard Chinese character input. The internal code used in mainland China is not compatible with Taiwan systems, but Singapore, and increasingly Hong Kong, use the same standard. The combined China/Singapore/Hong Kong market is a very promising market for U.S. PC software products. The trends in China's software are now at variance with the international market, however, and U.S. companies must make a bigger commitment to this market now or risk losing it completely to products compatible with U.S. software standards.

When China's 400 thousand users of personal computers (PCs) begin purchasing legitimate software rather than just copying it, China will represent a significant market for American software companies. The time is near. The agreement on intellectual property protection successfully concluded between the U.S. and China in January 1992, created new laws and regulations that, when fully implemented and enforced, protected American software in China. The emergence of an open, legitimate software market represents a significant opportunity for U.S. software companies.

Market Assessment To date, there has been no real market for PC software in China. Software has been a ubiquitous commodity that is copied freely. In assessing the potential size of a legitimate PC software market, one must analyze the types and quantities of PC software now in use in China.

China is developing much indigenous PC software, but over two thirds of PC software in use is still imported software or, more precisely, unauthorized copies of foreign software products. Most of these software products of foreign origin are modified for Chinese character input (hanzified).

As most of China's PC software is copied software, it is difficult to place a value on the potential market. In the absence of any statistical information whatsoever, the fair market value of the PC software acquired in the one year period from June 1, 1990 to May 31, 1991 has been estimated as $108 million. Nearly three quarters of this software has Chinese language software—about $49 million of "hanzified" foreign origin software and about 30.5 million of domestic Chinese software. The rest of the PC software is unaltered foreign origin software—$22.5 million of American software and $8.5 million of other foreign software.

Competitive Situation

Domestic Chinese Software China has some of the world's best software engineers and has developed many local software products. The ability of the Chinese to develop software in China is constrained mainly by the lack of a developed domestic software market. No matter how good the products are, it has been virtually impossible to profitably distribute them. They are subject to the same indiscriminate copying as imported software. Famous products like the CC-DOS Chinese character input system, developed by the Sixth Research Institute of the Ministry of Machinery and Electronics Industry (MMEI) were widely pirated int eh past, and the developers realized hardly any revenues for their efforts. Until software protection laws and regulation are fully implemented in China, China's software companies and research institutes will find it difficult to develop software for Chinese end-users without heavy subsidies from the government.

English language software is not appropriate for the China market and most PC software in use in China has been adopted for Chinese character input. The term "hanzified" is used to describe software that has been modified to accept "hanzi" (Chinese character) input. There is a standard double byte internal code for a set of about 7,000 characters called the "Guo Biao" or GB standard. Hanzified software in mainland China uses the GB internal code almost exclusively. The characters are usually displayed and printed as modern simplified Chinese characters. This Chinese character internal code is incompatible with the main systems in use in Taiwan. Hanzified software in mainland China uses the GB internal code almost exclusively.

Almost all of the hanzified PC software in China has been hanzified without the permission and support of the original developers. The Chinese do the hanzification work without access to source code, tool kits, or the assistance of the original developer. Not surprisingly, most of the hanzified software in China is full of bugs, and one or two versions behind the latest U.S. releases.

Wholesale copying of both imported and domestic software is still the norm in China. Swapping copied software among friends, although common in the West, occurs on a much larger scale in China. Since few individuals have their own PCs for home use, most of the copying takes place in institutional settings, such as ministries, local government bureaus, universities, research institutes, and corporations.

Efforts to educate Chinese about the value of intellectual property have succeeded in sensitizing Chinese end-users to the unacceptability of software piracy. Software protection is a very hot topic in China's computer industry press and has been the subject of many seminars. Software copying is becoming less open, but it is still very pervasive.

There is no case yet of any Chinese individual or organization having been prosecuted for pirating imported software. It appears there is also still no case of a Chinese organization undertaking a formal software audit and removing all unauthorized software.

Best Sales Prospects   According to the Ministry of Machinery and Electronics Industry (MMEI), China has an installed base of about 400,000 microcomputers.   This is a conservative estimate and others have estimated as high as 600,000.   In 1990, MMEI statistics indicate that 80,000 new microcomputers were purchased in China—60,000 were manufactured locally and 20,000 were imported.   The import figures are grossly understated and the actual number is believed to be about 40,000.   Most of the PCs purchased in China since 1990 have been 286 and 386 computers.   About a third of the current installed base is 286 or above.

The installed base for different types of PC software has been estimated as follows (16):

Operating System Software	400,000
Chinese Input Systems (software & firmware)	380,000
Word Processing Software	360,000
Spreadsheet Software	200,000
Database Management Software	160,000
CAD/CAM/CAE Software	40,000
Desktop Publishing (software & firmware)	25,000
Computer Languages	10,000

1. Operating Systems: MS-DOS is the de facto standard for PC operating systems in China.   There are some Unix and OS/2 users, but they are a small minority.   The Mackintosh computer and operating system has also not been popularized in China.   there is much interest in Windows, but, so far, Chinese end-users do not have any way to input GB standard Chinese characters in Windows applications.

To date, no Chinese PC computer manufacturer has purchased an OEM license to bundle operating system software and domestic microcomputers sold in the Chinese market.   It is difficult to impossible to find a Chinese company that is selling licensed operating system software.   Americans complain that no Chinese buy legitimate OS software.   Chinese end-users complain that no American companies distribute legitimate OS software in China.

2. Chinese Character Input Systems: There are over a hundred different methods for generating the GB code utilizing a standard computer keyboard.   China has not adopted any standards for character input, as the industry leaders believe the technology is still improving and a fixed standard may inhibit further development.

China's input methods may be broadly divided into three types: phonetic input, stroke/radical input, and numerical input.   The phonetic based input methods using China's standard "Hanyu Pinyin" romanization system are easiest to learn and most popular. Professional typists generally use stroke/radical based input systems, such as five stroke (wubi zixing) which are difficult to learn, but faster.   Numerical systems using telegraphic code of four-digit GB code are becoming less popular.   Most Chinese character input systems utilize several variations of the above input systems and let the user select their personal favorite.

The most popular Chinese character input system, historically, has been CC-DOS. As stated earlier, this software based input system has been widely copied in China and has not been a commercial success.

Efforts by other Chinese software developers to use software locks and key disk systems have also proved ineffective. Most new Chinese character input systems now use an add-in card with the Chinese character library and input system contained win Eprom memory. These cards, called "han-ka" in Chinese, sell for $350-700. Great Wall, Legend, and Jingshan make the most popular han-ka.

When used with the old 8086 computers, these han-ka are technically superior to software based Chinese input systems because they speed up character input by accessing the Chinese character library from electronic memory rather than from the hard disk. With the advent of 386 computers, however, software based systems can now load the character library in extended memory and operate equally fast. Han-kas now have no technical advantage over software input systems and suffer two significant disadvantages: they are more expensive because they utilize additional hardware, and they cannot be used with most laptop and notebook computers. Despite these shortcomings, han-kas seem to be displacing software based input systems.

The growing popularity of han-ka points to two unique factors in the China market: (1) embedding proprietary software in memory chips and selling it as an add-in card has been the only effective means of preventing software piracy, and (2) most Chinese work units are much more willing to allocate funds for the purchase of a tangible product like a han-ka than for an intangible product like computer software.

The Great Wall Han-ka is sold with the best selling Great Wall Computer. In fact, most of the major Chinese computer manufacturers under the leadership of the Ministry of Machinery and Electronics Industry (MMEI) offer their own Han-Ka bundled with their computers. Other companies not affiliated with MMEI (i.e. Legend, Syntone, etc.), have introduced han-ka that allow standard imported PCs to input Chinese characters and run hanzified software.

The Chinese character systems developed by the computer companies under MMEI use an independent display standard called "CVGA" (Chinese VGA). It is a 640 X 504 display and is not compatible with standard 640 X 480 VGA.

1st Eximport Corporation of Alhambra, California, a subsidiary of Beijing Sytone Corporation, has recently developed software for inputting GB standard Chinese character into Windows applications. Lingering concerns about software protection have delayed the introduction of this important new input system into China.

3. Word Processing Software: The trend in word processing in China differs greatly from the WP market in the North American/Western Europe market. No GUI word processors or even advanced character based word processors have yet been introduced into the Chinese market. Chinese end-users that need to do more than basic word processing, have leaped directly into Chinese desktop publishing systems.

Most Chinese end-users are still using simple text editors to do basic word processing. The most popular products include: HW, PE II, CCED, and XE. All of these are indigenous software products.

The only American wp software used for Chinese character word processing is Wordstar. Many Chinese users are still using unauthorized hanzified versions of early 80's Wordstar stripped of some English language functions such as spell checking.

Like the Japanese market, many Chinese end-users are using dedicated word processors. These sophisticated electronic typewriters have LCD screens that generally display about 8 lines of text and specialized keyboards which combine a standard qwerty keyboard with Chinese language function keys. The most popular is the Stone MS series. This is basically a Mitsui electronic typewriter that has Stone's wp software in internal memory and is assembled in China. Other Japanese companies are marketing Chinese language electronic typewriters in China.

4. Spreadsheet Software: Lotus 1-2-3 remains the most popular spreadsheet in China. It is mainly sold in its unauthorized hanzified versions. Lotus is now introducing its own hanzified product in China. Excel is also available in unauthorized hanzified versions. When Chinese character input for Windows is introduced, Excel 3 may take off. Other popular spreadsheets include Office, UFO, and other domestically developed products.

5. Database Management Software: The most popular database management systems in China are the unauthorized hanzified versions of Dbase II and III which comprise about 65 percent of the 160,000 database software users. Ashton-Tate has developed a new hanzified version of DBAse IV which is just being released in China as of this writing. Unauthorized hanzified versions of Foxbase are the second most popular database software in China. Informix and Oracle Also have a user base in China. Although Oracle's mainframe and mini relational database software is doing very well int he China market, the PC version of the Oracle has just been introduced and is not well established yet.

Chinese are developing several domestic database products, but none have really been popularized yet. Because of the unique features of Chinese language database management, the continued dominant position of American products cannot be taken for granted.

6. Desktop Publishing Software: The China Desktop Publishing (DTP) or "Paiban Xitong" market is not entirely analogous to the U.S. It is a distinctly two-tiered market, dominated by systems integrators that sell a complete DTP system rather than software only. DTP systems are generally sold with PC, VAG monitor, laser printer, and DTP software, which may be contained in part, or in entirety, on an add-in card.

Low-end Chinese DTP systems, like 909 and Bit, are sold for general office use and their functions are comparable to American DTP software like First Publishing or Finesse. The low-end Chinese DTP market niche, however, is more analogous to the U.S. market for high-end wp software, like WordPerfect, Word, or Amipro. High-end Chinese DTP systems are referred to as "Jimi Paiban Xitong" (precision DTP) and are analogous to professional DTP software, like Pagemaker.

No American DTP software has been popularized in China yet. The Twin Bridge Chinese Character Input System mentioned earlier, is compatible with Pagemaker 4.00 and has the potential to bridge the gap between English and Chinese DTP.

Although the DTP market is a relatively small segment of China's software market, it is also the fastest growing. It is included in this report because, of all the different software segments, the author believes that DTP is the best indicator of future trends. If DTP systems continue to utilize add-in cards, then it must be assumed that the state of software protection in China remains problematic.   If Chinese DTP does not move into the Windows environment, then it must be assumed that the Chinese PC software market is charting its own course far adrift from the mainstream American market.

The Future PC Software Market in China: Despite significant advances in software protection laws and regulations, China has a long way to go to educate computer users in China and enforce software protection. The market is embryonic, but growing. American PC software companies must now consider to what degree they wish to invest in this future market.

While the China market will probably remain separate and distinct from the Taiwan market for many years to come, products developed for the China market may also be marketed in Singapore now, and increasingly in Hong Kong in the future. Singapore also uses standard simplified Chinese characters and GB code. While Hong Kong mainly used traditional Chinese characters and Taiwanese input systems, China computing standards are becoming more popular. The combined China/Hong Kong/Singapore Chinese software market has great potential and merits a significant commitment of resources.

American PC software companies that wish to enter this market, must have products that accept double byte GB code input. Chinese prompts and help screens are also a strong plus. In the short term, PC software products will probably be sold mainly through OEM channels bundled with hardware.

If American companies do not actively participate in the emerging China PC software at this critical juncture, China will have to fill the void by developing its own software products and continuing to rely on Japanese hardware solutions (e.g. dedicated word processors). China's PC users will drift further from U.S. PC standards and rely on incompatible products like Chinese VGA, the han-ka, the Chinese DTP, the Chinese text processors, and the new generation of Chinese database software. Farsighted companies may wish to market good hanzified product in China now and help shape the future of this embryonic market.

CONSTRUCTION EQUIPMENT

In a country where the infrastructure needs quantum leaps in improvement to match the growth of industry in general, the need for construction equipment and, especially, highway construction equipment is huge.

Table 90 summarizes some statistics concerning the construction equipment industry (3).

Guangdong Province is an especially critical growth area for construction equipment as outlined in a Department of Commerce Report (17).

Table 90

Statistics Concerning the Construction Equipment Sector

A)	Three-letter ITA industry sector code:	CON
B)	Est. total market size (USD millions):	
	1991 -	$ 494
	1992 -	$ 543
	1993 -	$1,419
	1994 -	$1,994
	1995 -	$2,824
C)	Est. 1992-4 annual market growth rate:	10%
D)	Est. total imports (USD millions):	
	1991 -	$ 336
	1992 -	$ 370
	1993 -	$ 930
	1994 -	$1,395
	1995 -	$2,090
E)	Est. annual total import growth rate:	10%
F)	Est. imports from U.S. (USD millions):	
	1991 -	$ 33
	1992 -	$ 35
	1993 -	$ 84
	1994 -	$ 94
	1995 -	$103 (58)
G)	Est. annual growth of imports from U.S.:	5%
H)	China's receptivity to U.S. products in this sector (5 - High/1 - Low):	4
I)	Competition from local/third countries for U.S. firms (5 - Low/1 - High):	2
J)	Chinese market barriers to U.S. sales in this sector (5 - Few/1 - Many):	3
K)	Comments - factors for increased U.S. sales:	

- Heavy emphasis on infrastructure construction in Eighth Five-Year Plan, especially in energy (power, coal mines), transport (railroad, roads, bridges).
- Continued building boom in residential and commercial sectors.
- Loosening of credit.

L)	Most Promising Sub-sectors	1992 market size
	1. Dump trucks	$ 50 million
	2. Large earth-moving equipment	$100 million
	3. Road paving equipment	$ 30 million

Overview China's Guangdong Province—"the world's largest construction site"—will import $660 million of construction equipment over the next three years. Cradling Hong Kong on China's southern coast, Guangdong is the commercial center of China, the world's fastest growing economy. Guangdong's seemingly unstoppable development will attract $200 billion in public and private investment during the next twenty years. Although much of the necessary equipment can be sourced domestically, Guangdong must compete for it with other provinces which have less access to hard currency. There is also demand for specialized equipment using advanced technology which is not manufactured in China.

American manufacturer's share of the import market is under 10%. Although U.S. exports are increasing, improvement in market share will require aggressive marketing by suppliers.

Some estimates regarding the construction equipment market in Guangdong Province are shown in Table 91 (17).

Table 91

Some Data on Construction Equipment Markets in Guangdong Province

	Estimates: (US Dollars Millions)			(Percent Gain/Loss Est. Avg. Annual Real Growth - Next 3 Years
	1991	1992	1993	
Import Market	36 M	106 M	159 M	39%
Local Production	194 M	303 M	430 M	
Exports	N/A	N/A	N/A	
Total Market	230 M	409 M	589 M	27%
Imports From U.S.	5 M	7 M	8 M	16%
Exchanges Rates	$1=Y.5.5 $1=Y5.6 $1=Y5.7			

Future Inflation Rate Assumed = 8%

1992 Import Market Share:
USA: 7% M   JPN: 49% M   EC: 28% M   Other: 16% M

Receptivity Score (1-5): 3

Explanation of receptivity score: Guangdong end-users are not predisposed to purchase American construction equipment, but have shown strong interest when exposed to it. In general, they regard American equipment as reliable, but expensive.

Market Assessment Guangdong Province—"the world's largest construction site." One has only to take the three hour train ride from Hong Kong north to Guangdong's capital city, Guangzhou, to come to this conclusion. Every available area of its 69,000 square miles is under development with every conceivable type of project: transportation, utilities, housing, commercial property (17).

Over the next twenty year, some $200 billion will be spent on capital construction in Guangdong Province. Government-invested infrastructure projects include 32,500 miles of highway, twenty-two new power plants, 1,375 miles of railway, two subway systems, eleven airport projects and 560 million additional tons of port handling capacity. By 1995, the provincial government plans to invest $7.2 billion to increase per capita living space from the present 4 square meters to 11 square meters—and additional 60 million square meters of housing. Private capital is flowing in as well, financing many thousands of acres of factories, office complexes and shopping centers, in addition to infrastructure projects.

If current growth rates continue, investors in Guangdong should have no difficulty carrying out their ambitious plans. Guangdong's 1992 GDP of $39 billion—a 19.5% increase over 1991—was comparable to that of Singapore, an industrialized nation. Total investment in fixed assets for 1992 was $11.8 billion. Increased regionalization with Taiwan and Hong Kong should guarantee continued investment in Guangdong.

How does Guangdong's construction boom translate into equipment expenditures? The construction boom began in earnest in the late 1980s. In 1990, the total market for construction equipment, including imports and local production, was $192 million. In 1993 that figure should reach $589 million, a more than three-fold increase over three years. Imports as a share of the total market increased, also, from 15% in 1990 to 26% in 1992. Although the rates of increase in total market and imports are expected to decrease somewhat over the next three years, purchases of construction equipment and import share should continue to increase.

Many diverse entities in Guangdong import construction equipment. All are government bodies or state-owned companies under provincial, municipal or county administration. They include highway bureaus, ports, utilities and import/export companies, as well as contractors, which number approximately one thousand.

Competitive Situation Chinese manufacturers have the capability of supplying most types of basic construction equipment, but not in sufficient quantity to keep pace with Guangdong's development. In general, highly specialized, advanced equipment is unavailable on the domestic market. Some Chinese equipment, such as pavers and truck cranes, are regarded as having inferior quality. Recently, Chinese manufacturers have developed the capability of producing some products, such as tower cranes, previously available only from foreign suppliers.

Currently, imports comprise about one-quarter of the total Guangdong construction equipment market. Industry experts predict that proportion will increase as Guangdong's economic expansion continues.

Japanese companies have the largest per country market share. Komatsu, Kato and Hitachi have cornered the market on mid-sized excavators. Japanese companies market directly in China, and are represented by both Japanese trading houses and Hong Kong brokers. German, Swedish, French and Italian equipment is also imported, but to a lesser extent.

Approximately 50% of imported equipment currently in use is used equipment, mostly supplied by Hong Kong brokers. That proportion is expected to decline.

U.S. firms currently have a small share of the import market (75 estimated in 1992). The predominant American exporter to Guangdong is Caterpillar, which maintains a considerable share of the market for large bulldozers, excavators and loaders.

While end-users often express confidence in the quality of American equipment and a preference for doing business with Americans, several factors have kept American firms from gaining a larger market share. First, most end-users are not aware of the myriad types of quality equipment offered by American manufacturers. Secondly, purchasers worry about after sales service, particularly since few American manufacturers are represented in China. Third, they perceive American equipment as being more expensive than other foreign-manufactured equipment.

U.S. exports of construction equipment to Guangdong have increased during the past three years. However, market share is not likely to improve without aggressive marketing by U.S. firms.

Price and reliability are key to Guangdong purchasers of construction equipment. They are notably unimpressed with appearance and want reasonably priced, dependable equipment. As they expect equipment to wear out, they are generally unwilling to pay a premium for longer life. However, recent dissatisfaction with the longevity of Japanese equipment may present an opportunity for "total-life-cost" marketing.

Although very few end-users have import rights, they are increasingly making their own purchasing decisions. Therefore, it is essential to market directly to end-users. Concerns about after-sales service virtually require suppliers to have representation, with full service and parts capability, in China or Hong Kong. Hong Kong brokers successfully represent many American, Japanese and European exporters.

In the past, used equipment has been an attractive market opportunity, comprising 50% of the imported equipment currently in use. However, as consumers have had difficulty with servicing and buying power has increased, the market should diminish over time.

Market Access Import duties for the "best sales prospects" listed in Section D range from 12-30%. In addition, China assesses a value-added tax of 145 for most types of equipment. some types of construction equipment are subject to quotas or require import licenses. The value attributed to Chinese customs officials can be arbitrary and may vary between different ports of entry. In the future, tariffs may be reduced and market access problems mitigated as a result of bilateral agreements pursuant to Section 301 of the Omnibus Trade Act of 1988, as well as China's expected entry into GATT.

As indicated above, end-users increasingly make their own purchasing decisions, but many do not have the right to import themselves. Therefore, after the deal is concluded, they must contract with an importing authority to actually import the equipment. The importer may charge a commission of .5-1% for this service.

Guangdong Province, as China's top exporter, has more access to foreign exchange than any other province. However, restrictions on the availability and use of foreign currency may limit imports if comparable equipment can be obtained domestically.

Import payment practices are, for the most part, the same in China as in most other countries. Regardless of the source of financing, there are usually two common payment mechanisms: letters of credit and documents against payment.

Best Sales Prospects

Concrete Plants
Concrete Pavers
Concrete Saws
Concrete Pumps
Road Rollers
Pile Drivers
Tower Cranes
Truck Cranes
Drills
Loaders
Excavators
Service Elevators
Replacement Parts

Useful contacts:

Guangdong Construction Industry Association
305 Dongfeng Zhong Road
Guangzhou, Guangdong
Tel: (8620) 3330860, ext. 3506   Fax: (8620) 3335673

Guangdong Construction Machinery Company
707 Dongfeng Dong Road
Guangzhou, Guangdong
Tel: (8620) 7759689   Fax: (8620) 7762113

Foreign Economic Office
Guangdong Provincial Communications Department
27 Baiyun Road
Guangzhou, Guangdong
Tel: (8620) 3835348, ext. 336   Fax: (8620) 3831350

Guangdong Provincial Freeway Company
503 Yanjiang Zhong Road
Guangzhou, Guangdong
Tel: (8620) 3334810   Fax: (8620) 3323084

Third Import Department
Guangdong Machinery Import/Export Company
726 Dongfeng Dong Road
Guangzhou, Guangdong
Tel: (8620) 7770734   Fax: (8620) 7771703

Guangdong Electric Power Holding Company
757 Dongfeng Dong Road
Guangzhou, Guangdong
Tel: (8620) 7767888   Fax: (8620) 7770307

Import/Export Department
Guangdong Provincial Coal Machinery Industry Company
116 Yuehua Road
Guangzhou, Guangdong
Tel: (8620) 3331330, ext. 378   Fax: (8620) 3339732

China Coal Import/Export General Company Guangdong Branch
360 Huanshi Dong Road
Guangzhou, Guangdong
Tel: (8620) 3332075, 3331952   Fax: (8620) 3355864

Guangdong Petrochemical Industrial Development Company
116 Yuehua Road
Guangzhou, Guangdong
Tel: (8620) 3351594   Fax: (8620) 3354042

Guangdong Petrochemical Import/Export Trading Company
45 Guanglu Road
Guangzhou, Guangdong
Tel: (8620) 8850285, 8850287   Fax: (8620) 8850147

Sinopec Equipment Company Guangzhou Branch
3/F, 338 Dezhen Zhong Road
Tel: (8620) 3353174   Fax: (8620) 3353174

Guangdong Hydropower Material Company
39 Wende Road
Guangzhou, Guangdong
Tel: (8620) 3347034   Fax: (8620) 3347034

Chemical Machinery Department
Guangdong Yuehai Import/Export Company
470 Huanshi Dong Road
Guangzhou, Guangdong
Tel: (8620) 7779688, ext. 2013   Fax: (8620) 7765652

Material Management
No. 4 Shipping Affairs Engineering Bureau
Transportation Ministry
163 Qianjin Road
Guangzhou, Guangdong
Tel: (8620) 4412019, ext. 249   Fax: (8620) 4441842

Import/Export Department
Guangdong Engineering Technology Equipment Supply Company
118 Yuehua Road
Guangzhou, Guangdong
Tel: (8620) 3335737   Fax: (8620) 3338441

CYCLES (BICYCLES & MOTORCYCLES)

As anyone who has ever visited China can testify, the bicycle is the prime vehicle for moving the billion or so citizens from home to factory.

To a lesser extent in the PRC, motor scooters are important, although they are the vehicle of choice in Taiwan.

Some useful contacts in the bicycle industry include:

Anyang Bicycle Industrial Company
Beiguan District, Anyang
Henan Province 455000
Tel: 424292

Changzhou Jinshi Bicycle (Group) Company
Zhonglou, Changzhou
Jiangsu Province 213016
Tel: 602643

Qingdao Bicycle Industrial Company
Taidong, Qingdao
Shandong Province 266021
Tel: 333914

Shanghai Bicycle Plant
Yangpu District
Shanghai 200082
Tel: 5461544

Shanghai No. 3 Bicycle Factory
Yangpu District
Shanghai 200434
Tel: 5480155

Shaoxing General Bicycle Factory
Yuecheng, Shaoxing
Zhejiang Province 312000
Tel: 532300

Shenzhen Zhonghua Bicycle Company, Ltd.
Shatoujiao, Shenzhen
Guangdong Province 518020
Tel: 530203

Qingdao Hongxing Electric Appliance Company, Ltd.
Cangkou District, Qingdao
Shandong Province 266041
Tel: 443432

Shanghai Electric Appliance Company
Huangpu District
Shanghai 200002
Tel: 3216175

Shanghai General Washing Machine Plant
Zhabei District
Shanghai 200072
Tel: 6651800

Shanghai No. 1 Sewing Machine Factory
Luwan District
Shanghai 200023
Tel: 3773600

Shunde Xianhua Electric Appliance Manufactory
Shunde, Foshan
Guangdong Province 528311
Tel: 655118

Suzhou Xiangxuehai Electric Appliance Corporation
Jinchang, Suzhou
Jiangsu Province 215004
Tel: 333042

Tianjin Tianyang Washing Machine Company
Nankai District
Tianjin 300111
Tel: 767771

Xiechang Sewing Machine Factory
Xunui District
Shanghai 200232
Tel: 4387850

Yancheng Yanwu Electric Appliance (Group) Corporation
Yancheng
Jiangsu Province 224002
Tel: 225246

Yingkou Beifang Friendship Electric Appliance (Group) Company
Zhanqian, Yingkou
Liaoning Province 115001
Tel: 42601

Zhongshan Weili Washing Machine Plant
76 Sunwen Road East, Zhongshan
Guangdong Province 528400
Tel: 822363

Some useful contacts in the elevator industry include:

China Tianjin Otis Elevator Company, Ltd.
Hexi District
Tianjin Province 300210
Tel: 807147

China Schindler Elevator Company, Ltd.
6 Lugouqiao Nanli, Fengtai District
Beijing 100072
Tel: 3814477

Shanghai Mitsubishi Elevator Company, Ltd.
Minhang District
Shanghai 200240
Tel: 4303030

Some useful contacts in the refrigerator industry include:

Beijing Refrigerator Compressor Factory
Fengtai District
Beijing 100075
Tel: 761956

Changsha Refrigerator Plant
Changsha
Hunan Province 410118
Tel: 34531

China Refrigerator Industrial Company, Ltd.
Baiyun District, Guangzhou
Guangdong Province 510515
Tel: 7713668

China Yangzi General Refrigerator Works
Chuzhou
Anhui Province 239016
Tel: 22731

Hefei General Refrigerator Works
Zhongshi District, Hefei
Anhui Province 230001
Tel: 276815

Jilin General Refrigerator Factory
Jilin
Jilin Province 132105
Tel: 461771

Qingdao General Refrigerator Plant
Sifang District, Qingdao
Shandong Province 266032
Tel: 338888

Shanghai Refrigerator Plant
Changning District
Shanghai 200335
Tel: 2590400

Shangling Refrigerator Plant
Huangpu District
Shanghai 200135
Tel: 8855217

Shunde Huabao Air Conditioning Equipment Factory
Shunde, Foshan
Guangdong Province 528300
Tel: 225393

Shunde Zhujiang Refrigerator Factory
Shunde, Foshan
Guangdong Province 528303
Tel: 681175

Taizhou Chunian Refrigerator Equipment Company, Ltd.
7 Jiangtailu, Taizhou
Jiangsu Province 225300
Tel: 226088

Xinxiang Refrigerator Plant
Hongqi District, Xinxiang
Henan Province 453000
Tel: 353931

Some useful contacts in the television equipment industry include:

Beijing National Color Kinescope Company, Ltd.
Chaoyang District
Beijing 100015
Tel: 5007092

Dalian TV Set Factory
Shahekou, Dalian
Liaoning Province 116023
Tel: 491411

Fujian Hitachi TV Set Company, Ltd.
Taijiang, Fuzhou
Fujian Province 350004
Tel: 568897

Fuzhou Fuxin Kinescope Company, Ltd.
Taijiang District, Fuzhou
Fujian Province 350009
Tel: 558987

Hangzhou TV Set Factory
Xihu District, Hangzhou
Zhejiang Province 310012
Tel: 871424

Inner Mongolia TV Set Factory
Xincheng, Hohhot
Inner Mongolia 010010
Tel: 23251

Nanjing Television Set Factory
Qixia District, Nanjing
Jiangsu Province 210014
Tel: 432422

Nantong Television Set Factory
Nantong
Jiangsu Province 226006
Tel: 517107

Qindao TV Set Factory
Shinan, Qingdao
Shandong Province 266071
Tel: 363849

Shaanxi Broadcasting & TV Equipment Plant
Qindu, Xianyang
Shaanxi Province 712099
Tel: 319321

Shanghai No. 1 TV Set Factory
Xuhui District
Shanghai 200233
Tel: 4362603

Shanghai Yongxin Color Kinescope Company, Ltd.
Shanghai County
Shanghai 200237
Tel: 4701272

Shanxi Color Kinescope Plant
Qindu, Xianyang
Shaanxi Province 712099
Tel: 313130

Shijiazhuang TV Set Factory
Qiadong, Shijiazhuang
Hebei Province 050000
Tel: 632568

Suzhou TV Set Plant
Pingjiang, Suzhou
Jiangsu Province 215001
Tel: 773661

Tianjin TV Set Factory
Hexi District
Tianjin 300074
Tel: 352220

Wuxi TV Set Plant
Wuxi
Jiangsu Province 214064
Tel: 604721

Yunnan TV Set Factory
Panlong District, Kunming
Yunnan Province 650041
Tel: 22080

ELECTRIC POWER EQUIPMENT

By the early 1970s, major generator production centers in Harbin, Shanghai, Beijing, and Deyang (in Sichuan Province) had built both hydroelectric and thermal generators as large as 300 megawatts. There also were numerous small and medium-sized plants producing generators in the 3.2 to 80 megawatt range. As of 1986, China manufactured condenser type turbo-generating units with capacities of 6,000 to 300,000 kilowatts; back-pressure extraction generating units with capacities of 1,000 to 3,000 kilowatts; and hydroelectric power equipment consisting of generator equipment with an 18 million kilowatt capacity. Deficiencies showed in power generating equipment and transmission technology, and significant problems existed in direct-current transmission, particularly in converter technology. China continued to lack experience in design and production of high volt ampere transformers and circuit breakers (4).

Some of the salient statistics concerning the electric power system industry are given in Table 92 (3).

Table 92

Statistics Concerning Electric Power System Equipment

A)	Three-letter ITA industry sector code:	ELP
B)	Est. total market size (USD millions):	
	1991 -	$10,000
	1992 -	$11,000
	1993 -	$23,104
	1994 -	$40,989
	1995 -	$73,136
C)	Est. 1992-4 annual market growth rate:	10%
D)	Est. total imports (USD millions):	
	1991 -	$2,000
	1992 -	$2,400
	1993 -	$2,592
	1994 -	$2,980
	1995 -	$3,420
E)	Est. annual total import growth rate:	15%
F)	Est. imports from U.S. (USD millions):	
	1991 -	$1,039
	1992 -	$1,200
	1993 -	$ 864
	1994 -	$ 989
	1995 -	$1,186 (58)
G)	Est. annual growth of imports from U.S.:	7%
H)	China's receptivity to U.S. products in this sector (5 - High/1 - Low):	4
I)	Competition from local/third countries for U.S. firms (5 - Low/1 - High):	3

J)   Chinese market barriers to U.S. sales
     in this sector (5 - Few/1 - Many):   4
K)   Comments - Factors for increased U.S. sales:
     • Chronic power shortage and will spur new capacity additions of 10 gigawatt per year through
       90's.
     • Growing local funding puts premium on marketing ability.
     • Need gas turbines and pumped storage for peaking capacity.
     • China seeks foreign technology to develop local industry.

L)   <u>Most Promising Sub-sectors</u>   <u>1992 market size</u>
     1. Steam turbines, gas turbine generators $ 220 million
     2. Boilers $2,910 million
     3. Control, communication equipment $ 600 million

Market Overview   For a quarter of a century, rapid industrial growth in China was
facilitated by fast-growing energy supplies and low-priced electricity. In the late 1970s,
however, Chinese planners were faced with the prospect of dramatically reduced energy
growth rates and dramatically increased energy development costs.

Responding to heightened concerns of an impending "energy crisis," Chinese planners
adopted more flexible domestic and foreign economic policies to encourage energy
conservation and increased output of electricity and primary energy sources.

As a result of these policies, China's electric power sector has turned in a remarkable
performance in comparison to the gloomy forecasts of the late 1970's. After a short-lived
slowdown in the early 1980s during which China's electric power system began to modernize
and restructure, electricity generation grew by 7.4 percent per year between 1980 and 1987,
reaching a total 1987 output of 4,960 billion kwh in 1987.

In the 1980s (1980-1987), 35,000 Mw of power generating capacity were added to
China's electric power network. Additions to power generating capacity grew throughout the
period, with an additional 8100 Mw added in 1987.

During the sixth Five-Year Plan period (1981-1985), China expanded its electric power
transmission network by 80,000 kilometers. Programs to interlink regional grids and
provided long distance high voltage transmission systems to link large power stations at dams
and mine mouths were accelerated. Two thousands five hundred thirty-nine km of 500 kv
lines were installed.

The success of the electric power sector was an important factor in the ability of China's
industry to maintain one of the world's most rapid industrial growth rates. During the 1980s
industry as a whole grew by 11.2 percent, and the electricity-intensive industrial sector grew
by 10.4 percent—nearly matching its long-term growth rates.

During the 1980s, the Chinese market for electric power systems equipment has been
growing about 5 percent per year, reaching a total of nearly $6 billion in 1987. Of that
amount, over 60 percent, or about $4 billion, is spent on electric cable and wire and other
types of power transmission equipment. Electric power generation equipment accounts for
about 25-30 percent ($1.5 billion). The remaining 10-15 percent includes automatic controls,

coal handling equipment, pollution prevention equipment, and other power system auxiliary equipment.

China's very large and powerful domestic industry produces all types of electric power systems equipment. If only the largest factories that produce power generation and power transmission equipment, are counted, there are at least 661 factories that employ nearly one-half million workers. In 1987, China's domestic industry produced $1.1 billion and $3.4 billion in power generation and power transmission equipment, respectively.

In 1987, domestic factories held at least 80 percent of China's total market for electric power systems equipment. The actual dominance of domestic producers is somewhat higher because domestic output is valued in uneconomically low prices.

But while China's domestic factories are capable of producing very large quantities of virtually all types of equipment, most factories are using equipment and technologies that are two or three decades behind those of foreign manufacturers. China had only recently begun to produce power generating units largely than 250 Mw, and the great bulk of its transmission trunk line equipment is based on the 220 kv standard.

During the early 1980s, Chinese planners recognized the need to upgrade domestic production capabilities to meet new demands for much larger power stations and long distance high-voltage power transmission. They launched an ambitious program to import technology from foreign companies, and by 1988 Chinese factories had acquired an impressive array of technologies.

China utilizes a variety of methods to acquire technology. Some technology is purchased directly in the form of technology licenses. But in many cases, technology transactions are coupled with China's imports of power stations or large pieces of equipment. China also insists that most of its contracts include large training components that effectively transfer additional technology and industrial know-how.

In recent years, China's market for imported electric power systems equipment has run about $1.2 to $1.3 billion. Of this amount, approximately 35 percent is spent on power generating equipment (boilers and turbine generators), 45 percent on power transmission equipment, and 20 percent on auxiliary equipment.

An important development in China's relations with foreign companies in the electric power sector has been China's invitation to foreign organizations to jointly build modern thermal power plants. China has signed contracts for more than twenty plants, which will require China to import at least $5 billion worth of foreign equipment. These plants are expected to add a total of 15-20,000 Mw to China's power generating capacity by the early 1990's.

Chinese organizations have used a variety of ways to involve foreign companies. some power plants are being built utilizing private foreign investment (Day Bay nuclear plant and a thermal plant in Shenzhen): others are being financed by the World Bank, which has active hydro, thermal and transmission programs. In other cases, Chinese investment companies (HIPDC and CITIC) have invited companies to bid projects on a turnkey basis. These projects have been financed by China's aggressive and generally successful bids for bilateral soft loans and by the imaginative use of countertrade.

Low cost financing is a key factor in winning large power plant contracts. The French, Japanese, Italians, Spanish and British governments have aggressively supported their companies with heavily subsidized financing. Without such subsidies, U.S. companies often choose not to compete for such projects. When they do choose to compete, U.S. companies are forced to form an alliance with a foreign company or with one of their foreign subsidiaries to take advantage of such financing.

American companies have been moderately successful in the competition for power generation equipment sales, gaining about 20 percent of the import business. In the poor transmission segment of the market, American companies have obtained only about 10 percent of the business. Accurate estimates of the U.S. share of power system auxiliary equipment are not available, but American companies are thought to have achieved their best market penetration rates in these sectors.

American companies have been even more successful in licensing technology and forming co-production arrangements with Chinese domestic producers. American companies appear to have won one quarter to one-third of the technology transfer contracts in the power generation sector. American companies' share of technology transfer agreements in the power transmission sector has been far less—around 10 percent.

The demand for electricity in China will continue to outstrip supplies until the end of the century and beyond. As a result, Chinese officials plan a continuing aggressive program to expand and modernize the generation and transmission sectors. The market for all electric power systems equipment will expand by about 50 percent between 1977 and 1991. The demand for power generation equipment will expand least because current additions to power generating capacity are already approaching the goals set for the early 1990's. The demand for power transmission equipment will expand significantly beyond 1977 levels.

The market for imported electric power systems equipment will also expand int he 1977-1991 time period. However, because of China's aggressive program to modernize domestic factories, imported equipment, while rising in absolute terms, will decline as a share of the total market. The declining market shares will be greatest for electric power generation equipment. Domestic producers of automatic controls and other auxiliary equipment have not been as quick to adopt modern technology as domestic producers of power generation equipment. As a result, the foreign share of those markets should not decline in the immediate future. Foreign companies share of China's transmission market will depend on how aggressively China proceeds towards its goal of an integrated power transmission system.

Most of China's electricity (85 percent) is produced by large state-owned regional and provincial power administrations. Formerly, these administrations were bureaucratic organizations under the old Ministry of Water Resources and Electric Power. They are not under the general "guidance" of the Ministry of Energy, but are scheduled to be transformed into economic companies with more business autonomy. The regional and provincial power administrations are the primary end-users of electric power systems equipment.

A few large industrial complexes, such as the Baoshan Steel Works and large petrochemical complexes, have their own captive power plants. However, these plants are still linked to the regional grids and, at least until recently, used the resources of the regional power administrations for basic designs. The state-subsidized low prices for electricity produced in the large grids is a dis-incentive for large complexes to construct their own plants unless they have no alternative.

China uses few formal measures to protect its domestic industry. Tariff rates on electric power equipment are moderate, and non-tariff barriers are not a major problem. China has much more direct and powerful means to protect the domestic industry. The electric power sector has very little ability to earn foreign exchange, and the central planners who supply foreign exchange expended for imported equipment ensure that China buys very little equipment that could be produced in China. Moreover, important imports of foreign electric power system equipment are often conditioned on a foreign company's willingness to supply technology, industrial know-how, and training.

Chinese electric power organizations are a "tough sell," partly for historical, political, and cultural reasons. But most important, China is a poor country with limited foreign exchanges reserves. Without its own foreign exchange earnings, the electric power sector must rely on allocations from these reserves to purchase foreign equipment. In addition, since most important decisions are made by a complex bureaucracy, decision-making is often tortuously slow, the parameters of a proposed deal are ever-changing, and pressures to reduce costs are tremendous.

It is particularly difficult to sell engineering or consulting services to China's electric power sector. Chinese organizations have a bias against buying services unless they come bundled with equipment or a turnkey facility. With the exception of highly specialized small contracts, sales of engineering contracts are generally closely tied to complete power plant contracts or projects funded by the multilateral organizations. U.S. companies tend to be at a disadvantage because Chinese organizations emphasize low cost subsidized financing when awarding such contracts.

The decentralization of the Chinese economic system has made it relatively easy to locate and establish contact with China's end-users of electric power and equipment. Opportunities to advertise and exhibit abound. The problem for American companies is in deciding how much effort should be made to gain a share of the market. To stay in close contract with the market, many companies have offices in China. Marketing representatives may make regular trips to check on China's plans, and some companies have established sales and service relations with Chinese organizations. These costs are high. At the present time, most American companies are keeping a close eye on the market, but are being very selective about the projects on which they compete.

Market Assessment General trends in the electric power equipment market are reasonably clear. The insufficient electric power supply is one of the key constraints on economic growth in China. Chinese planners have placed a high priority on expanding their capability to generate and transmit electricity to end-users. China's current plan calls for China to generate 1,200 billion kwh by the year 2000, an annual rate of growth of 8.1 percent.

In response to the demands for more electricity, China has sketched its medium- and long-term goals for increasing electric power generation capacity. The official plan is to increase capacity by around 6.4 percent per year in the Seventh Five-year Plan and then accelerate construction of new generating capacity in the 1990s. During the Seventh Five-Year Plan, power generation capacity is to grow from 86,493 Mw in 1985 to 120,000-130,000 Mw in 1990. The planned annual additions to power generating capacity are, therefore, 7,000-8,000 Mw per year. The goal of the Eighth Five-Year Plan is a total increase in power generating capacity of 50,000-69,000 Mw, or an annual addition to capacity of 10,000-15,000 Mw. Then between 1995 and 2000, planners expect to add an additional 65,000-70,000 Mw to reach a total generating capacity of 240,000-270,000 Mw.

Chinese officials admit that less official attention and resources have been given to expansion and modernization of China's electric power transmission network. Most power transmission networks are connected by 110-volt lines, but 220-kv trunk lines grew from 28,462 km in 1980 to 46,056 km in 1986. In the early 1980s, installation of 500 kv systems began; they reached 2,539 km by 1986.

Current plans are to interlink the large power grids and to transmit power from large mine-mouth power plants and hydropower projects by expanding the 500 kv technology. Chinese planners hope to move to even more powerful transmission systems during the coming decade.

A second clear trend in the outlook for China's power system equipment market is the rising capabilities of domestic equipment suppliers. Chinese domestic manufacturers have aggressively sought modern technology and will be increasingly able to compete with foreign suppliers for much of the advanced equipment that will be needed.

Other factors that may affect the outlook for China's future power systems equipment market are less clear, and the 1991 estimates shown in Table 3.2-1 market are given in ranges to reflect those uncertainties. Nevertheless, these estimates indicate that the Chinese market for all electric power systems equipment from all sources will range from 6.5-8.5 billion by 1991.

All segments of the market will participate in this growth. Purchases of electric power generating equipment and of closely related controls and other equipment domestic production plus imports are expected to grow at a rate of 8-12 percent. We expect that by the early 1990s China will meet or exceed its goal of adding around 10,000 Mw of power generating equipment per year. We further expect that the value of the equipment (in real terms) will grow even more rapidly because more sophisticated, and hence more costly, equipment will be needed.

The wider range in the market projection for electric power transmission equipment (from $4 to $6 billion) reflects greater uncertainties about how aggressively China will move to interlink regional grids with 500 kv lines. In the long run, China's development of large mine-mouth thermal power plants and huge hydroelectric projects will require the more sophisticated and powerful transmission lines. However, many of these projects appear to have been delayed in favor of "quick fix" solutions that use smaller coal-burning thermal plants closer to end-users, and these require less sophisticated power transmission systems.

The ranges for projected market shares of domestic and foreign suppliers are even wider, reflecting greater uncertainties. Most important is the extent to which China's domestic industry will be able to digest and apply the technologies acquired in the past five years. China's factories have enough basic manufacturing capacity to produce great quantities of equipment, and many facilities have acquired the necessary technologies to produce the kinds of equipment that Chinese utilities intend to stall over the next decade. The range in Table 3.2-1 indicates that there remains a good deal of uncertainty on how quickly Chinese factories can combine their old production facilities with the new technologies to produce the desired equipment.

A second key question concerns the amount of foreign exchange that will be available to support the electric power sector. The utilities themselves are generally at a disadvantage in obtaining foreign exchange. They are required to sell electricity for uneconomically low prices (although most of their inputs are made available at low prices), and their revenues are predominantly, if not entirely in yuan, which are not convertible into foreign exchange. In the recent past, their foreign exchange shortages have been overcome partly because the central government has made development of the electric power sector a priority. In addition, the Chinese have financed electric power plants through a variety of flexible means including direct foreign investment, foreign exchange under the control of local governments, bilateral and multilateral loans, and countertrade. These programs have been far more successful than most observers would have predicted, and it is possible that success will breed more success as local governments continue to use such means to acquire power generating capabilities on their own or in joint ventures with the central government. Such an optimistic scenario is not assured, however, because already there are signs that some entities will find using such programs more difficult as their dept repayment and countertrade obligations grow.

Despite these uncertainties, China's market for imported electric power systems equipment can be expected to grow modestly from current levels. We project that foreign suppliers' sales to China in 1991 will grow to $1.3 to $1.6 billion, although the foreign share of the market will fall from around 25 percent in 1986 to around 20 percent in 1991.

Domestic Industry Competition The most significant competition in the market for electric power system equipment will come from China's own domestic industry. Domestic industry's competitive position vis-a-vis the rest of the world will improve in the next few years—partly because the Chinese government supports it through priority investment allocation and a process that offers domestic industry substantial protection from foreign competition.

As befits a huge, albeit poor, continental economy, China's domestic machinery industry has the quantitative ability to supply most of the needs of China's electric power industry. Unlike small, underdeveloped economies, China's huge domestic economy allow Chinese factories to achieve sufficient economies of scale to produce most types of equipment.

Nevertheless, Chinese technology in the electric power sector failed to keep pace with the rest of the world. For domestic and international political reasons, China's leaders for two decades (1957-1977) cut themselves off from the outside world and emphasized that domestic industry must self-reliantly support China's economic objectives. After an infusion of Soviet technology in the 1950s, Chinese electric power generation and transmission technology improved only marginally over the following twenty years. In comparison to the outside world, Chinese capabilities fell further and further behind.

In terms of its ability to produce huge quantities of relatively unsophisticated products, China's electric power equipment sector was a great success. Despite its almost total isolation from the rest of the world, the industry provided Chinese electric power utilities with sufficient equipment to support a 9.5 percent annual rate of industrial growth between 1957 and 1977. By the late 1970s, the electric power equipment industry was able to produce more than 6,000 Mw of power generating sets per year.

A key question in the development of China's domestic production capabilities is the ability of the Chinese factories to absorb and utilize the technology acquired from foreign countries. In the late 1970s and early 1980s, the Chinese began to seek foreign technology along with its imports of electric power equipment. By the end of 1987, China had signed as many as 200 separate technology transfers, joint ventures, or co-production contracts with foreign companies in the electric power field. Of these contracts, power generation technology accounted for about half, power transmission for one-third, and controls and auxiliary equipment for 10 percent.

American companies have been the leaders in electric power technology transfers to China, with approximately one-quarter to one-third of all contracts signed between 1981 and 1988. Japan stands second with about 15 percent, while the UK and West Germany have approximately 10 percent each.

Table 93 shows China's seven leading foreign suppliers of power generation and transmission equipment. Foreign trade statistics do not provide accurate estimates of auxiliary electric power equipment (18).

Japan is China's dominant supplier of electric power systems equipment. In all years, American manufacturers have placed second to Japan, although the value of American shipments is generally only one-quarter that of Japanese suppliers. In recent years, West German manufacturers active in licensing technology to China have challenged American suppliers for second place.

Table 93

China's Leading Suppliers of Electric Power System Equipment

	1984	1985	1986	1987
Japan	108.5	309.5	580.7	479.6
United States	27.0	95.5	102.6	143.4
Germany	17.7	43.2	97.8	80.8
Italy	2.4	5.9	15.6	54.7
France	7.3	41.3	51.6	42.2
United Kingdom	11.1	11.5	15.7	21.1
Canada	0.8	10.7	6.1	19.9

Italian and French manufacturers follow in fourth and fifth places, respectively. Italian manufacturers have enjoyed the most rapid rate of growth in recent years. Italian success is due, at least in part, to the Italian government's soft loan program that provides support to China's electric power.

Some useful contacts in the power industry include:

Datun Coal & Electricity Company
Pei County, Xuzhou
Jiangsu Province 221611

East China United Power Corporation
181 Nanjing Donglu
Huangpu District
Shanghai 200002
Tel: 3290000

Fujian Power Bureau
Fuzhou
Fujian Province 350004
Tel: 568897

Guangxi Power Bureau
Minzhulu, Nanning
Guangxi Province 530023
Tel: 203414

Guizhou Power Industrial Bureau
Nanming, Guiyang
Guizhou Province 550002
Tel: 25904

Harbin Steam Turbine Plant
Dongli, Harbin
Heilongjiang Province 150046
Tel: 281404

Huazhong (Central China) Power Administration Bureau
Donghu, Wuhan
Hubei Province 430040

Inner Mongolia Power Administration Bureau
Yuquan, Hohhot
Inner Mongolia 010020
Tel: 27211

North China United Power Corporation
33 Zaolin Qianjie, Guanganmennei
Beijing 100053
Tel: 3263377

Northeast China Power Corporation
18 Ningbolu, Heping District
Shenyang
Liaoning Province 110006
Tel: 3112405

Northwest Power Administrative Bureau
Shangdelu, Xincheng District, Xi'an
Shaanxi Province 710004
Tel: 25061

Shandong Province Power Bureau
Shizong, Jinan
Shandong Province 264000

Sichuan Province Power Administrative Bureau
17 Erduan Dongfenglu, Chenghua District
Chengdu
Sichuan Province 610061
Tel: 441212

Xinjiang Power Industry Bureau
Tianshan District
Xinjiang 830002

Yancheng Jianghui Power Group Company
Yancheng
Jiangsu Province 224001
Tel: 225193

Yunnan Power Bureau
157 Dongfeng Donglu, Kunming
Yunnan Province 650041
Tel: 63907

Some useful contacts in the power transmission industry include:

Baoding Transformer Plant
Xinshi District, Baoding
Hebei Province 071056
Tel: 37971

Beijing Heavy Electric Machinery Plant
Shijingshan District
Beijing 100039
Tel: 810361

Shenyang Transformer Plant
Tiexi District, Shenyang
Liaoning Province 110025
Tel: 551211

Some useful contacts in the cable industry include:

Chengdu Cable Plant
Wuhou District, Chengdu
Sichuan Province 610041
Tel: 582711

Harbin Cable Plant
Daowai, Harbin
Heilongjiang Province 150020
Tel: 486422

Kunming Cable Plant
Xishan, Kunming
Yunnan Province 650100
Tel: 81041

Shandong Cable Plant
Xinti
Shandong Province 271200
Tel: 223012

Shanghai Cable Plant
Yangpu District
Shanghai 200093
Tel: 5487200

Shanghai Wire & Cable (Group) Company
Hongkou District
Shanghai 200002
Tel: 3234559

Shenyang Cable Plant
Tiexi, Shenyang
Liaoning Province 110025
Tel: 554471

Shenyang Wire Factory
Shenhe, Shenyang
Liaoning Province 110013
Tel: 722340

Sichuan Cable Plant
2 Hongji Xinlu, Jinjiang District
Chengdu, Sichuan 610061
Tel: 441712

Tianjin Cable General Works
Nankai District
Tianjin 300112
Tel: 766112

Xiangtan Cable Plant
Xiangtan
Hunan Province 411101
Tel: 22711

Zhengzhou Electric Cable Plant
Zhongyuan District, Zhengzhou
Henan Province 450006
Tel: 446605

ELECTRONIC COMPONENTS

The electronic component category is close in definition to the "Process Controls—Industrial" which is dealt with later in this chapter. To some extent, it also comes close to the "Telecommunications Equipment" category which is also dealt with later in this chapter.

U.S. exports are highly competitive in price and quality and are preferred by Chinese end-users. Major competitors in this market are Japanese, Germany and other major players in the telecommunications field. Local firms are trying to reclaim high-tech market share by setting up more joint ventures.

Promising sub-sectors:

- Microprocessors (general purpose and function specific)
- Microcontrollers (general purpose and function specific)
- Other high-end semi-conductors (memory, advanced logic, programmable logic, and advanced linear products).

Some data on this industry segment are as follows:

A. Rank: 12
B. Name of Sector: Electronic Components
C. ITA or PS&D Code: ELC

	1993	1994	1995
D. Total Market Size	1,600	1,840	2,117
E. Total Local Production	1,350	1,548	1,780
F. Total Exports	300	340	390
G. Total Imports	550	632	727
H. Total Imports from U.S.	280	320	370
I. Exchange Rate		8.6	8.6

ELECTRONICS PRODUCTION AND TEST EQUIPMENT

In 1987, China's electronics industry was about ten to fifteen years behind those of the industrialized nations. Key problems were the inability to transfer technology from research to production and continued reliance on hand labor. Also, impatience to reach Western standards sometimes proved counterproductive. For example, instead of buying a complex item such as a microprocessor abroad, China chose to develop its own, at great expense.

In 1985, the electronics industry consisted of approximately 2,400 enterprises, 100 research institutions, four institutes of higher learning, and twenty secondary vocational schools. The industry employed some 1.4 million people, including 130,000 technical personnel. Besides the approximately 2,000 kinds of electronic components and large-scale integrated circuits produced by the industry, it made 400 varieties of electronic machinery, including electronic computers, television broadcast transmitters and receivers, and radar and communications equipment. In the 1980s, China made great strides in the production of consumer electronic products, such as televisions, radios, and tape recorders.

Table 94 gives some of the important statistics for the electronics production and test equipment industry (3).

Table 94

Statistics for Electronics Production and Test Equipment Industry

A)	Three-letter ITA industry sector code:	EIP
B)	Est. total market size (USD millions):	
	1991 -	$360
	1992 -	$400
	1993 -	$550
	1994 -	$630
	1995 -	$725
C)	Est. 1992-4 annual market growth rate:	5%
D)	Est. total imports (USD millions):	
	1991 -	$100
	1992 -	$120
	1993 -	$360
	1994 -	$424
	1995 -	$490
E)	Est. annual total import growth rate:	9%
F)	Est. imports from U.S. (USD millions):	
	1991 -	$ 38
	1992 -	$ 40
	1993 -	$150
	1994 -	$173
	1995 -	$200 (58)
G)	Est. annual growth of imports from U.S.:	10%
H)	China's receptivity to U.S. products in this sector (5 - High/1 - Low):	4

I)   Competition from local/third countries
     for U.S. firms (5 - Low/1 - High):   3
J)   Chinese market barriers to U.S. sales
     in this sector (5 - Few/1 - Many):   4
K)   Comments - factors for increased U.S. sales:
     • Bright spots include oscilloscope sales and semiconductor manufacturing equipment.
     • Consumer electronics demand is high.
     • More sophisticated production equipment is needed.

L)   <u>Most Promising Sub-sectors</u>   <u>1992 market size</u>
     1. Oscilloscopes $10 million
     2. SMT production equipment $11 million
     3. Ion implanters $15 million
     4. Electron beam equipment $15 million

M)   Some additional comments as of 1995 are as follows (58):
     • U.S. high-end products are very competitive in the market.
     • Major U.S. foreign competitors are: NEC, Thompson, Philips, Siemens, and the government
       owned Ministry of Electronics.
     • Chinese companies are focusing efforts on technology acquisition. Some of the technology
       transfers are occurring through joint ventures, although some technology has been illegally
       copied from foreign companies.
     • Monies allocated by the central government in this industry area is given in priority order to
       the military, government owned industry, and then to private industries.
     • Best sub-sector prospects within this sector include:
       - Semi-conductor manufacturing
       - Automotive equipment
       - Aviation
       - Telecommunications manufacturing

<u>Overview</u> The overall prospects for exports of American printed circuit boards (PCB) and
PCB manufacturing equipment to China are good. The market in southern China seems
strong. China produces at least five to six million square meters of PCB annually according
to official statistics. It is possible that the actual figure is much higher, because observer
interviewed admit that the large demand for PCB products, and high import duties on the
manufacturing equipment to make them, have encourage smuggling of that equipment (duties
for PCB manufacturing equipment go as high as 38%, including the Unified Industry and
Commerce Tax, or "Gongshang Tongyi Shui." Many end-users can escape part of this
assessment however).   Seventy to eighty percent of China's total documented PCB
production, about four million square meters, is used in consumer products such as
televisions, tape recorders and radios. Items like computers and telecommunications switches
absorb the remaining 20 percent. Documented production of double and multilayered PCP's
reaches only six to seven hundred thousand square meters, but is also probably
underestimated (21).

Chinese firms plan to expand and diversify production of PCB's for industrial equipment, with specific plans to increase manufacturing and exports of high standard single-sided PCBs. China also plans to increase production of double-sided and multilayered PCBs for domestic use.

Demand for PCBs for use in consumer products will probably continue to expand, although it will be difficult to track because the government has tended towards limiting "excessive" consumerism; therefore it may under report consumer product-related PCB production. However, there are specific, ambitious plans for the expansion of the telecommunications industry. Three joint venture enterprises produce central office switches, and AT&T may establish a new one soon in the wake of their February 1993 agreement to provide technology and equipment. The operations in existence all presently import CKD and SKD kits for local assembly. In order to reduce costs, telecommunications authorities would like to localize double-sided PCB production for these ventures.

Market Assessment Market demand is strong, both by factories that are set up as wholly-owned companies and wholly-owned ventures, as well as by large Chinese state organizations.

The market for PCB equipment and technology is highly competitive. Some Japanese firms are unwilling to sell high-end equipment to Chinese enterprises due to potential downstream competition by these firms in the future. Many such firms, however, successfully sell used equipment. For U.S. firms willing to sell more advanced equipment, this supposed reticence by Japanese firms could represent a market opportunity.

The largest potential growth in the market is from foreign invested electronic production firms, mostly in Fujian, Shanghai and Guangdong. Many of these firms would like to evolve from importing PCB semi-knockdown kits to complete production in China.

The booming domestic market for finished electronic goods is another source of growth for this industry. Several new industry sectors require high volumes of high standard PCBs. As mentioned above, the telecommunications industry would benefit from domestically produced indigenous PCBs for central office switches and PBXs. The local computer industry would also benefit from domestic production of PCBs for standard locally-assembled computers.

China is also beginning to produce flexible PCBs use in camera and other consumer goods manufacturing. So there is solid, lasting demand, based partly on consumer production, for more advanced equipment to increase production quantity and quality.

Many observers believe that demand for PCB equipment and materials will continue to grow. However, a number of factors may limit this growth. First, environmental protection authorities may eventually gain the power to limit production of facilities that are heavy polluters (probably not a short run consideration). Second, the high cost of advanced technology may limit expansion of state enterprises. In the past, a PCB manufacturing facility cost only US $3 to 4 million. Some factories, such as large TV factories could afford the cost. But now a PCB factory requires at least a US $10 to 50 million in investment: the state recently spent US $12 million for the Shanxi No. 704 factory, for example. It may be difficult for other facilities to be granted such generous investment.

Competitive Situation There are 400 PCB manufacturing facilities in China according to MMEI. The ministry considers 212 of these facilities to be of "national importance." This term is undefined, although it should be noted that an official from the China Electronics Corporation (CEC, MMEI's major manufacturing arm) has defined "important" as contributing to national industrial and defense goals instead of "excessive consumerism." This may not be the whole story though, as it is believed that many "less important" facilities are simply very small or manufacture low-standard products.

The 212 primary manufacturers are reportedly located in every province and region except Tibet. They are under the jurisdiction of fourteen different ministries and other government groups, including the Ministry of Machinery and Electronics Industry, the Ministry of Aero-Space Industry, and the Chinese Academy of Sciences.

China began to produce PCBs in the 1980s. DuPont was one of the first companies to sell PCB manufacturing equipment to China. Some Japanese companies, such as Panasonic, also have a well-established presence in China.

Although production responsibilities are spread through many ministries, MMEI controls all regulations and licenses in this sector. MMEI is also the major producer, as its subordinate factories, many of which belong to CEC, supplied 4.5 million square meters of PCB last year.

Some figures are available which indicate the most active areas of China are Guangdong Province and the Shanghai region. In 1990, 67 percent of all double-sided and multi-layered PCBs were manufactured in Guangdong Province. In the same year, 67 percent of all single-sided PCBs were manufactured in Shanghai municipality and the surrounding provinces of Jiangsu and Zhejiang. The Shanghai No. 20 Radio Factory, for example, annually produces 800,000 square meters. Their production line was imported from Panasonic and has been considered a model for all PCB producers. The Shanghai Vacuum Company has the manufacture capability of producing 500,000 square meters of PCB annually.

China lacks advanced technology in this field, hence the perception that most expansion of manufacturing capability will come from equipment imports. Most Chinese state-owned enterprises produce normal single-sided PCBs, with hole not smaller than 0.5mm. Joint venture enterprises use imported equipment which can produce 16 to 20 layered PCBs. At the moment, there are only ten Sun or equivalent work stations known to be imported for use in China's PCB factories, according to MMEI. In the laboratory (but not yet in production), some Chinese factories can produce 40 layer PCBs sized 450x450 mm, with 0.13 mm lines and 0.1 mm holes. In China there are more than twenty joint venture enterprises that manufacture PCBs. Most joint venture enterprises or new PCB manufacturing facilities are located in southern China.

Many Chinese PCB factories use some U.S. imported manufacturing equipment. there is also equipment from other countries including Italy, Japan, Germany, and Israel.

It has not been able to obtain figures on the U.S. market share, but it is probably substantial and may even be the largest in China.

Imported SMT equipment seems concentrated in China's southern provinces of Guangdong and Fujian. The big names in SMT from third countries are Tescon (Japan) and Siemens. Japanese companies are believed to control a significant share of this market, but figures are difficult to obtain, partly because many factories do plug-in business. Consumer product factories, especially those making televisions and audio equipment, have plug-in shops. U.S. firms are believed to have substantial exports to China of plug-in machines, but lag in SMT equipment.

We believe that the Chinese central government has no plans to meet the demand for PCB equipment with domestic production. But MMEI may have plans to manufacture certain key items in China by setting up foreign joint ventures. The tendency of Chinese government officials in other fields of electronics have been to pick one foreign firm with the best technology and price and enter into a joint venture emphasizing technology transfer. For example, Universal Company sold nothing in China before 1990, according to MMEI officials, when it was identified as a favored party with which to do auto insertion business, based partly on technology transfer considerations. In 1990 and 1991, Universal accomplished US $10 million annually in exports. This market had previously been dominated by Panasonic.

Japan's Tesson has a joint venture in Sichuan making radial inserters for television PCB assembly. Their equipment is said to be preferred because of a desire to keep the inserters on-line twenty-four hours a day, and because maintenance is simpler than for some other machines. More sophisticated equipment may eventually be purchased from the U.S.

Guizhou's Number 4506 factory manufactures SMT equipment in cooperation with Siemens (no further details). They have received significant financial support from MMEI, possibly indicating a military or other central government-oriented mission.

MMEI plans to set up twenty model production lines in different sectors during the Eighth Five-Year Plan (1991-5). One of them is an SMT PCB line at the Number 4506 Factory in Guizhou, and another will be in Shanghai. It means the MMEI will select the best equipment possible, and direct other factories to copy their scheme. Obviously, bids for this line will be highly contested. An Italian firm, Pulin (no further information) reportedly has more than ten joint ventures in China; this may be exaggerated. One source says that they concentrate on equipment sales, which in the eyes of this source, makes them a "poor" partner.

Most joint venture enterprises are located in Guangzhou Province, but at least one is in Dalian (the Dalian Taipingyang Duoceng Yinzhiban Chang or the Dalian Pacific Multilayer PCB Factory); two are in Tianjin, Tianli and Pulin; two in Shanghai, Shanghai Bell and Pulin. Some factories in Guangdong include Shantou Chaoshen, Guangzhou Pulin, Guangzhou Fafa, Shenzhen Xinhua, Dongguan Huiye, and Dongguan Wansi. Most of them can produce 50 thousand square meters of multilayer PCB annually. Some, like Fafa, are said to be capable of producing 180 thousand square meters PCB.

Market Access Some observers assert that since the secret promulgation of a vaguely worded 1985 directive by MMEI, it has been difficult to import any single-sided PCB equipment. This directive mandated that forty products, including PCB equipment, be limited or halted. Since that time, officials have made it known informally that limits are directed only against single-sided PCB equipment. It is possible to import more advanced equipment such as double-sided, SMT, and auto-insert machines, but import licenses are still required.

PCB manufacturing equipment was not a commodity freed from import licenses and duties as a result of the U.S.-PRC Market Access Talks in late 1992. But a few Chinese officials tell us informally that this situation may change for the better for U.S. and other exporters of PCB manufacturing equipment when China eventually accedes to the GATT. The standard duty rate for PCB equipment is 38%. But many end-users can escape some or even all of this assessment without smuggling. Universities, institutes and new high technology enterprises can receive a 50% duty reduction. If a semiconductor enterprise imports other equipment, they reportedly receive 100% duty relief (no further information). This still leaves some amount of motivation in the economy to smuggle, however, for those making imports which do not qualify or for those who do not want to hazard a system characterized by many as inefficient, corrupt, inconsistent, and time consuming.

MMEI is struggling to keep control of the import of PCB equipment and the production of PCBs even as Guangdong seems to be increasing its undocumented imports: MMEI controls not only import licenses, but also seeks to control negotiations for the purchase of PCB equipment. This is referred to as "lianhe duiwai, tongyi chengjiao" (consolidated negotiations with foreigners). The more traditional-minded officials believe that this allows for lower equipment prices: consolidating such dealings lends better to central planning than allowing the market to run free. For example, MMEI's China National Electronics Import Export Corporation (CEIEC) is the only firm with the right to import auto-insertion machines, and there may be other unpromulgated import restrictions.

China has a limited (but growing) system of independent agents or distributors, so U.S. companies have used other methods for penetrating China's market. Other possibilities include:

- Use the services of a U.S. (or third country) trading company. Many of these trading companies are willing to handle American products. Trading companies with offices in southern China will likely be the most effective.
- Use the services of a Hong Kong-based agent or distributor. Many Hong Kong agents and distributors are very active in China and have an extensive network of Chinese contacts.
- Establish a representative office in China. This is a good, if expensive, way to maintain a continued visibility in China. Some U.S. companies form joint ventures with a Chinese enterprise to provide after sales service for the U.S. company's products in China.
- Establish a manufacturing joint venture with a Chinese partner.
- Establish a technology transfer relationship with a Chinese partner. Although many U.S. companies have engaged in successful technology transfer arrangements with Chinese enterprises, the U.S. partner should be aware that intellectual property rights protection in China is newly established and untested.

In addition, U.S. companies should be aware that, although China has no requirement for countertrade provisions in imports, a foreign company willing to consider countertrade may sometimes gain the competitive edge.

Finally, Chinese end-users often require extensive technical assistance and training as part of the sales package. American companies, in general, have a good reputation in China for following through with technical assistance and training.

Best Sales Prospects:

    a. CAD/CAM work stations and software
    b. Optical analysis instruments (AIO)
    c. Digital control drilling machines
    d. Testing machines
    e. SMT equipment
    f. Cleaning machines
    g. Soldering systems

Key Contacts:

Chinese government trading organizations in this sub-sector:

Note: all telephone numbers should be preceded by the country code and city code. Unless otherwise specified, the Beijing numbers below are preceded by 86-1.

Ministry of Machinery and Electronics Industry (MMEI)
46 San Li He Road
Beijing 100823
Fax: 3295474

Department of Microelectronics and Basic Products
Device and Components Division
Fax: 3295474
Special Electronic Equipment Division

China Electronics Corporation (CEC)
27 wan Shou Lu
Beijing 100846
Fax: 8221835, 8213745
Department of International Cooperation

China National Electronics Import/Export Corporation
No. 23a Fuxing Road
P.O. Box 140
Beijing 100036, China
Tel: 8219532, 813510   Fax: 8223907, 8212352

China National Technical Import/Export Corporation
Jiu Ling Building
21 Xi Sanhuan Beilu
Tel: 8494916   Fax: 8414877

China Machinery Equipment Import and Export Corporation
16 Fuxingmenwai Dajie
Beijing 100045
Tel: 3268157   Fax: 3261865

Some useful contacts in the electronics industry include:

Beijing Mudan Electronic (Group) Ltd.
Haidian District
Beijing 100083
Tel: 2017031-4179

Beijing Philips Corporation Ltd.
Haidian District
Beijing 100081
Tel: 8414448

Hainan Electronic Company
Haikou
Hainan Province 570003
Tel: 72037

Hongguang Electronic Tube Plant
Jianshe Nanzhilu, Chenghua District
Chengdu, Sichuan Province 610051
Tel: 443723

Huafa Electronic Company, Ltd.
Luohu, Shenzen
Guangdong Province 518031
Tel: 352205

Huaqiang Sanyo Electronic Company, Ltd.
Luohu, Shenzhen
Guangdong Province 518031
Tel: 365390

Modern Electronic (Shenzen) Industry Company, Ltd.
Luohu, Shenzen
Guangdong Province 518026
Tel: 363660

Shenzhen Konka Electronic Company, Ltd.
Shangbu, Shenzhen
Guangdong Province 518053
Tel: 770869

Wuxi Huajing Electronic (Group) Company
Wuxi
Jiangsu Province 214061
Tel: 607123

Xiamen Overseas Chinese Electronics Company, Ltd.
Xiamen
Fujian Province 361006
Tel: 621091

Zhong'ou Electronics Industrial Company, Ltd.
No. 1 Eling Road, South Fuizhou
Guangdong Province 516000
Tel: 260720

Some useful contacts in the radio industry include:

Changzhou General Radio Factory
Tianning District, Changzhou
Jiangsu Province 213001
Tel: 442241

Chengdu No. 1 Radio Factory
22 Sanduan, Nanyihuanlu
Wuhou District, Chengdu
Sichuan Province 610041
Tel: 581066

Guangzhou Broadcasting Equipment Factory
Baiyun District, Guangzhou
Guangdong Province 510410
Tel: 6627653

Hefei No. 2 Radio Factory
Dongshi District, Hefei
Anhui Province 230011
Tel: 483700

Liaoning No. 8 Radio Factory
Xinfu District, Fushun
Liaoning Province 113006
Tel: 773084-281

Liaoyuan Radio Factory
Xinhua District, Xinxiang
Henan Province 453059
Tel: 222234

Nanjing Radio Factory
Xuanwu, Nanjing
Jiangsu Province 210002

Shanghai Broadcasting Equipment Factory
Changning District
Shanghai 200050
Tel: 2512010

Shanghai No. 18 Radio Plant
Xuhui District
Shanghai 200032
Tel: 4311200

Shanghai No. 4 Radio Factory
Xuhui District
Shanghai 200030
Tel: 4387521

Xi'an No. 1 Radio Factory
Lianhu, Xi'an
Shaanxi Province 710054
Tel: 751862

ENVIRONMENTAL CONTROL

In 1992, the People's Republic of China (PRC or China) experienced a 25% industrial growth rate and its urban population growth rate rose by 20%. This rapid growth has had a devastating affect on the environment. In the cities, the air is heavily polluted by particulates and sulfur dioxide due to the country's dependency on coal. In 1989, China was ranked the third largest source of both greenhouse gas emissions (8.5%) and industrial emissions of carbon dioxide (2,288.6 billion tons). These numbers have increased dramatically since that time. Solid waste piled outside of cities has leaked toxins into the ground water, and the water in many rivers dies not meet bathing standards, much less drinking. In the rural areas, misuse of the water supply, fertilizers, and pesticides has multiplied the water pollution problem. Also, poor farming practices in irrigation and drainage have destroyed millions of hectares of land, turning them into salt beds (50).

All this is to say that China has a potential ecological disaster on its hands. Of primary concern is the water supply; total waste water reached 36.65 billion tons per year in 1992 (not including township and village industry enterprises), an increase of 9% from 1991. This number is expected to rise to 132.86 billion tons per year with PRC's modernization drive. Along with industrial pollutants, sewage is a significant problem. These problems have created the need for a dramatic increase in Chinese municipal waste water treatment equipment and technology. In 1992, the total waste water treatment investment was estimated at US $2,948.9 million; this number is projected to rise 30% in 1993. The U.S. now holds roughly 4% of that market. Because of the ambiguity of numbers given to USFCS by several sources, specific figures are not available on municipal waste water treatment.

Although the Chinese government is aware of the necessity of becoming more ecologically conscious, China's Eighth Five-Year Plan (1991-1995) has budgeted only .85% of the GNP for environmental pollution control. This percentage falls short of the 1.5% estimated to be needed by China's National Environmental Protection Agency (NEPA). The government has begun utilizing foreign loans to introduce advanced equipment and technologies in the waste water treatment sector. These loans have come from the World Bank, the Asian Development Bank (ADB), the United Nations Development Program (UNDP) and Environmental Protection (UNEP), the Global Environment Facility (GEF), and financial institutions in Japan, Austria, Canada, Germany, Australia, and France.

The governing of this particular industry is highly decentralized with authority mostly vested in the industrial ministries: the Ministry of Water Resources (MOWR), the Ministry of Construction (MOC), the Ministry of Machinery and Electronic Industry (MMEI), the State Planning Commission, and the State Oceanographic Administration (SOA).

Overview   Sustained attention to the various aspects of pollution control has been a development of fairly recent vintage in modern day China. During the 1950s and 1960s, basic emphasis was on production—both agricultural and industrial. In the 1970s, however, appreciation grew as to the need to place greater emphasis on environmental protection and resource recovery, culminating in 1979 in passage of the Law on Environmental Protection of the People's Republic of China (for trial implementation) (22).

Subsequently, both the Sixth Five-Year Plan (1981-1985) and the Seventh Five-Year Plan (1986-1990) have emphasized environmental protection as a "major task of socialist modernization." The Sixth Five-Year Plan made available approximately 17 billion yuan for environmental protection programs (of which about 70 percent was earmarked for equipment and instruments and the Seventh Five-Year Plan earmarked approximately 33 billion yuan (roughly 8.9 billion 1988 dollars) of which about 55 percent was designated for equipment and instruments. The Seventh Five-Year Plan explicitly noted:

> The state stipulates that the various funds earmarked for environmental protection must be guaranteed and may not be diverted for other uses.

In consequence, the overall market for pollution control equipment and technology was projected to increase about 45 percent during the current Plan period, from approximately Y2.750 billion ($937 million) in 1985 to roughly Y4 billion ($1.1 billion) in 1990.

Some data published recently (58) on the overall pollution control market are hard to reconcile with the figures in this text, but may be helpful in indicating trends in the 1993-1995 period.

	1993	1994	1995
A. Total Market Size	508	577	658
B. Total Local Production	280	336	403
C. Total Exports	2	2.1	2.2
D. Total Imports	230	243	257
E. Total Imports from U.S.	47	50	53
F. Exchange Rate		8.6	8.6

Within these totals, the market for water pollution control equipment is projected to increase from $442 million in 1985 to $504 million in 1990, that for air pollution control equipment from $274 million in 1985 to $368 million in 1990, that for waste pollution control equipment from $120 million to $150 million, and that for noise pollution control equipment from $102 million to $123 million.

Overall it is estimated that water pollution control equipment will account for roughly 46 percent of the market during the Plan period, air pollution control equipment 30 percent, waste pollution control equipment 13 percent, and noise pollution control equipment the remaining 11 percent.

Domestic production is projected to account for a major share—roughly 86 percent—of the overall $5 billion market for pollution control equipment which is expected to develop during the Five-Year Plan period. Within this total, it is estimated that domestic production will account for approximately 85 percent of the market for water pollution control equipment, 82 percent of the market for air pollution control equipment, 90 percent of the market for waste pollution control equipment, and 93 percent of the market for noise pollution control equipment.

The overall value of imports in 1985 was $138 million; the total was projected to reach $162 million in 1990, an increase of approximately 20 percent. Over the Five-Year Plan period it is estimated that water pollution control equipment will account for about 47 percent of the imports, air pollution control equipment 39 percent, waste pollution control equipment nine percent, and noise pollution control equipment five percent.

Japan, the United States, and Hong Kong/Macao are the primary exporters of pollution control equipment to China, followed by West Germany and the U.K. In 1986, the last year for which data are available, Japan held approximately 37 percent of the import market, the U.S. 17 percent, Hong Kong/Macao 9 percent, West Germany 6 percent and the U.K. 3 percent.

Although future import market shares will be somewhat dependent on external circumstances, including the degree to which the dollar may appreciate or depreciate against Japanese and European currencies, it is projected that the overall order in 1990 will remain approximately the same, although Japan's market share should decrease somewhat and that of the U.S. and Hong Kong/Macao increase slightly. It is estimated that in 1990 Japan will hold about 27 percent of the larger import market, the U.S. 19 percent, Hong Kong/Macao 13 percent, West Germany 6 percent, and the U.K. 3 percent.

Demand for imported technology is growing, Chinese planners seeing the import of technology as a desirable alternative to equipment and instrument imports, both in the sense of avoiding continuing foreign exchange expenditures in the future and of strengthening the capabilities of domestic industry.

Although they have increased in recent years, exports of Chinese pollution control equipment are relatively limited because of the fairly backward nature of the equipment. For the immediate future it is anticipated that exports will remain limited; as the quality of domestic production improves output will probably be retained at home as an import substitute. Total exports are projected to average $20 million—$25 million a year.

It is estimated there are approximately 4,000 plants in China—few of them specialized—which produce pollution control equipment. A substantial number of subordinate to individual Ministries—such as those for chemicals, metallurgy, coals, and the like, and produce in substantial measure for plants under the control of the respective Ministries.

It is estimated that about 70 percent of the market is represented by industrial facilities and about 30 percent by governmental facilities, i.e., hospitals, public utilities other than power, and the like. Transportation and ferrous metals are the principal industrial consumers of pollution control equipment and municipalities and public utilities the principal governmental users.

To date the United States has been particularly successful in the sale to China of equipment for monitoring air quality. Trade sources indicate that although American equipment in general is appreciated for its high technological content, sales have occasionally been held back by high prices and an unwillingness to bargain, uncertain delivery dates, and uncertainties about the adequacy of post-sale service. Although Japanese products may have a somewhat lower technological content, they are cheaper, after-service is good, and delivery of product more certain.

Trade sources suggest the following as among the actions which would assist American manufacturers of pollution control equipment and technology to increase their share of the Chinese market (22):

1. Greater emphasis on contacts with Chinese technical personnel and on technical exchange programs, seminars, symposiums, and lectures.
2. Broader participation in exhibitions and trade shows.
3. Greater flexibility in sales practices, including willingness to bargain and to explore other than cash sales.
4. Participation in cooperative ventures.
5. Expanded budgets for a variety of development activities.
6. Greatly improved after-sale service, with more acceptable time and cost parameters.

Air Pollution Control   The Chinese market for air pollution control technology, instruments, and equipment is the second largest of the four discrete pollution control equipment sub-markets, accounting for about 30 percent of the overall market (23).

The growth in domestic production of air pollution control instruments and equipment is well illustrated if production is measured in yuan rather than in dollars in order to smooth out the effects of variations in exchange rates:

**Domestic Production of Equipment
and Instruments for Air Pollution Control**

	(Y 1,000,000)
1985	659
1986	734
1987	832
1988	931
1989	1,061
1992	1,379

Although domestically-produced equipment and instruments do not as a rule measure up to international standards, they nevertheless command about 82% of the local market. This percentage is projected to remain fairly constant through 1992, although the size of the market will grow substantially. Imports are estimated to have totalled about $51 million in 1987 and are projected to approximate $78 million in 1992, or roughly a 53% increase. In both years, imports are estimated to include about 50% equipment and 50% instruments.

Available data indicate that exports of Chinese air pollution control equipment and instruments totalled about $10 million in 1987. It is estimated that exports may reach $14 million in 1992. As the quality of domestic production improves, output will probably be retained at home as an import substitute.

As noted earlier, the Seventh Five-Year Plan (1986-1990) projects expenditures of about Y33 billion ($8.9 billion) for pollution control equipment and instruments. Roughly Y13.1

billion ($3.5 billion) appears to be earmarked for the prevention and control of air pollution. It is not possible to predict with accuracy the amounts which may be provided in the Eighth Five-Year Plan, but increases may be anticipated.

Demand for air pollution control equipment and instruments is driven by two imperatives: the need to upgrade existing facilities and the need to provide for new facilities.

The burning of coal, which is the basis for 70%-75% of China's energy supply, is the principal source of atmospheric pollution, followed by industrial dust and poisonous and harmful gases arising from industrial operations.

Illustratively, it is estimated that about 23 million tons of man-made dust are generated in China each year, some 17 million resulting from coal burning. Again, of 14.6 million tons of SO2 emitted into the atmosphere, 13 million are reportedly generated by coal burning. U.N. data estimate that China annually generates about 10% of the world's fossil energy carbon emissions.

In a recent survey of sixty cities, it was reported that the average density of suspended particles in the air per day was 2.2 times national Standard Two (300 micrograms/m3). Forty-five cities had experienced acid rain.

In another investigation involving seventy-two cities, the daily average content of sulphur dioxide was found to exceed State limits in all seventy-two, in some cities by four or five times.

In consequence of this situation, the Seventh Five-Year Plan calls for sustained emphasis on improvement of air pollution control measures.

Illustratively, it is reported that only seventy of industrial enterprises throughout the country are able to meet state standards for the amount of waste gas discharge. Progressively heavier fines are to be levied to assure improvement. As one device for encouraging recycling emissions from power plants, the UNDP is sponsoring a project in Shanghai to develop methods for using fly ash discharged by coal burning power stations as an ingredient in the manufacture of cement and concrete blocks.

In attempting to curb air pollution in cities, resulting from the residential use of coal, it was reported that in 1985 about 24% of urban dwellers were being supplied with gas as contrasted with 15.2% in 1980 and that centrally heated residential areas totalled 55 million square meters as contrasted with 18 million square meters in 1980. Continuing efforts are underway to curb pollution. For example, twenty-nine selected cities are expected to reduce suspended particles in the air by 1990 from 860 micrograms/m3 to below 500 micrograms/m3 in northern cities and from 450 micrograms/m3 to 300 micrograms/m3 in southern cities. As one step to this objective, selected cities are enjoined to supply residents with processed coals, as in briquettes, until gas supplies and central heat can be provided.

Recent passage of a new Air Pollution Prevention Law was designed to stress the importance of air pollution control. In consequence, there appears to be ample justification for estimating that the market for air pollution control technology, instruments, and equipment will continue to grow through 1992.

About two-thirds of the market is for equipment (23).

Water Pollution Control Unprecedented industrial expansion in China has served to place tremendous strains on the already grossly inadequate municipal waste water treatment systems in the major cities. As a result, of the 37 billion tons of industrial and residential waste water that flows annually from China's 467 cities, less than 10 percent is treated by the 70 or so waste water treatment facilities across the country before it is discharged. The worst sources of industrial water pollution in order of importance to Chinese authorities are: 1) paper making factories; 2) printing and dyeing factories; 3) chemical factories (especially medium and small sized enterprises); 4) electroplating factories; and 5) town and township enterprises. These and other factories drain more than 130,000 tons of poisonous chemical substances into China's waterways every year including 5,400 tons of mercury, 204 tons of cadmium, 2,020 tons of chromium, 1,209 tons of arsenic, 13,400 tons of phenol, 7,000 tons of cyanide, and over 100,000 tons of oil compounds. Specific industrial water pollution treatment targets have been established in the Eighth Five-Year Plan (1991-1995). Initial efforts will be directed at treating the waste water discharges of some 3,000 factories located primarily in the nation's big cities. Consisting mostly of large, state-run enterprises, these factories are responsible for 70 percent of the total national industrial sewage. The domestic production of water pollution equipment and instruments accounts for approximately 85 percent of the entire water pollution control market. The financing package associated with complete sewage treatment plant technology is a critical factor in determining what equipment is ultimately chosen. In fact, most of the water pollution control projects landed by third countries have included bi-lateral concessionary financing terms along with the project proposal. Projects funded by multi-lateral development agencies through tenders subject to international competitive bidding procedures represent the best chance for U.S. companies to compete for large projects on the basis of technical merit (24).

The Chinese government has estimated that there are 30,000-60,000 chemicals present in various concentrations in the major waterways in China (50). A list of the major pollutants and their quantities are:

	1991	1992	% Change
Industrial Waste Water	25,435	25,640	0.8%
(all figures in millions of tons)			
Heavy metal discharge	1,252	1,516	17.4%
Arsenic	675	872	22.6%
Cyanides	2,745	3,579	23.3%
Volatile Phenols	5,249	6,425	18.3%
Petrol Pollutants	61,952	65,076	4.8%

In 1990, 75% of waste water was generated by industries and 25% by domestic waste. Chinese statistics say these figures changed to 70% and 30% in 1991 and some experts believe the ratio will soon be at 50/50 ratio. The sewage disposal problem is tremendous. Sixty percent of human waste from public bathrooms in Beijing, the second largest city in China, leaves the city via the sewage system; 40% is transported out of the city by cart.

Much of this sewage removed by cart is piled and fermented and used as "night soil," fertilizer for the farming areas of China. In 1992 total sewage reached 12.21 billion tons. Of this figure, 18.5% was treated, up 3.6% from 1991.

In the rural areas misuse of the water supply, fertilizers, and pesticides have multiplied the water pollution problem. Also, poor farming practices in the areas of irrigation and drainage have destroyed millions of hectares of land, turning them into salt beds. In 1992, 50 million people and 30 million heads of cattle faced a drinking water shortage in rural north and northeastern regions (50).

Noise Pollution Control The Chinese market for noise pollution control technology, instruments, and equipment is the smallest of the four discreet pollution control equipment sub-markets, accounting for about 11% of the overall market (25).

Although domestically-produced equipment and instruments do not, as a rule, measure up to international standards, they nevertheless command almost 93% of the local market. This percentage is projected to remain fairly constant through 1992, although the size of the market will grow substantially. Imports are estimated to have totaled about $7.56 million in 1987 and are projected to approximate $10 million in 1992, or roughly a 34% increase. In both years imports are estimated to include about 78% instruments and 22% equipment.

The Seventh Five-Year Plan contains some broad injunctions respecting noise pollution: industrial enterprises are enjoined strictly to control fixed sources of noise and to take other noise control measures; and municipalities are enjoined to strengthen their problems for management of noise control, to strengthen the control of traffic noise, and to study technology for comprehensively harnessing environmental noise emanating from specified areas.

China: Standard of Environmental Noise in Industrial Enterprises

A. New or Rehabilitated Enterprises -

Maximum Hours in Working Day	Noise Limit (dB(A))*
8	85
4	89
2	91
1	94

B. Existing Enterprises

Maximum Hours in Working Day	Noise Limit (dB(A))*
8	90
4	93
2	96
1	99

*Note: Highest level may not exceed 115 dB(A)
Source: "Hygiene Standard for Noise in Industrial Enterprises," People's Republic of China.

China: Standard of Environmental Noise in Urban Areas

	Leq in (dB(A))	
Applicable Areas	Daytime	Nighttime
Special Residential Areas	45	35
Residential, Cultural and Educational Areas	50	40
First Type Mixed Areas	55	45
Second Type Mixed Areas and Commercial Centers	60	50
Concentrated Industrial Areas	65	55
Both Sides of Heavily Trafficked Roads	70	55

Source: "Standard of Environmental Noise of Urban Areas," People's Republic of China.

With respect to the quality of equipment, the noise pollution control manufacturing industry was directed to bring technology and quality by the end of the Plan up to the international standards of the early 1980s. Specific improvements are to be made in sound suppressor and in the quality of acoustical materials and enclosures.

In the light of the above, there appears ample justification for estimating that the market for noise pollution control technology, instruments, and equipment will continue to grow through 1992.

It is estimated that about 70% of the market for hardware will be for equipment and 30% for instruments.

Market Assessment Available Chinese statistical data (22) divide the overall environmental control industry sector into eleven sub-sectors and the government sector into six sub-sectors, as follows:

Industry Sector

Mining
Ferrous Metals
Non-Ferrous Metals
Chemical
Petrochemical
Light Industry
Textiles
Power
Transportation
Construction
Other

Government Sector

Central
Prefectural
Municipal
Medical/Research Institutions
Public Utilities
Other

The Transportation and ferrous metals sub-sectors are the principal industrial users of pollution control equipment and the municipal and public utilities sub-sectors the principal government sector users. Overall, the chemical industry sub-sector is estimated to be the principal user of water pollution control equipment, ferrous metals of air pollution control equipment, municipal government of waste pollution control equipment, and transportation of noise pollution equipment.

Table 95 shows estimated Chinese expenditures by category for pollution control equipment.

Table 95

China: Estimated Expenditures for Pollution Control Equipment by Major User Sectors

For 1992 in Millions of US$

Industry Sector

Mining	28.69	34.90	13.76	9.50	86.85
Ferrous Metals	40.98	44.42	16.06	4.22	105.68
Non-Ferrous Metals	32.78	25.38	11.47	3.48	73.11
Chemical	53.27	22.21	9.16	2.85	87.49
Petrochemical	36.88	22.21	10.32	2.10	71.51
Light Industry	45.08	12.70	6.88	1.27	65.93
Textiles	49.18	9.52	5.73	8.45	72.88
Power	24.59	38.07	12.62	12.67	87.95
Transportation	28.69	36.07	8.03	33.79	106.58
Construction	24.59	41.25	13.76	8.45	88.05
Other	45.71	30.58	6.90	18.81	102.00
Sub-Total	410.44	317.31	114.69	105.59	948.03

Government Sector

Central	22.13	23.47	5.91	6.98	58.49
Prefectural	23.95	16.43	11.23	6.57	58.18
Municipal	46.10	34.03	23.63	13.96	117.72
Medical Institutes	18.40	8.22	7.68	1.62	35.92
Public Utilities	49.79	24.65	5.32	7.80	87.56
Other	24.03	10.56	5.31	4.13	44.03
Sub-Total	184.40	117.36	59.08	41.06	401.90
TOTAL	594.84	434.67	173.77	146.65	1,349.93

Note: 1987, 1992   U.S. $1=Y3.72

Sources: China National Environmental Protection Industry Association. Field Interviews (22).

Competitive Situation Since sustained emphasis on utilization of pollution control equipment is a fairly recent development in China, the associated manufacturing industry is still rather backward and fragmented (22).

It is estimated that about 4,000 factories, substantially all of which are also producing other types of equipment and instruments, produce pollution control equipment. About 2,600 are members of the China National Environmental Protection Industry Association.

By and large pollution control equipment manufacturers fall into one of two categories: plants under the cognizance of one of the major Ministries—Coal, Chemicals, Metallurgy,, etc.—which produce equipment and instruments for other enterprises under the control of the same Ministry; and plants under cognizance of other units of government—such as provinces or municipalities—which produce equipment and instruments for use in localized areas.

In either event, few plants are what might be called specialized manufacturers. The great majority produce a wide variety of disparate equipment including pollution control equipment; some are integrated manufacturers and users; a small number are subsidiaries of research institutes.

Overall it is estimated that roughly two-thirds of the 4,000 plants in China produce instruments and meters and about one-third equipment. Some of the largest instrument factories—all of which produce a wide variety of instruments and meters—including environmental protection devices—are:

Beijing Analytical Instrument Factory
Wenquan, Haidianqu
Beijing 100095
Tel: 255-8728   Fax: 255-2854

Foshan Analytical Instrument Factory
97 Jianxin Lu, Foshan
Guangdong Province 528000
Tel: 333-2758   Fax: 335-2490

Shanghai Analytical Instrument Factory No. 3
77 Fenjang Lu
Shanghai 20031
Tel: 437-5460   Fax: 471-8772

Beijing Analytical Instrument Factory is the largest in China and has imported some advanced technology and equipment from West Germany. Shanghai Analytical Instrument Factory has imported technology and components from Japan. All the factories reportedly recognize shortcomings in their equipment, including low reliability and short service life, and are desirous of importing advanced technology from abroad.

Three of the largest water purification equipment factories are:
Beijing Chaoyang Water Processing Equipment Factory
Shanghai Water Processing Equipment Factory
Taiyuan Waste Water Processing Equipment Factory
Among leading producers of air pollution control equipment are:
Xuan Hua Metallurgical Environmental Protection Equipment Factory (Hebei)
Shanghai Metallurgical Mine Mechanical Equipment Factory
Shanghai Wujing Dust Removing Equipment Factory
Harbin Environmental Equipment Factory
Producers of noise pollution control equipment include:
Fengtai Noise Control Equipment Factory (Beijing)
Jinshan County Silencer Factory (Shanghai)
Shanghai #2 Noise Control Equipment Factory
Producers of waste pollution control equipment include:
Hao Xian No. 2 Environmental Protection Device Works
Tianjin Hazardous Chemical Disposal Factory
Tianjin Industrial Purifying Equipment Factory

Overall, it is recognized that the level of pollution control equipment in China is not very advanced, that production techniques are cumbersome, and that foreign technology in particular is required if equipment and instrumentation are to meet the requirements of progressively more stringent regulations.

It should be noted that, in past years, the centralized aspects of economic planning have served to de-emphasize both product quality and R&D.

Since, for the most part, manufacturing plants were serving a captive audience—either other plants under the control of the same Ministry or other plants within the same geographical entity—there was little incentive for the types of improvement which might have been engendered by a competitive situation. At the same time, since many plants were responsible for the production of a wide variety of instruments or equipment, there was little opportunity to benefit from economies of scale in production of pollution control equipment or to initiate relevant R&D. Furthermore, the country's research institutes—which might have provided internally-developed concepts for product improvement—in general were not an integral part of the manufacturing process and did not tend to focus their attention on applied research.

Hopefully, the import of technology from abroad will tend to raise the level of product quality and efficiency of production. To address the R&D problem, the State Council has promulgated a set of "Regulations to Promote Reform in the Scientific and Technological Management System." The regulations provide for integration by 1990 of a number of research institutes, many now under the Chinese Academy of Sciences, with large manufacturing enterprises to assure that more applied research is undertaken.

As earlier noted, imports account for only a limited share of the Chinese market for pollution control equipment, holding about 15% of the $884 million overall market in 1987 and projected to hold about 14% of the $1.350 billion market in 1992.

Within the four sub-sectors of the market, the import percentage varies somewhat (22):

Imports as Percentage of Sub-Sector Pollution Control Markets
(1987, 1992)

Sub-Sector	1987	1992
Water	14.8%	14.3%
Air	19.3%	17.9%
Waste	11.9%	10.7%
Noise	7.8%	6.9%

Japan was the principal exporter of pollution control equipment to China in 1986, the last year for which data are available, followed by the United States, Hong Kong/Macao, West Germany, and the United Kingdom. In 1986, Japan held approximately 37% of the import market, the U.S. 17%, Hong Kong/Macao 9%, West Germany 6%, and the U.K. 3%.

Major export countries were expected to remain unchanged in 1990, although the market share of Japan was expected to fall somewhat because of appreciation of the yen against the U.S. dollar and the market shares of the U.S. and Hong Kong/Macao to rise slightly.

Japanese exporters serve all market segments; in particular, instruments and meters are will accepted by Chinese end-users. China is also a significant importer of complete plants from Japan; the imported capital equipment is usually fitted with Japanese-made pollution control equipment. Illustratively, major equipment recently imported from Japan by the Baoshan Iron and Steel Works was completely fitted with appropriate pollution control equipment. As a result, dust in working areas was reportedly reduced to 20-21 tons per square kilometer per month in 1987—30 percent of the average for the metallurgical industry as a whole.

Mitsubishi Heavy Industries of Japan is supplying a flue gas desulphurization system for the Luohuang Power Plant in Sichuan, which was expected to go into operation in 1990. The plant, reportedly, is the first in China consuming high-sulphur coal which can treat exhaust gas so as fully to meet environmental protection requirements.

Japan benefits from a strong marketing presence in China, its proximity, and a willingness to provide concessionary financing. On the other hand, its products are not believed to be as technically advanced as those of the U.S. and West Germany and prices have become less competitive of late because of the appreciation of the yen against the dollar.

West German products are considered to have a high technological content, but to be relatively costly, a factor which has been exacerbated by the appreciation of the mark against the dollar.

Sales by Hong Kong/Macao have been basically of products with a low technological content and have largely represented low cost items. A growing percentage appear to represent transshipment from other countries which are shown in Chinese statistics as originating in Hong Kong/Macao.

In one of the few direct foreign investments in the environmental protection industry, SMEKRU of Denmark has established the Shanghai SMEKRU Municipal Engineering Company. The company plans to be active in design, construction, equipment supply, and consultation with respect to treatment of waste water, solid wastes, and air pollution.

An innovative approach was revealed recently with the decision by Chinese environmental authorities to accept an offer by a Canadian company to assist in the establishment of an international environmental technologies development center in Beijing. The center was reported to be the first joint Chinese-foreign project on environmental technologies.

The agreement was signed by the Chinese Research Academy of Environmental Sciences, the China National Environmental Protection Industry Association, and RIA Environmental Technologies of Vancouver.

According to the announcement, RIA will donate $350,000 to the center. The center will establish a data bank on environmental technologies, which will bring together in Beijing pertinent data from around the world.

The center will act as a paid consultant to clients in China and elsewhere, will help organize the transfer of appropriate technologies to China, and will encourage the development of new technologies in China.

The center plans to sponsor seminars and symposia to provide assessments of promising environmental technologies and will help train engineers and administrators. It will also produce and sell video tapes and publications relating to environmental protection.

Such a strategy tends to fit in well with the Chinese government's approach to economic cooperation, which emphasizes the introduction of new technology and the concept of cooperative effort. It appears to be the government's thinking that (1) cooperative projects provide better understanding of the application of new technologies; (2) value and quality can be better appreciated; (3) training can be facilitated; and (4) after-service and maintenance requirements can be better understood.

The Swedish Government has recently provided $300,000 to underwrite a feasibility study of the technical renovation of the Nanshi Water Treatment Plant in Shanghai. The study will be carried out by the Viak Ab Company of Sweden.

The German Machinery and Plant Manufacturers Association and the Federal Environmental Agency recently sponsored a five day seminar in Beijing which brought together thirty West German and 300 Chinese experts to discuss environmental protection technology. Ten West German companies exhibited advanced environmental protection equipment (22).

The U.S. held approximately 2.5% of the Chinese market for environmental protection instruments and equipment in 1986 and it was projected to hold about 2.7% in 1992. This represented 17% of the import market in 1986 and was projected to represent 19% of the market in 1992 (22).

It is recognized that a limited number of U.S. companies have developed strategies and committed resources. Nevertheless, there is a general impression in the market place that the marketing efforts of American companies have not been comparable to those of Japanese and German entrepreneurs.

Chinese trade sources suggest the following as among U.S. weaknesses insofar as the Chinese domestic market is concerned:

1. Absence of adequate research on the Chinese market;
2. Insufficient budgets for development activities;
3. Lack of sufficient contacts with Chinese technical personnel, despite the importance of such personnel in the decision-making process;
4. Insufficient participation in exhibitions and consequent failure to become better known to potential buyers;
5. Insufficient participation in seminars;
6. Absence of adequate after-sales networks, coupled with insufficient training at the time of sales;
7. Unwillingness to modify equipment to meet customers' requirements;
8. Marketing techniques which have not been adapted to the Chinese environment;
9. Uncertainties arising from the application of U.S. export control regulations;
10. Inflexibility of trade practices, including high costs and unwillingness to bargain;
11. Inadequate number of cooperative ventures;
12. Lack of patience.

It was pointed out, for example, that Japanese companies go to great efforts to establish close and lasting relationships with their customers. Between 1981 and 1986, illustratively, 651 Japanese experts provided free consulting services to 130 factories of all types. Customer personnel are not infrequently invited to Japan for training in Japanese factories and are provided with free lodging and a daily stipend. Feasibility studies are provided free of charge as a basis for encouraging the import of new equipment. As a matter of course, products are adapted to local requirements.

Trade recommendations as to efforts which might assist U.S. manufacturers to improve their presence in the Chinese market and further improve market share are essentially the reciprocal of the above, and include:

1. More adequate market research;
2. Expanded budgets for a variety of development activities;
3. Much greater emphasis on contacts with Chinese end-users and their technical personnel and on technical exchange and training programs, seminars, symposiums, and lectures;
4. More comprehensive participation in exhibitions and trade shows;
5. Development, with Chinese partners, of training centers and after-sales networks;
6. Greater flexibility in sales practices, including willingness to explore other than cash sales;
7. Greater participation in cooperative ventures;
8. Establishment of agency relationships and sales networks;
9. Greater willingness to tailor products to specific user requirements;
10. Greater consistency in the application of U.S. export control regulations.

U.S. equipment is recognized for its high level of technology, its reliability, and its durability. Drawbacks, as noted above, include comparatively high costs, lack of willingness to modify products to meet local requirements, and an uncertainty as to the availability of adequate after-service.

Insofar as technology is concerned, Joy Technology signed a $1 million transfer agreement with the Harbin Environment Equipment Company. The agreement will provide technology to manufacture systems for eliminating various types of industrial pollution and particularly covers technology for the design and manufacture of baghous flue gas desulphurization systems and electrostatic precipitators designed for the fossil-fueled electric utility industry. The agreement also calls for Joy's Western Precipitation Division to train Chinese engineers in the United States and China.

Best Sales Prospects   Based on existing and projected markets and related import penetration, the following listing summarizes apparent opportunities for export to China of various categories of pollution control instruments and technology. In a number of instances, interviewees expressed interest int he joint production with American companies of such types of environmental control equipment.

China: The Market for Pollution Control Technology, Instruments, and Equipment—Items Offering Best Sales Prospects for U.S. Suppliers (22)

Water
   Mobile laboratories
   Alarm and warning devices
   Special purpose pumps

Oil/water separators

Equipment for tertiary treatment of waste water (primarily chemical and biological sewage
 treatment)

Membrane separation equipment

Ionizing radiation systems

Mobile waste water treatment systems

Waste water recycling/reuse equipment

Point-of-use water treatment process equipment

Air

Multiple use analytical instruments

Mobile metering instruments and warning devices

Dry dust collection and comprehensive utilization equipment and technology (particularly for blast
 furnaces)

Gas collection and comprehensive utilization installations

Gas desulphurization and recovery systems

Waste

Hazardous waste analyzing equipment (including chromatographs, atomic absorption analyzers,
 atomic absorption spectrometers, infrared scanners)

Hazardous waste emergency treatment equipment (including high expansion foam, nuclear waste
 recovery systems)

Hazardous and other waste processing and resource recovery equipment (particularly including
 chromatographs

Noise

Turbine silencing systems

Acoustic radar

Useful Contacts: To make inquiries on a particular project, industry, or product, a company
should start with the appropriate ministry or corporation. In general, the company should
first contact the department within the ministry or corporation responsible for dealing with
foreign companies. In a ministry, this department will usually be known as the Foreign
Affairs Bureau or the International Cooperation Bureau. In a corporation, it will usually be
known as the Foreign Affairs or International Cooperation Department. The foreign affairs
department can then either arrange a meeting or direct the company to the appropriate
department in charge of the product or project.

For companies making their first contact with a ministry or corporation, the foreign
affairs department may often require an introduction of the company from an American
organization they are already familiar with before they will agree to a meeting. In this case,
the American Embassy commercial section, the US-China Business Council, or trade agents
or consultants can act as go-betweens.

Once a company has established a relationship with officials relevant to projects it is
interested in, contact can usually be made directly with the official instead of through the
foreign affairs department.

Contact information for major Chinese ministries and corporations follows. All the addresses are in Beijing unless otherwise indicated. If telephoning or faxing from overseas, first dial the (86-1) prefix.

National Environmental Protection Agency (NEPA)
Contact: Deputy Director of Waste Water Administration Department
No. 115 Xizhimmennei, Nan Xiao Jie
Beijing 100035
Tel: 832-9911   Fax: 832-8013

Ministry of Construction
Contact: Deputy Division Chief of Municipal Construction Department
9 Sanlihelu, Haidian District
Beijing 100835
Tel: 839-3160   Fax: 831-3669

Ministry of Water Resources
Contact: Deputy Director of Department of Foreign Affairs
1 Baiguanglu' Ertiao, Xuanwu District
Beijing 100761
Tel: 327-322 X5641/326-0495   Fax: 326-0365

Ministry of Agriculture
Contact: Division Chief of Department of Environmental Protection and Energy
11 Nongzhanguan Nanli
Beijing 100026
Tel: 507-4220   Fax: 500-2448

China National Council of Light Industry
Contact: Division Chief of Environmental Protection
B22 Fuchengmenwai Dajie, Xicheng District
Beijing 100833
Tel: 839-6526   Fax: N/A

Ministry of Machinery
Contact: Deputy Director of Industry Development Department
46 Sanlihe, Xicheng District
Beijing 100823
Tel: 859-4947   Fax: 859-5474

Ministry of Chemical Industry
Contact: General Manager of Environmental Protection
No. 1 Yiqu Zhongjie

Tel: 204-8510   Fax: 204-8510

China International Engineering Consulting Corporation (CIECC)
Contact: Chief Engineer of the Department of Social Benefits
32 Chegong Zhuang Xilu, Haidian Qu
Beijing 100044
Tel: 841-5511 X3414   Fax: 841-7301

China National Machinery Import/Export Corporation (CMC)
Mailing Address: P.O. Box 49, Erligou, Xijiao
Office Address: 3A Beiwa Lu, Haidian Qu
Beijing 100044
Tel: 841-1642   Fax: 842-1956

China National Technical Import/Export Corporation (CNTIC)
Contact: Chief of 1st Business Department
No. 21 Xisanhuan Beilu
Beijing 100081
Tel: 840-4831   Fax: 840-4833

China National Chemical Construction Corporation (CNCCC)
Contact: Manager of Department of Foreign Liaison
Building 16, Hepingli, Qiqu
Beijing 100013
Tel: 421-4043   Fax: 421-5527

China National Machinery & Equipment Import/Export Corporation (EQUIMPEX)
16 Fuxingmenwai Dajie
Beijing 100045
Tel: 326-8208   Fax: 362-375/306-1865

THE FOOD PROCESSING/PACKAGING EQUIPMENT INDUSTRY

Some salient statistics on the food processing and packaging equipment industry are given in Table 96 (3).

Table 96

Statistical Data on Food Processing/Packaging Equipment Industry

A)	Three-letter ITA industry sector code:	FPP
B)	Est. total market size (USD millions):	
	1991 -	$ 720
	1992 -	$ 800
	1993 -	$1,419
	1994 -	$1,619
	1995 -	$1,851
C)	Est. 1992-4 annual market growth rate:	8%
D)	Est. total imports (USD millions):	
	1991 -	$164
	1992 -	$180
	1993 -	$591
	1994 -	$709
	1995 -	$850
E)	Est. annual total import growth rate:	7%
F)	Est. imports from U.S. (USD millions):	
	1991 -	$ 10
	1992 -	$ 15
	1993 -	$ 41
	1994 -	$ 45
	1995 -	$ 50 (58)
G)	Est. annual growth of imports from U.S.:	2%
H)	China's receptivity to U.S. products in this sector (5 - High/1 - Low):	3
I)	Competition from local/third-countries for U.S. firms (5 - Low/1 - High):	1
J)	Chinese market barriers to U.S. sales in this sector (5 - Few/1 - Many):	3
K)	Comments - factors for increased U.S. sales:	

  - China will invest $4 billion to update its food processing and packing facilities in the Eighth Five-Year Plan.
  - Upgrades are needed both to improve quality in the domestic market and to be competitive in international markets.

L)	Most Promising Sub-sectors	1992 market size
	1. Cereals & Oilseeds Processing Machines	$140 million
	2. Food Processing Machines	$180 million
	3. Food Packaging Machines	$100 million

Overview At present China processes only 5-1 percent of its food output. Strengthening and modernizing the food processing/packaging industry has been a key goal of both the Sixth and Seventh Five-Year Plans, and China is now engaged in a serious effort to increase its export of processed/packaged foods. But in spite of widespread Chinese efforts to develop this sector, technology is still well below world standards. Since the quality of domestic food processing/packaging machinery does not produce products up to international standards, Chinese plants which wish to export their food products must import many of their food processing and packaging machines. And because high grade packaging materials are scarce in China, these must often be imported as well (27).

Market Assessment - Fruit and Vegetable Processing Equipment China's first cannery was established in Shanghai in 1906. In the next few years, other canneries were established in China's coastal cities. Today, China has canneries throughout the country, but most of its leading food processing plants are still in coastal cities. China now has 170 canneries which produce food for export, and 70 percent of these are in coastal areas. Canned foods are among China's most important light industrial export products. China now exports over US $500 million worth of canned food products every year. In 1987, canned food exports totalled 530,000 tons, worth about $500 million. By 1990, China planned to export 600,000 tons of canned food annually, worth over $600 million.

Canned vegetables are China's most important processed food export. China is now the world's top exporter of canned mushrooms. Other important exports include canned asparagus, broad beans, pineapple, oranges, water chestnuts, tomato ketchup, and green soy beans. Besides canned vegetables, China also exports canned meat, canned aquatic products, canned poultry, canned fruit juice, dried fruit, and jam.

Chinese planners believe that development of the food processing industry is a good way to speed up development of China's rural economy because of its strong links to agriculture. National planners believe China can continue to be a successful exporter of canned foods for a number of reasons. First, labor costs are low. Labor costs in the canned food industry are reportedly fifteen times higher in Taiwan than on the mainland. Second, China can supply most of the raw materials domestically.

Growth potential in China's canned food exports depends on three factors: the price of raw materials and packaging; on Chinese producers' understanding of foreign consumers' tastes; and on foreign restrictions on imports of food products. Because of inflation, domestic prices of canned foods have risen. But export prices have not changed very much, because competition among Chinese canned food exporters has kept prices down.

China also has a developing frozen food industry, mostly for the export market. Frozen food exports have increased markedly over the past few years, and are gaining on canned foods as an important export product. In 1987, for example, China exported almost $2 million worth of "quick frozen foods," (almost 2,000 metric tons). This category included frozen vegetables, frozen fruits, and specialty foods like frozen dumplings. From 1987 to 1988, exports of frozen prawns to the U.S. increased by 100 percent. In 1987 the U.S. imported US $42 million worth of frozen prawns from China. Most of China's frozen foods, however, are exported to Japan, with lesser amounts going to Hong Kong and other Southeast Asian countries (27).

The development of China's food processing sector will be constrained by three major factors: 1) the shortage of reasonably priced raw materials; 2) the existing low levels of technology in the sector; and 3) the lack of sufficient foreign exchange to import modern food processing equipment to upgrade Chinese factories.

China does not have a stable production base for the raw materials needed by its food processing industry. Many Chinese food processing facilities face rising prices for raw materials (fruits, vegetables, meats, etc.). Since the central government eased controls on food prices, the prices of many agricultural products have risen dramatically. Sometimes, peasant suppliers refuse to sell their produce to processing plants at all, preferring to sell to the more profitable fresh market. Because of this, many Chinese food processing/packaging enterprises face rising prices for the fruits and vegetables they process.

Related to this problem are the frequent shortages of raw materials. China is a developing country, and its per capita supplies of foodstuffs is still low. Therefore, even in the best years, China's food processing industry has difficulties finding enough raw materials for its factories. Raw materials are especially scarce in China's dairy, liquor, and processed sugar industries. In the dairy sector, for example, China's milk production is still very low, and demand for dairy products far exceeds available supply. China's per capita grain supply is also relatively low, and some Chinese planners believe the liquor industry consumes far too much of the nation's available grain supply. Because China must now import much of its refined sugar from abroad, Chinese planners would like to increase domestic capacity in this sector. But China's low production of sugar cane and sugar beets will hinder growth in this area.

With the exception of a few industries (such as the beer industry and the dairy products industry) most of the technology in China's food processing sector is below world standard. In order to upgrade its food processing industry, China must import advanced technology and equipment. But, although food processing is considered a key industry to China's development, in recent years the sector has been allocated very little foreign exchange by central authorities. Food processing is therefore in a "Catch 22" situation: the industry is expected to earn the foreign exchange it needs through exports; but the industry cannot export until it has the foreign exchange to upgrade its facilities.

Market Assessment - Meat and Poultry Processing Equipment The market in China for U.S. meat and poultry processing equipment is good. In recent years, meat production in the PRC has increased about 9 percent per year, and the need for processing equipment has grown steadily. China's consumption of meat products has increased as living standards have improved. The government has set the goal of increasing per capita annual meat consumption from 23.7 kilograms (1990) to 25 kilograms (2000). This means that meat production, and processing, must be raised to 32 million tons per year by 2000. While shortages of foreign exchange in some parts of the PRC limit enterprises' ability to purchase meat packaging and processing equipment, there should be sales and investment opportunities for U.S. firms in this sub-sector, particularly for those Americans willing to help the Chinese export processing equipment, meat products, or both (30).

The meat processing industry is highly decentralized, with many major decisions being made at the provincial or county level. While plants are widespread in China, the area of major activity are the cities of Shanghai, Tianjin, and Dalian, and the provinces of Jiangsu, and Zhejiang. The provinces of Hunan, Hubei, Henan, Hebei, and Shandong are the major meat-producing provinces of the PRC.

Market Assessment - Food Packaging China's packaging industry began only about seven years ago, but by 1987, its total output value was 20.5 billion Yuan. China now has over 6,000 packaging enterprises, employing 1.17 million people. China can now adequately package non-food products ranging from fertilizers to furniture for its own domestic use and for some export markets (27).

The most important packaging sub-sector in China, however, is the food packaging industry. This industry also has the most exacting special requirements. Although some technologies (e.g. Chinese bottling, capping and filling technologies) are adequate for domestic needs, many other foodstuffs have special packaging requirements, which Chinese packaging technology cannot meet. This problem is especially acute with export food products. Many foreign consumers insist on high standards of sanitation and an attractive appearance and China's food packaging industry is still struggling to meet these standards.

Although China's packaging industry grew at a rate of 15 percent between 1986 and 1987, growth has slowed since then. One of the major constraints to growth has been a lack of raw materials (primarily pulp, paper and high grade plastics). For example, each year the industry must import 350,000 tons of plastic, over 740,000 tons of packaging paper, and 80 percent of its galvanized iron needs.

China's canning industry has been affected by continued shortfalls in metal production, and by continued problems with quality control in the metallurgy industry. Only one factory in China (in Wuhan) produces the high quality galvanized iron needed by the canning industry. Because of such shortfalls, China has been forced to import large quantities of tin plate and aluminum sheeting for its food processing and packaging industries. But these purchases have absorbed large amounts of scarce foreign capital, and in 1988 the Chinese government raised import taxes on tin plate, and recently restricted imports of aluminum sheeting for pop-top cans for domestic use. As a result, factories are finding it harder and harder to find reliable and reasonably priced supplies of tin plate and aluminum sheeting.

Shortages of raw materials exist throughout the packaging sector. As in food processing, the Chinese food packaging industry lacks sufficient foreign exchange to import all the raw materials it needs. In 1988, the packaging industry needs US $400 million worth of imported packaging materials, but foreign exchange shortages limited imports to only half of that required. Chinese experts estimate that the demand for packaging materials will increase by over 60 percent between 1988 and 1989. But because of insufficient foreign allocations, the food packaging industry may face a shortfall of over US $300 million worth of imported packaging materials.

In theory, food packaging is an export led industry, in which foreign exchange earned from exported products can be used to import more advanced machinery and equipment. In practice, however, foreign exchange earned from exports of processed foods, often goes directly to the food processor. Factories which package the products (and thus increase the product's value) may receive no share of the foreign exchange earnings. For example, about 25% of the cost of producing a bottle of export quality Maotai liquor is absorbed by the packaging factory. The packaging plant must buy imported glass and paper, but often receives none of the foreign exchange earned through the exports of the product.

By the end of 1988, China's packaging industry was in a crisis. Almost half of the country's plastic packaging lines had stopped because of shortage of raw materials. Industry managers were desperately seeking foreign exchange allocations from the government to import the needed raw materials, but had little success. One frustrated manager accused the central government of "whipping the horse to run but being reluctant to give it grain."

China's food packaging industry is highly decentralized, and this may make it difficult to target market opportunities in this sector. China's food processing enterprises tend to make independent decisions on importing new equipment or developing new packaging technology without consulting China's national packaging organizations (27).

China National packaging Association (CHINAPAK): CHINAPAK was established in 1980 to coordinate national efforts to upgrade China's packaging industry. CHINAPAK now has about 38 branches throughout China which oversee the distribution of packaging machines, packaging materials, and containers all over the country. CHINAPAK controls central government funds earmarked for development of China's packaging industry, especially those funds for upgrading export packaging. CHINAPAK controls distribution of these funds and allocation of these funds among provinces. CHINAPAK also acts as a national clearing house for information about importing packaging equipment and materials, and controls the distribution of foreign exchange for importing packaging machinery and packaging materials (such as plastics, resins, paper and pulp).

CHINAPAK also operates sixteen production facilities of its own, and is involved in about 270 cooperative ventures with other Chinese enterprises. In some cases, CHINAPAK has invested in Chinese factories which package goods for export. In other cases, CHINAPAK actually helps manage the factory. CHINAPAK ventures include plastic and paper packaging, metal cans, printing (e.g. for labels), and storage drums. CHINAPAK also has close relations with fifty-seven packaging and packaging material research centers, two packaging engineering institutes (in Jilin and Hunan), and thirty-seven universities which offer courses of study in packaging.

Since 1980, CHINAPAK has imported packaging machinery and equipment, and in 1985 the organization started to export such goods as well. Some of CHINAPAK's import/export activities are conducted from the offices of its U.S. representative, UNIAM Company of New Jersey.

China National Packaging Corporation (CNPC): CNPC was originally an association for packaging experts from various Chinese industries. CNPC directly supervises sixteen subsidiary companies, with 10-20 factories directly under their administration. Of these, six are located in Sichuan Province and three are located in Zhejiang Province. CNPC members import packaging equipment and materials through CHINAPAK or through their own industrial ministry.

China Packaging Technology Association (CPTA): This organization is responsible for setting policies and standards for the industry. There are twenty-eight smaller associations under the aegis of CPTA, and an additional fifteen or so "specialty organizations" which set policies for specific types of packaging. These organizations are usually staffed by specialists from various industrial ministries, and usually focus on packaging activities within these ministries.

China International Packaging Import/Export Corporation (CIPIEC): CIPIEC is under the aegis os the Ministry of Foreign Economic Relations and Trade (MOFERT), and most of its activities involve exports. CIPIEC does import packaging materials, however, because its export products require a higher grade of packaging than is available domestically in China. Some of CIPIEC's import/export activities are conducted from the offices of a Hong Kong subsidiary. The responsibilities of CIPIEC and those of CNPC sometimes overlap, but CNPC tends to focus on domestic packaging activities, and CIPIEC tends to focus on exports.

Opportunities in China's Food Processing/Packaging Industries(27)

1) Meat processing - Canned pork, canned chicken and canned beef have become important food exports from China. Most Chinese canned meat products go to Asian customers, with smaller amounts going to European customers. U.S. companies should note that Chinese processed, chilled and frozen meat cannot be exported to the U.S. The USDA Food Safety Inspection Service is corresponding with the Chinese Commodity Inspection Bureau on this matter, but resolution appears to be a long way off. Meat processing plants are widespread in China, but major areas of activity are Shanghai, Sichuan, Jiangsu, Tianjin, Dalian (Liaoning Province), and Zhejiang.

   A) Canned and frozen pork are the main processed meats in China, but canned beef appears to be a growing sector in some areas of the country. In China's northeast, for example, Heilongjiang Province plans to develop its beef cattle industry—with an eye to exporting meat products to the Soviet Union in the future.

   B) Chinese meat producers who want to enter the Japanese market will need to import specialized cutting and packaging equipment to produce and package the cuts demanded by Japanese consumers. For example, China does not produce the modern equipment needed to cut and package either primal cuts of pork and beef, or the specialty chicken parts which Japanese consumers prefer.

   C) Processed meat for pet foods may be another possible area for U.s. trade or investment. Chinese meat processing may be able to produce satisfactory products for the large pet food markets in the U.S. and in Europe.

2) Milk products (processing and packaging): This is a big growth area for domestic sales in China. Fresh, powdered, and reconstituted milk, ice cream, and yogurt products are becoming more and more popular with Chinese consumers. Prices for

milk and yogurt are controlled in China, so companies cannot pass on increased packaging expenses to the consumer. Therefore, packaging equipment which uses domestically produced materials will be especially welcome in this sector. Areas of particular growth in China's dairy industry include Inner Mongolia, Zhijiang, Liaoning, Jilin, and Heilongjiang.

3) Prepared foods (e.g. soups, instant noodles, baby food): China's demand for prepared foods is growing as living standards rise. The country has a small prepared food industry now, but it offers consumers little variety, and Chinese processing plants would like to expand their production lines. China also has a small baby food industry, which is not able to meet rapidly growing demand.

4) Processed food production equipment suitable for duplicate use: China has a number of food processing plants which can vegetables in season, and can meat products (usually pork) at other times of the year. Such plants are interested in purchasing equipment which can be easily converted from one use to another. Although such plants may be found throughout China, some areas of the country (e.g. Sichuan, Hubei and Guangxi) are noted for their production of canned vegetables, and may be particularly receptive to duplicate-use food production equipment.

5) China's beer industry: China produces 6.5 million tons of beer annually, and is now the world's fifth largest beer producer (after the U.S., West Germany, the Soviet Union, and Britain). China's export beer industry is an especially promising market, for this sector has a good potential for earning foreign exchange through its export sales. The Chinese beer industry is a rapidly growing one. Certain provisions in China's complex price structure favor this industry, so the industry has been able to retain control of its export earnings and to use these earnings to upgrade its facilities. China's beer industry seeks modern technology and equipment, and is very interested in acquiring high quality food additives needed for its export products.

6) Sugar industry: Chinese planners would like to increase the country's sugar refining facilities, though development of this sector will be constrained for some time by insufficient domestic production of sugar cane and sugar beet.

7) Frozen foods: China began to develop its frozen food industry only a few years ago. China has begun to export frozen vegetables, and is interested in upgrading its technology in this field. China's frozen foods industry focuses on the export market. Most frozen foods are exported to Japan, with lesser amounts to Hong Kong and other countries. Although China exports large quantities of frozen shrimp to the U.S., it should be noted that Chinese frozen meat cannot be exported to the U.S. because of USDA regulations. Most of China's frozen food plants are located along the seacoast, in Fujian, Guangdong, Zhejiang and Shanghai. These areas are closer to overseas consumers than inland provinces, and are rich agricultural areas, with surplus aquatic and agricultural products suitable for freezing and exporting.

8) Specialty food packaging equipment: China's domestic food packaging equipment does not yet produce sanitary, attractive food packaging up to international standards. To increase exports of processed foods to developed countries, China will have to import more modern food packaging equipment.

A) Sealing machines for plastic bags: China's packaging industry has improved its sealing machine technology in recent years, but electric heating components, breakable parts (e.g. ring belts), and sealing for automatic components are still below world standards.

B) Plastic packaging material: Plastic packaging is lightweight and sturdy. It is very suitable packaging material for export foodstuffs, and China wants to modernize this packaging sub-sector. China already has a number of plastic packaging machines in place, but plants have trouble acquiring the special types of packaging material required by these machines (e.g. certain types of plastic films needed for wrapping raw meat and prepared foods). This problem is especially acute for export products. China's domestic industry for polyethylene and polyprophelene is developing rapidly, but China still must import large quantities of these plastics for its food industry.

C) Composite cans: To save scarce foreign exchange, and to minimize use of scarce tin plate, China's packaging industry has recently imported seventeen production lines for composite cans. These cans are produced from a mix of kraft board, plastic and aluminum, and can be used for solid, liquid and powdered foods, and for medicines and chemical products. China has imported composite can production lines from the U.S., France and Sweden, and has installed them in Hunan, Jilin, Zhejiang, Sichuan, Hubei, Liaoning, Heilongjiang, and Shanghai. Total output from the seventeen lines imported so far is expected to be 350 million cans each year.

D) Alternative packaging materials: Because China has severe shortages of high grade pulp, paper and plastic film, it is looking for alternatives to traditional packaging materials. For example, China has developed a new non-toxic polyvinyl chloride which can be used to wrap candy and cigarettes, and has developed a packaging paper made from straw pulp. Packaging technologies which use such alternative packaging materials should be favorably received in China.

E) Three piece can electric-resistance welding equipment: Many Chinese canneries have imported electric-resistance welding equipment for can making, which makes the welded seam stronger, eliminates lead contamination of canned foodstuffs, and saves on tin plate and solder tin.

F) Bottling technology: The technology of China's bottling industry is not up to world standards, although it is considered adequate for most domestic needs. Chinese bottling plants would like to upgrade their technology. But with the exception of beer and liquor, few Chinese bottled drinks are exported. So it may be difficult for bottling plants to earn the foreign exchange needed to import advanced technology.

G) Bundlers: Chinese bundling technology is below world standards in terms of adaptability, strength, range of readjustment, and reliability. Chinese packaging plants would like to upgrade their technology in this sub-sector.

    H) Shaping-filling-sealing machines: China's bag-shaping technology is only at early 1970's standards. China would like to upgrade its measuring equipment, and improve the capabilities of its paper and plastic box-making machines.

9) China's food processing/packaging industries are expected to finance imports of machinery and equipment mainly through export earnings. Therefore, Chinese food processing entities which earn large revenues through exports may be promising targets for U.S. marketing efforts.

Competitive Situation U.S. food processing/packaging companies are relative latecomers to the China market. Swiss, Italian, Spanish, West German and Japanese competition is already well-established in China. Dutch, British, Australian, French and Canadian companies are also active in this sector. Many Chinese food processing/packaging enterprises are simply not aware of what U.S. companies have to offer. Furthermore, many foreign competitors are assisted by generous concessionary loan programs sponsored by their home governments. Such programs are not available to U.S. companies.

Market Access

1) Problems in penetrating China's market—

Although there are many good opportunities for U.S. companies in China's food processing/packaging industry, U.S. companies wishing to enter the market should be aware of the following special problems:

    A) China's trade and investment climate has changed markedly since the events of June 1989. Some observers now question China's commitment to the sorts of economic reforms which would attract foreign traders and investors.

    B) China is now engaged in a program of serious economic retrenchment. This means that many Chinese organizations are now finding it very difficult to acquire the foreign exchange necessary to import U.S. goods and equipment in many industrial sectors (including food processing/packaging). U.S. companies should be aware that this tight money situation may continue for some time—many analysts say that it may be two to five years before the situation eases.

    C) U.S. companies should also be aware that patent protection is still a very weak concept in China. Some U.S. companies have sold a single machine to a Chinese enterprise, only to find that the enterprise later produced a similar machine of its own for sale on the Chinese market.

2) Flexible approach to marketing in China—

U.S. companies which take a flexible approach to marketing or investing in China stand the best chance to penetrate the Chinese market. Specific suggestion include:

    A) Be prepared to invest a good deal of time at the front end. In many cases, it takes months (even years) to get an agreement signed.

    B) Look at the broader marketing picture. For example, consider joint ventures and co-production for export to the wider Asian market. Chinese labor costs are substantially lower than many other areas in East Asia (including Taiwan and Hong Kong), so establishing labor-intensive operations within China for export goods makes sense.

C) Be willing to consider a flexible payment format. Chinese enterprises have traditionally preferred to pay in product through some type of barter trade arrangement. The recent economic retrenchment and continued shortages of forcing exchange, makes this type of arrangement more attractive than ever to Chinese enterprises.

Best Sales Prospects - Fruit and Vegetable Processing (29)

1. High-speed, automatic equipment for large, export-oriented firms for the processing/production of:
   a) Baby food (milk, powder, biscuits, strained fruits and vegetables, rice powder, soybean powder).
   b) Fruit and vegetable juices (what the Chinese call "healthy foods").
   c) Flour.
   d) Soybean powder and other vegetable protein products.
   e) Sugar.
   f) Additives (e.g. citric acid, dry yeast, pigments).
   g) Instant noodles and other convenience foods.
   h) Mushrooms and similar products.
   i) Corn, potato, starch, and denatured starch.
   j) Edible oil and margarine.
   k) Candied fruit, pickles.
   l) Bean products.
   m) Wine.
2. Freezing and cold storage equipment.
3. Sterilizing equipment.
4. Irradiation, ultrasonic, infrared and other food preservation technologies.
5. Small to medium-scale semi-automatic machinery for small and medium-scale food processing firms to prepare those products for local markets.

Best Sales Prospects - Meat and Poultry Processing (30)

1. Complete sets of medium and high-grade automated domestic livestock slaughtering equipment.
2. Pork processing machinery (smokehouses, injectors for ham, tenderizing machines for ham, and cooking houses).
3. High-speed, automatic equipment (e.g. sifter, steamers, strainers, mixers, canners, packers, and control monitors).

4. Freezing and cold storage equipment. (Note: While there appears to be enough very basic refrigeration equipment in China, there is a continuing need for quick freezing systems.)
5. Pre-processing control equipment packages, which include recovery systems, magnetic separators, recording thermometers, sterilizing systems, extractors, dryers, and coolers.
6. Irradiation, ultrasonic, infrared and other food preservation technologies.
7. Small to medium-scale semi-automatic machinery for small and medium-scale food processing firms to prepare those products for local markets.
8. Sausage processing equipment (fillers, sealers, high temperature/high pressure sterilization equipment).
9. Animal feeding/feedmill machines.
10. Pigs' blood processing equipment.
11. Slaughterhouse waste material processing equipment.
12. Special cutting and packaging equipment to prepare the prime cuts of pork and beef and specialty chicken parts demanded by Japanese buyers.
13. Poultry feeding technologies.
14. Poultry vitamin pre-mixes and trace minerals.
15. Micro-ingredient scales and other pre-mix equipment.
16. Pig confinement system technology and equipment.
17. Livestock transportation equipment and technology.
18. Meat and poultry baby food production machinery. (Note: The baby food division of Heinz Foods holds a strong 15 percent of the Chinese market. About 15 million babies are born every year in the PRC, and local firms cannot keep up with the demand.)

Best Sales Prospects - Guangdong Province

The best sales prospects for food processing and packaging equipment in Guangdong Province are set forth as the following (28):

The Guangdong Food Industry Association (GFIA) states that while the Eighth Five-Year Plan applies to China's food processing industry as a whole, Guangdong's needs are more "market" driven than centrally-planned by Beijing. The following are what Guangdong Food Industry Association believes to be Guangdong's needs (28):

1. High-speed, automatic equipment for "large, export-oriented firms for the processing/production of:
    a) Instant noodles and other convenience foods.
    b) Fruit and vegetable juices (what the Chinese call "healthy foods").
    c) Additives (e.g. citric acid, dry yeast, pigments).
    d) Baby food (milk, powder, biscuits, strained fruits and vegetables, rice powder, and soybean powder).
    e) Bakery and confectionery products.
    f) Preservatives for fruits and vegetables.
    g) Flour.

    h)   Candied fruits and pickles.
    i)   Bean products.
    j)   Corn, potato starch, and denatured starch.
    k)   Edible oil and margarine.
2. Freezing and cold storage equipment.
3. Paper packaging (outside), printing/labeling equipment:
    a)   Convenience and instant foods.
    b)   Jelly-type candy (crush-proof).
    c)   Medicine.
4. Sealing machinery: forming/filling.
5. Pressurized packaging for beauty products.
6. Meat processing for smaller portions.
7. Slaughtering equipment.
8. Cannery and bottling for convenience foods.
9. Irradiation, ultrasonic, infrared and other food preservation technologies.
10. Small to medium-scale semi-automatic machinery for small and medium-scaled food processing firms to prepare products destined for the local market.

Useful contacts in China

    U.S. food processing equipment firms can work with Guangdong's industry associations, for example:

Guangdong Food Industry Office
North 16-2 Tiansheng Village, Huanshi Road East
Guangzhou, Guangdong, China 510060
Tel: (86)(20) 3309120 Fax: (86)(20) 3338655

Guangzhou Food Industry Office
Room 301, E/F, Building No. 5
Guangzhou Government Courtyard, Fuqian Road
Guangzhou, Guangdong, China 510032
Tel: (86)(20) 3314304

Shenzhen Food Industry Association
Room 410, Zhongchu Plaza, Ba Guasi Road
Shenzhen, Guangdong, China 518029
Tel: (86)(755) 2262552 X410 Fax: (86)(755) 2262552 X555

Active Food Processors:

Star Lake Gourmet Powder Company, Inc.
Duanzhou, 3rd Road, Zhaoqing
Guangdong 526060
Tel: (758) 2809856   Fax: 239449

Guangdong Xinhui Candy and Biscuit Factory
32 Zhengcheng Road North, Huicheng
Xinhui, Guangdong 529100
Tel: (7646) 663836   Fax: 612878

Guangdong Nanhai Lishui Refrigeration Factory
Binjiang Road, Lishui Town
Nanhai, Guangdong 528244
Tel: (757) 462403   Fax: 562586

Guangzhou Fushouxian Health Care Products Factory
H.M. Guangzhou Company (GITIC Group)
9/F, 30 Zhongshan 1 Road
Guangzhou, Guangdong 510600
Tel: (20) 7700814   Fax: 7765524

Guangdong Luofushan Jiutianguan Mineral Water
Beverage Factory
46 Huangcheng Road
Boluo, Guangdong 516100
Tel: (752) 660539   Fax: 626979

Kwong Ming Overseas Chinese Foodstuff Company, Ltd.
Kwong Ming Overseas Chinese Livestock Farm
Shenzhen, Guangdong 518107
Tel: (755) 7731010   Fax: 7730005

Guangzhou Baiyun Food Industry Corporation
Da Jin Zhong Road
Guangzhou, Guangdong 510440
Tel: (20) 6660267

Guangzhou Food Products Company
17 Xiao Mei Da Street
Liwan Road North
Guangzhou, Guangdong 510315
Tel: (20) 8815085

Zhujiang Beer Company
Xin Gang Road East
Guangzhou, Guangdong 510315
Tel: (20) 4451136 Fax: 4451043

Guangzhou Dairy Company
49 Dongchuan Road
Guangzhou, Guangdong 510100
Tel: (20) 3815677

Shenbao Enterprise Ltd.
10 Tianbei Dong, Wenjin Road North
Shenzhen, Guangdong 518020
Tel: (755) 5532859

Huolibao Company
3 North Shatou Street, Fuhua Road
Futian District
Shenzhen, Guangdong 518033
Tel: (755) 3307041 Fax: 3307905

Foshan (Area Code: 757)

China National Cereals, Oils and Foodstuffs I/E Corporation
Guandong Branch Foshan Office
5 Shengtang Hou Jie
Renmin Xi Lu
Fax: 224150

Fenjiang Foodstuffs Factory
Weiguo Lu
Foshan 528000
Tel: 2286246

Foshan Haitian Flavouring Food Company
16 Wensha Lu
Foshan 528000
Tel: 2285281, 2286328   Fax: 2282234

Guangdong Foshan Seafood Enterprise Ltd. (JV)
2/F, 4 Gongzheng Lu
Foshan
Tel: 2287963, 2223779   Fax: 2223779

Foshan Machinery & Equipment I/E Company
Blk 1, 22 Weiguo Xi Lu
Tel: 2285573, 2222644, 2224166   Fax: 2221825

Nanhai Foodstuffs I/E Company of Guangdong
12 Guiyanxisan Road
Foshan 528200
Tel: 632805 Fax: 359395

Guangzhou (Area Code: 20)

China National Machinery I/E Corporation
Guangdong Branch
61 Yanjiang Road West
Guangzhou, Guangdong
Tel: 8885531

Guangdong Aquatic Products I/E Corporation
547 Nanhua Dong Lu
Guangzhou 510223
Import Department: 4421294   Trading Department: 4421296
Fax: 4429483

Guangdong Native Produce I/E Corporation (Group)
108 Jiangnan Dadao Zhong
Guangzhou 510240
Tel: 4420056   Fax: 4420738

China National Cereals, Oils and Foodstuffs I/E Corporation
Guangdong Branch Guangzhou Office
163 Renmin Nan Lu, Guangzhou
Office: 8882620, 8883503
Canned Goods: 8887660   Fruits Department: 8883058

Foshan Cereals, Oils and Foodstuffs I/E Branch Guangzhou Office
Jiaokoucun, Fangcuqu
Tel: 87891851, 8891972, 8891313

Guangdong Aquatic Products Factory
Xingang Dong Lu, Guangzhou
Tel: 4429746
Exhibition and Sales Department
209 Zhongshan Si Lu
Tel: 3333183

Guangdong Cereals and Oils I/E Corporation
2 Qiaoguang Lu
Guangzhou 510116
Business Office: 3334154 Packaging: 3330768
Fax: 3341345

Guangdong Feed Development Corporation
28 Huanghua Road
Guangzhou 510050
Tel: 3336163, 3349953 Fax: 3349204

Guangdong Foodstuffs (Group) Corporation
4 Yongshengzhongsha, Donghu Xi Lu
Dongshan 510100
Fax: 7762081

Guangdong Foodstuffs I/E Corporation
59 Yanjiang Xi Lu
Guangzhou 510130
Aquatic Products: 8861220 Confectionery: 8861885
Fax: 8862716

Guangdong Improved Variety Introduce Service Corporation
6/F Xinglong Building, 1 Shidaigang
Lujing Road, Guangzhou 510050
Tel: 3353124, 3353149 Fax: 3351785

Guangmei Foods Company Ltd. (JV)
Siheng Lu, Yuancun
Tianhequ 510655
Tel: 5525846 Fax: 5525117

Guangxi Cereals & Oils I/E Corporation
Guangzhou Company
128 Liuersan Lu 510130
Tel: 8885454   Fax: 8862549

Guangzhou Aquatic Product I/E Company
2/F, 47 Yanjiang Xi Lu 510130
Tel: 8889763   Fax: 8861802

Guangzhou Brewery
63 Xizeng Lu, Xicun 510160
Tel: 6664983

Guangzhou Canned Food Industry Corporation
(Guangdong Cannery)
Siheng Lu, Yuancun 510655
Tel: 5525785   Fax: 5525388

Guangzhou Cereals, Oils and Foodstuffs I/E Corporation
Baiyun Company
74 Guangyuang Xi Road
Guangzhou 510400
Tel: 6678174   Fax: 6665955

Guangzhou Foodstuff Industry Corporation
119 Yide Dong Lu 510120
Tel: 3338243, 3338153

Guangzhou Foodstuffs Corporation
17 Xiaomei DaJie
Liwan Lu 510170
Tel: 8816474, 8815085

Guangzhou Yazhou Soda Water Factory
6 Tianhe Lu
Tel: 7775453, 7750303

Hebei Province Cereals, Oils and Foodstuffs I/E Corporation
Guangzhou Office
13 Xicunwai Jie, Yi Xiang
Liuhua Lu 510160
Tel: 6662553, 6662174

Lingnan Biscuit Factory
16 Jiangjundong, Zhongshan Liu Lu
Tel: 3334886

Nei Mongol Cereals, Oils and Foodstuffs I/E Corporation
Guangzhou Branch
980 Jiefang Bei Lu 510400
Tel: 6678090, 6662120, 6663895

Shaanxi Cereals, Oils & Foodstuffs I/E Corporation
Guangzhou Office
109 Danan Lu 510115
Tel: 3332006, 3344539, 3331559, 7765372

Yunnan Cereals, Oils and Foodstuffs I/E Corporation
Guangzhou Office
206 Binjiand Xi Lu 510235
Tel: 4413092, 4448202

Zhujiang Beer (JO) Company
Xingang Dong Lu 510235
Tel: 4413092, 4451045

China National Packaging I/E Corporation
Guangdong Branch
5/F, 2 Qiaoguang Lu 510116
Tel: 3334985, 3331212, 3341701   Fax: 3341694

Guangzhou Branch
2/F, STI Bldg., Guangdong Science Hall
Lianxin Lu 510033
Tel: 3332069, 3331876, 3330705, 3330706, 3343873
Fax: 3340508

Guangdong Machinery & Equipment Company
185 Yuehua Lu 510030
Tel: 3334979, 3344244

Guangdong Machinery & Equipment I/E Corporation
59 Zhanqian Lu 510010
Tel: 6661398, 6665515, 6661383   Fax: 6677082

Guangdong Packing and Food Machinery Technical Development Center
82 Uangxiang Lu 510130
Tel: 8886462

Guangzhou Machinery & Equipment I/E Corporation
4/F Dongfeng Mansion
534 Dongfeng Dong Lu
Tel: 3337647 Fax: 3348553

Guangzhou Machinery I/E Corporation
7-8/F, 255 Dongfeng Xi Lu 510181
Tel: 3343244, 3343954, 3337787, 3332910, 3343455

Huizhou (Area Code: 752)

Guangdong Aquatic Products I/E Corporation
Huizhou Branch
4/F, 1 Nanmen Road
Huizhou 516001
Tel: 232624, 228467

Huiyang Foodstuffs I/E Company of Guangdong
26 Huangcheng Xiyi Road
Huizhou 516001
Tel: 233137 Fax: 225427

Huizhou Brewing Company Ltd. (JV)
9 Eling Nan Lu 516001
Tel: 2226933 Fax: 2235917

Huizhou Foodstuffs I/E Company of Guangdong
6 Zhongshan Dong Lu 516001
Tel: 2224244, 2233731, 2233511, 2234658, 2232290
Fax: 2233731

Jiangmen (Area Code: 7682)

China National Machinery and Equipment I/E Corporation
Guangdong Branch Jiangmen Office
26 Xiqu Dadao 529000
Tel: 3354391, 3351153, 3353339, 3352891, 3351462
Fax: 3351462

Jiangmen Biscuits Factory
47 Jianshe Lu 529000
Tel: 3333726, 3334194

Jiangmen Cereals and Oil I/E Company of Guangdong
7 Gangkou Lu 529051
Tel: 2232138, 2233621, 2232087, 2235095
Fax: 3353323

Jiangmen Water Company
Gaochengshan
Tel: 332943

Jiangmen Foodstuffs I/E Company of Guangdong
70 Yuejin Road
Jiangmen 529051
Tel: 332165   Fax: 351005

Shantou (Area Code: 754)

Shantou Aquatic Products I/E Corporation Shantou Company
322 Anping Lu 515011
Tel: 2273424, 2275176   Fax: 2271044

China National Cereals, Oils and Foodstuffs I/E Corporation
Guangdong Foodstuffs Branch Shantou Office
4-12 Huaian Heng Jie
Tel: 2272144

China National Cereals, Oils and Foodstuffs I/E Company of Guangdong
Yongfa Building, Jinshe Road East
Shantou 515041
Tel: 264484   Fax: 265040

Shantou Cold Storage Plant
25 Honglingjin Lu 515031
Tel: 2251858, 2232192

Shantou Fish Sauce Factory
Guanghua Lu
Tel: 2273323

Shantou Foodstuffs I/E Company of Guangdong
25 Jinsha Road, Middle
Shantou 515041
Tel: 253452   Fax: 253431

Shantou Suburb Natural Beverage Factory
Hudi Lu, Xiaqi 515064
Tel: 2221324, 2233286

China National Machinery I/E Corporation
Guangdong Branch Shantou Office
20 Nanhai Lu
Tel: 2275771, 2272778

Shantou Machinery & Equipment I/E Company of Guangdong
43 Dahua Lu 515031
Tel: 2230945, 2287017   Fax: 2252110

Guangdong Fruits & Vegetable I/E Company of Guangdong
9 Chunxing Road
Shantou 515041
Tel: 251433   Fax: 250306

Shaoguan (Area Code: 751)

Shaoguan Cereals, Oils and Foodstuffs I/E Company of Guangdong
Yigongli, Najiao
Shaoguan 512023
Tel: 885034   Fax: 885064

Shenzhen (Area Code: 755)

Nanlian Food Company Ltd.
Nanhai Oil Development Area
Nantou Houhai
Tel: 6692277, 6660499 X-201-3
Shekou: 9923118

Shenzhen Aquatic Products Development
Shennan Dong Lu
Tel: 2239408

Shenzhen Cereals Corporation
12 Hubei Lu 518001
Tel: 2225110, 2225109, 2222295
Fax: 2225109

Shenzhen Food Company Store Trade Industry Branch
Taoyuan Lu
Sungangqu 518020
Tel: 2263082-7

Shenzhen Foodstuffs Corporation
6 Dayuan, Fenghuang Lu 518003
Tel: 5530791   Fax: 5530791

Shenzhen Food and Beverage Industrial Company
36 Dongmen Zhong Lu 518001
Tel: 2223820, 2227057

Shenzhen Fruit & Vegetables Trading Company
153 Shennan Dong Lu 518001
Tel: 2222557, 2239975   Fax: 2239980

Shenzhen Hanlong Food Industry & Trading Company
66 Jiefang Lu
Tel: 2223987

Shenzhen Mineral Water Factory
5 Zhenhua Lu 518031
Tel: 3351522, 3351727

Shenzhen Aquatic Products Corporation
212 Renmin Road North
Shenzhen 518000
Tel: 2229159   Fax: 2222810

Shenzhen SEZ Foodstuffs Trading (Group) Corporation
5/F Ocean Building
66 Dongmen Bei Lu 518003
Tel: 5533871, 5533864, 553873   Fax: 5533733

Shenzhen SEZ Foreign Trade Group
Cereals, Oils and Foodstuffs I/E Corporation
Foreign Trade Shichu Building
Dongmen Nan Lu, Wenjindu 518002
Tel: 2234645, 2239596, 2239586, 2228691
Fax: 2234407

Shenzhen Salt Company
2F, 110 Renmin Bei Lu 518001
Tel: 2231207, 2223460, 2236103-5

Shenzhen Tri-Well Food (JV)
10 Tianbeidong 518020
Tel: 5534743, 5529376   Fax: 5529456

Wingming (Shenzhen) Food Factory
86 Jiefang Lu 518020
Tel: 2223509

Yunshen Edible Fungua Company (JV)
Room 2102-3 North Blk, Financial Center
Tel: 2246256, 2238509, 2246400 X2102-3
Fax: 2246256

China National Machinery I/E Corporation
Shenzhen Branch
9/F Foreign Trade Shichu Building
Dongmen Nan Lu
Tel: 2234422/4, 2234425, 2234645   Fax: 2236324

Shenzhen Wahtong Packaging Machinery Company Ltd.
24-1 Hongli Lu 518028
Tel: 2264136

China National Cereals, Oils and Foodstuffs I/E Corporation
Shenzhen Branch
4 Hongling Building, Hongling Road
Shenzhen 518030
Tel: 2247320

China National Cereals, Oils and Foodstuffs I/E Corporation
Guangdong Branch Shunde Office
31 Changdi, Rongqi
Tel: 82017, 82254   Fax: 41345

Guangshen Foods Corporation Ltd.
27 Fuhua Road, Futian
Shenzhen 518000
Tel: 3365745, 3367046

Zhanjiang (Area Code: 759)

Canton Bay Cereals & Oils United Trade Company
Building 9, Baiyuan Lu
Chikan
Tel: 3337110, 3337092

China National Cereals, Oils and Foodstuffs I/E Corporation
Guangdong Branch, Zhanjiang Office
3 Renmin Dong Yi Lu, Xiashan
Tel: 2222534, 2224355 X273, 2224565

Nanlian Food Company Ltd., Zhanjiang Branch
P.O. Box 26, Potou
Tel: 2223111 X52314

Zhanjiang General Cannery
Chikan
Tel: 3339622, 3339521, 3339709

Guangdong Salt Industry Machinery Plant
10 Jichang Lu
Tel: 2224501

Zhanjiang Machinery Plant
1 Jianshe Lu, Xiashan 524012
Tel: 2229941   Fax: 2228471

Zhanjiang Sugar Industry Machinery Factory
19 Kangning Lu
Chikana 524033
Tel: 3333400, 3333963

Zhaoqing (Area Code: 758)

Gaoyao Foodstuffs I/E Company of Guangdong
11 Kangle Road, Duanzhou District
Zhaoqing 526020
Tel: 229077, 220167   Fax: 231017

Zhaoqing Biscuit Factory
Duanzhou San Lu
Tel: 2232276, 2233694

Zhaoqing Brewery (JV)
Sanrongxia, Xijiao
Tel: 2232479

Zhaoqing Foodstuffs I/E Company
22 Jiangbin Xi Lu 526020
Tel: 2232141, 2236339, 2231088, 2224326, 2236326
Fax: 2231199

Zhongshan (Area Code: 7654)

Zhongshan Aquatic I/E Company of Guangdong
1 Huayuan Dajie, Zhongshan Lu
Shiqi 528400
Tel: 8822737, 2280882 X223 Fax: 8821207
Zhongshan Food and Drink Corporation
118 Yuelai Lu 528400
Tel: 8821234

Zhongshan Foodstuffs I/E Corporation of Guangdong
Renmin Lu, Shiqichengqu
Tel: 8822717, 8822771, 8822179, 8823257

Zhongshan Machinery Equipment and Agricultural Machinery I/E Company
of Guangdong
Zhongshan Bridge East, Shiqi 528400
Tel: 8823668, 8821212   Fax: 8823668

Zhongshan Packing & Printing Industrial Company
Qiguan Dong Lu, Shiqi
Tel: 8825301, 8828074, 8822298

Zhongshan Sugar, Tobacco and Wine Company
Zhongshan Lu, Shiqi 528400
Tel: 8822670

Zhongshan Water Company
34-2 Liantang Lu 528402
Tel: 8822429, 8823925

Zhuhai (Area Code: 756)

Guangdong Aquatic Products I/E Corporation Zhuhai Office
167 Fenghuang Lu, Xiangzhou 519000
Tel: 2222678 Fax: 2224907

Guangfeng I/E Trade Company
Room D, 5/F, Blk. 25, Yinhai Xincun
Tel: 8885233 Fax: 8886593

ZKW Enterprise (Group) Company Ltd. (JV)
Nanshan Industrial Zone 519000
Tel: 3332101-2, 3332105, 3332109
Fax: 3332110

Zhuhai Beverage Factory
Shishan Lu, Xiangzhou 519000
Tel: 2222879

Zhuhai Beverage No. 2
Qianshan Town 519070
Tel: 6611134

Zhuhai Cereals, Oils and Foodstuffs I/E Corporation
13 Jiaoyu Lu, Xinagzhouqu 519000
Tel: 2226324, 8886953, 2228669, 2225070, 8886942

Zhuhai Machinery & Equipment I/E Company of Guangdong Branch
Zhuhai Sub-Branch
41 Cuixiang Lu 519000
Tel: 2228251, 2228255 Fax: 2228252

Some useful contacts in the meat processing industry include:

Beijing Meat Processing Plant
Fengtai District
Beijing 100075
Tel: 762331

Beijing Shunyi Meat Packing Plant
Shunyi County
Beijing 101300
Tel: 9424518

Beijing No. 3 Meat Processing Plant
Haidian District
Beijing 100085
Tel: 2017460

Chongqing Meat Processing Plant
Jiulongpo, Chongqing
Sichuan Province 630082
Tel: 622381

Luoyang Meat Processing Plant
Xigong District, Luoyang
Henan Province 471001
Tel: 338074-225

Nanjing Meat Processing Plant
Xiaguan District, Nanjing
Jiangsu Province 210011
Tel: 801411

Shanghai Dachang Meat Processing Plant
Luoheqiao, Nandalu
Shanghai 200436
Tel: 6681641

Shanghai Longhua Meat Processing Plant
Xuhui District
Shanghai 200232
Tel: 4365407

Tianjin Meat Processing Plant
Dongjiano, Jianjin 300300
Tel: 490383

Wuhan Meat Processing Plant
Jiang'an District, Wuhan
Hubei Province 430011
Tel: 501265

Zigong Meat United Processing Plant
Dongxingsijie, Xigong
Sichuan Province 643000
Tel: 222577

Some useful contacts in the sugar industry include:

Guangdong Dongguan Sugar Mill
Zhongzang District, Dongguan
Guangdong Province 511700
Tel: 812121

Guangdong Shitou Sugarcane Chemical Plant
Nancun Town, Panyu, Guangzhou
Guangdong Province 511443
Tel: 4763322

Guangdong Zini Sugar Mill
Shawan Town, Panyu, Guangzhou
Guangdong Province 511487
Tel: 4732015

Guigang Sugarcane Chemical Plant
Guigang, Yulin
Gaungxi Province 537102
Tel: 4012

Jiangmen Sugarcane Chemical Manufactory
Jiangmen
Guangdong Province 529075
Tel: 351611

Nanhai Sugar Refinery
Nanhai County, Foshan
Guangdong Province 528212
Tel: 56699

Panyu Meishan Machine-Made Sugar Factory
Huangge Town, Panyu, Guangzhou
Guangdong Province 511400
Tel: 4971305

Zhangzhou Sugar Mill
Zhangzhou
Fujian Province 363000
Tel: 227353

Zhongshan Sugar Mill
Zhongshan
Guangdong Province 528400
Tel: 824890

HYDROELECTRIC POWER

Hydroelectric power is discussed separately from other electric power systems because of its special nature.

<u>Overview</u> China has one of the world's largest hydroelectric power markets. China will spend over two billion dollars a year, over twenty billion during the 1990s to trouble current capacity via the addition of over 40,000 megawatts by the year 2000. Imports will total about seven billion dollar this decade (20).

Primary import opportunities include those for power generation equipment for special needs such as pumped storage projects and very high or very low head dams, for construction equipment, and for engineering and design services. China will import wherever domestic capacity or technology is lacking or where foreign financing mandates international bidding or foreign sourcing.

Major hydropower projects are approved by central government authorities and funded by a combination of provincial and central government funds along with international loans. The World Bank is lending around three hundred million annually for hydropower projects. China's provincial level Electric Power Bureaus are generally project owners. Provincial design institutes and local governments have a growing influence in decision-making.

General contracting services and power plant equipment are typically sold to the end-user (project owner); construction equipment and materials are generally sold to general contractors, whether Chinese or foreign. Sales to international general contractors follow familiar patterns. For sales to the end-user, however, the complex decision-making process and pressure for local content make it imperative to develop effective in-country contacts, including contacts at the provincial level in the project's home province. Co-production deals, technology transfer agreements, and joint ventures are frequent components of a long-term marketing strategy for China.

China's electric power industry operates under the auspices of the Ministry of Electric Power (MOEP). There is a separate Ministry of Water Resources (MWR) which takes the lead on overall planning for each river system. MWR plays a key role in dam site selection and reservoir flooding, flood control, navigation, and irrigation matters. MOEP would take the lead on dam and power plant construction and operation.

China's electric power system is comprised of seven large electric power grids, each managed by a regional Electric Power Administration (dian guan ju), and several more provincial grids which are separately administered. These grids report to the Ministry of Electric Power (MOEP). Each province (and the cities of Beijing, Tianjin, and Shanghai which have province-level status) has a provincial Electric Power Bureau (dian li ju) which owns and operates the province's electric power plants, including hydroelectric power plants. At the municipal level are the electric utility companies (fa dian ju). The Electric Power Administrations, which run the grids, purchase power from the provincial Electric Power Bureaus, which run the plants, and sell power wholesale to the municipal electric utilities, which handle distribution and sales to the final customer.

In recent years, provincial electric power development corporations have been established as enterprises operating directly under the provincial electric power bureaus. These corporations are typically the project owners. The typical owner of a power plant is a state-owned corporation which has a certain degree of autonomy, is an independent accounting entity (that is, it keeps its own set of books and operates as a regulated profit-making corporation), and tends to act in its own interest, subject to the regulatory constraints under which it operates. A separate corporation may be set up for the development and operation of large projects as exemplified by the Ertan Hydroelectric Development Corporation. These local corporations nominally report to the Ministry of Electric Power, especially with respect to "business" (ye wu) matters such as technology and approval for major expansion plans. They are, however, strongly influenced by their local provincial governments which control their financial affairs and certain personnel matters and which are, increasingly, principal sources of investment funds for a new project.

There is a trend for the province which is to be the primary beneficiary of a new power plant to bear an increasing share of the cost. Thus, wealthy Guangdong Province, relatively self-sufficient in foreign exchange, might finance virtually all of a thermal power plant itself with little coming from the central government. Because of the huge capital investment required for hydroelectric projects, however, even in Guangdong, the central government will continue to play an important role in all but the smallest projects.

Market Assessment Defining the market in terms of generation equipment versus dams is the first step. The "hydroelectric power" sector refers to a type of major project which generates demand in many product categories. This report provides information on both the power plant and dam construction aspects of hydroelectric power, thus covering opportunities in the following areas:

Power Plant (usually only a few percent of entire project):
- hydraulic turbine and generator sets
- control systems
- excitation systems
- sub-station transformers and switchgear

Civil Construction (including dams):
- consulting/engineering/contractor services
- construction equipment
- construction materials

China currently has some 37,000 MW of hydroelectric capacity. China must spend about twenty-five billion dollars on hydropower, to more than double capacity to some 80,000 MW by the year 2000. Eighteen thousand MW is now in design and construction, 16,000 MW more is in the Eighth and Ninth Five-Year Plans (1991-2000), with another 10,000 MW coming from many small, locally-funded projects. Imports will run 20%-30%, approximately seven billion dollars (averaging $700 million per year, an increase from $400 million in 1992).

China's Power Generating Capacity (gigawatts)

Year	Thermal	Hydro	Total
1950	0.8	0.2	2.0
1960	10.0	1.9	11.9
1970	17.5	6.2	23.8
1980	45.6	20.3	65.9
1985	60.6	26.4	87.1
1990	99.9	37.0	136.0
1995 (planned)	147.0	47.0	194.0
2000 (planned)	170.0	80.0	250.0

China's current total installed generating capacity, hydro and thermal stands at 136,000 MW, with hydro accounting for a about a quarter. The Eighth and Ninth Five-Year Plans (FYP) call for a 115,000 MW increase in total capacity, with hydro representing very ambitious 30-40% of the growth. Total spending on electric power generation and transmission was nearly eight billion dollars in 1991. While most of the increase will still rely on the development of coal-fired plants, capitalizing on China's vast coal reserves, China will try to increase the proportion from hydropower. At 370,000 MW, China claims the world's largest hydropower reserves. Electric power is, and will remain, in chronic short supply, despite ambitious investment plans, as burgeoning industrial and consumer demand will continue to outstrip supply well into the foreseeable future. Water conservation and flood control are also high priorities in this land with its history of flood and famine. Plans to exploit those vast hydroelectric reserves will make China one of the largest markets in the world for hydropower construction and equipment. There are eighty centrally-funded hydropower projects in various stages of planning and construction, totalling about 100,000 MW, including thirty projects between 1,000 and 3,000 MW, seven over 3,000 MW, and the monster Three Gorges Project, the world's largest at 17,680 MW. These hydropower projects will be built as fast as funding will permit, and represent decades of construction and investment. Opportunities should also abound for investment in the electric power-intensive electro-chemical and metallurgical fields, areas not covered by this report.

Only a small fraction of the total spending on hydropower will be for imported goods and services. China has developed its industrial capabilities so most "standard" projects can be constructed and equipped with virtually no imported equipment or supplies, except advanced control systems. Three factors will determine the size of the import market: technology, capacity and financing.

China needs to import equipment or design services, in three project categories:

1. technically demanding projects, including high head dams (over 200 meters), large capacity turbine generator sets (over 300 MW), heavy silting situations, very extensive tunneling requirements (requiring imported tunnel boring machines), and exceptionally large concrete handling requirements (requiring imported high speed cable cranes and concrete refrigeration equipment).
2. bulb turbines required in low-head dams which China doesn't produce.

3. <u>pumped-storage projects</u> requiring pump/turbine and motor/generator sets which China currently does not produce.

Technology-driven import opportunities are moving targets. As China's own technical level increases, pressure for domestic procurement will tend to limit the import market. For example, current pumped-storage projectors call for co-production of part of the equipment in China; future projects will likely require a smaller imported component as Chinese capabilities grow.

There is also a gray area in technology-driven imports. China may be able to supply a serviceable product, but project owners may be reluctant to use it because of concerns for quality, technical specification, or delivery. For example, owners may prefer large bulldozers (over 300 hp), excavators (over ten cubic meters), and large dump trucks (over 40 tons), which China doesn't currently make, and will use imports if their funding permits. Otherwise, owners will use the less-preferred, but still serviceable, local products.

While China's level of technology is increasing, the manufacturing capacity in some fields; generators, turbines, steel plate, reinforcing bar, and lumber (for concrete forms) to name a few, are currently inadequate. Imports will close the gap.

China is seeking to increase its international borrowing for major projects. China will use imported services and equipment more extensively on projects financed by international loans. International procurement is typically a condition of the loan. Loans from multinational lending institutions, principally the World Bank, require international competitive bidding, Government-to-government "soft" loans (in which the United States does not participate) usually specify procurement from the donor country. Japan's large Overseas Economic Cooperation Fund (OECF), is "untied" aid which also requires international competitive bidding.

China's internal currency, the renminbi, is not yet convertible and the use of foreign exchange is carefully managed by the government. International loan proceeds (in foreign currencies) are carefully allocated to priority projects, and items within those projects, perceived as having greatest justification for imports. Only about 30 percent of hydropower projects are financed by significant levels of international loans. These are the larger or more technically demanding projects for which imported material, equipment, or know-how are most urgently needed. (Since they are the larger projects, they represent more than 30% of total investment.) International loans cover an average of 30% of the cost of those internationally-funded projects; these funds are applied to the urgently-needed imports. The balance of the funding comes from the central government and, increasingly, local governments. Since Chinese priorities in the usage of foreign loans are primarily based on technical need and industrial capacity, technology and capacity still are the primary factors determining which products China will import. In short, China imports when technology and capacity constraints make it necessary and financing makes it possible.

China's current industrial policies and foreign exchange strategy favor developing domestic industry and careful conservation of foreign exchange, thus favoring domestic procurement over imports. Many import barriers, tariffs. import licensing, and restrictions, are used to implement these policies. As a result, many U.S. suppliers face a gradually shrinking export market as these import barriers go up, even though the overall market continues to grow. For many firms, therefore, a strategy of local investment, of "becoming an insider," seems to be the best way to preserve a long term presence in the China market. There is a range of such "insider" strategies: development of local sales and service agents, technology licensing, manufacturing joint ventures, and wholly foreign-owned ventures. A decision of whether and how to take such a step requires thorough study and careful evaluation.

Another important market distinction is who the customer is: the project owner or the general contractor. Generally, it is the owner who selects design consultants, construction general contractors, and main power plant equipment. The general contractor (Chinese or foreign), in turn, will select suppliers for construction materials and equipment.

Project owners are typically provincial-level Electric Power Bureaus (Dian Li Ju). Key players who influence the owners' vendor-selection decisions include the provincial, regional, and central design institutes, and plants under the Ministry of Machinery and Electronics Industry (MMEI). MMEI represents the interests of Chinese manufacturers, which are both competitors and potential partners.

The following three brief cases illustrate several aspects of China's hydropower market.

Yantan: This is a 1,200 MW (4x300 MW) project. The project received only minimal international funding, including a $52 million World Bank loan and a $2 million Norwegian soft loan. The World Bank funds were used primarily for imported construction materials such as steel reinforcing bar over 30 mm diameter, high-strength steel plate, and lumber for concrete forms and framing timbers. In addition, a $2.6 million dollar control system was imported. The conventional power plant equipment was supplied by Chinese vendors, as was most of the engineering, construction, and the balance of the construction materials and equipment. Yantan represents a low-level import opportunity.

Ming Tombs Pumped Storage: This is an 800 MW (4x200) pumped storage project near Beijing, with a total investment of $500 million, $100 million of the investment is provided by Japan's OECF untied loan program. The remaining $400 million is for civil works and local procurement and is provided by central and Beijing municipal funds. Most of the $75 million equipment package was procured through international competitive bidding, under OECF rules. Several international consortia bid on the project. In some case, foreign bidders offered co-production packages in partnership with a Chinese equipment manufacturer in order to lower cost and incorporate an element of local content. Civil works are to be provided by Chinese contractors. The pump/turbine sets this project features, which China currently cannot produce, are the primary reason this project calls for substantial imports.

Ertan Dam: Ertan will be a 240 meter high double curvature arch ferro-concrete dam with a 3,300 MW (6x550 MW) power plant. Projected costs total $1.2 billion for civil works and $400 million for equipment. Foreign exchange for imported services, materials, and equipment, comes to about $600 million, or just over one-third of the cost. Half the foreign funds are supplied by a $300 million World Bank loan, the other half by the Chinese. There are two main civil works contracts. The contract for the underground work was let to general contractors Impreglio and Dumuz, and Italian-French consortium. The contract for the dam construction was let to the German firm Hausmann in a consortium with the Chinese contractor, Gezhouba. The American firm, Harza, was involved from an early date in project planning and design. One-third of the $1.2 billion civil works cost, or $400 million, is for hard foreign currency items. These items include construction equipment, materials (steel, wood, cement), and, professional fees and labor, each approximately one-third of the total. The remainder, roughly $800 million, is set aside for local procurement. About half the $400 million power plant cost is for imported equipment. Power plant equipment will be separately tendered by the owners, the Ertan Hydroelectric Development Corporation, established in 1987 by the State Planning Commission, to build and operate the project. Chinese funds come from both the central government and Sichuan Province, where the dame is located. The project's scale, technical complexity, turbine-generator size, and the involvement of World Bank loans are the primary reasons for the substantial imports.

In the case of the hydropower as with most other industrial development areas, Guangdong Province is something of a special case (19).

Guangdong's phenomenal growth, exemplified by a 28% increase in industrial output during the first eight months of 1992, has strained its inadequate power supply. Despite a massive construction program, supply persistently lags behind demand, by as much as 30-40%, according to official estimates. Because of this shortfall, Guangdong purchases electricity from Hong Kong $3.3 billion kwh in 1991) and conducts frequent brownouts, resulting in factory shutdowns. (Some large factories have their own backup generators.)

Guangdong's growth has been achieved by attracting foreign investment to build a manufacturing base for export abroad and to other provinces. As industrial production has increased, so have disposable incomes and expectations for a better lifestyle. This has caused an increase in household electricity consumption from 2.06 billion kwh in 1980 to 5.16 billion kwh in 1991. Per capita household consumption more than doubled in the same period, from 39 kwh to 81 kwh. An increase of 31% was seen in 1991 over 1990, as China's economic austerity program ended and consumers stepped up their purchases of audio-video appliances, refrigerators, washing machines and air conditioners.

As Guangdong's economy continues to accelerate, electricity consumption will certainly increase. In 1991, Guangdong's per capita electric consumption was approximately 670 kwh. This compares with over 3,000 kwh in nearby Hong Kong and over 10,000 kwh in the United States.

Over the past several years, Guangdong has worked hard to close the power gap and meet future needs. In 1985, Guangdong had only 3,900 megawatts of installed capacity. By 1992, installed capacity more than doubled to approximately 10,000 mw. However, current per capita installed capacity of approximately 0.16 kilowatts lags far behind Taiwan and Hong Kong, which in 1992 reached 0.85 kw and 1.42 kw respectively. (The U.S. has approximately 2.8 kw per capita installed capacity.) In order to realize its ambition of becoming the "fifth small dragon" (joining Hong Kong, Taiwan, Singapore and South Korea), Guangdong plans to achieve 1.0 kw per capita installed capacity by 2010. Economic planners assume Guangdong's population will reach 80 million by then, requiring 80,000 mw of installed capacity. This will be achieved in the following increments: 1995, 17,000 mw; 2,000, 32,000 mw; 2010, 80,000 mw.

In order to reach these targets, Guangdong leaders have identified power as one of the province's two top priorities the other is transportation) and will continue to invest billions in power plant construction. Using conservative figures of $600/kw for thermal and $2,000/kw for nuclear, Guangdong will invest, in 1992 dollars, at least $80 billion over the next eighteen years.

Guangdong's current installed base is approximately 20% hydro and 80% thermal. Officials estimate 41% of Guangdong's hydro potential has been tapped. Most of the thermal power plants are coal fired; the rest are oil (mostly residual oil, limited diesel and crude oil), fired steam or gas turbine or combined cycle. Daya Bay, Guangdong's first nuclear plant, is scheduled to come on line next year. Guangdong will use 30% of the electricity Daya Bay generates—the rest will be sold to Hong Kong. Daya Bay is a joint venture between the Chinese central government, Guangdong Province and Hong Kong's China Light and Power Company.

Between now and 2000, Guangdong will primarily build thermal plants. After that, the province plans to concentrate on nuclear plants. The central government recently approved Guangdong's second nuclear power plant (in Yangjiang), as well as two major thermal plants (in Taishan and Zhuhai). A relatively small investment in hydro plants is planned, including some interprovincial projects in neighboring provinces.

Nearly half of Guangdong's installed capacity is supplied by its twenty-five municipalities, which will continue to play a key role in Guangdong's power development. At least half are building new plants, ranging from 10 mw diesel units to 360 mw combined cycle plants to a 1200 (4x300) mw coal-fired plant, which is being built by Guangzhou, the capital city.

Guangdong's primary fuel is coal, which is in great abundance in China. However, there are several problems associated with coal use: air pollution, ash disposal (particularly as land is becoming an expensive commodity), transportation difficulties from mines in China's interior and slow construction schedules for coal-fired steam turbine plants. Most municipalities, driven by a desire to get plants on lone as soon as possible, opt for diesel, gas turbine or combined cycle plants. The province, however, plans to stay with coal until it shifts to nuclear around 2000. New provincial thermal projects will probably have to import coal until the transportation problems can be worked out.

Competitive Situation   Nearly all the factories that supply this market are under the jurisdiction of the Ministry of Machinery and Electronics Industry (MMEI). The two largest hydraulic turbine and generator manufacturers are the Dongfang Electrical Machinery Works in Sichuan and the Harbin Electric Machinery Works in Heilongjiang. A third is the Tianjin Power Equipment Manufactory. Other producers include the Chongqing Hydro Turbine Plant, Sichuan; the Hangzhou Electric Equipment Works, Zhejiang; the Shaoguan Water Turbine Plant, Guangdong; the Liuzhou Water Turbine Plant, Guangxi, and the Nanping Electrical Machinery Works, Fujian.

In the past, foreign suppliers have generally not been in direct competition with Chinese producers. Those projects funded by international loans generally called for international competitive bidding in which Chinese producers rarely competed. Chinese producers, rather, have more often played the role of consortium partner or subcontractor. As they gain experience and upgrade capabilities, they will become more active as competitors in the China market, either directly or in consortia with foreign competitors.

In some sub-sectors, construction for example, Chinese competitors are very active: Impreglio, the successful contractor on the Ertan project, is in a consortium with the Hydropower Construction Eighth Bureau, one of fifteen contractors under the Water Conservancy and Hydro Power Construction General Corporation in Beijing.

In the context of China's current industrial policy guidelines, which seek to encourage the transfer of technology to develop China's industry and impose protective import barriers to nurture those developing industries, long-term participation in the China market would require a local presence. According to Chinese statistics, over 30,000 Sino-foreign joint ventures of all types in China have been approved,and over 16,000 are in operation. Forming joint ventures, or wholly-foreign-owned ventures, is clearly a strategy followed by many firms. That is a very big step for most companies, however, and requires very careful groundwork. In the case of the core power plant equipment, turbines and generators, there are certain practical obstacles. One is that there are so few qualified producers in China, and the existing ones are engaged in a broad array of activities. It may be feasible to take on the entire Chinese firm in a joint venture, and impractical to carve out a portion for a separate joint venture of the "one factory, two systems" variety because the physical plant is so intertwined with other operations. There are also policy and regulatory barriers. Some firms, or MMEI, their supervising ministry, may not approve a joint venture for some key firms which the authorities believe can prosper on their own or via technology licensing and co-production contracts with foreign suppliers, rather than in joint ventures. Nevertheless, creatively exploring the possibilities for a joint or wholly-owned venture may be the right strategy for firms with adequate resources and the long term vision to carry them through.

It is not feasible to comprehensively cover the entire field of foreign competitors in the many product areas involved in the hydroelectric sector. However, in the core power plant equipment area, the familiar international competitors are active, including Mitsubishi Heavy Industries, Hitachi, Toshiba, Voith, Elin, Alsthom, and Siemens.

Voith Hydro U.S.A., formerly Allis Chalmers, is a competitor in both conventional hydraulic turbines as well as pumped-storage pump/turbines. General Electric's Canadian operation is also an active competitor in the hydropower sector in China.

U.S. firms are active in many other sub-sectors, including engineering consulting, construction equipment, and construction materials. These areas, especially engineering consulting and construction equipment, offer the greatest potential for significant growth in U.S. participation in China's hydropower sector.

While technical specifications and product quality are primary considerations, most world-class competitors meet these requirements. Price and commercial terms are thus the most common determinants of competitive success. In this respect, U.S. firms do find themselves at a competitive disadvantage in competition on projects funded by competitors' government-financed soft loans. Such projects are in the minority in this field, however. The World Bank is active, with about $300 million per year of loans for hydropower. In addition, Japan's OECF, which provides untied low-interest financing, is active in hydropower projects. Projects funded by these sources procure via international competitive bidding. U.S. firms have proven successful in such competitions. More aggressive use of Eximbank financing would generally improve the competitive position of U.S. suppliers.

Another key competitive factor is the ability to influence favorably the specifications which emerge from the long planning and design stage. Some firms have patiently laid the groundwork for several years by developing cooperative and exchange relationships with key design institutes, project offices, and Chinese manufacturers. Other firms have established joint ventures in China which include active local marketing operations. Bailey Controls is an example of the latter.

Market Access Hydropower development is one of China's top priorities. China has neither the funds nor the industrial capacity to meet her goals without foreign participation. International borrowing and the imports financed by that borrowing are integral parts of China's development strategy. There is, therefore, a positive environment for exports of the full range of products and services.

There remains, however, a key caveat to this open door: China will first attempt to meet needs first from domestic production—for design services, dam construction, construction equipment and materials, and power plant equipment. China will turn to imports both when international financing mandates open tenders and when local capabilities are inadequate. Even when China decides to import, MMEI's agenda of development of domestic industry will tend to press for local content, co-production, and technology transfers as part of the price of admission to the China market. Thus protectionism and manipulation of vendors to transfer to technology continue to be intrinsic to China's open door policy in this sector.

Many firms, as noted, have developed market entry strategies around the concept of becoming insiders, usually via investment in a joint venture. While there are relatively few policy barriers to investment in most of the sub-sectors covered here—China generally welcomes and encourages foreign investment in industries in need of an infusion of foreign technology and know how—there are many obstacles to plan, negotiate, establish and profitably operate a venture in China. These obstacles consist primarily of a lack of transparency in China's laws and regulations, which translates to excessive bureaucratic interference, an undeveloped industrial infrastructure which tends to raise operating costs, and, a frequent lack of shared vision between Chinese and foreign partners which may lead to confusion, disagreement, and stalemate. However, realism, proper planning, careful structuring, persistence and a stomach for frustration have generally paid off in profitable and successful joint venture operations.

Best Sales Prospects

Hydropower projects create demand for many product categories. Following are the most promising:

Civil Construction

Construction Equipment
- bulldozers
- dump trucks
- excavators
- backhoes
- graders, levellers, scrapers
- tractor shovel loaders
- winches and hoists
- cable cranes
- mobile cranes
- tower cranes
- drilling machinery
- tunnel boring machines
- lifting/handling/loading machinery
- conveyers (belts, etc.)
- industrial, off-highway trucks
- concrete pourers, finishers
- concrete refrigeration equipment

Generally, higher-end equipment with greater capacity or of a higher technology level are more likely import candidates.

Engineering and Consulting Services

Generally, foreign engineering and consulting services will be in greatest demand when particularly challenging technical difficulties occur or on very large and complex projects.

Construction Materials
- steel plate
- reinforcing bar
- lumber, wood
- cement
- concrete additives

Construction materials are likely to follow international financing or reflect special needs.

Power Plant Equipment

Power Generation and Transmission Equipment
- hydraulic turbines
- generators
- generator excitors

- transformers
- switchgear

Technically-demanding, high-head turbines, low-head, bulb turbines, turbine/generator sets exceeding 300 MW, and pumped storage equipment are the highest priority for equipment imports. Switchgear opportunities are especially pronounced in the case of underground power plants and sub-stations where dead-tank type SF-6 switchgear is used, or in the case of transmission voltages of 500 kV and above.

Control Systems

Control systems are one of the best prospects for U.S. vendors. The design of local products is not sufficiently advanced to meet requirements, and there is a trend towards integrated control systems, which Chinese vendors cannot currently supply.

Useful contacts:

Chinese Government Agencies: Related to End-Use Industry

Foreign Cooperation Department, Ministry of Electric Power
137 Fuyou Street, Xicheng District
Beijing PRC 102031
Tel: 86-1-602-3875

Hydropower Exploitation Department, Ministry of Electric Power
2 Baiguanglu Ertiao, Xuanwu District
Beijing, PRC 100761
Tel: 86-1-654-131 x288

Department of Foreign Affairs, Ministry of Water Resources
1 Baiguanglu'ertiao, Xuanwu District
Beijing, PRC 100761
Tel: 86-1-327-3322

Organizations Related to Project Finance

The World Bank, China Office
Diaoyutai State Guesthouse
Beijing, PRC
Tel: 86-1-831-2227

Department of International Business
State Energy Investment Corporation (SEIC)
91 Wukesong Road
Beijing, China 100039
Tel: 86-1-821-1376

Department of Hydro-Power Development
State Energy Investment Corporation (SEIC)
91 Wukesong Road
Beijing, China 100039
Tel: 86-1-821-3014
(SEIC handles State-allocated funds for the energy sector.)

Division of Public Relations
China International Trust and Investment Corporation (CITIC)
19 Jian Guo Men Wai Da Jie
Beijing, PRC 100004
Tel: 86-1-500-2625

Department of International Cooperation
Huaneng International Power Development Corporation
Beijing, PRC
Tel: 86-1-202-4466 x291

Chinese Government Agencies: Related to Producing Industries

International Cooperation Department
Ministry of Machinery and Electronics Industry
Sanlihe, Xicheng District
Beijing, PRC 100823
Tel: 86-1-867-447

Chinese Government Agencies: Other

Office of the Leading Group of Major Technological Equipment (OMATE)
State Council of the People's Republic of China
22 Xi An Men Street
Beijing, China 100017
Tel: 86-1-65-2272

First Comprehensive Industrial Department State Planning Commission
38 Yuetannanjie
Beijing, China
Tel: 86-1-809-1405

Technology Import/Export Department
Ministry of Foreign Economic Relations and Trade (MOFERT)
28 Donghouxiang, Andingmenwai, Dongcheng District
Beijing, PRC 100011
Tel: 86-1-519-7356

(MOFERT approves large investment projects, handles international loans, and administers imports licenses.

Electric Power Grid Administrations

(This agency operates the interprovincial grids, buys power from the power plants and sells to the provincial grids.)

Central China Electric Power Administrative Bureau
Liyuan, Donghu
Wuhan, Hubei Province, PRC
Tel: 86-27-812612

East China Electric Power Administrative Bureau
181 Nanjingdonglu
Shanghai, PRC
Tel: 86-21-211010

Division of Foreign Relations
North China Electric Power Administrative Bureau
32 Zao Lin Qian Jie, Bai Guang Lu, Xuanwu District
Beijing, PRC 100053
Tel: 86-1-366-131

Division of Foreign Relations
Northeast Electric Power Administrative Bureau
7 Wuduan, Wu Ma Lu
Shenyang, Liaoning Province, PRC
Tel: 86-24-361290

South China Power Grid Office
174 Tian He Lu
Guangzhou, Guangdong Province, PRC
Tel: 86-20-765533

Provincial Electric Power Bureaus

(These agencies operate the provincial grids, purchase power from the regional grid, and own and operate the power plants, either directly or through subordinate corporations.)

Division of Foreign Relations
Sichuan Provincial Electric Power Industry Bureau
17 Erduan, Dong Feng Lu
Chengdu, Sichuan Province, PRC   610061
Tel: 86-28-441212

Yunnan Provincial Electric Power Industry Bureau
158 Dong Feng Dong Lu
Kunming, Yunnan Province, PRC   650041
Tel: 86-871-25908

Qinehai Provincial Electric Power Industry Bureau
47 Sheng Li Lu
Xining, Qinghai Province, PRC   810008
Tel: 86-971-53356

Guangxi Regional Electric Power Industry Bureau
6 Min Zhu Lu
Nanning, Guangxi Autonomous Region, PRC   530023
Tel: 86-771-23414

Division of Foreign Relations
Guangdong Department of Water Conservancy and Electric Power
39 Duo Bao Lu
Guangzhou, Guangdong Province, PRC   510151
Tel: 86-20-815362

Guizhou Provincial Electric Power Industry Bureau
1 Bin He Lu
Guiyang, Guizhou Province, PRC   550002
Tel: 86-851-25908

Hubei Provincial Electric Power Industry Bureau
45 Xu Dong Lu, Wuchang District
Wuhan, Hubei Province, PRC
Tel: 86-27-814712

Hebei Provincial Electric Power Industry Bureau
5 Fu Qiang Da Ji
Shijiazhuang, Hebei Province, PRC 050011
86-311-48921

Division of Foreign Relations
Hunan Department of Water Conservancy and Electric Power
62 Shao Shan Lu
Changsha, Hunan Province, PRC 410007
Tel: 86-731-31195

Division of Foreign Relations
Jiangxi Provincial Electric Power Industry Bureau
111 Yong Wai Zheng Jie
Nanchang, Jiangxi Province, PRC
Tel: 86-791-227021

Heilongjiang Provincial Electric Power Industry Bureau
157 Dong Da Zhi Jie
Harbin, Heilongjiang Province, PRC
Tel: 86-451-34131

Liaoning Provincial Electric Power Industry Bureau
7 Wuduan, Nan Wu Ma Lu
Shenyang, Liaoning Province, PRC
Tel: 86-24-361617

Division of Foreign Relations
Fujian Provincial Electric Power Industry Bureau
1 Sheng Fu Lu
Fuzhou, Fujian Province, PRC 350001
Tel: 86-591-555121

Division of Foreign Relations
Zhejiang Department of Water Conservancy
7 Mei Hua Bei
Hangzhou, Zhejiang Province, PRC 310009
Tel: 86-571-26153

Shaanxi Northwest Electrical Administration
57 Shang De Lu
Xi'an, Shaanxi Province, PRC 710004
Tel: 86-29-25061

Gansu Provincial Electric Power Industry Bureau
306 Xi Jin Dong Lu, Qilihe District
Lanzhou, Gansu Province, PRC 730050
Tel: 86-931-34311

Tibet Department of Industry and Electric Power
14 Lin Kuo Bei Lu
Lhasa, Tibet Autonomous Region, PRC 850000

Xinjiang Regional Electric Power Industry Bureau
5 Jian She Lu
Urumqi, Xinjiang Autonomous Region, PRC 830002

Hainan Provincial People's Government Hai Fu Lu
Haikou, Hainan Province, PRC 570004
Tel: 86-750-42268

Chinese Electric Power Design Institutes

Division of Foreign Relations
Electric Power General Design Academy (Ministry of Energy)
65 An De Lu, De Sheng Men Wai
Beijing, PRC 100011

Water Conservancy and Hydropower Design Academy (Ministry of Energy)
Liu Pu Kang
Beijing, PRC 100011
Tel: 86-1-401-1177

Water Conservancy and Electric Power Scientific and Technological Information
Research Institute (Ministry of Energy)
Liu Pu Kang
Beijing, PRC 100011
Tel: 86-1-401-2244

Central South Surveying and Design Academy (Ministry of Energy)
Guitang
Changsha, Hunan Province, PRC
Tel: 86-571-882-824

East China Surveying and Design Institute (Ministry of Energy)
Nan Da Jie
Xi'an, Shaanxi Province, PRC
Tel: 86-29-719-606

Chengdu Prospecting Design Institute (Ministry of Energy)
1 Huan Hua Bei Lu, Qingyanggong
Chengdu, Sichuan Province, PRC
Tel: 86-28-669-023

Division of Foreign Relations
Kunming Surveying and Design Institute (Ministry of Energy)
14 Bai Ta Lu
Kunming, Yunnan Province, PRC
Tel: 86-871-22093

Division of Foreign Relations
Guiyang Surveying and Design Institute (Ministry of Energy)
78 Jie Fang Lu
Guiyang, Guizhou Province, PRC
Tel: 86-851-26919

Chinese River Basin Administration Authorities

Division of Foreign Relations
Yangtze River Water Conservancy Commission (Ministry of Water Resources)
1155 Jie Fang Da Dao
Wuhan, Hubei Province, PRC
Tel: 86-27-27911

Yellow River Water Conservancy Commission (Ministry of Water Resources)
11 Jin Shui Lu
Zhengzhou, Henan Province, PRC
Tel: 86-371-22971

Pearl River Water Conservancy Commission (Ministry of Water Resources)
Guangzhou, Guangdong Province, PRC

Songhua and Liao Rivers Conservancy Commission (Ministry of Water Resources)
Changchun, Jilin Province, PRC

Huai River Water Conservancy Commission (Ministry of Water Resources)
Bengbu, Anhui Province, PRC

Chinese Consulting Engineers

Li Shang Wu, International Cooperation Department
China International Engineering Consulting Corporation
Che Gong Zhuang Xi Lu
Beijing, PRC 100044
Tel: 86-1-841-7306

Chinese Society of Hydroelectric Engineering
1 Second Lane, Bai Guang Lu
Beijing, PRC

Hydroelectric Power Project Offices

Ertan Hydroelectric Development Corporation
Hua Pai Fang, Xi Men Wai
Chengdu, Sichuan Province, PRC
Tel: 86-28-668-312

Office of the Leading Group for Three Gorges Project Feasibility Studies
(Ministry of Water Resources)
1 Bai Guang Lu Er Tiao, Xuanwu District
Beijing, PRC 100761
Tel: 86-1-367-931

Chinese Consultants

International Cooperation Department
China International Engineering Consulting Corporation
Che Gong Zhuang Xi Lu
Beijing, PRC 100044
Tel: 86-1-841-7306

China International Economic Consultants
CITIC Building, 2nd Floor
19 Jianguomenwai Dajie
Beijing, 100004

Consultec
China Economic and Trade Consultants Corporation
B-12 Guanghua Road
Jianguomen Wai
Beijing, China 100020

Key Trading Companies

China National Technical Import and Export Corporation (CNTIC)
3A Wanshousi
Suzhou Jie Street, Haidian District
Beijing, China 100081

Hydropower Department
China National Machinery & Equipment I/E Corporation (CMEC)
16, Fu Xing Men Wai Street
Beijing, China 100045
Tel: 86-1-326-8177

China National Machinery Import and Export Corporation (CMC)
Er Li Gou, Xi Jiao
Beijing, China 100044
Tel: 86-1-831-7733 x4050

Key Contacts in Guangdong Province

Power Bureau
757 Dongfeng East Road
Guangzhou, China
Tel: (8620) 7767888   Fax: (8620) 7770307

Electric Power Design Institute
Technology Department
846 Dongfeng Middle Road
Guangzhou, China
Tel: (8620) 7756416   Fax: (8620) 7766160

Electric Power Test & Research Institute
73 Meihua Road
Guangzhou, China
Tel: (8620) 7767888 x23406   Fax: (8620) 7753850

Planning Commission
305 Dongfeng Middle Road
Guangzhou, China
Tel: (8620) 3330860 Fax: (8620) 3353542

Foreign Economic Relations & Trade Commission
Foreign Investment Division
305 Dongfeng Middle Road
Guangzhou, China
Tel: (8620) 3330860 Fax: (8620) 3332347

Guangdong Machinery Import & Export Corporation
Second Import Department
61 Yanjiang West Road
Guangzhou, China
Tel: (8620) 8862776, 8862326 Fax: (8620) 8861527

Guangdong Information Center
305 Dongfeng East Road
Guangzhou, China
Tel: (8620) 3330860 x3237 Fax: (8620) 3339723

Guangdong International Trust & Investment Company
Room 2101, GITIC Plaza
339 Huanshi East Road
Tel: (8620) 3311888 x72101, 3318297 Fax: (8620) 3318152

Guangzhou Municipality

Municipal Planning Commission
Energy Division
1 Fuqian Road, Building No. 1, Room 222
Guangzhou, China
Tel: (8620) 3330360 x3642 Fax: (8620) 3322714

Guangzhou General Power Development Company
757 Dongfeng East Road
Guangzhou, China
Tel: (8620) 7767888 Fax: (8620) 7770307

Municipal Economic Commission
Energy Office
1 Fuqian Road, Building No. 4, Room 601
Guangzhou, China
Tel: (8620) 3330360 x3837   Fax: (8620) 3322714

Municipal Hydroelectric Bureau
Wenming Road, Xiansi Street
Guangzhou, China
Tel: (8620) 3344244   Fax: (8620) 3342008

Guangzhou Zhujiang Electrical Power Company Ltd.
Panyu City, Guangzhou
Tel: (8620) 4988602 x2133   Fax: (8620) 4988601

Dongguan Municipality

Municipal Power Bureau
Dongguan, Guangdong, China
Tel: (867620) 231788 x107   Fax: (867620) 224292

Foshan Municipality

Municipal Economic Commission
Foshan, Guangdong, China
Tel: (86757) 335719, 334344   Fax: (86757) 322379

Panyu Municipality

Economic Commission
Panyu, Guangdong, China
Tel: (8620) 4823129   Fax: (8620) 4838375

Zhongshang Municipality

Municipal Power Bureau
Zhongshan, Guangdong, China
Tel: (86755) 802134   Fax: (867654) 808658

Shenzhen Special Economic Zone

Shenzhen General Power Corporation
Shenzhen, Guangdong, China
Tel: (86755) 323041   Fax: (86755) 323091

Zhuhai Special Economic Zone

Municipal Economic Commission
Electricity Supply Office
Zhuhai, Guangdong, China
Tel: (86756) 229458   Fax: (86756) 224874

INSURANCE

Overview With a fifth of the world's population, and a rapidly growing economy, China constitutes a large potential market for foreign and domestic insurers. The stakes are enormous: USD 4.3 billion in premium incomes (23.8 billion yuan at the official exchange rate) were collected last year by the People's Insurance Company of China (PICC). This is equal to 1.0 percent of the country's GNP. Analysts expect this market to grow 25 percent each year until the year 2000. Total premium incomes should reach USD 40 billion within seven years (54).

China is gradually seeking to open the insurance sector to foreign participation. At present, only two foreign insurance companies, American International Assurance (American International Group) and Tokyo Marine, have been granted licenses to sell insurance, and these are restricted to the Shanghai area. While the market remains substantially closed, many U.S. insurance companies have established representative offices in 1994, and several are pressing hard to be allowed to open branch offices in the near future.

Insurance is high on the list of service sectors the U.S. government is actively seeking to open in China. U.S. insurance companies have a high reputation, but face strong competition from Japanese, European, and Canadian competitors (58).

The following tabulation gives some idea of the trends in the insurance industry in China.

	1993	1994	1995
Total Sales	9,107	11,839	15,391
Total Local Sales	8,867	11,539	15,016
Sales by Foreign Firms*	240	300	375
Sales by U.S. owned Firms	48	60	75
Exchange Rate	8.6	8.6	

*Note: Consists of local premiums by foreign insurance company branch plus re-insurance with foreign companies.

Market Assessment The state monopoly, PICC, has heretofore dominated the market. However, a committee made up of representatives of the People's Bank of China (China's Central Bank) and the PICC is currently writing a new insurance law. The new law was expected to be published in April or May, 1994. Although drafts of the law are not yet available, it is expected that the legislation will loosen PICC's monopoly status.

Because of China's "opening up" policy, as well as its willingness to open its services industry in return for entrance into the General Agreement on Tariffs on Trade (GATT), analysts expect the new law to allow foreign companies greater access to the insurance market in China. American insurance companies—long considered the best in the world in terms of service and management—could find considerable opportunities in this new, vast market.

When the Communist Party ascended to power in 1949, PICC became the sole state insurer in China. For thirty-six years, the PRC did not allow the existence of other insurance companies. According to Mao Zedong's socialist principles, the state theoretically provided fair and equal compensation for workers and state companies.

Under these conditions, the PICC became a giant, lucrative monopoly. The firm is owned by the state and reports to the cabinet through the PBOC. Although other, mainly state-run, insurance firms have since been allowed to open businesses, PICC's four decade status as a state monopoly has earned them over 90 percent market share.

It is difficult to overstate PICC's size and influence. They control approximately 95% of the insurance industry, operating 4,200 branches and employing a total workforce of 110,000. PICC's most profitable operations are auto, property, industrial, life, and cargo insurance. Yet PICC has created policies for just about anything that could possibly be insured (about 400 types of insurance in all). This includes pig and cow insurance, and bicycle insurance. PICC also offers education and marriage insurance, which covers wedding and tuition costs if one's parents prematurely pass away.

PICC plays a key role in setting premium rates in cooperation with the PBOC. These rates are supposed to fluctuate in accordance with the market. Publication of premium rates is mandatory for all companies, including companies presently emerging as the PICC's competitors. PICC freely publishes its rates on auto, life, and property insurance (some samples are enclosed with this report). However, PICC prices more complex types of insurance in accordance with risk, volume of business, and other conditions, with published rates serving only as "guidance." According to the PICC, this system ensures "fair and free competition" in the market.

Under the present law, PICC is granted numerous other competitive advantages. For example, all insurance companies must cede 30% of revenues to PICC for reinsurance. The law does not allow foreign companies to offer reinsurance. China's GATT negotiators claim that this restriction on foreign companies offering reinsurance may soon be abolished. However, PICC officials claim that they are unaware of such proposals. They defend the present law, maintaining that PICC is the only insurance company large enough to offer reinsurance and insurance to high risk businesses.

PICC generally sells insurance through its own market staff, paid by salary, not commission. After the recent passage of a new "Unfair Competition Law," Chinese law does permit commissions to be offered if they are publicly disclosed. Other insurance firms in China have found that commissions can serve as a powerful marketing tool, as in the United States. PICC officials, however, state that they have no desire to change their salary-based system.

PICC does not offer insurance brokerage services. In fact, the provisional insurance law presently in effect does not cover the subject of brokerage, and no companies have been allowed to offer insurance brokerage services in China. Nonetheless, at least one foreign brokerage firm has established a representative office here. In addition, a few companies offer consulting services. For example, the English firm, Sedgwick and Sedgwick, has obtained a license to consult on reinsurance and intermediation which, in effect, may serve as the equivalent to insurance brokerage services. PICC officials have stated that the eventual introduction of the insurance law may permit international brokers to become active in the market.

Critics accuse PICC of using numerous methods to defend their influence. For instance, competitors have noted that PICC has moved to draft regulations which may require the purchase of their policies. They have also been known to spend long periods of time to process claims, or only compensating claimants with a fraction of total awards. PICC officials, on the other hand, maintain that as the biggest, most reputable insurance company in China, they offer the best service and possess the most experienced staff.

PICC has been making money. According to a senior economist at PICC, the company operated with an astounding profit margin of 40% in 1992, with total assets valuing 48 billion RMB. These profits are returned to the Chinese government. PICC deposits profits directly into the central government treasury. Certain funds are also invested in property.

PICC Chairman and President, Li Yumin, claims that PICC contributed 6 billion yuan in profits and taxes to the state treasury during the Seventh Five-Year period. PICC has not limited its operations to China and is presently aggressively expanding beyond PRC borders to become a significant multinational corporation. PICC has seventy foreign affiliates, subsidiaries, or branches, including a joint venture (with American International Group ((AIG)) in the United States. According to published reports, its Hong Kong branch handles nearly 20 percent of the island's insurance business. PICC has announced plans to open group companies in Southeast Asia, Europe, and the United States, hoping to become a "big name" in the world insurance market by the year 2000.

Competitive Situation For all of PICC's entrenched dominance in the Chinese insurance market, the industry has not been immune to change. Deng Xiaoping's call for the opening up of China through a "socialist market economy" in the mid-1980s, spurred the publication of the Provisional Insurance Law in 1985 which allowed the establishment of other firms.

To understand the Chinese insurance market, it is important to realize that two other state-owned firms, Pingan and Tiapingyang (Pacific) are rapidly growing. In addition, one independent American company, the American Insurance Group, has been given a limited mandate to compete for business in the Shanghai market. In addition, several government ministries and other state-owned firms are making tentative steps to enter at least some segments of the insurance business. Since PICC has fixed insurance prices for all of China, these companies (theoretically) compete on the basis of service.

PICC's most notable domestic competitors are the Ping An and Pacific Insurance companies. Ping An, based in Shenzhen, was founded in 1988 and has expanded quickly to include thirty-five branches. Its main areas of operation are life (38% of business), property (35%), and cargo (35%). Ping An reported a gross income of RMB 1.2 billion in 1992. Ping An recently established a joint venture in Shanghai with the Shanghai Trust and Investment Corporation (SITCO), the Shanghai Branch of the Industrial and Commercial Bank of China, and the Shanghai Jiu Shi Corporation.

Pacific Insurance, based in Shanghai, is China's second largest insurance company. China's Bank of Communications owns Pacific, providing it with significant leverage. The Executive Vice President of the Bank of Communications serves as Chairman of Pacific Insurance. PICC has also been growing quickly, insuring autos, property, marine equipment, aviation, and satellites. Both Pingan and Pacific are potentially very significant competitors in the Chinese insurance market.

As noted above, other government ministries have found niches in the insurance market. According to published reports, the Ministry of Labor has developed insurance for those workers of collective enterprises who do not enjoy lifelong welfare benefits given by the PICC. The Ministry of Civil Affairs offers home, crop, and property insurance to farmers. The Ministry of Personnel is trying to open an insurance business which does not yet seem to be well defined.

The China International Investment and Trust Corporation (CITIC) has just announced plans to open an insurance company. CITIC is 100 percent owned by the Chinese government and its profits are returned to the state. CITIC will reportedly gear its operations to cover import and export credits, as well as life insurance. Despite all these forays into the insurance market, however, efforts by various ministries to enter the insurance market will most likely be limited to areas directly under their jurisdiction over the short and medium term. Over the longer term, the new law—expected in April or May of 1994—will determine access to the market.

Lured by China's huge potential market, several forcing firms have established operations or have applied to open offices. Foreign insurance companies have discovered that PICCs hold on the market and bureaucratic regulations have made business difficult.

For instance, the Provisional Insurance Law stipulates that a foreign firms must open a "representative office" in China for a total of three years prior to the establishment of a service branch. (PBOC officials have declared that this regulation will not change with the new insurance law.) In addition, the present law only permits foreign companies to enter the market as joint ventures or as branches of foreign insurance firms in Shanghai. As a result, foreign companies may have to enter joint ventures with their present or future competitors, who possess the power to cease operations at any time.

Nonetheless, American insurers have tried to break into the market. The boldest foray by a foreign insurance company into the Chinese market has come from the American International Group (AIG). In October, 1992, AIG launched an insurance business in Shanghai—the first time a foreign company has been permitted to operate an insurance business in China since 1949. AIG deposited USD 8 million in the PBOC and has working capital of USD 2 million.

Its subsidiary, the American International Assurance Company (AIA), offers property, casualty, and liability insurance to foreign wholly-owned subsidiaries, foreign joint ventures, and joint technical cooperation ventures. AIA also provides foreign tourists and Shanghai residents with life insurance policies, including personal accident and medical coverage. The firm can accept payments in RMB or foreign currencies. AIA's business is limited to the jurisdiction of Shanghai.

Many industry representatives considered AIG's move an unprecedented coup in the Chinese insurance market—a foreign company allowed to operate fully-owned venture, able to circumvent China's dual currency system by accepting RMB, and permitted to sell insurance to both Chinese and foreigners. Insurers who wish to follow their lead should understand that it was not an easy or quick task. To gain state approval of their venture, AIA had to set up a representative office and Beijing and lobby the People's Bank of China. AIA spend considerable time and money meeting with PBOC and other government officials and gaining broad-based support.

After winning PBOC's consent in Beijing, AIA had to wage a similar campaign in Shanghai to win local approval for their operations. A longtime investor in Shanghai, AIA had the connections and influence to obtain permission to open business—a decade after first coming to China. Their mandate to do business in Shanghai does not imply a right to expand to other provinces or municipalities.

Prospective insurers should understand that the "opening up" of Chinese markets has brought macro-economic problems, as well as opportunities. Some regions or municipalities have obtained a high degree of economic autonomy. For instance, the British firm, Sedgwick and Sedgwick, has recently won "national approval" from the PBOC to offer insurance consulting services in China. Yet when Sedgwick went to Shanghai and Shenzhen for local approval, they were reportedly rebuffed and not allowed to open an office. The firm is still seeking local approval for its business.

Prospective insurance companies should understand that local regulations could prevent the realization of a truly national insurance market. Optimists in the insurance industry hope that nest year's insurance law will allow for a national, systematic framework. Cynics fear that the law will be vague, allowing powerful provinces to interpret it as they wish. Above all, prospective insurers should understand that doing business in China requires two stages of approval: at Beijing and at the local level.

Continental is another American insurer with a representative office in China. Continental has been in Beijing since 1980, but has not yet been permitted to sell insurance directly. Continental plans to work mostly with the multi-national corporations in this market. Continental also hopes to take advantage of the "triangular trade" between China, Hong Kong, and Taiwan.

Other firms such as Aetna, Prudential, Chubb, and Cigna are considering opening offices in China. Hong Kong, Taiwan and U.K firms have also set up representative offices. The Japanese are known to have a large presence in China, though the Chinese have not yet permitted any Japanese firm to open a branch office. Rumors abound, however, that the PBOC will soon allow a large Japanese insurer to open a branch in the near future.

Market Access The People's Bank of China (PBOC) is now preparing a law which seeks to establish a systematic legal framework for the insurance market. In line with China's opening up policy, foreign companies expect the new law to allow them greater access into the Chinese market. Although the PBOC has said that it would welcome foreign participation in the industry, foreign firms have expressed two major concerns about the new law.

1) Vagueness

Foremost, companies fear that the new law, like many other Chinese laws, will be vague. This could allow provinces and municipalities to interpret the regulations differently, making uniform, national coverage difficult. As one foreign insurance executive commented, "To some powerful provinces, the law could be no more than any piece of paper."

Vagueness in the law could also lead to unfairness in the market. Without a detailed law which maintains uniform standards, the new law could result in disorder in the market. Companies predict that there will have to be a considerable body of regulations issued by the PBOC which complement the law. This process will take time.

2)   *Vested Interests*

Companies also fear controversy within the Chinese government. At issue are fundamental differences between the PBOC and PICC on the future orientation of the market. Industry watchdogs characterize PBOC authorities as genuine reformers who wish to open the insurance market to foreign firms. The PBOC is especially cognizant of the benefits of free competition and China's policy mandate to enter the General Agreement on Tariffs and Trade.

PICC officials, on the other hand, are naturally concerned with their post-monopoly status. PICC officials state their intention to compete with all new entrants. They are in the process of greatly improving their standards. Moreover, they have many competitive advantages earned by many years of experience.

Future Prospects   Despite all these worries, nearly all sources in China, from PICC representatives to their competitors, to analysts and investors, all agree on one thing: the potential of the insurance market. Virtually all sectors of the insurance field have room for growth. Boosted incomes and high savings rates (38% of GNP) have given the Chinese people money to invest, especially on insurance policies which can protect their families and newfound private wealth.

Prospects for life insurance are very good. The PICC estimates that only 100 million people (less than 10 percent of the total population) currently have long term life insurance. Most life insurance policy holders are government officials. Thus, nearly a fifth of the world's population remains uninsured. In such a large market, there is great possibility. The economic boom should also aid the growth of other sectors of the insurance industry, particularly automobiles. In just slightly over a decade, automobiles have begun to clog the streets with daily traffic jams, as more and more Chinese can afford cars. More cars mean profits for insurance companies, for 80% of China's provinces mandate insurance for car owners.

Economists also note China's emergence as a dominant player in international trade which has led to an explosion in the shipping industry. Trading firms will require cargo insurance to cover their goods. Trade between "Greater China" (China, Hong Kong, and Taiwan) has been growing quickly in the past several years, and China's eventual entrance into GATT should further increase trade with Europe and the West.

Increased trade with the West should also benefit liability insurance. (At present, China's first medical liability case is winding its way through the courts.) Because most Western companies mandate insurance before signing contracts, liability insurance should boom. Moreover, western firms should seek the insurance companies they trust, such as AIA, Continental, and other American firms. It should be expected that more sophisticated Chinese firms will soon engage in similar insurance practices.

Finally, the market for property insurance should improve. As China moves from socialism to a market economy, private property increases at a very rapid rate. The Chinese corporate and individual property owner will want to insure these new assets. In addition, construction has been growing very rapidly, and hotels and department stores have been sprouting up in urban areas. This trend should continue, especially in the coastal cities.

In sum, the insurance industry in China offers great potential benefits, despite many uncertainties in the market. If and when the market opens up, however, it is likely to be big enough for many firms to prosper.

Key Contacts:

Insurance Corporations:

People's Insurance Company of China
Foreign Affairs Division, Administration Department
410 Fechengmennei Dajie
Beijing 100034
Tel: 6011870   Fax: 6011869, 6011870

American International Group Inc.
Jing Guang Center #3407
Hujialou, Beijing 100020
Tel: 5013388 x3407   Fax: 5012878
Shanghai #: 021-279-7168   Shanghai Fax: 021-279-8569

The Continental Corporation
Beijing Liaison Office
Room 901, Chains City Hotel
4 Gong Ren Ti Yu Chang Dong Lu
Beijing 100027
Tel: 5007602   Fax: 5007668

Government Organizations:

People's Bank of China
Financial Administration Department
Fuxing Men Xicheng District
Beijing 100800
Tel: 6016422; 6016718

People's Bank of China
Foreign Affairs Department, Foreign Financial Institutions
32 Cheng Fang Street
West District, Beijing, China
Tel: 601-6711   Fax: 601-6704

LABORATORY AND SCIENTIFIC INSTRUMENTS

Table 98 presents some of the pertinent statistics for the Laboratory and Scientific Instruments sector (3).

Table 98

Statistics for the Laboratory and Scientific Instruments Sector

A)	Three-letter ITA industry sector code:	LAB
B)	Est. total market size (USD millions):	
	1991 -	$300
	1992 -	$320
	1993 -	$450
	1994 -	$550
	1995 -	$660
C)	Est. 1992-4 annual market growth rate:	5%
D)	Est total imports (USD millions):	
	1991 -	$200
	1992 -	$210
	1993 -	$250
	1994 -	$300
	1995 -	$360
E)	Est. annual total import growth rate:	5%
F)	Est. imports from U.S. (USD millions):	
	1991 -	$100
	1992 -	$110
	1993 -	$150
	1994 -	$180
	1995 -	$207 (58)
G)	Est. annual growth of imports from U.S.	5%
H)	China's receptivity to U.S. products in this sector (5 - High/1 - Low):	4
I)	Competition from local/third-countries for U.S. firms (5 - Low/1 - High):	3
J)	Chinese market barriers to U.S. sales in this sector (5 - Few/1 - Many):	4

K) Comments - Factors for increased U.S. sales:
- Modernization of technology and industry continues to be a development priority.
- Technical transfer is a priority under the Eighth Five-Year Plan.
- Many Chinese institutions want the newest and best equipment.

L)	Most Promising Sub-sectors	1992 market size
	1. Industrial instruments	$50 million
	2. Scientific instruments	$40 million

Major foreign competitors are Advantest and Anritsu (Japan), R&S, Marconi, and Siemens (Germany). In many cases Japanese equipment, technically comparable to U.S. products, is significantly cheaper in China.

There are many small Chinese manufacturers who produce low-end goods. Many of the factories are located in Shenzhen and other parts of Guangdong.

U.S. products pose minor difficulties for end-users because of different electrical standards in China. Japanese and German products, in comparison, are not hindered by conversion difficulties (58).

MACHINE TOOLS AND METALWORKING EQUIPMENT

Overview In 1986, about 120 major enterprises produced most of China's machine tools. Many of the large plants were in the east, north, and northeast, particularly in Beijing, Shanghai, Xhenyang, Harbin, and Tianjin. In the early and mid-1980s, a number of agreements with foreign manufacturers aimed to help China upgrade its machine tool industry. The Shanghai municipal government also asked assistance from the World Bank in preparing and financing a comprehensive modernization scheme for the Shanghai machine tool industry.

Overall, the machine tool industry was based on 1960s technology. Many of the tools had a service life of only five to seven years, compared with twelve to fifteen years in industrialized countries. The tools were generally unreliable and were poorly suited for precision work because of outdated design, low quality purchased components, substandard manufacturing facilities and a lack of production-management expertise (4).

Table 99 summarizes some of the statistics concerning the machine tool and metalworking equipment industry (3).

Table 99

Salient Statistics for the Machine Tools/Metalworking Equipment Sector

A)	Three-letter ITA industry sector code:	MTL
B)	Est. total market size (USD millions):	
	1991 -	$2,200
	1992 -	$2,250
	1993 -	$2,590
	1994 -	$3,560
	1995 -	$4,214
C)	Est. 1992-4 annual market growth rate:	3%
D)	Est. total imports (USD millions):	
	1991 -	$ 800
	1992 -	$ 820
	1993 -	$1,900
	1994 -	$2,500
	1995 -	$2,944
E)	Est. annual total import growth rate:	3%
F)	Est. imports from U.S. (USD millions):	
	1991 -	$225
	1992 -	$250
	1993 -	$210
	1994 -	$270
	1995 -	$345 (58)
G)	Est. annual growth of imports from U.S.:	2%
H)	China's receptivity to U.S. products in this sector (5 - High/1 - Low):	4
I)	Competition from local/third-countries	

	for U.S. firms (5 - Low/1 - High):	2
J)	Chinese market barriers to U.S. sales	
	in this sector (5 - Few/1 - Many):	4
K)	Comments - factors for increased U.S. sales:	

- Chinese enterprises will upgrade machine tools to boose efficiency.
- Forging, casting, rolling and heat treatment will receive priority.

L)	Most Promising Sub-sectors	1992 market size
	1. Metalworking lathes	$600 million
	2. Casting machinery	$400 million
	3. Forging and pressing machines	$500 million

Market Assessment During the Eighth Five-Year Plan (1991-1996), China will stress the modernization of its energy, metallurgical, transportation, agricultural machinery and communications industries. This modernization program will require high quality machine tools. However, China can only meet about 60% of its domestic demand for metalworking machine tools; the remainder will have to be imported. U.S. companies face stiff competition from Japanese and European competitors (who often have access to attractive concessionary loan packages offered by their own governments). Nevertheless, U.S. metalworking machine tools enjoy a good reputation in China, and may U.S. machine tool companies have discovered ways to successfully compete in this market (33).

With an overall market approaching USD 1.5 billion, China's market for machine tools is the fifth largest in the world (after the USSR), Germany, the U.S.A. and Japan). Metalworking machine tools (e.g., metal cutting and metal forming machine tools) make up a majority of this market.

Although China itself produces a large number of machine tools, Chinese factories can meet only about 60% of domestic machine tool demand. The basic problem is a miss match between consumer demand and the items produced: most domestically produced machine tools are based on relatively simple technology, but Chinese customer want to buy more modern, sophisticated machine tools. For example, China's production of numerically controlled (NC) machine tools is only 1.5% of the total output of the industry. (In developed countries, this proportion can be as high as 25%.) As a result of this miss match, China's stockpiles of unwanted machine tools continue to mount.

Another problem is one of quality control and standards in China's machine tool industry. Many of the machine tools China produces, are not as carefully engineered or manufactured as those of advanced industrialized countries. Many Chinese consumers prefer the higher levels of accuracy and efficiency, and longer useful life of imported machine tools.

During the Eighth Five-Year Plan (1991-1995), Chinese central planners want to meet 70-80% of China's domestic demand for machine tools (compared with about 60% now). Planners also want to improve China's competitive position in the world machine tool market. Specifically, the planners want to upgrade China's machine tools' products spectrum (while maintaining the same total level of output); increase machine tool exports; improve standardization of product quality; and improve management of machine tool factories.

Multilateral donor organizations will also be active in China's machine tool sector during the Eighth Five-Year Plan. The United Nations Development Program (UNDP) will assist China with a USD 12 million project to upgrade China's machine tool industry. Sixty percent of the UNDP fund will be used for training and consulting services, the remainder will be used to improve equipment. In another example, the World Bank is involved in an ongoing program to upgrade Shanghai's machine tool industry. The Bank is also doing a feasibility study on a similar program for Shenyang (Liaoning Province).

U.S. products are considered to be of consistently high quality, but most analysts admit privately that German, Swiss, and Japanese high end products are just as good. Taiwan products at the lower end are regarded favorably, too.

U.S. products have suffered from lack of exposure in the market. In contrast Taiwaness, German, Japanese, and Italian firms have actively marketed their products. German and Italian training facilities have long been established in Tianjin and Beijing respectively. Taiwanese firms reportedly won the largest foreign market share because of extensive personal connections in the mainland.

Major competitors in this market are Taiwanese (22%), Japanese (21.5%), and Germany (18%). Mainland and Taiwanese products are mostly cheap, low-end products and do not compete with high technology tools produced by U.S. and other foreign exporters.

Many Chinese machine tool factories were originally designed through Soviet, Czechoslovakian, or Bulgarian partnerships. These now wholly Chinese owned factories are looking to improve their very low levels of technology through foreign cooperation.

U.S. firms are hindered by the unavailability of soft loans that are commonly provided to other foreign firms. U.S. products are also generally more expensive than Japanese goods of similar quality, and U.S. export license review seems to be more stringent and lengthy than those of other nations.

As of 1995, the best sub-sector prospects within this sector include automotive, aircraft and aerospace, natural resource extraction and exploitation, communications, and electronics production (58).

Best Sales Prospects

CNC machine tools now comprise about 40% of China's total machine tool imports. And high precision machine tools, EDM machines, transfer machines and special purpose machine tools together account for another 40% of imports. We expect this pattern to continue into the Eighth Five-Year Plan.

Best sales prospects include:

- large scale and precision machining centers with horizontal and vertical spindles.
- mould machining centers with CNC copying functions.
- FMC and FMS large scale and precision EDM and wire cutting EDM.
- large scale CNC turning machines and turning centers.

- multi-axis simultaneously controlled CNC copying milling machines with horizontal and vertical spindles.
- CNC copying milling machines.
- high performance and precision transfer machines.
- automatic line, heavy duty, large scale CNC machines (heavy duty horizontal and vertical turning machines, large scale floor-type milling and boring machines).
- precision external, internal, forming and special purpose grinding machines.
- high precision gear grinding machines with worm grinding wheels.
- gear grinding machines with plate grinding wheels.
- large scale and precision CNC jig-grinding machines.
- grinding machines for ball bearings.
- automatic line, various special purpose CNC turning and grinding machines (crankshaft turning and grinding machines, camshaft turning and grinding machines, roll grinding machines).
- CNC flame cutting machines.
- high-speed precision presses and transfer presses.
- CNC pressing, and punching and bending machines.
- CNC equipment and programmable controller.
- CAD/CAM technology.

The overall market for used machine tools is promising. The U.S., Germany, and Japan already supply used machine tools to China's automotive industry. In general, Chinese are interested in used heavy duty large scale machine tools.

<u>Key useful contacts:</u>

Department of Machine Tools and Tools
Ministry of Machinery and Electronics Industries (MMEI)
Sanlihe Road, Beijing, China 100823
Tel: 867345   Fax: 867745

China National Machine Tool Corporation (CNMTC)
19 Fang Jia Alley, An Nei
Beijing, China 100007
Tel: 401-4855, 485-431   Fax: 401-5657

International Cooperation Department
China Machine Tool and Tool Builders' Association (CMTBA)
26 South Yue Tan Street
Beijing, China 100825
Tel: 868261 x2668   Fax: 8013472

Beijing Machine Tool Research Institute
Xiwen Village, Miyun Reservoir
Beijing, China 101512
Tel: Miyun telephone exchange, number 2448   Fax: 3017831

China Machinery Engineering Society
Beijing, China 100823
Tel: 863-597

Machine Tools Branch
China Chamber of Commerce for Import/Export of
Machinery and Electronics Products
127 Xuan Wu Men Xi Da Jie
Beijing, China 100031
Tel: 601-5627

Beijing No. 1 Machine Tool Plant
Chaoyang District, Beijing 100022
Tel: 5022981

MACHINERY

The machinery industry has been a leading priority since the founding of the People's Republic. The industry expanded from a few small assembly and repair facilities before 1949 to a large, widely distributed machine building sector producing many kinds of modern equipment. However, as of 1987, the overall level of technology was still relatively backward. In the late 1970s and early 1980s, China intended to use large scale imports to modernize the machinery industry, but later decided that limiting imports to critical areas would be less costly. The former Ministry of Machine Building Industry's plans called for about 60 percent of the industry's products in 1990 to reach the technological level of the industrialized countries during the 1970s and 1980s. Products built to international standards received priority in allocation of funds, materials, and energy.

In 1987 the machinery industry was distributed throughout the country. Nearly all counties and towns had one or more machine factories. Major machinery centers were Shanghai, Tianjin, Shenyang, Beijing, Harbin, Changchun, Taiyuan, Luoyang, Wuhan, Chongqing, Chengdu, Xi'an and Lanzhou.

The machinery industry was selected by the State Council to lead the way in management reform. China's leaders realized that the quality of machinery would determine the success of modernization in all areas of the economy. The industry's extreme compartmentalization (a legacy of the Maoist obsession with self-reliance) showed a lack of communication among government offices or within regions. Skilled managers also were lacking (4).

Some useful contacts in the machinery industry include:

Beijing General Gear Works
Chaoyang District, Beijing 100022
Tel: 7717722

Beijing Renmin General Machinery Plant
48 Dongsanhuan Nanlu
Chaoyang District, Beijing 100021
Tel: 781831

Chang'an Machinery Manufactory
Jiangbei, Chongqing
Sichuan Province 630023
Tel: 751921

Changfeng Machinery Plant
Anning District, Lanzhou
Gansu Province 730070
Tel: 67111

Changhong Machinery Plant
Mianyang, Sichuan Province 621000
Tel: 23032

Changjiang Machinery Manufactory
Gulou, Nanjing
Jiangsu Province 210009
Tel: 306678

Changling Machinery Plant
Weibin District, Baoji
Shaanxi Province 721006
Tel: 314433

Changzheng Machinery Plant
Baishagongnong District, Daxian
Sichuan Province 636452
Tel: 22970-401

Dalian Heavy Machinery Plant
Shahekou, Dalian
Liaoning Province 116022
Tel: 404201

Dongfang Electric Machinery Plant
Shizhong, Deyang
Sichuan Province 618000
Tel: 221209

Harbin Bearing Plant
Xiangfang, Harbin
Heilongjiang Province 150030
Tel: 55011

Harbin Electric Machinery Plant
Dongli District, Harbin
Heilongjiang Province 150040
Tel: 282625

Hebei Zhangjiakou Coal Mining Machinery Plant
Qiaodong, Zhangjiakou
Hebei Province 075025
Tel: 213291

Hengyang General Metallurgical Machinery Plant
Hengyang, Hunan Province 421002
Tel: 31011

Huanghe Machinery Manufacturing Plant
Xincheng, Xi'an
Shaanxi Province 710043
Tel: 331766

Huashan Machinery Plant
Xincheng, Xi'an
Shaanxi Province 710043
Tel: 335131-2204

Huizhou Precision Machine Company, Ltd.
No. 1 Eling Road, South, Huizhou
Guangdong Province 516000
Tel: 233114

Inner Mongolia No. 1 Machinery Plant
Qingshanqu, Baotou
Inner Mongolia 014032
Tel: 33011-4238

Inner Mongolia No. 2 Machinery Plant
Qingshanqu, Baotou
Inner Mongolia 014033
Tel: 33071

Jialing Machinery Plant
Shapingba, Chongqing
Sichuan Province 630032
Tel: 961991

Jiangling Machinery Plant
Jiangbei, Chongqing
Sichuan Province 630021
Tel: 752461

Jincheng Machinery Plant
Baixia District, Nanjing
Jingsu Province 210002
Tel: 646161-779

Laiyang General Power Machinery Plant
10 Wulong Beilu, Laiyang
Shangdong Province 265200
Tel: 831122

Liuzhou Engineering Machinery Plant
Liuzhou, Guanxi Province 545007
Tel: 335631

Nanfang Power Machinery Corporation
South District, Zhuzhou
Hunan Province 412002
Tel: 21151

Nanjing Chenguang Machinery Plant
Qinhua, Nanjing
Jiangsu Province 210012
Tel: 624471-252

No. 1 Heavy Machinery Plant
Eulan Ergi, Qiqihar
Heilongjiang Province 161042
Tel: 82901

No. 2 Heavy Machinery Plant
Shizhong District, Deyang
Sichuan Province 618013
Tel: 223909

Northeast Machinery Plant
Dadong, Shenyang
Liaoning Province 110045
Tel: 893834

Qinchuang Machinery Plant
Xincheng, Xi'an
Shaanxi Province 710043
Tel: 335771

Shanghai Electric Machinery (Group) Company
Huangpu District, Shanghai 200002
Tel: 3216390

Shanghai Electric Machinery Plant
Minhang District, Shanghai 200040
Tel: 2561057

Shanghai Gangkou Machinery Works
Nanshi District, Shanghai 200127
Tel: 8838400

Shanghai General Machinery (Group) Company
Hongkou District, Shanghai 200080

Shanghai Heavy Machinery Plant
Minhang District, Shanghai 200240
Tel: 4301141

Shanghai Xinzhonghua Machinery Plant
Minhang District, Shanghai 200240
Tel: 4301161

Shenyang Heavy Machinery Plant
Tiexi, Shenyang
Liaoning Province 110025
Tel: 555711

Taiyuan Heavy Machinery Plant
Hexi District, Taiyuan
Shanxi Province 030024
Tel: 666921

Tinjiang Electrical Machinery Factory
Jianshe Road, North, Chengdu
Sichuan Province 610067
Tel: 336613

Xi'an Power Machinery Manufacturing Company
Fengdeng Beilu, Lianhu District, Xi'an
Shaanxi Province 710077
Tel: 44805

Xiamen Engineering Machinery Works
Kaiyuan District, Xiamen
Fujian Province 361004
Tel: 224313

Xiangtan Electric Machinery Plant
Xiangtan, Hunan Province 411101
Tel: 21922

Xingtai Metallurgical Machinery Roller Plant
Qiaoxi, Xintai
Hebei Province 054025
Tel: 223911

Xuzhou Engineering Machinery Group Corporation
4 Kuangshan Donglu
Gulou, Xuzhou
Jiangsu Province 221006
Tel: 61361

MEDICAL EQUIPMENT

Table 100 summarizes some of the salient statistics concerning the medical equipment industry in China (3).

Table 100

Salient Statistics for the Medical Equipment Sector

A)	Three-letter ITA industry sector code:	MED
B)	Est. total market size (USD millions):	
	1991 -	$1,040
	1992 -	$1,100
	1993 -	$ 730
	1994 -	$ 850
	1995 -	$1,000
C)	Est. 1992-4 annual market growth rate:	8%
D)	Est. total imports (USD millions):	
	1991 -	$210
	1992 -	$230
	1993 -	$400
	1994 -	$500
	1995 -	$630
E)	Est. annual total import growth rate:	8%
F)	Est. imports from U.S. (USD millions):	
	1991 -	$ 50
	1992 -	$ 54
	1993 -	$164
	1994 -	$185
	1995 -	$230
G)	Est. annual growth of imports from U.S.:	8%
H)	China's receptivity to U.S. products in this sector (5 - High/1 - Low):	4
I)	Competition from local/third-countries for U.S. firms (5 - Low/1 - High):	3
J)	Chinese market barriers to U.S. sales in this sector (5 - Few/1 - Many):	3
K)	Comments - factors for increased U.S. sales:	

- High quality and good reputation of U.S. medical instruments.
- Many top Chinese doctors are U.S. educated and prefer U.S. equipment.
- Competition from the Germans and others are intense; the Germans invite Chinese doctors for training to promote equipment sales.
- Track developments in World Bank and other foreign agencies' medical research programs in China for sales opportunities.

L)	Most Promising Sub-sectors	1992 market size
	1. Ultrasonic diagnostic equipment	$100 million
	2. Computer tomography scanners	$100 million
	3. Electro-medical apparatus	$200 million

Overview As the Chinese economy continues to grow, and with it the expectations of the Chinese people, there is mounting pressure for improved health care (35). Furthermore, China's demographic profile is aging. In the future this will increasingly strain an already deficient medical network. As China moves toward fulfilling this increased demand, its medical industry will provide some attractive opportunities for U.S. medical equipment suppliers during the remainder of the Eighth Five-Year Plan (1991-1995).

The scale of the Chinese market for medical equipment, combined with the technological constraints of Chinese manufacturers, makes the market for high tech American equipment look strong for the foreseeable future. In 1992, the United States controlled 33% of the import market.

China has been deregulating hospitals. They are increasingly individually responsible for their own budgets. This includes both generation of income and expenditures. This new competitive environment is leading to a need for better facilities to draw fee-paying patients.

There are still sizeable barriers to free trade. These should be somewhat eased as the market access agreement signed last year is gradually implemented. Foreign exchange availability remains a serious problem.

Market Assessment China's market for medical equipment is expanding steadily. This growth was fueled by the population's increasing affluence and a strong demand for improved medical care.

Estimated 1993 import market shares:

U.S.	33%
Japan	31.5%
Germany	13.5%
Other	22% (France, U.K., Italy, Canada, Sweden)

Competitive Situation The 1990s should continue to be a decade of rapid growth for the Chinese health care system, thus also a decade of rapid growth for China's medical equipment industry. Due to the technological constraints on domestic suppliers, the market for high end imported medical technology should remain strong for the foreseeable future.

The Chinese medical equipment industry is composed of roughly 420 companies employing over 140,000 people. Most of these firms are small or medium-sized, employing an average of 320 people. A lack of technology and related manufacturing know how limits these firms to the production of mid-level instruments and apparatus. Except in isolated instances, American firms will probably not find it cost effective to compete with Chinese firms in low and mid-technology levels. The Chinese are able to cheaply meet basic demand in these areas of the market.

This is not to suggest there will be no domestic competition in the high technology arena. As in most other areas in the economy, the Chinese government is aware of the need for advanced technology within the medical industry and is actively encouraging joint venture production and technology transfer in this sector.

Foreign competition in China is fierce (34). Major suppliers continue to build their presence in China's high growth potential market. Joint venture production in the medical industry is estimated to be 20-25% of the total Chinese market. Major foreign players who have established representative offices of joint venture production in China include (35):

Name	Product Categories
Analogic Devices	MRI equipment, ultrasound, fetal monitoring
Siemens	X-ray, cross sectional imaging, nuclear medicine CT, MRIs
Nihon-Kohden	patient monitoring ECG
Hitachi	patient monitoring ultrasound
Hellige	bedside monitors, patient monitoring systems
China Hewlett-Packard	imaging systems, cardiology, patient monitoring, ultrasound
Marquette	ultrasound, patient monitoring, carbon dioxide monitoring
Acuson	ultrasound
Toshiba	X-ray, ultrasound
Baxter Healthcare	surgical instruments, oxygen/blood gas monitors
General Electric	CT scanners, X-ray, radiotherapy, MRA systems, ultrasound, nuclear medicine equipment
Shanghai Johnson & Johnson	adhesive bandages
Aloka	ultrasound

Since the modernization of China's health care system began in the 1980s, the above firms and numerous others have been supplying China with the equipment this modernization drive requires. Firms from the United States, Germany, and Japan have been the major players. These three countries account for nearly 80% of the import market. They are expected to maintain their dominance of the market, but their respective market shares relative to each other is expected to change.

In 1985, the United States controlled 17.5% of China's import market for the medical industry. By 1992, the U.S. share had grown to roughly 33%, with gross sales of US $145 million. During this time period, the German market share also grew, though not as dramatically, to 13.5%. The Japanese were quick to enter the Chinese medical market and have developed an early lead. Since then, however, their share has fallen sharply from its peak of 65% in 1985 to a more realistic 31.5% today.

The Chinese have the ability to manufacture most low technology medical equipment on their own. As such, the American manufacturer would do well to concentrate on the high tech areas where there is little or no domestic competition. In addition to quota, licensing, and substitution restrictions, foreign exchange difficulties make the purchase of imported gods which have a domestically produced equivalent relatively unattractive.

There are roughly three group of government run hospitals: public, military and industrial. Public hospitals are further subdivided according to the level of government to which they are responsible. This ranking broadly corresponds to the size of the institution and the degree of its technical sophistication. It also served as a good indicator of a facility's financial position and purchasing power.

- Central Government
- Provincial/Municipal/Autonomous Region
- City
- Country/District
- Township/Village/Neighborhood

At the Central Government level, the health system is administered by the Ministry of Public Health (MOPH). This includes clinics, hospitals, and medical colleges. MOPH reports directly to the State Council. It sets policy and supervises medical institutions and coordinates medical research. There are thirteen national medical colleges, each of which has two or three teaching hospitals.

MOPH does not directly manage institutions at the Provincial level and below. These are funded and administered by their respective local government's public health authority.

The organizations which use large quantities of medical equipment can generally be divided into seven categories:

- General Hospitals
- Specialized Hospitals
- University Medical Centers
- Medical Research Institutes/Laboratories

- Traditional Chinese Medical Hospitals
- General Clinics
- Health Care/Disease Prevention Centers

Because of difficulties involving demand, patient volume, and foreign exchange, only the first four on the above list are likely to be buyers of high tech American medical equipment. Traditional Chines medicine hospitals, for example, do not require imported equipment. Those further down the list are just too small to easily justify such purchases.

Institutions at the central government or provincial levels, and perhaps at the city level in some cases, should be considered prospective end-users of advanced imported medical equipment. Institutions at the city level and below are often not big enough or well enough funded to shop for such items.

The People's Liberation Army (PLA) operates its won network of three hundred hospitals and four medical colleges, providing care for China's 3.1 million servicemen and their families. These institutions tend to be well-funded and very well equipped. The PLA's health care network is highly centralized. All major acquisitions are through the Logistics Health Administration.

A relatively small number of hospitals are administered by Ministries of the central government or large state-owned enterprises. Each ministry has a medical service bureau which is responsible for the planning, finance, and administration of a small health care network for its own employees. Major decisions on investments are generally made at the highest levels of these bureaus or above.

Although the hospitals are still nominally funded by the state, there is a clear and definite shift away from the state paying for medical care. This has had a profound affect on the Chinese medical industry. Medical care in China used to be another handout from the government, rationed on the basis of political and bureaucratic status. Today the situation is reversing. Hospitals are increasingly responsible for generating revenue. More importantly, they are allowed to keep much of the revenue they generate. This has created a competitive environment among Chinese hospitals which did not previously exist. In order to meet their budgets they must increasingly compete for patients. In order to be competitive, they must modernize their facilities.

Best Sales Prospects

Equipment Category	Product
Electro-medical apparatus scanners	B-mode ultrasonic sector; doppler ultrasound apparatus; cardiac defibrillating and monitoring apparatus; kidney lithotripters; electrocardiographs; patient monitoring systems; pulmonary testing systems.

Radiological apparatus	X-ray machines (800 mA and up, those used for angiography); CT scanners; MRI systems.
Clinical Laboratory equipment	Ultraspeed centrifuges; multi-functional biochemical analyzers; liquid/gas chromatographs; blood gas analyzers.
Mechano-therapy and respiration equipment	Carbon dioxide incubator; medium-range ventilators and anesthesia equipment; heart-lung machines; physical therapy equipment.
Medical and surgical instruments	Endoscopes; cardiac catheters.

Useful key contacts:

Import/Export Corporations

China National Medicine and Health Products Import/Export Corporation
L Suite, Huiyuan Apartments
8 Anding Road, Anding Menwai
Beijing 100101
Fax: 491-7462; 491-7476

China National Medicine and Health Products Import/Export Corporation
U.S. Branch
1044 Route 23, Suite 102
Wayne, New Jersey 07470
Tel: 201-633-6606 Fax: 201-633-6336

China National Medical Equipment & Supplies Import/Export Corporation
44 Bei Heyan, Huohai
Beijing 100725
Tel: 403-4433 x392, 350 Fax: 401-2327

China National Pharmaceutical Foreign Trade Corporation
38A, Beilishi Lu, Xizhimenwai
Beijing 100810
Tel: 831-6572 Fax: 831-6571

China National Medicine Corporation
38-A Beilishi Lu, Xizhimenwai
Beijing 100810
Tel: 831-3234, 831-8311

China National Medical Equipment Industry Corporation
Business Development Division
2 Bei San Huan Zhong Road
Beijing
Tel: 201-3407, 202-4222 x275

China National Machinery Import and Export Corporation
(Machimpex)
Import Building, Erligou, Xijiao, Beijing 100044
Fax: 831-4143

China National Instruments Import and Export Corporation
(Instrimpex)
Import Building, Erligou, Western Suburb, Beijing
Fax: 831-8380, 831-5925

Trade Associations

China Chamber of Commerce of Medicines & Health Products Import & Export
Building 12, Jianguomen Wai Street
Beijing, China 100022
Tel: (861) 500-4433 x2099   Fax: 506-2325

Government Organizations

Ministry of Public Health
Department of Foreign Affairs
44 Bei Heyan, Huo Hai
Beijing 100725
Tel: 401-4338   Fax: 401-4332

State Pharmaceutical Administration
38 (a) Beilishi Lu
Beijing, China 100810
Foreign Affairs Bureau, Zhang Yajun
Tel: 831-334 x1002   Fax: 831-5648
Planning Bureau, Zhang Ruqi
Tel: 831-3344 x0712   Fax: 831-8696

Economic Coordination Bureau, Tang Hong
Tel: 831-3344 x0609

Ministry of Foreign Technology and Economic Corporation
2 Dongchang 'An Street, Dongcheng District
Beijing, China 100731
Tel: 519-8804   Fax: 519-8904

Foreign Medical Trading Firms

The East Asiatic Company Ltd. (EAC)
35 Dongzhimenwai Street
Beijing 100027
Tel: 467-8888   Fax: (861) 467-2200, 467-2500

U.S. China Industrial Exchange Incorporated
#7 Xiao Piafang Hutong
Beijing, China 100010
Tel: 512-6662   Fax: 512-9903

End-user Hospitals

Asia Emergency Assistance
1010, 10/f China World Tower, CWTC
1 Jianguomenwai Dajie
Beijing, China 100004
Fax: 505-3526

Beijing Chest Diseases Hospital
Wenquan, Haidianqu
Beijing, China 100095

Beijing Emergency Medical Center
103 Qianmen Xi Dajie
Beijing, China 100004

Cardiovascular Institute and Fuwai Hospital
167A Beilshi Lu
Fuchengmenwai, Beijing, China 100037

Guangdong People's Hospital
Zhongshan Er Lu
Guangzhou, China 510080

Guangzhou Overseas Chinese Hospital
Shipai
Guangzhou, China 5103632

Cancer Hospital
Dongfeng Dong Lu
Guangzhou, China 510060

Dahua Hospital
Baoging Lu
Shanghai, China 200031

Huashan Hospital (Shanghai Medical University)
12 Wulumugi Zhong Lu
Shanghai, China 200040

Shanghai First Maternity and Infant Health Hospital
536 Changle Lu, Jinganqu
Shanghai, China 200040

Shanghai Children's Hospital
2 Kangding Lu
Shanghai, China 200041

Tianjin Childrens Hospital
1 Tonglou Dajie, Hexiqu
Tianjin, China 300074

Tianjin First Center Hospital
162 Munan Dao
Hepingqu, Tianjin, China 3000504

METALLURGICAL EQUIPMENT (INCLUDING FOUNDRY)

Much equipment in the metallurgical industry was based on Japanese designs of the 1930s and Soviet designs of the 1950s. Two-thirds of the major equipment at Anshan, one of the largest plants in China, was built during the 1930s and 1950s. In general, major metallurgical equipment was more technologically advanced than instruments and control systems. Measuring and monitoring instruments, essential to quality control, were in short supply.

Most of the iron- and steel-making equipment in general use was domestically produced. This included blast furnaces based on Chinese improvements to old Soviet designs, ore-beneficiation plants, open-hearth furnaces, electric furnaces, and a wide range of steel-finishing equipment. To achieve a higher technological level, various pieces of equipment were imported because China had not assimilated the technology necessary for domestic production. In most instances, the industry imported only the main equipment, neglecting necessary control instruments and auxiliary technologies (4).

Overview   During the Eighth Five-Year Plan (1991-1996), China will stress the modernization of its metallurgical industry—and this modernization program will require high quality foundry equipment. It is not likely that China's domestic foundry equipment manufacturers will be able to meet the country's growing demand. (The technology levels of domestic foundry equipment is generally low, and quality often does not reach international standards.) Therefore, much essential foundry equipment will be imported. U.S. companies face stiff competition from Japanese and European competitors (who often have access to attractive concessionaire loan packages offered by their own governments). Nevertheless, U.S. foundry equipment enjoys a good reputation in China, and a good number of U.S. companies have discovered ways to successfully compete in this market (36).

China has thirty-eight foundry machinery factories, with thirty of these specializing in foundry equipment. Major foundry machinery producers are located in Qingdao (Shandong), Baoding (Hebei), Luohe (Henan), Suzhou (Jiangsu) and Chongqing (Sichuan). China now produces over 260 different types of foundry machinery. However, much of this equipment lags well behind international standards of the 1990s.

During the Eighth Five-Year Plan (1991-1996), China's central planners want to upgrade the foundry industry. Since China's domestic foundry equipment industry cannot meet the nation's need for modern foundry machinery, much of the machinery will have to be imported.

Multilateral donor programs will also encourage the development of China's foundry industry. For example, the United Nations Development Program (UNDP) will assist China with a USD 12 million project to upgrade China's machine tool industry. Part of the funds will be used to modernize China's foundry industry.

The China National Machine Tool and Tool Builders' Association (CNMTBA) estimates that total annual output of metal castings in China is about 10 million tons—though most of this output does not meet the quality standards of developed countries. China's Eighth Five-Year Plan (1991-1996) calls for development of the country's metallurgical industry. For example, China plans to upgrade the facilities of several major iron and steel bases, in order to bring these bases up to the level of the more modern Baoshan Iron and Steel complex.

Since China treats foundry equipment as part of its machine tool sector, U.S. foundry equipment vendors will want to direct their China marketing efforts at major machine tool organizations as well as metallurgical facilities.

Competitive Situation

1. Domestic Production At present, much of China's domestically produced foundry equipment does not meet international standards of the 1990s. As a result, domestic production can only satisfy part of China's need for modern foundry equipment (see "Market Assessment").

But although most Chinese foundry equipment has not yet reached international quality levels, China does have modest, but growing exports in this sector. During the Eighth Five-Year Plan, Chinese authorities want to double the value of China's machine tool exports, and we expect that the foundry equipment sub-sector (if not able to double its export value) will at least see steady export growth.

2. Imports and U.S. Market Position We expect a modest (2-3%) growth in imports over the next three to five year (see "Statistical Data"). U.S. exporters will continue to meet their major competition from Japanese and German companies. In addition, French, Swiss, Swedish and British companies will continue to be competitive in rolling mill equipment and technology.

3. Competitive Factors U.S. foundry equipment manufacturers enjoy a good reputation with Chinese end-users, but Chinese buyers often look to tied soft/mixed loans to help finance their purchases. Here, U.S. exporters often find themselves at a serious disadvantage with competitors from Japan and Europe, because these competitors are sometimes able to use extremely attractive concessionaire loan packages offered by their own governments. (The "war chest" of the U.S. Eximbank is only used to match such offers in unusual cases where the offering government violates OECD rules concerning notice requirements or minimum grant percentages.)

U.S. companies can help their competitive position by familiarizing themselves and their customers with the Eximbank programs which are available to them. For example, Chinese buyers also show interest in export credit programs—such as those offered by Eximbank and the export-import banks of other countries. Eximbank has been very active in China and is able, under certain circumstances, to offer credit at the "OECD consensus rate" (currently 9.3 percent).

Best Sales Prospects

Best sales prospects include:

Melting and secondary refining:

-- Hot blast cupolas.
-- Holding furnaces for iron and non-ferrous metals.
-- Electric arc furnaces (including direct arc furnaces).
-- Electronic beam melting technology.
-- Plasma melting technology.
-- Powder injection metallurgy.
-- Electroflux refining furnace and process.
-- Secondary refining process and equipment for molten metal (including ladle metallurgy, vacuum treatment, ephosphorization and desulphurization for molten iron and steel).
-- Automatic metered pouring furnaces.
-- Inoculation, modification and nodularization of molten iron (equipment and processes).

Sand preparation and reclamation:

-- Sand preparation plant.
-- Metering and transportation equipment for loose material.
-- Sand mixers (including greensand, drysand and no-bake sand).
-- Sand reclamation equipment for resin-bonded sand and silicate-bonded sand.
-- Automatic greensand moisture control equipment.
-- Sand properties automatic control apparatus.
-- Cooling equipment for molding sand.

Molding, casting and knockout:

-- Modern high pressure molding machines and lines (including extrusion molding lines).
-- Air impact or air impulse molding lines.
-- V-process molding lines.
-- Automated molding lines for flexible production.
-- No-bake molding lines.
-- Shell molding lines.
-- Centrifugal casting machines for ductile iron pipes and centrifugal casting.
-- Die casting machines and automatic control equipment.
-- Low pressure die casting equipment and processes.
-- Horizontal continuous casting equipment and processes for ferrous and non-ferrous metals.
-- Lost wax casting equipment and processes.
-- Plaster casting.

-- Cavityless casting.
-- Shakeout machines (including cooling drum).
-- Cooling equipment for used sand.

Coremaking

-- Resin coating sand equipment.
-- Shell core machines and processes.
-- Hot and cold box core machines.
-- Warm box or the Q-process core machines.
-- Fast setting cold box shooters.

Fettling and coating:

-- Shot blast machines and cabinets.
-- Robots for gate and riser cutting, grinding operations.
-- Continuous cleaning drums.
-- Automatic cleaning lines for mass production.
-- Coating equipment and productions lines for castings.

Pattern making:

-- Pattern making equipment.
-- New pattern making materials.
-- Pattern design technology.

Melting control:

-- CO_2, SO_2 analyzers.
-- Spectrometers.
-- Hydrogen, nitrogen and oxygen microanalyzers.
-- Thermal analyzers for quick CE determinations.
-- Quick determinations for nodule count.
-- Automatic control for cupola blast.

Metallurgical quality control and metallurgical microanalysis:

-- Optical metallographic microscopes and image analysis systems.
-- Electron microprobe and scanning electron microscope analyzers.
-- X-ray diffractometers and fluorescence.
-- X-ray spectrometers.
-- X-ray defect detectors.
-- Linear accelerators.

-- Magnetic particle flaw detectors.
-- Fluorescent flaw detectors.
-- Ultrasonic flaw detectors.
-- Various non-destructive testing instruments for detection of physical properties of metals.

Pollution control:

-- Dust and hazardous gas extraction equipment for foundry processes.
-- Noise control equipment.

Foundry supplies:

-- Organic binders.
-- New silicate and other inorganic binders.
-- Mould and core washers.
-- Innoculants, nodification and nodularization agents, etc.
-- Metal filters.

Materials testing:

-- Sand testing machines.
-- Hardness testers (for metal).
-- Hardness testers (for sand molds).

Miscellaneous: quality control equipment and instruments and microprocessors for foundry process country.

Used foundry equipment: Overall, the market for used machinery is good. Chinese will often seriously consider buying used equipment in order to save scarce hard currency.

Useful Key Contacts:

Department of Machine Tools and Tools
Ministry of Machinery and Electronics Industries (MMEI)
Sanlihe Road
Beijing, China 100823
Tel: 867345 Fax: 867745

China National Machine Tool Corporation (CNMTC)
19 Fang Jia Alley, An Nei
Beijing, China 100007
Tel: 401-4855, 485-431 Fax: 401-5657

International Cooperation Department
China Machine Tool and Tool Builders' Association (CMTBA)
26 South Yue Tan Street
Beijing, China 100825
Tel: 868261 x2668   Fax: 8013472

Foundry Machinery Builders' Association (FMBA)
(also called Jinan Foundry and Metalforming Machinery Research Institute)
Number 646, Jing Shi Road
Jinan 250022, China
Tel: 37351

China Foundry Association (CFA)
277 Wang Fujing Street
Beijing, China 100740
Tel: 5126679, 558821 x320, x347   Fax: 5126675

Beijing Machine Tool Research Institute
Xiwen Village, Miyun Reservoir
Beijing, China 101512
Tel: Miyun telephone exchange, 2448   Fax: 3017831

China Machinery Engineering Society
Beijing, China 100823
Tel: 863-597

Machine Tools Branch
China Chamber of Commerce for Import/Export of
Machinery and Electronics Products
127 Xuan Wu Men Xi Da Jie
Beijing, China 100031
Tel: 601-5627

Some useful contacts in the non-ferrous metals industry include:

Baiyin Non-Ferrous Metal Company
Baiyin, Gansu Province 730900
Tel: 22560

Beijing Non-Ferrous Metal Industrial Corporation
Xuanwu District, Beijing 100053
Tel: 3021527

Daye Non-Ferrous Metal Company
Xialu, Huangshi
Hubei Province 435005
Tel: 392027

Fankou Lead & Zinc Mine
Renhua County, Shaoguan
Guangdong Province 512325
Tel: 880531

Huize Lead & Zinc Mine
Huize County, Qujing
Yunnan Province 654211

Huladao Zinc Plant
Huladao, Jinxi
Liaoning Province 121009
Tel: 201431

Jiangxi Copper Industrial Corporation
Guixi, Yingtan
Jiangxi Province 335424
Tel: 771913

Jiangxi Non-Ferrous Metal Processing Factory
Yiyang County, Shangrao
Jiangxi Province 334400
Tel: 22527

Jinchuan Non-Ferrous Metal Company
Jinchuan, Jinchang
Gansu Province 737100
Tel: 5230

Lanjiang Smeltery
Lanxi, Zhejiang Province 321100
Tel: 222411

Luoyang Copper Processing Plant
Jianxi, Luoyang
Henan Province 471039
Tel: 222411

Shanghai Non-Ferrous Metal Company
Hongkou District, Shanghai 200080
Tel: 3254100

Shaoguan Smeltery
Shaoguan, Guangdong Province 512024
Tel: 772985

Shenyang Metal Smeltery
Tiexi, Shenyang
Liaoning Province 110025
Tel: 551411

Shenyang Non-Ferrous Metal Processing Factory
Sujiatun District, Shenyang
Liaoning Province 110102
Tel: 982521

Taiyuan Copper Industrial Company
Nancheng, Taiyuan
Shanxi Province 030012
Tel: 773136

Tianjin Electrocopper Factory
Dongjiao, Tianjin 300240
Tel: 621173

Tongling Non-Ferrous Metal Corporation
Tongguanshan, Tongling
Anhui Province 244001
Tel: 34367

Wuhu Smeltery
Sihe District, Wuhu
Anhui Province 241009
Tel: 51988

Yunnan Metal Smeltery
Xishan, Kunming
Yunnan Province 650102
Tel: 81131

Yunnan Tin Industrial Company
Geiju City, Yunnan Province 661400
Tel: 6152

Zhongtiaoshan Non-Ferrous Metal Corporation
Yuanqu County, Yuncheng
Shanxi Province 043700
Tel: 23001

Zhouzhou Metal Smeltery
North District, Zhuzhou
Hunan Province 412004
Tel: 31431

MINING EQUIPMENT

Table 101

Salient Statistics for the Mining Industry Equipment Sector

A) Three-letter ITA industry sector code: MIN
B) Est. total market size (USD millions):
    1991 - $1,590
    1992 - $1,829
    1993 - $1,362
    1994 - $1,867
    1995 - $2,598
C) Est. 1992-4 annual market growth rate: 15%
D) Est. total imports (USD millions):
    1991 - $ 295
    1992 - $ 339
    1993 - $ 665
    1994 - $ 997
    1995 - $1,496
E) Est. annual total import growth rate: 15%
F) Est. imports from U.S. (USD millions):
    1991 - $180
    1992 - $198
    1993 - $136
    1994 - $156
    1995 - $180 (58)
G) Est. annual growth of imports from U.S.:   10%
H) China's receptivity to U.S. products in
    this sector (5 - High/1 - Low):   4
I) Competition from local/third countries
    for U.S. firms (5 - Low/1 - High):   4
J) Chinese market barriers to U.S. sales
    in this sector (5 - Few/1 - Many):   4
K) Comments - factors for increased U.S. sales:
    • High quality of U.S. equipment and services.
    • U.S. vendors developing greater familiarity with market.
    • Strong emphasis by Chinese government on mining, especially for coal, in Eighth Five-Year
       Plan.
    • Demand for more energy in China translates into greater demand for coal and the equipment
       to mine it.

L) Most Promising Sub-sectors	1992 market size
1. Open-pit mining equipment (trucks, power shovels, etc.)	$100 million
2. Boring and sinking machinery	$ 20 million
3. Parts for boring and sinking machinery	$ 15 million
4. Parts for derricks	$ 10 million

Overview   China offers a potentially large market for U.S. manufactured open pit and underground mining equipment and mining related services. The Chinese government has made mining development one of the priority areas of the Eighth Five-Year economic plan. Many new mines are being developed, and equipment and services are being upgraded in older mines (37).

The major force creating this market is the fact that China's coal supply falls far short of meeting demand. Furthermore, there is a strong need to export minerals to acquire foreign exchange. Needs include not only digging and moving equipment, but also services (e.g. computerized systems) designed to improve mine safety and efficiency. Development of this market is directly related to other markets—e.g. sales to China of railroad equipment needed to improve the transportation of minerals from mines to coastal ports, sales to China of coal-utilizing power plants, etc.

A range of factors will influence changes in this market vis-a-vis U.S. sales prospects. First is the availability or non-availability to U.S. firms of funding. Japan will continue to play a very important role in financing all kinds of projects and, directly or indirectly, the purchases of U.S. equipment and services. A third important factor is who in China will control the mines—the central government or local/regional entities. A fourth factor which influences changes in this market, albeit indirectly, is whether China will be able to improve its transportation system. There are shortages of train, cars, and track.

Mining—particularly coal mining—is so important to the PRC that national leaders have, on occasion, put their personal stamp on major projects (e.g. Deng Xiao Ping's endorsement of the Antaibao project).

While the central government frequently supports big projects and purchases, state-owned mines cannot meet the markets' demands, and so more and more private or semi-private mining operations are developing. State-owned coal mines are under the jurisdiction of the Ministry of Energy (MOE). Minmetals, the government agency controlling mines, has set mining priorities, policies and import purchase requirements. However, in recent years, due to the decentralization of decision-making, more and more purchasing decisions are made at the mines themselves. If the central government loosens controls over mining equipment and services purchases, U.S. firms may be able to increase sales. However, decentralization has also led, in some cases, to bureaucratic inertia. The U.S. executive selling into this market must make certain that whatever entity he or she is dealing with has the funds and authorization to make the purchases in question.

Market Assessment Market demand for mining equipment and services is driven primarily by coal mining. Demand for coal far outstrips supply in China. This is primarily because of artificially low, government set prices and bottlenecks in the country's transportation system, not only because production is low at the mines themselves. Domestic demand is expected to increase about 50 percent between now and the year 2000. Short-term prospects for sales of coal abroad have recently been weak—about USD 30 per ton, compared with almost USD 609 per ton a decade ago. However, since Japan reportedly plans 10,000 MW of additional coal-fired power capacity by the year 2000, and since Taiwan and the ASEAN countries are expected to double their coal requirements by the mid to late 1990s, the prospects in the future for increases in demands for U.S. coal mining equipment look good. The increased Japanese capacity alone will require an extra 15 to 18 million tons of coal per year. This is about double the entire 1990 output of the Antiabao mine.

A number of other factors affect prospects for marketing U.S. equipment and services. First, China is heavily dependent upon coal; about three-quarters of the nation's energy is from this source. Such heavy dependence creates a rather solid demand base. Furthermore, the country's reserves—some two trillion tons—are huge. There is enough to last for about 2,000 years. PRC coal production has almost doubled between 1980 and 1990—from about 600 million metric tons (MMT) to around 1.1 billion metric tons annually.

New projects also affect market prospects. In early 1990, the central government started to invest one billion yuan (about USD 200 million) in the Jungar Coal Mine in Inner Mongolia. This is the PRC's largest open-cast coal mine. (Almost all government coal mines are underground operations.)

Still another factor affecting demand is the aging of the PRC's equipment. Only about 1/3 of China's mines are fully mechanized. Equipment bought in 1983, when the coal mining industry in China was overhauled, is beginning to wear out and will need to be replaced. Conclusion: Demand for U.S. equipment and services in this sub-sector should be quite strong. However, because the central government artificially sets coal prices very low, many of the big mines operate in the red and do not have extra funds to purchase U.S. or other foreign equipment.

A field related to coal mining in which the Chinese have expressed interest is methane recovery technology. One source estimates that China's coal reserves contain about four trillion cubic meters of methane.

Demand for U.S. equipment and services in the non-coal mining area varies to some extent relative to major new national projects. For example, in 1993, work to expand the PRC's largest nickel production facility, in Gansu Province, is scheduled to be completed. The Jinchuan Nonferrous Metals Corporation there has signed many contracts with foreign firms for mining machines. Total production during the first quarter of 1991 of the ten major non-ferrous metals—copper, aluminum, lead, zinc, nickel, tin, antimony, mercury, magnesium, and titanium—was up about 11 percent over the first quarter of 1989, suggesting that orders for more machinery in this area could be in the offing. Some of the new orders could be associated with the development in Inner Mongolia of big zinc, lead, copper, silver, and molybdenum mines. China's plans to double its steel production by the year 2000 can provide opportunities for U.S. firms to sell mining equipment for iron ore, chrome, magnesium, and gold. In early 1991, CNNC proposed to the Japan-China Nonferrous Metals Group of the Japan International Trade Promotion Association (JITPA), that they undertake eight joint venture mineral resources development projects in China. If JITPA approves even some of these plans, the demand for heavy U.S. mining equipment could increase dramatically. Included are copper (reserves 226 million tons), lead/zinc (200 million tons), titanium sponge (7,000 tons/year), lithium salt (1,600 tons/day), aluminum, and rare metal sand operations.

The principal government end-user groups are as follows:

Electrical power plants throughout the nation.

China National Coal Development Corporation (CNCDC).

Ping Shuo First Coal Corporation (PSF), CNCDC.

China National Local Coal Mines Development Corporation (CNLCMDC).

China National Coal Import and Export Corporation (CNCIEC), which handles almost all of China's coal exports.

China National Nonferrous Metals Industry Corporation (CNNC).

Beijing General Research Institute of Mining and Metallurgy (BGRIMM).

Private and semi-private (joint venture) end-users include:

Antaibao Coal Mine, Shanxi Province. This is a long shot as a potential significant end-user; it depends on how much additional capital the new managers infuse into the mine. Mines in regions where ordinary citizens need the gas for heating and cooking are the primary end-users of recovered methane equipment and services. (Figures for the percentage of consumption and percentage of imports consumed by the above end-users are not available.)

Private or semi-private demand for mining equipment and services is growing, since public-sector mines cannot meet the demands of the market. This may create opportunities for U.S. sales that did not exist before, but the U.S. firm must be cautious about trying to sell to entities which may not have foreign exchange and/or may not have the authority to make significant equipment purchases.

In general, U.S. equipment and services in this sub-sector are some of the best in the world and are well-regarded in the PRC.

The centralization/decentralization situation as it affects the mining equipment and services sub-sector is, as of mid-1991, confused in China. In 1989, for example, the government introduced the "divide the pot and eat" policy, under which coal consumers could invest in coal production. In 1990, however, there was the beginning of a return to centralization, contested, of course, by the provinces.

Centrally-controlled coal mines account for about 50% of China's coal production, but this percentage will undoubtedly decrease, since the government mines will probably continue to be unable to meet the targets set in the Eighth Five-Year Plan; local mines will make up more and more of the difference. In the mid-1980s, there were about 80,000 mines owned by provinces, counties, towns, and individuals.

According to some analysts, big coal mining operations in China require a centralized infrastructure and fuel supply. Since, by the late 1980s, the mines' bureaucracy was anarchic, operation and expansion of existing locations was very difficult. Weak authority over decision-making on (a) provision of enough fuel oil, (b) the supply of enough coal transporting rail cars, and (c) the timely completion of rail links to seaports reportedly was a major factor in the decision by foreign investors in the Antaibao mine to decide to sell their shares in that operation.

Competitive Situation

1. Domestic Production Chinese-made equipment is, to a gradually growing extent, a source of competition for U.S. imports locally. It dominates the low-technology part of this sub-sector market, and Chinese capabilities to produce higher technology equipment are slowly increasing. However, there is a continuing need for medium and high-tech equipment from abroad. One example—Chinese equipment in Antaiboa's coal washing plant reportedly did not operate well. The Coal Science Academy, Pingdingshan Coal Dressing Design Academy, Chinese Mining University, Northeast China College of Engineering, Luoyang Mining Machinery Plant, Sino-Japanese Joint Investment Chengcheng Electronics Company, and the East China Coal Company System are all engaged in developing and producing new mining equipment for this sub-sector. For there to be an increase in the number of joint ventures producing mining equipment there would probably have to be both (1) a much stronger market for the products of China's mines, leading to heavy demands for more equipment, and (2) a big push by the Chinese government to encourage joint ventures in this field. At present, neither (1) nor (2) seems to be operative.

2. Imports Imports play an important role in meeting total market demand in the mining area. The extent to which they are a source of competition with locally-produced equipment depends, to a certain degree, on one's perspective. If one is with a Chinese enterprise needing top quality equipment, a direct and immediate purchase from abroad is probably desirable. If one is with a Chinese ministry charged with securing foreign technology transfers and encouraging local production through joint ventures or by Chinese firms alone, a local purchase is probably preferable.

The reasons for the three year growth figure includes the following: First, the Chinese government is emphasizing the further development of mining—particularly coal mining—in the Eighth Five-Year Plan. Second, foreign firms, including U.S. companies, are becoming more skillful and sophisticated in selling mining equipment and services in China. Third, the Chinese are under pressure to "buy American," and mining equipment is clearly a sub-sector where significant purchases should be possible.

Imports do not meet market demand in this sub-sector. Very few or none of the pieces of equipment imported from abroad are re-exported.

There have been some shifts in Chinese policy and practice in sourcing from market vs. non-market economies but, to some degree, this is now a moot question, since many of the Eastern European economies have become partially or wholly market-oriented and that of the U.S.S.R. is in a state of confusion and transition. Low cost equipment has been sold to China from the former Soviet camp countries for decades, the quantity increasing during periods of political warming; relations between the PRC and all eastern European countries are reasonably good now, so purchases of both services and equipment have probably increased recently. Eastern European countries have considerable mining experience.

Examples of imported equipment and technology are the following: USSR, plans for a coal works site in Shanxi; valves, control systems, pumps and a feasibility study for a slurry pipeline; coal dressing factory; Czechoslovakia, technology and equipment; France, a gasification plant; Japan, coal handling machinery; UK, a coal preparation plant.

3. U.S. Market Position and Share Imports from the U.S. have increased for the reasons cited above—U.S. experience, Chinese need, and pressures on the Chinese to buy U.S. products. As long as U.S. companies maintain their technological superiority, and as long as China has the foreign exchange to pay for our products, the U.S. position in this market should remain good. As local capabilities to produce equipment and provide services gradually improve, the U.S. and other foreign suppliers will have to give up the lower end of the market. The U.S. position vis-a-vis third country suppliers depends heavily on the availability to third country competitors of mixed credit financing, U.S. government (FCS and other agencies) support for U.S. sales efforts, and the willingness of competing nations' governments to continue high pressure, low cost sales programs for their own products.

Prominent U.S. suppliers in this sub-sector include Joy Manufacturing Company, Mine Safety Appliances Company, Montana College of Mineral Science and Technology, Philadelphia Mixers Company, Euclid, WABCO, Allis Chalmers, and Rexnord. These and other U.S. firms have supplied coal conversion technology, heavy trucks, drilling assistance and equipment, gasification equipment, and a wide variety of other skills and items.

Prominent third country suppliers in this market include USINOR SR (France), Hong Kong Industrial Trading Company, Ltd., (former) East German Government, Japanese Government, Shichester Diamond Services Ltd., subs. of De Beers Consolidated Mines Ltd. (South Africa), National Research Institute for Metals (Japan), Broken Hill Proprietary Company Limited (BHP) (UK), Kreditanstalt fur Wiederauf Bank (FRG), Energy Department of the Ministry of Trade and Industry (Japan), Funke, Huster and Company (FRG), City Resources (Asia) Company Ltd. (HK), NA Company (HK), Metal Mining Agency of Japan, Japan International Cooperation Agency, Magran Marble Industrial Corporation, Ltd. (Macao), Tamrock Company (Finland), Murphy Group (Australia), Reliance Group (HK), Agency of Natural Resources under MITI (Japan), NA Company (France), Plenty Mixers (UK), Orion Yhtyma Oy Normet (Finland).

4. Competitive Factors There are a number of reasons why certain firms get business in this market. First in importance are price and credit availability. The final price is often determined by the availability (or lack) of mixed credit financing, plus the offering of "sweeteners." U.S. firms are, in some cases, teaming up with Japanese firms to promote sales in China, the U.S. firm providing the equipment or technology while the Japanese provide the financing. The Japanese, and other foreign, loan factor, is very important; if Japanese loans are truly as advertised, then U.S. firms will continue to play a strong role in this market. Another factor related to financing is the studies of the U.S. Trade and

Development Program (TDP). These studies can lead to U.S. contracts. TDP programs are, at present, suspended in China.

Quality is another reason why certain firms secure contracts in this area. U.S. mining equipment is generally considered second to none in the world. Chinese mines, geological conditions, weather, and terrain bear, in many cases, a close resemblance to those in the U.S. Related to this is reputation. A number of U.S. mining equipment and services firms already have good "guan-xi" (relationships) with Chinese officials and engineers. Some Chinese in the PRC bureaucracy, or at the mines themselves, may already have formed alliances—open or secret—with U.S. or certain third country firms. This situation gives such companies an inside track on mining equipment contracts.

Service and, in particular, the provision of spare parts, is another important factor in securing contracts. Active selling at the mine site has been cited by a foreign equipment salesmen as a critical factor in getting the mining equipment business. Salesmen who prefer the high life of Beijing to going out to the mines themselves, are probably losing big sales.

Environmental concerns are gradually attracting more concern from Chinese enterprises and officials. As a result, the import climate for methane-recovery technology is good; the Chinese have shown strong interest in equipment and services in this area.

U.S. firms can improve their competitive standing in this sub-sector by developing a thorough understanding of what mixed credits may be available to them and to their foreign competitors by inviting—when appropriate—potential Chinese buyers to the U.S.A. to see equipment in operation, by developing a close liaison with the local American Chamber of Commerce, U.S.-China Business Council representative, and FCS officers, by patiently engaging, over a long period of time, in detailed research, by developing, again over an extended period of time, close relations with Chinese buyers, and by visiting the mines.

Market Access

1.   Import Climate   Trade regulations do not appear to constitute important impediments to doing business in this particular market. Business seems to be demand-driven, so the major "impediments" are indirect—e.g. lack of international demand for minerals, inability to transport the minerals to Chinese ports from the mines, below market, state-determined prices for minerals, and similar issues. The general character of the PRC's centrally-controlled economy is, perhaps, the biggest impediment to more business, as is simple lack of credit locally. Recent economic austerity program and credit crunch may be easing somewhat, the central authorities are not moving as fast as U.S. companies would like to liberalize overall business conditions and free up credit.

A factor which can be either an impediment or an incentive depending upon the particular circumstances is the problem of centralization vs. decentralization of mining operations and control in China. The mid-1980's trend toward decentralization was followed, in the late 1980s and 1990, by a trend toward centralization. Now, forces in the provinces and at the mines themselves are demanding a stronger share in business decisions. The situation is, thus, in flux. Another factor which can cut both ways, is the growing sources of funds—at the central, provincial, municipal, and mining enterprise level. Proliferation can mean more money is available to purchase U.S. equipment. It can also mean more confusion. A major "incentive" int he market right now is the government's emphasis on mining expansion. Even without the special emphasis, however, the market is still a promising one since it is "basic infrastructure" and may thus be somewhat immune to the ups and downs of the general Chinese economy.

The best way to cope with these problems and benefit from the built-in "incentive" int his market is hard work, combined with patience and lots of "hands-on salesmanship.

"Meeting Chinese technical or safety standards" does not seem to be an issue in this sub-sector since, in general, foreign equipment technical levels are higher than local ones.

2. Distribution and Business Practices in this Sub-sector There are at least two practices in this market which can affect sales of U.S. equipment and services. First, the Chinese sometimes express the wish to keep their equipment standardized to save money on operational training and spare parts. U.S. mining equipment is already standard in some parts of China's mining industry, and U.S. firms should take advantage of this fact.

Second, the Chinese sometimes state that they want to buy the most modern, top quality mining equipment money can buy. When this is the case, U.S. products generally have the edge over cheaper, but lower quality mining equipment from, for example, eastern Europe.

Practices in this market which may impede the sales of U.S. equipment include the following: First, the Chinese occasionally ignore the technical superiority of U.S. equipment, preferring to buy from another country which can offer a larger and/or more advantageous mix of credits and soft loans.

Second, the Chinese sometimes buy from others because U.S. companies are not aggressive or personal enough in pressing their sales. In certain cases, U.S. firms have mistakenly thought that deals were finalized when, in fact, competitors were hard at work undoing what should have been a U.S.-Chinese contract. Some U.S. companies which are new-to-market do not understand that, to the Chinese, face-to-face contacts are extremely important. Telephone calls or communications by fax are no substitute for frequent meetings in China itself. And visits directly to the mines where equipment is to be used can be a critical factor in making sales.

Third, where very high-tech mining equipment is involved, the Chinese may simply lack the knowledge required to make a sound purchase judgement.

What should U.S. firms emphasize? Their experience in the mining field—probably longer and deeper than that of any of our competitors; the top quality of U.S. equipment and excellent follow-up with spare parts and servicing; and the very competitive prices U.S. firms can offer when the playing field is level.

What should U.S. firms look out for? One problem is that certain Chinese, nominally working for a Chinese governmental organization, are, in fact, secretly in league with a foreign company. Another problem is the Chinese inviting U.S. bids simply to bid down the prices of foreign competitors, who will ultimately win through the provision of soft loans. A third problem used to be the Chinese unwillingness, in some cases, to expend scarce foreign exchange on follow-on service, support, or spare parts agreements. In one recent and large sale of U.S. mining equipment, however, the Chinese buyer and the U.S. seller were wise enough to insist that spare parts and follow-on servicing and training be an integral part of the entire contract. Fourth, U.S. sellers of extremely heavy or complex machinery or haulers should make certain that there are adequate railroad facilities to move the equipment to the site where it is needed or, alternatively, that roadways are suitable for such a movement.

An ongoing problem in China is that intellectual property protection is backward and flawed. While this issue has not had much impact on the sales of mining equipment so far, U.S. companies should be cautious about how and with whom they share technology which Chinese joint venture (JV) partners or others could pirate. An additional difficulty is the tendency of some foreign business and government competitors to engage in disguised or open bribery and payoffs. A further problem is that the U.S. firms are sometimes unaware of the critical role played by superior, silent Chinese partners to a deal. These partners need to be identified and kept informed of all developments as the business relationship evolves. Including a trusted, third party, such as CITIC (the China International Trust and Investment Corporation), can prove valuable in resolving disagreements. Another issue—U.S. firms' tendency to want to sign too quickly and expect payoffs in a short period of time. The U.S. company entering the China market should develop a patient, long-term attitude toward the market and expect to make money only after an extended period of time.

There is, on occasion, a need to train Chinese engineers or mechanics in the use of American mining equipment. It is generally wiser to bring U.S. specialists to China to train people locally than to send the Chinese to the U.S. Reason—operating conditions in the PRC are very different from those in the U.S. However, including training trips to the U.S. may help win the contract.

3. Financing U.S. firms need to be flexible on matters relating to financing in the mining equipment market. Investment and financing sources are extremely varied—central government, local or provincial government, local mining authorities, international public institutions, private and public banks, etc. Since many of the PRC's coal mines are losing money, the central government's willingness or unwillingness go give big equipment purchases the go ahead is frequently a key factor in whether sales can be made. In April 1990, Japan reportedly loaned China USD 1.13 billion for equipment sales and construction of coal projects. The World Bank may be showing greater willingness to provide financing for projects in China. The U.S. embassy advises companies which are interested in a China World Bank project to travel to the PRC early in the process to contact the concerned officials in the Chinese government. The U.S. embassy can assist in identifying which Chinese organizations are involved in the project. World Bank bids in China are tendered by the International Tendering Corporation through public advertisements. The embassy can make arrangements to purchase World Bank tenders on a cost basis.

Dealing with small, local mines can present to U.S. suppliers both opportunities and problems in the financing area. On the one hand, such mines can sell at higher prices than can government mines and are, therefore, often more profitable. Extra cash for purchases of U.S. equipment may be available. On the other hand, such small operations may not have central government organizations' financial backing; the risks could be greater.

In more and more trade deals with China, U.S. firms are teaming up with Japanese companies, the latter providing the technology or equipment while the latter provides the financing. In 1989, the Japanese extended a USD 800 million loan to develop, in Inner Mongolia, the Junggar project. Although the Japanese Export-Import Bank is financing this project, there is a possibility that some funds will be available to purchase non-Japanese equipment. Japanese banks were among the thirty-nine or so banks involved in financing the Antaibao mine.

While Chinese interest in methane-recovery technology from the U.S. is strong, financing purchases in this area has been, at least for one U.S. company, a problem. That firm was reportedly offered rugs and coal by the Chinese in exchange for U.S. technology. The World Bank, Japan's Overseas Economic Cooperation Fund (OECF), the United Nations Environment Program (UNEP), and the United Nations Development Program (UNDP) are, according to one source, considering methane recovery-related projects in the PRC.

Best Sales Prospects

Equipment most needed from abroad includes:

-- Heavy hauling trucks
-- Power shovels
-- Boring machinery
-- Tunneling machinery (420 needed replacing in early 1991, according to one report)
-- Sinking machinery
-- Parts for boring machinery and sinking machinery
-- Derricks
-- Parts for derricks
-- Coal cutting equipment
-- Hydraulic pumps
-- Loading equipment
-- Coal washing equipment/technology (Note: Some or all of Antaibao's Chinese-made coal washing equipment has reportedly failed to operate well.)
-- Coal extractors (201 needed replacing in early 1991, according to one report)
-- Aircraft (small) for reaching remote mining sites
-- Programmable exchange systems for mines
-- Microwave systems (for remote mines)
-- Satellite earth stations
-- Environmental equipment to clean up coal slurry water and discharged gangue
-- Moving screen jigger systems
-- Numerical control air valves
-- Re-vibration jiggers
-- Sorters
-- No pressure feeding swirlers
-- Authigenic medium swirlers

-- Flotation machines
-- Power coal slurry sorting equipment
-- Wire, spiral, and high-frequency vibrating screen systems
-- Spiral dumping filter-type centrifuge systems
-- High speed centrifuges
-- Vacuum filters
-- Pressurize filter systems
-- Belt-type vacuum filter systems
-- Concentrator systems
-- Rolling tube dryers
-- Pulverizers and roller breakers
-- Pump systems
-- Chute conveyor systems
-- Bucket hoist systems
-- Resonant feed systems
-- Jiggers combined with automation systems
-- Flotation machines combined with automation systems
-- Ash measurement devices
-- Heat output measurement devices
-- Car loaders and counting systems
-- Computer central control systems
-- Sensors
-- Copper mining machinery (some was being overhauled in early 1991, according to a newspaper report)
-- Equipment to treat sulfide ores
-- Flash flotation and column flotation technology
-- Railroad equipment, technology, cars (Note: upgrading the transportation of minerals is just as important for China as improving the way minerals are actually mined)
-- Methane recovery-related technology, including prospecting, monitoring, drilling, hydraulic fracturing, and pumping equipment, gas appliances, pipelines, and storage tanks

Unless stated otherwise, the equipment wanted by the Chinese and listed above should be new. Much used U.S. equipment would, in our judgement, be quite suitable for Chinese conditions, and it certainly would be cheaper. However, in most cases, the Chinese, perhaps for reasons of "face," want their equipment new and sometimes even state-of-the-art.

Services most needed from abroad include:

-- Safety systems (computerized)
-- Monitoring systems (computerized)
-- Redesigning of old mines and old mine machinery
-- Advice on how to clean the air and water of discarded coal slurry and gangue
-- Computer-aided management efficiency development

-- Scientific mining-related research
-- Methane recovery-related consulting services and software

Key Contacts in Central Government

SPC (State Planning Commission)
38 Yuetan Nan Jie Xichengqu 100824
Foreign Economy and Trade Department
Tel: 8091455

MOER (Ministry of Energy Resources)
137 Fuyou Jie Xichengqu 100031
Coal Department
Tel: 654131 x330

MCI (Ministry of Chemical Industry)
Liupukang Andingmenwai 100723
Technical Department
Tel: 2019933 x739; Also
CMB (Chemical Mines Bureau)

NSTC (National Science and Technology Commission)
54 Shanlihe Lu Xichengqu 100862
Multipurpose Planning Department
Tel: 8012583

MOC (Ministry of Communications)
10 Fuxing Lu Haidianqu 100845
Technical Department
Tel: 365816

MOFERT (Ministry of Foreign Economic Relations and Trade)
2 Dong Changan Ji Dongchengqu 100731
Technical Import/Export Department
Tel: 5128261, 5129523
Administration Department of Foreign Investment
Tel: 5129320
MINMETALS (China National Metals and Minerals Import/Export Corporation)
China National Metal Products Import/Export Corporation)
SINOCHEM (China National Chemical/Export Corporation)
CNTIEC (China National Technical Import/Export Corporation)

MOGMR (Ministry of Geology and Mineral Resources)
International Cooperation Department
64 Funei Da Jie 100812
Tel: 658561 x368   Fax: 22531 MGMRC CN
China National Geology Technology Import/Export Corporation (under MOGMR)
China Geology and Gem Minerals Corporation (under MOGMR)

MMI (Ministry of Metallurgical Industry)
Department of Foreign Affairs
46 Dongshi Xida Jie 100711
Tel: 557031 x4110
China Metallurgical Construction Corporation (under MMI)
China Gold Corporation (under MMI)

Key Contacts - Regional

Some useful contacts in the mining industry include:

Dachang Mining Bureau
Nandan County, Hechi
Guangxi Province 547000
Tel: 285832

Fengfeng Mining Administration Bureau
Fengfengkuang, Handan
Hebei Province 056201

Fushun Mining Administration Bureau
Xinfu, Fushun
Laoning Province 113008
Tel: 583889

Fuxin Mining Administration Bureau
Haizhou District, Fuxin
Laoning Province 123000
Tel: 053152

Hanxing Metallurgical Mining Administration Bureau
Congtai District, Handan
Hebei Province 056032
Tel: 23951

Huaibei Mining Administration Bureau
Huaibei, Anhui Province 235006
Tel: 21112

Huainan Mining Administration Bureau
Tianjia'an, Huainan
Anhui Province 232001
Tel: 44334

Jixi Mining Administration Bureau
Jiguan, Jixi
Heilongjiang Province 158100
Tel: 22421

Kailuan Mining Administration Bureau
Lunan, Tangshan
Hebei Province 063018
Tel: 223811

Luoyang Mining Machinery Plant
Jianxi District, Luoyang
Henan Province 471039
Tel: 222711-4575

Panzhihua Mining Administration Bureau
West District, Panzhihua
Sichuan Province 617066
Tel: 8774

Pingdingshan Mining Bureau
Pingdingshan, Henan Province 467000
Tel: 222212

Pingxiang Mining Administration Bureau
Chengguan District, Pingxiang
Jiangxi Province 337003
Tel: 333123

Qitaihe Mining Administration Bureau
Taoshan, Qitaihe
Heilongjiang Province 154600
Tel: 72234

Shenyang Mine Administration Bureau
Xinchengzi, Shenyang
Liaoning Province 110122
Tel: 463619

Shuangyashan Mining Administration Bureau
Jianshan, Shuangyashan
Heilongjiang Province 155103
Tel: 22656

Shuichng Coal Mining Administration Bureau
Zhongshan District, Liupanshui
Guizhou Province 553000
Tel: 22961

Shuiroushan Coal Mining Administration Bureau
Changning, Hengyang
Hunan Province 421513
Tel: 24141

Tiefa Mining Administration Bureau
Diaobingshangjie, Tiefa
Liaoning Province 112700
Tel: 66013

Xinwen Mining Administration Bureau
Xintal, Shandong Province 271233
Tel: 332516

Xishan Mining Bureau
Hexi, Taiyuan
Shanxi Province 030053
Tel: 666294

Xuzhou Mining Administration Bureau
235 Huaihai Xilu, Xuzhou
Jiangsu Province 221006
Tel: 53940

Yanzhou Mining Administration Bureau
Jining, Shandong Province 273500
Tel: 2260

OIL AND GAS FIELD MACHINERY AND SERVICES
Table 102 summarizes some of the salient statistics for the oil and gas field machinery and services area.

Table 102

Salient Statistics for the Oil and Gas Field Machinery and Services Sector

A) Three-letter ITA industry sector code: OGM

B) Est. total market size (USD millions):

1991 -	$4,000
1992 -	$5,000
1993 -	$5,500
1994 -	$6,050
1995 -	$6,655

C) Est. 1992-4 annual market growth rate: 10%

D) Est. total imports (USD millions):

1991 -	$500
1992 -	$600
1993 -	$750
1994 -	$820
1995 -	$990

E) Est. annual total import growth rate: 10%

F) Est. imports from U.S. (USD millions):

1991 -	$200
1992 -	$220
1993 -	$250
1994 -	$275
1995 -	$305 (58)

G) Est. annual growth of imports from U.S.:   10%

H) China's receptivity to U.S. products in this sector (5 - High/1 - Low):   4

I) Competition from local/third countries for U.S. firms (5 - Low/1 - High):   4

J) Chinese market barriers to U.S. sales in this sector (5 - Few/1 - Many):   4

K) Comments - factors for increased U.S. sales:
- Offshore and Tarim Basin discoveries will bring future investment in production and pipeline facilities.
- Energy is among highest development priorities and U.S. technology and equipment widely admired.
- Recent opening of East China Sea to foreign exploration and production and some evidence that foreign risk-sharing investment in northern and western onshore exploration may be opened up.

L)	Most Promising Sub-sectors	1992 market size
	1. Onshore equipment and services	$1,000 million
	2. Offshore production equipment and services	$1,000 million
	3. Major pipeline projects	$1,000 million
	4. Geophysical instruments and secondary recovery equipment	$ 200 million

Some useful contacts in the area of steel pipe manufacture (for oilfield use, for example) are:

Anshan General Steel Pipe Plant
Lishan, Anshan
Liaoning Province 114031
Tel: 612175

Boaji Oil Steel Pipe Factory
Weibin District, Baoji
Shaanxi Province 721008
Tel: 312244

Hengyang Steel Tube Mill
Hengyang, Hunan Province 421001
Tel: 22151

Shandong Yantai Steel Pipe Mill
Yanti, Shandong Province 264000
Tel: 242485

Shanghai Steel Tube Plant
2950 Xixianlu
Shanghai 200940
Tel: 6672257

Tianjin Seamless Steel Pipe Plant
Hexi District, Tianjin 300220
Tel: 282931

PACKAGING EQUIPMENT

China's whole packaging industry (including its paper packaging industry) was very undeveloped until the early 1980s. Over the past decade, Chinese producers have come to a growing realization of the importance of packaging in sales promotion, particularly for export markets. By 1987, the total output value of China's packaging industry was 20.5 billion Yuan. China now has over 6,000 packaging enterprises, employing 1.17 million people (38).

But China's packaging industry is, in a way, a victim of its own success. Because demand far exceeds supply, the industry has emphasized output volume over product quality or production efficiency. And with customers willing to buy its poorest quality products, China's packaging industry has felt little need to stress research and development work.

Nationwide, China's paper packaging sector suffers from outdated plant technology and a severe shortage of vital raw materials, such as paperboard and wide corrugated board. In this highly decentralized industry, many packaging plants must provide their own raw materials. Even relatively small plants must often devote a portion of their plant space to manufacturing the paperboard and corrugated board they need for box making.

Chinese planners are emphasizing technology and equipment which can stretch the country's scarce wood resources to meet rapidly increasing demands for paper packaging. For example, China is interested in acquiring extensible bag technology (which increases the durability and strength of both wood and non-wood based paper bags).

Chinese exporters have also been using more paper as they come to understand the importance of packaging for export marketing. Much of this export quality packaging must be manufactured from imported materials. For example, most of China's domestic cardboard box linerboard is made from non-wood materials which fall apart easily under hot and humid conditions. This poses a distinct problem in export packaging for China's customers in Southeast Asia.

Table 102 summarizes some of the salient statistics for the packaging equipment industry (3).

Table 102

Salient Statistics for the Packaging Equipment Sector

A)	Three-letter ITA industry sector code:	PKG
B)	Est. total market size (USD millions):	
	1991 -	$200
	1992 -	$224
C)	Est. 1992-4 annual market growth rate:	12%
D)	Est. total imports (USD millions):	
	1991 -	$ 30
	1992 -	$ 40
E)	Est. annual total import growth rate:	33%

F) Est. imports from U.S. (USD millions):

    1991 - $ 6

    1992 - $ 9

G) Est. annual growth of imports from U.S.:   50%

H) China's receptivity to U.S. products in
this sector (5 - High/1 - Low):   3

I) Competition from local/third countries
for U.S. firms (5 - Low/1 - High):   2

J) Chinese market barriers to U.S. sales
in this sector (5 - Few/1 - Many):   3

K) Comments - factors for increased U.S. sales:

- China's export drive requires better quality packaging which will require imported packaging equipment.
- China National Packaging Corporation is aggressively seeking contacts with U.S. firms.

L) Most Promising Sub-sectors   1992 market size

    1. Bottle and canning equipment $50 million

    2. Agricultural products packaging equipment $45 million

    3. High speed packaging machinery $25 million

PAPER AND PAPERBOARD

Overview In the early 1980, China's serious shortage of productive forests combined with outdated technology to create a shortage of pulp and paper at a time of increasing demand. From 1981 to 1986, the annual growth rate of paper production was 7.3 percent. In 1986, however, only 20 percent of paper pulp was made of wood; the remainder derived from grass fiber.

China's more than 1,500 paper mills produced approximately 45.4 million tons and over 500 different kinds of machine-made paper in 1986. Approximately 1 million tons of pulp and paper were imported annually. In 1986, China focused on pollution control, increased product variety, reduced use of fiber and chemical ingredients, and more efficient use of energy as measures to improve production. China also sought foreign assistance to achieve these goals (4).

Table 103 summarizes some of the salient statistics for the paper and paperboard industry (3).

Table 104

Salient Statistics for the Paper and Paperboard Sector

A)	Three-letter ITA industry sector code:	PAP
B)	Est. total market size (USD millions):	
	1991 -	$6,500
	1992 -	$6,600
C)	Est. 1992-4 annual market growth rate:	3%
D)	Est. total imports (USD millions):	
	1991 -	$610
	1992 -	$620
E)	Est. annual total import growth rate:	1%
F)	Est. imports from U.S. (USD millions):	
	1991 -	$120
	1992 -	$130
G)	Est. annual growth of imports from U.S.:	2%
H)	China's receptivity to U.S. products in this sector (5 - High/1 - Low):	4
I)	Competition from local/third countries for U.S. firms (5 - Low/1 - High):	4
J)	Chinese market barriers to U.S. sales in this sector (5 - Few/1 - Many):	3
K)	Comments - factors for increased U.S. sales:	

- From 1990 to 1991 exports from U.S. to China jumped 82%.
- This market is erratic. Sales to China declined for a few years prior to 1990.
- Modern industry requires far higher quality in paper than is generally available in China.

L)	Most Promising Sub-sectors	1992 market size
	1. Newsprint	$1,200 million
	2. Kraft liner board	$1,800 million
	3. Waste paper	$1,500 million

China's pulp and paper industry is relatively undeveloped. With a rising standard of living, Chinese consumers are now demanding higher quality paper products, but country-wide demand still far exceeds supply. In addition, demand for higher quality paper is increasing among Chinese exporters, who have come to understand the importance of packaging for export marketing. The fundamental constraint to the growth of China's papermaking industry is the lack of a stable domestic supply of good quality raw materials. In recent years, the U.S. has become one of China's major suppliers of pulp and paper (including wastepaper), and China's two leading pulp and paper importers have both established representative offices in the U.S. Although this sector is a promising one, U.S. companies should be aware of a number of special problems which fact foreign companies in the China market. For example, there are still a number of unanswered questions about the long-term effects of China's economic retrenchment policies on foreign trade and investment (38).

Only about one-third of China's mills are centrally controlled by the Ministry of Light Industry, but these mills are responsible for two-thirds of China's total paper production. Those mills which are not under the aegis of the Ministry of Light Industry tend to be small operations which use straw as their raw material for production.

1. Forest Resources According to official Chinese statistics, China's total forest land base is 124.65 million hectares (approximately 308 mill acres). This represents about 13 percent of the total land area of China. China's national forestry goal is to increase the commercial forest estate to 20 percent of the land mass by the year 2020.

Most of China's forest lands are located in the northwestern provinces of Heilongjiang and Jilin, and in the southwestern provinces of Yunnan, Guangdong and Sichuan. China's national forests include 9,141 million cubic meters of timber inventory. Mature commercial forests contain an inventory of about 2,622 million cubic meters, with an additional 1,109 million cubic meters on open forest lands or on lands with scattered trees. Much of the mature timber inventory—possibly as much as one-half of the total—is presently inaccessible. Approximately 55 percent of the total inventory consists of softwoods such as Larch, Red Pine and firs. The remaining 45 percent consists of hardwoods such as Eucalypti, poplar and birch.

According to FAO estimates, total wood production in China was 266.9 million cubic meters in 1986. Of this, about 174 million cubic meters was used as fuelwood.

China loses approximately 0.5 million hectares (.12 million acres) of forest lands each year from overcutting, illegal cutting, and clearing for agriculture, mining, or building construction. In 1987, a very large forest fire occurred in northern Heilongjiang Province, near the Soviet border. A total of 1.14 million hectares (2.82 million acres) suffered damage. Of this, 440,000 hectares of trees were destroyed.

Losses in current timber processing are estimated to total at least 18 million cubic meters per year. China is making an effort to cut some of these losses through more efficient processing procedures.

2. Shortage of Raw Materials The fundamental constraint to the growth of China's papermaking industry is the lack of a stable domestic supply of good quality raw materials. Sixty percent of China's paper is made from non-wood fibers such as bagasse (sugar cane residue), bamboo, wheat straw, waste paper and chips. Only 20 to 25 percent of China's pulp is wood-based—and half of this is imported. Although Chinese goals call for increased domestic fiber content in Chinese paper products, most Chinese papermaking plants lack the technology to produce adequate paper products with locally available pulp.

Because domestic supplies of high quality pulp are in short supply, China is forced to import large quantities of pulp each year from the U.S. and other countries. Much of this imported pulp is blended softwood kraft pulp. China meets its needs for other pulps through its own domestic production of unbleached hardwoods and through substitutes.

China is seeking to maximize use of its own domestic pulp resources (which tend to be lower quality, non-fiber pulps like rice straw) by mixing domestic pulps with high quality imports. One recent proposal calls for an export-led development approach to China's papermaking industry, in which Chinese factories would manufacture export-quality specialty papers based on a blend of imported pulp and locally-available cotton pulp.

3. Recycling Wastepaper To conserve domestic resources of virgin pulp, and to cut back on pulp import expenditures, China has begun to emphasize wastepaper recycling (26). China has also begun to import high-quality wastepaper (much of it from the U.S.) to blend with its own lower-grade domestic pulps. According to the U.S. Department of Commerce, 1988 U.S. exports of scrap paper and paperboard to China were worth $14.2 million. Chinese wastepaper importers are particularly interested in two types of wastepaper which the U.S. has in abundance. First, Chinese want lower quality wastepaper such as old corrugated boxes from grocery stores—this type of wastepaper is relatively inexpensive, but still can be recycled into new cardboard boxes with adequate strength for most Chinese uses. Second, Chinese want old newspapers with a high wood pulp content. (Much domestic Chinese newsprint is low grade printing paper made from ground wood and chemical pulp and cannot be easily recycled.)

4. Effects of Economic Retrenchment on the Pulp and Paper Industry Faced with an overheated economy, China's planners instituted a nationwide economic retrenchment program in late 1988. The resulting slowdown in the economy has affected China's pulp and paper industry in several ways. In an ironic twist, because of the severe paper shortages of 1989 (the first year of the austerity program), many Chinese organizations began to stockpile supplies. As a result, in early 1990, China was facing a temporary paper glut, with unsold paper piling up in paper mills throughout the country.

For example, having survived several nationwide paper shortages in early 1989, many newspaper printing houses stockpiled newsprint as a precautionary measure at the end of the year. But, at the same time, the Chinese government stopped publication of over 500 newspapers and magazines, and limited the size of some newspaper editions. As a result, China's market for newsprint declined sharply in early 1990, as publishing houses used up their 1989 stockpiles of newsprint.

China's market for copper plate printing paper also declined. Because of the austerity program, many copper plate customers turned to less expensive technologies to save money. In addition, the national government restricted calendar purchases by Chinese organizations (which had previously bough large numbers of expensive calendars to use as gifts). This new government sanction contributed to the declining demand for copper plate printing paper. In 1990, the demand for copper plate printing paper was expected to be about 150,000 tons (down from 180,000 tons per year before 1988).

Slowdowns in other industries also affected national demand for paper. For example, the slowdown in China's construction industry has greatly decreased the demand for paper-based cement wrapping. Demand has also dropped for paper used by the electronics industry. Chinese electronics enterprises had imported large quantities of this paper in 1988, before the austerity program began. But the austerity program affected the electronics industry severely: in 1989, industry demand for paper dropped to 2,000 tons (from 7,500 tons in 1988).

5. Under Capitalization of the Industry For many years, China's papermaking industry has been chronically under capitalized by the central government. In 1987, investment for technical renovation of the papermaking industry was only 2 percent of total light industry investment for such renovation. Shanghai's papermaking industry is still using equipment dating back to the 1930s, and the city estimates it needs 2.15 billion yuan over the next five years to modernize its papermaking industry.

Much of the growth in China's papermaking industry has come from local investments. During the 1980s, 70 percent of total capital construction investment in the papermaking industry came from local authorities who set up collectively owned factories. This local investment is expected to decrease sharply in 1990, however, as China moves towards greater economic re-centralization and as local authorities grapple with the nationwide economic austerity program and credit crunch.

6. Pricing Policy Growth of China's pulp and paper industry has also been constrained by an irrational price system, under which the price of raw materials (such as timber, or pulp) has gone up, while the price of widely produced paper products like newsprint and textbook paper has been kept artificially low. One result has been frequent shortages of newsprint and textbook paper because of papermakers' reluctance to produce such unprofitable paper products.

Because demand for many types of paper is far outstripping supply, the Ministry of Light Industry has set targets for a major readjustment of China's papermaking industry during the Eighth Five-Year Plan. Targets include six major papermaking sub-sectors:

a) Newsprint - The Plan calls for an annual 7.8 percent increase in production of newsprint from 1991-1995. Newsprint output as a proportion of total papermaking industry output will increase from 4.6 percent in 1995, to 5.5 percent in 2000, and 7 percent in 2020. Papermaking facilities will be urged to use domestically available raw materials such as bagasse, bluish dogbane and other bast-fiber plants to make newsprint.

b) **Relief printing paper** - Production of relief printing paper, including paper for offset printing, will increase during the Plan. The current goal is for relief printing paper to comprise 10 percent of total paper output.

c) **Writing paper** - Because copying machines and other modern office equipment has reduced the need for writing paper, the proportion of writing paper production under the Plan will be reduced from 10 percent in 1990, to 9.7 percent in 1995, 9.5 percent in 2000 and 8.4 percent in 2020.

d) **Paperboard** - The Plan calls for annual production increases, especially in packaging materials such as high-strength paperboard and white paperboard. According to the Plan, paperboard should make up 43.4 percent of total industry output by 1995.

e) **Household Use Paper** - Chinese planners expect per annual capita consumption of household use paper, especially of medium- and low-grade toilet paper, to reach 0.57 kg by 1990, 08 kg by 1995, and 1.2 kg by 2000. Under the Plan, production of household use paper would increase from approximately 5 percent of total paper output in 1990, to 5.7 percent 1995, and 7 percent in 2000. The Plan also calls for the production of more varieties of household use paper for Chinese consumers.

f) **Higher Quality Paper Pulp** - One priority under Plan will be to increase China's production of paper pulp, especially medium- and long-staple pulp. Wood pulp will be used mainly for manufacturing high- and medium-grade paper and paperboard. Major cities will receive an allocation of straw and reed pulp to be used to supplement wood pulp for this purpose.

China's development priorities in its paper industry include the following:

1) Raw materials -
   Increase production of wood, and of long and medium non-wood fibers (e.g. bamboo, kenaf, and Chinese alpine rush).
   Encourage joint ventures in which timber is supplied by the foreign partners.

2) Organization -
   Severely limit the number of small, inefficient paper mills, and close mills which generate high amounts of pollution.

3) Technology and Equipment -
   Update technology relating to straw-pulping, disposal of used chemicals and wastewater, recycling of wastepaper, bleaching, and energy saving equipment.

4) Production -
   Emphasize production of newsprint, relief printing paper, paperboard, household paper (especially medium and low grade toilet paper), paper for textbooks and packaging.
   Increase production of commercial pulp (to increase the production of cardboard for packaging).

Competitive Situation Besides the U.S., several other countries are major suppliers of pulp and paper products to China. These countries include Canada, New Zealand, Sweden, Finland, Mexico, Chile, and the Soviet Union. China's major suppliers of papermaking technology and equipment are the U.S., Sweden, Finland, Austria, Norway, France, Japan, and Britain. Finnish companies have been especially active in China. Many of these foreign competitors are assisted by generous concessionaire loan programs sponsored by their home governments. Such programs are not available to U.S. companies.

Only two organizations (CNPPC and CHINAPACK) handle most of China's pulp and paper imports. Because there only are two major players, new-to-market U.S. companies will find it relatively easy to identify major industry contacts (not always an easy thing to do in China). However, U.S. companies may also find that it is just as easy for their competitors to identify the same contacts.

Chinese pulp buyers appear to have thoroughly researched foreign suppliers and have a sophisticated knowledge of the regions (and the specific companies) which can best meet their pulp import needs. Both CNPPC and CHINAPACK have opened representative offices in the U.S., and have established business relations with a number of prominent U.S. pulp and paper companies.

Chinese Imports of Forest Products (Timber, Plywood, Pulp) In 1987 and 1988, China imported about 7 million and 10 million cubic meters of timber respectively. But in the first eleven months of 1989, China's timber imports were down 36 percent from the same period in 1988. Extending this pattern over the whole year, China's total 1989 timber imports may have dropped to below 6.5 million cubic meters.

In recent years, imports of softwood lumber have averaged 130 thousand cubic meters (almost all from British Columbia). Sixty-five percent of China's imports in tropical hardwood plywood come from Malaysia; and 35 percent come from Indonesia. Except for pulp and paper, China has not imported significant volumes of processed wood products in recent years.

During the 1980s, China emerged as the U.S.' second largest trading partner in forest products. In 1988, the U.S. exported over USD 615 million worth of forest products to the PRC. Chinese importers prefer the longer fiber kraft pulp of the U.S. Pacific Northwest, Canada, and Northern Europe, but the Chinese do buy some shorter U.S. southern pine blended kraft pulp as well.

Imports of Pulp and Paper In 1987 imports of paper and cardboard were 1.3 million tons. But this dropped sharply to 1 million tons in 1988. Because of the current economic retrenchment, 1989 import figures were expected to be even lower. China's pulp imports for 1987 and 1988 were .8 million tons and 1.1 million tons, respectively. Overall, 1989 pulp imports were expected to drop somewhat from 1988 levels.

In 1989 decreases were due, in large part, to China's current policy of economic retrenchment, which has made it very difficult for many Chinese enterprises to come up with the cash to pay for imports. However, foreign industry specialists note that Chinese imports of pulp and paper have gone through a number of ups and downs in the past. For example,

1988 saw a sharp decrease in Chinese imports of kraft linerboard, which mirrored a similar pattern in the early 1980s. This up-and-down pattern may be a partial result of China's highly centralized import purchasing structure for pulp and paper which is not always fine-tuned to actual conditions of industry supply and demand.

Best Sales Prospects

I.   Pulp and Other Wood Products
   - Blended softwood kraft pulp
   - Needle bleached soft kraft
   - Dissolving pulp (for rayon, glasseine paper)
   - Mechanical pulp
   - Fluff (for tissues and sanitary products)
   - Particleboard and fiberboard

II.   Wastepaper

   - Less expensive grades of wastepaper (such as used corrugated cardboard boxes from grocery stores)
   - Recycled newspapers, especially those with high wood pulp content

III. Paper

   - Newsprint, especially newsprint with a high wood pulp content
   - High speed offset press newsprint
   - Kraft linerboard
   - Bleached paperboard for the food packaging industry
   - Office paper for the communications, computer and electronics industries
   - High quality writing paper
   - Boxes made of corrugated paper linerboard and paperboard
   - Printing paper for magazines, and cigarette wrappers
   - Plasticized printing paper for magazines

Useful Contacts:

China National Pulp and Paper Corporation (CNPPC)
82 Dong An Men Jie
Beijing
Tel: 557 881/ 550 293/ 512 2321/ 552 163/ 550 472
Fax: 557519

China National Pulp and Paper Corporation (CNPPC) is under the aegis of the Ministry of Foreign Economic Relations and Trade (MOFERT). This organization handles about 80 percent of all China's imports of pulp and paper, and also purchases plywood, fiberboard, kraft linerboard and newsprint. CNPPC has a number of representatives in several overseas locations, including the U.S. and Japan.

U.S. Representative Office of CNPPC

Amicell Incorporated/Tri-Union (U.S.A.) Incorporated
6 Stamford Forum
Stamford, CT 06901
Tel: (203) 353-1474 Fax: (203) 353-1482

China National Packaging Import and Export Corporation
(CHINAPACK)
28 Dong Hou Xiang
An Ding Men Wai, Beijing
Tel: 421-1747/ 421-2204/ 421-6661   Fax: 421-2124

CHINAPACK was established in 1980 to coordinate national efforts to upgrade China's packaging industry. CHINAPACK imports packaging machinery and equipment, packaging materials, containers and package printing equipment. CHINAPACK is responsible for supplying packaging materials for all of China's export products. CHINAPACK is China's largest importer of paper, and second largest importer of pulp. CHINAPACK has established representative offices in the U.S., Japan, the Netherlands, Canada, Australia, Singapore and Hong Kong.

CHINAPACK U.S. Subsidiary

UNIAM Corporation
25 Broad Avenue
Palisades Park, NJ 07650
Tel: (201) 941-9758   Fax: (201) 941-9799

Ministry of Light Industry
Department of Paper
Number 2 B, Fu Waidajie
Beijing, China 100833
Tel: 890751, 867262

The Ministry of Light Industry coordinates China's paper industry policy, production plans, and administration. It is also in charge of major projects.

China Paper Industry Development Corporation
Number 12, Guanghua Lu
Beijing, China 100020
Tel: 500-4461/ 592-561 Fax: 500-4461

China Paper Industry Development Corporation is responsible for developing new raw materials for the paper industry. It has forty-seven member factories, including five joint venture plants. The Corporation does some development work itself in new raw materials for the paper industry.

China Pulp and Paper Import/Export Company
(China National Light Industrial Products Import/Export Corporation)
82 Dong An Men Street
Beijing, China 100747
Tel: 552163 Fax: 557519

Imports and exports paper products.

China Packaging Technology Association
31 East Chang An Avenue
Beijing, China 100005
Tel: 512 4133 Fax: 512 4128

This organization has no subdivision specializing in paper products. One individual (Mr. Li Peng) serves as general coordinator for the Association's paper related activities. The Association owns and operates a number of paper packaging plants and packaging printing plants. The Association also owns one papermaking factory, as well as some forest lands in the U.S. The Association has organizational links with CHINAPACK.

China Technical Association of the Paper Industry
12 Guanghua Lu
Beijing, China 100020
Tel: 5002880

The Technical Association helps coordinate China's papermaking activities. The Association focuses on technical training and technical exchange activities and does not operate any factories.

Printing and Printing Equipment Industry Association of China
Number 6 Dongshang Hutong
Dong Dan
Beijing, China
Tel: 512 3289

The Printing Association is a membership organization of individual printing plants. It coordinates activities in China's printing industry, including the development and purchase of printing equipment and supplies.

Ministry of Forestry
Hepingli
Beijing, China
Tel: 463-061, 421-3061

The Ministry of Forestry has primary responsibility for managing China's forest lands, harvesting timber within the State Plan, reforesting farmlands, and planning future production levels. The Ministry also handles a significant share of domestic solid wood processing.

China Timber Import and Export Corporation (TUSHU)
82 Dong An Men Street
Beijing, China
Tel: 512 4765, 512 6928   Fax: 512 4788

China Timber Import and Export Corporation (TUSHU) is under the aegis of the Ministry of Foreign Economic Relations and Trade (MOFERT). Through its subsidiary office in Settle (SUNDRY), this organization handles most wood imports (and almost 100 percent of the softwood long imports) from the United States. Some wood imports are also handled by the China International Trust and Investment Corporation (CITIC), by the Chinese military, and by a few enterprises which earn their own foreign exchange.

Some useful contacts in the paper industry include:

Beijing Papermaking and Packing Industry Corporation
Dongcheng District
Beijing 100028
Tel: 4082331

Fujian Qingzhou Paper Mill
Sha County, Sanming
Fujian Province 365506
Tel: 22910

Guangzhou Paper Mill
Haizhu District, Guangzhou
Guangdong Province 510281
Tel: 4448900

Jiamusi Paper Mill
Dongfeng District, Jiamusi
Heilongjiang Province 154005
Tel: 282

Jilin Paper Mill
Changyi District, Jinlin
Jilin Province 132002
Tel: 478301

Jincheng Paper Mill
Jin County, Jinzhou
Liaoning Province 121203
Tel: 820030

Minfeng Paper Mill
Jiaxing, Zhejiang Province 314000
Tel: 280971

Nanping Paper Mill
Nanping, Fujian Province 353000
Tel: 23224

Qiqihar Paper Mill
Longsha District, Qiqihar
Heilongjiang Province 161005
Tel: 37931

Shanghai Paper Manufacturing Company
Jing'an District, Shanghai 200002
Tel: 3212433

Shixian Paper Mill
Tumen, Yanbian
Julin Province 133101
Tel: 864

Yingkou Paper Mill
Zhanqian, Yingkou
Liaoning Province 115001
Tel: 42721

Yueyang Paper Mill
Yueyang, Hunan Province 114002
Tel: 222622

PETROLEUM

Overview A rudimentary petroleum refining industry was established with Soviet aid in the 1950s. In the 1960s and 1970s, this base was modernized and expanded, partially with European and Japanese equipment. In 1986, Chinese refineries were capable of processing about 2.1 million barrels per day. By 1990, China plans to reach 2.5 million barrels per day.

In the 1970s, China constructed oil pipelines and improved ports handling oil tankers. The first oil pipeline was laid from Daqing to the port of Qinhuangdao; 1,150 kilometers long, it became operational in 1974. The following year the pipeline was extended to Beijing; a second line connected Daqing to the port of Lüda and branched off to the Democratic People's Republic of Korea. A pipeline from Linyi in Shandong Province to Nanjing was completed in 1978, linking the oilfields of Shengli and Huabei to ports and refineries of the lower Chang Jiang region. In 1986, plans had been made to construct a 105-kilometer pipeline linking an offshore well with the Chinese mainland via Hainan Island (4).

Table 105

China Petroleum Statistics (52)

Output of Selected Refined Products

Commodity (in tons)	1991	1992
Crude Oil (refinery input)	113,627,500	120,802,000
Finished Gasoline	23,448,100	26,227,900
Distillate Fuel Oil	59,424,900	61,887,600
Petrochemical Feedstock	8,053,500	8,209,600
Lubricants	1,727,100	1,872,100
Petroleum Coke	1,578,800	1,590,070
Waxes	669,900	682,700
Asphalt and Road Oil	3,114,100	3,374,400
Hydrocarbon Solvents	504,200	548,600

Source: SINOPEC

Imports and Exports of Crude Oil

	Quantity in Tons	
Year	Imports	Exports
1991	5,972,471	22,237,537
1992	11,360,000	21,510,000
1993(E)	15,000,000	19,000,000

China is rich in energy resources, yet lacks ready energy supplies to meet its economic development needs. Despite high proved or likely reserves of coal, oil and gas, and other energy sources (including hydropower and uranium) and rapid development of the energy sector, especially in the last decade, supply lags severely behind in demand, with government estimates of the demand shortfall at 25-30 percent. The state imposed pricing policy has three tiers ranging from one-fourth the world price, up to the world price. This has created disincentives to investment and encouraged wasteful excess demand. The oil and gas sector has also been plagued by lack of incentives for high technology drilling, compounded by a general shortage of investment funds due to an aversion to accept foreign investment in some of the most promising areas.

China's critical need for energy has forced the pace of reform in the oil and gas sector and created new opportunities for U.S. exploration, processing, equipment and service companies. Over the past year, the Chinese have opened up onshore and offshore areas to exploration by foreign companies and have increased cooperation in downstream as well. Chinese purchases of U.S. equipment and services have also been significant over the past year. In the area of price reform, Chinese officials hope to eliminate the lower controlled price in 1994.

While opportunities for outside participation in the petroleum sector continue to increase, deeper reforms would be in the interest of both U.S. Companies and the PRC. When petroleum products are included in the calculation, China may have become a net importer of oil and gas during 1993. The Chinese want to increase output of crude oil from the 142 million tons produced in 1992 (about 2.8 million bbls/day) to at least 165 million tons by the year 2000 (the president of China national petroleum company cites a goal of 200 million tons for the year 2000—or four million barrels per day), with a corresponding increase in refining capacity. China can only achieve these ambitious goals by opening major new fields to exploration, further involving foreign companies in enhanced oil recovery (EOR) operations in existing fields, encouraging large outside investments in processing and distribution, rationalizing the pricing structure and assuring foreign participants a return on investment (52).

The oil and gas industry is heavily weighted toward petroleum production. At the same time, oil consumption is dwarfed by coal which provides about 70 percent of primary energy supply. Natural gas make up no more than three percent of primary energy supply. Natural gas production was 14.9 billion cubic meters in 1991 and 15.1 bcm in 1992. More than 80 percent of China's natural gas production is used to make chemical fertilizers; the remainder is piped to Shanghai for household consumption. Oil, on the other hand, serves a wide variety of uses in industry and transport.

The oil and gas sector is almost exclusively government-owned with a high degree of central government control. While the petroleum sector has changed significantly during the past decade of reforms, and government entities now have a limited number of joint ventures with foreign firms and the PRC continues to open up more areas to exploration by foreign companies, the oil and gas industry within China has not been opened to private businesses as has been the case recently in other areas, and it has never been linked to the collective (as opposed to the state-owned) economy. Traditionally, energy has been regarded as one of the key resources, which Chinese leaders have consistently said must remain under government control. Increasingly, however, there is a greater willingness to allow internal reforms, coupled with a greater degree of foreign participation in the energy sector.

China ranks tenth in the world in proven reserves (47). These deposits, located both offshore and onshore, are estimated to be about 24 billion barrels of oil. The offshore oil deposits are located in the East and South China Seas. The onshore oil deposits include China's oldest producing oilfields and are located in the northeast region.

Since 1988, China's crude oil production has remained level at about 2.8 million barrels per day (b/d). Between 1980 and 1988, oil production increased from 2.1 million b/d to 2.8 million b/d. According to officials at the U.S. Department of Energy (DOE) and the East-West Center, China has been unable to increase its oil production beyond 2.8 million b/d because of its aging oilfields and the absence of adequate capital financing.

China hopes to increase production with the use of enhanced oil recovery technology and the exploitation of new oilfields. According to officials at the East-West Center and DOE, China's total oil production is expected to increase to 2.9 million b/d by 1995 and to 3.1 million b/d by the year 2000.

The Major Onshore Oilfields Over 70 percent of China's total petroleum production comes from three oilfields, all around thirty years old. Six of the top seven producing oilfields are in two geologic basins in northeast China—the Songliao Basin (Daqing) and the Bohai Basin (Shengli, Liaohe, Zhongyuan, Huabei, and Dagang). The only top producer outside of the northeast is the Karamay Oilfield in Xinjiang's Junggar Basin. The Chinese communists' first major oil find in 1956, Karamay still ranks number four among China's oilfields, producing six percent of total output (52).

Given the age of these fields and the high rate of drilling, all of the major current oilfields are likely to see declining production in the short to medium term, and some are already in decline. CNPC has attempted to stabilize production as much as possible and has long used secondary recovery techniques to prolong the life of the fields. It has already begun to use enhanced oil recovery (EOR) technology on an experimental basis for some of its most important older fields, including Daqing and Karamay, and is now looking to expand the use of EOR. Nevertheless, most observers expect to see significant declines in production at current fields within the next ten years, and also believe without significant new production China will be a net importer of crude oil by 1995. In a recent interview, CNPC's Wang Tao said that when imports of petroleum products are factored into the equation, China wind up a net importer of petroleum for 1993 once all the data are in. At the same time, some outside experts believe that the traditional fields could produce beyond expectations if CNPC were willing to fully involve outside firms in an all out effort to apply EOR techniques.

The oil in China's northeast tends to be heavy and has a high wax content—in some fields as high as 50 percent. The quality of the oil has tended to make both refining and pipelines expensive. Given northeast China's bitter winter temperatures, high pour point temperatures for crude oil produce major problems for pipelines (some of Liaohe's oil has such a high pour point temperature that it can be sculpted into figures at room temperature).

CNPC constitutes each oilfield as a Petroleum Administration Bureau (PAB). Until recently, all revenues went to the central CNPC administration, which then provided budgets for the fields. In 1991, CNPC gave the PAB's far greater autonomy. Most fields now retain their revenues and have to cover all current costs and investment themselves. CNPC has retained greater control over the three main producers—Daqing, Shengli and Lioahe—and possible Karamay, as well. These fields turn over more of their profits, but in return receive direct investment from the center. These funds, often for expensive items like ear technology, van be quite significant. Nevertheless, as a portion of CNPC investment, funds for enhancement of existing fields are undoubtedly dwarfed by investment in the development of new fields.

The PAB's in China's older fields suffer from heavy labor-related costs. They are extreme examples of the old work unit (*danwei*) system, which in many other sectors of the economy is slowly evolving into commercial rather than social organizational structures. The PAB's provide essentially cradle-to-grave services for their employees and families. Because no cities existed near the oilfields, the old ministry of petroleum built cities itself, including roads, transportation, schools, housing, medical facilities, stores, etc. All these facilities continue to be administered by the PAB's.

While factories in urban areas are increasingly divesting themselves of extraneous facilities, other PABS are trapped by their remote locations. They have traditionally provided employment to everyone living in their areas who needed a job (i.e., spouses and adult children of their employees). With no alternate sources of employment in the area, some PABS find it difficult to divest themselves of excess staff. Many have expanded downstream into petrochemicals. Some are also finding new life by servicing the new oilfields in the northwest (Tarim and Turpan-Hami Basins).

Given the problem of excess labor and the prospect of having to import a million barrels of oil a day in the year 2000, CNPC has established two subsidiaries to pursue overseas oil exploration activities. Sino-American Petroleum Development Corporation (SAPDC) won a bid from Peru to raise the recovery rate of an existing field, and will bid for more blocks. Asian-Australian Petroleum Development Corporation (AAPDC) focuses on Asia and Oceania. CNPC has made investments in Canada, and is looking at exploration and development in India and Papua New Guinea. The Daqing PAB is negotiating for exploration rights to two fields in Irkutsk, in eastern Siberia.

Potential New Fields The current slogan in the Chinese oil industry is, "stabilize the east—develop the west." Many in both the Chinese and western oil industries see great potential for China's Tarim Basin. Although there has been some minor work done in Tarim for decades, major work in this area did not begin until the late 1980s. The wells in Tarim, which is located in the Taklamakan Desert, one of the world's most inhospitable regions, produced 888,848 tons in 1992. CNPC hopes to produce 10 million tons annually from the Tarim (approximately 200,000 barrels/day) by the year 2000 (52).

Unlike most of the oil in China proper, CNPC officials say that much of the oil in Tarim is very light, with low sulfur and low wax content. CNPC officials will not divulge their reserve estimates, and estimates given by Chinese economists of 18 billion tons of reserves

(126 billion barrels) seem rather high—particularly as foreign oil industry analysts typically estimate all of China's proven reserves to be in the 25-30 billion barrel range. Nevertheless, there is widespread consensus that Tarim may have major potential.

Tarim oil, however, is not easily recovered. The geological structures are complex and the surface conditions worse than perhaps any other onshore oil basin in the world. The Taklamakan Desert is infamous in history as a desert from which no one returns. Unlike other deserts there are no oases in its interior—only around the rim. The sand is particularly fine—considerably finer than that of the Arabian Peninsula—making drilling and site construction difficult. Surface temperatures are exceedingly hot in summer and cold in winter. Moreover, the oil is relatively deep—as deep as 6,000 meters—making drilling technically difficult and very expensive.

CNPC's subsidiary, the Tarim Petroleum Exploration and Development Bureau (TPEDB) has made significant progress in developing fields in the Lunnan area to the west of its headquarters at Korla, Xinjiang, and also in Tazhong, in the center of the basin. Nevertheless, TPEDB officials admit they have not yet found "the big one."

Transportation is one of the major headaches for Tarim developers. The remote area is on average over 2,500 km from China's major cities. There had been talk of building a pipeline of that length to refineries in Luoyang, but TPEDB officials acknowledge that production would have to rise considerably above current levels for such a long pipeline to be economically feasible. TPEDB built a 250 km pipeline, which went online in July 1992, from the Lunnan fields to the railhead at Korla, so that current production can then be transported by rail to China proper. While planners would eventually like to see a pipeline, rail is viewed as a feasible alternative unless production surpasses Karamay.

At the same time, very large investments in Tarim only make economic sense if there will be transportation infrastructure—ideally a large pipeline to the eastern consuming regions—in place to move large quantities of oil. Because the decision on a major pipeline has not yet been made, and both construction and exploration efforts could easily extend into the beginning of the next century, it is highly unlikely that Tarim can solve China's petroleum shortfall in the next few years.

The Turpan-Hami or Tuha Basin close to Urumqi, Xinjiang's capital, is also a promising site for oil development. While a much smaller basin than Tarim, it does not pose the same technical or transport problems. Production is still fairly low (approaching 1.4 million tons in 1993) but it is expected to increase rapidly in the next few years. Tuha is on the Urumqi-Lanzhou rail line, and there are no plans to build a pipeline.

Both Tarim and Tuha oil developers have chosen not to follow the pattern of the older fields of building entire cities at the fields themselves. They have chosen to place their headquarters in existing cities and to hire service teams from older fields to do the actual work in the fields. The PABS compete for work at these sites in a bid system. Workers go to Xinjiang without their families, work very hard when there and then are given generous leave terms to return to their families in China proper. TPEDB officials believe this system is much more cost effective than building cities in the desert. The system also allows CNPC to maintain reserve employment at the older fields and continue to use their service infrastructure despite declining output. Huabei PAP, for example, has been extremely active in sending teams to Tarim.

The Offshore Picture CNOOC divides itself into four main subsidiary companies: two for the South China Sea (Nanhai East Oil Corporation in Guangzhou and Nanhai West Oil Corporation in Zhanjiang), and one each for the East China Sea (East Offshore Oil corporation in Shanghai) and the Bohai Gulf (Bohai Oil Corporation in Tianjin). It also has a smaller company in Hainan. The four subsidiaries work closely with foreign companies, and most companies find the relationships quite satisfactory. The central office in Beijing is also actively involved in international contracting.

CNOOC faces the same price barriers as were discussed above for CNPC. Thus, most international investors find themselves forced to find foreign buyers for their oil or gas finds. For oil this does not prove to be a great difficulty, although for natural gas the problem can be greater.

Because international cooperation accounts for such a large portion of CNOOC's business and much of its production is exported, CNOOC is in far better financial condition than CNPC. CNOOC, unlike CNPC, publishes an annual report. Although such numbers are not entirely reliable in China, it reported total profits in 1992 of rmb 29.27 million (just over USD 5.0 million at the official exchange rate).

Although some exploration and experimental drilling had occurred earlier, offshore development did not really begin to get underway until China's policy of openness to the outside world in the 1980s allowed for cooperation with foreign oil companies. CNOOC and its predecessor, the ministry of petroleum, have successfully completed four rounds of bidding for blocks in the South China Sea, the Bohai Gulf and the East China Sea. Since the early 1980s, the number of wells CNOOC drills itself has increased significantly since the early 1980s, and by all accounts CNOOC's technical abilities have improved even more.

While a number of firms were disappointed with their finds in the South China Sea, the area has shown promise for several of the major oil companies. The ACT Group (Agip, Chevron and Texaco) brought their wells in the Pearl River Mouth Basin onstream in November 1991 and expect peak production to be approximately 1.5 million tons annually. U.S. firms Amoco, Phillips and Pecten have also had some success in the South China Sea area.

A number of firms are now involved in exploration and development in the Bohai Gulf area. U.S. firm, Texaco, signed a major exploration contract for a block in Bohai in 1991. Bp and the Japanese National Oil Company had signed similar contracts earlier. Bohai produced 940,000 tons of crude oil in 1991, mainly from CNOOC's own wells.

The largest contract signed offshore was the sales contract for gas from the Yacheng 13-1 field south of Hainan Island between producers CNOOC, Arco and Kuwait National Petroleum Corporation and purchaser China Light and Power and Esso in Hong Kong—the contract is to supply 2.9 billion cubic meters/year to China Light and Power for power generation. The plan calls for an 800 km pipeline to Honk Kong and a smaller offshoot line to Hainan Island. The sales agreement culminated a nine year effort by Arco to find an appropriate customer for the gas first discovered in 1983.

Market Assessment Between 1985 and 1992, exports of crude oil accounted for a significant but declining share of Chinese production—from 24 to 15 percent overall. China's crude oil exports reached a high in 1985 of about 610,000 b/d and steadily declined to about 430,000 b/d in 1992, a decrease of about 30 percent. According to DOE, China ranked about seventeenth as a world oil exporter (500,000 b/d). The top three world oil exporters were Saudi Arabia, Iran, and the former Soviet Union. Daily exports from these countries were about 4.8 million b/d, 2.2 million b/d, and 2.2 million b/d, respectively.

The three largest export markets for Chinese crude oil are the United States, Japan, and Singapore. According to the East-West Center, exports to the United States in 1985, for example, totalled about 90,000 b/d, but by 1992 had declined by 20 percent, to about 72,000 b/d. China's exports to Singapore also declined by 74 percent, from about 170,000 b/d in 1985 to 45,000 b/d by 1992. On the other hand, exports to Japan between 1985 and 1992 increased by 14 percent, from 221,000 b/d to 252,000 b/d.

Petroleum exports are a major part of China's total foreign exchange earnings, but have fallen in importance relative to other exports since 1985, when 26 percent of gross foreign exchange earnings came from petroleum. In 1992, oil exports accounted for only about 4 percent of China's total foreign exchange earnings, amounting to about $3.8 billion in foreign exchange revenues.

The major contributing factor to the increase in imports is the demand for oil by China's transportation sector. According to officials at DOE, there is a great demand for oil to operate motor vehicles (taxis, trucks, and buses). This sector's need for oil is projected to grow at about 7 percent annually between 1985 and the year 2000, according to the Petroleum Industry Research Foundation. Oil consumption for purposes other than transportation will also continue to increase. For example, the East-West Center estimates that as China's overall economy continues its robust growth, the demand for oil will increase, reaching 4.8 million b/d by the year 2000. Although more conservative in its estimate, DOE also projects an increase in China's oil consumption. It estimates demand will rise to 3.2 million b/d by the year 2000 and to 4 million b/d by 2010.

Energy experts at DOE and the East-West Center project that China's oil consumption will continue to increase and that by 1995 China will become a net importer of oil. Between 1980 and 1992, China's imports of crude oil increased from about 8,000 b/d to 227,000 b/d, while consumption of oil increased from 1.8 million b/d to 2.7 million b/d. Between 1991 and 1992, crude oil imports increased by 91 percent. Imports of crude oil are expected to reach about 400,000 b/d by 1995 and 1.2 million b/d by the year 2000. China imports crude oil mostly from neighboring countries such as Indonesia and Malaysia, but also from the Middle East. In 1991, for example, it imported about 53,000 b/d of crude oil from Oman and about 1,000 b/d from Iran.

OPEC's long-term hopes are pinned on one region: China and its Asian neighbors. While growth in oil demand in Europe and the United States is expected to be flat over the next decade, Asian demand is expected to grow by the year 2000 by 5 million barrels a day, according to Fereidun Fesharaki, energy expert at Hawaii's East-West Center. China's oil consumption alone is growing 10 percent a year. In 1990, China exported 500,000 barrels a day. By 2000 it will be importing 1.3 million barrels a day, or the equivalent of virtually all of Kuwait's export production. (China, no doubt, will be increasingly tempted to pay for this by selling arms.)

Competitive Situation   Oil represented about 18 percent of China's 1992 overall energy consumption. Coal remains the primary source of energy and represented about 75 percent of total energy consumption in 1992. Coal will continue to be China's primary source of energy into the next century. By 2010, for example, China will still rely on coal to meet about 75 percent of its energy needs, according to DOE. Notwithstanding the central importance of coal, oil is an important energy source and will remain so for some time into the future (see Figure 11).

Market Access   As China's rapid economic growth has increased its demand for oil, China has encouraged foreign investment in order to obtain the capital and technology needed to expand exploration and production. While exact information is not available on China's domestic investment in its oil industry, U.S. energy experts told us that China lacks the financial resources to increase investment in oil exploration and production activities. U.S. oil companies, however, have invested more than $1 billion in China's petroleum sector since 1978.

To encourage foreign investment in its oil industry, in early 1993 the Chinese government announced that it would allow foreign oil companies to bid competitively for exploration and production contracts in previously closed areas in northwest China and other onshore areas. Several U.S. oil companies have signed agreements with Chinese officials, and some are discussing potential exploration and production activities. In addition, China has made other reforms to encourage foreign investment. For example, it reduced the amount of oilfield royalties that foreign firms must pay from 12.5 percent for all oilfields to an adjustable rate for various production levels of the fields.

The G.A.O. (47) contested ten U.S.-owned companies based on a list provided by the American Petroleum Institute to obtain their perspectives on China's petroleum industry. All of the U.S. oil companies we interviewed are either currently investing or considering investing in China either in onshore or offshore oilfields within the next five years. Eight of the companies we interviewed said they had invested in China's oil industry beginning as early as 1978. As of December 1992, these oil companies had investments ranging from $10 million to $200 million or more each. Five of the companies individually had $200 million or more invested in China. Most of the oil companies we interviewed said they were primarily involved in exploration.

Officials of the ten U.S. companies contacted cited the following factors that make China's oil industry an attractive investment opportunity:
- China has abundant crude oil reserves (roughly equal to those of the United States).
- China's relatively unexplored Tarim Basin is believed to contain large potential reserves of crude oil
- China's population and rapidly growing economy create a large and growing demand for energy, including oil.

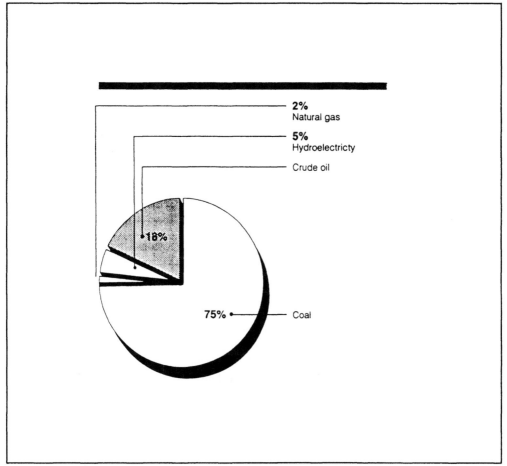

Figure 11: China's Overall Energy Consumption, 1992
Source: Lawrence Berkeley Laboratory in Reference (47).

- China has had about fifteen years of experience in conducting business with U.S. oil companies.

U.S. oil companies contacted, both those presently investing in China and those considering doing so, said that the following factors discourage investment in China's oil sector:

- The companies' earlier onshore and offshore oil exploration and production efforts in China were not fully successful. China had opened several onshore tracts to foreign investors in 1985. Those companies investing in these tracts did not recover sufficient oil to make their investments profitable.
- China's proposed oil tracts in the Tarim Basin offered for bid are not considered the best geologically, and the basin's remote location makes exploration and transportation costly.
- China continues to control oil prices. Although China has paid international prices for oil to foreign companies producing offshore, some companies are not sure whether China will be willing to pay international market prices for oil produced by foreign companies onshore. If China does not pay international market prices, oil production and transportation may be too costly for foreign companies.
- China's past contract terms may have not been adequate for continued foreign investment. Some oil company officials said that China needs to improve its contract terms in order to continue to attract foreign investment for the Tarim Basin.
- China's government gives preferential treatment to its government-owned corporations over foreign companies. Several oil company officials said they found it difficult to do business in China because foreign companies are not treated equally. For example, some U.S. oil companies consider the tracts offered for foreign investment in the Tarim Basin to be less geologically desirable than other tracts in that region.

According to the Wall Street Journal for May 18, 1994 has decided on a new price and marketing strategy. It appears to have the overall purpose of enduring the financial health of China's two oil giants, China National Petrochemical Corporation (SINOPEC), the country's leading refiner, and China National Petroleum Corporation (CNPC), the leading oil producer. Low international oil prices have cut into their margins and led to uncontrolled imports, reducing their market share.

Documents dated April 4 and implemented piecemeal since the beginning of May call for a new centrally directed price and distribution system. The order sets a new two-tier price for Chinese crude oil, ranging from 700 yuan ($81) to 1,250 yuan ($144) a ton, depending on whether the oil is produced within or outside the central plan. That's roughly an increase of 100%, and is seen as a major boost for CNPC.

The new system also dictates prices for some refined products that are well above the international spot market price. Gasoline will wholesale for $277 a ton and diesel for $218 a ton. Not all new prices have taken effect.

China's two leading oil distributors, Sinochem and Unipec, will handle all imports and license retailers under the regulations. The monopoly will force foreign oil companies to work through the two conglomerates to sell oil products in China, threatening retail networks built up by the foreign firms. The documents suggest that central authorities will also close or take over many small-scale Chinese retailers and distributors that had thrived on selling low-cost imports.

The new regulations come into effect even as China seeks to increase the role of foreign oil companies in helping to solve its energy woes. In the past year, China has invited companies to explore onshore sites, including the potentially oil rich Tarim Basin in Xinjiang Province, and opened up new offshore exploration areas.

Sinopec has also opened the refining sector to foreign investment in a bid to raises output. Royal Dutch/Shell Group, for one, plans a $5 billion joint venture refinery in Nanhai, Guangdong Province.

Foreign oil company officials said they want to wait to see how long the new regulations will last and how the Chinese will implement them before commenting on their companies' business prospects. But many acknowledged that the regulations have already impacted sales and prompted a wait-and-see attitude about large-scale new investments, particularly those involved in downstream production and distribution.

Useful Contacts China's State Council has the overall responsibility for the Chinese oil industry, while subordinate government corporations under the Council administer its functions. In early 1993, these administering corporations' functions were as follows:

- The Ministry of Foreign Trade and Economic Cooperation is responsible for establishing and implementing foreign trade policy.
- The China National Petroleum Corporation is responsible for exploration and development of onshore and shallow water offshore oilfield areas, and natural gas fields. When China opened eleven southern provinces to foreign investors in 1985, China National Petroleum Corporation established the China National Oil and Gas Exploration and Development Corporation to negotiate and sign oil exploration contracts in the Tarim Basin and other oilfield areas.
- The China National Offshore Oil Corporation controls all deep offshore operations and manages foreign oil company investment in Chinese deep waters.
- The China National Petrochemical Corporation manages oil refining and marketing of refined products.
- The China National Chemicals Import and Export Corporation manages oil exporting and importing.

The Chinese government has also established two joint venture companies: (1) China United Petroleum Corporation (China Oil)—a joint venture between China National Chemicals Import and Export Corporation and China National Petroleum—and (2) China United Petrochemical Corporation—a joint venture oil trading company between China National Petrochemical Corporation and China National Chemicals Import and Export Corporation. Both China Oil and United Petrochemical Corporation handle oil trading, overseas investments, foreign investment in China's exploration and development sector, and Chinese investment abroad.

The Ministry of Energy (MOE)   The MOE was abolished in March 1993, and Ministries of Coal Industry and Electric Power were created.   The State Planning Commission also provides advice to the State Council on energy policies.

The new structure of the oil industry is shown in Figure 12 (47).

The China National Petroleum Corporation (CNPC)   The China National Petroleum Corporation (CNPC) is the major producer of crude oil in China.   It produced 99 percent of China's crude oil output in 1990, over 98 percent in 1991, and more than 97 percent in 1992; and will continue to produce over 90 percent of crude for the next decade and possibly far beyond.   CNPC, whose Chinese name is actually the China National Petroleum and Natural Gal General Corporation, was formed during a reorganization of the former Ministry of Petroleum in 1988.   It controls all onshore oil fields and shallow water offshore fields (up to five meters depth).   Its major production comes from a number of older oil fields, most notably the Daqing oil field in northeast China, which produces almost 40 percent of China's annual oil output.

By changing from a ministry to a company, CNPC was supposed to rationalize its operations and become less bureaucratic.   However, the transition is not yet complete. CNPC still has many of the prerogatives of a ministry, especially since its president—currently Wang Tao—is considered to be at ministerial level within the Chinese government.   In addition to carrying out it commercial operations, CNPC continues to be the major supplier of policy advice on oil and gas issues to the State Council.   Moreover, since CNPC sells much of its oil below market prices, the company operates very much as state planners direct, rather than as a business reacting to market forces.   Much of CNPC's work involves such arcana as distributing quotas both to oil fields and consumers.   Needless to say, lower-than-market-prices act as a severe disincentive to exploration, to developing costlier wells and to maximizing production from current fields.

CNPC's oilfields are administered by eighteen petroleum administration and exploration bureaus.   There has been a great deal of discussion in recent years as to whether the various oilfields should be allowed to operate more independently by, for example, setting their own prices and making independent investment decisions.

CNPC's President Wang said in August that he expected by 1995 to transform the petroleum administrations bureaus into "enterprise groups which will operate in line with the requirements of world market economy."   At present, many smaller, less profitable oilfields are now left on their own, with not investment from the center.   The large profitable oilfields, including Daqing, Shengli and Liaohe, continue under active central government control, as do promising new areas in Xinjiang.

In addition to its crude oil production, CNPC itself is a strong vertically integrated company.   It produces a large part of its equipment and machinery through its own manufacturing plants.   CNPC's wholly-owned subsidiary, China National Oil Development Corporation (CNODC) is the contracting agent for cooperation with foreign companies.   In addition to the southern provinces which had been opened to foreign participation earlier, on February 17, 1993, CNPC announced that it was opening up the southeastern sector of the

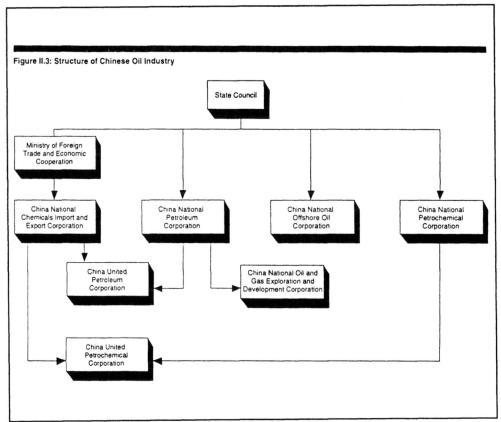

Figure II.3: Structure of Chinese Oil Industry

Figure 12: Structure of Chinese Oil Industry
Sources: Petroleum Argus and East-West Center

Tarim Basin, and areas in north and east China. In addition, ten developed oilfields were chosen as candidates for cooperation with foreign firms.

The China National Offshore Oil Corporation (CNOOC)   The China National Offshore Oil Corporation (CNOOC) was formed in 1982. It controls all offshore oil and gas fields of a depth beyond five meters. CNOOC's oil production in 1992 was 3.87 million tons. CNOOC operates a number of oilfields itself, but has far greater foreign involvement than CNPC. Offshore bidding began in China in 1982. Thus far, four rounds of bidding have been completed, and the South China Sea is under active development. The fourth round of bidding for two areas in the East China Sea was announced on June 30, 1992. Winners announced thus far in that round are Texaco, Agip, Maersk, Chevron, Maxus, Exxon, Japex, Teikoku, Shell China and Pecten International, and Cluff Oil of Hong Kong. Exploration is was expected to commence in early 1994.

CNOOC appears to have less clout within the Chinese government than the larger CNPC. Its President, Wang Yan, is ranked as equivalent to a Vice Minister. CNOOC is more a purely commercial operation than CNPC. Its great success thus far has not been in producing oil and gas—although CNOOC expects offshore production to reach 4.6 million tons this year and 10 million tons by 1997—but in attracting foreign investment. From 1982-1992, foreign firms spent USD 2.25 billion on exploration and USD 814 million on development offshore.

The China Petrochemical International Corporation (SINOPEC)   SINOPEC (the China Petrochemical International Corporation is the major refiner and producer of petrochemical products in China, producing almost 90 percent of total refinery output. It was formed in 1983 and has operated very much as part of the planned economy with its inputs determined by state planners (and by the production of CNPC) and its output determined by the interaction between quotas and the non-market prices it faces. SINOPEC's output figures account for the oil and gas that it purchases (from CNPC, CNOOC or SINOCHEM), refines and then sells, and not oil that it refines on a service contract basis. Some crude oil is purchased directly from the oilfield by the end-user, and then SINOPEC (or another refiner) refines it under a service contract. SINOPEC is divided into seventy-two production units, of which thirty-seven are refineries. Observers point out that while SINOPEC has modernized its equipment, now output prices often make it unprofitable for it to use some of its most advanced refining equipment and processes.

In recent years SINOPEC has invested heavily in new equipment for both refining and petrochemicals (including petrochemicals then used for enhanced oil recovery). U.S. firms have been active in selling equipment and plants to SINOPEC, and more recently have shown heightened interest in downstream joint ventures in this area. Such opportunities do exist. A number of European oil firms are building ethylene plants in China, which are due to come online in the next few years. On September 27, 1993, SINOPEC and Amoco Corporation signed a general protocol to facilitate the two companies exploring joint ventures in refining and petrochemicals. Other U.S. companies are interested in refining, processing and marketing opportunities.

As with offshore and onshore exploration, it appears that the downstream industry will increasingly welcome foreign participation. China's objectives are to expand and modernize its refining capacity, both to upgrade the competitiveness of its plants and to be able to utilize a broader mix of imported crudes. Again, as has occurred upstream, the increased openness of the Chinese to foreign participation will not only provide opportunities for large companies willing and able to make major investments, but will also open up new markets for small and medium equipment and service companies.

China National Chemicals Import/Export Corporation (SINOCHEM) SINOCHEM (the China National Chemicals Import and Export Corporation) is an import/export company under the Ministry of Foreign Trade and Economic Cooperation, MOFTEC). It trades in oil and gas as part of its international chemicals trade. The quantities of oil and gas it imports and exports are determined by state planners. Until recently, it was the only company legally engaged in the import and export of petroleum and petrochemical products from onshore sources. In January 1993, SINOCHEM and CNPC formed China National United Oil Corporation (originally "SINOIL," but changed to China Oil more recently), authorized to import and export crude, refined products, and petrochemicals; and to import telecommunications equipment used in e and d, engage in oil refining and petrochemicals production, and to explore and develop overseas oilfields and make other foreign investments related to the petroleum industry. In February 1993, SINOCHEM and SINOPEC formed China International United Petroleum and Chemical Corporation (UNIPEC), which is authorized to import both crude oil (for SINOPEC's refineries) and petroleum products. CNOOC engages in production sharing agreements that include direct exports from offshore. There are reports that some localities import refined petroleum products outside of the purview of SINOCHEM, UNIPEC or China Oil.

Contact names and addresses:

The following are the addresses and telephone numbers for the major organizations involved in oil and gas in China:

> **China National Petroleum Corporation**
> **International Bureau**
> **P.O. Box 766, Liu Pu Kang**
> **Beijing 100724 P.R.C.**
> **Tel: 86-1-201-6107 Fax: 86-1-209-4806**

> **China National Offshore Oil Corporation**
> **International Liaison Department**
> **Jingxin Building 23/F, Jia 2, North Dongsanhuan Road**
> **Chaoyang District, Beijing, P.R.C. 100027**
> **Tel: 86-1-466-3696 Fax: 86-1-466-2994**

SINOPEC International
No. A-6 Huixin Dongjie
Chaoyang District
Beijing 100029 P.R.C.
Tel: 86-1-422-5533   Fax: 86-1-421-6972

SINOCHEM
Erligou, Xijiao
Beijing 100044 P.R.C.
Tel: 86-1-831-7733   Fax: 86-1-831-6017

China National United Oil Corporation
Exhibition Centre Hotel
No. 135 Xizhimenwai Street
Beijing 100044 P.R.C.
Tel: 86-1-835-0975   Fax: 86-1-835-0989

Some useful contacts in the oil refinery industry include:

Anshan Oil Refinery
Tiexi District, Anshan
Liaoning Province 114011
Tel: 44321

Gangzhou Oil Refinery
Xinhua District, Gangzhou
Hebei Province 061000
Tel: 242811

Harbin Oil Refinery
Taiping District, Harbin
Heilongjiang Province 150056
Tel: 72522-651

Jinan Oil Refinery
Gongye Nanlu, Jinan
Shandong Province 250101
Tel: 43622

Jingmen Oil Refinery
Jingmen, Hubei Province 434539
Tel: 31501

Jiujiang Oil Refinery
Jiujiang, Jiangxi Province 332004
Tel: 224911

Lanzhou Oil Refinery
Xigu, Lanzhou
Gansu Province 730060
Tel: 56011

Linyuan Oil Refinery
Datong, Daqing
Heilongjiang Province 163813
Tel: 348489-488

Luoyang Oil Refinery
Jili, Luoyang
Henan Province 471012
Tel: 337171

Qianguo Refinery
Qian Gorlos County
Jilin Province 131100
Tel: 3921

Shijiazhuang Oil Refinery
Chang'an, Shijiazhuang
Hebei Province 050032
Tel: 552901-14

PHARMACEUTICALS

A short term sales potential for Western medicines in China is substantial. Total pharmaceutical imports in 1992 reached $319 million, of which Western prescription medicines accounted for $128 million. China will continue to import Western pharmaceutical products which are used to treat the leading causes of death because its domestic production does not meet market demand. Although China has significantly increased its production of antibiotics during the past five years, similar drugs which are produced abroad are considered to be superior in quality and efficacy. It is difficult to gauge market potential for specific drugs because detailed information on domestic production was not available.

Chinese doctors are knowledgeable about Western drugs, urban residents enjoy increasing levels of disposable income, and patients are receptive to Western drugs. Market access is expected to improve as China eliminates quotas on certain pharmaceutical products in 1995. Although the criteria for issuance of an import registration certificate are not entirely clear, domestic production capability continues to play a role in deciding whether an import registration certificate will be issued.

Long term sales potential is more difficult to predict. Nevertheless, with a rapidly expanding economy, an increase in per capita income, and greater emphasis on health, growth of the market undoubtedly will be substantial. Sales deriving from the production of plants built through foreign investment are likely to exceed the potential for pure imports. Production by foreign invested enterprises ("FIE") is causing dynamic growth in the market. Some FIE's have reported that after a product is introduced, increased awareness has actually caused market demand to grow. Chinese trade policy continues to encourage foreign investment over purchases from foreign sources in order to foster self-sufficiency and conserve foreign exchange.

This section pertains to prospective business opportunities for sale and manufacture of pharmaceuticals, defined as Western drugs which are prescribed by a qualified physician. Traditional Chinese medicines and Western medicines which can be purchased without a prescription are not within the scope of this section.

The health care system is organized vertically along governmental, industrial and geographical lines. The Ministry of Public Health, the People's Liberation Army, and industrial ministries all administer their own systems (including clinics, hospitals and medical colleges) which are designed to serve their employees. Provincial, township and county governments maintain their own hospitals and village clinics which are utilized by government employees and workers who are employed by township and village enterprises. In 1990, 208,734 health care institutions served all patients.

Prior to the initiation of economic reforms about ten years ago, provision of health care was offered primarily through communes. Emphasis was placed on preventive care and traditional Chinese medicine. Since the elimination of the commune system, health care is no longer free. Health care subsidy programs have emerged which cover the medical expenses of about 20-25 percent of China's population. There are more than 800 million Chinese, whose access to the health care system depends upon their ability to pay because they are not employed by an organization which offers medical care subsidies.

The government medical subsidy system offers full benefits to about 25 million civil servants, but does not cover their dependents' medical costs. The labor subsidy system provides complete coverage to about 75 million workers employed by State-run enterprises; fifty percent of their dependents' costs are covered. Seventy-nine million workers employed by collective, township or village enterprises receive subsidized medical benefits through a variety of schemes which feature co-payment requirements and ceilings on reimbursements.

Individuals who do not receive medical care subsidies are less likely to purchase higher priced imported Western medicines. Patients in urban areas are generally insured and have more income to spend on medical care. In the fourth quarter of 1992, average income increased in real terms for urban residents by 8.8 percent and for rural residents by 5.9 percent. Therefore, it is possible that people who do not receive medical care subsidies will be able to afford to purchase Western drugs.

SPAC (State Pharmaceutical Administration of China) is a government department which reports directly to the State Council. SPAC is responsible for managing the industry's production and distribution, policy development, research and development, establishment and enforcement of national standards and quality controls, examination and inspection of pharmaceuticals which are produced in China and imported, and coordination of imports and exports.

SPAC is divided into nine bureaus: planning, policy and regulation, science and education, quality administration, economic coordination, machinery and equipment, personnel and labor, foreign affairs bureau, and general office. Provincial and local level pharmaceutical administrations are managed by SPAC. SPAC supervises five specialized national corporations: China National Pharmaceutical Supply and Marketing Corporation, China National Pharmaceutical Industry Corporation, China National Medicine Corporation, China National Pharmaceutical Foreign Trade Corporation, and China National Medicines and Health Products Import/Export Corporation (these State trading enterprises are prospective sales agents). SPAC is also affiliated with several research institutes and publishing organizations.

The primary function of MPH (Ministry of Public Health) is to set public health policy, supervise medical institutions and coordinate medical research. MPH plays a secondary role in the regulation of drug importation. MPH's Department of Pharmaceutical Administration is primarily involved with certification of drug efficacy.

Market Assessment

1. Market Demand

a. Policy Developments

For the period 1991-2000, the Chinese government has allocated 26 billion RMB (USD 4.5 billion) for investment in capital construction and technical renovation of manufacturing facilities. During the Eighth Five-Year Plan (1991-1995), China plans to increase overall production of the medical industry by 8.5 percent annually; domestic sales are expected to increase by 7 percent, output of drugs by 3.5 percent, and exports by 6.5 percent per year.

Prospects for foreign sales and investment are good. Chinese doctors are knowledgeable about Western drugs, urban residents enjoy increasing levels of disposable income, and the industry has great potential, but requires more advanced production technology and equipment.

b. Research and Development

On January 11, 1993, the State Science and Technology Commission announced the establishment of a leading group on new drug research and development. The objective of the leading group is to concentrate effort and finances on coordinating research. Deputy Director Hui Yongzheng stated that China's previous pharmaceutical research system concentrated on copying foreign drugs in order to shorten the time required for new drug development. This research system is fragmented and experiences difficulty in transferring basic research results to industrial application. The meeting in January was convened to announce a new direction for pharmaceutical development.

Further information on China's research and development plans was not available from SPAC and MPH. Both organizations were reluctant to offer any general information about specific existing projects or resources which are committed to research and development.

c. Diseases

China is able to produce several types of Western medicines to treat major illnesses. However, domestic production does not meet the entire market demand. New drugs which are more effective and less toxic are needed. Advanced drugs are generally imported because domestic producers lack the technology which is required to produce many of the drugs. Foreign experts believe Chinese production technology lags more than ten years behind Western production technology.

Although some of the diseases listed below in Table 106 are treated with traditional Chinese medicine, many Chinese doctors believe that such preparations are ineffective for short term treatment. Sales opportunities for Western drugs which treat these diseases are vast, but may be limited by lack of sufficient foreign exchange, cost to the patient, and import substitution policies which protect domestic producers.

Table 106

Death Rate for Ten Major Diseases in China (1990)

Urban Areas		Rural Areas	
Disease	Death PCT	Disease	Death PCT
malignant tumor	21.88	respiratory	24.82
cerebrovascular	20.83	malignant tumor	17.47
cardiovascular	15.81	cerebrovascular	16.16
respiratory	15.76	cardiovascular	10.82
injury/toxicosis	6.91	injury/toxicosis	10.65
digestive	4.02	digestive	5.01
endocrine, immunity		neonatal	2.51
nutrition	1.74	tuberculosis	1.85
urinary/reproductive	1.58	infectious not above	1.76
neonatal	1.51	urinary/reproductive	1.48
tuberculosis	1.20		
Total	91.24	Total	92.53

Population in 1990: 1.1 billion
Source: <u>China Statistical Yearbook</u> (Beijing: State Statistical Bureau, 1991).

d. Aging Population

An interview with the SPAC revealed that the Chinese government is concerned about the medical system's ability to treat diseases associated with aging or which occur in the older portion of the population. The following table suggests a substantial portion of the population may require Western medicine for treatment of serious diseases during the next ten years. By the year 2000, 29,769,000 people will be over the age of fifty (not accounting for those who die during the next seven years).

Population by Age (1990 1:1,000)

Age	People	Age	People
0-09	11106.3	50-59	8741.7
10-19	21785.7	60-69	6045.0
20-29	23014.5	70-79	2909.0
30-39	17011.9	80-84	537.1
40-49	11302.6	85+	233.8

2. End-User Profile

Prospects for foreign sales are good. Chinese doctors are knowledgeable about Western drugs, urban residents enjoy increasing levels of disposable income, and patients are receptive to Western drugs.

Both Chinese doctors and patients tend to view Western pharmaceuticals as being of higher quality and more effective than domestic products. Although imported drugs are typically twice the price of locally produced alternatives, they are preferred by many urban Chinese even if cheaper domestic brands are available.

Medical China, a group of medical consultants based in Hong Kong, has conducted a comprehensive study of demand for various pharmaceuticals. The firm interviewed doctors and pharmacists from 150 hospitals and pharmacies throughout China and concluded that most physicians demonstrated extensive knowledge of Western antibiotics and were receptive to introducing them to China.

The interviews revealed that doctors prescribe Western drugs based upon their assessment of quality, efficacy and cost to the patient. The study demonstrated that in these rural areas where income is lower and knowledge of Western medicines is less prevalent, Chinese patients were more likely to first request traditional Chinese medicines. However, in urban areas, patients were more aware of the efficacy of foreign drugs and were in a better position to pay for them because their medical care costs are subsidized.

Recent 1993 statistics on personnel in health care institutions are not available. However, the China Statistical Yearbook for 1991 indicates that there may be future increases in demand for Western medicines which is correlated to changes in Chinese medical practices. Between 1988 and 1990, the number of doctors who practice Western medicine increased from 1,251,000 to 1,389,000 respectively for both years, while doctors of traditional medicine decreased 471,000 and 459,000 respectively. (The ratio of average number of doctors per person in China is 1.5 to 1,000.) The number of physicians which practice both Chinese and Western medicine was 1,617,000 and 1,763, 000 respectively. According to the same source, pharmacists of Western medicine numbered more than pharmacists of Chinese medicine in 1990, 236,000 and 170,000 respectively.

One may also infer from these statistics, that if health care institutions become more oriented toward Western medicine for treatment of certain diseases, hospitals and pharmacies will be more willing to stock them. The cost of maintaining sufficient stock and consistency of supply will probably be key factors.

2. Imports   Total pharmaceutical import value reached USD 318,715,437 in 1992. Importation of medicaments containing Chinese traditional medicine in 1992 accounts for more than half of total imports and are valued at USD 177,344,826. Other items which are included in the import statistics but are beyond the scope of this report, include adhesive dressings and plasters, suture materials, x-ray preparations, dental preparations and contraceptive preparations; accounting for USD 13,140,885 of the import value. Total importation of pharmaceuticals within the scope of this report accounted for approximately

USD 128,231,000 in 1992, after subtracting both traditional Chinese medicines and other items.

According to MPH, competitive products from Japan, Germany and Italy enjoy a greater market share because firms from these nations have a long trade relationship with China. Some hospitals in China were established by these countries in the 1900s. The institutions and doctors have maintained contacts with these nations since that time.

The following tabulation (58) gives an idea of the trends in the total pharmaceutical market and in imports (in millions of $US):

	1993	1994	1995
Total Market Size	6,640	8,100	8,250
Total Local Production	7,000	8,500	9,000
Total Exports	860	980	1,180
Total Imports	500	580	700
Total Imports from U.S.	28	32	40

Competitive Situation

1. Domestic Production

a. Products

During the past five years, China has focused on the production of antibiotics and basic medicines used to treat acute or endemic diseases. Data on domestic production of specific drugs or types of drugs was not available from public sources. Such data may be available from Chinese contacts for a fee.

Antibiotics: During the Seventh Five-Year Plan, China emphasized increasing the production capacity and quality of antibiotics. According to the SPAC, antibiotics currently account for 15% of total pharmaceutical production in China. The overall supply of the most common antibiotics appears to meet 90% of the demand. However, China cannot produce the most advanced penicillin or third and fourth generation cephalosporin. China also continues to import bulk preparations required to make antibiotics and to supply 900 factories which are devoted to bulk production.

Anti-Cancer Drugs: Adriamycin (generically known as xorubicin HCI) is a broad spectrum anti-cancer drug used primarily for treatment of various tumors, lung cancer and gastric cancer. Haimen Pharmaceutical Factory is the only domestic producer of the drug. In 1987, construction began on the Haimen Factory in Jiaojiang City, Zhejiang Province. Drug production began in 1991. In 1980, the Chinese government decided to develop domestic production for this drug in an effort to reduce the cost for importation of the drug to treat over 1.8 million cancer patients. The Huaming Pharmaceutical Factory in Zantou also expected to produce 1.5 million bottles of xorubicin HCl annually. The drug will cost fifty percent less an imported doxurubicin.

b. Domestic Producers

More than 2,000 factories are involved in the production of Western medicines in China. The SPAC has identified thirty-six key enterprises which are the largest and most profitable domestic producers. The producers described below were selected by the SPAC Economic Cooperation Division as the most prominent factories during our interview.

i.   Huabei (North China) Pharmaceutical Factory

Located in Shijiazhuang City, Hebei Province, Huabei is a leading producer of antibiotics, sulfa drugs, vitamins, and bulk preparations. Huabei produces ninety products, including one-sixth of China's total antibiotic output each year. Since its establishment in 1958, the factory is now considered to be one of the most technologically advanced due to its importation of the pharmaceutical industry's first fully computerized production line. The factory has adopted the international GMP (Good Manufacturing Practices) standards. The factory employs 10,000 people.

ii. Shanghai No. 3 Pharmaceutical Factory

Located in Shanghai Municipality, the factory has been one of China's primary antibiotic manufacturers since 1951. Its other main products are penicillin, erythromycin, neomycin, oxacillin, piperacillin, cephalothin, cephamamdole nafate, and cephaperazone. Sixty percent of its production is exported annually, earning more than USD 8 million. The factory employs more than 2,000 people.

In 1990 Shanghai No. 3 broke ground for a new plant, called the Zhejiang Branch Factory, which will have an output value of USD 60 million per year. The project is comprised of two parts—USD 36.5 million was invested for cephalosporin production and USD 10.5 million was invested to increase tetracycline output. The value of imported foreign technology and equipment is expected to be USD 8 million. The tetracycline factory will produce 365 tons per year, of which two-thirds will be exported. When the cephalosporin factory is completed in 1993, it will be China's largest producer with capacity to produce 76 million injection bottles and sixty-five tons of intermediate preparations.

iii. Xinghua Pharmaceutical Factory

Located in Zibo City, Shandong Province, the factory annually produces 5,000 tons of bulk and 20,000 tons of other chemical materials used in the preparation of final products. It exports the material to over forty countries and earns USD 10 million each year. The factory employs 4,800 people.

iv. *Northeast Pharmaceutical Factory*

This is forty year old factory is a large scale, comprehensive enterprise, producing stock drugs, bulk and preparations. Located in Shenyang City, Liaoning Province, the factory produces over sixty varieties of chemicals and semi-finished preparations. The factory produces approximately 5,000 tons of pharmaceutical products including bulk and powder. During 1986-1995, the factory will emphasizing production of vitamins and cephalothin and developing ten new drugs. In 1987, its total export value reached USD 24.8 million. The factory employs 93,000 people.

v. *Baiyunsan Pharmaceutical Factory*

Located in Guangzhou, Guangdong Province, the factory produces medicant preparations and final products for treatment of colds, heart disease, and stomach disorders. The factory exports its products primarily to the U.S., France and Brazil. The factory was established in 1975 and employs 5,000 people.

vi. *Harbin Pharmaceutical Factory*

Located in Harbin, Heilongjiang Province, the factory was established in 1958 and employs more than 4,000 people. The factory is a major producer of penicillin, sulfa drugs, erythromycin, and other preparations. It is a leading exporter, but no statistics on its exports volume are available.

vii. *Shandong Jining Antibiotic Factory*

Located in Jining City, Shandong Province, the company employs 3,000 people. It produces benzylpenicillin sodium, streptomycin sulphate, oxytetracycline base, mitomycin, lincomycin hydrochloride and other antibiotic extractions.

c. *Foreign Investment*

During the Eighth Five-Year Plan, China plans to increase production of penicillin and bulk medicines. By 1995, the production goal is 5,000 per year for each type of product. To attain this goal, China plans to acquire foreign capital and import foreign technology and production equipment. SPAC officials have confirmed that China's research and development program has not been sufficiently funded to support development of the latest technologies.

Foreign pharmaceutical producers will continue to play an important role in minimizing China's cost of technological development through technology licensing. Now that China offers administrative protection for pharmaceutical drugs which were patented abroad between 1986 and 1993 and are to be produced in China, the investment environment is much more attractive. Effective intellectual property protection will ensure parties which are not licensees will not be allowed to manufacture or sell the product in China.

According to SPAC officials, China plans to become self-sufficient in production of all antibiotics during the Eighth Five-Year Plan. Achievement of this goal will continue to depend upon acquisition of foreign technology and investment capital. China primarily relies upon the importation of cephalexin, cefazolin, and cephradine to meet domestic demand. Joint venture production of these three drugs presents a good investment opportunity.

Two new production lines will be set up for penicillin; one at the Shandong Pharmaceutical Factory and the other at the Northeast Pharmaceutical Factory. the cost is estimated to be 500 million RMB (USD 87 million) to achieve a production goal of 1,000 tons per year. Two existing factories will be renovated to produce bulk preparations. These factories, Harbin Pharmaceutical Factory and North China Pharmaceutical Factory, have been assigned a production goal of 2,000 tons per year.

Other foreign investment opportunities exist for production of drugs to treat illnesses commonly found in the elderly such as heart disease, cancer, bone brittleness, and alzheimer disease. New methods of drug administration such as controlled release medicines, skin patches, nasal sprays, and inhalation preparations are also targeted for foreign investment by SPAC officials.

China is relying heavily on foreign investment to upgrade the technological level of the pharmaceutical industry. No statistics are available on production by foreign-invested enterprises ("FIE"), both joint ventures and wholly-foreign owned enterprises, which would currently account for a certain percent of domestic production and a certain percent of pharmaceutical exports. The information may be purchased from SPAC. The major FIEs are listed below.

i.   Glaxo Pharmaceuticals, Ltd. (Britain): The joint venture produces Ventolin, a bronchi dilator for asthma treatment, in cooperation with two Chinese partners; the Southwest No. 3 Pharmaceutical Factory in Chongqing and the China National Pharmaceutical Foreign Trade Corporation.

ii.   Otsuka Pharmaceutical Company, Ltd. (Japan): The joint venture produces intravenous solutions in cooperation with the China Pharmaceutical Industrial Corporation in Tianjin.

iii. Janssen Pharmaceutical NV (Belgium): The joint venture produces anesthetic and anti-internal parasite medicine in cooperation with Hanjang Pharmaceutical Factory in Shaanxi Province.

iv.   Swedish Pharmaceutical Consortium (Sweden): The joint venture produces cardiovascular medicines for hypertension and angina pectoris, medicines for treatment of asthma and bronchitis, and nutritious intravenous solutions in Wuxi, Jiangsu Province. The Chinese partner is comprised of three Chinese entities; China National Pharmaceutical Industry Corporation, Mashan District

Industrial Corporation, and Jiangsu Provincial Pharmaceutical Corporation.

v. Ciba-Geigy AG (Switzerland): The joint venture produces cardiovascular drugs, antibiotics, and anti-rheumatic drugs in cooperation with the Beijing General Pharmaceutical Corporation and the Beijing No. 3 Pharmaceutical Factory.

vi. Abbott International Ltd. (U.S.A.): The joint venture produces diagnostic reagents in cooperation with Shanghai Medicine Industry Research Institute and Ningbo Pharmaceutical Factory.

vii. American Enterprise Inc. (U.S.A.): The joint venture produces lincomycin in cooperation with Zhejiang Tian Pharmaceutical Company.

viii. Fluor Daniel Inc. (U.S.A.): Plans to participate in upgrading pharmaceutical plants in Shanghai and Zibo, Shanxi Province. Project contracts were signed in 1990.

ix. HAQ Biomedical Inc. (U.S.A.): The joint venture produces diagnostic kits in cooperation with Zhanjiang Municipality Scientific Committee.

x. ICN Pharmaceuticals Inc. (U.S.A.): Signed an agreement to produce ribavirin, an anti-hepatitis drug, with China National Medical Corporation in 1989.

xi. IVAX Corporation (U.S.A.): Plans to produce six different medicines in cooperation with Kunming Pharmaceutical Factory. The contract was signed in March 1992.

xii. Merck & Company (U.S.A.): Licensed technology to produce recombivax HB, a hepatitis B vaccine, to the National Vaccine and Serum Institute and the Shenzhen Biotechnology Corporation. Ground breaking occurred in April 1993.

xiii. New Brunswick Scientific Inc. (U.S.A.): Agreed to produce new pharmaceutical products and equipment in cooperation with East China University of Chemical Technology in Shanghai.

xiv. Pfizer International Inc. (U.S.A.): The joint venture plans to produce antibiotics in cooperation with the Dalian Pharmaceutical Factory in Liaoning Province. Factory construction began in May 1990.

xv. E.R. Squibb and Sons (U.S.A.): The joint venture produces antibiotics, vitamins, and medicines for cardiovascular and dermatological diseases in cooperation with Shanghai Pharmaceutical Industry Corporation. The joint venture began operation in 1985. In 1990, Squibb spend USD 4.9 million to expand its manufacturing facilities.

xvi. SmithKline Beecham Corporation (U.S.A.): The joint venture produces tagamet, diazide, zental, contact, ectotrin, ridaura to treat ulcers, hypertension, intestinal parasites, colds and allergies, pain, and rheumatoid arthritis respectively, in cooperation with Tianjin Pharmaceutical Industry Corporation. Operation began in 1987.

xvii. Warner-Lambert Company (U.S.A.): The joint venture produces empty hard gelatin capsules, used in delayed release preparations, in cooperation with China International Pharmaceutical Cooperation Corporation in Suzhou. Production began in 1989.

xviii. Meiji Seika Kaisha Ltd. (Japan): The joint venture, Huaming Pharmaceuticals Company, Ltd., produces doxorubicin, an anticancer drug in cooperation with the Tuobin Pharmaceutical Company in Shantou.

2. Competitive Factors

a. Efficacy and Price

As noted above under "end-user profile," doctors prescribe Western pharmaceuticals according to a prioritized criteria. Consideration is first given to quality and efficacy, then cost. Many Chinese doctors have received medical education abroad and are particularly interested in scientific articles and clinical trial studies which demonstrate product efficacy. Retail prices continue to be controlled by the state for domestic products. However, the retail price for imported pharmaceuticals is not controlled.

b. Consistent Supply

Product availability is an import criteria for stocking domestic and foreign drugs. Hospitals which frequently encounter disruption in supply will probably be reluctant to continue stocking the product.

Level three wholesalers do not have a financial incentive to stock expensive foreign products. Because they are required to meet transaction quotas, there is a aversion to stocking high priced products. Foreign manufacturers should closely supervise sales agents which work with the wholesalers to ensure sufficient supply.

c. Marketing Strategy

In addition to utilizing the distribution system described below, it is important to generate demand for imported Western pharmaceuticals. Domestic producers primarily rely upon the standard distribution system and spend little time or effort on marketing. Because antibiotic producers have enjoyed a situation where market demand exceeded supply, it has not been necessary to independently create marketing channels.

Because hospitals are now responsible for their own profits, they have a greater financial interest in what types of drugs are sold by their pharmacies. Doctors are now free to prescribe drugs from pharmacies within or without the hospital pharmacy. Therefore, it is in the best interest of the hospital to give greater weight to the doctor's requests to stock particular drugs.

The Medical China study mentioned above also concluded that Chinese doctors are receptive to receiving new product introductions from pharmaceutical sales people. Many Chinese doctors are well informed about Western medicines and others have received medical education abroad. Chinese doctors are sensitive to sales people which exhibit a patronizing attitude during sales visits and seminars.

Other promotional activities which should be considered include seminars, distribution of free samples, widespread distribution of product literature, advertising in medical journals, and labeling products in Chinese and English.

d. Advertising

Advertising in Chinese medical journals may be an effective means of generating interest in new to market products. Approval must be sought from the Chinese government prior to commencement of an advertising campaign. China's Drug Administration Law does not permit advertisement of drugs unless approved by the local health bureau. Article 44 requires the text of the advertisement to be consistent with the package insert approved by the Ministry of Public Health or the local health bureau. Article 43 provides that an application submitted by a foreign company for advertisement of drug in China should be accompanied by certification issued by the country of production, package insert, and other relevant information.

e. Packaging

Packaging in the Chinese and English language is desirable from a marketing perspective. The Drug Administration Law sets forth specific requirements in Article 37. Although the law does not specifically require the information to be presented in the Chinese language, it would be difficult to convince the authorities that the packaging was in compliance with the law if no Chinese translation is provided. The "package insert should give the name and strength of the product, name of the manufacturer, the PRC government certification number, the lot number, principal ingredients, indications, dosage, contraindications, adverse reactions and precautions."

Market Access

1. Distribution Channels

a. System Description

Product distribution is controlled by a three-tier system which is managed by the China National Corporation of Medicine (CNCM). The system serves the pharmaceutical needs of 208,734 health care institutions, which includes 62,454 hospitals. Hospitals above the county level, numbering 13,489, are most likely to stock Western drugs.

On level one, five national level stations, located in Beijing, Shanghai, Shenyang, Guangzhou, and Tianjin, allocate products to level two. Level two is comprised of 218 provincial level stations which sell to level three. Level three is comprised of 2,300 stations which are located on the county or municipality level. On level three 76,000 retail distribution entities facilitate the work of the other three levels. (At each level, a State controlled price mark up is permitted for distribution of domestic and foreign products.)

Subsequent to decentralization of distribution in the mid-1980s, factories are now authorized to sell directly to hospitals and pharmacies. Factories which do so are also permitted to add on the distribution mark-ups and garner grater profits. Although some independent networks have arisen, most producers continue to use the standard distribution system in order to avoid problems with transportation and bureaucratic barriers. FIEs typically take a diversified approach by establishing independent networks in the urban areas and using the standard distribution system to reach customers in the inland areas.

b. Sales Representation

Hospitals and pharmacies typically do not have import authority. Therefore, they are not in a position to directly sign procurement contracts, deal in foreign exchange, or handle import formalities. Their pharmaceuticals are usually obtained through State Trading Entities (STEs) and the pharmaceutical distribution system described above.

As discussed below in the section on import certification, the importation of pharmaceuticals is highly regulated. Article 11 of the "Provisions Governing Importation of

Drugs," expressly require that an enterprise authorized to engage in foreign trade must obtain a separate business license for handling international drug sale/purchase transactions from the DAB or provincial level units in order to deal in this product. Only properly registered foreign trade units are authorized to contract and handle the import quality testing process. The Provisions also provide for civil and criminal penalties to be imposed according to the provisions of the "Drug Administration Law" for failure to comply with the requirements of the "Provisions."

Article 27, the Drug Administration Law, requires Chinese purchase contracts for drugs which have not been previously imported to be approved by the Ministry of Public Health. The Chinese importer must present the contract along with the drug package insert, clinical trial and new drug approval certification, and technical content and quality information. This process is separate from the procedures discussed below concerning import permits.

In the past, almost all pharmaceutical products were only imported through the Medical and Health Products Import/Export Corporation (MEHECO), which is supervised by SPAC. However, because the trade regime has been decentralized, there are now several STEs which are authorized to import and export pharmaceutical products. Note the list of STEs below in the "key contacts" section.

STEs are previously State-run enterprises which are now only loosely supervised by the State and are responsible for their own profits and losses. STEs continue to play an important role in implementing the state import plan. The typical STE is a buyer agent. This means that they procure goods upon the request of domestic companies lacking authority to engage in foreign trade.

The advantage of engaging the services of an STE is that companies organized on the national level or provincial have a great deal of experience with international trade transactions. STEs have also cultivated contacts with relevant government agencies which administer the import control apparatus, including import licenses, quotas and other restrictions. Such contracts are critical to timely implementation of the contract. STEs are also familiar with the process of obtaining letters of credit and understand the foreign exchange control system.

The disadvantage of appointing and STE as sales agent is that these firms are typically "order takers." Although some STEs are becoming more progressive, American firms should not assume that STEs will actively undertake marketing efforts by designing strategies which are uniquely suited to the Chinese market.

As a result of economic reform programs which have introduced profound changes in the establishment of companies and management of labor, many independent, private enterprises have been established. These firms have "spun-off" previously state-run enterprises of different types—factories, STEs, research institutes, consulting companies and government organizations.

These companies are characterized as independent because they do not play a role in the implementation of the state plan. They are typically capitalized by a combination of private funds and state funds or solely private funds. All such entities are responsible for their profits and losses.

The advantage of appointing this type of company as a sales agent is that it may have a keener financial interest in aggressively marketing your product. Some of these private enterprises have established relations with an entity which has foreign trade authority. When the negotiations reach the contractual stage, the foreign trade entity then signs the contract and implements the importation procedures as required by the Chinese government.

The disadvantage of working with this type of company is that the company may not be authorized to engage in foreign trade. Therefore, the company may perform limited services and must entrust final contract negotiations to an authorized trade enterprise. Even if such companies have received authorization to engage in international trade, the company may lack the critical contacts which implement the import control apparatus, may be unsophisticated in marketing techniques and methods of payment.

One important point of caution merits particular attention by new to market firms. The Chinese restrictions on legal capacity to contract are complicated and unique to socialist nations. Any American firm seeking to appoint a Chinese national as sales agent should ask to see their business license and an English translation of the text. Inspect this document to assure that the individual or enterprise is authorized to engage in business and that the scope of the activity includes the type of product that they propose to sell for your firm.

If the agent does not have a business license or the scope of the business license does not comport with the requirements of the sales agreement, then the agreement will be unenforceable. The agent's signature on the agreement will not make it enforceable because the agent lacks legal capacity to undertake obligations in connection with activities which he/she is not authorized to engage in. For more information about legal issues which pertain to sales agent agreements, please see a separate report on this topic. The report is available from the National Trade Data Bank, the US&FCS offices in China or the China Desk at the U.S. Department of Commerce.

A third means of securing sales representation is to engage the services of a trading company which has established a resident office in China. Such resident offices are not allowed to engage in direct profit-making activity but they can provide other useful services.

Resident representative offices lack legal capacity to sign contracts because such activity is beyond the scope of their business registration and approved activity. This means that a resident representative may engage in market research, product introduction to end-users, liaison and initial negotiations. At the final contract signing stage, the contract is signed by an individual who is not the registered representative or the contract must be signed abroad.

This may be a convenient arrangement for companies which are new to the market or new to exporting. Successful sales in China requires knowledge of the relevant industry, Chinese business practices and law, and language competency.

c. *Terms of Payment*

Typically, international sales contracts are conducted using Chinese contract forms. Most of these forms stipulate payment shall be via letter of credit, opened through the Bank of China. Bank of China still does not permit foreign banks to confirm the letter of credit. China generally has a good reputation of honoring its letters of credit. However, the Bank of China is particularly unwilling to honor documents containing discrepancies between the terms of the letter of credit and shipping documentation.

Payment via the documentary collection process is similar to the letter of credit method, except that there is no absolute guarantee that the buyer will honor the documents which will be presented to the bank. The Bank of China generally does not undertake an active role in collecting payment from the buyer in the event that the buyer is unwilling to tender payment. For more information about dispute resolution mechanisms in China, please see a separate report which is available from US&FCS.

2. Import Regulations

a. Import Substitution and Quotas

The Chinese government administers a complex network of non-tariff import barriers. Pharmaceutical products are heavily regulated by the Ministry of Public Health and subject to quota and import license barriers.

The U.S.-China market access agreement requires China to eliminate import substitution policies. Although quotas and import permits should not be subject to import substitution policies, there will be a period of readjustment during which the following criteria will continue to be applied to bulk and finished preparations. Import permit approval is currently based on whether domestic alternatives are available in sufficient quantities to meet demand, whether the imported drug is to be used to treat a priority disease, and whether the drug meets certain efficacy standards. In the past, import permit applications and renewals have been declined in order to protect domestic producers from foreign competition.

Pursuant to the requirements of the market access agreement, quotas will be gradually increased year by year and eliminated by December 31, 1995 for the following drugs: penicillin, streptomycin, erythromycin, antibiotics, and acylicamides.

b. Import Quality Testing and Import Certification

American exporters of pharmaceuticals should obtain a copy of the "Provisions Governing the Importation of Drugs" (hereinafter referred to as the "Provisions"). These regulations were issued by the Ministry of Public Health as Decree No. 6 on August 6, 1990 and became effective on January 1, 1991. The Provisions set forth three documents which must be obtained prior to importation: a) quality testing report, b) clinical testing certificate for first-time importation, and c) import registration certificate or single import permit.

The Provisions state all pharmaceuticals are subject to quality testing at the port of entry. Chapter III of the Provisions explains the procedure for quality testing at the port of entry. The "Sampling Regulations on Imported Drugs" and the "Sampling Regulations on Imported Medical Material" govern the testing process. Article 11 of the Provisions states that the process of obtaining a quality testing report may only be handled by a Chinese importer which is a signatory to the drug purchase contract, authorized to engage in foreign trade and properly registered with the Drug Administration Bureau.

A favorable quality testing report is issued depending on whether the drug is properly labeled, safe, effective, and needed in domestic clinical practice. In addition, the drug must meet the specifications of the PRC Pharmacopoeia, or the Ministry of Public Health specifications or pharmacopoeias generally used in international commerce.

The Provisions provide for administrative review of the testing report. Objections must be raised within ninety days by the importing unit. If the importer objects to the result of the administrative review, it may seek re-examination of the report through arbitration by the National Institute for the Control of Pharmaceutical and Biological Products.

Article 9 of the Provisions requires trial in China for pharmaceuticals which are imported to China for the first time. Clinical testing shall be conducted in China according to the requirement of the Drug Administration Bureau (DAB) of the Ministry of Public Health. American firms should also be aware of the "Rules Governing the Registration and Clinical Trial of Foreign Drugs in China" and the "Rules Governing the Approval of Clinical Trial of Foreign Drugs" which were both issued by the Ministry of Public Health on February 2, 1988.

These Rules explain the procedures for clinical trial. Fifty to three hundred cases, in addition to the control group, may be required depending upon the status of drug registration abroad. The clinical trial is conducted by a hospital or institution which is designated by the DA. The applicant is allowed to propose candidates which will undertake the clinical trial. The clinical trial certificate must be included with other supporting documentation and be attached to the application for the import certificate. Upon approval of the clinical trial results, the applicant must pay a USD $3,000 fee.

In addition to passing quality inspection and clinical trial, an importer must also obtain a "registration certificate for importee drugs" (hereinafter referred to as an "import permit") before the pharmaceutical may be imported. The Provisions do not set forth criteria for issuance of the import permit nor do they provide for administrative review.

Either a foreign manufacturer or an agent may submit the import permit application to the DAB. The provisions require that an application form be completed in duplicate and the following materials must be attached along with Chinese language translations.

- FDA certification
- patent registration in the foreign country
- trial samples of the pharmaceutical to be imported
- technical data
- Chinese clinical trial certificate

The import permit is generally issued within three months. Upon approval, the import permit will be issued after the applicant pays a $500-1,000 permit fee. It is valid for three years from the date of issuance and may be renewed within six months prior to expiration. Documentation of FDA approval and technical specifications must be attached to the import permit renewal application.

In some cases, a drug may be imported without an import permit. The Chinese importer may submit an application for a "single permit for drug importation" if the drug is in short supply or is needed due to special requirements. The importer must submit an application to the provincial health departments, which then forward the application to the DAB. The permit is limited to a single transaction for a specific quantity of drugs.

Sales Prospect Areas For Medical and Pharmaceutical Equipment

1. Electro-medical apparatus

    -   electronic medical equipment (electrocardiographs, electroencephalographs, electromyographs, pacemakers, etc.)
    -   ultrasonic equipment
    -   laser equipment
    -   electro-medical equipment for Chinese medicine
    -   complete patient monitoring systems
    -   infusion equipment

2. Radiological apparatus

    -   x-ray apparatus and parts/accessories
    -   apparatus based on the use of other radioactive substances, and parts/accessories (CT scanners, magnetic resonance imaging systems, Pet scanners, gamma cameras, linear accelerators, Cobalt-60 radiotherapeutic equipment, etc.)]

3. Mechano-therapy and respiration apparatus, orthopaedic appliances and artificial parts of the body

    -   artificial respiration apparatus (such as ventilators) including high pressure oxygen cabin
    -   anesthesia equipment
    -   mechano-therapy, massage apparatus
    -   heart-lung machines
    -   dialysis equipment
    -   orthopaedic appliances, surgical belts, trusses, etc.
    -   protheses and components (artificial limbs, etc.)
    -   artificial organs
    -   hearing aids and other appliances worn or carried to compensate for a defect or disability

4. Medical and surgical instruments

    -   surgical instruments including syringes, forceps, etc.

-   diagnostic instruments such as stethoscopes etc.
-   optical instruments including endoscopy apparatus

5. Clinical laboratory equipment

    -   blood gas analyzers, blood cell counters
    -   biochemical analyzers
    -   centrifuges
    -   gas or liquid chromatographs
    -   spectrophotometers, osmometers
    -   liquid scintillation counters, etc.

6. Pharmaceutical equipment

    -   production and processing equipment for:
        •   sterilization
        •   chromatographic separation
        •   fermentation
        •   milling, crushing, dispersing and mixing
        •   filtration and molding
        •   sieving and sorting
        •   purification
        •   granulating and heating
        •   vacuum mixing
        •   tablet presses and dies

    -   packaging equipment for:
        •   ampoule and vial filling
        •   blister and bubble packing
        •   capsule filling and closing
        •   tube filling and sealing
        •   coding and labelling

    -   quality control equipment for:
        •   capsule and tablet inspection
        •   weighing devices
        •   leakage detection
        •   others

Table 107 lists the best sales prospects for drugs in China (39).

Table 107

Best Sales Prospects for Drugs

1. Cardiovascular
2. Drugs and inhalants to treat respiratory diseases
3. Cancer drugs
4. Analgesic drugs and preparations
5. Bulk preparations for manufacture of antibiotics

Key Contacts

Import/Export Corporations

China National Pharmaceutical Foreign Trade Corporation
38A, Beilishi Lu, Xizhimenwai
Beijing, China 100810
Tel: 831.6572 Fax: 831.6571
Note: Several provincial branches exist.

China National Medicine Corporation
38A, Beilishi Lu, Xizhimen
Beijing, China 100810
Tel: 831.32344, 831.8311

China National Medicines and Health Products Import/Export Corporation
12 Jianguomenwai Dajie
Beijing, China 100022
Tel: 500.3344 Fax: 513.7988
Note: Several provincial branches exist.

Trade Association

China Chamber of Commerce of Medicines and Health Products Importers/Exporters
12 Jianguomenwai Dajie 12/F
Beijing, China 100022
Tel: 500.1542, 500.3344 Fax: 500.1150

Government Organizations

State Pharmaceutical Administration
38 (A) Beilishi Lu
Beijing, China 100810
Foreign Affairs Bureau, Zhang Yajun
Tel: 831.3344 x1002, DL 831.5648   Fax: 831.5648
Planning Bureau, Zhang Ruqi
Tel: 831.3344 x0712, DL 831.8966   Fax: 831.8696
Economic Coordination Bureau, Tang Hong
Tel: 831.344 x0609

Ministry of Public Health
Pharmaceutical Administration
Houhai Beiheyan
Beijing, China
Tel: 403.4433 x311

China Trademark Agency
1 Fuxingmenwai Jie
Beijing, China 100860
Tel: 801.344 x1821, 1802   Fax: 801.0208

China Patent Agency
1 Fuxingmenwai Jie
Beijing, China 100860
Tel: 801.3344 x1906, 408.2233 x424   Fax: 801.1207, 801.1069

Huake Intellectual Property Consultancy Center
State Pharmaceutical Administration of China
A38, Beilishi Lu
Beijing, China 100810
Tel: 831.3344 x0908   Fax: 831.6577

Medical Associations

Anti-Tuberculosis Association
42 Dongsi Xidajie
Beijing, China
Tel: 553.685

Chinese Medical Association
42 Dongsi Xidajie
Beijing, China
Tel: 513.3311

China Pharmaceutical Association
42 Dongsi Xidajie
Beijing, China
Tel: 551768

China Red Cross Society
53 Ganmian Hutong
Beijing, China
Tel: 512.4447

Some useful contacts in the pharmaceutical industry include:

Beijing Pharmaceutical Factory
Chaoyang District, Beijing 100020
Tel: 5022077

Hangzhou Minsheng Pharmaceutical Factory
Gongshu, Hangzhou
Zhejiang Province 310011
Tel: 874824

Harbin Pharmaceutical Factory
Nanyang, Harbin
Heilongjiang Province 150086
Tel: 63496

Jining Antibiotic Factory
Shizong, Jining
Shandong Province 272121
Tel: 213961

Nanfang Pharmaceutical Factory
Luohu District, Shenzen
Guangdong Province 518029
Tel: 360199

Northeast General Pharmaceutical Works
Tiexi, Shenyang
Liaoning Province 110026
Tel: 520133

Shanghai Sino-American Pharmaceutical Company, Ltd.
Minhang District, Shanghai 200024
Tel: 4302740

Shijiazhuang North China Pharmaceutical Factory
Chang'an, Shijiazhuang
Hebei Province 050015
Tel: 551133

Southwest Synthetic Pharmaceutical Factory
Jiangei County, Chongqing
Sichuan Province 631137
Tel: 754728

Tianjin Smith Kline and French Laboratories Ltd.
Dongliao, Tianjin 300163
Tel: 470622

Wuhan Pharmaceutical Factory
Qiaokou District, Wuhan
Hubei Province 540035
Tel: 332281

Xian Janssen Pharmaceutical Company Ltd.
Xincheng, Xi'an
Shaanxi Province 710043
Tel: 334455

Xinhua Pharmaceutical Factory
Zhangdian, Zibo
Shandong Province 255005
Tel: 214223

PLASTIC MATERIALS AND RESINS

Table 108 summarizes salient statistics for the plastic and resins industry (3).

Table 108

Salient Facts on Plastic Material and Resins Sector

A)	Three-letter ITA industry sector code:	PMR
B)	Est. total market size (USD millions):	
	1991 -	$4,000
	1992 -	$5,000
	1993 -	$5,500
	1994 -	$5,650
	1995 -	$5,700
C)	Est. 1992-4 annual market growth rate:	10%
D)	Est. total imports (USD millions):	
	1991 -	$1,800
	1992 -	$2,000
	1993 -	$4,089
	1994 -	$4,084
	1995 -	$3,964
E)	Est. annual total import growth rate:	10%
F)	Est. imports from U.S. (USD millions):	
	1991 -	$230
	1992 -	$250
	1993 -	$451
	1994 -	$433
	1995 -	$424 (58)
G)	Est. annual growth of imports from U.S.:	5%
H)	China's receptivity to U.S. products in this sector (5 - High/1 - Low):	4
I)	Competition from local/third countries for U.S. firms (5 -Low/1 - High):	3
J)	Chinese market barriers to U.S. sales in this sector (5 - Few/1 - Many):	3
K)	Comments - factors for increased U.S. sales:	

- Large investment in petrochemical intermediates (ethylene, styrene monomer) and in polymer production reflect drive toward self-sufficiency and presage a shrinking share for imports, an insider position via investment is a coping strategy.
- Engineered plastics and proprietary compounds will be more attractive niches than price-based commodities.

J)	Most Promising Sub-sectors	1992 market size
	1. Engineered plastics/composites	
	for consumer and industrial goods	$500
	2. Very specialized plastics	$500

Some useful contacts in the plastics industry include:

Foshan No. 2 Plastics Factory
Foshan, Guangdong Province 528000
Tel: 229988

Foshan Wuxi No. 3 Plastic Factory
Foshan, Guangdong Province 528000
Tel: 212635

Some useful contacts in the rubber industry include:

Beijing No. 1 Rubber Plant
Haidian District, Beijing 100039
Tel: 82199 22381

Hangzhou Rubber Plant
Jianggan District, Hangzhou
Zhejiang Province 310016
Tel: 653939

Hualin Rubber Plant
Mudanjiang, Heilongjiang Province 157032
Tel: 29704

Nanfang Rubber Group
Guilin, Guanxi Province 54101
Tel: 225030

Ningxia Yinchuan Rubber Plant
Xincheng, Yinchuan
Ningxia Province 750011
Tel: 76491

Qingdao No. 2 Rubber Plant
Cangkou, Qingdao
Shandong Province 266041
Tel: 443321-551

Qingdao No. 6 Rubber Plant
Taidong District, Qingdao
Shandong Province 266021
Tel: 335611

Qingdao No. 9 Rubber Plant
Shinan, Qingdao
Shandong Province 266002
Tel: 266471

Qingdao Tongtai Rubber Plant
Taitong, Qingdao
Shandong Province 266021
Tel: 333431

Rongcheng Rubber Plant
Yatou Town, Rongcheng
Shandong Province 264300
Tel: 572628

Shanghai Dafu General Rubber Plant
Changning District, Shanghai 200051
Tel: 2517479

Shenyang No. 3 Rubber Plant
Tiexi District, Shenyang
Liaoning Province 110025
Tel: 455-233

PLASTIC PRODUCTION MACHINERY

Table 109 summarizes salient statistics for the plastic production machinery industry (3).

Table 109

Salient Statistics on Plastic Production Machinery Sector

A)	Three-letter ITA industry sector code:	PME
B)	Est. total market size (USD millions):	
	1991 -	$600
	1992 -	$700
C)	Est. 1992-4 annual market growth rate:	5%
D)	Est. total imports (USD millions):	
	1991 -	$100
	1992 -	$110
E)	Est. annual total import growth rate:	5%
F)	Est. imports from U.S. (USD millions):	
	1991 -	$20
	1992 -	$30
G)	Est. annual growth of imports from U.S.:	5%
H)	China's receptivity to U.S. products in this sector (5 - High/1 - Low):	2
I)	Competition from local/third countries for U.S. firms (5 - Low/1 - High):	2
J)	Chinese market barriers to U.S. sales in this sector (5 - Few/1 - Many):	4

K) Comments - factors for increased U.S. sales:
- Consumer spending is growing.
- Agricultural plastic sheet—a major market.
- Market is decentralized, fragmented, concentrated in coastal and southeastern provinces, placing a premium on marketing and service network.

L)	Most Promising Sub-sectors	1992 market size
	1. Packaging materials	$ 70 million
	2. Agriculture sheeting equipment	$ 80 million
	3. Consumer goods manufacturing equipment	$100 million

PORT DEVELOPMENT

Overview China offers a potentially large market for U.S. manufactured port development equipment and services. The Chinese government has made port expansion one of the priority areas of the Eighth Five-Year economic plan. Many new ports are being constructed.

The major force creating this market is the fact that China's facilities for shipping fall short of meeting demand. There is a strong need to increase exports to acquire foreign exchange. Development os this sub-sector market is directly related to other markets of interest to U.S. business, e.g. sales to China of railroad and road construction equipment needed to improve transportation from the interior to coastal ports, expansion of U.S.-China shipping in U.S. bottoms, etc.

A range of factors will influence changes in this market vis-a-vis U.S. sales prospects. First is the availability or non-availability to U.S. firms of funding. Japan will continue to play a very important role in financing all kinds of projects and, directly or indirectly, in the purchases of U.S. equipment and services. Next is the U.S. government's position on continuation of most favored nation trading status for China. A third important factor is who in China will ultimately control port development—the central government or local/regional entities. A fourth factor which would lead to a significant expansion of the PRC's coastal shipping facilities is the development of direct Taiwan-PRC trade.

PRC port development got off to a slow start. From 1949 to around 1979, only one deep water berth was built per year. The year of the first call of a China Ocean Shipping Company (COSCO) vessel at an American port, Seattle, was 1979 and was also a year of dramatic change in the pace of construction of China's coastal facilities. Between 1979 and 1988 U.S.-China trade increased some six times, from USD 2.3 billion to USD 14 billion. Increasing emphasis was placed on port development during the Seventh Five-Year Plan (1986-1990). For example, between 1986 and 1990, Fujian Province launched more than forty harbor building projects. Eleven of these were for deep water berths. During roughly this same period of time, the province spent RMB 900 million on port construction. With these new projects came a dramatic expansion of overall Chinese trade; a significant example of this was the launching of direct PRC-South Korean trade. U.S. government agencies became more active, as well.

Market Assessment

1. Market Demand

Market demand for port development equipment and services is increasing primarily because of China's seemingly insatiable need to expand trade. Existing port facilities are not adequate to move today's huge amounts of products into and out of the country, not to mention increasing amounts of products in the future.

U.S. firms should be aware of China's port development plans. Future planning by PRC authorities can be divided into two parts—the 1991 to 1995 Eighth Five-Year Plan period and the 1991 to 2000 ten year development program period. By the year 2000, China hopes to have about 2,000 coastal ports, 1,200 of them deep water ports.

From 1991 to 2000, harbors will be built and/or expanded in seven areas:

1. The Northeast. Key ports - Dalian and Yingkou (both in Liaoning Province). Others - Dandong and Jinzhou.
2. North China. Key ports - Tianjin and Qinhuangdao. Others - Wangtan and Huanghua (all in Tianjin area).
3. Shandong Province. Key ports - Qingdao and Yantai. Others - Shijiu, Longkou, Weihai, and Penglai.
4. Jiangsu and Zhejiang Provinces. Key ports - Shanghai, Lianyungang, and Ningbo. Others - Nantong, Zhangjiagang, Zhenjiang, Nanjing, and Wenzhou.
5. Fujian Province. Key ports - Fuzhou and Xiamen. Others - Meizhou Bay and Quanzhou.
6. South China (all in Guangdong Province, except Beihai, in Guangxi Province). Key ports - Guangzhou, Shenzhen, Shantou, and Zhangjiang. Others - Beihai, Fangcheng, Zhuhai, and the Pearl River Delta area.
7. Hainan Province. Key ports - Haikou and Yangpu. Others - Basua and Sanya.

Examples of the above development plans are as follows: Yantian; by the year 2000, this port is slated for forty-eight deep water berths. Fujian; between 1991 and 1995, this province plans ten deep water berth projects. The provincial authorities are reportedly prepared to earmark RMB 300 million for these projects. Among them are the following:

-- Mawei Port in Fuzhou: 370,000, 100,000, and 20,000 ton capacity wharves.
-- Meizhou Bay: 35,000 and 10,000 ton capacity wharves.
-- Dongdugang, Xiamen: Second phase of the construction of four deep water berths.
-- Dashikeng, Longhai, Zhangzhou City: One 10,000 ton capacity wharf.

Expanding trade is the basic goal of port development. Related to this is the construction of large vessels. At present, only the ports of Dalian and Shanghai have facilities where ships over 100,000 dead weight tons (DWT) can be built. As of February 1991, there was a backlog of five years of orders to China's shipyards for more and bigger vessels. Port development authorities are thus being pressed, not only by the central government and trading officials, but also by shipbuilders, to speed up construction activities along the coast.

Some pertinent questions to be asked are as follows:

A. *What are some other projects, related to port development, in which U.S. firms might be interested?*

A primary category is expansion of connecting, inland transportation links-major highways and railroad lines. Building these vital links must keep pace with port development; otherwise existing bottlenecks, which are already costing China millions of dollars in losses every year, will be exacerbated. The Chinese authorities must rationalize their use of railroad cars entering port areas. At times (e.g. when cars were needed to transport coal from the Antaibao mine to the sea), the mining, railroad, and port authorities failed to cooperate, and the losses to business, and China, were immense.

B. *What PRC and U.S. government policy changes might affect market prospects for U.S. companies in the port development sub-sector?*

The PRC government's crackdown on pro-democracy demonstrators in June, 1989 led to the suspension of the U.S. Trade and Development Program's (TDP's) China feasibility studies; the crackdown also led to more frequent and critical reviews by Congress of China's most favored nation trading status. Uncertainties about MFN cloud the trading and investment picture in China for many U.S. businesses. The TDP suspension has hurt U.S. sales to the PRC in a number of areas, including port development. The studies often led to big sales by U.S. firms. Similar studies continue to be made, but by others. For example, the Pudong branch of the Industrial and Commercial Bank of China has decided to provide a USD 15 million loan for technical studies associated with the renovating of Shanghai's wharf, which handles one-fifth of the PRC's imported bulk shipments of grain and sugar. The target date for the completion of this project is 1994. Had the Shanghai wharf studies been done under TDP auspices, the planning could have been geared toward U.S. specifications and toward U.S. sales.

U.S. perceptions of the overall political climate in China will also have a bearing on U.S. sales and U.S. government programs supporting such sales. Should there arise a perception that the PRC's political climate had become more repressive, Congress would predictably seed to withdraw or heavily condition China's MFN eligibility.

Any Chinese central government policies tending to erode significantly confidence in a smooth and stable Hong Kong post-1997 transition could impact on port development and China trade. About 60 percent of PRC-origin container trade is conducted with Hong Kong bills of lading. Eighty percent of the remaining forty percent, which is shipped with PRC bills of lading, is actually trans-shipped through Hong Kong. These figures show the overwhelmingly dominant role Hong Kong plays in China trade. No port on the China coast can match Hong Kong's excellent natural topography, superior port facilities, and cheap, efficient labor.

Another PRC government policy change which could affect port development marketing relates to the elimination of the China National Foreign Trade Transportation Corporation (Sinotrans) as middleman for most shipping. If the Chinese government were to permit American and other foreign shipping concerns (e.g. Sealand Services or American President Lines - APL) to accept bookings directly from Chinese exporters, overall foreign trade could expand significantly. Sinotrans presently monopolizes most or all shipping transactions, including the setting of prices and issuing and signing bills of lading. This redundant Chinese bureaucracy imposes tariffs for its "services." These tariffs could be eliminated if Sinotrans were abolished; this is unlikely, however, under present conditions.

Several U.S. government policy changes might affect U.S. firms' port development activities in China. For example, if the U.S. lifted its military equipment-related sanctions against the PRC, certain U.S. naval equipment might hypothetically be licensed for sale and might lead to the expansion of PRC navy-related activity. This would be particularly true at the port of Dalian, where China builds submarines and warships. (Note: Dalina is the number one port in the entire PRC in terms of value of exports, and it has ambitious plans to put in as many as eighty deep water berths in nearby Dayao Bay. Half a mountain near the bay has been pushed into the sea to form a gigantic field, where future facilities will be sited. City officials have a "can-do" attitude.)

If the U.S. government joins hands with a consortium of U.S. companies engaged in port development and forms a government-industry consortium, U.S. sales to China could increase. Reason: The Chinese authorities prefer to deal with consortia or conglomerates in big development projects, rather than with a scattering of foreign companies.

If the U.S. government should move to cut or stop sales of key imports from China, port development could be indirectly affected. For example, 75 percent of Sealand's income in U.S.-China trade comes from exporting garments from the PRC. A sudden drop in the volume of garments sold to the U.S. would probably result in a cut in Sealand's trade with China.

Finally, if the U.S. Maritime Administration (MARAD) and the U.S. Federal Maritime Commission (FMC) insist that China grant U.S. container shippers the same rights and privileges that the U.S. grants Chinese shipping companies like COSCO, and if these demands are met by the PRC, trade could expand, resulting in pressure for more, bigger, and better port facilities.

C.   What other developments could affect this market?

One would be the discovery of significant deposits of oil in the Bohai Gulf or any other area adjacent to China's coastline. The Dalian shipyard is engaged in the production of oil drilling ships, oil drilling platforms, oil production modules, and shuttle tankers. U.S. suppliers of equipment and services related to such production should be prepared to move into this market quickly if big deposits of oil are discovered offshore.

Enormous port construction activity would ensue if Japan decided to finance a mammoth cross-mountain pipeline from the Tarim Basin oil fields to the sea. Oil reserves at Daqing, China's primary source of petroleum, are dwindling. Some U.S. experts believe that, eventually, the PRC will be forced to build this pipeline and collateral port facilities.

2. End-Users

The principal government-related end-user groups in China are the port authorities of the cities of the seven regions listed above. The larger and more sophisticated facilities, listed as "key ports," are those which generally import the most foreign equipment. The private sector, as it relates to port construction, is relatively small in the PRC. Nevertheless, more and more municipalities and port authorities, particularly in southern China, are acting as if they were "private sector" operations, with relatively limited connections with the central government in Beijing. While the U.S. firm selling to southern ports can generally expect a much looser, free-wheeling, red tape free business environment than the firm selling to northern port authorities, there are exceptions. For example, the municipal leaders of the northern port city of Dalian have assured U.S. officials that they have the determination, authority, and energy to act pretty much on their own. Another aspect to the picture are "sister city" relations. For example, Shenzhen has established such relations with Houston.

These informal ties, welcomed by, but not directly under the control of the central government, are a sign of growing decentralization and/or "privatization" of parts of the Chinese economy. The result, for U.S. firms, is a rather mixed picture, with some authorities appearing to be independent of the central government and others less so. The prudent U.S. executive will cover all bases, checking regulations, restrictions, and rules not only in the port locality but also in Beijing.

The receptivity score is 3 because, while U.S. equipment and services in this sub-sector are some of the best in the world and are well regarded in the PRC, most port development work is done locally; the bulk of the foreign work is undertaken by nearby Hong Kong and Japanese companies.

The Chinese are receptive to manufacturing joint ventures and technology transfer arrangements. Most joint ventures are located along China's east coast, where the infrastructure is relatively developed. While there may be potential for U.S.-Chinese joint ventures in the field of port construction, such developments are presently in a very early stage, and useful evaluation cannot yet be made.

Competitive Situation

1. Domestic Production

Port development equipment made in China dominates most of this sub-sector market—certainly the low technology part of the market. While China is working hard to upgrade domestic production, it still has a long way to go, and, for several decades, there will be a continuing need or medium- and high-tech equipment from abroad. Domestic firms, particularly those which require foreign currency and foreign technology inputs, generally welcome establishing joint ventures with companies from abroad.

2. Imports

Imports play an important role in meeting total market demand in the port development sub-sector. The extent to which they are a source of competition with locally-produced equipment depends, to a certain degree, on one's perspective. If one is with a Chinese enterprise or port authority needing top quality equipment, a direct and immediate purchase from abroad is probably desirable. If one is with a Chinese ministry charged with securing foreign technology transfers and encouraging local production through joint ventures or by Chinese firms along, a local purchase is probably preferable.

There are at least three reasons for present growth trends. First, the Chinese government is putting special emphasis on port development. Second, foreign firms, including U.S. companies, are becoming more skillful and sophisticated in selling equipment and services in China. Third, the Chinese are under pressure to "buy American."

Very few or none of the pieces of equipment imported from abroad for this sub-sector are re-exported.

Sourcing from market vs. non-market economies: This is now a moot matter, since the Eastern European economies have become partially or wholly market-oriented and/or are in a very fluid transitional period.

When Hong Kong, which presently accounts for a substantial percentage of China's port development equipment and services imports, becomes part of China in the year 2000, the PRC's foreign import pattern will obviously change.

3. U.S. Market Position and Share

U.S. port equipment and services exports to southern China have increased in recent years in large part because of the concerted efforts by FCS Guangzhou. FCS officers from the Consulate General visited regional ports many times, set up calls at the ports for high-level Washington visitors, met repeatedly with local Chinese officials, and used unique and creative ways to promote American interests through the Shenzhen-Houston sister city relationship.

The U.S. position in the port development sub-sector should remain good as long as U.S. companies maintain their technological superiority, China has the foreign exchange to pay for our products, there is stability in the PRC, our companies can secure mixed credit financing equal to that of third country competitors, and the U.S. government (FCS and other agencies) gives vigorous support for U.S. sales efforts.

Prominent U.S. suppliers in this sub-sector include Caterpillar, Hyster, Bechtel, Ch&E, GEHL, Mi-Jack, Casco/General Railway Signal, and Marinette Marine.

4. Competitive Factors

There are a number of reasons why certain firms get business in this market. Technical superiority, reputation, price, credit availability, good "guan.xi" (relationships) with Chinese authorities, and geographical proximity are all key factors. With respect to reputation and technical superiority, U.S. equipment is generally considered second to none in the world; everything else being equal, U.S. companies should be able to secure many port development contracts in China. With respect to price—this is often determined by the availability (or lack) of mixed credit financing, plus the offering of "sweeteners." U.S. firms are, in some cases, teaming up with Japanese firms to promote sales in China, the U.S. firm providing the equipment or technology while the Japanese provide the financing. The Japanese loan factor is very important; if Japanese loans are truly untied, as advertised, then U.S. firms will continue to play a strong role in this market. Another issue related to financing is the studies of the U.S. Trade and Development Program (TDP). These studies can lead to U.S. contracts. TDP programs are, at present, suspended in China.

Vigorous sales promotion is another reason why certain firms—Japanese in particular—get business in this sub-sector market. First, the Japanese are continuing to conduct feasibility studies, such as the one for the giant Yantian port. Second, they invite large delegations to Japan, frequently on all-expense-paid "study tours." In some cases, family members are invited to come along. Third, the Japanese follow up with calls on Chinese officials in the particular port city several times each month.

There are two other ways U.S. firms may be able to improve their business prospects in this sub-sector market. First, they can emphasize their environmental consciousness. Citizen and government awareness of water, land, and air pollution is slowly increasing in the PRC, and American companies, used to very strict regulations at home, should be able to use their "good neighbor" reputation to their advantage. Emphasis on environmentalism took a giant leap in neighboring Taiwan when the political system there became more democratic. U.S. firms should watch China carefully to determine whether similar political changes would be helpful for American sales.

Second, the U.S. is known to support democratic development in China. While this factor may not presently help American firms secure contracts, it could, in the future, if China takes a dramatic turn toward a more open system. Firms seen as "friends of democracy" may, in the future, have a better chance to secure contracts than those with very close ties with the old communist leaders. In the long run, political developments in the PRC could be far more important than any strictly business-related factors for U.S. firms contemplating entering the China market.

For the time being, U.S. firms can improve their competitive standing in this sub-sector by developing a thorough understanding of what mixed credits may be available to them and to their foreign competitors, by inviting—when appropriate—potential Chinese buyers to the U.S.A. to see equipment in operation, by developing a close liaison with the local American Chamber of Commerce, U.S.-China Business Council representative, and FCS officers, by patiently engaging in detailed research, by developing over an extended period of time, close relations with Chinese buyers, and by visiting the ports.

Market Access

1. Import Climate

Trade regulations do not appear to constitute important impediments to doing business in this particular market. Nevertheless, U.S. firms should be familiar with Chinese port and shipping rules. These include the "PRC Rules of Control of International Ocean-Shipping of Containers." These regulations, promulgated by the State Council in its sixty-eighth decree, dated December 5, 1990, can be found in English on pages seven through nine of the English-language "China Economic News" (No. 3) of January 21, 1991. Topics covered include the control of cargo transportation, delivery and liability, and shipping-related penalties. U.S. firms should also be familiar with the provisions of the 1988 U.S.-China Maritime Agreement which, among other things, gives U.S. companies two new rights—to establish feeder service from the PRC and to establish representative offices in the PRC. In general, the question of "meeting Chinese technical or safety standards" is not a significant issue, since foreign equipment technical and safety levels are nearly always higher than local ones.

As far as U.S. government regulations are concerned, American companies wishing to export very high-tech port development products to China should work closely with the U.S. Department of Commerce Bureau of Export Administration (BXA) to ensure that the equipment falls within BXA guidelines. Recently, some of the guidelines relating to China have been liberalized.

What are some impediments to doing business in the PRC, and how can these difficulties be handled?

Doing business in China has never been easy. A complex system of market and administrative controls restricts the access of foreign firms to the market. Business people must conduct thorough feasibility studies and endure a sometimes protracted and costly negotiation and approval process. Raw material and transportation bottlenecks must be overcome.

Nevertheless, the port development sub-sector market is still a promising one. Ports are part of China's "basic infrastructure," and port development may, therefore, be somewhat immune from the ups and downs of the general economy. The best ways to cope with market problems are hard work, patience, knowledge of the territory, and lots of hands-on salesmanship. More specifically, U.S. firms can

-- use the services of a U.S. or third country trading company to help them.

-- use the services of a Hong Kong-based agent or distributor. Many Hong Kong agents and distributors are very active in China and have an extensive network of Chinese contracts.

-- establish a representative office in China. Some U.S. companies form joint ventures with Chinese enterprises to provide after-sales service for the U.S. company's products in China.

-- establish a manufacturing joint venture with a Chinese partner. The U.S. partner will have to consider the special issue of repatriating profits when it considers a joint venture in the PRC.

-- establish a technology transfer relationship with a Chinese partner. The U.S. partner should be aware that the PRC's legal structure offers rather weak intellectual property rights protection.

2. Distribution and Business Practices in this Sub-sector

There are at least two practices in this market which can aid sales of U.S. equipment and services. First, the Chinese sometimes express the wish to keep their equipment standardized to save money on operational training and spare parts. American firms should take advantage of this fact in areas where U.S. equipment is already standard.

Second, the Chinese sometimes state that they want to buy the most modern, top-quality equipment money can buy. When this is the case, U.S. products generally have the edge over cheaper, but lower quality equipment from third countries.

Practices in this market which may impede the U.S. sales, include the following: First, the Chinese occasionally ignore the technical superiority of U.S. equipment, preferring to buy from another country which can offer a larger and/or more advantageous use of credits and soft loans. Second, the Chinese sometimes buy from others because U.S. companies are not aggressive or personal enough in pressing their sales. In certain cases, U.S. firms have mistakenly thought that deals were finalized when, in fact, competitors were hard at work undoing what should have been a U.S.-Chinese contract. Some U.S. companies which are new-to-market do not understand that, to the Chinese, face-to-face contacts are extremely important. Telephone calls or communications by fax are no substitute for frequent meetings in China itself. And visits directly to the ports where equipment is to be used can be a critical factor in making sales. Third, where very high-tech equipment is involved, the Chinese may simply lack the knowledge required to make a sound purchase judgement.

What should U.S. firms look out for in this sub-sector market?

First, sellers of very heavy or complex machinery, haulers, trucks, or cranes should be certain that there are adequate facilities to move the equipment to the site where it is needed. The Chinese roads or railroads in the port area may be too small or weak. Second, American firms should be careful about intellectual property protection. It is both backward and flawed in the PRC. Another problem is the habit of some foreign firms and governments to engage in disguised or open bribery. A final issue—the tendency of some American to sign quickly, rush back to the home office, and hope for immediate returns. The U.S. company entering this market should develop a patient, long-term attitude and expect to make money only after an extended period or time. China's progress is still slowed by inefficiency, poor management practices, and lack of technical expertise, though companies will sometimes find that such problems are offset by one of the nation's biggest single advantages for foreign business—low labor costs.

Chinese end-users often require extensive technical assistance and training as part of the sales package. It is generally wiser to bring U.S. specialists to China and train people locally than to send the Chinese to the U.S. Reason: PRC operating conditions are very different from those in the U.S.

What should U.S. firms emphasize?

-- Their experience in the port development field—probably longer and more extensive than that of any of our competitors.

-- The top quality of U.S. equipment and excellent follow-up with spare parts and servicing.

-- The very competitive prices U.S. firms can offer when the playing field is level.

-- The broad variety of equipment and services American companies can offer in this field. For example, Qinghuangdao, one of China's largest ports, has traditionally handled mainly coal and oil. However, the variety of cargoes is increasing; grain, timber, fertilizer, cement, ores, and fodder. U.S. firms, used to working in the immense and highly complex American market, are familiar with handling a wide variety of cargoes. They should be in a stronger position than their competitors to sell the sophisticated and specialized equipment China needs.

What should U.S. firms look out for?

One problem is that certain Chinese, nominally working for a Chinese governmental organization, are, in fact, secretly in league with a foreign company. Another problem is the Chinese' inviting U.S. bids simply to bid down the prices of foreign competitors, who will ultimately win through the provision of soft loans.   A third problem—U.S. sellers of extremely heavy or complex machinery or haulers should make certain that there are adequate railroad facilities to move the equipment to the site where it is needed or, alternatively, that roadways are suitable for such a movement.   The intellectual property protection problem has already been mentioned.   An additional difficulty is the tendency of some foreign business and government competitors to engage in disguised or open bribery and payoffs.   A further problem is that the U.S. firms are sometimes unaware of the critical role played by superior, silent Chinese partners to a deal.   These partners need to be identified and kept informed of all developments as the business relationship evolves.   Including a trusted, third party, such as CITIC (the China International Trust and Investment Corporation), can prove valuable in resolving disagreements.   Another issue-U.S. firms' tendency to want to sign too quickly and expect payoffs in a short period of time.   The U.S. company entering the China market should develop a patient, long-term attitude toward the market and expect to make money only after an extended period of time.

There is, on occasion, a need to train Chinese engineers or mechanics in the use of American equipment.   It is generally wiser to bring U.S. specialists to China to train people locally than to send the Chinese to the U.S.   Reason: Operating conditions in the PRC are very different from those in the U.S.

3. Financing

U.S. firms need to be flexible on matters relating to financing in the port equipment and services market.   Financing sources are extremely varied—central government, local or provincial government, local mining authorities, international public institutions, private and public banks, etc.

Chinese buyers often look to tied soft/mixed loans to help finance their purchases.   Here, U.S. exporters often find themselves at a serious disadvantage with competitors from Japan and Europe, because these competitors are sometimes able to use extremely attractive concessionary loan packages offered by their own governments.   (The "war chest" of the U.S. Eximbank is only used to match such offers in unusual cases where the offering government violates OECD rules concerning notice requirements or minimum grant percentages.)

U.S. companies can help their competitive position by familiarizing themselves with the Eximbank programs which are available to them.   For example, Chinese buyers also show interest in export credit programs—such as those offered by Eximbank and the export-import banks of other countries.   Eximbank has been very active in China and is able, under certain circumstances, to offer credit at the "OECD consensus rate" (9.3 percent as of mid-1991).

The World Bank is actively involved in China port development.   The invitation to bid on equipment for the Xinsha terminal project of Huangpu port earlier this year was part of a USD 88 million World Bank loan procurement.   The U.S. Embassy advises companies which are interested in a China World Bank project to travel to the PRC early in the process to contact the concerned officials in the Chinese government. The U.S. Embassy can assist in identifying which Chinese organizations are involved in the project.   World Bank bids in

China are tendered by the International Tendering Corporation (ITC) through public advertisements. The Embassy can make arrangements to purchase World Bank tenders on a cost basis. For more information, contact the Second Business Division, ITC, China National Technical Import and Export Corporation, Wanshousi 3A, Suzhou Street, Halidan District, Beijing, China.

Another important financial institution, the Asian Development Bank (ADB), tentatively proposed a USD 100 million China port development project in 1989. The project was to be targeted at the building of three deep water berths at Dandong, Yantai, and Shantou ports. As or early 1991, the ADB planned to lend USD 20 million to Yingkou's newly-established Bayuguan harbor for the purchase of freight loading and unloading equipment.

In more and more trade deals with China, U.S. firms are teaming up with Japanese companies, the latter providing the technology or equipment while the latter provides the financing. Shenzhen's Yantian port project, phase I, is being financed by a USD 100 million Japanese soft loan (thirty years, 2.5 percent interest, ten year grace period). These funds can be used for construction material and equipment only. In 1989 financing—57 billion yen (about USD 440 million)—for expansion of the port of Qingdao, including loading and unloading equipment and automatic control facilities for two coal terminals, came from the Japanese Overseas Economic Cooperation Fund.

Imports into China often require import licenses and approval to spend foreign exchange. However, if the Bank of China (BOC) or another state-owned bank issues a letter of credit (LC), the U.S. seller can usually be sure that necessary approvals have been obtained.

Most BOC LC's are sight LC's. Payment is made only after the Chinese bank which issued the LC has received the export documents. This means a minimum of ten to twenty days waiting before the U.S. exporter can collect payment for goods delivered. (For example, a U.S. exporter would arrange for all export documents to be shipped to the BOC, and then would have to wait for a BOC review of the documents before being paid.)

A second common Chinese payment practice affects large equipment sales and technology exports to the PRC. For such sales, Chinese buyers typically make a ten to twenty-five percent down payment, then pay 70 to 75% on delivery and the remaining 10-15% on installation. However, at the time of the initial down payment, Chinese buyers often require a standby letter of credit (SLC) from the seller's bank, guaranteeing the return of the down payment if sales terms are not met. A problem arises when a small U.S. exporter does not have a credit line sufficient to cover the required SLC. (Note: This special provision does not usually apply to sales of commodities or to sales of simple goods.)

Countertrade: The PRC has no legislatively mandated countertrade requirements. Common forms of business with the PRC now include countertrade, compensation trade, leasing, and technology licensing arrangements. A foreign company willing to consider countertrade may sometimes gain the competitive edge.

Hard currency: China's central government exerts strict control over foreign exchange allocation, and foreign exchange controls constitute a significant non-tariff barrier. Most of the PRC's imports and exports are handled by a relatively small number of state-owned trading companies authorized to transact business involving foreign exchange. Moreover, Chinese regulations for foreign-invested enterprises require that the remittance of profits, the purchase of imported components or raw materials, and the payment of compensation to foreign personnel be done in foreign currency. If such a company has a shortage of foreign currency (usually because it is having difficulty exporting its products), it may be unable to carry out these transactions. While foreign invested enterprises can now get foreign currency at local currency swap markets, it involves the payment of a premium which affects the profitability of the firm.

Best Sales Prospects

1. Breaker excavators
2. Multi-purpose cranes (40 ton)
3. Portal crane (16 ton)
4. Rubber tire crane
5. Front forklift truck
6. Forklift truck (44, 16, 5, 3, and 2.5 ton)
7. Tire mounted crane (40 and 16 ton)
8. Tractors for containers
9. Pushing-collecting machines
10. Bulk packaging machines
11. Tugboats (3200 and 1600 HP)
12. Pilot boats
13. Transporting boats
14. Computer equipment systems
15. Telecommunications equipment for port use
16. Dragline excavators
17. Road rollers
18. Bulldozers
19. Road graders
20. Tire loading trucks
21. Mixers
22. Asphalt mixers
23. Locomotives
24. Highway/railway vehicles
25. Container bridges
26. Container trailers
27. Container front cranes
28. Container forklift trucks (25, 30.5, and 40 ton)
29. Small forklift trucks (2, 2.5, and 3 ton)
30. Side forklift trucks
31. Straddle carriers
32. Container tired gantry cranes
33. Container track gantry cranes
34. Bucket wheel ship unloaders

35. Continuous bucket ship unloaders
36. Belt ship unloaders
37. Grab bucket ship unloaders
38. Suction type pneumatic ship unloaders
39. Continuous belt ship loaders
40. Bucket wheel reclaimers
41. Giant belt systems
42. Pushing-collecting cabin cleaners
43. Giant coal terminal control systems
44. Mineral loaders
45. Tower seaport cranes (60 ton)
46. Timber loaders
47. Multi-purpose level luffing cranes (40 ton)
48. Level luffing cranes (16 ton)
49. Towing and fire control boats (3200 HP)
50. Towing boats (3200 HP)
51. Pilot boats
52. Vibrating rollers (18 ton)
53. Motor graders (150 HP)
54. Wheel loaders (3.2 and 1.5 CM)
55. Dump trucks (20 ton)
56. Trucks (5 ton)
    Note: U.S. companies should try offering either new or used equipment.

Key Contacts

COSCO (China Ocean Shipping Company)
International Cooperation Section
6 Dong Changan Jie
Beijing 100004
Tel: 5121188 x4452 Fax: 5122408

CSTC (China Shipbuilding Trading Company, Ltd.)
Multi-planning Section
#10 Yuetan Bei Xiao Jie
Beijing 100830
Tel: 8312560 Fax: 8313380

CSSC (China State Shipbuilding Corporation)
Economic Cooperation Section
#5 Yue Tan Bei Jie
Beijing 100037
Tel: 8317618 Fax: 8313380

Dalian Port Development Project
c/o Office of Foreign Affairs
Dalian City
#1 Stalin Square
Dalian 116002
Tel: 333728

CHEC (China Harbor Engineering Company
#10 Fuxing Road
Beijing
Tel: 4216722, 4219323   Fax: 4216722

NSNC (New Seas Navigation Corporation)
10/F, #1040 Suzhou Road
North Shanghai
Tel: 253920

COES (China Ocean Engineering Services, Ltd.)
#10 Fuxing Road
Beijing
Tel: 5005599 x3503, 3504, 3505

MOC (Ministry of Communications)
Engineering Administration Bureau
Port Construction Division
#10 Fu Xing Road
Beijing 100845
Tel: 3260673, 3265544 x2620, 2654

MOA (Ministry of Agriculture)
International Cooperation Bureau
c/o Fisheries Policy, Fisheries Port Bureau
#11 Nong Zhen Guan Nan Li
Beijing 100026
Tel: 5004363, 5002448

ADB (Asian Development Bank)
Loan Utilization Office
Yingkou Harbor Bureau
Bayuquan District, Yingkou
Liaoning 115007
Tel: 51600 x2366   Fax: 0417-42497

Yingkou Harbor Administration Bureau
Zhanqian District
Yingkou, Liaoning
Tel: 42800 x122

Yingkou New Port Economic Zone
General Development Corporation
Bayuquan District, Yingkou
Liaoning 115007
Tel: 51043   Fax: 0417-51777

POWER TRANSMISSION EQUIPMENT

Table 110 gives some salient statistics for the power transmission equipment industry (3).

Table 110

Salient Statistics for the Power Transmission Equipment Sector

A) Three-letter ITA industry sector code: PTE
B) Est. total market size (USD millions):
   1991 - $1,000
   1992 - $1,200
C) Est. 1992-4 annual market growth rate: 10%
D) Est. total imports (USD millions):
   1991 - $120
   1992 - $150
E) Est. annual total import growth rate: 8%
F) Est. imports from U.S. (USD millions):
   1991 - $20
   1992 - $30
G) Est. annual growth of imports from U.S.:   8%
H) China's receptivity to U.S. products i
   this sector (5 - High/1 - Low):   4
I) Competition from local/third countries
   for U.S. firms (5 - Low/1 - High):   3
J) Chinese market barriers to U.S. sales
   in this sector (5 - Few/1 - Many):   3
K) Comments - factors for increased U.S. sales:
- China's protectionist import substitution policies are particularly marked in this sector.
- Strategy is to become an insider via investment, or focus on slow-to-localize high tech peripherals.
- Growing role of local funding for projects puts premium on local marketing skills.

L) Most Promising Sub-sectors	1992 market size
1. Transformers	$300 million
2. Switchgear	$100 million
3. Transmission equipment: cable, towers, insulators	$300 million

Overview The Chinese market for electric power transmission equipment is more than twice as large as the market for power generation equipment (40).

Imports of power transmission equipment reached about $500 to $600 million in 1986 and 1987. Imports appear to have 20 percent share of China's market for this type of equipment. In fact, however, China subsidize prices for domestically-produced power transmission equipment. If Chinese prices were raised to reflect real costs, the share of foreign imports would probably drop to 10-15 percent.

Much of the new equipment is probably used to maintain and improve the existing network of transmission lines and substations. The Chinese system is extensive but is also relatively backward. Eighty percent of the system (in terms of kilometers) is composed of lines rated at 110-kv and below.

The lower priority assigned to power transmission network improvements in recent years also is reflected in the lower growth rate of power transmission equipment compared to power generation. In terms of the domestic currency (in order to eliminate the impact of foreign exchange rates changes), the domestic power transmission sector appears to have doubled in the last five years compared to a fourfold increase of the power generation sector.

Market Assessment Chinese planners have aggressive goals for expanding the power transmission network, particularly 500 kv lines. As one sector Chinese power official describes the Seventh Five-Year Plan (1986-1990): "The plan also stipulates the 8,000 kilometers and possibly a further 3,000 km of 500 kv lines to be commissioned. Under this arrangement, about 10,000 km of 500 kv lines will be under construction during this period."

Other Chinese specialists optimistically forecast that by the year 2000, China will tie its seven major regional grids together and give China a national integrated power system (NIPS) with a total installed capacity of more than 200 gigawatts. Two officials of the authoritative Electric Power Research Institute wrote that in the last few years of the 1980s, China will complete three 500 kv lines. One will tie Northeast China to the North China Grid; the second will connect Northwest China to North China; and the third will link Southwest China to the grid in South China. These lines will join the 500 kv line that is now being built between the Central China grid, which contains the hydro-power stations on the Yangzi River, and East China. In the 1990s, the NIPS would be completed, with additional 500 kv lines connecting North China to Central China, Northwest China to Southwest China, and Central China to South China. Most observers believe this forecast is extremely ambitious. There are reasons to believe that implementation of these plans is likely to be delayed beyond the year 2000.

The 1991 market projection suggests that the outlook for China's electric power transmission equipment sector is much less certain that the outlook for China's electric power generation sector.

Over the five year period 1986-1991, it is expected that total expenditures on power transmission equipment will grow at least 50 percent, but that growth could reach 100 percent.

The outlook for imported equipment is even more uncertain. Overall growth of the transmission system will be rapid if China moves quickly to begin major new high voltage transmission projects (500 kv lines), and this will create a very favorable market for foreign imports. Under these conditions (very rapid growth), we believe that imported transmission equipment imports would rise to as high as $750 million or 50 percent higher than late 1980's levels.

If the actual growth in the transmission sector is more moderate (50 percent or so over five years), as we believe more likely, we anticipate that China's domestic industry would supply most of the needed equipment and imports would grow to only 20 percent or so beyond current levels. Even under these relatively pessimistic assumptions, the Chinese market for transmission equipment in 1991 is estimated to be at least $600 million.

Many of the reasons for the uncertainties affecting the power transmission equipment market are the same as those affecting power generation equipment—access to foreign exchange, shortages of primary energy sources to expand electricity generation, and the ability to officials to obtain a consensus on difficult political and economic decisions. In addition to these questions, there are others that are specific to China's plans for expanding the power transmission network.

The first problem is the apparent lack of consensus on just what kind of power transmission systems makes sense and how rapidly China should move towards the goal of a nationwide unified grid. Some Chinese journal articles emphasize the benefits of a national unified grid with power shared between grids with different power demands at different times of day, while others treat these benefits as decidedly secondary. Perhaps more important, Chinese specialists and Western advisors seem to be debating basic technical questions about the proposed national integrated system.

In the late 1980s to early 1990 time period, an even more basic factor is that China has been relatively slow in building the huge open pit coal mines and adjacent mine mouth thermal power stations that have been seen as primary sources of new power generating capacity in the 1990s. Emphasis seems to have shifted to building thermal power stations closer to electricity end-users, which has lessened the immediate need for state-of-the-art long distance high voltage transmission lines (40).

Competitive Situation   The powerful domestic equipment industry has the capability of turning out most products required for electricity transmission. This capability is evidenced by the fact that the domestic industry was the predominant source of equipment for the expansion of the domestic transmission system during the two decades of the 1960s and 1970s when China isolated itself from foreign economic relations.

In addition, the industry employs a work force of nearly 400,000 people, which creates strong political pressures to supply most of China's needs domestically. As is the case in the electric power generation equipment industry, the twin pressures of greatly expanded needs for modern equipment and the need to provide work for China's domestic factories have led to a vigorous program to provide China's domestic industry with modern technology.

The following paragraphs present an overview of the main elements of the power transmission equipment factories under China's Ministry of Machinery, China's primary system for electric power equipment production.

Transformers: One hundred twenty-seven plants under the Ministry of Machinery produce transformers under state contract. Of these, three are "backbone" enterprises that can produce 500 kv transformers and sixteen factories can produce transformers larger than 110 kv; but the great majority of factories produce small transformers rated at less than 35 kv. Total production in 1986 was 40.94 million kva of which the large enterprises produced 21.5 million kva, or 52.5 percent.

Porcelain: In 1986, sixty-nine enterprises produced porcelain products for electric power transmission. Of these, the most important firms numbered eighteen. Nine rated the distinction of "key central" enterprises and three were "backbone" enterprises that were capable of producing 330-500 kv porcelain products. According to 1986 statistics, the sixty-nine factories employed 47,192 workers. They turned out 83,570 tons of high tension porcelain products including 38,325 sets of 110-220 kv equipment.

Condensers: Over 100 factories produced condensers in 1986. Of these, twenty-five factories, almost certainly the largest and most sophisticated, belonged to the Ministry of Machinery system. Total condenser production in 1986 amounted to 15.41 million kvar. According to incomplete statistics, two factories produced more than 2 million kvar; three factories produced more than 1 million kvar; five factories produced between 500,000 and 1 million kvar; and six factories produced between 200,000 and 500,000 kvar while the remaining factories all produced less than 200,000 kvar.

Wire and Cable: In 1986 the Ministry of Machinery's system included 207 enterprises that produced electric wire and cable. This huge industry employed 146,400 workers, including nearly 6,500 engineers and technicians. The industry produced 101,00 km of electric power cable and 169,700 tons of aluminum wire with twisted steel core.

Japan has consistently held 50-60 percent of China's market for electric power transmission equipment. The U.S. share has been just short of 10 percent for the three most recent years for which detailed data are available. German manufacturers have done better than their American counterparts with a steadily rising market share that approached 12 percent in 1987. The Italian share jumped from 2.3 percent to 9.4 percent in 1987.

During the Seventh Five-Year Plan, China hopes to commission between 8,000 and 11,000 km of 500 kv transmission lines, and by the end of this century, the Chinese want to have transmission capabilities in the 500-1200 kv AC class. Foreign companies will play an important role in these accomplishments because the Chinese will need to rely on imported technology and equipment to meet these goals.

China's first high-voltage transmission line, the Pingdinghsan-to-Wuhan 500 kv line was engineered and designed by the Chinese, but foreign equipment, including thirteen sets of 500 kv circuit breakers, was used at the three substations at Pindingshan, Shuanghe, and Wuchang. Several foreign companies—Merlin-Gerin (France), Alsthom (France), HIT (Japan), Brown Boveri Company (Switzerland), and ASEA (Sweden)—were competing for that contract. The equipment and associated manufacturing technology were imported from Merlin-Gerin and ASEA.

The second transmission project was the Yuanbaoshan-Shenyang 500 kv line. The Chinese undertook this project themselves with the licenses from Pingdingshan, but they encountered a number of technical problems in producing the licensed equipment. China lacks adequate testing and research facilities for this advanced technology and has been forced to send some of its 500 kv AC products to the KEMA laboratories in the Netherlands for testing. China also lacks a high power laboratory that can perform all of the required 500 kv short circuit tests for this technology.

On subsequent projects the Chinese turned to imported foreign equipment to avoid delaying these important projects because of domestic production difficulties. For the

Datong-Beijing 500 kv line, they purchased General Electric substation equipment; and for the Xuzhou-Shanghai line, they approached and received a loan from the World Bank. The World Bank-funded project provided for the transmission of power from a 1300 Mw mine mouth, coal fired thermal power station at Xuzhou in Jiangsu Province to the East China power grid. This project utilized a bilateral loan for the Yangzi River crossing works, and assisted with the transfer of technology in 500 kv transmission line and substation design, construction, operation, and maintenance. The training component under the project included the establishment of a training center and the equipping of two technical schools in Nanjing and Shanghai for the operation and maintenance of 500 kv transmission lines and substations. This project was completed by the end of 1988. Gilbert/Commonwealth (U.S.) won the bid for engineering work on substations under the World Bank loan.

In high-voltage DC transmission where companies like Brown Boveri Company and ASEA are technically strong, major competition will come from Western Europe. All substation equipment for China's first high-voltage direct current line from Gezhuba dam to Shanghai was supplied by a Brown Boveri-Siemens consortium under a December 1984 contract that included a technology transfer component.

Competition from Chinese factories will be strong in the supply of low-technology transmission equipment, such as transformers, condensers, wire and cable, and porcelain products. Chinese equipment manufacturers are competent in the range of equipment necessary for 220 kv transmission lines, which were the standard trunk lines for the Chinese power grids before 1981, and they have begun initial production of their own 500 kv AC transmission system equipment at factories in Xian and Shenyang, with technology imported in the early 1980s from ASEA (Sweden), Brown Boveri (Switzerland), and Merlin-Gerin (France). However, foreign companies will still be called on to supply a large share of the 500 kv transmission equipment during the Seventh Five-Year Plan.

American involvement in China's electric power transmission market has been fairly limited. American companies hold only about 10 percent of the transmission equipment market and rank third in the number of technology transfer contracts signed. American companies accounted for about 20 percent of the technology transfer contracts signed, just behind West Germany and Switzerland.

Several American companies have been active, however. General Electric signed a seven year technology transfer deal with the Xian Rectifier Research Institute for high-power thyristors and diodes and a licensing agreement for surge arrestors with Xian Electric Manufacturing Corporation. McGraw Edison has also licensed transmission technology.

A number of engineering firms have conducted transmission studies. Bechtel conducted a study on a 500 kv transmission project from Shajiao to Jiangmen, and as mentioned above, Gilbert/Commonwealth was awarded the substation engineering work on the World Bank project. The Bonnevile Power Administration conducted a study of a 500 kv transmission project in cooperation with the U.S. Army Corps of Engineers.

In an attempt to help American industry get its foot in the door in this important area, the U.S. Trade and Development Program provided a $460,000 feasibility study grant for the expansion of the Xian High Voltage Apparatus Research Institute. Xian is one of China's two major centers for the electric power transmission, transformation, and distribution industries. Shenyang is the other. The feasibility study, conducted by Power Technologies, Inc., was completed in October 1986, but the project has stalled for lack of foreign exchange. If and when funding becomes available for the project, it is not certain that American companies will be competitive on the project.

Future advances by American companies will be limited because several key American companies are reducing their involvement in this market. Following its merger with ASEA/Brown Boveri, Westinghouse will be getting out of the international power generation and transmission business with the exception of nuclear power, and General Electric is pulling out of most phases of the transmission business. These American companies began their high-voltage work before the Europeans or Japanese, but then U.S. business atrophied, in part because of a downturn in power investment and in part because lines are so good that they do not have to be replaced. The European industry started later, when integrated power transmission made high-voltage economical. As a result, the European industry is still strong and has been active in pursuing business in developing countries.

GE and Schlumberger USA both still produce protective relays, and in fact, GE sold protective relays for the Tianshengqiao-Guangzhou transmission project as a subcontractor to the Nanjing Automation Research Institute under a Japanese loan. However, Westinghouse and GE have pulled out of circuit breaker and transformer business, which effectively leaves much of the transmission equipment market to the European and Japanese by default (40).

PRINTING EQUIPMENT

Overview During the Eighth Five-Year Plan (1991-1995), China expects to spend $60 million to import advanced printing technology and equipment. The efficiency of the printing industry would certainly benefit from use of computerized typesetting equipment and offset printing presses. Because China's import substitution policy creates serious barriers to importation of certain types of equipment and the targeted equipment may be procured through technology transfer or cooperative assembly arrangements, this may not be a profitable market for the direct sale of American printing equipment (41).

In the U.S.-China Memorandum of Understanding on Market Access signed on October 10, 1992, the Chinese Government confirmed that it has eliminated all import substitution regulations, guidance and policies and that it will not subject any products to any import substitution measures in the future. China's adherence to this commitment may positively influence direct sales of American printing equipment in China. Nevertheless, there may be a market niche for small rotary offset presses and ancillary equipment which would be compatible with both rotary and single sheet offset printing presses.

Market Assessment

A. Eighth Five-Year Plan (1991-1995

China's printing equipment industry operates under the supervision of the Ministry of Machinery and Electronics Industry. The printing equipment is manufactured by approximately 262 collective and state-owned enterprises. The leading sixty-four enterprises produce 80% of the industry's annual output.

Most of the smaller factories continue to produce traditional platemaking equipment, lead typesetting and platen press printing equipment, and simple post-print equipment which is used for folding, cutting, and binding.

Production of technologically advanced printing equipment is limited to only a few specially designated factories. These factories appear to have a state sanctioned monopoly on production of certain types of equipment because they are the "industry leaders."

The Printing Equipment Administrative Group plans to move toward nationwide use of computer typesetting systems. Many of the fifty-five major provincial level newspapers use this method in conjunction with rotary offset printing or sheet fed printing presses. Although the provincial newspapers adopted computer typesetting as the industry standard in 1990, several newspapers still have not procured the desired equipment. Most publishers of books, newspapers of limited circulation, and magazines still use traditional typesetting, presses and ancillary printing equipment.

The industry welcomes opportunities to discuss foreign investment, technology transfer or domestic assembly of foreign equipment. The Printing Equipment Administrative Group plans to spend US $60 million to acquire advanced technology during the Eighth Five-Year Plan.

B. Domestic Production

Total industrial output value for sixty-four out of 250 printing equipment manufacturers in 1988 was US $170,278,378 (exchange rate US $ 1:3.7 RMB) and US $189,097,297 in 1989. (No statistics are available for 1990-1192.) Although production output value increased, the number of units produced dropped slightly:

Equipment Type	Output	
	1988	1989
Platemaking Equipment	30,267	27,890
Printing Equipment	1,856	1,561
Binding Machinery	3,943	3,542

The Printing and Printing Equipment Industries Association of China estimates the annual production value of the sixty largest factories in 1991 was US $127 million, having an annual production capacity of 60,000 units. Because China imported US $117 million worth of printing equipment in 1990, it would appear that imports meet nearly 50% of overall domestic demand. No other detailed information is available on domestic production since 1989.

1. Pre-Print Equipment

a. Photo typesetting Equipment: China imported several of these units in the past few years, but plans to upgrade photo typesetting by utilizing color scanners which will be produced domestically. Currently, three factories produce 200 photo typesetting units per year. The Shanghai Optical Machinery Factory is the leading producer, accounting for one-half of China's annual production. It imported Japanese production technology in 1985. The two other manufacturers are Wuxi Photo Typesetting Factory and Jilin Optical Machinery Factory. Photo typesetting is primarily used by a few book publishers and packaging printers.

b. Color Scanners: This equipment will continue to be in great demand as China upgrades the technological level of the printing industry. However, these plans will not necessarily lead to increased imports of American equipment. In 1988, China purchased nearly 100 units and was only able to use 20% of them for various technical reasons. Chinese Customs statistics do not specify what types of platemaking equipment was imported in 1988, but the value of color scanners and other platemaking equipment was US $17 million. By 1990, total printing equipment imports dropped to US $12 million, of which color scanners accounted for approximately US $3.8 million. The number of color scanners imported by China dropped from thirty-seven in 1989 to twenty-four in 1990. In light of this experience, MMEI has approved cooperative production of color scanners by the Huabei Optical Instrument Factory. The factory contracted to assemble color scanner kits which are imported from the Hell Company, a West German concern.

The cooperative assembly project has already produced thirty units and MMEI expects it to import twenty to thirty more kits in 1992. China has previously imported color scanners from Japan, West Germany, Israel, and England.

   c. **Manual Lead Typesetting:** This equipment is still primarily used by book publishers, magazines, and newspapers of limited circulation. MMEI would like to see these publishers adopt computerized typesetting, but the funds for purchasing the equipment are not available at this time.

   d. **Computer Typesetting:** Several provincial newspapers now use this typesetting method. Approximately fifty units have been imported since 1988. The Shandong Weifang Computer Company is now the only domestic producer. It has established a cooperative assembly project with a Japanese or West Germany Company (MMEI was uncertain about the source of the kits). The <u>People's Daily</u> newspaper in Beijing purchased American computer typesetting equipment a few years ago but it is not operating very well. American manufacturers should be aware that the Chinese language software used by newspapers is not compatible with most computer typesetting equipment. This software is the industry standard, so requests for technical modifications should be expected. Due to this software problem, one additional import approval layer was added for this equipment to assure that all imported equipment will be compatible.

2. *Printing Presses*

   The two leading printing press manufacturers are Beijing Renmin General Machinery Plant ("Beiren") and Shanghai Renmin Printing Equipment Company. The former is the primary rotary offset printing press manufacturer and the latter is the primary sheet fed offset press manufacturer; but both factories produce both types.

   Although detailed information about the Shanghai factory was not available at the time this report was written, the interview with Beiren was informative. With respect to the degree of government involvement with production, Beiren would be considered a progressive enterprise. It is no longer state-owned, pays tax to the state and does not produce a set quota.

   The factory's production and product price is determined according to the law of supply and demand. During the next twelve years, it plans to spend US $15 million to procure foreign technology and production equipment.

   Beiren produces eleven different types of rotary offset printing presses. It also jointly manufactures single color sheet fed offset presses in conjunction with the Zeiser Company from West Germany. Its annual production capacity is approximately 800-1,000 units. This level production cannot meet market demand, being able to fulfill only about two-thirds of its orders. It currently has purchase orders for every unit to be produced through 1994. Each year Beiren produces 700 web or two-color rotary offset presses and 100 multicolor rotary offset presses. The average Chinese sale price is US $300,000-400,000. Although the product quality is inconsistent, it is very inexpensive compared to the average American price of US $900,000 to 1.5 million. German equipment is perceived to be most preferred on price, technological sophistication, and quality. Japanese equipment is considered to be next best on these criteria. According to Beiren, last year China imported 115 multicolor offset printing presses from Germany and Japan. Beiren will begin joint venture production of a West German Zeiser brand rotary printing press soon. The prototype was on display at CHINA PRINT '92.

3. *Post-Print Equipment*

MMEI believes China's demand for various types of post-print equipment used or folding, cutting, sorting, and binding is satisfied by domestic supply. Excess production capacity is exported primarily to Hong Kong, Sri Lanka, Singapore, India, and Malaysia.

Imports

1. Pre-Print Equipment: Between 1988 and 1990, the average U.S. market share was 4%. In 1988, the relative sales among the leading exporters to China (in US $ million) were: U.S. 2, compared to 5.5 for Japan and 3.8 for West Germany. In 1989, the U.S. export market share was 0.6, compared to 5.9 for Japan, 2.9 for Hong Kong, and 1.4 for Switzerland, U.K., and West Germany. In 1990, the U.S. export market was 0.5, compared to 4.5 for Japan, 2.6 for West Germany, and 2.6 for Hong Kong.

2. Printing Presses: During three years, the U.S. sold US $3.4 million out of US $189 million, which was 1%. In 1988, the comparative export earnings (in US $ million) were: 0.3 for the U.S., compared to 15 for West Germany, 12.5 for East Germany, 2.9 for Hong Kong and 2.8 for Japan. In 1989, the U.S. market share was 1.9, compared to 12.3 for West Germany, 8.8 for East Germany, 12.1 for Hong Kong, and 8.9 for Japan. In 1990, the U.S. market share was 1.2, compared to 29.9 for West Germany, 13 for East Germany, 16.2 for Hong Kong and 10 for Japan.

3. Post-Print Equipment: U.S. sales for this sub-sector during three years were US $6.2 million, which is 8% of the total. In 1988, the relative exports to China among the contenders (in US $ million) was: 2 for the U.S., 12.9 for West Germany, 8.3 for Japan, and 11 for Hong Kong. In 1989, the U.S. share was 3.2, compared to 2.1 for West Germany, 1.5 for Japan, 3.7 for Hong Kong, 2 for Switzerland, and 1.8 for Taiwan. In 1990, the U.S. share was 1, compared to 0.8 for West Germany, 1.8 for Japan, 3.2 for Hong Kong, 2.1 for Switzerland, and 114 for Taiwan.

Exports

The estimated value of China's export of printing equipment in 1991 was US $20 million. The equipment is primarily purchased by buyers in India, Thailand, Hong Kong, Russia, and Poland. According to Chinese Customs statistics, the total export value in 1990 was US $10.1 million: US $1.1 million for platemaking and typesetting equipment; US $3.7 million for printing presses and parts; and US $5.3 million for post-print equipment (41).

Competitive Situation

U.S. equipment technology is perceived to be superior, but too expensive. One American company has been successful in selling about ten units and is discussing the possibility of joint venture production in China. It is unfortunate that no American companies currently produce single sheet fed offset presses because China has decided that his type of press will replace it aging platen presses. One American company, Harris Graphics, has merged with the leading German manufacturer, Heidberg. Because web rotary offset printing presses are very efficient and require high quality paper, the Printing Equipment Administrative Group believes that such presses are only appropriate for use by provincial newspapers. The Administrative Group has decided that sheet fed offset presses are more flexible because the equipment can accommodate a variety of printing needs and does not require use of high quality paper. The Heidberg, a sheet fed offset press manufacturer from Germany, is the preferred supplier and has the largest market share in China.

The Chinese end-users and equipment manufacturers in the printing equipment industry have a strong preference for West German and Japanese equipment. Although a few American companies have successfully established assembly operations or technology transfer projects, direct sales opportunities are limited. Regardless of which type of purchasing arrangement is agreed upon, the seller should be aware that the Chinese buyer will often request a gratuitous trip to the United States before the contract is signed. Some companies have dealt with this request by offering a trip after the contract is signed and then building the trip cost into the equipment sales price. Because opportunities to travel to the U.S. are very limited, the Chinese buyer does not usually object to including the trip cost in the contract.

When confronted with complaints by the prospective buyer that the American equipment is too expensive, the seller should be aware that Japanese sales practices are very different than those employed by most American businesses. The Japanese sell the first few machines at a very low price with the expectation that prices can be raised in the future. Sometimes, Japanese companies even donate a few units to a prospective buyer if the anticipated future sales volume would permit the seller to recoup the loss later. Chinese buyers also believe the average sales price for American printing presses is approximately three times the price of a domestically produced machine and about one-third higher than prices offered by West German and Japanese suppliers.

After sales service is a very important Chinese purchasing criteria. The American seller should assure prompt service and thoroughly explain its customer service policies and training program. Although the American company may think it is very reasonable to first require an inspection report or return of defective parts before replacement equipment or parts are given to the Chinese buyer, the Chinese claim that most Japanese and European companies first replace the defective equipment or parts then deal with the defective goods. The Beijing Renmin General Machinery Plant claimed that it has had a few bad experiences with American service and prefers West German or Japanese equipment for this reason.

Market Access

A. Decentralization and the Market Economy Although decentralization has taken place with respect to production decisions for some printing equipment manufacturers, the importation of equipment appears to be highly regulated. Chinese end-users also do not have opportunity to spend hard currency and can only import through state-owned trading corporations.

B. Import Barriers China's foreign trade regime is guided by an import substitution policy. This means that if a product is manufactured in China, it will not receive import approval unless certain criteria are met. These criteria are designed to protect "infant industries." As discussed above, most of the "leading" factories which produce technologically advanced printing equipment are doing so through assembly of foreign kits, or through purchase of foreign technology, and are considered to be in the early development stage. Although a few factories produce sophisticated equipment, the majority do not.

Importation of rotary and sheet fed offset printing presses, color scanners, and computer typesetting equipment requires import approval. In addition, printing presses require an import license and color scanners are subject to a quota of thirty per year. The process of import approval is complicated. Before a product which is on the list of fifty-three "controlled products" can be imported, an application, MMEI's Third Department, MMEI's Administrative Group, the Import Examination Office (shencha ban), and the Ministry of Materials Supply.

Importation of single color offset presses is generally not approved because the equipment can be produced in China. Because China is able to produce a few multicolor rotary offset printing presses and color scanners, it is likely that domestic production capacity must be exhausted before import approval will be granted.

Best Sales Prospects

The key opportunities are for production of computer typesetting equipment; multicolor offset printing equipment; small sheet fed offset printing equipment for office use; large sheet fed printing equipment for production of books, newspaper and magazines; resin board making equipment; package printing equipment; and color scanning equipment. Because the quality of domestically produced equipment is inconsistent, quality inspection equipment is also desired.

In contrast to numerous technology transfer or assembly opportunities, the prospects for sale of sophisticated printing equipment is very limited due to import barriers. A market niche may exist for ancillary equipment which is compatible with both rotary and sheet fed offset printing equipment. China has a strong preference for sheet fed offset printing equipment because the paper used by circulation newspapers is generally not durable enough to be used on rotary offset printing equipment. Sales prospects for post-print equipment are limited due to excess domestic production capacity and increasing exports.

The Beijing Renmin General Machinery Plant is interested in producing small sheet fed offset presses for office use. It will be traveling to the U.S. sometime this year to visit with

American equipment manufacturers to discuss technology transfer or cooperative assembly in China.

China has developed Chinese-language software for use with computer typesetting equipment, but most imported equipment still requires technical adjustments to be compatible with it. Only one Chinese factory is currently assembling computer typesetting equipment. The desire to upgrade newspaper and book production may created an opportunity for the direct sale of the equipment, but the most promising prospect may be for cooperative assembly.

Useful Contacts

1. Chinese Import/Export Corporations

The Chinese economy does not operate on open market distribution channels which are typically found in capitalistic economic system. It is difficult to identify prospective sales agents or distributors in China's foreign trade system. The companies listed below are authorized state-owned foreign trade corporations which are buyers' agents, as opposed to sellers' agents.

China Machinery Import/Export Corporation
Erligou, Xijiao
Beijing, China 100044
Tel: 831.7733 x5160, 5161, 5162 (Import Department)
Fax: 831.4143

China Machinery & Equipment Import/Export Corporation
No. 16 Fuxingmenwai Dajie
Beijing, China 100045
Tel: 801.3462   Fax: 326.1865

China National Electronics Import/Export Corporation
No. 23A Fuxing Road
Beijing, China 100036
Tel: 821.9561, 813.043   Fax: 822.3907, 822.3914, 821.2352

China National Technical Import/Export Corporation
Erligou, Xijiao
Beijing, China 100044
Tel: 841.4847, 840.4970   Fax: 831.6696

China National Instruments Import/Export Corporation
Erligou, Xijiao
Beijing, China 100044
Tel: 831.7392, 831.2921 (Import Division)
Fax: 831.5925

Other Useful Contacts

Press and Publications Administration
No. 85 Dongsi Nandajie
Beijing, China 100703
Tel: 550.228

Printing and Printing Equipment Industries Association of China
6 Dong Sheng Hutong, Dongdan Ertiao
Beijing, China
Tel: 512,3289

Beijing Renmin General Machinery Plant
48 South Donghuan Road
Beijing, China
Tel: 771.5355, 771.6600 x358   Fax: 771.1389

Ministry of Machinery and Electronics Industry
Third Equipment Bureau
46 Sanlihe Road
Beijing, China 100823
Tel: 329.5120, 329.5119, 329.5118   Fax: 801.3867, 862.644, 329.5115

Zhonglian Printing Equipment Company Ltd.
49A Dongdan, Ertiao
Beijing, China
Tel: 550.459

PROCESS CONTROL EQUIPMENT

Table 111 gives some salient statistics for the Industrial Process Control Sector (3).

As noted in the table, the sector includes power plant instrumentation, chemical plant instrumentation and CAM (computer aided manufacturing).

Table 111

Salient Statistics for Process Control Industrial Sector

A)	Three-letter ITA industry sector code:	PCI
B)	Est. total market size (USD millions):	
	1991 -	$ 500
	1992 -	$ 600
	1993 -	$1,445
	1994 -	$1,332
	1995 -	$2,305
C)	Est. 1992-4 annual market growth rate:	8%
D)	Est. total imports (USD millions):	
	1991 -	$150
	1992 -	$180
	1993 -	$223
	1994 -	$258
	1995 -	$296
E)	Est. annual total import growth rate:	8%
F)	Est. imports from U.S. (USD millions):	
	1991 -	$ 40
	1992 -	$ 50
	1993 -	$ 56
	1994 -	$ 63
	1995 -	$ 72 (58)
G)	Est. annual growth of imports from U.S.:	8%
H)	China's receptivity to U.S. products i this sector (5 - High/1 - Low):	5
I)	Competition from local/third countries for U.S. firms (5 - Low/1 - High):	4
J)	Chinese market barriers to U.S. sales in this sector (5 - Few/1 - Many):	4
K)	Comments - factors for increased U.S. sales:	

- During the Eighth Five-Year Plan period, the Chinese government will give high priority to the development of high-tech equipment and processes which require much higher standards of industrial control.
- U.S. exports are very competitive. Fifteen percent of instrument sales are transferred as part of finished products/structures like power plants, chemical plants, etc. (58).

L)	Most Promising Sub-sectors	1992 market size
	1. Power plant instrumentation	$150 million
	2. Chemical plant/refinery process control	$100 million
	3. Numerically-controlled machine tools	$ 50 million

Overview The total size of China's industrial process controls market is estimated (1987) to be US $1.2 billion. Domestic production accounts for approximately 68% of this total, and foreign imports 32%. Chinese exports of process controls are currently less than 1% of the total market.

Projections for the development of China's process controls market roughly follow China's Seventh Five-Year Plan, which calls for a 9% annual growth rate in the machinery and electronics sector. The import market is projected to grow slightly faster than this, but this projection is highly dependent on how easily Chinese purchasers can gain foreign exchange currency, and on the severity of import barriers. Process controls imports decreased in 1987 for these reasons, and could decrease further despite growing demand if these problems remain.

Market Assessment It is difficult to obtain accurate figures for the overall industrial process control (IPC) market size in China, for several reasons. First, the United States appears to be the only country which makes regular distinctions between IPC and non-IPC use of products in its statistics. Second, the Chinese customs statistics are too broad for specific analysis of IPC products; they are at best useful for overall trends which bear on IPC production use. The only Chinese statistics directly applicable to the question are estimates made by government ministries. Third, many of the IPCs which enter China are not sold directly as IPCs, but as part of larger capital equipment, sold and installed by foreign contractors. The IPCs that control power plants, modern production and processing equipment, supplied through foreign companies, are often not displayed in IPC-related statistics; their costs are contained in the categories of the larger capital equipment.

In the past ten years, China has pursued the goals of modernization and development by adopting an "open door policy" toward foreign technology and investment. This program has gradually expanded from modest beginnings, and recent pronouncements suggest that the government intends to continue opening the door wider to foreign business. Between 1981 and 1986, the trend in growth may be summarized by saying that the technology import value roughly doubles from one year to the next.

The market for industrial process control (IPC) products has not grown so dramatically, but has enjoyed the same environment for growth. Purchases of imported IPCs are encouraged by the government, especially if the technology to manufacture the products is part of the transaction. If domestic IPC products are not available to meet the internal market demand, the opportunity to sell state-of-the-art IPC components with the associated technology is available. Sales of production equipment and technology, or investment in joint ventures to manufacture in China are generally preferred by the Chinese over direct sales of products, as these assist China in developing its own technical capabilities. The market for this kind of technology transfer can be expected to continue to grow.

Chinese ministry level planners are becoming more specific about which types of technology import are to be encouraged. This industry-wide planning can result in wide swings in policy. In past years, imports of assembly lines for domestic goods such as television sets, refrigerators, fans and washing machines were in high demand, as China wished to increase production capacity for these items. Most recently, however, as China has assimilated much of this technology, the demand for this type of foreign equipment has declined. This rise and fall of demand is expected to recur in other more advanced technologies as China's technological level advances. Government pronouncements, particularly the Seventh Five-Year Plan are a good indication of which sectors are currently in vogue. In the near future, among the sectors expected to receive most emphasis are the basic infrastructure industries including energy, transport, iron and steel, communications, petroleum, and specific high-tech industries such as electronics.

Domestic production figures are available for the IPCs which are controlled by the State Commission of Machine Building Industry (SCOMI). There are reported to be 1,000 companies that manufacture some type of IPC component; of this number, 300 are controlled through SCOMI (now replaced by Ministry of Machine Building and Electronics Industry, MMEI). According to SCOMI representatives, these 300 companies account for roughly 80% of the domestically produced IPCs. The other 700 factories are subsidiaries of specific companies and only produce for the parent company. The products produced are specific to the parent company's needs and these IPC shops do not sell into the export market, nor are the products available outside the parent factory.

Competitive Situation Competition between foreign supplying countries varies with the sub-sectors of the process controls market. The U.S. is strongest in the high-technology end of the market, including scientific instrumentation and distributed process control systems. Demand for advanced technologies will continue for as long as China is unable to match foreign technological standards. The U.S., Japan, and Western European countries taken as a group each hold roughly 30% of the import market. Although the U.S. is gaining in some specific fields, it has lost a few percent of overall market share per year, notably to West Germany and Japan.

Market Access Major Chinese end-users of industrial process controls include the metallurgical, power generation, machine building, chemical and petroleum industries. Other light industry typically lacks the money to automate their equipment with foreign products. Much depends on the export potential of the industry for access to foreign currency (e.g. the petroleum industry, which ordinarily can afford foreign equipment, but now lacks funds due to the drop in world oil prices) and the importance of the industry to national development interests. One especially fast-growing field is the nuclear industry, where demand for process controls and test instrumentation is expected to grow at over 30% annually for the next several years.

As China emphasizes reduction of imports and development of its technological base, trade barriers are imposed on some direct sales, but technology transfer agreements and joint ventures are encouraged. Some foreign companies are developing long-term strategies used on this trend, including the establishment of joint manufacturing facilities and service centers in major locations. This had proved successful for companies which can afford the long-term investment, and the trend toward this kind of investment and away from complete reliance on direct sales is likely to continue.

Best Sales Prospects

Detailed estimates of domestic IPC demand are available only for certain specific product sub-categories. Table 112 lists purchasing plans for representative IPC products in coming years (42).

Average annual demand growth rates correspond closely with the 9% Seventh Five-Year Plan overall annual growth rate for production in the machinery and electronics sectors. However, this does not rule out growth in the import market in coming years. Market sectors most likely to see growth in imports are those which require advanced technology and are being encouraged by the central government; nuclear industry test instrumentation is a good example of this, showing a spectacular 33$ annual growth rate from 1990-1995.

Table 112

Projected Demand Statistics for Selected IPCs, 1990-2000
(million US$)

Product Category	1990	1995	Annual Growth
Nuclear Industry Test Instrumentation	13.43	56.42	33%
Auto-Recording & Data Display Instruments	40.30	67.16	11%
Common Pressure Gauge	42.72	70.79	11%
Electromagnetic Flowmeter	5.37	8.06	8%
Electric Actuator	32.24	48.36	8%
Infrared Radiation Thermometer	4.03	5.91	8%
Precision Pressure Gauge	4.86	6.80	7%
Globe Regulating Valve	17.46	24.18	7%
Industrial Pt Resistance Thermometer	16.12	21.50	6%
Electronic Pneumatic Valve Locator	2.03	2.69	6%
Glass Rotometer	6.72	8.33	4%
Turbine Flowmeter	6.85	8.19	4%
Pneumatic Indicating Regulator	3.76	3.22	-3%
Pneumatic Diff. Pressure Transmitter	4.30	3.40	-5%

Source: Instrumentation Information Center of SCOMI.

Imports Into China The most reliable and detailed data for IPC imports to China are contained in the customs statistics of the various exporting countries. Total import market size estimates vary significantly depending which categories in these statistics are considered to fall within the process controls category.

We include figures for the following categories in our estimate of the IPC import market (42):

- Process variable instrumentation
- Liquid/gas variable controls
- Electro-mechanical controls
- Controllers and regulators
- Final control elements
- Physical/chemical instrumentation
- Radiation detectors
- Parts

These categories are available for the U.S. and Japan, which make up roughly two-thirds of the UPC import market. By allowing for the market share of the two countries, a total import market size may be estimated using the figures for the U.S. and Japan. The details of this estimate are given in Table 113.

Table 113

Estimate of Total IPC Import Market Size

	1985	1986
Estimated IPC import value (million US$):		
United States	117	109
Japan	75	110
Estimated market share of the U.S. and Japan together:		
	68%	64%
Estimated total IPC import market value (million US$):		
	284	342

Useful Contacts

Selected addresses of China representative offices.

AHS China, Ltd.
Tong Fang Hotel Room 2281
Guangzhou
Tel: 669900 x2281

Allied Signal China, Inc.
Lido Commercial Building
A-2, 5th Floor, Beijing
Tel: 5006763, 5006766

Asahi Trading Company, Ltd.
Beijing Hotel, Room 1436
Beijing
Tel: 5007766 x1436

Bailey Controls
41 Gulou West Street
Beijing
Tel: 441537 x37

China Hewlett-Packard, Ltd.
P.O. Box 9610
Beijing No. 2 Watch Factory, 4th Floor
San Huan Bei Road
Shuang Yu Shu, Beijing
Tel: 280567/280456

Conemsco Limited (LTV Energy Products)
Beijing Hotel Room 1009, Beijing
Tel: 5007766 x1009

Continental Trading Company
Yanjing Hotel Room 7004, Beijing
Tel: 868721 x7004

Control Data China, Inc.
Noble Towers Room 1701-1706, Beijing
Tel: 5122288 x1701-6, 5123717

Creusot-Loire International
Qianmen Hotel Room 609, Beijing
Tel: 333686

FMC Far East Ltd.
CITIC Building Room 2705, Beijing
Tel: 5002255 x2750, 5002251

General Processes Pte
Friendship Hotel Room 214, Tianjin
Tel: 31-4646, 31-0372

Global Technology, Inc.
Xiyuan Hotel Room 919, Beijing
Tel: 8313388 x919

Gokei Trading Corporation
Xinqiao Hotel Room 482, Beijing
Tel: 557731 x482

Gould Corporation
Friendship Hotel, Building 4, Suite 4604
Beijing
Tel: 890621 x4604, 4605

Hitachi, Ltd.
Xiyuan Hotel, Building 5
Beijing
Tel: 8313388

Honeywell, Inc.
Noble Towers, 14th Floor, Beijing
Tel: 5122288 x1408, 1409 or 5123677

Japan-China Machinery
Xiyuan Hotel Room 1414, Beijing
Tel: 8313388 x414

John Fluke Manufacturing Company
P.O. Box 9085
Noble Towers, 21st Floor, Beijing
Tel: 5122288 x2102 or 5123435

Kanematsu Gosho, Ltd.
Heping Hotel, Beijing
Tel: 554800

Koji Trading Company, Ltd.
Xinqiao Hotel Room 206, Beijing
Tel: 557731 x206

Kyoho Tsusho Kaisha, Ltd.
Yanjing Hotel, Room 1528, Beijing
Tel: 868721 x1528

Mannesmann AG
Karl-Heinz Palm
Xiyuan Hotel, Beijing
Tel: 896070

Marconi Electronics
Xiyuan Hotel, Building 1, Room 129
Beijing
Tel: 8313388 x129

Marumbeni Corporation
58 Maoming Nanlu Room 305, Shanghai
Tel: 372319 x305

National Council for US-China Trade
Suite 1136, Beijing Hotel
Tel: 5007766 x1136

Nippon Electric Company, Ltd.
Beijing Hotel Room 4090, Beijing
Tel: 5007766 x4090

Rockwell International
Lido Centre Block A-2, 5th Floor
Beijing
Tel: 5006665

Siemens AG
CITIC Building, Room 2101, Beijing
Tel: 5003338 x2110

Sperry China Services, Inc.
Zhaolong Hotel, Room 201, Beijing
Tel: 5002299

Taiyo Koeki Company Ltd.
Yanjing Hotel, Room 1628, Beijing
Tel: 868721 x1628

Tektronix China, Ltd.
Xiyuan Hotel, Room 102, Beijing
Tel: 8021657

Texas Instruments China, Inc.
CITIC Building, Room 7-05, Beijing
Tel: 5002255 x3750 or 5002705

Toyota Tsusho Kaisha, Ltd.
58 Maoming Nanlu, Room 536, Shanghai
Tel: 371195

United Nations (UNDP)
2 Dongqijie Sanlitun, Beijing
Tel: 523731

United Technologies
CITIC Building, Room 1603, Beijing
Tel: 5003094

US China Industrial Exchange, Inc.
Xiyuan Hotel, Room 2301, Beijing
Tel: 8313388 x835

Wang Laboratories
CITIC Building, Room 2301, Beijing
Tel: 5002255 x2310

Westinghouse Electric
Xuanwumen Hotel, 12th Floor
30 Qianmen Xi Dajie, Beijing
Tel: 34-2797, 34-1541

World Bank
Xiyuan Hotel, Building 3, 3rd Floor
Beijing
Tel: 8312227

Yamatake-Honeywell Company, Ltd.
Beijing Hotel, Room 6061
Beijing
Tel: 5007766 x6061

Yokogawa Electric Works
Yanjing Hotel, Room 9014, Beijing
Tel: 868721 x9014

Yokohama Machinery Trade
Minzu Hotel, Room 2310, Beijing
Tel: 658541 x2310

PROCESSED FOODS

The processed food industry can include seafood, dairy products and specialty foods. Table 114 summarizes some statistics for this overall area.

The text in this section of this volume focuses on fast foods as one fast growing segment described in a Department of Commerce report (31).

Table 114

Statistics on the Processed Food Industry

A)	Three-letter ITA industry sector code:	FOD
B)	Est. total market size (USD millions):	
	1991 -	$10,000
	1992 -	$11,000
C)	Est. 1992-4 annual market growth rate:	10%
D)	Est. total imports (USD millions):	
	1991 -	$500
	1992 -	$600
E)	Est. annual total import growth rate:	20%
F)	Est. imports from U.S. (USD millions):	
	1991 -	$50
	1992 -	$60
G)	Est. annual growth of imports from U.S.:	30%
H)	China's receptivity to U.S. products in this sector (5 - High/1 - Low):	4
I)	Competition from local/third countries for U.S. firms (5 - Low/1 - High):	4
J)	Chinese market barriers to U.S. sales in this sector (5 - Few/1 - Many):	3
K)	Comments - factors for increased U.S. sales:	

- U.S. fast food companies are aggressively, and successfully, penetrating the Chinese market.
- Almost all categories of specialty foods have shown dramatic increases in the past two years.
- There has been a dramatic increase in Chinese imports of U.S. specialty foods in most categories in the past two years.
- Increasing consumer spending power coupled with traditional Chinese emphasis on cuisine.

L)	Most Promising Sub-sectors	1992 market size
	1. Seafood	$1,000 million
	2. Dairy products	$ 100 million
	3. Specialty foods	$ 80 million

Overview - Fast Food Like most service industries in China, the market for fast food outlets, equipment, and related managerial skills is still in the early stages of development, but it is growing at a rapid clip. Many foreign fast food companies have established operations in China's more open urban centers; Beijing, Shanghai, Guangzhou and Shenzhen to name a few.   At present, roughly six or seven U.S. based firms have established approximately two dozen fast food outlets. These stores sell chicken, donuts, hamburgers, pizza, and ice cream. Chinese firms from Taiwan, and Hong Kong are expanding rapidly in the market. Also, many indigenous PRC competitors have been established.

American fast food companies have found that China is a difficult market. A number of factors restrain growth. First, lack of legal infrastructure inhibits the use of the normal franchise mechanism.   American firms are forced to enter into joint ventures in each individual market.   Second, operations in China must cope with a severe lack of foreign exchange.   Third, operations in China must purchase almost all supplies from the local market.   Finally, there is a severe lack of trained personnel in China to staff a modern restaurant operation.

This report deals with two distinct, but interrelated areas: fast food service and fast food production equipment.

Market Assessment for Fast Food Service As disposable income has increased, alternatives for spending have not increased at a commensurate pace. Fast food is considered to be a novel form of consumption. Single young workers in cities with salaries around US $100 per month are some of the best customers of fast food establishments.

Urban Chinese value very highly the service and cleanliness associated with modern fast food establishments.   Fast food ventures are generally considered to be superior to conventional informal Chinese eateries. Moreover, Chinese will often visit fast food outlets just for the novelty of Western cuisine. In many cases, Chinese middle class individuals have never had the opportunity to sample Western style food. A visit to the local McDonald's or Pizza Hut may even be their first brush with Western culture.   Price is a factor, but the Chinese will pay extra for the experience.

Brand names are also very important. Most fast food chains strive for an American image. The newness and popularity of American products, or products which suggest an American origin, is an unquantifiable, but very important factor affecting Chinese sales. The most obvious proof of the cultural attraction to American fast food is the proliferation of fast food firms with American sounding names. "Uncle Sam's," "Pioneer Chicken," "Brownies" and "Cowboy Noodles" are examples of outlets which have no known U.S. connection outside of their names.

Another significant factor is tourism. Foreign tourists have hard currency available and tend to gravitate toward known operations. This can be a significant strategic advantage, as it assists the balancing of hard currency and repatriation of profits. Although only 5-7% of McDonald's revenue is in Foreign Exchange Certificates (FEC), foreigners compose 11% of its clientele.   Domestic tourists also are likely to try foreign fast food chains for the experience of urban living. Domestic tourists make up 19% of McDonald's Beijing market.

Finally, marketing strategies directed at children may be particularly effective. Urban Chinese live under the "one child policy." This has created a social situation which boosts disposable income per family and leads to extravagant, by Chinese standards, spending on their "little emperors." As one former Vice-Minister said recently, "The children! They're eating money right out of their parents pockets!"

Competitive Situation - Fast Food There are an increasing number of American fast food joint ventures in China, including Kentucky Fried Chicken (KFC), Golden Skillet, McDonald's, Dairy Queen, and Pizza Hut. With a 20-25% market share, Americans make up the largest foreign group. Chinese firms from Hong Kong and Taiwan are in second place. Japanese firms have the next largest share. Major non-U.S. firms include Bonny Fried Chicken (Australia), Da Fa Fried Chicken (Thailand), and Yoshinoya (Japan). Indigenous PRC competition includes many local single store outlets, and a few multi-store chains such as Uncle Sam's, Pioneer Chicken, Tak Hsin, Fairwood, and California Noodle. Rong Hua Fried Chicken (PRC), is said to be a major competitor of KFC in some locations.

In this dynamic environment, the possibilities for the fast food companies which overcome the barriers for entry to the market seem enormous. These barriers, however, must be overcome before business can start on even a regional basis. The first of these is finding a suitable business partner. Second, the American firm must find suppliers for a large portion of its provisions. Third, the new entry into the China market must locate or train sufficient managerial expertise. Fourth, the firm must be structured in such a way that it can generate foreign exchange revenue.

Best Sales Prospects

There is a growing market for all sorts of food processing equipment in China, but some of the items most likely to have waiting markets may include (31):
1. Fast food fryers.
2. Fast food ovens.
3. Dairy processing equipment.
4. High speed, automatic equipment (e.g. sifters, steamers, strainers, mixers, canners, packers, control monitors).
5. Freezing and cold storage equipment. (Note: While there seems to be adequate basic refrigeration equipment in China, there is a continuing need for quick freezing system.)
6. Pre-processing control equipment packages (recovery systems, magnetic separators, recording thermometers, sterilizing systems, extractors, dryers, and coolers).
7. Irradiation, ultrasonic, infrared, and other food preservation technologies.
8. Small to medium sized semi-automatic machinery for small and medium scale plants serving local markets.
9. Hot dog/sausage making equipment (fillers, sealers, high temperature/pressure sterilization equipment).
10. Special cutting and packaging equipment for meat.
11. Micro-ingredient scales and other pre-mix equipment.

The Ice Cream Industry As described in the Wall Street Journal for September 19, 1994, Chinese traditionally don't eat dairy products. But in a country where workers think nothing of calling in sick with "heat stroke," ice cream has proved an exception. Some managers say they buy it in bulk to keep employees from falling asleep in sweltering offices.

In fact, 200 Chinese companies now churn out about a million metric tons of ice cream a year, a figure that industry experts estimate is growing by about 20% annually. A metric ton is equal to 2,204.62 pounds.

That has foreign ice cream makers salivating. But to grab a share of the market, they must persuade skeptical consumers—used to cheap, watery domestic offerings—that the cream is more important than the ice.

So far this year, food giants, such as Kraft General Foods, Inc., a unit of Philip Morris Company, Unilever NV and Nestle SA have announced multimillion dollar production arrangements in the country. They're vying for freezer space with U.S. brands already on the market, including TCBY, Bud's, Baskin Robbins and Meadow Gold, as well as the Mountain Cream label from Hong Kong. Most of these new competitors are seeking initially to gain a sales foothold in a particular city or region, rather than immediately tackling the distribution woes that make an all-China market illusive.

The Snack Food Industry Reliable statistics are not yet available on China's consumption, production, or trade of snack foods, but U.S. trade data clearly reflects the increasing demand for this high-value product. In the 1990-1993 period, U.S. exports of snack foods to China increased at an annual rate of 160 percent. Rising living standards and income, when combined with consumers interest in convenience and quality, are generating the demand for imported snack foods. Hong Kong remains an important conduit for these products, and it is likely that the above figures underestimated the actual sales of U.S. snack foods in China (58).

One particular category of interest is that of tree nuts (pistachios) which represents a total 1995 market size in China of $5,000 million $US. There is no local production in China. Of the $US 9,000 million worth of imports, some 90% come from the U.S. and about half of those are re-exported by China.

Pistachio imports grew by 28 percent in 1993. First quarter imports in 1994 suggest some slackening of growth. Snack size packaging with U.S. logos are proving to be very popular, although use of lower quality non-U.S. origin nuts in some cases may retard growth. U.S. almonds are also popular, with total trade at about one-tenth the level of pistachios. Most local "almonds" are actually apricot kernels. Pistachio exports are re-exports following splitting of shells or other processing. Import duty of 50 percent on pistachios continues to act as a constraint on increased imports (58).

PULP AND PAPER MACHINERY
Table 115 shows salient statistics concerning the pulp and paper machinery industry (3).

Table 115

Salient Statistics Concerning the Pulp and Paper Machinery Sector

A) Three-letter ITA industry sector code: PUL
B) Est. total market size (USD millions):
    1991 - $ 500
    1992 - $ 565
    1993 - $4,857
    1994 - $5,299
    1995 - $5,837 (58)
C) Est. 1992-4 annual market growth rate: 13%
D) Est. total imports (USD millions):
    1991 - $ 50
    1992 - $ 58
    1993 - $327
    1994 - $336
    1995 - $347
E) Est. annual total import growth rate: 16%
F) Est. imports from U.S. (USD millions):
    1991 - $10
    1992 - $13
    1993 - $58
    1994 - $59
    1995 - $60
G) Est. annual growth of imports from U.S.:   30%
H) China's receptivity to U.S. products in
    this sector (5 - High/1 - Low):   3
I) Competition from local/third countries
    for U.S. firms (5 - Low/1 - High):   3
J) Chinese market barriers to U.S. sales
    in this sector (5 - Few/1 - Many):   3
K) Comments - factors for increased U.S. sales:
    • Growth in office equipment use (computers, copiers).
    • Increased emphasis on packaging, especially for rapidly-growing exports.
    • Quality of paper needed is much higher than before in China.
    • Companies from Canada, Finland, and Northern Europe hold the largest foreign market share because their governments provide loans for China. U.S. export prices are undercut by competitors.

L) Most Promising Sub-sectors	1992 market size
1. Bag and envelope machines	$100 million
2. Particle board machines	$ 40 million
3. Pulping equipment	$ 30 million

Overview From 1980 to 1986, China's papermaking industry imported about USD 176 million worth of foreign technology and equipment. From 1986 to 1988, China imported USD 230 million worth of such technology and equipment. Chinese papermaking plants are interested in importing pulping equipment; chemical recovery systems; second hand equipment for treating wastepaper; and modern, high speed equipment for making hygienic paper, cigarette paper, paper for making color film, and special cardboard.

The market in China for U.S. wastepaper has potential. While it may be unstable and volatile in some parts of the PRC, in other parts (e.g. the Shanghai area), demand is strong and getting stronger. There is a great need in the PRC for materials other than domestic wood pulp for the manufacture of paper, cardboard, and related items. China needs a great deal more, and higher quality paper and packaging products; supply lags far behind demand.

The major force creating this market is the fact that China is losing its struggle to increase forest acreage. The Chinese government has made conservation of its forest resources a priority during the Eighth Five-Year economic plan. However, year by year more forests are lost to fires and cutting. One source indicates that China loses approximately 1/2 million hectares (about 1 1/2 million acres) of forests each year from overcutting, illegal cutting, and clearing for agriculture, mining, or building construction. Some statistics indicate that most small trees replanted in barren rural areas or mountainsides are not taking root. An expert notes that, since 1949, the government has planted 153 million hectares of trees; of these, only 25 million hectares of trees have survived. Each year 300 million cubic meters of timber are used, and only 200 million cubic meters are being replenished through planting. The timber shortages have meant that wood prices have skyrocketed—80 percent a year between 1985 and 1988. New forests which are surviving must, at all costs, be preserved, not only for industrial purposes but also to hold the soil and prevent destructive flooding. Unfortunately for China, there is no prospect that, within this decade, the situation will improve (26).

Another major force creating this market for U.S. exporters is the fact that, although the Chinese appear to be good at gathering, recycling, and reusing their wastepaper (otherwise known in the trade as "secondary fiber") and waste cloth, in fact, statistics show that such reuse is far below the average for most countries of the world. Recycling Chinese paper is very difficult since its wood content is already very low. Imported wastepaper, much higher in wood content, is relatively easy to recycle.

Best Sales Prospects

The kind of wastepaper most needed by Chinese enterprises is probably that with the highest wood pulp content. Less expensive grades (e.g. primarily used corrugated cardboard boxes such as those used in grocery stores) may also sell fairly well. Sales prospects related to wastepaper exports to China include (38):

-- second hand equipment for treating wastepaper.
-- recycling machines to make paper and paper board from wastepaper.
-- ink removing machines (better machines would enable Chinese pulp manufacturers to better prepare newsprint for recycling).
-- anti-pollution devices (the paper pulp industry is one of China's worst polluters).
-- technology for improving processes for producing non-wood fiber pulp (the PRC presently uses lime processing, sodium carbonate processing, calcium bisulfide processing, alkaline processing, sulphite pulping, and other methods).
-- pulp-making equipment.
-- cleaning, screening and beating equipment.
-- washing and boiling equipment.
-- boilers.

There are also needs for a variety of equipment other than that used in wastepaper recovery and handling. These needs include (38):

-- Pulping equipment.
-- Chemical recovery systems.
-- Modern, high-speed equipment for making hygienic paper, cigarette paper, paper for making color film.
-- Modern technology and equipment for making paper from non-wood sources such as bagasse.
-- Fourdrinier paper machines (to produce wider paper than is commonly available in China).
-- Corrugating machines.
-- Converters to fold linerboard and corrugated paper into boxes.
-- Second hand equipment for treating wastepaper.
-- Recycling machines to make paper and paperboard from wastepaper.
-- Machines to manufacture new types of paper containers such as paper drums, paper cans.
-- Machines to manufacture molded pulp products.
-- Extensible bag technology.
-- Chemical recovery and pollution abatement equipment for papermaking facilities.
-- Ink removal technologies (to remove ink from recycled paper).
-- Special use items (e.g. computerized control systems, specialty valves, drums, etc., for the papermaking industry).

Useful Contacts in China

CNPPC (China National Pulp and Paper Corporation)
82 Dong An Men Jie
Beijing
Tel: 557 881 or 550 293

CPIDC (China Paper Industry Development Corporation
#12 Guang Hua Road
P.O. Box 100020
Beijing
Tel: 500 4461 Fax: 01 500 4461

(Note: CPIDC is responsible for developing new raw materials for the paper industry. Its board members include representatives of at least forty major paper mills and corporations, at least three institutes connected with MOLI, plus the China National Light Industry Machinery Corporation.)

Import and Export Company of the Yalu Jiang Paper Mill
#612 Zhenzhu Road, Dandong City
Liaoning Province
Tel: 44941 x232

CHINAPACK (China National Packaging Import and Export Corporation)
28 Dong Hu Xiang, An Ding Men Wai
Beijing
Tel: 421 1747, 421 2204, 421 6661 Fax: 421 2124

(Note: CHINAPACK has a number of functions; it is China's second largest importer of pulp. Its U.S. subsidiary is the UNIAM Corporation.)

MOLI (Ministry of Light Industry)
Department of Paper/Paper Industry Bureau
#2 B, Fu Waidajie
Beijing 100833
Tel: 890751, 867262

Department of International Cooperation
#22-B Fuwai Dajie
Beijing 100833
Tel: 832 9631 Fax: 601 5851

CPTA (China Packaging Technology Association)
31 East Chang An Avenue
Beijing 100005
Tel: 512 4133 Fax: 512 4128

MOF (Ministry of Forestry)
Department of Foreign Affairs
Yuan Haiying, Hepingli
Beijing

CTI/EC (China Timber Import/Export Corporation)
#82 Dong An Men Street
Beijing

CPPI/EC/CNLIPI/EC (China Pulp and Paper Import/Export Corporation
China National Light Industry Products Import/Export Corporation)
82 Dong An Men Street
Beijing 100747
Tel: 552163   Fax: 557519
(Note: This company imports and exports paper products.)

SICF (State Investment Corporation of Forestry)
Beijing
Tel: 821 1373   Fax: 821 1677

Zhongyuan International Friendship Trade Corporation
Zhongnan Road
Wuchang, Wuhan
Tel: 813 771, 812 605   Fax: 027 711832

CITTC (China International Technology Trading Company)
#41 Xisongshu Hutong, Xicheng District
Beijing
Tel: 601 4574   Fax: 6013933

TUSHU (China Timber Import and Export Corporation)
82 Dong An Men Street
Beijing
Tel: 512 4765, 512 6928   Fax: 512 4788
(Note: This organization handles most of China's wood imports from the U.S. Its
U.S. subsidiary, in Seattle, is SUNRY.)

CNLIPI/EC
(China National Light Industry Products Import/Export Corporation - Limpex)
Dalian Branch
#110 Stalin Road, Dalian
Tel: 230712   Fax: 0411 808346

PUMPS, VALVES AND COMPRESSORS

Table 116 shows salient statistics for the Pumps, Valves and Compressors Segment (3).

Table 116

Salient Statistics for the Pumps, Valves and Compressors Sector

A)	Three-letter ITA industry sector code:	PVC
B)	Est. total market size (USD millions):	
	1991 -	$1,400
	1992 -	$1,500
C)	Est. 1992-4 annual market growth rate:	5%
D)	Est. total imports (USD millions):	
	1991 -	$ 250
	1992 -	$ 280
	1993 -	$1,300
	1994 -	$1,495
	1995 -	$1,719
E)	Est. annual total import growth rate:	5%
F)	Est. imports from U.S. (USD millions):	
	1991 -	$ 80
	1992 -	$ 90
	1993 -	$260
	1994 -	$299
	1995 -	$343 (58)
G)	Est. annual growth of imports from U.S.:	5%
H)	China's receptivity to U.S. products in this sector (5 - High/1 - Low):	3
I)	Competition from local/third countries for U.S. firms (5 - Low/1 - High):	2
J)	Chinese market barriers to U.S. sales in this sector (5 - Few/1 - Many):	4

K) Comments - factors for increased U.S. sales:
- Emphasis on chemicals and energy in Eighth Five-Year Plan.
- Chinese protectionist import substitution policies are barriers.
- U.S. exports are competitive in the pump and valve market. Foreign competitors are from Sweden, Germany and Japan.
- Italy, Japan, Germany and Korea are the major compressor exporters to China. The U.S. holds virtually no share in this sector.

L)	Most Promising Sub-sectors	1992 market size
	1. Chemical Plants	$210 million
	2. Petrochemical Plants	$240 million
	3. Oil and Gas Refineries	$320 million

RAILWAY EQUIPMENT

China's investment in the railroad industry during the Seventh Five-Year Plan was higher than that for any previous Five-Year Plan, with an 80 percent increase over the Sixth Five-Year Plan (1981-85).   The country allocated ¥10 billion to manufacture and purchase locomotives, and the remainder went to repair and rebuild obsolete equipment. During the Seventh Five-Year Plan, the Ministry of Railways set a production goal of 5,000 locomotives, including over 800 electric and over 2,000 diesel locomotives. The Ministry also planned to manufacture 110,000 freight and 10,000 passenger cars. Despite these ambitious domestic production targets, China had to rely heavily on imported technology to modernize its railroad rolling stock (4).

Some useful contact in the Railway Equipment Industry include:

Beijing Erqi Locomotive Plant
Fengtai District
Beijing 10072
Tel: 818408

Dalian Locomotive and Rolling Stock Works
Shahekou District, Dalian
Liaoning Province 116022
Tel: 402043

Datong Locomotive Plant
Datong, Shanxi Province 037038
Tel: 521124

Meishan Rolling Stock Plant
Mei County, Leshan
Sichuan Province 612162
Tel: 370568

Puzhen Locomotive and Rolling Stock Plant
Pukou District, Nanjing
Jiangsu Province 210032
Tel: 852424

Qiqhar Rolling Stock Plant
Tiefeng, Qiqihar
Heilongjiang Province 161002
Tel: 52769

Qishuyan Locomotive and Rolling Stock Works
Qishuyan District, Changzhou
Jiangsu Province 213011
Tel: 771711

Shenyang Rolling Stock Plant
Huanggu District, Shenyang
Liaoning Province 110135
Tel: 462257

Sifang Locomotive and Rolling Stock Works
Sifan District, Qingdao
Shandong Province 266031
Tel: 333174-412

Tangshan Rolling Stock Plant
Tangshan, Hebei Province 063035
Tel: 241912

Tianjin Car Works
Nankai District, Tianjin 300112
Tel: 764813

Xi'an Rolling Stock Plant
Weiyang District, Xi'an
Shaanxi Province 710086
Tel: 41379

Zhouzhou Electric Locomotive Factory
East District, Zhuzhou
Hunan Province 412001
Tel: 31331

Zhouzhou Rolling Stock Plant
East District, Zhuzhou
Hunan Province 412003
Tel: 23051

RETAIL

Overview China's retail market remains underdeveloped. Currency issues, poor legal infrastructure, fierce competition in the most attractive geographic area and tortuous distribution networks ensure that the entry of foreign companies into this sector will be difficult.

Nonetheless, as China's economy has slowly opened up, the market is expanding rapidly. U.S. and other foreign companies have started to open stores and sell goods. Foreign retailers are lured by a rapidly expanding class of urban residents with middle class income and values (55).

The Chinese economic boom has been the main force behind the retail growth. The average 9 percent annual growth rate of the Chinese economy since 1979 has resulted in higher disposable income—money that can be spent on retail goods. Average per capita income for rural residents soared from RMB 134 in 1978 to RMB 630 in 1990, an increase of 370 percent. The average annual salary of an urban employee rose 250 percent in the same period, from RMB 615 to RMB 2140. These increases have been particularly large in the cities of Guangzhou, Shanghai, and Beijing.

Boosted earnings have resulted in increased purchasing power. The Beijing Statistics Bureau estimates that the average amount a Beijing resident spends on discretionary shopping totals RMB 1,300-RMB 1,500 per year (USD 232-267 per year at the official exchange rate). Yet a recent study by the McKinsey Consulting Group claims that average purchasing power in China is almost 30 percent higher than described in official figures. In addition, China's high savings rate—38 percent of GNP (US $187 billion)—indicates that the Chinese have considerable reserves of money to spend.

China has at least five urban markets with an average annual income of USD 1,000 per person—a total of about 50 to 60 million people. These statistics indicate the growing consumer power of China's densely populated urban areas. The average figures, however, hide a great disparity in actual spending, even in the urban areas. For example, one market research firm calculated average annual family income at USD 3,240 in Shenzhen compared to approximately USD 1,260 in Shanghai or Beijing.

Many families which before could only afford food, clothing, housing and other basic necessities, leaving little to spare, can now consider buying what used to be seen as luxury items: color TVs, fashionable clothes, multi-speed bicycles or a trip to the local fast food outlet. Color TV, cable TV or VCR penetration in the urban areas is very high, up to 70 percent of households in some urban areas. Washing machines are owned by the majority of Chinese urban households. Similarly, more than 50 percent of Chinese urban residences have refrigerators.

These improvements have also begun to change the spending habits of Chinese consumers. Displaying wealth in communist China has become fashionable, particularly among younger Chinese who did not experience the Mao era or cultural revolution. Consumers seek goods such as flashy suits and brand name clothing as symbols of success. This new class of consumers has displayed a strong preference for imported goods, particularly those from Japan, Europe and the United States.

Boosted earnings and demand for good have led to rapid expansion of retailing in China. In the last six years, domestic retail sales have been growing at an average annual rate of 14 percent. Figures from the State Statistics Bureau showed that retail sales totaled 1.1 trillion RMB (USD 188 billion) in 1992, an increase of 15.7 percent from the previous year. One need only walk down a major street in a populated city to witness China's retail growth: Crowded department stores display the latest fashions, video equipment, and appliances, while street vendors hawk brand name clothes at discount prices, some of which violate U.S. trademarks.

Despite publicized attempts by Zhu Rongji to slow the pace of growth, retail sales are expected to grow another 20 percent in 1993 and 1994, according to a forecast by the State Planning Commission. Another positive indicator is that the government has recently begun to loosen the money supply, which should result in increased consumer spending.

Despite China's attempts at liberalization, the Chinese government still dominates the retail sector. Though most of the nation's 8.7 million retail enterprises are privately owned, the state still runs the largest operations. At the end of 1990, China had 280,000 state-owned retail enterprises, accounting for about 40 percent of all sales, according to the China Business Review. "Collectives" accounted for 34 percent of sales. Private enterprises were responsible for 19 percent of total sales.

These state-run industries maintain considerable control over the production and distribution of goods. Every product sold by retail enterprises must be approved by State commercial bureaus and other administrative departments, which categorize all products according to industry, manufacturing process, and nature of product—an incredibly time-consuming process for retailers who wish to sell a wide array of items.

Moreover, the state-controlled system has difficulty balancing the forces of supply and demand. A Ministry of Internal Trade investigation into about 700 major commodities found the supply and demand are balanced only 54 percent of the time, while 30 percent of the goods were piling up in storehouses (China Daily, November 9, 1992). Despite increases in sales volume, many state operations have remained unprofitable. Official figures indicate that about 30 percent of state and collectively run shops are operating in the red, incurring losses of RMB 75 million (USD 13 million) in 1991. In light of China's booming economy, such losses indicate major weaknesses in the government-run retail sector.

The problems of the state-controlled retail system are obviously manifest to even casual visitors: pay is minimal, even by Chinese standards; service is notoriously slow; shop keepers are generally unhelpful; and choice is limited. The shops have made very little attempt to introduce any modern equipment, software or management.

The shortcomings of the state system have led to a burgeoning of an informal society of "kiosk" owners. Many streets in China are now lined with thousands of these privately-owned kiosks. Each kiosk must pay the city a fee for registration and rental. They are then free to sell anything that they can legally acquire at any price. Generally, these small shopkeepers are micro-scale and sell only one type of good.

Another recent manifestation of the rigid system of state retailing is the "bonding" of state stores within a city or geographic area into informal networks. Through cooperation, state-owned store managers can improve their purchasing power vis-a-vis the state wholesale network.

Competitive Situation   In heated debate last year, Chinese leaders were divided bout allowing foreign firms into the retail market. Unwilling to relinquish state dominance in the market, conservatives evoked fears of allowing foreign businesses into China. They argued that foreign investment in the retail sector would erode the system of public ownership—the foundation of the socialist economy.

Liberal reformers, on the other hand, pushed to open the retail sector, hoping to lure technology and much-needed foreign exchange to China. These leaders argued that foreign competition would pressure state-owned retailers to increase efficiency. Moreover, they expressed hopes that opening retail markets would facilitate entrance into the General Agreement on Tariffs and Trade.

The resulting "Open Door" policy, established in the fall of 1992, struck a balance between these two factions. China now allows foreign retailers in China, but has mandated many restrictions. The thrust of the present government regulatory structure is as follows:

1. A Controlled Experiment   According to the Ministry of Internal Trade, foreign retailers can only open joint venture department stores in eleven major cities and zones: Beijing, Fuzhou, Tianjin, Shanghai, Guangzhou, Qingdao, Hainan, Shenzhen, Shantou, Xiamen, and Zhuhai. The combined population of the cities—among the wealthiest in China—is about 60 million people. The number of stores is limited to two per city. Ministry of Internal Trade officials are considering expanding the number of experimental areas, yet they insist the pace of change will be gradual.

2. No Wholly Foreign-Owned Stores   If foreign investors wish to open a retail business in China, they must set up joint ventures with Chinese enterprises. Chinese leaders hope that the joint venture structure will enable Chinese retailers to gain expertise from foreign partners. Foreign companies have complained that such a system puts them at the mercy of their Chinese partners, whom they often times consider to be their future competitors. However, the regulations do not require that Chinese partners be majority shareholders.

3. Retail Only, No Wholesale   Foreign-invested stores are allowed to sell imports and domestic goods to Chinese consumers, but are not allowed to engage in the wholesale business. There are also related restrictions on trucking and other distribution practices. Chinese policy-makers fear that allowing foreign companies to sell wholesale goods would constitute too great a shock for China's trade and distribution systems.

4. Balanced Sales of Domestic and Foreign Products   China requires foreign-invested stores to generate at least 50 percent of sales volumes from Chinese-made products. For every dollar worth of foreign goods sold, stores must sell at least an equal amount of Chinese products. This requirement clearly aims to prevent excessive imports and to protect Chinese-made goods.

5. Foreign Exchange Balancing and Export Promotion Like most other foreign ventures in China, retailers must balance their own foreign exchange. However, unlike other foreign ventures, retailers do not have a choice of methods to do this. To finance their own imports, the stores must export Chinese products. This requirement is designed to promote Chinese exports, a trade-off that China is demanding for allowing foreigners into its retail markets. In order to make sure foreign investors can satisfy this requirement, Chinese officials have stressed that they will only approve foreign retailers that possess substantial overseas distribution networks.

There is a great deal of ambiguity about this policy. For example, it remains unclear whether a firm can use past exports from China to balance future imports. Chinese officials would clearly prefer export increases to cover additional imports.

6. Tariff and Non-tariff Barriers Foreign retail outlets may offer a wide range of goods, but many imported products are subject to myriad import-license controls. These include quotas on automobiles and major household electrical appliances such as air conditioners and washing machines. Tariffs are also very high on most consumer good imports. Cosmetic duties are 120 percent.

Foreign Retail Ventures Foreign influence in China's retail industry increased substantially since 1989. Statistics are impossible to obtain, because they are maintained at the local level. However, it is clear that foreign retailers can be classified in a few major groups:

Department Stores Since foreign-invested stores can import directly from overseas, they can bypass China's import and wholesale agencies. This allows them to respond to the changing needs of consumers rapidly and cost-effectively. In contrast, state-owned retailers must absorb the cost of Chinese importers who serve as middlemen, as well as government taxes on these intermediaries.

Yaohan International's Department stores represent the boldest expansion by foreign retailers into China. Yaohan's joint venture in 1992 with the Shanghai No. 1 Department Store was the first foreign retail venture approved by the Chinese government. The store is a precursor to the Shanghai Yaohan, due to open in 1995, which will reportedly become the biggest department store in China.

Yaohan also opened a Beijing store in late 1992 in a joint venture with the China Venturetech Investment Corporation (CVIC). Yaohan occupies seven stories in a building in Beijing's main business district, employing 1,150 people. Japanese bankers estimate the store's turnover at RMB 1 million a day (USD 175,000). Yaohan has announced plans to open ten department stores across China by 2010.

Yaohan has demonstrated the importance of making the right business connections. Yaohan has forged ties with two Chinese enterprises with strong political connections and commercial experience: China International Trust & Investment Corporation (CITIC), the central government's main overseas investment arm, and China Venturetech Investment Company (CVIC), which helps finance Chinese businesses.

These connections have given Yaohan several advantages. Not only was Yaohan the first retail venture approved by the Chinese government; the company also reportedly received tax concessions and a license allowing the company to import a percentage of their merchandise without having to pay full import duties. Yaohan's reputation and long-term commitment to selling in China undoubtedly facilitated these arrangements.

In addition to the Yaohan group, numerous other foreign department stores are active in the China market. They include the following: Luftansa in Beijing; Sincere from Hong Kong in Shanghai; Chia Tai from Macao; Wing On from Hong Kong in Shenyang, Guangzhou and Wuhan; Seibu from Japan in Shenzhen; Dickson Concepts from Hong Kong in Shanghai; Goldlion from Hong Kong in Guilin; Singapore's Min Dian in Shanghai. There are no known department store ventures by either American or European groups at the present time.

Though it is too early to comment significantly on the success or failure of these ventures, some preliminary observations can be made. First of all, these ventures have received considerable attention among the Chinese. Almost all large department stores were packed with curious customers on their grand openings. Sincere's Shanghai store, for example, was reportedly crowded with 90,000 customers on its January, 1992 grand opening, and now averages 35,000 customers per day.

Foreign department stores have also reported problems with their preliminary marketing strategies. Chinese customers were far more discriminating and sophisticated than anticipated. While they clearly preferred Western goods, they would not simply buy "anything Western." Rather, they looked for quality at a good price.

Boutiques   There are a small, yet rapidly growing, number of foreign boutiques in China. Most have been opened by Hong Kong retailers, such as: Giordano, Fortune Duck, Bossini, Crocodile, Theme, the French Connection and Reno. A number of European brands are extensively sold through this channel, including Pierre Cardin. Several U.S. companies have also started boutique-like businesses. These include: Nike, Concord, Playboy and American Place. (American Place is owned and operated by the former Chairman of Macy's, Mr. Edward Finkelstein.) Each of these companies run independent retail outlets in China.

Other American companies have chosen to rent counter space on a long term basis in state or foreign owned department stores. These companies usually pay rent and a percentage of sales to the store owner. They generally sell a combination of imported and domestically produced branded merchandise. Examples of this type of retail activity include Walt Disney and Maiden Form.

Still others have licensed their products to third party owners of boutique retailers. For example, clothes from American designer, Donna Karan, will reportedly go on sale at a DKNY sportswear boutique in Shenzhen in late 1993. Many European luxury good firms have chosen this route to expand sales into the China market.

Generally speaking, these boutiques source the bulk of their merchandise from Chinese factories, rather than import. The factories, most of which are located in Guangdong Province, are mostly owned by Taiwan, Hong Kong or Korean entrepreneurs. These factories are geared to export high quality goods to the Japanese, American and European export market, a certain percentage of which spills over into the domestic market.

Due to high import duties and the foreign exchange problems mentioned above, retailers are forced to limit the amount of imported merchandise. Imported products are sold in local currency only for a very high premium, between 50 and 70 percent above the domestic retail price. This premium allows boutique retailers to pay for the hard currency costs associated with imports. Nonetheless, many Chinese consumers are willing to pay this premium for the prestige of owning foreign-made merchandise.

Franchises Franchising is an infant industry in China. Fast food operations such as McDonalds, Shakeys, Baskin-Robbins, KFC, and Pizza Hut are market leaders. American fast food restaurants currently control 20-25% of the Chinese market, are reporting impressive profits, and are part of a growing industry in China. (Please see FCS Beijing's fast food ISA for more information.)

Despite the obvious potential of franchising in China, there remain many serious obstacles. Foremost is the currency. A successful franchise in China must minimize hard currency costs by minimizing imports. Chinese firms also lack hard currency to pay franchise fees and, if sales are in RMB, to make royalty payments. Second, franchisers must be very cautious about their intellectual property. China lacks a trade secrets law and trade mark protection is not assured. Third, quality control is very uncertain. Given difficulties in finding local suppliers, it is difficult to guarantee that customers receive the same array and quality of goods at different operations. Fourth, all licenses and registrations are given by local governments. This makes it very difficult for foreign franchise operators to coordinate management across geographical jurisdictions.

As a result of the above barriers, most foreign franchise operators have chosen the joint venture model over the standard franchise relationship. A joint venture requires a much higher degree of foreign personnel, capital and management commitment than the traditional franchise model.

A number of American franchise firms have chosen Shenzhen as their gateway into the China market. They have set up wholly-or partly-owned franchise outlets in Shenzhen—the city immediately across the border from Hong Kong. Shenzhen has numerous advantages over any other city in China. Due to the city's unique legislative status, foreign companies are allowed to set up wholly-owned operations in the city. Also, duties for goods entering Shenzhen city limits are lower and, therefore, it is possible to move goods in from Hong Kong. In addition, it is possible for management to live in Hong Kong and commute to the outlet in Shenzhen. Many customers in Shenzhen pay in Hong Kong currency, which is convertible to U.S. dollars. It should also be noted that Shenzhen has a number of other very desirable features for foreign retail outlets. Disposable income is high in Shenzhen, on average several times the average in China. Also, advertising in Hong Kong spills over into the Shenzhen market as well. Franchise companies that have set up outlets in Shenzhen include: Unos Pizza, McDonalds, Toys "R" Us, Seven-Eleven and others.

From a national marketing strategy, an outpost in Shenzhen enables franchise or other retail outlets the opportunity to test the market at minimal risk. Also, a successful Shenzhen operation gives the company a training center to facilitate future expansion into the interior market of China.

Catalog and Mail Order   There is presently one mail order service in China. A Hong Kong businessman, Walter Wong Chung-shum, entered a joint venture with the Guangzhou Municipal Post Office in October, 1993. The acting director of the post office serves as the Chairman of Guangzhou New Living Mail Order Service. Mr. Wong serves as chairman and general manager. Guangzhou New Living Mail Order Service is a totally new concept for retailing in China. The company hopes to take advantage of the postal service, which is one of the few institutions that reach every corner of the country. At the same time, critics fear that the postal service in China is too inefficient to provide consistent service. The future of mail order in China is uncertain.

Telemarketing   Telemarketing has been introduced in China by satellite TV. The STAR service, run out of Hong Kong, is able to reach many Chinese households through a very extensive cable TV network. Advertisers are able to use this medium to introduce products which can be ordered by fax or mail. Payment must be made by hard currency credit cards.

Hindering the growth of this market are import duties and other import restrictions which create great uncertainty. Also, it should be noted that relatively few Chinese households have telephones. Thus, this marketing tool remains in its infant stage.

Supermarkets   At present, only a very small percentage of Chinese urbanites shop in modern supermarkets. Shanghai is definitely the leading city with regard to the development of supermarkets, with approximately one dozen locally run operations.

Beijing also has several supermarkets associated with department stores or other major retail developments. For example, the Welcome Supermarket, with two locations in Beijing, is managed by Hong Kong's Welcome Chain, but owned by the Chinese government. It is targeted at the foreign community in Beijing and wealthy Chinese. Welcome Supermarket accepts payment in both RMB and FEC.

Direct Marketing   Direct marketing was introduced to China by American companies. At first, the national level authorities in Beijing forbade the use of direct marketing techniques. However, American firms were able to find provincial level governments who were able to issue necessary permits. Most of the merchandise sold by direct marketing firms is produced in China—to avoid excessive tariff and other non-tariff barriers. Companies involved in direct marketing include: Avon, Amway and McCalls.

SHIPBUILDING

From 1961 to 1987, China's maritime fleet grew faster than that of any other country in the world. During that time, the merchant fleet tonnage increased by an average 13.6 percent each year. From 1982 50 1987, Chinese shipyards produced fifty-five ships, including bulk cargo vessels, freighters, tankers, container ships, partial container ships, and passenger-cargo vessels, with a total deadweight tonnage of more than 700,000 million tons. At the end of 1985, about 17 percent of China's merchant fleet was built domestically.

Some useful contacts in the shipbuilding industry include:

Dalian New Shipyard
Xigang, Dalian
Liaoning Province 116021
Tel: 330225

Dalian Shipyard
Xigang District, Dalian
Liaoning Province 116002
Tel: 237627

Guangzhou Shipyard
Fangcun, Guangzhou
Guangdong Province 510382
Tel: 8891712

Hudong Shipyard, Shanghai
Yangpu District
Shanghai 200129
Tel: 8847222

Jiangnan Shipyard
Luwan District
Shanghai 200011

Shanghai Shipyard
Huangpu District
Shanghai 200120
Tel: 8840451

Xingang Shipyard
Tanggu District
Tianjin 300456
Tel: 973995-8

Zhonghua Shipyard
Yangpu District
Shanghai 200090
Tel: 5432600

STEEL INDUSTRY

China, the world's fourth largest steel producer, has produced 66 million tons of steel in 1990, among which, crude iron output was close to 62 million tons, rolled steel output over 51 million tons, cast iron output 16.9 million tons. In 1991, China churned out 70 million tons of steel products. The major producers are Capital (Shoudu), located in Beijing, Anshan (located in Liaoning Province), Benxi (located in Liaoning Province), Panshihua (located in Sichuan Province), Wuhan (located in Hubei Province), and Baotou (located in Gangsu Province) Iron and Steel Companies (2).

In 1992, China churned out a record 80 million tons of steel, and imported around 6 million tons of steel, by far the largest figure in recent years. The total output of domestic iron ore was 200 million tons in 1992.

Although China has made a large investment in the steel industry and the quantity of steel production has greatly increased in recent years, yet the quality of some kinds of steel needs to be greatly upgraded. At present, about 60 percent of rolled steel is behind the international standard, and some kinds of steel cannot fully meet the requirement in terms of quantity and quality.

According to the Chinese authorities, China, in the next five years, will focus on these sorts of steel: pipe steel for the oil industry; steel for power stations; steel for the automobile industry; galvanized steel and alloy steel; steel for light industry and civil use; steel for the chemical industry as well as stainless steel, bearing steel and steel used for the electronics industry.

Before 1949, the iron and steel industry was small and dispersed; the Japanese had built the only modern steel facility just after World War I at Anshan, Liaoning Province. Although Japan eventually built nine blast furnaces in Anshan, total steel output by all plants never exceeded 1 million tons annually. Much of the Japanese equipment was either damaged in the Chinese Civil War (1945-49) or removed by the Soviets at the end of World War II (4).

Since the establishment of the People's Republic, considerable investment has consistently gone to expand steel output. Steel production, however, has been very sensitive to changes in economic policies and political climate (see Figure 13). Steel output rose steadily in the 1950s, when Soviet advisers helped establish the basis of the iron and steel industry, installing numerous Soviet-designed blast and open-hearth furnaces. The Great Leap Forward saw a significant increase in the number of primitive backyard furnaces producing poor quality pig iron; numerous new, small, modern plants; overuse of large plants; and exaggerated production reports. In 1961, the industry broke down. Nearly all small plants were closed, and output fell to less than half the amount reported for 1960. From 1961 to 1965, output gradually recovered as equipment was repaired; basic oxygen furnaces were purchased from Austria and electric furnaces from Japan. Production fell in 1967 and 1968 during the Cultural Revolution, but grew rapidly in the relative political stability from 1969 through the early 1970s. In the mid-1970s, political upheaval retarded output, as did the catastrophic Tangshan earthquake of 1976. The event severely damaged the Tangshan steel plant and the Kailuan coal mines. The latter are major sources of coking coal.   After 1976, output climbed steadily, reaching 34.5 million tons in 1979.   Steel production for 1986 was 50 million tons.

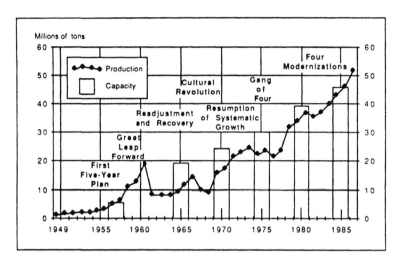

Figure 13:   Steel Production and Capacity, 1948-86 (4)

Steel was viewed as the cornerstone or "key link" of both the Great Leap Forward and the Four Modernizations programs (see Economic Policies, 1949-80, ch. 5).   But the post-Mao leadership was determined not to repeat the economically disastrous Great Leap Forward policies: in 1978 it called for a period of readjustment and as cutback in steel investment. It had set a goal, however, of producing 80 million tons of steel by 2000. Production targets were to be met by renovating and improving existing facilities, rather than building new ones. Improvements in existing plants reduced steel industry energy consumption from 73.8 million tons of coal in 1978 to 69.1 million tons in 1983, and production increased by 26 percent. The Chinese realized they would need outside assistance to fully modernize their steel industry.   They sought hardware, technology transfer, and managerial and planning assistance.

In 1987, China was the world's fifth largest producer of iron and steel, but lagged far behind developed countries in production methods and quality. Most steel capacity was in open hearth furnaces with basic oxygen furnaces, electric furnaces, and side blown converters.   Much of the iron and coking coal used in making steel was of low quality. Approximately 25 percent of the country's coal went for steel production in 1985. In 1985, capital construction, considered excessive by the Chinese, exacerbated existing shortages of rolled steel, and imports filled 25 percent of domestic demand (4).

The Ministry of Metallurgical Industry reported in 1985 that China had thirteen plants capable of producing at least 1 million tons per year. Accounting for approximately 65 percent of total production, these mills were built mostly during the 1950s. The Anshan plant was the oldest and most productive of all, producing 7 million tons per year. The next largest was in Wuhan. It was constructed in the 1950s with Soviet aid. China began construction in 1978 on its first integrated steel complex, the Baoshan iron and steel works in Shanghai, but the completion date moved from 1982 to 1985 and finally to 1988.

Besides the larger plants, about 800 smaller mills were dispersed throughout the country in 1985. They ranged from specialty mills producing 500,000 tons per year to very small operations under local jurisdiction or other ministries. Many of the smaller mills were legacies of the Great Leap Forward, when local authorities had hurriedly established their own steel making facilities. In the mid-1980s the government hoped to phase out these inefficient plants in favor of larger, more productive.

In the late 1980s, it was apparent that steel output would remain insufficient to meet the needs of the Four Modernizations. During the period covered by the Seventh Five-Year Plan, imports were expected to average 41 percent of domestic output. Thin rolled sheets, used to make such items as motor vehicles, washing machines, and refrigerators, were in extremely short supply. In 1984, China had to import about half its steel sheet and about 80 percent of its steel plate. Production of tubes and pipes also was inadequate, and approximately 50 percent of all tubes had to be imported. The country was most proficient in the production of steel bars, but it still had to import an estimated 1.8 million tons of rods and bars in 1984. In 1985, China imported a record 15 million tons of steel, more than two-thirds of it from Japan (4).

In 1992, China produced 3 million tons of cold rolled steel plates. Of this, the Baoshan Iron and Steel Works (Baogang) turned out 1.3 million tons, the Wuhan Iron and Steel Company (Wugang) produced 600,000 tons, the Anshan Iron and Steel Company (Angang) produced 700,000 tons, and the Yichang Company in Shanghai produced 120,000 tons. However, China required 3.5 million tons of cold rolled steel plates. Domestic producers mainly produce cold rolled steel plates more than 1 mm thick. China can only produce less than 200,000 tons of less than 0.5 to 0.6 mm thick cold rolled steel plates. More than 500,000 tons of this specification must be imported, mainly from Japan. Currently, the domestic market price for 0.5 to 0.6 mm cold rolled steel plates is $520 per ton, which is much higher than that of the imported price of $420 per ton and the state price of $245.

China planned to produce 381,000 tons of galvanized plate in 1992. Because of the innovation of its equipment, the output of Wugang was reduced from 188,000 tons in 1991 to 170,000 tons in 1992. Baogang and the Shanghai Metallurgical Bureau produced 200,000 tons and 11,000 tons, respectively. However, the estimated consumption of galvanized plate was 550,000 tons in 1992. The balance came from imports from Brazil, Japan, the Republic of South Korea, and European countries (48).

Wugang is the sole producer of cold rolled silicon steel sheet in China. It produced 120,000 tons in 1992. Consumption was about 240,000 tons of cold rolled silicon steel sheet in 1992. China continued to import cold rolled silicon steel plate to meet its demand.

The Ministry of Metallurgical Industry (MMI) planned to advance its iron and steel enterprises into a self-sufficiency stage to meet the demand of iron and steel by the late 1990s. First, two new factories will be under construction in Shangdong Province in the 1990s. Second, the Ministry will continue to organize and develop enterprise groups. The Ministry will support and promote the development of Angang, Baogang, Shoudou Iron and

Steel Corporation (Shougang), and Wugang enterprises into a stock sharing system held by legal persons and workers within the enterprises. Third, under the guidance of a unified state plan, the Ministry intends to coordinate with related departments and/or ministries to adopt the method of integrating the adjustment of price, merge the two price tracks, and decontrol the price and management within the enterprises. It gradually will reduce the number of iron and steel products produced under the mandatory plan and develop into a full market economy.

The iron and steel industry produced 72 Mmt of pig iron and 80 Mmt of crude steel in 1992. China plans to speed up the construction of large and medium size iron and steel projects and to continue the expansion of iron ore mining capacity to meet demand because of increased output and the variety of ferrous products. MMI is investing a large sum in iron ore mining. MMI is looking for foreign partners in the next several years to maintain a stable growth in the iron and steel industry. MMI planned to spend $1 to $1.2 billion or 20% of the total capital investment in the iron and steel industry to renovate old mines with latent production capacity and build new mines such as the Nanfen Mine in Benxi, Jian Chan in Taiyuan, Shuichang in Beijing, Bayanobo in Nei Mongol, and Qidashan in Anshan in 1995.

China's four largest steel producers have set their target of producing 10 Mmt/a of crude steel: Angang and Shougang by 1994, Baogang by 1998, and Wugang by 2000. The Ministry planned two 10-Mmt/a greenfield construction projects. One is Qilu Iron and Steel Corporation at Jining, Shangdong Province. The investment will come mainly from Shougang, while the state and Shangdong Provincial government will contribute some money. The output capacity of the complex was to be 5 Mmt/a of steel in 1997 and reach 10 Mmt/a in the year 2000. Jining is about 323 km west of Shijiusuo, which has two 100,000 ton berths. Reserves of iron ore deposits in Zhangjiawa, Hanwang, Changzhe in Shangdong Province and Huoqiu in Anhui Province are about 1.7 billion tons. Jining is a major coal production center. The second is a joint venture between China and Japan at Shijiusuo in Shangdong Province that has been on hold since its announcement in 1991.

Guangdong Provincial Planning Commission is seeking foreign cooperation to build the 10 Mmt/a Zhanjiang Steel complex at Donghai Dao in Zhanjiang Shi by 2010. The joint venture will have the Guangdong Provincial government and Baogang as partners. Foreign investment will be at least 49% of the total investment. Construction of the project will be in three phases, and the first phase construction was to get under way in 1995. Ore used by the complex will come from Australia, Brazil, India, and local mines.

In 1979, Shougang signed a contract of responsibility agreement with the state government. According to the agreement, the corporation will increase profits delivered to the Government by 7.2% annually and overall profits by 20% each year. Of the profits the corporation retained, 60% will be used in expanding production, 20% in increasing employees' wages and bonuses, and the rest for collective welfare. In 1992, the corporation used the expanding production fund to acquire domestic and overseas enterprises (42).

Shougang ranked fourth in sales volume of China's biggest industrial enterprises in 1991. In 1992, the corporation had received approval from the State Council to set up joint equity and cooperative projects, each with an investment of less than $100 million abroad and $200 million in the country. It also received approval to set up a bank with its financial system and business as the same as those of the China Trust Industrial Bank and to establish an international trade and engineering corporation. It also empowers sending personnel of the corporation abroad and inviting foreigners to work in China.

In October 1992, Shougang agreed to pay $312 million to purchase the Hierro Peru Iron Mine in Peru. Under the contract, Shougang agreed to pay $120 million in cash, invest $150 million over the next three years, and assume $42 million of Hierro Peru's debt. The corporation also has discussed the possibility of increasing the investment to $300 million, which would include building a steel plant at the port of San Nicolas. Shougang planned to increase the current mine annual output level of 2 Mmt to 10 Mmt and possibly to 15 Mmt. The mine has estimated iron reserves of 1.4 billion tons with an iron content of 51% to 57%. The corporation considered the investment in the Hierro Peru Iron Mine would be cheaper than importing the same amount of ore from Australia. In 1992, China purchased more than 300,000 tons of iron from the Hierro Peru mine.

In November 1992, Shougang purchased a U.S. steel mill owned by California Steel Company. The corporation will dismantle the plant and ship it to China for reassembly in Jining, Shangdong Province, as part of the first phase of construction of the Qilu Iron and Steel Corporation.

Shougang also invested $20 million to buy 51% of the stock of Tung Wing Steel (Holdings) Ltd. in Hong Kong. Tung Wing is a steel products dealer that is involved in trading, warehousing, and transport. The company's steel trading accounts for more than one-third of Hong Kong's total. Tung Wing would act as an arm for Shougang's import and export of steel products in and out of China.

Besides acquiring international enterprises, Shougang also added two domestic firms under its aegis. Shougang acquired No. 4 Metallurgical Construction Company in Guixi, Jiangxi Province, and No. 10 Metallurgical Construction Company in Huayin, Shaanxi Province, which were formerly under China National Nonferrous Metals Industry Corporation. Shougang will be responsible for paying debts while accepting all 16,000 employees into Shougang's staff. In December 1992, Shougang opened its own bank, Hua Xia Bank in Beijing. The bank has registered a capital of $174 million. The bank will conduct all the business as approved by the People's Bank of China and the State Administration of Exchange Control, as with other banks in China.

To improve productivity, Wugang planned to cut two-thirds of its 120,000 workers. If the targets are reached, the per capital output of iron and steel will be raised from 40 to 200 tons. This will enable the company to compete in the worldwide market. In the beginning of 1992, the company formed four subsidiary companies specializing in mining, equipment, manufacturing, and services. These companies absorbed 50,000 of the laid off workers. The service company is expanding its business into real estate, fast food machinery, and hotel management, and hopes to hire another 20,000 workers at the end of 1993.

Nippon Steel of Japan agreed to assist Wugang to build another electrical silicon sheet mill by doubling its silicon sheet production capacity from its current 100,000 mt/a level. Nippon Steel helped Wugang to build an electrical silicon sheet mill in 1979. An international bank group, including banks from Spain, France, and the United Kingdom, signed a contract for a $160 million syndicated loan to support the construction of the No. 3 steel plant for Wugang. The company will use export credit to purchase advanced equipment and technology from these countries.

Baogang and the Shanghai Iron and Steel Company, a steel products enterprise, merged in 1992. Boagang now has the capacity to produce 11.71 Mmt of steel. Coupled with the completion of a third phase construction project in 1998, steel output by Baogang will reach 15 Mmt/a. The major reason for the merger was to unify overall planning in the development of the steel industry in Shanghai. Baogang will be responsible for the overall planning and production by Shanghai Iron and Steel Company.

Kaiser Engineers completed a pre-feasibility study on a gas-based direct reduced iron plant in Western Australia's Pilbara region for a Sino-Australia joint venture project. The project intends to produce 2 Mmt/a of direct reduced iron; 50% of the output will be shipped to China. The project was estimated to cost about $1.1 billion.

Some useful contacts in the iron and steel industry include:

Anshan Iron & Steel Corporation
Tiexi, Anshan
Liaoning Province 114021
Tel: 723090

Bengxi Beitai General Iron & Steel Plant
Beitaizhen, Pingshan District
Benx Liaoning Province 117017
Tel: 231246

Bengxi Iron & Steel Corporation
Renminlu, Pingshan District
Benxi, Liaoning Province 117000
Tel: 243191

Changchen Special Steel Corporation
Jiangyou, Sichuan Province 621701
Tel: 22133

Changzhi Iron & Steel Company
Changzhi, Shanxi Province 046031
Tel: 22900

Chengde Iron & Steel Works
Shuangluan District, Chengdi
Hebei Province 067002
Tel: 444901

Chengdo Iron & Steel Works
Qingbaijiang District, Chengdu
Sichuan Province 610303
Tel: 903051

Chengdu Seamless Steel Tube Mill
Dongfeng Nanlu, Jinjiang District
Chengdu, Sichuan 610069
Tel: 443412

Chongqing Iron & Steel Corporation
Daduhe, Chongqing
Sichuan Province 630081
Tel: 624778

Chongqing Special Steel Plant
Shapingba, Chongqing
Sichuan Province 630032
Tel: 661961-2142

Dalian Steel Works
Gandingzi, Dalian
Liaoning Province 116031
Tel: 662112

Daxian Prefecture Steel & Iron Complex
Daxian, Sichuan Province 635002
Tel: 23366

Daye Steel Plant
Shihuiyao, Huangshi
Hubei Province 435001
Tel: 292043

Echeng Iron & Steel Works
Ezhou, Hubei Province 436002
Tel: 22821

Emei Ferroalloy Plant
Jiulizhen, Emeishan
Sichuan Province 614222
Tel: 2488

Fushun Iron & Steel Company
Wanghua District, Fushun
Liaoning Province 113001
Tel: 689605

Fushun Steel Plant
Wanghua, Fushun
Liaoning Province 113001
Tel: 686258

Guangzhou Iron & Steel Company, Ltd.
Fanglun District, Guangzhou
Guangdong Province 510730
Tel: 2212738

Guiyang Steel Works
Nanming District, Guiyang
Guizhou Province 550005
Tel: 5255223

Hainan Iron Mine
Qiongzhung Autonomous County
Hainan Province 572700
Tel: 22522

Hanoan Iron & Steel Works
Fuxing, Handan
Hebei Province 056015
Tel: 442267

Hangzhou Iron & Steel Works
Gongshu, Hangzhouo
Zhejiang Province 310022
Tel: 544301-3948

Harbin Steel Rolling Mill
Xianfang, Harbin
Heilongjiang Province 150030
Tel: 52446

Hefei Iron & Steel Company
Dongshi, Hefei
Anhui Province 230011
Tel: 482889

Heilongjiang Xilin Iron & Steel Complex
Xilin, Yichun
Heilongjiang Province 153025
Tel: 357

Henan Anyang Iron & Steel Company
Tiexi, Anyang
Henan Province 4554004
Tel: 331951

Hohhot Iron & Steel Works
Huimin District, Hohhot
Inner Mongolia 010050
Tel: 34961

Hunan Lianyuan Iron & Steel Works
Loudi, Hunan Province 417009
Tel: 313521

Jiangxi Xinyu Iron & Steel Works
Xinyu, Jiangxi Province 336501
Tel: 222701

Jiangyin Steel Works
68 Renmin Donglu, Jiangyin
Jiangsu Province 214400
Tel: 882239

Jilin Ferroalloy Plant
Changyi, Jinlin
Jilin Province 132002
Tel: 478326

Jinan Iron & Steel Works
7 Gongye Beilu, Jinan
Shandong Province 250101
Tel: 42896

Jinzhou Ferroalloy Factory
Taihe, Jinzhou
Liaoning Province 121005
Tel: 579261

Jiuquan Iron & Steel Company
Jiayuguan, Gansu Province 735100
Tel: 3294

Kunming Iron & Steel Company
Anning, Kunming
Yunnan Province 650302
Tel: 99530

Laiwu General Iron & Steel Works
Chengzipuzhen, Laiwu
Shandong Province 271104

Lanzhou Steel Works
Chengguan, Lanzhou
Gansu Province 730020
Tel: 498811

Liaoyang Ferroalloy Plant
Baita District, Liaoyang
Liaoning Province 111000
Tel: 33585

Linfen Iron & Steel Company
Linfen, Shanxi Province 041000
Tel: 6980

Lingyuan Iron & Steel Company
Lingyuan, Chaoyang
Liaoning Province 122500
Tel: 23212

Liuzhou Iron & Steel Works
Liuzhou, Guangxi Province 545002
Tel: 227322

Luoyang Steel Works
Luoyang, Henan Province 471023
Tel: 338601

Ma'anshan Iron & Steel Corporation
Yushan, Ma'anshan
Anhui Province 843003
Tel: 83449

Nanchang Iron & Steel Works
Nanchang, Jiangxi Province 330012
Tel: 331122

Nanjing Iron & Steel Works
Dachan, Nanjing
Jiangsu Province 210035
Tel: 791615

Nanjing No. 2 Iron & Steel Works
Yuhuatai District, Nanjing
Jiangsu Province 210041
Tel: 629146

Nanjing Steel Rolling Works
Jianye District, Nanjing
Jiangsu Province 210017
Tel: 628101-234

Panzhiuhua Iron & Steel Corporation
East District, Panzhihua
Sichuan Province 617167
Tel: 4261

Pingxiang Iron & Steel Works
Xiangdong, Pinxiang
Jiangxi Province 337019
Tel: 441423

Qindao General Iron & Steel Works
Cangkou, Qingdao
Shandong Province 266043
Tel: 446761

Qiqihar Steel Works
Eulan Ergi, Qiqihar
Heilongjiang Province 161041
Tel: 84951

Sanming Iron & Steel Works
Sanming Fujian Province 365000
Tel: 222075

Shaanxi Steel Plant
Xincheng, Xi'an
Shaanxi Province 710043
Tel: 335176

Shanghai Baoshan Iron & Steel Complex
Baoshan District, Shanghai 201900
Tel: 6648648

Shanghai Ferroalloy Plant
101 Changjiang Xilu
Shanghai 200431
Tel: 6672281

Shanghai No. 1 Iron & Steel Works
735 Changjianglu, Wusong District
Shanghai 200431
Tel: 3244100

Shanghai No. 10 Iron & Steel Works
Changning District, Shanghai 200052
Tel: 2596409

Shanghai No. 2 Iron & Steel Works
Yangpu District, Shanghai 200090
Tel: 5433911

Shanghai No. 3 Iron & Steel Works
Nanshi District, Shanghai 200126
Tel: 883980

Shanghai No. 5 Iron & Steel Works
332 Tongjilu, Shanghai 200940
Tel: 3209060

Shanghai No. 8 Iron & Steel Works
Putuo District, Shanghai 200060
Tel: 2564460

Shanghai Silicon Steel Plant
Yangpu District, Shanghai 200090
Tel: 5432590

Shanghai Xinhu Iron & Steel Works
Yangpu District, Shanghai 200082
Tel: 5416860

Shaanxi Taiyuan Iron & Steel Corporation
Beicheng, Taiyuan
Shaanxi Province 030003
Tel: 344984

Shaoguan Iron & Steel Works
Qusiang, Shaoguan
Guangdong Province 512123
Tel: 880134

Shaoxing Iron & Steel Works
Yuecheng District, Shaoxing
Zhejiang Province 312000
Tel: 532901

Shenyang General Iron & Steel Works
Sujiatun, Shenyang
Liaoning Province 110112
Tel: 984637

Shenyang Steel Rolling Mill
Tiexi District, Shenyang
Liaoning Province 110021
Tel: 551461

Shijiazhuang Iron & Steel Works
Chang'an District, Shijiazhuang
Hebei Province 050031
Tel: 554921

Shoudu Iron & Steel Corporation
Shijingshan District, Beijing 100041
Tel: 873586

Shuicheng Iron & Steel Company
Zhongshan, Liuanshui
Guizhou Province 553028
Tel: 29769

Suzhou Iron & Steel Works
Suzhou, Jiangsu Province 215151
Tel: 931447

Tangshan Iron & Steel Corporation
Lubei, Tangshan
Hebei Province 063016
Tel: 223991

Tianjin Iron Works
Shexian, Handan
Hebei Province 056404
Tel: 3397

Tianjin No. 1 Steel Rolling Mill
Hexi District,, Tiajin 300220
Tel: 282160

Tianjin No. 2 Rolling Mill
Beijao, Tianjin 300400
Tel: 592156

Tianjin No. 3 Steel Rolling Mill
Hebei District, Tianjin 300241
Tel: 661652

Tianjin No. 4 Steel Rolling Mill
Hedong District, Tianjin 300170
Tel: 414408

Tianjin No. 5 Rolling Mill
Hedong District, Tianjin 300182
Tel: 413160

Tianjin Special Steel Plant
Hexi District, Tianjin 300200
Tel: 282843

Tianjin Steel Plant
Hedong District, Tianjin 300180
Tel: 412709

Tianjin Steel Plate Mill
Hedong District, Tianjin 300180
Tel: 413206

Tonghua Iron & Steel Company
Erdaojiang, Tonghua
Jilin Province

Weiyuan Iron & Steel Plant
Weiyuan County, Neijiang
Sichuan Province 642469
Tel: 22187

Wuhan Iron & Steel Corporation
Qingshan, Wuhan
Hubei Province 430083
Tel: 663718

Wuxi Steel Plant
Nanchang District, Wuxi
Jiangsu Province 214026
Tel: 554112

Wuyang Iron & Steel Company
Wuyang District, Pingdingshan
Henan Province 462500
Tel: 822212-139

Xialu Iron & Steel Works
Xialu District, Huangshi
Hubei Province 435004
Tel: 222991

Xiangtan Iron & Steel Company
Xiangtan, Hunan Province 411101
Tel: 22255-2123

Xingtai Iron & Steel Works
Qiaoxi, Yingtai
Hebei Province 054027
Tel: 223927

Xining Steel Works
Chengbei District, Xining
Qinghai Province 810005
Tel: 54901

Xinjiang Bayi Iron & Steel Works
Toutunhi District, Urumqi
Xinjiang Province 830022
Tel: 371420

Xixing Iron & Steel Complex
Wuxi, Jiangsu Province 214151
Tel: 669861

Xuzhou Iron & Steel Works
Xuzhou, Jiangsu Province 221004
Tel: 37980

Yichang Bayi Steel Plant
Yichang, Hubei Province 443001
Tel: 551176

Yingrou Steel Plate Plant
Laobian District, Yingrou
Liaoning Province 115005
Tel: 45295

Zhangdian Iron & Steel Works
Zhangdian District, Zibo
Shandong Province 255007
Tel: 224123

Zhangjiagang Shalhou Iron & Steel Corporation
Shazhou County, Suzhou
Jiangsu Province 215625
Tel: 222801

Zhangjiakouo Xuanhua Iron & Steel Corporation
Xuanhua, Zhangjiakou
Hebei Province 075103
Tel: 312178

Zhuzhou Hard Alloy Plant
East District, Zhuzhou
Hunan Province 412000
Tel: 23851

Zhuzhou Steel Plant
North District, Zhuzhou
Hunan Province 412005
Tel: 32431

Zigong Hard Alloy Factory
Machongkou, Da'an District
Zigong, Sichuan Province 643011
Tel: 223821

Zunyi Ferroalloy Plant
Zunyi, Guizhou Province 563004
Tel: 3411

TELECOMMUNICATIONS EQUIPMENT

Table 117 summarizes some salient statistics for the telecommunications equipment sector (3).

In the telecommunications equipment sector, front runners in foreign sales to China are France's Alcatel Alsthom, which has about half of China's market for digital telephone switches, Sweden's Ericsson and America's Motorola, which together dominate the market for mobile telephones.

In the winter of 1992-93, AT&T signed a memo of understanding to cooperate with China in eleven areas of telecommunications and network computing. "This is a start," says William Warwick, chairman and CEO of AT&T's China Business Unit. "The opportunity for us is tremendous. It will grow as the Chinese market grows—dramatically." As one indication, Mr. Warwick explains that China currently has only 1.6 telephone lines per 100 people. By the year 2000 the Chinese plan to raise that to 10 lines per 100 and by 2020 to 42 lines per 100—the ratio in Japan today. (In contrast, the U.S. has 52 lines per 100.)

Table 117

Salient Statistics for the Telecommunications Equipment Sector

A)	Three-letter ITA industry sector code:	TEL
B)	Est. total market size (USD millions):	
	1991 -	$1,500
	1992 -	$1,800
	1993 -	$4,500
	1994 -	$5,900
	1995 -	$7,500 (58)
C)	Est. 1992-4 annual market growth rate:	20%
D)	Est. total imports (USD millions):	
	1991 -	$ 500
	1992 -	$ 600
	1993 -	$3,150
	1994 -	$4,200
	1995 -	$5,250
E)	Est. annual total import growth rate:	10%-20%
F)	Est. imports from U.S. (USD millions):	
	1991 -	$ 80
	1992 -	$ 80
	1993 -	$560
	1994 -	$700
	1995 -	$875 (58)
G)	Est. annual growth of imports from U.S.:	5%
H)	China's receptivity to U.S. products in this sector (5 - High/1 - Low):	4
I)	Competition from local/third countries for U.S. firms (5 - Low/1 - High):	3

J) Chinese market barriers to U.S. sales
    in this sector (5 - Few/1 - Many):   4
K) Comments - factors for increased U.S. sales:
    - A priority development sector.
    - USG has worked with industry to overcome impediments to sales of central office switching equipment.
    - Competing governments offer concessionary loans.
    - Growth in private (company/ministry) systems.

L) <u>Most Promising Sub-sectors</u>   <u>1992 market size</u>
    1. PBX, Digital switches $300 million
    2. Facsimile machines $ 50 million
    3. Cellular equipment $ 30 million
    4. Satellite Earth Stations $ 40 million
    Also listed without specifying an estimated dollar value are (58):
        Paging Networks with 10 million subscribers
        Network computer equipment
        CATV equipment

Overview Recent Chinese news releases boast that 95% of china's cities and villages are linked by telephone and that 261 cities have established automatic or semi-automatic dialing services. Without a good perspective on China's telecommunication network, this new might lead one to believe that China is quickly approaching western standards in communication service. A true perspective, though, would show that although improvements are not insignificant, China will still lag far behind developed countries, even some Asian developing countries, well into the 21st century (43).

Despite confusion over the precise meaning of the new policies of "socialist planned commodity economy," and even some media intimations of China's experiments with capitalism, China is still basically a politically planned economy. It is also determined to protect its infant industries from foreign competition. Foreign investment and technology transfer are the goal, even if it slows down development for some period of time. Imports will be possible only as long as domestic production is of insufficient quality or quantity to meet China's needs. Nevertheless, analysis of the 13th National Party Congress and other current trends indicates a relatively stable period of overall economic growth for China.

The Seventh Five-Year Plan (covering the years 1986 to 1990) calls for investing $5.4 billion in communications. However, authorities have announced that beginning with 1988 the state's share of the investment in the development of communications will drop from 35% to 19.4%, requiring more funds to come from local sources.

Leading the way in China's imports are three primary technologies for which China has not been able to transfer sufficient technology: digital switching, cellular mobile radio, and digital microwave. Five areas which will fact import restrictions are:

1. Digital transmission systems including optical fiber and microwave equipment (below 140 MBPS).

2. Office automation equipment including telex, telegraph, facsimile (FAX), photocopiers, and laser printers.
3. Analog communications equipment including frequency domain modulation (FDM) carrier systems under 4380 channels, microwave carrier systems under 1800 channels and crossbar switches under 10,000 lines.
4. Small capacity mobile radio systems.
5. Satellite ground receivers. This restriction, though, does not necessarily mean absolutely no imports, but may only mean quotas on the amount imported or additional tariffs.

This sector is of high priority and is heavily invested by the government. It is infected by politics because of the high value of equipment sales and because of the ministerial level competition with the Ministry of Posts and Telecommunications for industry control. There is a significant use of loans from sources such as Japan's OECF, the IMF, the ADB, and the World Bank (58).

Technology transfer is increasingly being required for the completion of sales contracts. Joint ventures are becoming more common in this sector.

Market Assessment Imports of telephone switching equipment should continue to grow over the next five years with an average growth rate of about 20%   A meeting in January 1988, announced that 700,00 lines of digital switching would be imported in 1988. Imports of second hand crossbar switching equipment will find greater acceptance now and actually appear to have become part of the national plan. The number of installed lines of private branch exchange (PBX) equipment is growing faster than that of central office (CO) switches, but imports of small PBXs may receive strong competition from domestic manufacturers in one or two years because of recent technology transfers.

The market for telephone, telegraph, telex, and FAX equipment should begin to decline in a few years as indigenous products begin to capture the market. There may be some growth in imports in 1988 due to imports of knockdown kits for telex and FAX equipment. Because of excess manufacturing capacity of telephone sets in China, imports in this area will be limited to sales associated with private automatic branch exchanges (PABX).

The market for fiber optic transmission products should continue to grow beyond 1988 due to China's inability to import the technology to manufacture 140 megabits per second (MBPS) optical fiber terminal equipment. However, excess domestic production capacity for optical fibers should lead to a decrease in imports. By 1993, China is expected to use primarily domestic products for fiber optic systems.

China has imported several cable manufacturing lines which will become operational over the next two years, making sales in this area very limited.

Pulse code modulation (PCM) products use European standards, so U.S. products must be adapted to meet this standard and to work in an environment which still includes paper insulated cables and electro-mechanical switches. Straight sales without a cooperative venture will be limited. China will continue to use FDM products until 1995, but imports in this area are unlikely.

Similar to the market for fiber optic transmission products, the market for microwave products is expected to continue slow growth beyond 1988 due to China's inability to import the technology for manufacturing 140 MBPS digital microwave systems. Other wireless communication products should begin a faster growth curve. Users of mobile radio products are expected to press for relaxation of import restriction in one to two years, possibly leading to large contracts at that time.

The market for broadcast transmission equipment should remain open because China desires to develop stereo AM radio and because imports of large transmitters are still needed. The market for transmission equipment of less than 1000 watts will probably be restricted to technology transfers.

Broadcast studio products, other than television cameras, should continue to see growth. TV cameras, which constitute 70% of this market, are presently imported mainly as knockdown kits from Japan. There will be a strong move to make production more indigenous.

China's data network is in its infancy. The market will grow, but since it is new and there are no patterns upon which to base projections, the amount and rate of this growth is difficult to predict.

The future for the telecommunications market in China is best summed up by the words of one of the interviewees who was surveyed for this report: "If handled correctly, China's telecommunication market is very large, but when handled incorrectly, it becomes a very small market."

The service is not great, but improving. Novelist Bette Bao Lord, wife of former American Ambassador to China, Winston Lord, illustrated the lack of telephones with a story about being called after midnight by Chinese acquaintances, but being tolerant of these jarring intrusions because it was the only time her callers could get a line. Since that 1987 anecdote, things have improved due to the growth described above: successful connections between cities on the first try run at about 20 percent, and within the best urban systems about 80 percent. The quality of today's conversations over the old wiring is still not up to western standard. However, China has come a long way from the late 1970s. In 1978, the only way for visiting Defense Secretary Harold Brown to call Washington fast was to use a secret phone center in the basement of the Great Hall of the People (Butterfield, p. 388).

Domestic Direct Dialing (DDD), at the end of 1992 was available in 1,745 cities. Ghat number is up from 1,116 cities in 1991. International Direct Dialing (IDD) is up from 573 to 698 cities in 1991 and 1992, respectively. One-hundred and ninety-six countries can be accessed on these systems.

Special calling services such as call waiting, conference calls, speed dialing, and callback dialing have been offered, but such services have not seen heavy demand. Consumers are more anxious to acquire a phone; the bells and whistles are of little concern (51).

Telecommunications Switching Equipment Imports of telephone switching equipment should continue to grow over the next five years even if China signs additional joint ventures in the near future. Manufacturing start up for a joint venture in switching equipment would take three to four years, thus not affecting much of the projected period. The largest potential negative influence on imports would be a decision by the government to halt imports. This is not considered likely because of the continued move toward decentralization. Imports of small size PABX equipment will effected by domestic manufacturers in the next one to two years. Import projections are based on an average growth rate of 20% per year. Over the last two to three years, the current growth rate has been much higher than 20%, perhaps 40-60%, but that is believed to be due to the opening of a new market. Growth should begin to slow down with increased difficulty in obtaining foreign currency. China's industrial development should allow for a 20% growth rate.

New imported digital switching equipment tariffs have been announced which appear to provide continued support for Shanghai Bell Telephone Manufacturing (SHBTM) and perhaps the PABX manufacturers. The new tariffs effect switches with less than a 5,000 line switching capacity. As of 1987, only eight cities had installed exchanges larger than 10,000 lines, however thirty-nine others were either waiting for approval or waiting to negotiate contracts. The metropolitan areas will probably exclusively import new digital exchanges, while the plans for the rural areas call for crossbar exchanges.

The PABX market should continue to grow. Numbers for the size of this market are difficult to obtain since most countries do not break out this category in their export statistics. China does not have good statistics on the market. It is possible, though, to estimate market size by comparing this market to the public switching market. The number of installed lines of PABX equipment is growing faster than that of central office equipment. The estimated market for PABX imports is in the hundreds of thousands of lines per year.

Telex and Facsimile Products The MPT and Ministry of Electronic Industry (MEI) are very interested in gaining control over this market because of the size of the market and the lower technology of the products. In a pattern, similar to what was done with consumer TV and radio sets, the Chinese have imported several production lines for these products. They are currently assembling from imported knockdown kits. In the future, they will use indigenous sources for more and more of the components until virtually all are sourced from within China. The projected growth in 1988 is due to the continued import of knockdown kits. By 1993, all but the more sophisticated components, are expected to be sourced from within China. At that time, the market is expected to be comprised of telex switching equipment, "high end" consumer products (for which China has not obtained manufacturing technology) and telephones associated with imported PABXs.

Import Statistics, Estimates and Projections for Telephones,
Telex, Telegraph and Facsimile
(in millions of dollars)

1986	1987	1988	1993
$150	$190	$230	$125

Wire and Fiber Optic Transmission Products The wire and fiber optic transmission market is expected to continue growing on beyond 1988 due to China's inability to import the technology to manufacture 140 MBPS optical fiber terminal equipment. Imports of fiber optic cable are expected to be restricted beginning in 1988, because China has imported manufacturing lines that can manufacture three to five times China's anticipated needs. There is not an equivalent over-abundance of fiber optic terminal products though. China's PCM product manufacturers are not yet manufacturing in quantity and are not expected to for another one or two years. By 1993, after domestic manufacturing has reached full capacity, China is expected to use domestic products wherever possible and imports will begin to decline. China has imported several wire cable manufacturing lines that will become operational over the next two years, making sales in this area very limited.

Import Statistics, Estimates and Projections
for Wire Transmission Products
(in millions of dollars)

1986	1987	1988	1993
$24	$40	$45	$20

Wireless Transmission Products Similar to fiber optic transmission products, the microwave market is expected to continue slow growth beyond 1988. This is due to China's inability to import the technology to manufacture 140 MBPS microwave equipment. China had signed a contract with NEC to manufacture digital microwave products and had expected to be able to meet its growing needs through this technology transfer. But, the Coordinating Committee on Exports to Communist Countries (COCOM) apparently has restricted the transfer of technology, so China will continue to import these products. Other wireless communication products are expected to begin a faster growth curve.

Mobile radio is expected to grow to 300,000 lines by 1990, but China's domestic manufacturers cannot manufacture sufficient quantities. The Chinese have technology transfers in small mobile radio systems including radio telephones. But some transfers are still awaiting COCOM approval. Others are assembly kits that may not lead to indigenous manufacturing in the future. China imposed import restrictions based on a belief that it could domestically manufacture the products. There is a wide gap between the market size and the manufacturing capacity, so the restrictions may change in the future. China will undoubtedly sign more technology transfers within the projected five year period, but imports are not expected to be greatly affected because of the need for imported parts for those technology transfers.

The Chinese made a large commitment to satellite/earth stations in the last few years. The Chinese feel capable of making their own analog C-band reception equipment, but do not express that same confidence in making transmitters nor digital satellite communications equipment. In 1995, China expects to add K-band. Currently, they are working to develop their own equipment. Straight purchases in K-band equipment would probably be in small quantities (perhaps as samples). China expects to wait to build this network until it has developed its own products or has imported the technology.

The Chinese like stereo AM radio and are working on developing stereo consumer receivers. They have selected C-QUAM and will soon begin setting up a network of transmitting stations. Large transmitters will probably continue to see sales, but China has technology transfers in several types of lower power transmission equipment (1000 watt and under) and hence this market should not be large other than for technology transfers.

Import Statistics, Estimates and Projections
For Wireless Transmission
(in millions of dollars)

1986	1987	1988	1993
$68	$67	$75	$90

Broadcast Studio Products TV cameras make up more than 70% of imports for the studio products category. They primarily come from Japan or Hong Kong (re-exports). Currently, most are assembled in China using knockdown kits. It is expected that because of the volume of imported TV cameras, China will also work hard to increase indigenous sourcing of components. The market for cameras is also expected to diminish as a result of market saturation. Most other products in this category should continue to see growth though, as China has not actively pursued importing the manufacturing technology for these products (amplifiers, mixer/control boards, loudspeakers and microphones).

Import Statistics, Estimates and Projections
For Broadcast Studio Products
(in million of dollars)

1986	1987	1988	1993
$21	$27	$30	$15

Data Communication Products There is a very strong drive at this time to develop data services to strengthen China's modernization drive. The current market is probably less than $5 million. By 1990, China is expected to be importing data multiplexing equipment and most other types of communication products. Perhaps by 1993, the market will be up to $10-20 million.

Communications Test Instruments The primary buyers of communications testing equipment in China are believed to be manufacturing research and development departments and academic institutes. It is not common for the telephone operating companies to buy test equipment to service the newly imported equipment. The Chinese have an attitude that the foreign company that supplies the communication equipment should guarantee the equipment for life. Since even technicians in operating companies in the U.S. have trouble understanding the sophisticated test equipment, it will probably be some time before Chinese operating companies are ready to use sophisticated test equipment.

Siemens (FRG) has a contract arrangement for knockdown kit assembly of microprocessor controlled PCM test equipment. Even with domestic assembly of these instruments, it is unlikely that sales will be substantial, perhaps only two to seven units per year.

Communications Service Industry It is not easy to obtain service industry contracts in China because the Chinese do not place a high value on information. The system in the past has been that what one location in China knows is free information to the entire country. China uses a significant portion of its technical talent to study the progress of technology in other countries. On-the-job training to upgrade workers' skills is not a high priority. The general attitude in China is that information and training should be free or cost very little. They find it difficult to pay for intangible goods.

Therefore, the service companies that are doing business in China find business difficult. They get most of their proceeds from "package deals" (e.g. some of Japan's loans required that NTT do a certain amount of consulting), or through indirect revenues (e.g. cable and wireless does consulting to improve communications between Hong Kong and China to increase the international calling), or through creative revenue generation (e.g. the Germans are giving satellite equipment to the Broadcast Ministry in exchange for the proceeds from selling TV advertisement time). If you can figure out a way to make money for your Chinese partner to pay you, then you might find business in the service industry. China's telecommunications network planning, installation, and maintenance are in great need of help, but when the help does not include hardware, they find it hard to pay.

Competitive Situation Japan is China's leading trading partner in telecommunications, with almost 25% of the import market. The United States appears to be second, although re-exports through Hong Kong account for about 20% of the market.

There are fifty-four wholly-owned Chinese manufacturers of central office switches. The largest producer, Zhu Hai Company, produced 125,000 lines in 1991. Combined there was a total of 9.5 mil. central office and PBX switches produced in 1991. All other domestic production is performed by five active joint ventures (51).

Switches with large capacity (10,000-20,000 lines or more) are generally desired by the large cities, but other smaller switches are often sought by local areas. It is difficult under current plans for the present domestic base to produce the 15 million lines needed per year. We have been unable to assess the exclusive manufacturing capacity of central office switches with any real consistency, but believe that there is a large gap between what is needed and what can be produced. Also, while China can produce switches domestically, parts imports will be necessary for the foreseeable future.

The most recent joint ventures have been with two North American Companies. In June of this year, Canada's Northern Telecom Ltd. signed an agreement with China's State Planning Commission to manufacture and sell central office switches as well as beginning a research center in Beijing. Earlier in February, SPC signed a similar agreement with American Telephone and Telegraph.

The joint ventures created before 1993 are between MPT and Alcatel in Shanghai (the largest and most successful), MEI and NEC in Tianjin, and MEI and Siemens in Beijing.

In 1992, the U.S. market share rested at about eight percent including Northern Telecom's Raleigh, North Carolina plant, which represents five or more percent of the total. These figures should rise markedly with this year's joint venture between AT&T and SPC. Also with speculation that Northern Telecom will be moving its headquarters to North Carolina, the U.S. market share will rise dramatically.

China's seemingly bottomless pit of a market makes planners who must approve switch purchases and JV's confident that they can demand technology transfer and good prices. U.S. firms have been slow to give in to these demands. Instead, European and Japanese firms have filled the top five positions in this sector. Two factors seem to lead the list of requirements for success here: 1) aggressive marketing and moves to position themselves here early with a big JV, and; 2) favorable technology transfer and pricing, seem to have worked well in establishing them as the dominant supplier. Behind Alcatel is NEC of Japan, Ericsson of Sweden, Fujitsu of Japan, and Siemens of Germany.

Market Access and Sales Prospects The three largest user groups for foreign products are the MPT, the MOR and the MRTV and their member provincial bureaus. The MPT, as head over the telecommunications industry in China, plans and administers interprovincial and international trunking systems, sets interconnection standards, oversees the MPT manufacturing industry and trains technicians and scientists for its industry. The MPT is responsible for all national aspects of public telecommunications and operations in China. Management of the long distance trunk routes, packet switching and international direct calling fall under the MPT. The MPT has not part in any of the independent networks such as the networks under the ministries of coal, petroleum, railroad, water and power, and the military.

Intra-provincial telecommunications networks are primarily administered by the provincial bureaus. The bureaus report more directly to their provincial or municipal governments than they do to the MPT (three municipalities and twenty-three provinces not including Taiwan and Hong Kong). Exceptions to this are projects funded either by the State or by the MPT.

The MOR has the second largest nationwide telecommunications network. Because the MOR's manufacturing and network is independent of the MPT's, the MOR does not seem to maintain a "buy Chinese products" attitude, but it does expect to continue developing and utilizing crossbar switching equipment, which represents a large share or MOR's manufacturing. The size of the MOR's manufacturing and installed network are much smaller than that of the MPT. The MOR's Seventh Five-Year Plan emphasizes the development of a digital network. This plan includes three major transmission projects:

1. Fiber optic systems from Datong to Qinghuangdao and from Beijing to Wuhan.
2. Digital microwave from Guangzhou to Hengyang and from Shanghai to Hangzhou.
3. Planning and testing of satellite communications for future development.

And three major business network projects:
1. Utilize foreign loans to improve and develop long distance switching offices in Beijing, Hangzhou, Guangzhou, and other locations.
2. Expand the existing network of facsimile machines from the current 300 machines to 2000.
3. Develop a public data network.

This plan is to include the following:
- $95 million for communications cable (4500 kmm of which 4000 km already contracted.
- $14 million for the long distance switching network (eight tandem exchanges along with transmission equipment).
- $14 million for the local telephone exchanges (160,000 lines).
- $108 million for the renovation and construction of wireless dispatch communications (11,000 km of renovation and 8,000 km of new construction).
- $3 million for improving telephone dispatch (10,000 lines/500 telephone exchanges).

The Ministry or Radio and TV was not formed as an independent ministry until 1982, when the importance of broadcasting became more apparent. There is a four level structure that exists within the broadcast hierarchy: national broadcast center level, the provincial level (including municipalities), county level and village level. Under this system, funding may come from any one of these levels. Most larger provincial broadcast bureaus have import/export offices for importing equipment. However, selection of purchases is generally made at the provincial level by planning organizations instead of by the import/export offices. When counties incorporate large cities, it is also possible that the large cities may directly fund purchases of imported equipment, but these purchases are still normally routed through the provincial import/export offices.

The MEI is an indirect user of foreign products, in that it imports large orders for other ministries. Orders are often organized through the MEI so that the MEI can help support the products' maintenance and service needs. Following this route gives China a more unified approach toward imports and facilities negotiating for the transferring of technology for the future. In addition, the MEI researches new fields and acts as a consulting organization for the other ministries.

Best Sales Prospects

Central Office Switches

With increases of 24% expected for the next two years, this is a leader in the telecommunications sector.

Private Branch Exchanges (PBX)

Private branch exchanges are smaller capacity switches used by such organizations as hotels, large businesses, and hospitals. These switches normally have the capacity of around

1000 lines. PBX's are produced by most of the large central office switch manufacturers. There are twenty-four domestic PBX manufacturers in China.

Paging Devices

The number of paging device subscribers reached 2.22 million. This was up from 1.04 million subscribers in 1991. This incredible growth is partially due to the fact that a pager is a convenient option for those who do not have telephones. As phone sets become more readily available and more affordable, the demand rate may steady out.

The Ministry of Industrial Standardization and Research, and Beijing Hualian Electric Company, will open domestic production of wide frequency radio paging transmitters (138-174 MHZ) in late 1993. Up to that time all transmitters have been imported (primarily from Motorola in the U.S.) at a cost of US $12,000-14,000. These transmitters will have a power output of 500 watts and a radius of 30 km; the same as Motorola pagers.

Production is estimated at 100 to 200 transmitters a year.

Cellular Telephones

Cellular telephones are popular. At the end of 1992, there were 177,000 cellular subscribers. That number represents a 376% increase over the 47,000 subscribers in 1991. This sector's major supplier of cellular network equipment is Ericsson.

The phenomenal expansion of this sector has created some problems however. The largest of which is the inconsistency in frequencies used throughout China. This variation makes the basic "Roaming" service provided to western cellular subscribers impossible.

Useful Contacts

The following two lists give addresses, telephone numbers and telex numbers for organizations which are involved with the telecommunications market in China. The first list gives ministry level organizations. For each ministry, there is a subordinate bureau in each province which is located int he provincial capital. The second list gives the major import and export corporations which are in charge of importing telecommunication equipment. Other organizations involved in trade and large projects are also included. Names of managers are given only for reference. It should be noted that if any of these ministries or organizations are contacted by telephone, the receptionist who answers the phone may not speak English.

I.   Relevant Ministries and Ministry Level Organizations

The Ministry of Electronics
Department of International Cooperation
Sanlihe, Beijing 100823
Tel: 86-1-329-4968   Fax: 86-1-8013867

The Ministry of Posts and Telecommunications
Department of External Affairs
13 West Changan Avenue
Beijing 100804
Tel: 6020540   Fax: 86-1-601-1370

China Electronics Corporation
Department of International Cooperation
Attn: Director General
27 Wanshoulu
Beijing 100846
Tel: 821-8528 x3781   Fax: 86-1-821-3745

II.   Import & Export Corporations and Other Trade Organizations

Beijing Guangda Corporation
Xiyuan Hotel, Building 6
Er Li Gou, Xijiao, Beijing
Tel: 89-0721 x601-618

China Aviation Technology Import & Export Corporation
67 Jiao Tong Street, Beijing
Tel: 44-2444

China Electronics Technology Import & Export Corporation
49 Fuxing Road, Beijing
Tel: 81-0910, 81-1188

China Great Wall Industrial Corporation
17 Wen Chang Hutong, Beijing
Tel: 89-3155, 65-1896

China National Communication Construction Corporation
13 West Chang'an Street, Beijing
Tel: 65-1886

China National Instruments Import & Export Corporation
P.O. Box 2811
Er Li Gou, Xijiao, Beijing
Tel: 89-0931

China National Machinery Import & Export Corporation
Er Li Gou, Xijiao, Beijing
Note: There is a branch office in every province. The largest is in Beijing:
China National Machinery Import & Export Corporation, Beijing Branch
190 Chao Yang Men Nei Street, Beijing
Tel: 55-6915, 55-3504

China National Posts and Telecommunication Industry Corporation
13 West Chang'an Street, Beijing
Tel: 66-1242

China National Posts and Telecommunication Materials Corporation
13 West Chang'an Street, Beijing
Tel: 66-1312

China National Technology Import Corporation
Er Li Gou, Xi Jiao, Beijing
Tel: 89-2116

China New Generation Corporation
P.O. Box 511, Beijing
Tel: 66-4714

TEXTILE FABRICS

China is a world famous and traditional textiles producing country. Textiles industry is the cornerstone of its national economy. In 1989, its output value and profit and taxes together accounted for one-tenth of the national total and its textiles export, a quarter of the national total exports (2).

Textile is one the major foreign exchange earners. In 1991, the Chinese textile exports came up to nearly $US 15 billion and plans to top $US 17.5 billion by the year 1995.

Table 118 gives some of the salient statistics concerning the textile fabrics sector in China (3).

Table 118

Salient Statistics Concerning the Textile Fabrics Sector

A)	Three-letter ITA industry sector code:	TXF
B)	Est. total market size (USD millions):	
	1991 -	$5,000
	1992 -	$5,650
C)	Est. 1992-4 annual market growth rate:	13%
D)	Est. total imports (USD millions):	
	1991 -	$1,500
	1992 -	$1,725
E)	Est. annual total import growth rate:	15%
F)	Est. import from U.S. (USD millions):	
	1991 -	$500
	1992 -	$600
G)	Est. annual growth of imports from U.S.:	20%
H)	China's receptivity to U.S. products in this sector (5 - High/1 - Low):	4
I)	Competition from local/third countries for U.S. firms (5 - Low/1 - High):	4
J)	Chinese market barriers to U.S. sales in this sector (5 - Few/1 - Many):	4
K)	Comments - factors for increased U.S. sales:	

- High quality fabric for high-priced exports.
- Colorful, lighter and stronger fabrics in increased demand.

	Most Promising Sub-sectors	1992 market size
L)	1. Cotton yarn and fabrics	$2,000 million
	2. Synthetic fibers	$1,500 million
	3. Wool and woven fabric	$ 150 million

Overview   China has a long and rich history in production of silk bast fiber, and cotton textiles. The earliest silk producer, China began exporting to West Asia and Europe around 20 B.C. Ramie, a grass used to produce woven fabrics, fish lines, and fish nets, was first cultivated around 1000 B.C. and is found in the provinces of Hunan, Hubei, Sichuan, Guangdong, Guizhou and the Guangxi-Zhuang Autonomous Region. Cotton spinning and weaving was the largest domestic industry in the late nineteenth and early twentieth centuries. After a respectable, but inconsistent performance from 1949 to 1978, textile production increased significantly with the introduction of the responsibility system (see Glossary) for agriculture in 1979. By 1979, supplies of textiles had improved, the cloth-rationing system (in force since 1949) had ended, and the industry had begun to flourish.

From 1979 to 1984, the output value of the textile industry rose approximately 13 percent annually. In 1984, China had about 12,000 enterprises producing cotton and woolen goods, silk, linen, chemical fibers, prints and dyed goods, knitwear, and textile machinery. Textile production was 15.4 percent of the country's total industrial output value in 1984. Textile exports in 1984 (excluding silk goods) totaled US $4.2 billion, up 21.7 percent over 1983, and accounted for 18.7 percent of the nation's total export value. By 1986, textiles had replaced oil as the top foreign exchange earner.

Traditionally, the coastal areas had the most modern textile equipment and facilities. Shanghai and Jiangsu Province were the nerve centers of the industry, accounting for 31.6 percent of the total gross output value for textiles in 1983. Other major textile areas were Shandong, Liaoning, Hubei, Zhejiang, and Hebei provinces.

After 1949, cotton textile production was reorganized and expanded to meet consumer needs. Cotton cultivation increased in the areas around the established spinning centers in the port cities of Shanghai, Qingdao, Tianjin, and Guangzhou. New spinning and weaving facilities opened near the inland cotton producing regions. In 1983, China produced 4.6 million tons of cotton, more than double the 1978 total.

China still was the world's largest silk producer in 1985, manufacturing approximately 422,000 meters of silk textiles. Shanghai and Jiangsu and Zhejiang provinces were the main silk centers. In 1985, China also produced approximately 125,000 tons of knitting wool, 218 million meters of woolen piece goods, 3.5 million tons of yarn, and 541,000 tons of chemical fibers.

The textile industry employed 7.45 million people in 1990, a significant increase from the 1985 figure of 5.7 million. Clearly, the textile industry ranks as a major employer, employing one-ninth of China's industrial labor force. SSB figures show that 24,584 enterprises were engaged in textile production in 1990, including 9,303 in the cotton industry, 2,109 producing woolen textiles, and 3,210 engaged in silk production.

Investment in textile production during the five years of the Seventh Five-Year Plan (1986-1991), exceeded 37.3 billion renminbi or about USD 6.8 billion. Textile machinery imports for the first half of 1992 have already matched figures for all of 1991.

Over the past dozen years, China has altered the structure of production and sales of textiles for both domestic and foreign markets. China did away with its system of cloth rationing in 1983, the year it claims it became self-sufficient in textile production. In 1984, the Ministry of Textiles decided to implement a series of reform measures which affected areas such as fabric pricing, raw material administration, domestic marketing and export regulations. That same year, the Ministry of Textiles introduced a system of farm-to-plant direct dealing for wool supplies. The Ministry of Commerce, in 1985, replaced its state monopoly purchasing system with a contract system and forbade any trading until all contracts had been fulfilled.

Per capita cloth output, according to China's state statistical bureau statistics, rose from 6.73 meters in 1952 to 16.63 meters in 1990, down somewhat from the 1988 peak of 17.06 meters.

China has also entered into a number of overseas joint ventures to produce textiles. For example, China has approached firms to establish joint ventures in Mexico, Guyana, Jamaica, Mauritius, Canada, Australia, The United Arab Emirates, Egypt, Nigeria, Panama, and even the U.S. at a trade zone in Texas.

While there is no shortage of unskilled or semi-skilled labor for China's textile and apparel industries, highly skilled technicians capable of handling increasingly sophisticated imported machinery are in demand. In fact, some provinces have "lured" technicians and managers away from successful ventures in China's coastal provinces to establish or improve production in other areas of the country.

In some cases, China's industry also suffers from an excess of workers as factories modernize and demand greater productivity from their workers. Under-employment is common, with sometimes as many as three or four persons employed where one should suffice. The government's sensitivity to unemployment has, in the past, precluded wholesale layoffs or firings. Many state-owned enterprises continued to employ workers in production of goods which had no market, a practice that China's government hopes to discontinue.

In terms of overall labor productivity as measured in output per person per year, textile employees averaged 18,191 Yuan or about USD 3,300 per year in 1990. This figure is about double that of an employee in the timber industry.

Market Assessment China's textile and apparel production was forecast to grow five percent per year between 1991 and 1995, according to Ministry of Textile estimates. This represents a decline from seven percent growth rates achieved between 1985 and 1991. Total textile and apparel production in 1991 stood at USD 38 billion. Ministry of Textiles estimates indicate China hopes production will reach USD 49 billion by 1995 and USD 62.5 billion by 2000. More than 8 million workers are employed in the garment and textile industries.

Textile and garment production not only satisfies basic domestic demand for China's 1.1 billion people, but also generated exports worth USD 16.8 billion in 1991, making textiles first among the country's foreign exchange earners. Chinese textile officials project that the country will export USD 17.5 billion in 1995 and between USD 20 and USD 23.5 billion by the year 2000. According to China customs administration statistics, in the six years between 1985 and 1990, China's textile and garment exports totalled USD 60.267 billion compared to USD 28.048 billion from 1979 to 1984. China's largest export markets are Hong Kong, Japan, the EC, and the U.S.

In the past, textile exports have outpaced garment exports. Chinese industry sources project that by 1995, the proportion will be reversed, with garments representing 65 percent of total textile industry exports. Garments currently account for 40 percent. Imports of synthetic fibers have risen dramatically, outpacing imports of natural fibers.

According to Ministry of Textiles officials, an uncertain international market climate couple with economic retrenchment in the domestic textile and apparel industry led one-third of China's textile and apparel enterprises to suffer losses in 1991.

Many Chinese government and business officials believe four major issues confront China's textile and apparel industry in the next five years. The domestic industry must be rationalized. Technological standards must be raised. The industry should be "optimized," i.e., increasing efficiency, improving quality, developing greater varieties of products. And overall management and control need improvement.

Remedies to these problems include giving priority to the development of chemical fibers and textile machinery and equipment. Plans call for the construction of large production bases for chemical fibers and the updating of existing factories through imports of foreign machinery. China's coastal production facilities are to focus on higher-value export oriented production, leaving the manufacturing of primary raw materials to less developed inland areas. The productive power of China's township enterprises has yet to be fully tapped and could show efficiency gains through expansion of technical and managerial expertise. Finally, the industry's export orientation would be emphasized and new markets sought.

Natural Fibers

Silk: Silk is the first textile that comes to mind when China is mentioned. Silk production has risen from 47,200 metric tons in 1986 to 56,600 metric tons in 1990. China is careful not to destabilize its market for silk through over-production. China has introduced a number of renovations to improve and expand its silk products, including blending silk with other fibers, cross-weaving, and jacquard weaving. According to the China Resources Silk Corporation, China's exports of silk materials account for 90 percent of the world total and 40 percent of the silk fabric.

Cotton: China's textile industries have sought to expand product development across the full range of textile products. In cotton and its blends, China claims improvements have been made in combed yarn, broad width cloth, high-count and densely woven fabrics, high density downproof fabric and denim products.

Wool: In the past few years, China's wool fabric industry claims it has made the transition from production of heavier, coarse wool fabrics to newer more marketable lightweight and soft fabrics, such as fine suiting, cashmere, gaberdine and angora blends.

Ramie: China's Ramie industry has also grown with the number of spindles in use growing from barely 75.000 in the early 1980s to more than 600,000 in 1992. Some 8,000 looms produce Ramie fibers for use in garments, furnishings and industrial applications.

Synthetic Fibers

While natural fibers continue to be important to China's textile industry, manmade fibers promise to be even more important to the industry's future. Output of manmade fibers rose from 450,000 tons in 1980 to 1.86 million tons in 1991. Chinese officials say they hope to raise total production to 2 million tons by 1995 and 2.6 million tons by the year 2000. Currently, China must annually import about 600,000 tons of chemical fibers to make up for insufficient domestic production.

Annual capital investment in chemical fibers by state-owned units rose dramatically from 1985 compared to 1990. In 1985, state-owned units invested about USD 120 million in chemical fibers compared to USD 400 million in 1990.

Beyond the usual range of manmade fibers, China has expanded into production of various synthetic fibers including cationic dyeable polyester, high tenacity-modulus vinyl fiber, high absorbency polyester fiber, PBT fiber and a number of fibers with special characteristics such as flame-retardant, duck down-like, anti-pilling, antistatic and composite fibers. New fiber experimentation includes aromatic, carbon, pre-oxidized, and phenolic fibers. The latter is claimed to be a neutron absorbing fiber for use in aviation and space technology.

Fiber Handling Processes

Spinning: In general, Chinese textile industries have sought to control the expansion of total production, decrease the number of outdated spindles and spinning looms in operation and increase productivity and technical levels of existing operations. As of 1991, 260,000 spindles were devoted to Schappe spinning of silk and about 180,000 looms were engaged in weaving silk fabric. Between 1986 and 1991, approximately USD 550 million was invested in upgrading machinery devoted to silk production. Upgrading of cotton fiber production has also followed suit. As a result, some three million cotton spindles and 26,000 cotton looms have been renovated, more than 3,000 combing machines have been added, and 10,000 shuttleless looms installed.

The number of spindles in the wool sector have increased from 1.68 million in 1986 to 2.66 million in 1991. Likewise, the number of looms producing wool cloth has increased from 25,700 to 33,600 in that same period.

China's textile industry has sought to improve its spinning capability by importing, and, in some cases producing, spinning machines and belated technologies. For example, a full range of dry spinning technologies has expanded the use of acrylic fibers. China has begun domestic production of hi-speed filament spinning and of spinning machines.

Weaving and Knitting: China has introduced ring frame, roving frame and rapier looms. Domestic production of the latter has already begun as has production of water/air jet looms. Domestic production of circular knitting machines and their subsequent widespread use has enhanced productivity and efficiency of knitting enterprises.

Finishing: In the area of after treatment of silk, China's industry says it has developed a new printing thickener as well as crease, shrink-resistance and low-temperature dyeing technologies. Chinese cotton textile producers say conventional printed, woven, and knitted goods have also experienced new developments. For example, mercerized and singed knitted fabric, warp-knitted fleece, knitted imitation fur and other middle-to-high grade fabrics can now be processed by various treatments such as shrinkproofing, resin and chintz finishing, embossing and coating. Important enhancements can be added which are anti-static or flame retardant.

China has begun to produce its own high temperature/pressure dyeing machines as well as flat screen and rotary screen printing machines and auto-levellers. It has also finished testing of open-width scouring and bleaching machines and large capacity jiggers and hopes to begin production line operations in the near future. China's textile machinery makers have also sought to develop automatic winding and automatic reeling machines.

Competitive Situation

Domestic Market: China's domestic market consumes slightly more than half of China's total textile production, according to the Ministry of Textile 1991 almanac. Domestic purchases of garments have risen more rapidly than purchase of textiles reflecting a shift form homemade to readymade garments, according to textile industry design officials. According to a recently published survey, Chinese spend an average of 14.9 percent of their earnings on clothing compared to 19.3 percent for a Hong Kong resident. Chinese officials believe the Chinese people will spend more money on clothing as income increases, though they are cautious about assigning proportions given the other shifts taking place in food, housing, medical care, etc.

China's domestic market experiences both shortages and excesses of supply. Sometimes these fluctuations are the result of increased domestic demand. At other times, they are the result of good shifting to export markets to earn higher prices overseas. According to a recent sample survey of China's domestic silk marketing firms conducted by the Ministry of Commerce, for example, thirty-three of fifty-one types of silk are in excess supply, sixteen are in balance, and two are in short supply.

Exports: China exported USD 16.732 billion worth of textiles in 1991, up 20,84 percent from 1990 according to China customs administration statistics. Textile exports accounted for 23.27 percent of China's total exports in 1991 and 22.3 percent of 1990s total.

In all but a handful of categories, China's textile exports averaged increases in the 30 to 40 percent range. Knitted and cotton cloth exports for 1991 amounted to USD 8.99 billion, up 31.42 percent. China exported 190,400 tons of cotton yarn in 1991 worth USD 472 million. Pure woolen fabric exports increased by 35.39 percent while their unit price fell by 5.85 percent. Blended woolen fabrics were up 37.31 percent, but unit prices dropped 1.1 percent. Silk fabric exports rose 13.34 percent over 1990 volumes, but foreign exchange earnings dropped by 7.43 percent.

Imports: China imported approximately USD 1.5 billion in textiles during the first six month of 1992 or a little less than the total for 1991 of nearly USD 1.8 billion. Imports of synthetics have surpassed imports of natural fibers. From January through June this year, China imported approximately USD 350 million in textiles from the U.S. Nearly two-thirds or USD 238 million of that total was in the form of raw cotton. The import sectors shrinking the most were those where domestic production came on stream or demand for the import declined as a result of market shifts toward higher value products.

Some useful contacts in the textile industry include:

Beijing Printing and Dyeing Mill
Chaoyang District, Beijing 100025
Tel: 5004477-181

Changzhou Dongfang Printing and Dyeing Mill
Tianning District, Changzhou
Jiangsu Province 213002

Hangzhou United Silk Printing & Dyeing Factory
Gongshu, Hangzhou
Zhejiang Province 310015
Tel: 817824

Hanzhou Silk Scouring & Dyeing Factory
Xiacheng, Hangzhou
Zhejiang Province 310004
Tel: 543441

Huangshi Cotton Textile Printing & Dyeing Mill
Huangshigang, Huangshi
Hubei Province 435002
Tel: 224921

Huzhou Silk Printing & Dyeing Mill
Huzhou, Zhejiang Province 313000
Tel: 224013

Jiamusi Textile Printing & Dyeing Mill
Yonghong District, Jiamusi
Heilongjiang Province 154004
Tel: 31312

Jiangxi Cotton Textile Printing & Dyeing Mill
Donghu, Nanchang
Jiangxi Province 330039
Tel: 331807

Jiangyin Dyeing & Printing Mill
1 Yinranlu, Jiangyin
Jiangsu Province 214400
Tel: 884160

Northeast No. 1 Printing & Dyeing Mill
Baqiao, Xi'an
Shaanxi Province 710038
Tel: 364811

Shanghai No. 1 Printing & Dyeing Mill
Putuo District, Shanghai 200060
Tel: 2552141

Shanghai Xinguang Underwear Dyeing & Weaving Mill
Hongkou District, Shanghai 200080
Tel: 5462250

Shanghai Yongxin Raincoat Dyeing & Weaving Mill
Xuhui District, Shanghai 200030
Tel: 4396630

Shanxi Textile Printing and Dyeing Mill
Hexi District, Taiyuan
Shanxi Province 030024
Tel: 666411

Shenzen Zhongguan Printing & Dyeing Company, Ltd.
10 F Real Estate Road, Renmin Roo
Shenzen Province 518001
Tel: 200942

Shijiazhuang No. 1 Printing & Dyeing Mill
Chang'an District, Shijiazhuang
Hebei Province 050011
Tel: 647986

Sichuan No. 1 Cotton Textile Printing & Dyeing Mill
Mashiqiao, Chenghua District, Chengdu
Sichuan Province 610053
Tel: 442912

Suzhou No. 1 Silk & Satin Scouring & Dyeing Mill
Canglang District, Suzhou
Jiangsu Province 215007
Tel: 551554

Weifang No. 2 Printing & Dyeing Mill
Weicheng District, Weifang
Shandong Province 261006
Tel: 232971

Wuxi Bleaching & Dyeing Plant
Wuxi Jiangsu Province 214008
Tel: 403851

Wuxi Silk Printing & Dyeing Mill
Beitang District, Wuxi
Jiangsu Province 214035
Tel: 669171

Xiangfan Cotton Textile Printing & Dyeing Mill
Xiangfan, Hubei Province 441002
Tel: 223290

Xiangtan Textile Printing & Dyeing Mill
Xiangtan, Hunan Province 411102
Tel: 21211

Yangzhou Printing & Dyeing Mill
Guangling District, Yangzhou
Jiangsu Province 225003
Tel: 232034

Zhengzhou Printing & Dyeing Mill
Zhongyuan District, Zhengzhou
Henan Province 450053
Tel: 448840

Some useful contacts in the textile mill category include:

Anqing Textile Mill
Anqing, Anhui Province 246018
Tel: 510810

Baotou General Textile Mill
Qinghan, Baotou
Inner Mongolia 014030
Tel: 57788

Chongchun Textile Mill
Chaoyang District, Changchun
Jiling Province 130011
Tel: 52235

Dalian Textile Mill
Ganjingzi District, Dalian
Liaoning Province 116033
Tel: 600991

Fuyang Textile Mill
Fuyang, Anhui Province 236089
Tel: 265002

Jinzhou Textile Mill
Jinzhou District, Dalian
Liaoning Province 116100
Tel: 4402

Nanning Cotton Textile Printing & Dyeing Mill
Nanning, Guangxi Province 530001
Tel: 333151

Puqi General Textile Mill
Jingquan, Puqi
Hubei Province 437321
Tel: 23471

Sichuan Langzhong Silk Mill
Lanzhong County, Nanchong
Sichuan Province 637400
Tel: 22811

Sulun Textile Mill
Ganglang District, Suzhou
Jiangsu Province 215007
Tel: 552504

Suzhou Dongwu Silk Mill
Pinqjiang District, Suzhou
Jiangsu Province 215005
Tel: 774691

Suzhou Zhenya Silk Mill
Pinjiang, Suzhou
Jiangsu Province 215005
Tel: 771601

Wuhu Textile Mill
Xinwu District, Wuhu
Anhui Province 241000
Tel: 32995

Wuhu Xinsheng Silk Mill
Wujiang County, Suzhou
Jiangsu Province 215228
Tel: 51018

Xinjiang Tianshan Woolen Textile Company, Ltd.
Xinshi District, Urumqi
Xinjiang Province 830000
Tel: 218805

Yancheng Textile Mill
Yancheng, Jiangsu Province 224001
Tel: 225352

Some useful contacts in the cotton mill industry include:

Baoding No. 1 Cotton Mill
Chaoyang District, Beijing 100025
Tel: 5072831-2395

Beijing No. 2 Cotton Mill
Chaoyang District, Beijing 100025
Tel: 5004499-291

Dezhou Cotton Mill
Dezhou, Shandong Province 253002
Tel: 21735

Handan No. 2 Cotton Mill
Congtai District, Handan
Hebei Province 056024
(#3 Mill @ 056025
#4 Mill @ 056026)
Tel: 310904
(#3 Mill @ 319095
#4 Mill @ 319096)

Hangzhou No. 2 Cotton Mill
59 Gongrenlu, Chengxiangzhen
Xiaoshan, Zhejiang Province 311200
Tel: 623911

Henan Huaxin Cotton Mill
Ji County, Xinxiang
Henan Province 453100
Tel: 64521

Henan Yubei Cotton Mill
Belguan, Anyang
Henan Province 455000
Tel: 423996

Jinan No. 1 Cotton Mill
Tianqiao, Jinan
Shandong Province 250033
Tel: 552044

Luoyang Cotton Mill
Xigong, Luoyang
Henan Province 471009
Tel: 338311-242

Nantong No. 1 Cotton Mill
Nantong, Jiangsu Province 226002
Tel: 544711

Nantong No. 2 Cotton Mill
Nantong, Jiangsu Province 226006
Tel: 517173

Nantong No. 3 Cotton Mill
Haimen County, Nantong
Jiangsu Province 226121
Tel: 05231-233247

Northwest No. 1 Cotton Mill
Weichang, Xianyang
Shaanxi Province 712000
Tel: 213960

Northwest No. 2 Cotton Mill
Qindu, Xianyang
Shaanxi Province 712000
Tel: 212823

Northwest No. 4 Cotton Mill
Baqiao District, Xi'an
Shaanxi Province 710038
Tel: 39032

Northwest No. 7 Cotton Mill
Qindu, Xianyang
Shaanxi Province 712000
Tel: 214945

Shaanxi No. 10 Cotton Mill
Weiyang District, Xi'an
Shaanxi Province 710086
Tel: 44971

Shanghai No. 12 Cotton Mill
Yangpu District, Shanghai 200090
Tel: 5432790

Shanghai No. 17 Cotton Mill
Yangpu District, Shanghai 20090
Tel: 5431010

Shanghai No. 19 Cotton Mill
Yangpu District, Shanghai 200090
Tel: 5430220

Shanghai No. 2 Cotton Mill
Putuo District, Shanghai 200060
Tel: 2564460

Shanghai No. 21 Cotton Mill
Changning District, Shanghai 200060
Tel: 2598441

Shanghai No. 22 Cotton Mill
Putuo District, Shanghai 200060
Tel: 2561401

Shanghai No. 31 Cotton Mill
Yangpu District, Shanghai 200090
Tel: 5433711

Shanghai No. 8 Cotton Mill
921 Songpulu, Shanghai 200940
Tel: 6671160

Shanghai No. 9 Cotton Mill
Yangpu District, Shanghai 200090
Tel: 5341575

Shanxi Jinhua Cotton Mill
Yuci, Jinzhong
Shanxi Province 030600
Tel: 26911

Shashi Cotton Mill
Shashi, Hubei Province 434003
Tel: 215391

Shashi Jingsha Cotton Mill
Shashi, Hubei Province 434001
Tel: 212291

Shijiazhuang No. 1 Cotton Mill
Chang'an District, Shijiazhuang
Hebei Province 050011
Tel: 647976

Shijiazhuang No. 2 Cotton Mill
Chang'an District, Shijiazhuang
Hebei Province 050011
Tel: 647941

Shijiazhuang No. 3 Cotton Mill
Chang'an District, Shijiazhuang
Hebei Province 050011
Tel: 648966

Shijiazhuang No. 4 Cotton Mill
Chang'an District, Shijiazhuang
Hebei Province 050011
Tel: 648986

Tianjin No. 1 Cotton Mill
Hejong District, Tianjin 300170
Tel: 414561

Tianjin No. 2 Cotton Mill
Hexi District, Tianjin 3000202
Tel: 281091

Tianjin No. 3 Cotton Mill
Hedong District, Tianjin 300170
Tel: 413915

Tiajin No. 4 Cotton Mill
Hexi District, Tianjin 300220
Tel: 282951

Wuhan No. 1 Cotton Mill
Hanyang, Wuhan
Hubei Province 430050
Tel: 442911

Wuxi No. 1 Cotton Mill
Nanchang District, Wuxi
Jiangsu Province 214031
Tel: 2235676

Wuxi No. 2 Cotton Mill
Chong'an District, Wuxi
Jiangsu Province 214008
Tel: 403612

Wuxi No. 3 Cotton Mill
Beitang, Wuxi
Jiangsu Province 214044
Tel: 224556

Zhengzhou No. 3 Cotton Mill
Zhongyuan District, Zhengzhou
Henan Province 450007
Tel: 448931

Zhengzhou No. 4 Cotton Mill
Zhongyuan District, Zhengzhou
Henan Province 450007
Tel: 447065

Zhengzhou No. 5 Cotton Mill
Zhongyuan District, Zhengzhou
Henan Province 450007
Tel: 448562

Zhengzhou No. 6 Cotton Mill
Zhongyuan District, Zhengzhou
Henan Province 450007
Tel: 448683

Some useful contacts in the synthetic fiber industry include:

Baoding United Chemical Fibre Plant
Xinshi, Baoding
Hebei Province 071055
Tel: 436736

Cixi Polyamide Fibre Company
Zhonghanzhen, Cixi
Zhejiang Province 315301
Tel: 825611

Dandong Chemical Fibre Industrial Company
Zhenxing, Dandong
Liaoning Province 118002
Tel: 61811

Foshan Polyester Filament Plant
Foshan, Guangdong Province 528000
Tel: 221819

Fujian Yong'an Chemical Fibre Plant
Yong'an Fujian Province 366016
Tel: 39101

Guangzhou Synthetic Fibre Plant
Baiyun District, Guangzhou
Guangdong Province 510160
Tel: 8814422

Hangzhou Chemical Fibre Plant
Xihu, Hangzhou
Zhejiang Province 310011
Tel: 888924

Heilongjiang Polyester Fibre Plant
Heping Road, Acheng
Heilongjiang Province 150316
Tel: 22663

Hubei Chemical Fibre Plant
Xiangyang County, Xiangfan
Hubei Province 441133
Tel: 2390

Jiangsi Chemical Fibre Plant
Donghu, Nanchang
Jiangsi Province 330006
Tel: 226600

Jilin Chemical Fibre Plant
Jilin, Jilin Province 132101
Tel: 338474

Kaiping Polyester Enterprise Group Corporation
Kaiping County, Jiangmen
Guangdong Province 529300
Tel: 23628

Kaishantun Chemical Fibre Pulp Mill
Longjing, Yanbian
Jilin Province 133417
Tel: 12

Liaoyang Petrochemical Fibre Company
Hongwei, Liaoyang
Liaoning Province 111003
Tel: 58882

Nanhai Polyester Filament Plant
Nanhai County, Fuoshan
Guangdong Province 528208
Tel: 50676

Nanjing Chemical Fiber Plant
Qixia District, Nanjing
Jiangsu Province 210038
Tel: 561011

Nantong Acetate Fibre Company, Ltd.
Nantong, Jiangsu Province 226008
Tel: 510512

Pingdingshan Polyamide Cord Fabric Plant
Pingdingshan, Henan Province 467000
Tel: 332922

Shanghai Chemical Fiber Company
Huangpu District, Shanghai 200002
Tel: 3218000

Sichuan Vinylon Works
Changshou County, Chongqing
Sichuan Province 631254

Wuxi General Synthetic Fibre Plant
Chong'an District, Wuxi
Jiangsu Province 214041
Tel: 410371

Xiamen Hualun Chemical Fibre Company, Ltd.
Xinglin, Xiamen
Fujian Province 361022
Tel: 679280

Xiamen Liheng Polyester Company, Ltd.
Xinglin District, Xiamen
Fujian Province 361022
Tel: 679450

Xinhui Polyamide Fiber Plant
Xinhui County, Jiangmen
Guangdong Province 529100
Tel: 669328

Xinhui Terylene Plant
Xinhui County, Jiangmen
Guangdong Province 529100
Tel: 663807

Xinxiang Chemical Fibre Plant
Beizhan, Xinxiang
Henan Province 453011
Tel: 353901

Yingkou Chemical Fibre Plant
Zhanqian, Yingkou
Liaoning Province 115001
Tel: 42501

Yizheng United Chemical Fibre Industrial Corporation
Xiangpu, Yizheng
Jiangsu Province 211416
Tel: 32235

Yuyao Chemical Fibre & Cotton Textile Mill
3 Fangzhilu, Yuyao
Jiangsu Province 315400
Tel: 622504

Zhongshan Polyester Fibre Plant Company, Ltd.
Zhongshan Port, Zhongshan
Guangdong Province 528400
Tel: 821394

TEXTILE MACHINERY

China's woolen and chemical fiber industries are the third and fourth biggest in the world, and its production scale of spinning machines, equipment, knitting and garment making are all among the largest in the world.

But the textile machines in use are half outmoded and need to be modernized. About one-fourth of the total 30 million cotton spindles and 200,000 of 800,000 looms need to be replaced. To modernize textiles industry, the Chinese authority has decided to take three years to eliminate 3 million outmoded spindles made before 1949. The first step is to modernize about one million spindles and looms. And technological renovation will take place mainly in 145 state-owned factories for cotton, wool, silk, garments and chemical fiber products and fabric for interior decoration. These factories form a national team to catch up with international standards (2).

Table 119 summarizes some of the salient statistics for the textile machinery industry in China (3).

Table 119

Salient Statistics Concerning the Textile Machinery Sector

A)	Three-letter ITA industry sector code:	TXM
B)	Est. total market size (USD millions):	
	1991 -	$2,000
	1992 -	$2,050
C)	Est. 1992-4 annual market growth rate:	4%
D)	Est. total imports (USD millions):	
	1991 -	$110
	1992 -	$150
E)	Est. annual total import growth rate:	10%
F)	Est. imports from U.S. (USD millions):	
	1991 -	$30
	1992 -	$32
G)	Est. annual growth of imports from U.S.:	11%
H)	China's receptivity to U.S. products in this sector (5 - High/1 - Low):	3
I)	Competition from local/third countries for U.S. firms (5 - Low/1 - High):	2
J)	Chinese market barriers to U.S. sales in this sector (5 - Few/1 - Many):	3
K)	Comments - factors for increased U.S. sales:	

- China is one of the world's major textile exporters, and textile exports are a major foreign exchange earner for China.

L)	Most Promising Sub-sectors	1992 market size
	1. Textile spinning/twisting machinery	$200 million
	2. Sewing machinery	$300 million
	3. Knitting machinery	$500 million

Overview   East China has been picked as an area of focus in the discussion of textile machinery in the text which follows.

Imported equipment and technology will play a pivotal role as East China's textile industry modernizes to compete in the international market. According to China's Eighth Five-Year Plan (1991-1995), the East China region will invest a total of USD 1.14 billion to restructure its textile industry, spending USD 260 million for imported equipment and technology, USD 420 million for plant and infrastructure construction and USD 460 million on domestic equipment for technical upgrade projects.

The East China region which includes Shanghai Municipality and the provinces of Jiangsu, Zhejiang, and Anhui, is China's principal textile production base. It contains 50 percent of the country's textile production capacity. As it invests in modernization over the next three years, the industry will develop its cotton and wool weaving, yarn spinning, garment assembly and chemical/synthetic fiber production. Imports will be concentrated on airjet looms, rapier looms, knitting machines, chemical fiber production equipment and technology to improve dyeing, printing and finishing techniques. East China also expects to develop its textile machinery industry through technology licensing agreements with foreign firms.

Shanghai will spend approximately USD 130 million on textile equipment imports. Zhejiang and Jiangsu will spend about USD 50 million and USD 80 million on equipment imports respectively.

U.S. companies are not aggressive in the market. Awareness of U.S. equipment, and, at 3 percent, the current U.S. market share, are both negligible. Potential end-users are drawn to the more active German, Italian and Japanese firms. Interested U.S. firms have also been unable to compete with the concessional loans provided by many European governments. U.S. equipment and technology is competitive in the dyeing and pre-treatment processes and should be able to expand market share. Foreign competitors dominate the market for weaving, spinning and knitting equipment.

Market Assessment   In 1991, the industry's profits dropped for the third consecutive year; 44 percent of the industry's firms lost money. Some of the problems facing the industry are: declining efficiency, outdated equipment, over-production, shortage of domestic raw materials, rising costs of cotton and a slowdown in the international market due to the worldwide recession. These problems are particularly ominous as China's textile industry exports generate 25 percent of the country's hard currency. The government estimates that total projected textile export earnings will reach USD 15 billion in 1992 and USD 17 billion by 1995. East China's textile exports grew from USD 3.74 billion in 1989 to an estimated USD 5 billion in 1992.

To maintain its international market share, the industry will modernize by eliminating outdated equipment (in particular an over capacity of spindles) and will reach international standards by upgrading quality and efficiency. For example, China has 350 workers per 10,000 spindles, while Italy has fifteen workers per 10,000 spindles. The labor-intensive nature of China's textile industry makes for inconsistent quality. The low worker productivity also offsets China's competitive labor costs.

1. Market Demand

China has approximately 40 million spindles, of which 13 million are outdated (1950s-1960s) and 3 million are antiquated (pre-1949). There are also approximately 860,000 looms, of which 250,000 are outdated. With 20.18 million spindles and 408,000 looms, the East China region possesses half of China's textile production capacity.

Shanghai has 2.5 million spindles, 1.1 million of which have been in continuous use since pre-1949. The Textile Ministry set targets for Shanghai to retire 600,000 spindles by 1996 (200,000 by 1993) and to replace 500,000 other spindles by 1996. China will produce the spindles domestically but will import equipment and technology to control spindle operations. The Ministry has not set targets for looms. To date, Shanghai has voluntarily removed 84,000 cotton spindles, 2,000 wool spindles and 1,526 looms.

Within Shanghai, enterprises in the new Pudong economic development zone will receive USD 66.8 million to import new equipment for ten large projects. These projects involve renovating five existing Pudong mills and constructing five new mills (relocated from the western bank of the neighboring Huangpu River).

In 1992, Shanghai will also invest in eighty additional technological upgrade projects, fifteen of which will rely upon imported textile equipment.

Jiangsu Province has over 5 million spindles which are operating at 85 percent capacity. Over the next three years, the province plans to replace 1 million spindles while retiring approximately 400,000 spindles.

2. End-User Profile

Shanghai currently has the largest concentration of textile production in China. Shanghai textile exports amount to 10% of China's total textile exports and 40% of Shanghai's total industrial output. The Shanghai textile industry includes twelve corporations (spinning & weaving, dyeing & finishing, knitting, toweling & bedsheeting, handkerchief, dyed yarn weaving, thread & ribbon,, chemical fibers, woolen & Jute, silk garment making, textile machinery and machine accessories), thirteen research institutes and three textile colleges. There are 540 factories (404 state-owned, sixty-nine collectively-owned, six collective-and state-owned and sixty-one Sino-foreign joint ventures). Its workforce exceeds 520,000.

The Jiangsu Provincial Textile Bureau includes more than 700 enterprises and produces one-third of Jiangsu's exports. The bulk of its imported equipment is from Germany, Italy and Japan. During the next three years, the Bureau plans to import equipment to improve labor productivity and raise quality rather than increase production volume.

Competitive Situation

1. Domestic Production

Local production of textile equipment is a priority area of development for the Textile Ministry with cooperation from the Ministry of Machinery and Electronics Industry. From 1991-95, East China will invest USD 740 million to purchase domestic equipment and further develop the domestic industry.

There are numerous manufacturers of textile equipment in East China. Probably the most aggressive of these manufacturers is the Shanghai #2 Textile Machinery Factory (Shanghai #2). Shanghai #2 was the first enterprise in the textile machinery manufacturing sector to receive government authorization for independent foreign trade. It was the first State enterprise in Shanghai to adopt the "comprehensive contract system" (direct authority to hire and fire and allow employees to choose jobs), and is one of the first enterprises to "go public" with a share holding system via the Shanghai Stock Exchange. The capital raised through the stock issuance will be used to import equipment and technology in four areas: Spinning, Automatic Cone Winding, Computer Integrated Manufacturing System (CIMS) and Flexible Machine System (FMS).

In the past, domestic manufacturers produced the majority of the Textile Industry's non-key equipment, relying upon imports primarily for key components. However, these manufacturers are now importing state-of-the-art technology through transfer agreements and joint ventures to manufacture their own machines. Shanghai has used technology transfer agreements eleven times since 1980. These agreements involved shuttleless looms, circular knitting machines, steam set machines, POY polyester spinning (Barmag of Germany), overflow dye machines (Brozzoli of Italy), and ring spinning (Zinser of Germany). To date, Shanghai also has sixty-one joint ventures with foreign firms. These joint ventures are expected to have a total output of USD 360 million in 1992.

While local textile manufacturers rate Shanghai #2 highly, they generally complain about the poor quality of locally-made textile equipment. Among their complaints about Chinese equipment are the lack of service guarantee and lower equipment efficiency, i.e. new Chinese looms have a waft rate of only 180 compared with a 1,000 waft rate for imported looms. As the number of enterprise authorized to import and export increases, local factories are exercising greater control over their equipment purchases. This will expand significantly the market for imported equipment.

2. Imports

Japan was the main supplier of imported textile equipment when China began importing equipment in 1978. According to local officials, "the Japanese were the closest and arrived first." In the 1980s, European, and to a certain extent, U.S. manufacturers entered the market. Within the past five years, Italy, Germany and Japan have captured approximately 80 percent of the market.

3. U.S. Market Share

The U.S. share in East China's imported textile equipment market is currently a minuscule 3 percent. U.S. manufacturers have a good reputation for quality and service but many industry contacts are unaware of U.S. suppliers and products for most of the equipment they want to buy. For example, the director of the Shaoxing Silk Printing Mill imports machines from Europe. He knows nothing about U.S. equipment and assumes there are not U.S. manufacturers whose equipment can process silk, rayon or other fine fibers. Generally, there is a belief that the U.S. textile industry is shrinking and that U.S. equipment does not exist or has not kept up with international development. In comparison, Italy has a reputation for having a highly competitive textile machinery industry that is very export oriented.

U.S. manufacturers and equipment which do have a market presence are:

Gaston County Inc. -	Scoring machines, Bridging machines and Rope Treatment Process machines
Maiden Corp. -	Dye Inspection/Testing machines
Gerber Corp. -	Lotting machines
Tube-Tex Corp. -	Pre-treatment Shrinkage machines
Other U.S. firms -	Computerized Color Matching systems, Bleaching machines and Starching machines.

U.S. firms are active in the emerging area of machine tools for textile equipment manufacturing. Two U.S. firms with a strong presence in the market are Cincinnati Milacron and Kearney & Trecker (K&T). The computer systems that accompany the textile machinery manufacturing process are dominated by U.S. firms such as DEC, UNISYS, HP and EDS.

A problem facing U.S. firms involves the process technology innovation of foreign competitors. An example of this is computerized testing machines linked to the factory's textile production line. Currently, a U.S. firm sells a testing machine which diagnoses a fabric's color composition. Both Japanese and Italian firms however, introduced new computerized technology at the 1991 Hanover textile fair offering multi-purpose machines that combine testing and dyeing (Japan) and testing and weaving (Italy). The end result is that the Japanese and Italians have positioned themselves to offer a "smart" system linking two previously separate operations into one.

4. Foreign Equipment/Competition

Japan, Italy and Germany are the three major foreign suppliers in East China. The Japanese have developed an extensive network for information and have hired Shanghai consultants to provide extensive market information. They have the best reputation for long-term involvement. For example, Shaoxing officials have traded with Japan for hundreds of years. In Shaoxing, Japanese companies finance the original equipment through compensation trade or even "loan" the equipment. However, parts must be purchased in cash which is where the Japanese firms make their profits. German companies have an excellent reputation for product quality and durability. Italian companies are very cost competitive, market directly to the factories and solicit information for product development and improvements. All three countries' companies sponsor technical seminars for potential customers, generally at local hotels.

Some textile industry contacts perceive that American firms do not offer Chinese companies their best prices. End-users prefer to source directly from the manufacturer but have found U.S. companies reluctant to quote prices. Moreover, when they do quote prices, the prices have been higher than those offered to American customers or Chinese-American trading companies.

5. Competitive Factors

Factors affecting imports include price, functions of the machine, durability, reputation, marketing and after sales service. The latter factor is especially important as the technical and qualitative distinctions between competing machines are becoming smaller and smaller.

Pricing considerations are often difficult to separate from financing and other terms. For example, two U.S. firms (Cincinnati and K&T), a German firm (Frikwerner) and an Italian firm (Mandori) competed on a Flexible Machine System, a contract valued at approximately USD 5 million. One of the U.S. firms would have won, except the German government offered a grant of approximately USD 650,000 (1 million DM) which paid for training and software development costs. This financing came from a scientific committee (BMFT) which is funded and supported by the Chinese and German governments.

Quality and durability are areas where firms have good reputations. Generally, U.S. and German equipment lasts about twenty years, while Japanese equipment lasts about five years. However, the U.S. recently lost the sale of a complete polyester factory to a German competitor with new models in operation. The American firm could only show plans for new models, the demonstration plants were fifteen to twenty years old.

The range of a company's product line is also very important. Chinese end-users prefer to purchase a whole line of equipment from one supplier. This helps the European and Japanese companies which tend to be more integrated than U.S. producers.

6. Marketing

Marketing is the most important aspect of doing business in East China. There are many marketing channels to reach the factory. Trade fairs, technical exchange seminars, trade publications (i.e. International Textile Bulletin), factory contact, bureau contact, and general reputation are all useful.

Common to all of these approaches are regular and consistent visits to develop strong relationships with Chinese end-users. U.S. companies have a reputation for seldom visiting China to display and introduce their equipment. In contrast, Japanese manufacturers spend an average of six months a year in China, while German and Italian manufacturers come every six months. Price, visits and technical seminars are especially important to enter the market. Chinese end-users are very reluctant to purchase equipment which is untried in China, particularly from new suppliers. Participation in trade shows is often very helpful for initial sales. Exhibitors sold 90 percent of their equipment at two recent trade exhibitions (ShanghaiTex '91 and Shanghai International Clothing Machine Exhibit—SICME '92). Once the first set of equipment is sold, reputation and references strongly influence future sales. A U.S. company recently exhibited a machine for sewing mattresses. The Shanghai Light Industry Bureau purchased it right off the exhibit floor. After a successful installation, other factories and Bureaus are now interested in purchasing the same machine.

East China contacts rely on the International Textile Machine Exhibition to identify new products, companies and technologies. The Exhibition is held every four years, most recently in Hanover, Germany (1991). Chinese industry sources noted that U.S. firms were not well-represented.

Trade exhibitions within China are also very important. These exhibits allow factory managers and engineers (key decision makers) a rare opportunity to meet face to face with foreign manufacturers. Participation in trade shows is important both to develop contacts and to sign contracts. Chinese authorities will after delay contract signing until the exhibition to boost the reputation of Chinese shows and to encourage participation. East China holds an equipment exhibition every year in Shanghai alternating between textile equipment (ShanghaiTex) and garment equipment (SICME). During the past four years, U.S. firms have had a very weak attendance at these fairs; only fourteen U.S. exhibitors participated in ShanghaiTex '91. Although Jiangsu officials attend the Shanghai exhibitions, they also sponsor their own shows in Nanjing. The following chart details recent exhibitions and the number of exhibitors:

	Total	Italy	Germany	HK	Japan	China	U.S.
SICME '92	78	1	3	24	19	24	0
ShanghaiTex '91	333	94	61	57	17	5	14
SICME '90	33	NA	NA	NA	NA	NA	NA
ShanghaiTex '89	361	109	71	64	11	0	18

Market Access

1. Import Climate

Through 1995, the Chinese Textile Ministry will give priority to imports and technical renovation projects (see the Best Prospects section). The State Council has announced it will not approve any projects expanding cotton or wool capacity during 1992-95 except foreign-funded joint ventures. It will allow projects to increase chemical fiber rolling and chemical fiber polymer production, but only those included in the State plan.

2. Import Approval Process

In Shanghai there are four main Chinese parties involved in successful sales of foreign textile equipment or technology—the factory, the Textile Bureau, the Economic Commission and the government import-export trading company. The two most important are the factory and the bureau; the trading company arranges payment and signs the contract, the Economic Commission approves transactions over USD 5 million. Equipment purchases include the following stages:

- The Bureau evaluates and approves the initial proposal from the factory.
- The factory begins technical exchanges and may visit potential foreign suppliers.
- The factory selects a manufacturer and together they submit a detailed feasibility study to the Bureau for approval.
- The factory chooses a Chinese government trading company to negotiate the trade and financing details. Several commonly used companies are:
  - China Machinery Import Export Corporation.
  - China Technology Import and Export Corporation.
  - China Textile Machine Technology Import and Export Corporation.
  - Shanghai Foreign Trade Corporation.
  - Shanghai International Technology Import and Export Corporation.
  - Shanghai Shenxing Technology Import and Export Corporation

This process indicates the importance of factory and bureau contacts. The end-user decides on a supplier long before the foreign trade corporation becomes involved in the project.

3. Distribution/Business Practices

China does not yet have an established system of independent agents or distributors. Foreign companies either establish a representative office in Hong Kong or in China or contract with an agent or distributor for marketing. Many foreign companies use Hong Kong or Taiwanese agents. They pursue the market aggressively, share a common language and culture and can provide service much more conveniently than U.S.-based companies. They also have experience with Chinese business practices and can provide the perks which are often essential to make the sale.

After-sales service and training are crucial to effectively market equipment. As Chinese end-users gain responsibility for purchasing and maintenance, they are becoming increasingly aware of the need for service. They are also very aware of the high cost of spare parts and service and are seeking ways to minimize these costs. Ideally, Chinese end-users want local access to maintenance and repair service and want to pay in local rather than in foreign currency.

Marketing strategies are very complex in this environment. Successful firms need to develop contacts and trade leads, conduct technical seminars and product demonstrations and provide after-sales service. Increasing numbers of local firms are available to provide some or all of these services.

4. Payment/Financing

There are generally three ways to acquire foreign equipment: direct imports, joint ventures and compensation trade. The method used in a particular project depends on the availability of foreign exchange and the priority of the project.

The decision on allocating foreign currency for importing new textile equipment is based on an official "export-agency" system. The Bureau administers this system and controls the foreign exchange earned by factories. According to this system, the more foreign currency a corporation earns, the larger is that corporation's allocation of foreign currency for imports. With the introduction of the shareholding system, however, more companies will raise foreign exchange through outside channels (i.e. Shanghai No. 2 Textile Machinery Corporation). When the Bureau allocates foreign exchange it channels it through Chinese banks to the factory. Factories with no allocation, or an insufficient allocation of foreign exchange often purchase imports using a combination of foreign exchange purchased in the swap markets (typically 30% of project cost) and loans from Chinese banks (typically 70% of project cost). In addition, sometimes Chinese trading companies sell imported equipment to Chinese factories for RMB, the inconvertible Chinese currency.

Most imports are financed by sight letters of credit (LCs) issued by the Bank of China or other state-owned banks. Payment is made only after the Chinese bank which issued the LC has received the export documents. This causes a minimum ten to twenty day delay before the U.S. exporter can collect payment for goods delivered.

For large equipment and technology sales, Chinese buyers typically make a 10 to 15 percent downpayment, then pay 70 - 75 percent on delivery and the remainder upon installation. At the time of the initial downpayment, however, Chinese buyers often require a Standby Letter of Credit from the seller's bank, guaranteeing the return of the downpayment if sales terms are not met. A problem arises when a small U.S. exporter does not have a credit line sufficient to cover the required standby LC.

Where possible, Chinese end-users prefer to obtain foreign equipment by entering into joint ventures with foreign companies (including, sometimes, with equipment suppliers themselves) rather than importing it directly. Shanghai requires the foreign joint venture partner to invest at least 25% of the total invested capital (with a minimum of joint venture investment of USD 100,000). The required foreign investment is often in the form of equipment. Joint ventures are subject to lower taxes than Chinese enterprises and offer other benefits to the Chinese investor such as the right to import cars and greater control of their foreign exchange earnings.

The option of using compensation trade appears to be gaining some support at the township level. Township factories are experiencing rapid growth and are seeking innovative forms of payment to import new equipment. An agreement between a Chinese weaving/dying mill and a Hong Kong trader is one example. The terms involve the exchange of USD 6.5 million in equipment for the factory's agreement to spin, weave, dye and print imported raw material from Hong Kong. The finished product will then be sold back to the Hong Kong trader at a set price. This agreement will last five years and will allow the factory to use its new machines' excess production capacity for its own benefit.

Foreign government financing has also played a role in securing sales for foreign manufacturers. In the past, Italy and England have provided low interest loans (3%-5%) with twenty year payment terms. Japan is another common provider of loans. Japanese loans carry interest rates at approximately half the commercial rate with terms of ten to fifteen years. The O.E.C.D. agreement not to offer concessional financing to commercially viable projects should preclude all textile projects from soft loans and grants. In addition, U.S. suppliers should be aware that the U.S. Import Export Bank provides export credits and working capital loans to support U.S. exports.

Best Sales Prospects

During China's Eighth Five-Year Plan (1991-95), there will be many opportunities to enter the East China market for imported machinery. Officials in Shaoxing, a city in Zhejiang Province, emphasized the need for jet spindles, jet looms, drying equipment and permanent press equipment and chemicals. In Shanghai, technical upgrade projects will require imported equipment in six key sectors: Cotton Spinning, Weaving and Preparing, Dyeing and Finishing, Wool Processing, Knitting and Garment Production and Accessories. The technical exchange projects are seeking cooperation in three broad categories: Textile, Printing and Dyeing and Other. Details on both technical upgrade and technical exchange projects with their respective planned equipment imports follow this section.

1. Technical Upgrade Projects

(i)   Cotton Spinning: To improve yarn quality by increasing the evenness of sliver and minimizing nap impurities.
-- Combined line of blowing and carding machines.
-- Roving frames.
-- Key components of ring spinning frames.
-- Combers.
-- Cone winders with splicers.

(ii)   Weaving and Preparing: To have high speed machines that can keep warp yarn tension constant.
-- Warping machines.
-- Signing machines.
-- Water jet looms
-- Air jet looms.
-- Projectile looms.
-- Rapier looms.

(iii)   Dyeing and Finishing: To improve detail processing, special finishing and small batch jobbing in large varieties.
-- Flat screen printing machines.

-- Rotary screen printing machines.
-- Duples printing machines.
-- Mercerizing ranges.
-- Raising machines.
-- Schreinering machines.
-- Coating machines.
-- Comprehensive shrinking machines.

(iv) Wool Processing: To improve yarn quality by increasing the evenness of sliver and strength of yarn, with a focus on worsted light fabrics, high quality sweaters and cardigans.
-- Wool spinning machines.
-- New model flat knitting machines.

(v) Knitting and Garment Production: To maintain current market position with modest investments in upgrade.
-- Circular knitting machines.
-- Embroidery machines.
-- Hosiery machines.
-- Steaming machines.
-- Ironing machines.
-- Computerized cutting machines.
-- Lagging and transporter conveyors.

(vi) Other Accessories.
-- Textile madeups.
-- Handkerchief production.
-- Thread and ribbon processing.
-- Zippers and button production.

2. Technical Exchange Projects

A. Textile
1. Automatic winding machines.
2. Development of fancy yarn products.
3. Development of air jet spinning.
4. Development of air spinning.
5. Development of air twisting-in device.
6. Spinning technology.
7. Introduction of continuous production cotton spinning workshops.
8. Technological introduction of new opening and picking equipment and automatic chute feeding system for cotton spinning.

9. Introduction of card's latest technology (i.e. dust sucking, autolevelling, automatic can changing and its stationary flat).
10. Connecting and conveying technology in drawing, sliver lap and combing process.
11. Rowing frame.
12. Spinning spindle (electrified spindle), metallic clothing, flat clothing and cylinder comb.
13. Development of slivering process equipment for wool spinning.
14. High speed double motor driven autoleveller.
15. Lacing frames.
16. Small size testing machines.
17. Spindle test device.
18. Drafting device.
19. Electronic slub catcher.
20. Air filtration system.
21. Analysis of the prospects for multi-phase looms.
22. Rapier looms.
23. Air jet looms.
24. Water jet looms.
25. Loom's weaving device.
26. Loom's dobby mechanics.
27. Double layer sizing machines.
28. Development of shuttleless looms.
29. Loom's shedding mechanics and its programming device.
30. Characteristics of electronic loom control.
31. Development of jacquard.
32. Integration of loom's production flow.
33. High speed warping machines.
34. Development of foreign sizing machines.

B. Printing and Dyeing

1. Finishing of Silk Fabric.
2. Automation of printing and dyeing workshops.
3. Fused Dyeing.
4. Foam finishing.
5. Foam finishing and cold pad-batch dyeing for circular knitting.
6. Modernized finishing of cotton fabrics.
7. Control technology for dyeing.
8. High quality wool yarn finishing process.
9. High quality wool yarn finishing process equipment.
10. Dyeing machines with small bath ratio.
11. Bobbin dyeing machine.

12. Low bath ratio treatment for rope fabric.
13. Development of Ager.
14. New printing technology for flat screen and rotary screen printing machines.
15. Special finishing.

C. Other

1. Circular flat bed machine.
2. Development of large diameter machines.
3. Computer flat bed machine.
4. Crocheting technology.
5. New hosiery machine technology.
6. Introduction of knitting machine technology in compound needles, compound motion and compound sinker.
7. Continuous treatment technology of circular knitting.
8. Dacron (Tetoron) imitation silk equipment for:
   i) Preparation system—winding, drawing, twisting and sizing machines.
   ii) Finishing equipment—craping machine and alkali reduction treatment equipment.
9. New silk warping machines.
10. Development of silk machinery technology.
11. Speed response system for garment production (i.e. hanger system).
12. Cap pressing machine.
13. Stereo pressing technology (i.e. vertical pressing trouser, vertical pressing shirts).
14. Analysis of garment machinery development trends.
15. Introduction of electro-mechanical integration products such as: electronic dobby, electronic jacquard, electronic weighing, frequency conversion speed regulation, electronic coloring, transponding thread and pattern preparing systems.
16. Analysis of the prospects for the international textile market.
17. Development of chemical fiber production process.
18. Concave screw knives.
19. Latest autoleveller.

Source: *Advance Press Conference for the East China Garment Processing Equipment 1992 Trade Show.*

Key Contacts

Director R&D Import Department
Shanghai Textile Industry Bureau
24 Zhongshan Road (E.1)
Shanghai, China 200002
Tel: 86-21-3233265   Fax: 86-21-3290982

Director Foreign Economic Cooperation Office
Shanghai Textile Industry Bureau
24 Zhong Shan Road (E.1)
Shanghai, China 200002
Tel: 86-21-3214590   Fax: 86-21-3290982

Executive Manager
Lianyungan Textile Factory
Southern YuDai River District
Xinpu, Lianyungang, China 222004
Tel: 86-518-413877   Fax: 86-518-413841

Deputy Director
Henan Textile Industry Bureau
Jian She Road
Zhengzhou, Henan Province, China 450007
Tel: 86-371-446433 x2124   Fax: 86-371-775281

Division Chief
Anhui Textile Industry Bureau
52 Lujiang Road
Hefei, Anhui Province, China 230061
Tel: 86-551-255479   Fax: 86-551-251980

Fujian Textile Industry Bureau
27 Dongda Road
Fuzhou, Fujian Province, China 350001
Tel: 86-591-553477

Planning and Construction Division Chief
Jiangsu Textile Industry Bureau
48 Zhongshan Dong Lu
Nanjing, China
Tel: 86-25-631435   Fax: 86-25-305328

Manager
Jiangsu Garment Equipment and Technical Service Center
117 Zhongyang Road
Nanjing, Jiangsu Province, China 210009

General Manager
Jiangxi Garment Company
116 Ba Yi Avenue
Nanchang, Jiangxi Province, China 330006

Senior Economist
Shandong Textile Industry Bureau
145 Wen Hua Dong Road
Jinan, Shandong Province, China 250014
Tel: 86-531-45911 x237   Fax: 86-531-615674

Deputy Division Chief
Zhejiang Light Industry Bureau
Mei Hua Bei Road
Hangzhou, Zhejiang Province, China 310009
Tel: 86-571-774971 x463   Fax: 86-571-774564

Deputy Manager
Shanghai Garment Company
614 Hankou Road
Shanghai, China 200001
Tel: 86-21-3205016   Fax: 86-21-3206680

Senior Engineer
Shanghai Textile Industry Design Institute
130 Chang Shou Road
Shanghai, China 200060
Tel: 86-21-2583020 x14   Fax: 86-21-2588184

Director
Shanghai No. 2 Textile Machinery Ltd.
265 Chang Zhong Road
Shanghai, China
Tel: 86-21-5318888   Fax: 86-21-5421963

Vice Director
Shanghai No. 11 Knitting Factory
96 Zhao Jia Bang Road
Shanghai, China 200020
Tel: 86-21-4372779   Fax: 86-21-4339466

Senior Engineer
Shanghai Cotton Mill No. 28
1028 Hunan Road
Shanghai, China 201204
Tel: 86-21-8840421   Fax: 86-21-8842024

Deputy Director
Shanghai No. 1 Printing & Dyeing Factory
1901 Suzhou Road West
Shanghai, China 200060
Tel: 86-21-2552141   Fax: 86-21-2535176

Manager
China Textile Machine Technology Import and Export Corporation
15 Pujiang Road, Pujiang Hotel, Room 315
Shanghai, China 200080
Tel: 86-21-3254564   Fax: 86-21-3207354

Some useful contacts in the textile machinery area include:

China Textile Machinery Plant
Yangpu District, Shanghai 200090
Tel: 5432970

Jingwei Textile Machinery Plant
Yuci City, Shanxi Province 030600
Tel: 22878

Shanghai No. 2 Textile Machinery Plant
Hongkou District
Shanghai 200434
Tel: 3423736

Zhengzhou Textile Machinery Plant
Jinshu District, Zhengzhou
Henan Province 450053
Tel: 3366491

CHAPTER 5

FOREIGN VENTURES

This final chapter of this volume will attempt to survey the spectrum of foreign involvement in industrial development in China as of 1995.

This is not intended to be an all-inclusive list of foreign involvement in China, but is intended to provide a panorama of timely information which could serve as a guide to involvement for future entrants. It is intended to present a broad view of very recent participation by various foreign (U.S. and other) concerns in China. Particular emphasis has been placed on reports of joint ventures between foreign companies and Chinese companies.

Foreign Company	Country	China Partner	Comments
Advanced Micro Device	U.S.A. (Sunnyvale, CA)	---	Plans to build $29 million semi-conductor plant in Suzhou in Jiangsu Province.
Airbus Industrie	France	---	Plans to invest $25 million in maintenance and training centers in China.
Air Products and Chemicals	U.S.A. (Allentown, PA)	Beijing Analytical Instruments Factory	Plans to build first helium storage and transfer facility in China to be supplied from U.S. and marketed to medical (MRI), research and electronic users.
		---	Built oxygen plant at Baoshan Iron and Steel Mill near Shanghai in 1991 with 2.4 million lb/day capacity and plans 4.8 million lb/day expansion by 1997.

Foreign Company	Country	China Partner	Comments
Air Products and Chemicals	U.S.A. (Allentown, PA)	Nanjing Chemical	Will build 1,500 ton/day air separation plant in Nanjing to supply Yangzi River Region.
		Various	Has established thirteen joint ventures with annual sales of $300 million as of 1994.
Akzo Nobel (and Kayaku Akzo of Japan)	Netherlands	Tianjin No. 2 Organic Chemical Plant	The new company, Tianjin Akzo Nobel Peroxides, will manufacture organic peroxides.
Albright and Wilson (British Subsidiary of Tenneco-U.S.A.)	U.K.	Hunan Resun Industrial Chemical Corp.	Will build a plant in Changsha to produce specialty sufactants for detergents and toiletries.
Alcatel NV (tele-communications unit of Alcatel-Alsthom SA)	Registered in Netherlands, but based in France.	Chinese National Postal & Telecom Industry Corp.	Joint venture is Shanghai Bell Telephone Equipment Mfg. Co. owned 32% by Alcatel and also having a Belgian government interest
		---	Alcatel said to have half of telephone switching market in China valued at $1.2 million annually.
Allied Industries International	Hong Kong	Jilin Chemicals	Jilin Petrochemicals is joint venture to produce acrylic acid and ethylene oxide.

Foreign Company	Country	China Partner	Comments
Allied Signal	U.S.A.	Dengfeng Motor Corp. (#2 car producer in China)	Plan to produce hydraulic braking systems.
		---	Will build $27 million plant in Shanghai to make turbochargers for diesel trucks and vans.
		---	Hopes to have half of China auto parts market by year 2000.
American Telephone and Telegraph (AT&T)	U.S.A.	Shenzen Posts and Tele-communications Bureau	Won $13 million contract to set up new ultrahigh speed digital transmission system.
Amoco Corp.	U.S.A.	Liaoyang Petrochemical	Amoco sold polypropylene technology license in 1978.
		Yanshan Petrochemical	Amoco sold purified terephthalic acid license in 1979.
		Yizheng Joint Corp.	Amoco made long-term PTA sales arrangements in 1980s.
		Yizheng Amoco Fabrics	$18 million venture produces PP fabrics for sale in China and export.
		Xunlum Co., Zhuhai	Plan 250,000 m.t. plant for terephthalic acid (PTA).
Anheuser-Busch Co.	U.S.A. (St. Louis, MO)	Tsingtao Brewery	Anheuser-Busch has purchased 5% stake.

Foreign Company	Country	China Partner	Comments
Anheuser-Busch Co.	U.S.A. (St. Louis, MO)	Zhongde Brewery, Wuhuan	Anheuser-Busch bought 80% stake in February 1995. Plans to start Budweiser beer production in mid-1995.
Asea Brown Boveri A.G.	Germany	---	Plan to build five coal and gas fired power plants.
		---	Plan to develop and build electric locomotives with Chinese partner.
Ashland Petroleum	U.S.A.	East Asia Carbon Fibers Material Co., Anshan, Liaoning Province	Ashland sold 450,000 lb/yr pitch-based fiber plant to China in 1994.
AST Research	U.S.A.	---	Operates a joint venture plant making personal computers in Tianjin.
		---	Also has a plant in Gonguan SEZ near Hong Kong.
		---	Entered China market for PC sales in 1985; has 31% of the China market in 1994.
Atomic Energy of Canada, Ltd.	Canada	---	China plans to buy two 685-megawatt Candu reactors.
B.A.S.F.	Germany	Jilin Chemical Industry Corp.	Plan to build a 15,000 ton/yr neopentyl glycol plant in Jilin Province in NW China.

Foreign Company	Country	China Partner	Comments
B.A.S.F.	Germany	Yangzi Petrochemical	Yangzi-BASF Styrenics will produce ethylbenzene, styrene and polystyrene as of 1997.
		Northeast General Pharmaceutical Factory	Plan plant to produce vitamins in Shenyang, primarily for animal nutrition.
		Jinling Chemical	Plan to produce polyester resins.
		China World Best Development Corporation and Pudong Development Bank	Will build plant in Qingpu County near Shanghai to produce nylon carpet fibers.
		Shanghai Dyestuffs	Shanghai BASF Colorants and Auxiliaries Co. plans $140 million plant to produce textile and leather dyes.
		---	Has unsaturated polyester plant at Nanjing which is slated for expansion.
Bayer A.G.	Germany	Shanghai Corp. of Pharmaceutical, Economic and Technical International Cooperation	Plan to produce animal health products.
		Shanghai Veterinary Pharmaceutical Works	Plan to produce animal health products to be marketed by SVPW.

Foreign Company	Country	China Partner	Comments
Bayer A.G.	Germany	---	Bayer-Shanghai Dental Ltd. founded in 1986 to produce synthetic resin teeth and other products.
		Wuxi Dyestuffs Factory	A new company, Bayer Wuxi Dyestuffs, will build $18 million plant to produce and disperse dyestuffs for the textile industry.
		Wuxi Dyestuffs Factory	Another new company, Bayer Wuxi Leather Chemicals Co. will make chemicals for the leather industry.
		Shanghai Coatings Corporation	Bayer Shanghai pigments will produce iron oxide pigments.
Becton, Dickinson & Co.	U.S.A. (Franklin Lakes, NJ)	---	Plans $15-25 deal to make medical devices in Suzhou-Singapore township.
Bell South Corp.	U.S.A.	China United Telecommunications Corp. (China Unicom)	Plan to set up cellular, wireless and long distance telephone networks in Beijing and Tianjin.
Bio-Technology General Corp.	U.S.A.	U.S.A.Shenzen Boda Natural Products Co.	Plan to market three anti-cancer drugs produced in China on worldwide basis.

Foreign Company	Country	China Partner	Comments
BOC (British Oxygen Company)	U.K.	Fushun Iron and Steel Corp.	Fushun BOC Industrial Gases will be BOC's seventh joint venture in China.
		Hualing Group	Will make gases and equipment.
		Shanghai Wusong	Plan to produce industrial gases.
Boeing Co.	U.S.A. (Seattle, WA)	Xian Aircraft Co.	Boeing is buying tail sections for its 737 jets with $300 million in contracts in hand.
		---	Boeing China Inc. is agent for jetliner sales to China with 14% of all Boeing sales in 1994 slated for China.
BP Chemicals (British Petroleum subsidiary)	U.K.	Daqing Technology Import & Export Corp.	Plan to produce maleic anhydride using Techniment (Italian) technology by 1996.
		---	Has exported acrylonitrile to China since 1973.
		Sinopec Sichuan Vinylon Works	Chengqing Municipality will be co-partner in $100 million acetic acid plant.
		Shanghai Wujing Chemical Complex	Using BP technology in acetic acid plant to come on stream in 1996.

Foreign Company	Country	China Partner	Comments
Cabot Corp.	U.S.A.	Shanghai Pacific	Will produce carbon black.
Chrysler Corp.	U.S.A.	---	Beijing Jeep Corp. produces 15,000 Jeep Cherokee sport utility vehicles per year. Also produces other sport utilities derived from a Russian chassis.
Ciba	Switzerland	Quingdao Dyestuffs Factory	Plan to produce disperse dyes for polyesters and leather chemicals at factory in Shandong.
		Shanghai Gao Qiao	Plan to produce antioxidants.
		Qingdao Pesticides	Plants produce insecticides.
Coca-Cola Company	U.S.A.	Shanxi Bureau of China's Ministry of Coal and Kerry Group of Malaysia	Will build $25 million bottling plant in Shanxi Province in North China.
Courtaulds	U.K.	Suzhou Resin Factory	Plan plant at Suzhou in Jiangsu Province to produce powder coatings for packaging.
		Chang Cheng Chemical of Taiwan	Has powder coatings plant started in 1991.
		---	A new powder coatings plant will start up near Shenzen in Guangdong Province in 1994.

Foreign Company	Country	China Partner	Comments
Degussa	Germany	Zhenya Carbon Black	Have inaugurated a $36 million joint venture with a capacity of 53,000 tons/yr.
		Jilin Chemical Industries	Will engage in organic chemicals production.
Digital Equipment Corp.	U.S.A.	Hunan Computer Factory	Plan to manufacture Chinese script computer terminals at a plant in Hunan Province.
Dow Chemical	U.S.A.	Zhejiang Chemical	Polyols project to be built at Ningbo near Shanghai.
DuPont (E.I. DuPont de Nemours & Co.)	U.S.A.	Liaoyang Petrochemical Fiber Co.	Plan a joint venture together with Rhone-Poulenc (France) to make nylon-6,6 salt at a 100,000 metric tons/yr rate.
		China Worldbest Development Corp.	Plan a joint venture to make and market Lycra spandex fiber in China.
		Shanghai Precision Photomask Corp.	Plan $16 million investment in electron beam facility to produce advanced photomasks for integrated circuit production.
		Asia Pacific Ag. Chemicals	Plant to be built to produce "Londax" rice herbicide in Shanghai.

Foreign Company	Country	China Partner	Comments
Ecogen	U.S.A. (Langhorne, PA)	China National Green Food	Plan to develop biopesticides for markets in China.
Energy Power Corp.	U.S.A.	---	Had $1.2 billion power plant in Guangdong Province approved in 1994 by Chinese government.
L.M. Ericsson	Sweden	---	Proves two-thirds of all cellular phone gear in China today and has four joint ventures operating.
Exxon	U.S.A.	Sinopec	Have installed lubricants additives plants at Lanzhou refinery.
Ferro Corp.	U.S.A.	Guangdong Foshan Ceramic Group	The joint venture, Foshan-Ferro Ceramic Materials, will make and market ceramic frits, glazes and colors.
FMC Corp.	U.S.A.	Shanghai Wusong	Will produce hydrogen peroxide.
Ford Motor Co.	U.S.A.	Shanghai Automation Instrumentation Company	Will produce electronic components including clock and radio products at first and possibly vehicle control products later.
Foster Wheeler Energy Corp.	U.S.A.	---	Received contracts in mid-1994 for two coal-fired steam generators in Hubei Province.

Foreign Company	Country	China Partner	Comments
Gallup, Inc.	U.S.A.	Japan Management Association	Studying brand loyalty and consumer attitudes in China.
General Electric Co.	U.S.A.	Shanghai Municipal Electric Power	GE will own and operate four 100 megawatt turbine generators at the Zhabei district power plant in Shanghai.
General Motors	U.S.A.	Jinbei Automotive Company	Plan to make small pickup trucks and sport utility vehicles in $100 million plant started in 1992, but deferred to 1995.
		China North Industries Group (Norinco)	Negotiating to produce a family-size automobile in China.
GE Plastics	U.S.A. (Pittsfield, MA)	M.C.I.	Setting up technical center in Shenzen and building a 20,000 ton/yr plant in Guangdong to produce polycarbonate plastics.
G. Heilman Brewing Co.	U.S.A. (La Crosse, WI)	Hong Kong Investments, Ltd.	Plan to produce Lone Star beer in twenty-three breweries throughout China.
GTE (General Telephone and Electronics)	U.S.A.	Unicom (a network being built by electronics, railway and power ministries)	Plan to build local, long distance and wireless network in China.
		China United Telecommunications Corp.	Joint venture plans to build the Unicom network.

Foreign Company	Country	China Partner	Comments
Heineken	Netherlands	Fraser & Neave of Singapore	Plan to form Asia Pacific Breweries, Ltd. to produce Heineken and local brands of beer.
Henkel	Germany	Siping Municipal Oils and Fats General Plant	Siping Henkel Detergents and Cleaning Products Co., Ltd. will produce 150 million lbs/yr of detergent powders in Siping in NE China
		---	Henkel has eight joint ventures in place and six more planned to double 1994 sales of $100 million.
		Shanghai Surfactant Factory and Shanghai Petrochemical	Plan to form Shanghai Henkel Oleochemicals to produce 30,000 tons/yr of surfactants.
Hiram Walker Wines and Spirits Ltd. (a unit of Allied Domecq PLC, the world's second largest wine and spirits producer)	U.K.	Qingdao Huaguan Wines & Spirits Co.	Plan $100 million joint venture to produce premium wines and spirits.
Hoechst A.G.	Germany	China National Tobacco	Involves $150 million acetic anhydride and cellulose acetate plant in Nantong, Jiangsu Province.
		China World Best Development & China National New Building Material Corp.	$30 million project to produce spun-bonded polyester fiber in Shanghai.

Foreign Company	Country	China Partner	Comments
Hoechst A.G.	Germany	Dongguan Chemicals & Dongguan City Automobile Co.	$5 million venture to produce automotive refinishing paints.
		---	Total Hoechst investment in China estimated at $300 million in 1994; plan to double by 1996.
Hoechst Celanese	U.S.A.	China National Tobacco	Will make acetate filter tow for cigarettes. Total investment in three plants to be $100 million.
		Guangzhou Synthetic Fiber Co.	Hoechst Guangzhou Masterbatch Co., Ltd. will build plant.
I.B.M.	U.S.A.	Ji Tong Communications Ltd.	Plan a national system for credit and debit cards, a computerized customs system and an intercity computer network.
I.C.I.	U.K.	---	Have built $25 million paint plant in Guangzhou, Guangdong Province
		---	I.C.I. has relatively low profile in China, perhaps since assets were seized by government in 1956.
		Shanghai Pacific	Plan to produce titanium dioxide.

Foreign Company	Country	China Partner	Comments
I.T.T. Corp.	U.S.A.	Zhenjiang Connector Factory	I.T.T.-Cannon unit to produce electronic connectors at plant in Zhenjiang near Shanghai.
I.T.T. Flygt A.B.	Sweden	Jinbei Automobile Co.	Will manufacture sewage and mining pumps.
KFC Holdings (A division of Pepsico, Inc.)	U.S.A.	---	Plan to expand chain of fast food outlets from 50 to 200 by year 1999.
Lion Nathan, Ltd.	New Zealand	---	Plan to build $235 million brewery in Suzhou-Singapore township.
ABB Lummus Crest, Inc.	U.S.A.	Sinopec Technology Co. (Beijing)	Planning to commercialize use of Sinopec-developed catalyst to produce ethylbenzene from dilute ethylene feed.
Mazda Motor Corp.	Japan	Fuzhou Solid Motors Corp. & Salim Group of Indonesia & Tomen Corp. of Japan	Plan to build plant in Fujian Province to produce pickup trucks starting in 1996 at a 10,000 unit/yr level.
McDonnell Douglas	U.S.A.	---	Building aircraft parts since 1979 including doors and horizontal stabilizers; also assembling kits sent from Long Beach, CA.

Foreign Company	Country	China Partner	Comments
Merck & Co.	U.S.A.	Hangzhou East China Pharmaceutical Co.	Will produce prescription drugs starting in 1995.
Microsoft Corp.	U.S.A.	Great Wall Electronics Group	Hope to develop Windows 95 software for China market.
Mission Energy	U.S.A.	Lippo Group of Hong Kong	Together with Bechtel Enterprises plan to build a 700-megawatt power station in southern Fujian Province facing the strait of Taiwan.
Mitsubishi Petrochemical Engineering	Japan	---	Doing feasibility study for billion dollar coal-chemical complex at Baotou.
Mitsubishi Heavy Industries and MitsubishiEngineering and Shipbuilding	Japan	China National Technical Import and Export	Mitsubishi to furnish $100 million worth of fertilizer equipment for phosphate fertilizer plant in southwest Guizhou Province.
Mitsui	Japan	China Merchants Ltd.	See entry under PPG Industries.
Monsanto	U.S.A.	Jiangsu Chemical Pesticide Group	Will produce heat transfer fluids in Suzhou.
Morgan Stanley Group Inc.	U.S.A.	People's Construction Bank of China and others including China National Investment and Guarantee Corp.	Plan to form China International Capital Corp. as China's first investment bank.
Motorola, Inc.	U.S.A.	China United Telecommunications Corp.	Will supply mobile cellular phones for Guangzhou Province.

Foreign Company	Country	China Partner	Comments
Nippon Sanso	Japan	---	Has established Shenyang Nissan Gas to produce oxygen-enriched air by absorption to supply plant of Shenyang Toyo Steel.
NorskHydro	Norway	Suzhou Huasu Chemical	Plan to produce PVC resin and film.
Northern Telecom		Beijing University of Posts and Telecommunications	Bell Northern Research, the RD division is opening a lab in Beijing
	Canada	Bank of China and Philips Electronics Southeast Asia Holding NV	Will produce very large integrated (VLSI) circuits.
		Seven partners including Guangdong Posts and Telecom Authority	Will set up company to build switches for Chinese phone networks.
Owens Corning Fiberglass Corp.	U.S.A.	---	Plan to produce fiberglass insulation in Changchun; earlier plastic pipe venture failed due to failure to assess domestic competition.
Peugeot-Citroen	France	---	New assembling Citroen ZX from kits in Hubei Province and planning full-scale local production.
Phillips Chemical	U.S.A.	Shanghai Petrochemical	Will build a 100,000 ton/yr linear polyethylene plant at Jinshanwei.

Foreign Company	Country	China Partner	Comments
Pitney Bowes	U.S.A.	---	Has $29 million contract to begin automating China's 55,000 post office branches.
PPG Industries and Mitsui-Japan	U.S.A.	China Merchants, Ltd.	Will build automotive paint plant at Tianjin.
PPG Industries	U.S.A.	Lianyungyang Chemical Fertilizer and Nanchang Chemical Industrial Material Factory	Will produce auorphous silica.
Raytheon	U.S.A.	---	Has Raytheon China Co. subsidiary supplying air-traffic control systems to a number of sites in China.
Rhone-Poulenc	France	Liaoyang Petrochemical Fiber and DuPont (U.S.)	Plan to produce nylon 6,6 fiber.
		Wuxi Chemicals Industry	Rhone-Poulenc Specialty Chemicals Wuxi Co. will produce specialty surfactants.
		Xinghuo Chemical Works	Have formed Rhone-Poulenc Xinghuo Quality Sealants to produce 4 million lbs/yr of silicone sealants for the construction industry.

Foreign Company	Country	China Partner	Comments
Rhone-Poulenc	France	Jilin Chemical Industry Corporation	Suzhou Rhone-Poulenc Anli Specialty Chemicals Company is joint venture to produce acrylic warp-size chemicals.
Roche	Switzerland	Shanghai Sunve	Plan to produce vitamins.
Rockwell International Corp.	U.S.A.	China North Industries Corp.	Has converted a small arms factory into a sewing machine factory.
Rohm and Haas	U.S.A.	Beijing Dongfang Chemical Plant	Plan to produce acrylic emulsions.
Royal Dutch Shell	Netherlands	China Aviation Oil Supply Corp. and Tianjin Harbour Nanjiang Development Co.	Plan $26 million oil storage and transport facility at port of Tianjin.
Sandoz	Switzerland	Tianjin No. 5 Dyestuffs Factory	Will build $30 million plant to produce dyestuffs.
Scott Paper Co.	U.S.A.	Shanghai Paper Corp.	Plan to make and sell Scott tissue products.
Siemens A.G.	Germany	---	Plan a joint venture to build and operate a coal-fired power station in Hanfeng. The project cost is $1 billion and Siemens will have a 40% stake.
Smith Kline Beecham		China National Biological Products Corp. and Shanghai Institute of Biological Products	Plan to make and market SKB's "Havrix" hepatitis A vaccine.

Foreign Company	Country	China Partner	Comments
Sprint	U.S.A.	China Ministry of Posts and Telecommunications	Will build lines from Beijing and from Shanghai to connect Chinese subscribers to Internet.
Unigene Laboratories	U.S.A.	Qindao General Pharmaceutical Co.	Plan to make a drug to treat osteoporosis.
Unilever PLC	U.K.	Sumstar	The joint venture, Wall's (Beijing) Co. has Beijing ice cream factory; will build second near Shanghai.
		Zhangjiakou Detergents	Will produce and market fabric detergents.
		Shanghai Toothpaste Factory	Plan to expand market for local and international toothpaste brands.
Upjohn	U.S.A.	Suzhou Pharmaceutical Factory No. 4	Building a $30 million antibiotics and steroids factory.
Wal-Mart Stores, Inc.	U.S.A.	Ek Chor Distribution System Co. of Hong Kong, a unit of C.P. Pokhand Co., a Thailand-based company.	Plan to open stores in Hong Kong first and Shanghai and Shenzen later.

Foreign Company	Country	China Partner	Comments
Westinghouse Electric Co.	U.S.A.	Harbin Electrical Equipment Co.	Plan to make steam turbines.
		Shanghai Heavy Machinery Co.	Plan to make steam turbines.
		---	Will provide two steam turbine power plants for Jiangsu-Ligang Electric Power Co.
		Longyuan Power Technology Exploitation Corp.	Will renovate and modernize steam turbine generators.
		Huaneng Power International, Inc.	Building four generators for coal-fired power plants in Liaoning Province.
Xerox Corp.	U.S.A.	Shanghai Movie & Photograph Industrial Corp.	Has about half of China's desktop copier market.
Yaohan Group	Japan	Shanghai No. 1 Department Store Co.	Plan to build "Nextage Shanghai" Shopping Center—a $200 million investment the size of thirty-four football fields. Will include retail, sports and entertainment complexes.
Yukong Ltd.	South Korea	Sinopec	$80-100 million project will produce polyols in Tianjin municipality.

Foreign Company	Country	China Partner	Comments
Zeneca	U.K.	Nantong Pesticide Factory and Nantong Petrochemicals Corp. and Jiangsu Agrochemicals Co.	Will produce paraquat herbicides in Nantong near Shanghai.
		Sino-Pharm	Zeneca Sino-Pharm Development and Consulting Co. will help to modernize the Chinese pharmaceutical industry.

REFERENCES

1. Kirschner, E. M., Peaff, G., Reisch, M. S., Storck, W. J. & Thayer, A. M., <u>Chem & Eng News</u> (July 25, 1994) 10-14.

2. Economic & Social Commission for Asia and the Pacific, "Guidebook on Trading With the People's Republic of China," Fourth Edition, New York, United Nations (1993).

3. International Trade Administration, Office of the PRC & Hong Kong, "Country Marketing Plan—China," Report PB93-160,299, Washington, DC, National Technical Information Service (1993).

4. Federal Research Division, Library of Congress, "China—A Country Study," Ed. by Worden, R. L., Savada, A. M., & Dolan, R. E., Supt. of Documents, U.S. Government Printing Office (1988).

5. International Trade Administration, Office of the PRC & Hong Kong, "The China Business Guide," Report PB94-143,021, Springfield, VA, National Technical Information Service (1994).

6. Comtois, C., "Transport & Territorial Development in China, 1949-1985," Publication CRT-627, Montreal, Centre de Recherche Sur Les Transports, Universite de Montreal (April 1989).

7. International Trade Administration, Office of the PRC and Hong Kong, "Industry Sector Analysis: Port Development," Report PB93-160,547, Springfield, VA, National Technical Information Service (1993).

8. China Statistical Information & Consultancy Service Center (CSICSC), "China's Leading Companies (Including Special Economic Zones & Coastal Cities)," Secaucus, NJ, Hualin International, Inc. (1992).

9. International Trade Administration, Office of the PRC & Hong Kong, "Guangdong 1992 Economic Overview," Report PB94-143,013, Springfield, VA, National Technical Information Service (1994).

10. International Trade Administration, Office of the PRC & Hong Kong, "Industry Sector Analysis: Agricultural Machinery," Report PB93-160,349, Springfield, VA, National Technical Information Service (1993). (Superseded by Reference #53.)

11. International Trade Administration, Office of the PRC & Hong Kong, "Industry Sub-sector Analysis: Automotive Industry," Report PB93-233,252, Springfield, VA, National Technical Information Service (1993).

12. International Trade Administration, Office of the PRC & Hong Kong, "Industry Sector Analysis: Air Traffic Control (ATC) Equipment," Report PB94-143,047, Springfield, VA, National Technical Information Service (1994).

13. International Trade Administration, Office of the PRC & Hong Kong, "Industry Sector Analysis: Avionics & Support Equipment in East China," Report PB94-143,070, Springfield, VA, National Technical Information Service (1994).

14. International Trade Administration, Office of the PRC & Hong Kong, "Industry Sector Analysis: Ground Support, Airport Equipment & Services," Report PB93-160,455, Springfield, VA, National Technical Information Service (1993).

15. International Trade Administration, Office of the PRC & Hong Kong, "Industry Sector Analysis: Building Materials," Report PB94-143,062, Springfield, VA, National Technical Information Service (1994).

16. International Trade Administration, Office of the PRC & Hong Kong, "International Market Insight: PC Software Market," Report PB93-160,497, Springfield, VA, National Technical Information Service (1993).

17. International Trade Administration, Office of the PRC & Hong Kong, "Industry Sub-sector Analysis: Construction Equipment in Guangdong," Report PB93-233,278, Springfield, VA, National Technical Information Service (1993).

18. International Trade Administration, Office of the PRC & Hong Kong, "Industry Market Research: Electrical Power Systems—Market Overview & Business Environment—China," Report PB93-160,372, Springfield, VA, National Technical Information Service (1993).

19. International Trade Administration, Office of the PRC & Hong Kong, "Industry Sector Analysis: Electrical Generating Equipment in Guangdong Province," Report PB93-160,364, Springfield, VA, National Technical Information Service (1993).

20. International Trade Administration, Office of the PRC & Hong Kong, "Industry Sector Analysis: Hydroelectric Power," Report PB94-143,054, Springfield, VA, National Technical Information Service (1994).

21. International Trade Administration, Office of the PRC & Hong Kong, "Industry Sector Analysis: Printed Circuit Board Equipment," Report PB-93-182,665, Springfield, VA, National Technical Information Service (1993).

22. International Trade Administration, Office of the PRC & Hong Kong, "Pollution Control—Market Overview," Report PB93-160,323, Springfield, VA, National Technical Information Service (1993).

23. International Trade Administration, Office of the PRC & Hong Kong, "Industry Market Research: Pollution Control—Air Pollution—China," Report PB93-160,513, Springfield, VA, National Technical Information Service (1993).

24. International Trade Administration, Office of the PRC & Hong Kong, "Industry Sector Analysis: Urban Water Sanitation—China," Report PB93-160,653, Springfield, VA, National Technical Information Service (1993). (See also Reference #50.)

25. International Trade Administration, Office of the PRC & Hong Kong, "Industry Market Research: Pollution Control—Noise Pollution—China," Report PB93-160,521, Springfield, VA, National Technical Information Service (1993).

26. International Trade Administration, Office of the PRC & Hong Kong, "Industry Sector Analysis: Wastepaper—China," Report PB93-160,646, Springfield, VA, National Technical Information Service (1993).

27. International Trade Administration, Office of the PRC & Hong Kong, "Industry Sector Analysis: Food Processing & Packaging Machinery," Report PB93-160,406, Springfield, VA, National Technical Information Service (1993).

28. International Trade Administration, Office of the PRC & Hong Kong, "Industry Sector Analysis: Food Processing Equipment in Guangdong Province," Report 94-143,039, Springfield, VA, National Technical Information Service (1994).

29. International Trade Administration, Office of the PRC & Hong Kong, "Industry Sector Analysis: Fruit & Vegetable Processing Equipment—China," Report PB93-160,430, Springfield, VA, National Technical Information Service (1993).

30. International Trade Administration, Office of the PRC & Hong Kong, "Industry Sector Analysis: Meat and Poultry Processing Equipment—China," Report PB93-160,463, Springfield, VA, National Technical Information Service (1993).

31. International Trade Administration, Office of the PRC & Hong Kong, "Industry Sub-sector Analysis: Fast Food & Equipment," Report PB93-233,237, Springfield, VA, National Technical Information Service (1993).

32. International Trade Administration, Office of the PRC & Hong Kong, "Industry Sector Analysis: Petrochemical Industry in East China," Report PB93-160-539, Springfield, VA, National Technical Information Service (1993).

33. International Trade Administration, Office of the PRC & Hong Kong, "Industry Sector Analysis: Metal Working Machine Tools—China," Report PB93-160,489, Springfield, VA, National Technical Information Service (1993).

34. International Trade Administration, Office of the PRC & Hong Kong, "Industry Market Research: Medical & Pharmaceutical Equipment—Market Environment & Market Overview—China," Report PB93-160,471, Springfield, VA, National Technical Information Service (1993).

35. International Trade Administration, Office of the PRC & Hong Kong, "Industry Sub-sector Analysis: Medical Equipment," Report PB93-233,260, Springfield, VA, National Technical Information Service (1993).

36. International Trade Administration, Office of the PRC & Hong Kong, "Industry Sector Analysis: Foundry Equipment—China," Report PB93-160,422, Springfield, VA, National Technical Information Service (1993).

37. International Trade Administration, Office of the PRC & Hong Kong, "Industry Sector Analysis: Open Pit/Underground Mining Equipment—China," Report PB93-160,505, Springfield, VA, National Technical Information Service (1993).

38. International Trade Administration, Office of the PRC & China, "Industry Sector Analysis: Pulp & Paper Industry—China," Report PB93-160,331, Springfield, VA, National Technical Information Service (1993).

39. International Trade Administration, Office of the PRC & China, "Industry Sector Analysis: Pharmaceutical—China," Report PB93-182,657, Springfield, VA, National Technical Information Service (1993).

40. International Trade Administration, Office of the PRC & Hong Kong, "Industry Sector Analysis: Electrical Power Systems—Transmission Equipment Market," Report PB93-160,380, Springfield, VA, National Technical Information Service (1993).

41. International Trade Administration, Office of the PRC & China, "Industry Sector Analysis: Printing Equipment—China," Report PB93-160,554, Springfield, VA, National Technical Information Service (1993).

42. International Trade Administration, Office of the PRC & Hong Kong, "Industry Market Survey: Process Controls—Overview & Business Regulations—China," Report PB93-160,562, Springfield, VA, National Technical Information Service (1993).

43. International Trade Administration, Office of the PRC & Hong Kong, "Industry Market Research: Telecommunications—Overview—China," Report PB93-160,612, Springfield, VA, National Technical Information Service (1993).

44. International Trade Administration, Office of the PRC & China, "International Market Insight—Textile Industry Profile—China," Report PB93-160,638, Springfield, VA, National Technical Information Service (1993).

45. International Trade Administration, Office of the PRC & Hong Kong, "Industry Sector Analysis: Textile Equipment—China," Report PB93-160,620, Springfield, VA, National Technical Information Service (1993).

46. U.S. Department of Agriculture, Economic Research Service, Situation & Outlook Series, "China," Publication 94-4 Washington, DC, (August 1994).

47. U.S. General Accounting Office, "U.S. Government Policy Issues Affecting U.S. Business Activities in China," Report GAO/GCD 9A-94, Washington, DC, (May 1994).

48. U.S. Bureau of Mines, "Mineral Industries of Asia & the Pacific," Published as Vol. 3 of The Minerals Yearbook, U.S. Department of the Interior, Washington, DC, (1992).

49. Hargreaves, D., Eden-Green, M. and Devaney, J., "World Index of Resources & Population," Brookfield, VT, Ashgate Publishing Company (1994).

50. International Trade Administration, Office of the PRC & Hong Kong, "Industry Sector Analysis: Municipal Waste Water Treatment," Report PB94-173,549, Springfield, VA, National Technical Information Service (1994).

51. International Trade Administration, Office of the PRC & Hong Kong, "Industry Sector Analysis: Telecommunications Central Office Switches," Report PB-173,531, Springfield, VA, National Technical Information Service (1994).

52. International Trade Administration, Office of the PRC & Hong Kong, "Special Topic Report: Oil, Gas Industry Profile," Report PB94-173,515, Springfield, VA, National Technical Information Service (1994).

53. International Trade Administration, Office of the PRC & Hong Kong, "Industry Sector Analysis: Agricultural Machinery," Report PB94-173,507, Springfield, VA, National Technical Information Service (1994).

54. International Trade Administration, Office of the PRC & Hong Kong, "Industry Sector Analysis: Insurance," Report PB94-173,499, Springfield, VA, National Technical Information Service (1994).

55. International Trade Administration, Office of the PRC & Hong Kong, "Industry Sector Analysis: Retail," Report PB94-173,523, Springfield, VA, National Technical Information Service (1994).

56. International Trade Administration, Office of the PRC & Hong Kong, "1993 Shenzen's Investment Guide & U.S.-China Business Center Pamphlet," Report PB93-192,995, Springfield, VA, National Technical Information Service (1993).

57. International Trade Administration, Office of the PRC & Hong Kong, "Industry Sector Analysis: Solid Waste," Report PB94-210,853, Springfield, VA, National Technical Information Service (1994).

58. International Trade Administration, International Market Research Division, "Country Commercial Guide: China, Fiscal Year 1995," Springfield, VA, National Technical Information Service (1994).

59. Blum, H. R., "China's "New" Chemical Industry," Chemistry & Industry, pp. 763-69 (October 3, 1994).

INDEX

Printed and bound by CPI Group (UK) Ltd, Croydon, CR0 4YY

08/05/2025

01864823-0004